Pearson New International Edition

THINK Public Relations
Wilcox   Cameron   Reber   Shin
Second Edition

PEARSON

Pearson Education Limited
Edinburgh Gate
Harlow
Essex CM20 2JE
England and Associated Companies throughout the world

Visit us on the World Wide Web at: www.pearsoned.co.uk

© Pearson Education Limited 2014

 ISBN 10: 1-292-02528-X
ISBN 13: 978-1-292-02528-5

British Library Cataloguing-in-Publication Data
A catalogue record for this book is available from the British Library

Printed in the United States of America

Table of Contents

1. What is Public Relations?
Dennis L. Wilcox/Glen T. Cameron/Bryan H. Reber/Jae-Hwa Shin 　　　　　　　　　　　　　　**1**

2. The Growth of a Profession
Dennis L. Wilcox/Glen T. Cameron/Bryan H. Reber/Jae-Hwa Shin 　　　　　　　　　　　　　　**25**

3. Careers in Public Relations
Dennis L. Wilcox/Glen T. Cameron/Bryan H. Reber/Jae-Hwa Shin 　　　　　　　　　　　　　　**53**

4. Today's Practice: Departments and Firms
Dennis L. Wilcox/Glen T. Cameron/Bryan H. Reber/Jae-Hwa Shin 　　　　　　　　　　　　　　**73**

5. Research and Campaign Planning
Dennis L. Wilcox/Glen T. Cameron/Bryan H. Reber/Jae-Hwa Shin 　　　　　　　　　　　　　　**95**

6. Communication and Measurement
Dennis L. Wilcox/Glen T. Cameron/Bryan H. Reber/Jae-Hwa Shin 　　　　　　　　　　　　　　**123**

7. Public Opinion and Persuasion
Dennis L. Wilcox/Glen T. Cameron/Bryan H. Reber/Jae-Hwa Shin 　　　　　　　　　　　　　　**147**

8. Managing Competition and Conflict
Dennis L. Wilcox/Glen T. Cameron/Bryan H. Reber/Jae-Hwa Shin 　　　　　　　　　　　　　　**175**

9. Ethics and the Law
Dennis L. Wilcox/Glen T. Cameron/Bryan H. Reber/Jae-Hwa Shin 　　　　　　　　　　　　　　**195**

10. Reaching Diverse Audiences
Dennis L. Wilcox/Glen T. Cameron/Bryan H. Reber/Jae-Hwa Shin 　　　　　　　　　　　　　　**221**

11. The Mass Media
Dennis L. Wilcox/Glen T. Cameron/Bryan H. Reber/Jae-Hwa Shin 　　　　　　　　　　　　　　**243**

12. The Internet and Social Media
Dennis L. Wilcox/Glen T. Cameron/Bryan H. Reber/Jae-Hwa Shin 　　　　　　　　　　　　　　**265**

13. Corporate Public Relations
Dennis L. Wilcox/Glen T. Cameron/Bryan H. Reber/Jae-Hwa Shin 　　　　　　　　　　　　　　**289**

14. Events and Promotions
Dennis L. Wilcox/Glen T. Cameron/Bryan H. Reber/Jae-Hwa Shin **313**

15. Global Public Relations
Dennis L. Wilcox/Glen T. Cameron/Bryan H. Reber/Jae-Hwa Shin **335**

16. Government and Politics
Dennis L. Wilcox/Glen T. Cameron/Bryan H. Reber/Jae-Hwa Shin **357**

17. Entertainment, Sports, and Tourism
Dennis L. Wilcox/Glen T. Cameron/Bryan H. Reber/Jae-Hwa Shin **379**

18. Nonprofit, Health, and Education
Dennis L. Wilcox/Glen T. Cameron/Bryan H. Reber/Jae-Hwa Shin **401**

Index **425**

What is Public Relations?

What is Public Relations?

A Busy Day

Cierra is an account executive in a San Francisco public relations firm. When her workday begins at 6 A.M., her East Coast colleagues, with their three-hour head start, have already been filling her e-mail inbox. As she drinks her coffee, she checks e-mails as well as RSS feeds (Really Simple Syndication—an online content aggregating system). Then she scans feeds from blogs covering industries she represents for her clients and checks her clients' websites. By 9 A.M., Cierra is on her way to her downtown office via light rail; wasting no time, she monitors the news and her e-mails on her smartphone during her commute. Her New York colleagues have sent her a schedule for a client's West Coast media tour. She makes some minor adjustments to the tour, since she knows the Bay Area journalists better than her Manhattan counterparts do. Next she turns her attention to a news release about a client's new mobile phone app. She finishes the edits, gives it a once-over, and e-mails it to the client for approval. An electronic news service will deliver the release to newspapers across the country as soon as the release is approved.

In her office, Cierra gets a visit from the firm's student intern. In going through news clippings to monitor client-related industries, the intern has identified some news about pending government environmental regulations that have the potential to negatively impact a client's reputation. One legislator used the client as an example of why the regulations are needed. Cierra sends several high-priority e-mails and sets up a meeting with the client.

Cierra's next activity is a brainstorming session with staff to generate creative ideas about a campaign to raise funds for the local art museum. She finds this client to be one of her most challenging. Nonprofits compete for volunteers and members as well as financial donations, especially in a lean economy. When she returns to her office, there are a number of telephone messages. A reporter called for background information on a story; a graphic designer has finished a brochure; a catering manager wants to finalize arrangements for a reception; and a client has asked her to attend a video news release taping.

Cierra lunches late with a client who seeks her counsel on how to announce employee layoffs, a situation fraught with ethical issues. After lunch, Cierra treks to a client pitch appointment, using her computer tablet en route to check databases and gather information about the prospective client's industry. She also checks online news updates to determine if anything is occurring that involves or affects her other clients. At 6 P.M., as she winds down from the day's hectic activities, she reviews stories from a clipping service about one of her accounts, an association of California vintners. She is pleased to find that her feature story, which included recipes, wine pairings, and color photos, appeared in several daily newspapers.

1 **Based on the description of Cierra's day, how would you define public relations if a friend asked you what you were studying in this class?**

2 **What role do the Internet and social media play in Cierra's day?**

3 **How does Cierra interact with journalists and use news coverage to inform her work throughout the day?**

Ask Yourself

> What Is Public Relations?

> What Are the Components of Public Relations?

> How Does Public Relations Differ from Journalism?

> How Does Public Relations Differ from Advertising?

> How Does Public Relations Differ from Marketing?

> How Can an Integrated Approach to Public Relations Benefit an Organization?

The Challenge
OF PUBLIC RELATIONS

As the chapter-opening scenario illustrates, the challenge of public relations (PR) is multifaceted. A public relations professional must have skills in written and interpersonal communication, research, negotiation, creativity, logistics, facilitation, and problem solving.

Individuals who seek a challenging career at the center of what's happening in modern organizations will find public relations to their liking. Owing to the variety of tasks—ranging from brochure layout to focus groups and polling data analysis—and the chance to work for clients and companies across the gamut of profit, non-profit, and government sectors, more and more people like Cierra are choosing the field of public relations every year.

CNN.com lists "public relations specialist" as one of the top 50 professions for job opportunity and salary potential. The U.S. Bureau of Labor Statistics (BLS) predicts "much faster than average" growth for the public relations profession. Between now and 2018, the BLS predicts a very healthy 24 percent job growth in the field.

 think Which skills make PR professionals successful?

" Public relations specialists are concentrated in large cities, where...communications facilities are readily available and where many businesses and trade associations have their headquarters. Many public relations consulting firms, for example, are in New York, Los Angeles, San Francisco, Chicago, and Washington, D.C., according to the U.S. Bureau of Labor Statistics. "

Global SCOPE

Public relations is a well-established academic subject that is taught throughout the world. Large numbers of students around the globe study public relations as a career field. In the United States, more than 300 universities have sequences or majors in public relations, and approximately 100 European universities offer studies in the subject. Many Asian universities are offering new graduate and undergraduate public relations programs—from India to Singapore to China. Student demand is increasing dramatically.

The public relations field is most extensively developed in the United States, where organizations are projected to spend almost $8 billion annually by 2013 on public relations, according to estimates by Veronis Suhler Stevenson, a specialty banker in the communications industry.

While the U.S. dominates the public relations market, *The Holmes Report* (holmesreport.com), an annual agency industry listing, reflects the global power of PR. Agencies in Belgium, Brazil, Canada, China, France, Germany, Italy, Japan, Sweden, and the UK were among the top 50 agencies in 2011 according to income, which ranged from $531.5 million to $21.8 million among those top agencies.

Alan VanderMolen, Edelman's Asia-Pacific president told *AdWeek* that he envisions growth of 23 percent in Asian revenue in the next five years. Major growth is occurring in the Asian public relations industry for several reasons. China is emerging as the "new frontier." Since opening to market capitalism, China's economy has been increasing at the rate of 8 percent annually. The public relations industry is sharing in this growth. The China International Public Relations Association (CIPRA) reports there are now 20,000 practitioners in the country and annual spending on public relations has reached $2.2 billion.

Other Asian nations, such as Malaysia, South Korea, Thailand, Singapore, Indonesia, and India, are rapidly expanding their free-market economies as well, which creates a fertile environment for increased public relations activity. Latin America and Africa also present growth opportunities.

> "By geography, India and Korea are on fire. By sector, tech is hot and so is digital. I haven't been this excited about the market in a long time."
> **Alan VanderMolen, Edelman's Asia-Pacific President**

A VARIETY OF **definitions**

People often define public relations by referring to some of its most visible techniques and tactics, such as coverage in a newspaper, a television interview with an organization's spokesperson, or the appearance of a celebrity at a special event. Knowing what professionals do every day is important, but it does not suffice as a definition.

Public relations is a process involving numerous subtle and far-reaching aspects beyond media coverage. It includes research and analysis, policy formation, programming, communication, and feedback from numerous publics (for example, employees, consumers, investors–basically any stakeholder is a "public" for an organization). Its practitioners operate on two distinct levels—as advisers to individual clients or to an organization's top management, and as technicians who produce and disseminate messages in multiple media channels.

A number of formal definitions for public relations have been formulated over the years. In *Effective Public Relations*, Scott M. Cutlip, Allen H. Center, and Glen M. Broom state that "public relations is the management function that identifies, establishes, and maintains mutually beneficial relationships between an organization and the various publics on whom its success or failure depends." This approach represents the current belief that public relations is more than persuasion. Public relations should foster open, two-way communication and mutual understanding,

You can grasp the essential elements of effective public relations by remembering the following words and phrases that make up public relations activity: deliberate . . . planned . . . performance . . . public interest . . . two-way communication . . . strategic.

DELIBERATE. Public relations activity is intentional. It is designed to influence, gain understanding, provide information, and obtain feedback.

PLANNED. Public relations activity is organized. Solutions to problems are discovered and logistics are thought out. The activity is systematic, requires research and analysis, and takes place over a period of time.

PERFORMANCE. Effective public relations is based on actual policies and performance. No amount of public relations will generate goodwill and support if an organization is unresponsive to community concerns.

PUBLIC INTEREST. Reputable public relations activity is mutually beneficial to the organization and the public; it provides for the alignment of the organization's self-interests with the public's concerns and interests.

TWO-WAY COMMUNICATION. Public relations is more than one-way dissemination of informational materials. It is equally important to solicit feedback.

STRATEGIC MANAGEMENT OF COMPETITION AND CONFLICT. Public relations is most effective when it is an integral part of decision making by top management. Public relations involves counseling and problem solving at high levels, not just the dissemination of information after a decision has been made by other leaders.

It isn't necessary to memorize any particular definition of public relations. It's more important to remember the key words used in the definitions that frame today's modern public relations.

think How can PR help to foster a mutually beneficial relationship between an organization and its public?

while complying with the principle that an organization changes its attitudes and behaviors in the process. It is a two-way process because change and accommodation occur for the organization—not just the target audience.

Although definitions of public relations have long emphasized the building of mutually beneficial relationships between the organization and its various publics, a more assertive definition has emerged over the past decade.

Glen T. Cameron, of the Missouri School of Journalism, defines public relations as the "strategic management of competition and conflict for the benefit of one's own organization—and when possible—also for the mutual benefit of the organization and its stakeholders or publics." This definition casts the public relations professional first and foremost as an advocate for the employer or client, but acknowledges the importance of mutual benefit when circumstances allow. It does *not* imply that the public relations professional acts only in the self-interest of the

Direct-delivery video company Netflix made both customers and investors unhappy; when it increased prices by 60 percent, its stock price tumbled by 50 percent. An e-mail apology from the CEO was judged by many as being insincere. The company eventually acknowledged its communication failure.

employer without due regard to honesty, integrity, and organizational transparency. Indeed, an ethical framework always guides the PR professional in his or her work.

PUBLIC RELATIONS AS A process

Public relations is a process—a series of actions, changes, or functions that bring about a result. A number of attempts have been made to capture the public relations process, several of which are summarized here to provide a sense of how work in public relations unfolds. One way to describe the public relations process, and to remember its components, is to use the RACE acronym, which was first

articulated by John Marston in his book *The Nature of Public Relations*.

Diffusion-of-knowledge theorists call public relations people "linking agents." Sociologists refer to them as "boundary spanners," because they act to transfer information between two systems. As the concluding lines of the official statement on public relations by the Public Relations Society of America (PRSA) note: "The public relations

think How does research inform the actions that PR professionals take?

practitioner utilizes a variety of professional communication skills and plays an integrative role both within the organization and between the organization and the external environment."

"No matter the situation, exceptional communications practices do not change. Do what you know. People forget the basics.

Lisa Davis, vice president of corporate affairs at MedImmune

PR, Advertising, and Marketing Combine Forces to Change the Reputation of "Junk" Food

As you will learn in this chapter, public relations shares qualities with, but is distinct from, advertising, marketing, and journalism. However, public relations often joins forces with these professions to educate key publics. That's the strategy that the public relations firm Ketchum and word-of-mouth and social media marketing firm Zócalo Group adopted in an award-winning campaign for Frito-Lay.

Frito-Lay was concerned that snack foods like its Lay's potato chips, Fritos and Tostitos corn chips, and SunChips multigrain chips suffered from the "junk food" label. They wanted to educate "influencers" about the healthy ingredients in Frito-Lay products. Ketchum and Zócalo conducted pre-campaign research and found that 92 percent of people said the most powerful influencers in purchase decisions are family, friends, and experts. The research also showed that only 30 percent of influencers believed that Frito-Lay offered healthy snacks. A focus group identified "good fats/simple ingredients" as the most convincing message in shifting influencers' perceptions. Frito-Lay had removed unhealthy trans fats from its snacks years ahead of the competition, according to Ketchum's situation analysis. And products like Fritos had simple ingredients—"corn, corn oil and salt—that's it." The message was good but it wasn't enough; to make sure that consumers did not think the company was trying to promote chips as health foods, Frito-Lay also consulted with nutrition experts and developed educational materials about smart snacking.

To communicate their message about Frito-Lay's ingredients and smart snacking, Ketchum and Zócalo identified nutrition, health, and food experts as prospective influencers. They also reached out to bloggers and online "brand fans." Educational roundtables were held at national conferences attended by influencers—the Society for Nutrition Education and the American Dietetic Association. Booths were set up at blogger conferences, including the Healthy Living Summit and the SocialLuxe Lounge. Direct mail was employed to distribute new product "sneak peeks" to journalists, bloggers, and health professionals. Similarly, brand fans were sent "fan packs." In both instances, educational materials were included in the packages.

These same influencers—journalists, bloggers, and health professionals—were invited to production plants to see the food being made firsthand. Registered dietitians representing grocery chains were hosted at a two-day workshop to determine how best to get the good fat/simple ingredients message into their stores.

Online resources included YouTube videos featuring a Frito-Lay chef offering recipe and chip pairings. SnackSense.com and LicensetoSnack.com were developed as centers for product information and snacking research.

At the conclusion of the influencer campaign, 90 percent of the health professionals who were reached by the program became Frito-Lay advocates. Plant tours resulted in 130 participants tweeting or blogging about what they learned. Thirteen hundred brand fans signed up to be evangelists for the brand. Each fan boasted an average following of 10,000 people.

In this innovative and successful campaign, traditional public relations tactics like media relations and educational activities such as plant tours were paired with word-of-mouth marketing by brand fans and health experts to create a synergy that raised the reputation of Frito-Lay snacks from junk food to sensible snack. In 2011, Ketchum, Zócalo, and Frito-Lay won a PRSA Silver Anvil for the campaign.

1 What publics were identified as "influencers" in this case? Do you think some would be more influential than others? If so, why?

2 Which tactics in this PR Casebook would you identify as public relations and which as marketing?

3 What research was conducted? How was research essential to a successful campaign?

The public relations process also may be conceptualized in several steps. The PR Casebook example is detailed in the steps outlined here in this figure.

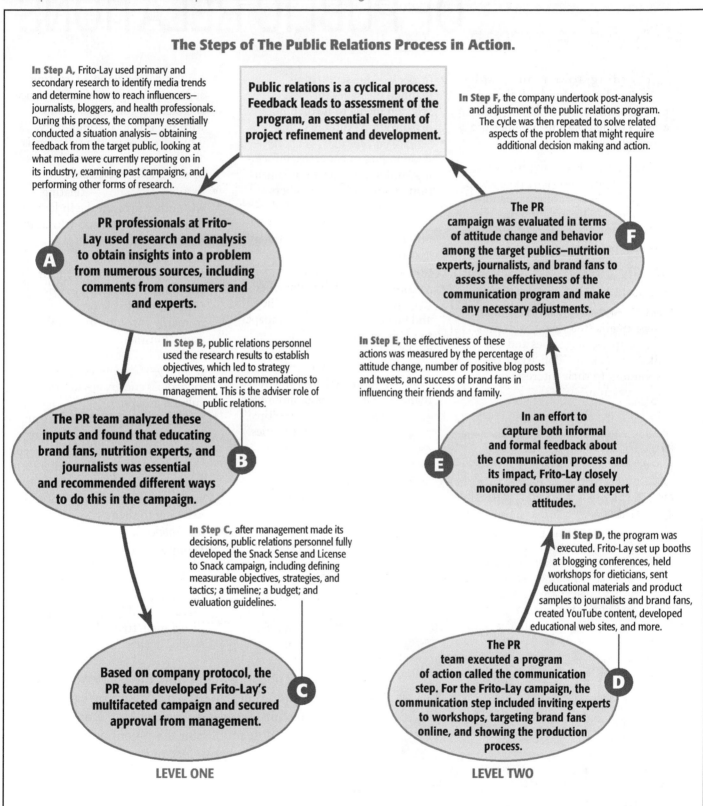

The Steps of The Public Relations Process in Action.

In **Step A**, Frito-Lay used primary and secondary research to identify media trends and determine how to reach influencers—journalists, bloggers, and health professionals. During this process, the company essentially conducted a situation analysis— obtaining feedback from the target public, looking at what media were currently reporting on in its industry, examining past campaigns, and performing other forms of research.

Public relations is a cyclical process. Feedback leads to assessment of the program, an essential element of project refinement and development.

In **Step F**, the company undertook post-analysis and adjustment of the public relations program. The cycle was then repeated to solve related aspects of the problem that might require additional decision making and action.

A PR professionals at Frito-Lay used research and analysis to obtain insights into a problem from numerous sources, including comments from consumers and and experts.

F The PR campaign was evaluated in terms of attitude change and behavior among the target publics—nutrition experts, journalists, and brand fans to assess the effectiveness of the communication program and make any necessary adjustments.

In **Step B**, public relations personnel used the research results to establish objectives, which led to strategy development and recommendations to management. This is the adviser role of public relations.

In **Step E**, the effectiveness of these actions was measured by the percentage of attitude change, number of positive blog posts and tweets, and success of brand fans in influencing their friends and family.

B The PR team analyzed these inputs and found that educating brand fans, nutrition experts, and journalists was essential and recommended different ways to do this in the campaign.

E In an effort to capture both informal and formal feedback about the communication process and its impact, Frito-Lay closely monitored consumer and expert attitudes.

In **Step C**, after management made its decisions, public relations personnel fully developed the Snack Sense and License to Snack campaign, including defining measurable objectives, strategies, and tactics; a timeline; a budget; and evaluation guidelines.

In **Step D**, the program was executed. Frito-Lay set up booths at blogging conferences, held workshops for dieticians, sent educational materials and product samples to journalists and brand fans, created YouTube content, developed educational web sites, and more.

C Based on company protocol, the PR team developed Frito-Lay's multifaceted campaign and secured approval from management.

D The PR team executed a program of action called the communication step. For the Frito-Lay campaign, the communication step included inviting experts to workshops, targeting brand fans online, and showing the production process.

LEVEL ONE

LEVEL TWO

The Components
OF PUBLIC RELATIONS

According to a monograph issued by the Public Relations Society of America (PRSA) Foundation, public relations includes the following components:

- *Counseling*—Providing advice to management concerning policies, relationships, and communications.
- *Research*—Determining the attitudes and behaviors of groups to plan public relations strategies. Such research can be used to generate mutual understanding or influence and persuade publics.
- *Media Relations*—Working with mass media (television, web sites, newspapers, magazines and the like) by seeking publicity or responding to their interests in the organization.

- *Publicity*—Disseminating planned messages through selected media to further an organization's interests.
- *Employee/Member Relations*—Responding to concerns, informing, and motivating an organization's employees or members.
- *Community Relations*—Undertaking activities within a community to maintain an environment that benefits both an organization and the community.
- *Public Affairs*—Developing effective involvement in public policy and helping an organization adapt to public expectations. The term "public affairs" is also used by government agencies to describe their public relations activities and by many corporations as an umbrella term to describe multiple public relations activities.
    - *Government Affairs*—Relating directly with legislatures and regulatory agencies on behalf of an organization. Lobbying can be part of a government affairs program.
    - *Issue Management*—Identifying and addressing issues of public concern that affect an organization.

- *Financial Relations*—Creating and maintaining investor confidence and building good relationships with the financial community. This aspect of public relations is also known as investor relations or shareholder relations.
- *Industry Relations*—Relating with other firms in the industry of an organization and with trade associations.
- *Development/Fund-Raising*—Demonstrating the need for and encouraging the public to support charitable organizations, primarily through financial contributions.
- *Multicultural Relations/Workplace Diversity*—Communicating with individuals and groups in various cultural groups.
- *Special Events*—Stimulating an interest in a person, product, or organization by means of focused "happenings" as well as other activities designed to encourage interacting with publics and listening to them.
- *Marketing Communications*—Employing a combination of activities designed to sell a product, service, or idea, including advertising, collateral materials, publicity, promotion, direct mail, trade shows, and special events.

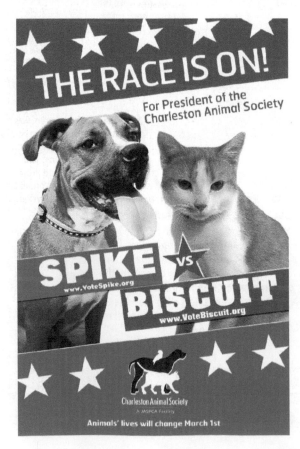

Working with a public relations firm, the Charleston (SC) Animal Society (CAS) organized a mock election campaign—Spike versus Biscuit—to raise awareness for the animal shelter. Spike the dog and Biscuit the cat announced platforms as they ran for president of the organization. The "candidates" produced posters, announced key endorsements, made campaign appearances, maintained Facebook diaries, and made YouTube commercials. The campaign raised awareness for a new $11 million adoption center and increased animal adoption rates in the Charleston area.

Beware of Bamboozling Bloggers

Many public relations firms and professionals are doing their best to reach out to social media sites and the blogosphere. But the best intentions can fail if these new media are not handled correctly. For example, the interest of food bloggers and mommy bloggers was naturally piqued when they received an invitation to dinner at the intimate Italian restaurant Sotto Terra, hosted by Food Network celebrity chef George Duran.

Suzanne Chan, the blogger mom behind Mom Confessionals wrote, "We were promised a delicious Italian four-course meal and scintillating conversation on the latest food trends with other foodies. I was salivating at the thought of this meal...." Both bloggers and the hosts were unpleasantly surprised however when, the food they were served was not prepared by a chef but was instead Marie Callender's frozen lasagna from ConAgra Foods.

Employees from Ketchum recorded diner

Chef George Duran

reaction to the lasagna and Marie Callender's Razzleberry Pie with hidden cameras. While the public relations firm may have expected the foodies to express pleasant surprise when the truth was revealed, the bloggers instead wrote about the event being a "sham" and "bait and switch."

Bloggers have become important citizen journalists, product/service/food reviewers, and influential opinion leaders. Naturally, public relations professionals want to woo such leaders, but just like other journalists, bloggers must be handled with care.

ConAgra and Ketchum reported that most attendees had fun at the event. But even a verbal few who feel they were duped can cause an uproar and at least momentarily sully your organization's reputation.

Deborah Silverman, head of the PRSA Board of Ethics and Professional Standards, called the incident "unfortunate." Ketchum has a strong reputation for ethical public relations but public relations practitioners must remember that bloggers wield substantial influence among their loyal readers. After all, that's why PR pros enlist bloggers' support. But PR missteps can take on what may seem like disproportional importance when those missteps fly instantly around the blogosphere.

PR blogger Bob Conrad (thegoodthebadthespin. com) offers six observations about dealing with bloggers: 1) Genuinely engage bloggers on their blogs rather than spamming them with press materials; 2) target bloggers appropriately; 3) understand that bloggers can be more influential than traditional journalists; 4) monitor and contribute to blogs, always keeping your client's or organization's needs in mind, 5) do your own blogging; 6) be helpful, transparent, honest, and genuine rather than trying to pitch to bloggers.

1 How are bloggers different from traditional journalists? How are they similar?

2 Hidden camera surprises have often been used in advertising. Was the Italian meal stunt ethical?

HOW PUBLIC RELATIONS
DIFFERS FROM **journalism**

Writing is a common activity of public relations professionals and journalists. And both go about their jobs in many of the same ways: They interview people, gather and synthesize large amounts of information, write in a journalistic style, and produce good copy on deadline. In fact, many reporters eventually change careers and become public relations practitioners.

This has led many people, including journalists, to draw the incorrect conclusion that there is little difference between public relations and journalism. For these misinformed people, public relations is simply being a "journalist-in-residence" for a non-media organization. In reality, despite sharing techniques, the two fields are fundamentally different in scope, objectives, audiences, and channels.

Scope

Public relations, as stated earlier, has many components, ranging from counseling to issues management and special events. Journalistic writing and media relations, although important, are only two of these elements. In addition, effective practice of public relations requires strategic thinking, problem-solving capability, and other management skills.

Objectives

Journalists gather and select information for the primary purpose of providing the public with news and information. Professors David Dozier and William Ehling state that in journalism, "communication activities are an end in themselves." Public relations personnel also gather facts and information for the purpose of informing the public, but their objective is different. Public relations communication activity is a means to the end—a way of managing competition and conflict in the best interests of the practitioner's employer. In other words, the objective is not only to inform, but also to change people's attitudes and behaviors so as to further an organization's goals and objectives.

Whereas journalists are objective observers, public relations personnel are advocates. Harold Burson, chairman of the Burson-Marsteller public relations firm, makes the following point:

To be effective and credible, public relations messages must be based on facts. Nevertheless, we are advocates, and we need to remember that. We are advocates of a particular point of view—our client's or our employer's point of view. And while we recognize that serving the public interest best serves our client's interest, we are not journalists. That's not our job.

Audiences

Journalists write primarily for a mass audience—readers, listeners,

The channels that public relations professionals employ may combine mass media outlets—newspapers, magazines, radio, and television. They may also include direct mail, pamphlets, posters, newsletters, trade journals, special events, and messages shared via blogs, social media networks, or websites.

What is Public Relations?

12

Why is it important that journalists remain objective?

or viewers of the medium for which they work. By definition, mass audiences are not well defined. A journalist on a daily newspaper, for example, writes for the general public. A public relations professional, in contrast, carefully segments audiences based on various demographic and psychological characteristics. Such research allows public relations messages to be tailored to audience needs, concerns, and interests for maximum effect.

Channels

Most journalists, by nature of their employment, reach audiences through one channel—the medium that publishes or broadcasts their work. Public relations professionals use a variety of channels to reach their target audiences.

b t w ...

China has the fastest-growing public relations market in the world. The country, with more than 1.3 billion people, now has approximately 20,000 public relations practitioners and 3,000 public relations firms. Among them are a host of international public relations firms in residence, whose presence reflects China's emergence as a major economic power.

The Economist reported that in 2010, public relations revenues rose 33 percent to $242 million. The China International Public Relations Association (CIPRA) estimated even higher revenues, and the industry continues to experience double-digit growth every year. The growth of Chinese public relations began to take off in the early 1990s as the country started to develop a market economy. Its gross domestic product (GDP) has rapidly expanded in recent years, and the central government has given a boost to the public relations industry by initiating significant mass media reforms, which in turn have resulted in a friendlier environment for business news and product publicity.

China also has joined the World Trade Organization (WTO), which has led to more public relations activity by international companies that are competing fiercely for customers around the globe. The biggest development, according to *The Economist,* is the soaring demand for public relations among Chinese companies as they actively seek local consumers, foreign investment, and international outlets for their goods.

Undoubtedly, China's public relations practitioners will become leaders in the practice of digital public relations. Blogger Chris Lee of planetcontent.co.uk, reported on a statement by Ogilvy PR officials in 2011 that there are an estimated 470 million Internet users in China, and half of those access the web on mobile devices. Lee notes that China is the only Asian country in which people typically have more online than offline friends. Trust in Internet sources is high—45 percent of Chinese trust online reviews, and trust in bloggers is "huge," according to Lee. Microblogging is popular, Lee writes, and you can say more in 140 Mandarin characters than you can in 140 English-language characters. This all suggests a potentially receptive audience in China, ready for digital, social media, and online public relations campaigns.

HOW PUBLIC RELATIONS DIFFERS FROM advertising

Just as many people mistakenly equate publicity with public relations, there is also some confusion about the distinction between publicity (one area of public relations) and advertising.

Although publicity and advertising both use mass media to disseminate messages, the format and context are different. Publicity—information about an event, an individual or group, or a product—appears as a news item or feature story in the mass media. Material is prepared by public relations personnel and submitted to news

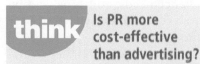

think **Is PR more cost-effective than advertising?**

departments for consideration. Reporters and editors, in their crucial role as gatekeepers, determine whether the material will be used or simply thrown away.

Advertising, in contrast, involves paid space and broadcast time. For example, organizations and individuals may contract with the advertising department of a mass

media outlet for a full-page ad or a 60-second commercial. An organization writes the advertisement, chooses the type style and graphics, and controls where and when the advertisement runs. In other words, advertising involves renting space in a medium, where the advertiser has considerable control over the final message. The lion's share of revenues for all mass media comes from the sale of advertising space.

Other differences between public relations and advertising are summarized in the nearby table.

The major disadvantage of advertising is its cost. For example, a full-page color ad in the national edition of *Parade* magazine, which is distributed weekly in 610 newspapers to a circulation of 67 million, costs as much as $1 million. Costs for advertising campaigns that appear on network television can run multimillions of dollars. For this reason, companies increasingly use one tool of public relations—product publicity—that is more cost-effective and often more credible because the message appears in a news context. Product publicity is news coverage of a product or service. While the message is not as controlled as purchased advertising space, it is believed to be more credible. One national study, for example, found that almost 70 percent of consumers place more weight on media coverage than advertising when determining their trust of companies and buying a product or service.

Advertising	Public Relations
Advertising works almost exclusively through mass media outlets.	Public relations relies on a number of communication tools—social media, brochures, special events, speeches, news releases, feature stories, etc.
Advertising is addressed to external audiences—primarily consumers of goods and services.	Public relations presents its message to specialized external publics (stockholders, vendors, community leaders, environmental groups, and so on) and internal audiences (employees).
Advertising is readily identified as a specialized communication function.	Public relations is broader in scope than advertising, dealing with the policies and performance of the entire organization, from the morale of employees to the way telephone operators respond to calls.
Advertising is often used as a communication tool in public relations.	Public relations' activity often supports advertising campaigns.
Advertising's function is primarily to sell goods and services.	Public relations' function is to help an organization thrive in complex, competitive environments. This goal calls for dealing with economic, social, and political factors that can affect the organization.

HOW PUBLIC RELATIONS DIFFERS FROM marketing

Public relations is distinct from marketing in several ways, although the boundaries between marketing and public relations often overlap. Both deal with an organization's relationships and employ similar communication tools to reach the public. They also share the ultimate purpose of ensuring an organization's success and economic survival. Public relations and marketing, however, approach this task from somewhat different perspectives.

Public relations is concerned with building relationships and generating goodwill for the organization; marketing is concerned with customers and selling products and services. Public relations does support sales, but additionally deals with a broad array of publics beyond customers. As James E. Grunig, editor of *Excellence in Public Relations and Communication Management*, explains:

[T]he marketing function should communicate with the markets for an organization's goods and services. Public relations should be concerned with all the publics of the organization. The major purpose of marketing is to make money for the organization by increasing the slope of the demand curve. The major purpose of public relations is to save money for the organization by building relationships with publics that constrain or enhance the ability of the organization to meet its mission.

Grunig also points out a fundamental difference between marketing and public relations in terms of how the public is described. Marketing and advertising professionals tend to speak of "target markets," "consumers," and "customers." Public relations professionals talk about "publics," "audiences," and

"stakeholders"—that is, groups that are affected by or can affect an organization. According to Grunig, "Publics can arise within stakeholder categories—such as employees, communities, stockholders, governments, members, students, suppliers, and donors, as well as consumers."

Philip Kotler, professor of marketing at Northwestern University and the author of a leading marketing textbook, calls public relations the fifth "P" of marketing strategy, the original four Ps being product, price, place, and promotion. As he wrote in *Harvard Business Review*, "Public relations takes longer to cultivate, but when energized, it can help pull the company into the market."

When public relations is used to directly support an organization's marketing objectives, it is called

The goal of public relations is to attain and maintain accord and positive behaviors among social groupings on which an organization depends to achieve its mission. The fundamental responsibility of public relations as a management process is to **build and maintain a hospitable environment** for an organization.

The goal of marketing is to attract and satisfy customers (or clients) on a long-term basis to achieve an organization's economic objectives. The fundamental responsibility of marketing as a management process is to **build and maintain markets** for an organization's products or services.

VS

Old Spice was looking to leverage the popularity of its "Old Spice Guy" Isaiah Mustafa to publicize a new advertising campaign. An interview with Oprah via Skype, two appearances on *The Ellen DeGeneres Show,* coverage in *Entertainment Weekly* and USATODAY.com, and more resulted in an unbelievable 2 billion-plus impressions.

> "In its market-support function, public relations is used to achieve a number of objectives. The most important of these are to raise awareness, to inform and educate, to gain understanding, to build trust, to make friends, to give people reasons to buy, and, finally, to create a climate of consumer acceptance.

Thomas Harris, *The Marketer's Guide to Public Relations*

marketing communications. This capacity was identified as a component of public relations earlier in the chapter.

Thomas Harris coined the term "marketing public relations" in his book *The Marketer's Guide to Public Relations*. He writes:

> I make a clear distinction between those public relations functions [that] support marketing, which I call marketing public relations (MPR), and the other public relations activities that define the corporation's relationships with its non-customer publics, which I label corporate public relations (CPR).

Dennis L. Wilcox (one of the authors of this text), in *Public Relations Writing and Media Techniques* (seventh edition), lists eight ways in which public relations activities contribute to fulfilling marketing objectives:

1 **Develop** new prospects for new markets, such as people who inquire after seeing or hearing a product release in the news media

2 **Provide** third-party endorsements—via newspapers, magazines, radio, and television—through news releases about a company's products or services, community involvement, inventions, and new plans

3 **Generate** sales leads, usually through articles in the trade press about new products and services

4 **Pave** the way for sales calls

5 **Stretch** an organization's advertising and promotional dollars through timely and supportive news releases

6 **Provide** inexpensive sales literature—articles about a company and its products can be reprinted as informative pieces for prospective customers

7 **Establish** a corporation as an authoritative source of information on a given product

8 **Help** sell minor products that don't have large advertising budgets

TOWARD AN INTEGRATED PERSPECTIVE: strategic COMMUNICATION

Although well-defined differences exist among the fields of advertising, marketing, and public relations, there is an increasing realization that an organization's goals and objectives can be best accomplished through an integrated approach, not just through marketing but through all communication functions. This understanding gave rise in the 1990s to such terms as *integrated marketing communications*, *convergent communications*, and *integrated communications*.

Several factors fuel the trend toward integration:

1 Downsizing and reengineering of organizations have led to consolidated departments and reduced the number of staff members dedicated to various communication functions. As a result, one department, with fewer employees, is expected to do a greater variety of communication tasks.

2 Organizational marketing and communication departments are making do with tighter budgets. To avoid the high cost of advertising, many organizations are looking for alternative ways to deliver messages. These efforts may include building buzz by word-of-mouth, targeting influentials (i.e., "opinion leaders" or "trend setters"), web marketing, grassroots marketing, media relations and product publicity, and event sponsorship.

3 There is a growing realization that advertising, with its high costs, isn't the silver bullet that it used to be. Part of the problem is the increasing

"We're beginning to see research that supports the superiority of PR over advertising to launch a brand. A recent study of 91 new product launches shows highly successful products are more likely to use PR-related activities than less successful ones…. PR creates the brand. Advertising defends the brand."

Al and Laura Ries, *The Fall of Advertising and the Rise of PR*

clutter of advertising (one estimate is that the average U.S. consumer is exposed to 237 ads each day, or about 86,000 each year) and advertising's general lack of credibility among consumers.

The concept of integration reflects the increasing sophistication of organizations as they seek to use a variety of strategies and tactics to convey a consistent message. Think of a golfer with a variety of clubs in her bag. She may use one club (public relations) to launch a product, another club (advertising) to reinforce the message, and yet another club (Internet marketing) to actually sell the product or service to a well-defined audience.

Strategic communication requires grit and determination—but more specifically GRRIT—to successfully integrate advertising, marketing, and public relations:

G lobal/multicultural
R esearch based
R elationship focused
I nternet/new media oriented
T oolbox-driven tactics

GRRIT enables professionals to battle for success on behalf of an organization across a broad range of goals—from increased sales or better community relations, to brand loyalty or long-term donations for worthwhile causes.

4 It is now widely recognized that the marketing of products and services can be affected by public and social policy issues. For example, environmental legislation influences packaging and the content of products, a proposed luxury tax on expensive autos affects sales of those cars, and a company's support of Planned Parenthood or health benefits for same-sex partners may spur a product boycott.

The impact of such factors, which have not traditionally been considered by marketing managers, has led many professionals to suggest that organizations should do a better job of integrating public relations and public affairs into their overall marketing considerations.

Jack Bergen, senior vice president of corporate affairs and marketing

Starbucks raised awareness of environmental issues. The company noted that the typical person who replaces paper cups with a coffee mug saves seven trees each year. As part of a larger awareness campaign, Starbucks gave 1.2 million customers a free cup of coffee on a single day if the customer brought in his or her own mug.

for Siemens Corporation, agrees that organizations should do a better job of integrating public relations and public affairs into their overall marketing considerations. In an interview with *PRWeek*, he noted that public relations is the best place for leading strategy in marketing: "In developing strategy, you have multiple stakeholders. PR

people understand the richness of the audiences that have an interest in the company; advertising just focuses on customers. Strategy is the development of options to accomplish an objective. PR people can develop these as they have the multiplicity of audiences and channels to use to reach them."

The concept of integration is less controversial than its implementation. It makes sense for an organization to coordinate its messages and communication strategies, but considerable discord arises on exactly how to accomplish this.

According to the consulting firm Osgood O'Donnell & Walsh, "The single biggest obstacle is company structure." In an article for *The Strategist*, the firm's principals wrote, "The communications functions—corporate communications, advertising, investor relations, and governmental affairs—are usually in different silos within companies, and interaction between their leaders is, for the most part voluntary (i.e., not required by senior management) and informal."

In some organizations, the marketing department has the dominant voice, and public relations is relegated to a support function in terms of techniques instead of playing a role in overall strategy development. This often means that public relations is responsible only for tactical work, such as creating product publicity, planning event promotions, and arranging media interviews at trade shows. Problems also arise in other organizations

What Would You Do?

Managing Competition

Yogurtini is a relatively new player in the burgeoning frozen yogurt business, and it faces stiff competition in the marketplace from more established brands such as TCBY, Pinkberry, and Red Mango. You have just been hired to help the company out with its public relations efforts.

The first Yogurtini was founded in Tempe, Arizona. There are now 15 stores in eight states, with 13 more locations "coming soon." In these stores, customers personalize their servings by filling their own cups with anywhere from 10 to 16 flavors and choosing from 65 toppings. Yogurtini promotes the concept: "Swirl it, top it, weigh it, pay it."

Imagine that research shows that the typical Yogurtini customer is a woman between the ages of 24 and 35, who brings her friends and family members with her to the shop. The company has decided to do an integrated communications program for the next year that would involve public relations, advertising, and in-store marketing promotions. The focus will be on enhancing the visibility of its stores at the local level and making Yogurtini a distinct brand among the clutter of other frozen yogurt franchises in the community. Do some brainstorming. Which ideas and activities would you suggest? Remember—you need to be creative because you don't have a big budget.

when advertising agencies attempt to do integrated programs. In many such cases, 90 percent of the communication budget is spent on advertising and 10 percent or less is spent on public relations.

Fortunately, such stories are becoming rarer as an increasing number of organizations have begun to emphasize the team approach to integrated communications. Experts in the various disciplines (advertising, public relations, direct promotion, marketing) now typically work as a team from the very beginning of a project. The role of public relations in the marketing mix is essentially defined by competition in the marketplace—competition between brands, competition for market share, and even competition for the loyalty of consumers.

9 Ways Public Relations Contributes to the Bottom Line

It is often said that public relations is a management process, not an event. Patrick Jackson, active in PRSA national leadership and a leading public relations counselor for many years, formulated this chart to show how public relations can contribute to the success of any organization.

PROCESS	PRINCIPAL ACTIVITIES	OUTCOMES
1 Awareness and information	Publicity, promotion, audience targeting	Pave the way for sales, fund-raising, stock offerings
2 Organizational motivation	Internal relations and communication	Build morale, teamwork, productivity, corporate culture
3 Issue anticipation	Research, liaison with audiences	Provide early warning on issues, constituency unrest, social/political anticipation
4 Opportunity identification	Interact with internal and external audiences	Discover new markets, products, audiences, methods, allies, issues
5 Crisis management	Respond to (or prevent) issues, coalition building	Protect position, retain allies and constituents, keep normal operations going despite battles
6 Overcoming executive isolation	Counsel senior managers	Encourage realistic, competitive, enlightened decisions
7 Change agent	Interact with internal and external audiences, research	Ease resistance to change, promote smooth transition
8 Social responsibility	Research, mount public interest projects and tie-ins, promote volunteerism/philanthropy	Create reputation, earn trust
9 Influencing public policy	Foster constituency relations, build coalitions, lobby, promote grassroots campaigns	Ensure public consent to activities, products, policies; remove political barriers

summary

What Is Public Relations?

- Terms found in most definitions of public relations include deliberate, planned, performance, public interest, two-way communication, strategic management of competition, and conflict management function.

- Public relations is well established in the United States and throughout the world. Growth in this sector is currently strong in Europe and Asia, particularly China.

- The public relations process can be described with the RACE acronym: research, action, communication, evaluation.

What Are the Components of Public Relations?

- Public relations work includes counseling, media relations, publicity, community relations, governmental affairs, employee relations, investor relations, development/fund-raising, special events, and marketing communications.

- Bloggers need to be handled with care when it comes to social media and public relations. Many bloggers are citizen journalists and public relations practitioners should be honest and transparent with them.

How Does Public Relations Differ from Journalism?

- Although writing is an important activity in both public relations and journalism, the scope, objectives, and channels are different for journalism and public relations.

How Does Public Relations Differ from Advertising?

- Publicity is just one area within public relations. Publicity employs mass media to disseminate messages, as does advertising, although the format and context differ for PR and advertising.

- Publicity goes through media gatekeepers, who make the ultimate decision whether to use the material as part of a news story. Advertising involves paid space or time and is separate from news/editorial content.

How Does Public Relations Differ from Marketing?

- The functions of public relations often overlap with those of marketing. However, the primary purpose of public relations is to build relationships and generate goodwill with a variety of publics, whereas marketing focuses on customers and the sale of products and services.

- Public relations can be part of a marketing strategy. In such cases, it is often called marketing communications.

How Can an Integrated Approach to Public Relations Benefit an Organization?

- An organization's goals and objectives are best achieved by integrating the activities of advertising, marketing, and public relations to create a consistent message.

- Integration requires teamwork and the recognition that each field has strengths that complement and reinforce one another.

questions
FOR REVIEW AND DISCUSSION

1 There are many definitions of public relations. Of those found in this chapter, which do you think best reflects reality? Why?

2 Why is public relations so difficult to define? How would you define it based on what you know now?

3 Which of the steps in the public relations process do you think are most important to a successful campaign? Why?

4 Feedback is considered an important part of the public relations process. Why?

5 How do social media offer both opportunities and obstacles for public relations practitioners?

6 Many people think of public relations practitioners simply as "in-house journalists." What are some of the major differences between public relations and journalism?

7 How should public relations practitioners work with bloggers? How do bloggers differ from journalists?

8 What are the pros and cons of using public relations versus advertising to raise awareness about an organization's product or service?

9 It has been asserted that public relations creates brands, whereas advertising can reinforce and defend a brand. Do you agree? Why or why not?

10 How does James Grunig differentiate between publics and stakeholders? How might this differentiation be useful in developing PR strategies?

11 How can PR fulfill marketing objectives?

12 Describe the concept of integrated communications (IC), which some people also call integrated marketing communications (IMC). Which four factors have led to the growth of integrated campaigns?

MySearchLab®

More Than Words: How to Really Redefine the Term "Public Relations"

Posted by Steve Radick | December 9, 2011

www.comPRehension.prsa.org

Trade organizations like PRSA have the responsibility to promote professionalism within their disciplines by keeping members on the cutting edge.

The PR toolbox of tactics may have little to do with a broad definition of public relations. What do you think?

Edward Bernays didn't think that propaganda is a dirty word. Do you think attitudes have shifted over the years? Some public relations scholars still contend that there's little difference between public relations and propaganda. Other scholars argue that propaganda is unethical, but PR is not.

Indeed, even with an ever enlarging toolbox of tactics and media, public relations must remember to focus on the "relations part."

While revisiting definitions may be important, because public relations focuses on relationships and the management thereof, actions do matter.

There's big news in the public relations industry this week as the Public Relations Society of America (PRSA) recently announced that they are embarking on an international effort to modernize the definition of public relations. Chartered in 1947, PRSA is the world's largest and foremost organization of public relations professionals and boasts a community of more than 21,000 members across the United States. Their current definition of public relations — *"public relations helps an organization and its publics adapt mutually to each other"* was last updated in 1982, before Twitter, before Facebook, hell, even before you had a computer at your desk. Technology has changed a lot over the last 30 years. So to have the ways in which organizations and their publics relate to one another, it's definitely time for a change.

Unfortunately, ever since the days of **Edward Bernays**, public relations has had its roots in "managing the message." Public relations grew out of propaganda, spin and manipulation — no wonder we've had an image problem for the last 100 years! Too many public relations practitioners have become so focused on the message that they have totally forgotten the *relations* part of public relations. As **The Cluetrain Manifesto** taught us way back in 1999 (also before social media), "public relations does not relate to the public; companies are deeply afraid of their markets."

PRSA (disclaimer: I've been a member of PRSA or PRSSA since 2000.) should take this same advice while redefining the definition of public relations. The words might end up being totally accurate and insightful, but if public relations practitioners don't also change their actions, the perception of the industry will never change. I hope that all PRSA members would realize the perception of public relations is about more than words — it's about actions.

What is Public Relations?

And with that, here are ten actions that I'd like to become part of the new definition of public relations:

1. Instead of spamming my email pitches to massive distribution lists, **I will put in more than ten seconds of effort** and personalize it to the reporter/blogger/writer/anchor/editor I'm contacting.

2. I will stop being a yes-man for my clients and actually provide the **expert** communications counsel I'm (hopefully) being paid to provide.

3. I will learn how to speak with an actual **human voice** instead of the voice of mission statements, brochures and marketing pitches.

4. I will not forget the *relations* in public relations and will try to develop real relationships with the members of the media I work with **instead of treating them like pawns that can be manipulated**.

5. I will stop snowing my clients and inflating my value through the use of ambiguous outputs like hits, impressions and ad equivalency, and instead focus on the **outcomes** that public relations has helped accomplish.

6. I can no longer be the man behind the curtain, ghostwriting messages and press releases while I hide behind my brand or organization. I will take responsibility for my **strategies** and **tactics**.

7. Regardless of my age, I will recognize that keeping up with and understanding technology is now a job requirement.

8. Likewise, I will stop assuming that social media IS public relations and vice versa. Social media is becoming a much larger aspect of public relations and present practitioners with new tools to use, but they are **not one in the same**.

9. Public relations cannot exist in a vacuum — I realize that my public relations efforts will be more effective if I **collaborate and communicate regularly** with marketing, advertising, strategy, operations and other groups throughout the organization.

10. And finally, I will recognize that good public relations isn't about manipulating media coverage — it's about helping an organization **create and maintain stronger relationships** with all of its stakeholders.

Redefining "public relations" is a crucial first step, but changing the perception of public relations will require more than words — it will require a shift in the thinking and the actions of thousands of public relations professionals. Let's start modeling the behaviors we hope to instill in all public relations practitioners and start taking public relations from messages to actions.

Text Credits

Credits are listed in order of appearance.

Reprinted by permission of Harold Burson.

Photo Credits

Credits are listed in order of appearance.

Dmitriy Shironosov/Shutterstock;
Ilja Mašík/Shutterstock;
Bangalore Office India/Alamy;
Michael Tercha/MCT/Newscom;
Lana Sundman/Alamy;
Charleston Animal Society;
WireImage/Getty Images;

Harry Vorsteher/Media Bakery;
ZUMA Press/Newscom;
(bl) Monkey Business Images/Shutterstock;
(br) Konstantin Chagin/Shutterstock;
Robin Platzer/Twin Images/LFI/Photoshot/
Newscom;
(br) ZUMA Press/Newscom; (bl) Stephen

Coburn/Shutterstock;
(tc) Vitaly Korovin/Shutterstock; (bl) WimL/
Shutterstock

Tactics image: Petr Z/Shutterstock
Tablet image: Falconia/Shutterstock

The Growth of a Profession

The Growth of a Profession

The Advancement of Women

The history of public relations is also a story about the contributions of women to the profession. Today, women such as Beth Comstock, chief marketing officer and senior vice president of General Electric, have made notable contributions and achieved high-level executive positions. Comstock leads GE's sales, marketing, and communications functions, after a succession of publicity and promotion roles at GE, NBC, CBS, and Turner Broadcasting.

The success of women like Comstock, of course, is due in part to the pioneering efforts of many women in the field. Among those sometimes unsung heroes are Doris Fleishman, Betsy Plank, and Inez Kaiser. One of the first female pioneers in the business was Doris Fleishman, the wife and business partner of Edward L. Bernays, who is often referred to as the "father of modern public relations."

In 1920, Fleishman went to Atlanta (in place of her husband) to promote media coverage of the NAACP convention in Georgia's newspapers. It was the first NAACP convention held in the South, and PR historian Susan Henry says it was important to have Fleishman handle this sensitive situation because her style was less antagonistic than Bernays's. Ever the trailblazer, Fleishman compiled and edited *An Outline of Careers for Women: A Practical Guide to Achievement* in 1928.

Betsy Plank, who broke the glass ceiling in the early 1960s by becoming vice president of public relations for Illinois Bell in Chicago, also opened doors for women in the field. She is referred to as "the First Lady in public relations" because she was the first female to become president of the Public Relations Society of America. In her later years, she was the "godmother" of the Public Relations Student Society of America (PRSSA) and a strong advocate for public relations education. Today, her legacy is being carried out by the Plank Center for Leadership in Public Relations at the University of Alabama.

Inez Kaiser blazed a new trail in 1962 by becoming the first African American woman to head a public relations firm with national clients. She was also the first African-American woman to join the Public Relations Society of America, the first African-American inducted into the Hall of Fame for Women in Public Relations, and the first African-American woman to join the Kansas City Chamber of Commerce. She is honored today by the public relations division of the Association for Education in Journalism and Mass Communications (AEJMC) with a scholarship in her name for graduate students of color.

1 How are the attitudes of society reflected in the comparatively short list of female heroes in public relations?

2 What sort of obstacles do you think early female pioneers faced in the field? Do you think those obstacles still exist?

3 Do you think the obstacles faced by women are or were similar or different to those that multicultural practitioners faced?

Ask Yourself

> Which Key Events and Individuals Shaped the History of Public Relations?

> What Are the Trends in Today's Practice of Public Relations?

> In What Ways Is Public Relations Evolving and Growing as a Professional Practice?

> What Are the Major Professional Public Relations Organizations and What Do They Do?

A Brief History
OF PUBLIC RELATIONS

The practice of public relations is not new. In ancient epochs, practitioners used public relations tactics to manage conflict and to gain a competitive advantage over rival individuals or points of view.

Ancient Beginnings

The roots of public relations stretch back to the civilizations of Babylonia, Greece, and Rome. Ancient civilizations used persuasion to promote the authority of governments and religions. Of course, these efforts were not known as "public relations" at the time, but the techniques would certainly be familiar to public relations practitioners today: interpersonal communication with opinion leaders, public speeches, written and visual communication, staged events, publicity, and other tactics.

It has often been said that the Rosetta Stone, which provided a key for modern translation and understanding of ancient Egyptian hieroglyphics, was basically a publicity release touting the pharaoh's accomplishments. Similarly, the organizers of the ancient Olympic Games used promotional techniques to enhance the perception of athletes as heroes in much the same way as we do in the modern Olympic Games. Then, as now, athletes competed on and off the field for the hearts and minds of sports fans, employing public relations tactics such as public appearances and media interviews.

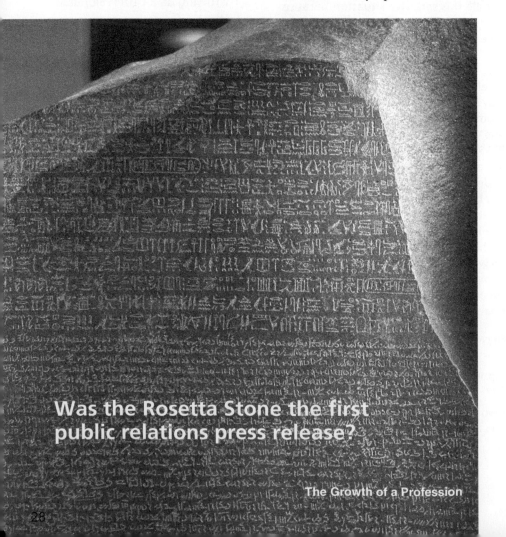

Was the Rosetta Stone the first public relations press release?

think Can you think of a modern instance of a religious or political organization using public relations to promote a position to the public?

Politician Julius Caesar had ambitions to become emperor of the Roman Empire. To that end, he organized elaborate parades whenever he returned from winning a battle to burnish his image as an outstanding commander and leader. After Caesar became a consul of Rome in 59 BCE, he had clerks make records of senatorial and other public proceedings and post them on walls throughout the city. These *acta diurna*, or "daily doings," were among the world's first newspapers.

The concept of conflict is likewise not a new theme in the practice of public relations. Pope Urban II persuaded thousands of followers to serve God and gain forgiveness for their sins by engaging in the Holy Crusades against the Muslims. Six centuries later, the Church was among the first to use the word *propaganda*, when Pope Gregory XV established the College of Propaganda to supervise foreign missions and train priests to propagate the faith.

Public Relations in Colonial America

To promote immigration to America, in 1584, Sir Walter Raleigh sent back to England glowing accounts of what

During the Renaissance (in the fifteenth and sixteenth centuries), Florentine and Venetian bankers practiced the fine art of investor relations. They were probably the first, along with local Catholic bishops, to promote the concept of corporate philanthropy by sponsoring such artists as da Vinci, Michelangelo, Titian, and Tintoretto.

was in reality a swamp-filled Roanoke Island. (Eric the Red adopted the same persuasive tactic, circa 985 CE, when he discovered a land of ice and rock and named it Greenland.) Spanish explorers publicized the never-discovered Seven Cities of Gold and the fabled Fountain of Youth to lure prospective adventurers and colonists to the New World.

Public relations played an active role in building support for the conflict that led to American independence—engaging in what modern public relations practitioners term *conflict positioning*. The Boston Tea Party, which *PRWeek* has called the "the greatest and best-known publicity stunt of all time," was orchestrated by Samuel Adams, a man who understood that symbolism can sway public opinion. The colonists threw crates of tea leaves from a British trade ship into

Boston Harbor to protest excessive British taxation on items such as tea, and the rest is history.

Thomas Paine's persuasive writing was similarly instrumental in bringing lukewarm citizens into the Revolutionary movement. His pamphlet titled "Common Sense" sold more than 120,000 copies in three months in 1776. Influencing the makeup of the new political system were the *Federalist Papers*, 85 letters written by Alexander Hamilton, James Madison, and John Jay.

The Age of the Press Agent

The 1800s was a period of growth and expansion in the United States, an era that featured growing competition for consumer attention and loyalty. It also was the golden age of the press agent—a publicist who works

for recognition of an organization or individual. The period was the age of hype, in which organizations employed the media and various tactics to promote individuals, causes, products, and services.

Press agents succeeded in glorifying Davy Crockett as a frontier hero to draw political support from Andrew Jackson and made a legend out of frontiersman Daniel Boone. John Burke was the press agent who made Buffalo Bill's Wild West Show a household phrase throughout the United States. Buffalo Bill and Annie Oakley were the rock stars of their age.

These old-time press agents and the people they represented played on the gullibility of the public and its desire to be entertained. Advertisements and press releases were exaggerated to the point of being outright lies. Doing advance work for an attraction, press agents would drop tickets on the desk of a newspaper editor along with the announcements. Generous publicity generally followed on the heels of these gifts, and the journalists and their families flocked to the free entertainment with little regard for the ethical considerations that largely prohibits such practices today.

It is no surprise, then, that today's public relations practitioner, exercising the highly sophisticated skills of evaluation, counseling, communications, and influencing management policies, shudders at the suggestion that public relations grew out of press agentry. And yet some aspects of modern public relations have their roots in the practice.

Public Relations Grows as America Grows

Just as they were used to lure colonists to seventeenth-century America, publicity and promotion were employed in the nineteenth century to populate the western United States. Land speculators distributed pamphlets and publicity that described almost every community as "the garden spot of the West," which one critic of the time called "downright puffery, full of exaggerated statements, and high-wrought and false-colored descriptions." One brochure about Nebraska, for example, described the territory as the "Gulf Stream of migration … bounded on the north by the 'Aurora Borealis' and on the south by the Day of Judgment." Other brochures were more down-to-earth but still stretched the truth, describing the fertile land and abundant water, and touting the opportunity to build a fortune.

American railroads, in particular, used extensive public relations and press agentry to attract settlers and expand their operations. People and communities were needed throughout the western United States to provide a business opportunity for rail companies. Consequently, such companies as the Burlington and Missouri Railroad took it upon themselves to promote western settlement. To lure settlers from Britain, the Burlington and Missouri Railroad set up an information office in Liverpool that distributed fact sheets and maps and placed stories in the local press. In addition, the railroad promoted lectures about migrating to the American West.

Near the end of the nineteenth century, the Atchison, Topeka and Santa Fe Railway launched a campaign to entice tourists to the Southwest. It commissioned dozens of painters and photographers to depict the dramatic landscape and portray romanticized American Indians weaving, grinding corn, and dancing.

A wave of industrialization and urbanization swept the nation after the American Civil War. New concentrations of wealth led to concerns about business practices. In 1888, the Mutual Life Insurance Company hired a journalist to

b t w …

Phineas T. Barnum, the great American showman of the nineteenth century, was the master of what historian Daniel Boorstin calls the *pseudoevent*—a planned happening that occurs primarily for the purpose of being reported. Barnum used flowery language and exaggeration to promote his various attractions in an age when the public was hungry for entertainment.

Barnum knew the value of opinion leaders and third-party endorsement. Through his press agentry, Tom Thumb became one of the sensations of the century. Standing just over 30 inches tall, Thumb was exceptional at singing, dancing, and performing comedy monologues. Barnum made Thumb a European phenomenon by introducing him to society leaders in London. An invitation to Buckingham Palace followed, and from then on Thumb played to packed houses every night.

Another Barnum success was the promotion of Jenny Lind, the "Swedish Nightingale." Barnum promoted her and her beautiful singing on a national tour in the United States, making her a pop icon even before the American Civil War. Barnum filled auditoriums on opening nights by donating part of the proceeds to charity. As a civic activity, the event attracted many of the town's opinion leaders, whereupon the general public flocked to attend succeeding performances. This tactic is still employed today by entertainment publicists.

Henry Ford was the first major industrialist in the United States, and he was among the first to use two basic public relations concepts. The first was the notion of positioning—the idea that credit and publicity always go to those who do something first. The second idea was the importance of being accessible to the press.

In 1900, Ford obtained press coverage of the prototype Model T by demonstrating it to a reporter from the *Detroit Tribune.* By 1903, Ford was receiving widespread publicity by racing his cars—a practice still used by today's automakers ("Win on Sunday; sell on Monday"). Ford hired Barney Oldfield, a champion bicycle racer and a popular personality, to drive a Model T at a record speed of about 60 miles per hour. The publicity from these speed runs gave Ford financial backing and a ready market.

Ford became a household name because he was willing to be interviewed by the press on almost any subject, including the gold standard, evolution, alcohol, foreign affairs, and even capital punishment.

write news releases designed to stave off criticism and improve its image. In 1889, Westinghouse Corporation established what is thought to be the first in-house publicity department. In 1897, the term public relations was first used by the Association of American Railroads in a company listing.

The Rise of Politics and Activism

The nineteenth century also saw the development and use of public relations tactics on the political and activist front. Amos Kendall, a former Kentucky newspaper editor, became an intimate member of President Andrew Jackson's "Kitchen Cabinet"; he could be considered the first presidential press secretary.

Kendall sampled public opinion on issues, advised Jackson, and skillfully interpreted the

Carrie Nation employed dramatic tactics in her campaign against liquor.

president's rough-hewn ideas, molding them into powerful speeches and news releases. He also served as Jackson's advance agent on trips, wrote glowing articles that he sent to supportive newspapers, and is believed to be the first person to use newspaper reprints in public relations campaigns. Almost every complimentary story or editorial written about Jackson was reprinted and widely circulated. Article reprints are still a standard tactic in PR practice.

Supporters and leaders of causes such as abolition, suffrage, and prohibition of alcohol also employed publicity to maximum effect throughout the nineteenth century. One of the most influential publicity ventures for the abolition movement was the publication of Harriet Beecher Stowe's *Uncle Tom's Cabin.* Amelia Bloomer, a women's rights

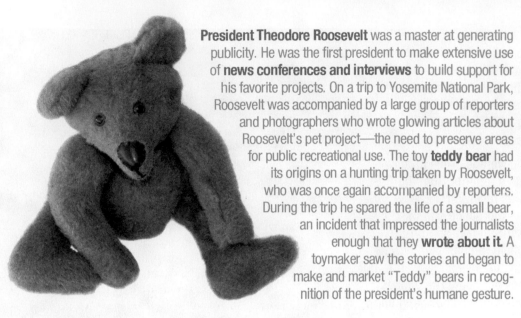

President Theodore Roosevelt was a master at generating publicity. He was the first president to make extensive use of **news conferences and interviews** to build support for his favorite projects. On a trip to Yosemite National Park, Roosevelt was accompanied by a large group of reporters and photographers who wrote glowing articles about Roosevelt's pet project—the need to preserve areas for public recreational use. The toy **teddy bear** had its origins on a hunting trip taken by Roosevelt, who was once again accompanied by reporters. During the trip he spared the life of a small bear, an incident that impressed the journalists enough that they **wrote about it.** A toymaker saw the stories and began to make and market "Teddy" bears in recognition of the president's humane gesture.

advocate, garnered plenty of media publicity by wearing loose-fitting trousers in protest of the corset. Noted temperance crusader Carrie Nation became nationally known by invading saloons and destroying the liquor bottles and bars with an axe.

Activists like these have used public relations tactics throughout history. In the 1860s, naturalist John Muir wrote in the *New York Times* and other publications about the importance of protecting the Yosemite Valley in California. In 1889, he worked with the editor of *Century Magazine*, Robert Underwood Johnson, to promote a campaign requesting congressional support for Yosemite National Park. This activist public relations campaign succeeded—and generations of people have enjoyed the benefits of a protected Yosemite.

Modern Public Relations Comes of Age

As the use of publicity gained acceptance, the first publicity agency, known as the Publicity Bureau, was established in Boston in 1900, with Harvard College as its most prestigious client. George F. Parker and Ivy Ledbetter Lee opened a publicity office in New York City in 1904. Public relations practice continued to evolve in the 1900s, as business leaders and politicians increasingly

employed public relations tactics. This growth also provided an opportunity for the rise of the independent counselor.

Although public relations practitioners through the ages have been thoughtful about their communication approaches, the idea of public relations as a strategic endeavor really took hold in the early twentieth century. The Georgia-born, Princeton-educated Ivy Ledbetter Lee was the first public relations counselor. He began as a journalist, became a publicist, and soon expanded that role to become the first public relations counsel.

When Lee opened his public relations firm, he issued a declaration of principles that signaled a new practice model: public information. His emphasis was on the dissemination of truthful, accurate information rather than the distortions, hype, and exaggerations that characterized press agentry. Lee's declaration, which stemmed from his journalistic orientation, read, in part:

> This is not a secret press bureau. All our work is done in the open. We aim to supply news…. In brief, our plan is, frankly and openly, in behalf of business concerns and public institutions, to supply to the press and the public of the United States prompt and accurate information concerning subjects which is of value and interest to the public.

Lee began by handling media relations for the Pennsylvania Railroad, but is best known for his work for John D. Rockefeller, Jr. Lee was hired to provide strategic counsel in the wake of the vicious strike-breaking activities known as the Ludlow Massacre at the Colorado Fuel and Iron (CF&I) company mine in 1914.

Through a *muscular approach* to public relations—that is, by employing careful strategy and a broad array of tactics—Lee prevented the United Mine Workers from gaining a foothold in the CF&I mines. Through strategic counsel, Lee provided both his client and the miners with some level of success and satisfaction and put their conflict to rest. See the PR Casebook box in this chapter to learn more about Lee's innovative work in the wake of the infamous Ludlow Massacre.

Lee continued as a counselor to the Rockefeller family and its various companies, but he also counseled a number of other clients, too. For example, he advised the American Tobacco Company to initiate a profit-sharing plan, the Pennsylvania Railroad to beautify its stations, and the movie industry to stop inflated advertising and develop a voluntary code of censorship. He also was retained by the New York subway system in 1916 to foster public understanding and support.

Under Ivy Lee's direction, the Interborough Rapid Transit Company (IRT) took an innovative approach, communicating directly with its passengers through pamphlets, brochures, and posters "to establish a close understanding of its work and policies." Designed to resemble the front page of a newspaper, *The Subway Sun* and *The Elevated Express* announced the introduction of coin-operated turnstiles; informed commuters about the opening of the 42nd Street shuttle between Grand Central Station and Times Square; asked riders to not block the doors; and urged them to visit the city's free swimming pools.

Ivy Lee is remembered today for four important contributions to public relations:

- Advancing the concept that business and industry should align themselves with the public interest
- Dealing with top executives and carrying out no program unless it has the active support of management
- Maintaining open communication with the news media
- Emphasizing the necessity of humanizing business and bringing its public relations down to the community level of employees, customers, and neighbors

Another PR innovator was George Creel. A former newspaper reporter, Creel was enlisted by President Woodrow Wilson to organize a massive public relations effort to unite the nation and to influence world opinion during World War I. Wilson accepted Creel's advice that hatred of the Germans should be downplayed and that loyalty and confidence in the government should be emphasized. The newly formed Committee on Public Information publicized the war aims and Wilson's ideals—to make the world safe for democracy and to make World War I "the war to end all wars."

By demonstrating the success of these techniques, this massive publicity effort had a profound effect on the development of public relations. It also awakened awareness of the power of mediated information to change public attitudes and behavior. This realization, coupled with postwar analysis of British propaganda devices, resulted in a number of scholarly books and college courses on the subject. Among these was Walter Lippmann's classic book *Public Opinion* (1922), in which he pointed out how people are moved to action by "the pictures in our heads."

Edward L. Bernays was one of several individuals who served on the Creel Committee and went on to become a successful and widely known public relations counselor. Bernays, through brilliant campaigns and extensive self-promotion, was known as the "father of modern public relations" by the time of his death in 1995 at the age of 103.

Bernays, who was the nephew of Sigmund Freud, conceptualized a model of public relations that emphasized the application of social science research and behavioral psychology to formulate campaigns and messages to change people's perceptions and encourage certain behaviors. In contrast to Lee's public information model, which emphasized the distribution of accurate news, Bernays's model essentially focused on advocacy and scientific persuasion. His process involved listening to the audience, but the sole purpose of

Lee's posters explained the need for fare increases in the 1920s, extolled the fast direct train service to baseball games at Yankee Stadium and the Polo Grounds, and supplied information on how to get to other city institutions. Today, more than 90 years later, Lee's idea of communicating directly to passengers is still being used by public transit systems around the world.

Lee Advises Rockefellers and Coal Industry

IVY LEDBETTER LEE served as a pivotal and controversial figure when the Colorado Fuel and Iron Company (CF&I) took on striking miners in an incident that became known as the Ludlow Massacre.

Public relations scholar Kirk Hallahan has called the Ludlow Massacre "one of the most important episodes in the early development of public relations." Hallahan writes:

"On April 20, 1914, a gun battle broke out between striking miners and the Colorado state militia at the temporary camp set up by strikers outside the mines at Ludlow. Three strikers and one militiaman were killed. However, the real tragedy was revealed when 11 women and children were found dead in one of the many earthen storage pits dug below the tent colony. ... The incident sparked 10 days of widespread violence in the surrounding coal fields, resulting in at least 53 deaths."

The Rockefeller family owned 40 percent interest in CF&I and therefore became a logical, high profile target for union leaders. Coloradoans went to New York to petition John D. Rockefeller, Jr. When he refused to see them, pickets formed outside Rockefeller's New York offices and his home in Tarrytown, NY. As the problem escalated, Ivy Lee was hired as a consultant. His first course of action was to talk Rockefeller out of combating the negative publicity with advertisements. Lee later said, "I advised him that would be in the highest degree unwise, and that no money should be used in any way, directly or indirectly, to influence the attitude of the press on the subject." This stance was consistent with Lee's Declaration of Principles, which stated in part, "All our work is done in the open. We aim to supply news. This is not an advertising agency."

Lee traveled to Colorado to do some firsthand research. He talked to striking miners, politicians, mine supervisors, and military officers. His goal was to assess public opinion to inform his public relations tactics. After his trip, he suggested that the mining company president write an open letter thanking miners for their loyalty during the strike. The letter was published as a poster to be used in the mining camps and as a flyer to be distributed to the miners' homes. A clipping service was also hired to collect newspaper articles from papers across the country. The content of the articles was analyzed and summarized so Lee could keep his thumb on the pulse of the press.

Among Lee's tactics was dissemination of a series of informational bulletins titled, "The Struggle in Colorado for Industrial

John D. Rockefeller, Jr., was portrayed in the press as being seriously concerned about the plight of the workers, and his visit to Colorado resulted in policy changes and more worker benefits. Here, he watches children of miners marching into school.

Freedom." The leaflets were distributed to opinion leaders and journalists across the country. They were compiled into a booklet and distributed to 40,000 people. Hallahan wrote, "Virtually all the material ... drew on information from various reputable sources in government and the community and was provided to Lee by CF&I or Rockefeller officials."

At multiple points, Lee, Rockefeller and CF&I officials were called to testify at government hearings. Lee frequently wrote the testimonial statements for Rockefeller and CF&I. At one of these hearings, it was revealed that there were several factual errors in the leaflets Lee had compiled and distributed. Hallahan surmises that Lee may not have aggressively verified material or perhaps he was simply careless. Controversy arose around the claim that Lee may have deliberately misled opinion leaders and journalists with the content.

Eventually, Lee convinced John D. Rockefeller, Jr. to visit the Colorado mines himself. This trek generated reams of positive publicity as Rockefeller was photographed talking to miners. He even donned a mining helmet and wielded a pickax.

Despite the controversies surrounding the handling of the Ludlow Massacre and striking miners, Lee's work is often pointed to as the beginning of modern industrial public relations. Hallahan summarizes, "To his credit, Lee was an individual of character, who believed in the decency of humanity and had faith in the ability of people to think rationally and discern truth when given the necessary facts."

1 How did Lee conduct research during this campaign?

2 What tactics other than publicity did Lee employ?

3 Do you think it was ethical of Lee to take on such a cause? Why or why not?

gathering feedback was to formulate a better persuasive message.

Bernays became an important spokesperson for the "new" public relations with the publication of his 1923 book *Crystallizing Public Opinion*. His first sentence announced: "In writing this book I have tried to set down the broad principles that govern the new profession of public relations counsel." In the pages that followed, Bernays outlined the scope, function, methods, techniques, and social responsibilities of a *public relations counsel*—a term that was to become the core of public relations practice.

Journalist Larry Tye credits Bernays, who was named by *Life* magazine in 1990 as one of the 100 most important Americans of the twentieth century, with developing a unique approach to solving problems. Instead of thinking first about tactics, Bernays would always think about the "big idea" on how to motivate people. For example, when the bacon industry wanted to promote its product, Bernays came up with the idea of having doctors across the country endorse a hearty breakfast. No explicit mention was made of bacon, but sales soared anyway as

Over the course of his long career, Edward L. Bernays had many successful campaigns (some controversial) that have become classics.

Lucky Strike Cigarettes.

Bernays found that while smoking was seen primarily as a man's activity, women smoked cigarettes as an expression of liberation and power. Based on his research, he labeled cigarettes women's "Torches of Freedom" and planted the idea with some socialites that they should be seen smoking cigarettes when they strutted their fashion in New York's 1929 Easter Parade. Journalists reported on the event and smoking became a more acceptable—even fashionable—activity among women.

Procter & Gamble's Ivory Soap. Procter & Gamble sold its Ivory Soap bars by the millions after Bernays came up with the idea of sponsoring soap sculpture contests for school-age children. In the first year alone, 22 million schoolchildren participated in the contest, which ran for 35 years.

Light's Golden Jubilee. To celebrate the fiftieth anniversary of Thomas Edison's invention of the electric light bulb, Bernays arranged the attention-getting Light's Golden Jubilee in 1929. It was his idea that the world's utilities would all shut off their power at one time, for one minute, to honor Edison. President Herbert Hoover and many dignitaries were on hand for the event, and the U.S. Post Office issued a commemorative two-cent postage stamp.

think What are the key differences between the approaches advocated by Lee and Bernays?

people took their doctors' advice and started eating the quintessential hearty breakfast—bacon and eggs.

Bernays had a powerful partner in his wife, Doris E. Fleischman, who was a talented writer, an ardent feminist, and, at one time, the Sunday editor of the *New York Tribune*. Fleischman was an equal partner in the work of Bernays's firm, interviewing clients, writing news releases, editing the company's newsletter, and writing and editing books and magazine articles.

Public Relations Expands in Postwar America

During the second half of the twentieth century, the practice of public relations became firmly established as an indispensable part of America's economic, political, and social development.

The booming economy after World War II produced rapid growth in all areas of public relations. Companies opened public relations departments or expanded existing ones. Government staffs increased in size, as did the PR staffs of nonprofits such as educational institutions and health and welfare agencies. Television emerged in the early 1950s as a national medium and as a new challenge for public relations professionals. New counseling firms sprang up nationwide.

The growth of the economy was one reason for the expansion of public relations. Other factors also played key roles, including the following:

- Dramatic increases in urban and suburban populations
- The advent of "big business," "big labor," and "big government"
- Scientific and technological advances, including automation and computerization
- The communications revolution

and proliferation of mass media
- The dawn of a new bottom-line financial consideration approach to decision making, which replaced the more personalized deliberations of previous, more genteel, times

Many people felt bewildered by rapid change, cut off from the sense of community that characterized previous generations. They sought power through innumerable pressure groups, focusing on causes such as environmentalism, working conditions, and civil rights. Public opinion, registered through new, more sophisticated methods of polling, became increasingly powerful in both opposing and effecting change.

As their physical and psychological separation from their publics grew, American business and industry turned increasingly to public relations specialists for audience analysis, strategic planning, issues management, and even the creation of supportive environments for the selling of products and services. Mass media also became more complex and sophisticated, and demand for specialists in media relations grew in tandem.

By 1950, an estimated 17,000 men and 2,000 women were employed as practitioners in public relations and publicity. In 1960, the U.S. Census counted 23,870 men and 7,271 women in public relations, although some observers put the figure at approximately 35,000. Since 1960, the number of public relations practitioners has increased dramatically; it now stands at more than 300,000 nationwide.

Evolving Practice and Philosophy

Thanks to breakthroughs in social science research, the focus of public relations shifted during the first half of the twentieth century from press agentry and a journalistic approach to the psychological and sociological effects of persuasive communication on target audiences. The 1960s saw Vietnam War protests, the civil rights movement, the environmental movement, interest in women's rights, and a host of other issues come to the fore of American consciousness. Anti-business sentiment was high, and corporations adjusted their policies in an effort to generate public goodwill

> "In my philosophy, public relations is fundamental to a democratic society where people make decisions in the workplace, marketplace, the community, and the voting booth. Its primary mission is to forge responsible relationships of understanding, trust, and respect among groups and individuals—even when they disagree.
>
> Betsy Plank, "the First Lady of public relations"

4 Classic Models OF PUBLIC RELATIONS

James Grunig and Todd Hunt presented this typology of public relations practice in their 1984 book *Managing Public Relations*. Although all four models are practiced today in varying degrees, the two-way symmetric model is considered the "ideal" mode of practice.

Press Agentry/Publicity

Press agentry/publicity entails one-way communication, primarily through the mass media, to distribute information that may be exaggerated, distorted, or even incomplete to "hype" a cause, product, or service. Its purpose is advocacy; little or no research is required. P. T. Barnum was a noted historical figure during this model's heyday. Sports, theater, music, and film—think of the classic Hollywood publicist—are the main fields in which this model is employed today.

Public Information

One-way distribution of information, not necessarily with a persuasive intent, is the purpose of the public information model, which is based on the journalistic ideal of accuracy and completeness. The mass media serve as the primary channel for dissemination of the information. There is fact finding for content, but little audience research regarding attitudes and dispositions. Ivy Lee, a former journalist, is the leading historical figure who was instrumental in this model's implementation. Government, nonprofit groups, and other public institutions still rely on this practice model today.

Two-Way Asymmetric

Scientific persuasion is the purpose, and communication is two-way in this model, albeit with imbalanced effects. The model has a feedback loop, but its primary purpose is to help the communicator better understand the audience and persuade it to accept the practitioner's message. Research is used to plan activities and establish objectives as well as to learn whether objectives have been met. Edward L. Bernays was the leading historical figure during the two-way asymmetric model's beginnings. Marketing and advertising departments in competitive businesses and public relations firms are the primary places in which this practice model is found today.

Two-Way Symmetric

Gaining mutual understanding is the purpose of the two-way symmetric model, in which communication is two-way, with balanced effects. Formative research is used to learn how the public perceives an organization and to determine what consequences actions/policy might have on the public. Evaluative research measures whether public relations efforts have improved public understanding. The goal of this "relationship building" is to identify policies and actions that are mutually beneficial to both parties. Edward L. Bernays, later in his career, supported this model. Today educators and professional leaders are the main proponents of this model, which is practiced in organizations that engage in issue identification, crisis and risk management, and long-range strategic planning.

and understanding. As a result the idea of issues management was added to the job description of the public relations manager. It marked the first expression of the idea that public relations should do more than persuade people that corporate policy was correct.

During this period, the idea emerged among business managers that perhaps it would be beneficial to have a dialogue with various publics and adapt corporate policy to suit their particular concerns. James Grunig, in his interpretation of the evolutionary models

 How do the different models of public relations reflect the times in which they were developed?

of public relations (see the nearby box), labeled this approach *two-way symmetric communication* because it involves balance between the organization and its various publics; that is, the organization and the public influence each other.

The 1970s was an era of reform in the stock market. The field of investor relations boomed. By the 1980s, the concept that public relations was a management function

was in full bloom. The practice was actively moving toward the strategic approach. Public relations practitioners endorsed the concept of management by objective (MBO) as they sought to convince higher management that public relations did, indeed, contribute to the bottom line.

An awareness of reputation, or perception, management began to dominate in the 1990s. Burson-Marsteller, one of the largest public relations firms in the world decided that its business was not public relations, but rather "perception management." Other firms declared that their business was "reputation management." The idea of "public relations as conflict management" is directly linked to the notion of reputation management. In the current era, public relations people work to maintain credibility, to build solid internal and external relationships, and to manage issues. Inherent in this conceptualization is the idea that public relations personnel should enhance corporate social responsibility (CSR) by employing research to do (1) environmental monitoring, (2) public relations audits, (3) communication audits, and (4) social audits.

By 2000, a number of scholars and practitioners were beginning to view the practice of public relations as "relationship management"; the basic idea is that public relations practitioners are in the business of building and fostering relationships with an organization's various publics. Relationship management builds on James Grunig's idea of two-way symmetric communication, but goes beyond it by recognizing that an organization's publics are, as Stephen Bruning of Capital University notes, "active, interactive, and equal participants of an ongoing communication process."

The dialogic (dialogue) model of public relations that has emerged

When faced with contractual obligations to pay bonuses to top-performing executives while simultaneously laying off assembly-line workers because product demand is down, how does one balance moral and business obligations and manage the public and media reaction?

CLASSIC CAMPAIGNS
Show the Power of Public Relations

During the last half of the twentieth century, a number of organizations and causes used effective public relations to accomplish highly visible results. *PRWeek* convened a panel of public relations experts and came up with some of the "greatest campaigns ever" during this time period.

- **THE CIVIL RIGHTS CAMPAIGN.**
Martin Luther King, Jr., was an outstanding civil rights advocate and a great communicator. He organized the 1963 civil rights campaign and used such techniques as well-written, well-delivered speeches; letter writing; lobbying; and staged events (nonviolent protests) to turn a powerful idea into reality.

- **SEAT BELT CAMPAIGN.** In the 1980s, the U.S. automotive industry got the nation to "buckle up" by engaging in an extensive public relations campaign. Tactics included winning the support of news media across the country, interactive displays, celebrity endorsements, letter-writing campaigns, and several publicity events, such as buckling a 600-foot-wide safety belt around the iconic Hollywood sign in the hills of Los Angeles.

- **STARKIST TUNA.** Negative media coverage threatened the tuna industry when dolphins were getting caught in fishermen's nets. StarKist led the industry in changing fishing practices with conferences, videos, and an Earth Day coalition. Approximately 90 percent of the U.S. public heard about the company's efforts, and StarKist was praised as an environmental leader.

- **UNDERSTANDING AIDS.** This successful health education campaign changed the way that AIDS was perceived by Americans. In addition to a national mailing of a brochure titled Understanding AIDS, grassroots activities specifically targeted African Americans and Hispanics.

- **MACY'S THANKSGIVING DAY PARADE.** For more than 85 years, the Macy's department store has sponsored the Macy's Thanksgiving Day Parade. Viewing the parade has become a holiday tradition for many American families. In addition, it was the centerpiece of the 1947 film *Miracle on 34th Street* (which has been remade four times and was turned into a Broadway musical as well).

since 2000 is an extension of relationship management. Although healthy long-term relationships with various publics are always the end goal, moral obligations and other forces within an organization sometimes require professionals to make difficult decisions. Considerations of investors, employees, citizens, and activists inevitably come into conflict on occasion. Public relations professionals should have their fingers on the pulse of their various publics so that they can help executives make decisions—decisions that are often difficult because they are intended to deal with conflict.

The concept of dialogue places less emphasis on mass media distribution of messages and more on interpersonal channels. Michael Kent and Maureen Taylor, for example, say that the Internet and World Wide Web are excellent vehicles for dialogue if websites are interactive.

Although there has been a somewhat linear progression in public relations practice and philosophy as the field has expanded, today's practice represents a mixture of the various public relations models. The Hollywood publicist/press agent and the public information officer for the government agency are still with us. Likewise, marketing communications, which almost exclusively uses the concept of scientific persuasion, and two-way asymmetric communication persist. However, when it comes to issues management and

Michael Kent and Maureen Taylor of the University of Oklahoma wrote in a *Public Relations Review* article that a "theoretical shift, from public relations reflecting an emphasis on managing communication, to an emphasis on communication as a tool of negotiating relationships, has been taking place for some time."

relationship building, the two-way symmetric and dialogue models are now generally considered to be the most appropriate.

Trends IN TODAY'S PRACTICE OF PUBLIC RELATIONS

Technological and social changes have continued to transform aspects of public relations practice during the first decade of the twenty-first century. The feminization of the field, the search for more ethnic and cultural diversity, and other trends will shape the practice in the years to come.

Feminization of the Field

In terms of personnel, the most dramatic change has been the transformation of public relations from a male-dominated field to one in which women now constitute more than 70 percent of practitioners. The shift has been going on for several decades. In 1979, women made up 41 percent of the public relations workforce; by 1983, they had become the majority (50.1 percent). A decade later, the figure stood at 66.3

percent. By 2000, the proportion of jobs held by women had leveled off at about 70 percent, where it remains today. In contrast, women account for approximately 60 percent of the U.S. workforce, according to the U.S. Bureau of Labor Statistics. The national organizations also reflect this feminization trend. About 75 percent of the membership in the International Association of Business Communicators (IABC) is female, and the Public Relations Society of America (PRSA) says that more than 60 percent of its members are women.

About two-thirds of all majors in journalism and mass communications programs are now women, and 70 to 75 percent of public relations majors are female. It's worth noting that women also constitute the majority of students in law school,

veterinary programs, and a number of other academic disciplines.

Despite this trend toward feminization of the public relations profession, salary and job description disparities between men and women persist in the field. A number of studies have shown that the majority of women in public relations earn less money than their male counterparts and are usually found at the tactical level of public relations practice rather than the management/counseling role. Tellingly, the Arthur W. Page Society, whose membership is made up of senior-level communication executives, remains majority male, but the percentage of women in the organization increases every year.

Still, some women in public relations have become the top

> **"Surveys and focus groups continue to [show] … that, although the public relations profession is almost 70 percent women today, men are often favored for hiring, higher salaries, and promotions to management positions."**
>
> University of Maryland professors Linda Aldoory and Elizabeth Toth, in the *Journal of Public Relations Research*

communications officers of their corporations. In spite of their success, Professor Emeritus Larissa Grunig of the University of Maryland is concerned about highlighting women who have made it to the top, calling it "compensatory feminism." According to Grunig, the success of a few individuals can give the false idea that across-the-board progress is being achieved.

These arguments and concerns have somewhat dissipated over the years. That public relations is a high-status profession may still be debated, but the power and influence of women in the PR management suite are clearly stronger today than they have ever been. Also, salaries remain fairly high compared to those found in other female-dominated fields, such as nursing or teaching.

Statistics and surveys note the persistence of a gender gap in salaries and reveal that there continue to be fewer women than men in senior management. A number of reasons for these stubborn trends have been offered, but recent research seems to indicate that the biggest factor is years of experience in the field. Youjin Choi of Dongguk University, Seoul, Korea, and Linda Childers Hon of the University of Florida found that "[t]he number of years of respondents' professional experience was the single significant predictor of income." Linda Aldoory and Elizabeth Toth found years of experience to be a significant factor in income inequity, but cited evidence that gender and interrupting a career also have an effect on salaries and job advancement.

The organizational environment may affect a woman's rise to top management as well—a theory called the *structionalist perspective*. Toth argues that more women than men fulfill the technician role—a less powerful role than the managerial role—because of different on-the-job experiences. Choi and Hon also point to organizational structure as a problem, noting that women in many organizations are excluded from influential networks, have a paucity of role models, and must work in male-dominated environments.

Choi and Hon, however, did find that organizations (such as many public relations firms) where women occupied 40 to 60 percent of the managerial positions are "gender integrated" and more friendly environments for the advancement of women than male-dominated organizational structures. In other words, those organizations committed to gender equity are the organizations that practiced the highest quality public relations.

---

think In addition to the benefits inherent in pursuing a culture of fairness, what might be another reason it would be in the best interest of a public relations firm to have a diverse staff?

A number of reasons have been cited to explain the major influx of women into the field of public relations:

- Women find a more welcoming environment in public relations and see more opportunities for advancement than in other communications fields, such as newspaper work.

- Women can make more money in public relations than in comparable traditionally female-dominated fields, such as teaching and social work (although they still make less than men in the field, on average).

- A person can start a public relations firm without a lot of capital.

- Women are thought to have better listening and communication skills than men and are often perceived to be more sensitive than men in facilitating two-way communication.

The Importance of Diversity

According to the U.S. Census Bureau, minorities now constitute 36 percent of the 312 million people in the United States. The fastest-growing, and now largest, minority group in this country is Hispanics. Hispanics currently account for 16 percent of the U.S. population, compared with 13 percent for blacks/African Americans. Asian/Pacific Islanders make up 5 percent, and Native Americans constitute 1 percent of the population.

The number of minorities in public relations falls considerably short of reflecting the percentage in the general population. One major goal of the industry is to somehow make the field of public relations more representative of the population as a whole.

Many public relations employers express the desire to hire more minority candidates, but they have difficulty doing so because they receive so few applications. One thorny problem that has yet to be overcome in this regard is the education pipeline. In a *PRWeek* survey, 41 percent of white, 80 percent of black, and 56 percent of Hispanic respondents strongly agreed that their organizations had a hard time recruiting ethnic minorities, while 31 percent of whites, 84 percent of blacks, and 49 percent of Hispanics strongly agreed that their organization had a hard time retaining them once they were successfully recruited. When asked what kept them from recruiting and retaining minorities, 44 percent of white, 62 percent of black, and 46 percent of Hispanic respondents indicated there were not enough minority role models and 26 percent of whites (50 percent of non-whites) said their organization was not active enough in recruiting minorities.

The percentage of ethnic group members in public relations has improved over the past decade, and many companies are now making a concerted effort to attract more minorities. Hispanics, in particular, because of their collective spending power, constitute a major audience for marketers and source of public relations specialists. Reaching major ethnic audiences can require specialized knowledge and messages tailored to their particular cultures and values.

As part of their efforts to attract more minority members to the public relations profession, PRSA (www.diversity.prsa.org) and other major public relations organizations are increasing minority scholarships, organizing career fairs, and giving awards to local chapters that institute diversity programs. PRSA informs members of diversity issues by including news from the Hispanic PR wire and Black PR wire on its website home page (www.prsa.org).

In addition, groups such as the National Black Public Relations Society (BPRS), the Hispanic Public Relations Association (HPRA), and the Asian American Advertising and Public Relations Association (AAAPRA) are being asked to help public relations firms and companies identify qualified job applicants. Leaders of these minority associations say that employers must make a greater effort to recruit minorities to public relations by going to traditionally black colleges, participating in more college career fairs, enlisting the aid of college professors to identify good candidates, and even placing job ads in publications that reach a variety of ethnic groups.

The globalization of public relations has also created a strong need for employees from diverse cultural backgrounds. Firms need staff who possess multiple-language skills, personal knowledge of other nations, and sensitivity to the customs and attitudes of others. Knowledge of Spanish and Asian languages, such as Chinese, will be especially valuable in coming years.

> "Having a diverse workforce is imperative to the success of any PR agency trying to reach out to diverse audiences. However, the PR workforce does not currently represent the ethnic-minority community in the United States. Therefore, the active recruitment and retention of multicultural talent in PR is necessary to create a diverse employee roster and ensure your agency is equipped to effectively engage all audiences."
>
> Stephanie Howley, SVP of human resources, Cohn & Wolfe, in *PRWeek*

The Hispanic population in the United States is expected to be 30 percent of the total population by 2050. The Hispanic consumer market is estimated to be worth $1.3 trillion by 2014, according to the Selig Center for Economic Growth at the University of Georgia.

Diversity Shows Up in Social Media Use

Diversity is an important issue in public relations for many reasons. Perhaps chief among them is the disparity between how ethnic groups use social media differently. Knowing about how different groups use different media is key to harnessing the power of social media in campaigns designed to target all members of society.

For example, according to socialmediatoday.com, 36 percent of Hispanics and 33 percent of African Americans access social media on mobile phones, but only 19 percent of whites do. Of course these numbers change by the day, if not the hour. And ethnic minorities are currently the majority to make weekly visits to social media sites including Facebook, YouTube, and Twitter.

Manny Ruiz, co-publisher of the Hispanic PR Blog and *PapiBlogger*, told *PRWeek* that "Multicultural youths are in many places in a short time and want to see, touch, taste, feel, and hear to form their opinions. This is why social media, live events, and various consumer engagement activities that reach multiple touchpoints often succeed [with them]."

When Estée Lauder launched a new product line designed for Hispanic consumers, the company enlisted mobile ads, a microsite, product videos, Facebook, and Twitter to get samples of the products into consumers' hands.

Robert Jackson, U.S. marketing director for McDonald's, told *PRWeek*, "One thing where African Americans are leading is social media, so we are incorporating more social and Web-based marketing into our media mix to make sure we are reaching the consumer in the most relevant environments."

Despite all the hype about the importance of reaching ethnic publics via social media however, at least one study found that remarkably few brands use Spanish-language Facebook fan pages to reach Hispanic customers. Of 184 brands, only 34 had any kind of Spanish-language presence on Facebook, according to a study by business network Latinum.

This is true despite the fact that there are only about 2 percent fewer Spanish-language Facebook fans than English-language fans. Andy Hasselwander, a vice president at Latinum, explained to *Advertising Age*: "On Facebook there's a big opportunity to engage. For brands willing to put up Spanish-language Facebook pages, there's a huge payoff."

Because diverse publics seem to be disproportionate users of social media, it is prudent to include such tactics in any campaign to broaden its appeal and impact.

1 What brands have you observed to be especially good at employing social media in their campaigns?

2 Why do you think minorities disproportionately use social and mobile media?

3 Imagine you are developing a health communication campaign for urban African American youth. What media would you use? What if the campaign were aimed at Hispanic youth? Asian American youth?

Some companies are working hard to court a growing multicultural market. For example, as flu season hit in 2011, Kleenex began a campaign to raise brand awareness among Hispanics. The campaign enlisted children to be *Atrapa-Estornudos,* or "Sneeze Catchers." Children were encouraged to go to the Spanish- or English-language website www.kleenex.com/Atrapaestornudos/Index.aspx, where they could become certified Sneeze Catchers by answering five questions. One question was "As a Kleenex® Brand Sneeze Catcher, you promise to help keep stuff off your hands by: a) Using

Kleenex® facial tissues with Sneeze Shield, b) Wiping them on your jeans, or c) Wiping them on your friend's shirt."

Children could also play online games and download a Sneeze Catcher's activity booklet. Parents were engaged by being required to approve their child's participation, thereby giving their children access to the activity booklet.

PRWeek reported that Kleenex experienced a one-point market

share increase among Hispanics overall and a four-point market gain in four cities where the majority of campaign activities were focused.

Other Major Trends in Public Relations

A number of issues will likely influence the practice of public relations in the coming years.

Transparency. Instant global communications, corporate finance scandals, government regulation, and the increased public demand for accountability have made it necessary for all society's institutions, including business and industry, to be more transparent in their operations. Half of all World-Class Brands said they were focusing most of their social media efforts on mobile tools. Likewise, 50 percent said that their increased use of smartphones and tablets would change their approach to social media.

An ever-broadening social media toolbox. The social media boom began with the advent of weblogs or "blogs" in the late 1990s. MySpace and Facebook emerged shortly thereafter and nearly simultaneously (August 2003 and February 2004, respectively). Facebook

became the largest worldwide social network in mid-2008. Google+ was introduced in 2011 and offers many of the features of Facebook and MySpace, but Google claims that its "circles" feature groups' social networks, offering users additional privacy and promoting sharing.

The development of YouTube provided an easy platform for video blogs or "vlogs," while Flickr allowed for easy photo sharing. Tools like Tumblr and Twitter have substantially advanced blogging. Tumblr is a blogging site that combines several of the features of the sites mentioned above. It allows easy sharing of text, photos, links, music, and video from both computers and mobile devices. Twitter, a microblogging platform, was founded in March 2006 as a means of allowing friends, celebrities, causes, and companies to tell each other what they're doing in real time.

This expanding social media toolbox provides both opportunities

and challenges for public relations practitioners. Opportunities include the ability to communicate directly with stakeholders, unfettered by gatekeepers; challenges include keeping up with messages and critics in real time.

Increased emphasis on evaluation. Public relations professionals will continue to improve measurement techniques for showing management how their activities actually contribute to the bottom line.

Managing the 24/7 news cycle. The flow of news and information is a global activity that occurs 24 hours a day, seven days a week. As a consequence, public relations personnel must constantly update information, answer journalists' inquiries at all hours of the day, and be aware that any and all information is readily available to a worldwide audience. New media and technology make it possible to disseminate news and information all day long, but the effect is often

one of overwhelming information overload. A major challenge to today's practitioners is figuring out how to cope with the cascade of information and how to give it shape and purpose so it has relevance to multiple audiences.

New directions in mass media. The power of the traditional media isn't what it used to be. In the United States, circulation of daily newspapers dropped almost 9 percent in the first quarter of 2011. In a survey by the Pew Research Center, 66 percent of consumers said they use television as their primary news source. Forty-one percent said they use the Internet as their main source for national and international news. Network evening news ratings for ABC, CBS, and NBC fell from a combined 52 million viewers per night in 1980, according to the Pew Project for Excellence in Journalism, to 22 million viewers per night in 2011, according to the Nielsen Company. In short, there have been

1 million fewer viewers of these broadcasts each year, even though the U.S. population is growing by about 2.8 million people each year.

Public relations personnel are expanding their communication tools to account for the fact that no single mass medium is now a proven vehicle for reaching key publics. One resulting change has been the shift to electronic preparation of media materials. An International Association of Business Communicators (IABC) study found that electronic news-

departments have disappeared, but increasingly such tasks as media relations, annual reports, and sponsored events are outsourced to independent public relations firms.

The importance of lifelong learning. Given the rapid additions to knowledge in today's society, public relations personnel will need to continually update their knowledge base just to stay current. New findings in a variety of fields are emerging that can be applied to public relations practice. These fields include behavioral genetics, evolutionary social psychology, economics, the physics of information, social network analysis, and semiotic game theory. In

> ## Half of all World-Class Brands said they were focusing most of their social media efforts on mobile tools. Likewise, 50 percent said that their increased use of smartphones and tablets would change their approach to social media.
>
> A spring 2011 online survey by Weber Shandwick and Forbes of 1,897 senior executives from high-revenue companies in 50 countries

letters, e-mail notices, websites, and CDs or DVDs have largely replaced print materials in this realm.

Outsourcing to public relations firms. Outsourcing is now almost universal. This is not to say that in-house corporate public relations

addition, the need to specialize in a particular field or area of public relations will likely intensify because it's becoming almost impossible for a generalist to master the detailed knowledge required for such areas as health care and financial relations.

TABLETS Change the Way People Consume News

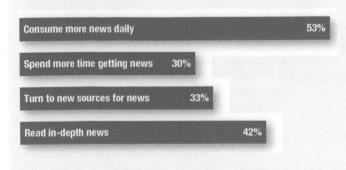

Consume more news daily	53%
Spend more time getting news	30%
Turn to new sources for news	33%
Read in-depth news	42%

The Pew Research Center Project for Excellence in Journalism found that 53 percent of tablet users consume news daily on their tablets, 30 percent spend more time getting news than they did before owning a tablet, 33 percent turn to new sources of news on their tablet, and 42 percent regularly read in-depth news articles on their tablet.

A Growing
PROFESSIONAL PRACTICE

Public relations as a profession faces several criticisms—practitioners are sometimes accused of being unethical, spinmeisters, or worse. One way that the profession has chosen to address such criticism is through the education of practitioners about issues related to professional practice. By "professional" practice, we mean that public relations practitioners should have a common set of ideals and expectations for what is acceptable in practice. For public relations to be considered a respected profession, many practitioners argue, it must have guiding standards like those that govern lawyers, doctors, teachers, nurses, accountants, and other professions.

The Public Relations Society of America

The largest national public relations organization in the world is the Public Relations Society of America (www.prsa.org). PRSA is headquartered in New York City. It has more than 21,000 members and about 110 chapters nationwide. It also has 14 professional interest sections that represent such areas as business and industry, counseling firms, independent practitioners, the military, government agencies, associations, hospitals, schools, non-profit organizations, and educators.

PRSA has an extensive professional development program that offers short courses, seminars, teleconferences, and webcasts throughout the year. In addition to workshops and seminars, PRSA holds an annual meeting and

publishes *Tactics*, a monthly tabloid of current news and professional tips, and the *Strategist*, a quarterly magazine with in-depth articles about the profession and issues related to practice. The organization also sponsors the Silver Anvil and Bronze Anvil awards to recognize outstanding public relations campaigns.

PRSA is the parent organization of the Public Relations Student Society

think What are the advantages of joining a professional organization—to the individual and to the profession as a whole?

of America (PRSSA), whose website can be found at www.prssa.org. PRSSA is the world's largest preprofessional public relations organization, with almost 300 campus chapters and more than 10,000 student members. The student groups offer career-related programs at the local chapter level and provide mentoring and networking with the local professional PRSA chapter. PRSSA makes available a national publication, *Forum*, and sponsors a national case study competition to encourage students to exercise the analytical skills and judgment required for public relations problem solving. After graduation, PRSSA members are eligible to become associate members of PRSA.

The International Association of Business Communicators

The International Association of Business Communicators (IABC)

(www.iabc.com) is the second-largest organization of communication and public relations professionals, with more than 15,000 members in 80 nations.

Headquartered in San Francisco, IABC has similar objectives as the PRSA. It holds year-round seminars and workshops and an annual meeting. The organization also has an awards program, known as the Gold Quill, that honors excellence in business communication.

The IABC publishes *Communication World*. IABC also sponsors campus student chapters, but these groups are not comparable to PRSSA in size or organizational structure.

The International Public Relations Association

Based in London, the International Public Relations Association (IPRA) (www.ipra.org) is global in scope. IPRA has 1,000 members in 80 nations. Its membership is primarily senior international public relations executives, and its mission is "to provide intellectual leadership in the practice of international public relations by making available to our members the services and information that will help them to meet their professional responsibilities and to succeed in their careers."

IPRA organizes regional and international conferences to discuss issues in global public relations. It also reaches its widespread membership through its website and *Frontline*. IPRA issues "Gold Papers" on public relations practice and conducts an annual awards competition (Golden World Awards).

Professionalism, LICENSING, AND ACCREDITATION

Is public relations a profession? Should its practitioners be licensed? Does the accreditation of practitioners constitute a sufficient guarantee of their talents and integrity? These and related questions remain the topic of ongoing discussion within the public relations profession.

> "We act as publicists, yet we talk of counseling. We perform as technologists in communication, but we aspire to be decision makers dealing in policy."
>
> John F. Budd, Jr.

Professionalism

Among public relations practitioners, there are considerable differences of opinion about whether public relations is a craft, a skill, or a developing profession. Certainly, at its present level, public relations does not qualify as a profession in the same sense that medicine and law do. Public relations does not have prescribed standards of educational preparation, a mandatory period of apprenticeship, or state laws that govern admission to the profession. Adding to the confusion about professionalism is the difficulty of ascertaining what constitutes public relations practice.

At the same time, there is a rapidly expanding body of literature about public relations—including this text and many others in the field. The two major scholarly publications serving the field are *Public Relations Review* and *Journal of Public Relations Research*. Substantial progress is also being made in developing theories of public relations, conducting research, and publishing scholarly journals.

The Institute for Public Relations (www.instituteforpr.org) and the Strategic Communication and Public Relations Center at the University of Southern California's Annenberg Center (www.annenberg.usc.edu/sprc) are commonly regarded as the two major "think tanks" in the public relations field. Other research centers include the Plank Center for Leadership in Public Relations at the University of Alabama (www.plankcenter.ua.edu) and the Arthur W. Page Center for Integrity in Public Communication at Penn State University (http://pagecenter.comm.psu.edu/).

Licensing

Proposals that public relations practitioners be licensed were discussed even before PRSA was founded 60 years ago. One proponent, Edward L. Bernays, believed that licensing would protect the profession and the public from incompetent, shoddy opportunists who do not have the knowledge, talent, or ethics required of public relations professionals.

Under the licensing approach, only those individuals who pass rigid examinations and tests of personal integrity could call themselves "public relations" counselors. Those not licensed would have to call themselves "publicists" or adopt some other designation. So far, the opponents of licensing seem to have carried the day. Today, there is no particular interest on the part of the public relations industry, the

Arguments for Licensing	Arguments Against Licensing
Advocates say licensing would be beneficial to the profession because it would:	Opponents of licensing say that it won't work because:
• Define public relations	• Any licensing in the communications field would violate the First Amendment; civil and criminal laws exist to deal with malpractice
• Establish uniform educational criteria	• Licensing is a function of state governments, but public relations people often work on national and international levels
• Set uniform professional standards	• Licensing ensures only minimum competence and professional standards, not high ethical behavior
• Protect clients and employers from imposters	• The credibility and status of an occupation are not necessarily ensured through licensing
• Protect qualified practitioners from unethical or unqualified competition	• Setting up the machinery for licensing and policing would be very expensive to taxpayers
• Raise practitioners' overall credibility	

The Qualities of a Professional

Regardless of whether licensing is required, many professionals and PRSA itself promote the idea that the most important thing is for individuals to act like professionals in the field. A professional practitioner should have the following qualities:

- A sense of independence
- A sense of responsibility to society and the public interest
- Concern for the competence and honor of the profession as a whole
- A higher loyalty to the standards of the profession and fellow professionals than to the employer of the moment

Unfortunately, a major barrier to professionalism is the attitude that many practitioners themselves have toward their work. As James Grunig and Todd Hunt note in their book *Managing Public Relations,* practitioners tend to hold more "careerist" values than professional values. In other words, they place higher importance on job security, prestige in the organization, salary level, and recognition from superiors than on the values just listed. For example, 47 percent of the respondents in a survey of IABC members gave a neutral or negative answer when asked if they would quit their jobs rather than act against their ethical values. In addition, 55 percent said they consider it "somewhat ethical" to present oneself misleadingly if that is the only means of achieving an objective. Almost all agreed, however, that ethics is an important matter, worthy of further study.

On another level, many practitioners are limited in their professionalism by a "technician mentality." These people narrowly define professionalism as the ability to do a competent job at executing the mechanics of communicating (preparing news releases, brochures, newsletters, and so on) even if the information provided by management or a client is in bad taste, is misleading, lacks documentation, or is just plain wrong.

Some practitioners defend the technician mentality, arguing that public relations people are like lawyers in the court of public opinion. Everyone is entitled to his or her viewpoint, the argument goes, and whether the public relations person agrees or not, the client or employer has a right to be heard. Thus, they say, a public relations representative is a paid advocate, just as a lawyer is. The flaw in this argument is that public relations people are not lawyers, who operate in a court of law where judicial standards are applied.

Ultimately, courts are increasingly holding public relations firms accountable for information disseminated on behalf of a client. Clearly, it is no longer acceptable to say, "The client told me to do it."

---

consumer movement, or even state governments to initiate any form of legislated licensing. An alternative to licensing is accreditation.

 think How might licensing change how public relations professionals do business?

APPLY YOUR KNOWLEDGE

What Would You Do?

Keeping an Eye on Trends
In this chapter, we have identified a number of trends in public relations, including the feminization of the field and the drive for a more diversified workforce. Other trends include the decline of the mass media, the importance of lifelong learning, and the public's demand for organizational transparency.

Select one of these issues and do some additional research. Write a short paper or make a presentation from the standpoint of what a public relations professional should know about this issue and how it may affect working in public relations.

Accreditation

The major effort to improve standards and professionalism in public relations around the world has entailed the establishment of accreditation programs. This means that practitioners voluntarily go through a process by which a national organization "certifies" that they are competent, qualified professionals.

PRSA began its accreditation program more than 40 years ago. A testing process for members provides the opportunity to earn Accredited in Public Relations (APR) status. Other groups have also established accreditation programs.

When it developed a program for its members in 1965, PRSA was one of the first public relations organization to offer accreditation. Candidates are required to take a preview course (available online), complete a "readiness" questionnaire, and show a portfolio of work to a panel of professional peers before taking the written exam, which is available at test centers throughout the United States. In addition, the member must have five years of professional experience.

To date, approximately 5,000 practitioners have earned APR status, or 18 percent of the PRSA's membership. Approximately 10 percent of IABC's 15,000 members have earned its ABC designation.

summary

Which Key Events and Individuals Shaped the History of Public Relations?

- Although *public relations* is a twentieth-century term, the roots of this practice go back to ancient Egyptian, Greek, and Roman times.

- The American Revolution, in part, was the result of such staged events as the Boston Tea Party, and the publication of the *Federalist Papers* helped cement the federal system of the new government.

- The 1800s were the golden age of the press agent. P. T. Barnum used many techniques that are still employed today. In addition, the settlement of the American West was driven in large part by promotions created by land developers and U.S. railroads.

- From 1900 to 1950, the practice of public relations was transformed by individuals such as Henry Ford, Ivy Lee, George Creel, and Edward L. Bernays. They moved the profession from press agentry toward a more journalistic approach of distributing accurate public information.

- From 1950 to 2000, organizations found it necessary to employ public relations specialists to communicate effectively with the mass media and a variety of publics. This was the age of scientific persuasion, management by objective, and strategic thinking.

What Are the Trends in Today's Practice of Public Relations?

- A major trend in public relations has been the influx of women into the field. Women now account for roughly 70 percent of public relations practitioners in the United States.

- The public relations workforce is still overwhelmingly Caucasian. Efforts are being made to diversify the workforce to better represent society as a whole.

In What Ways Is Public Relations Evolving and Growing as a Professional Practice?

- Four classic models of public relations are the press agentry/publicity, public information, two-way asymmetric, and two-way symmetric models. Although all four models are practiced today in varying degrees, the "ideal" one is the two-way symmetric model.

- An expanding social media toolbox provides both opportunities and challenges. Opportunities include the ability to communicate directly with stakeholders; challenges include the difficulty of keeping up with messages and critics in real time.

What Are the Major Professional Public Relations Organizations and What Do They Do?

- Professional organizations such as PRSA, IABC, and IPRA play an important role in setting standards and providing education and networking opportunities for public relations professionals.

- Despite some arguments in support of the move, public relations professionals are not currently licensed. Accreditation programs for practitioners, with continuing education, is an attractive alternative.

questions
FOR REVIEW AND DISCUSSION

1 Which concepts of publicity and public relations practiced by P. T. Barnum should modern practitioners consider using? Which should they reject?

2 What four important contributions did Ivy Lee make to public relations?

3 The Boston Tea Party has been described as the "greatest and best-known publicity stunt of all time." Would you agree? Do you believe that staged events are a legitimate way to publicize a cause and motivate people?

4 Describe briefly the publicity strategies employed by Henry Ford.

5 Cite an example from a campaign of Edward Bernays discussed in this chapter that illustrates the following quote : "Instead of thinking first about tactics, Bernays would always think about the "big idea" on how to motivate people".

6 Summarize the major developments in the philosophy and practice of public relations from the 1920s to 2010.

7 James Grunig outlined four models of public relations practice. Name and describe each one. Do these models help explain the evolution of public relations theory?

8 Modern public relations is described as "relationship management." How would you describe this concept to a friend? A newer concept suggests that the purpose of public relations is to establish a "dialogue" with individuals and various publics. How does establishing a dialogue differ from managing relationships?

9 Females now constitute the majority of public relations personnel. Why do you think this is the case?

10 Should public relations practitioners be licensed? What are the pros and cons of licensing?

11 Why do some people say that "technician mentality" undermine efforts to establish professional standards in public relations?

MySearchLab®

Women make great strides in PR

September 5, 2011 12:19 pm, The Financial Times by Rebecca Knight

As women entered the business workforce following the Women's Liberation movement of the 1960s, public relations was a safe and somewhat easy way to get a foot in the door.

Public relations is a growing profession at the same time that many other mass communications professions are on the wane. The use of online and social media as public relations tools has greatly increased the demand for savvy public relations pros.

The "glass ceiling" that exists in many industries has been cracked in public relations. Women increasingly have access to leadership opportunities in PR.

In PR, when we talk about technicians, we are talking about those who create the media kit. When we talk about managers, we're talking about those who develop strategies that technicians implement.

Women in senior roles are more common in firms and nonprofits than they are in corporations.

Fiske's statement could be said to stereotype women's skill set. Do you agree or disagree with this stereotype? Why?

The public relations industry is dominated by women. In 1970, according to Ragan's PR Daily, women comprised only 27 per cent of the US public relations workforce. Today, close to three-quarters of the members of the Public Relations Society of America are female; in the UK, about 64 per cent of those employed in PR are female.

Also, women in the US with bachelor's degrees in journalism or mass communication disproportionately specialise in advertising and PR, which have more opportunities for full-time employment than other parts of the industry.

But unlike many fields where women dominate at entry level and in the junior ranks but are noticeably absent at the managerial and principal levels, in PR they are increasingly seen in managerial roles.

According to the most recent data from the PRSA national committee on work, life and gender, women and men are enacting the role of manager at the same rate for the first time since these figures were first collected in 1979. ("Enacting" the role means that respondents said they performed activities that researchers classify as carried out by a "manager", as opposed to a "technician" or a "specialist" – both of which are more junior-level jobs.)

Rosanna Fiske, chief executive and chairwoman of the PRSA, says: "We have seen a rising number of women leaders at the agency level, and an increasing number become independent practitioners who are setting up their own shops. But we have not seen this happen at the corporate level.

"So, yes, we are seeing changes, and yes, we have seen a number of women rise to the top. But I wish there were more of them."

Fiske believes more women gravitate to the field because PR jobs require skills that tend to come by women naturally, such as empathy, listening and multitasking.

"PR is about communication, and women are born communicators," she says. "PR is also about relationship building, and there is a lot of research in cultural anthropology that shows that this is a strength of women."

Another reason women are drawn to PR careers is that they are often more conducive to the balance of work and family. "There's a lot more flexibility in this industry," says Fiske. "It's not an eight-to-five job where you have to be chained to a desk."

In spite of these advances, women still face double standards. Consider a recent conversation I had with Christine Deussen, president of Deussen Global Communications, a small PR shop based in New York that specialises in wine, spirits and hospitality. A few months ago, she received a thank-you note from one of her top European clients, a man.

"He opened with something like, 'When I was first assigned my Deussen team, I was worried because it was all women. I didn't know if they were up to the job.' He went on to say thank you, and by the end, it was such a beautiful note," says Deussen. "But I do think perceptions are funny. I was surprised that even today someone might see an all-female team as lightweight."

She says she had always wanted to start a company, but admits perhaps she was "a little blind" to the barriers that women face in business.

"I'm 42. I grew up in an age where little girls and boys were treated equally," she says. "We had Title IX requirements [that disallow gender discrimination in the US] for sports. My mother was an entrepreneur. I went to Barnard [the women's college in New York]. I always thought, if I wanted to start a business, of course I could do that. I went into it a little blind, but in this case I think ignorance is bliss."

Public relations is a 24/7 job, but that doesn't mean that it's inflexible. So, while there are times you'll put in 20-hour days, there are also down times when you can catch up on your work/life balance.

Why do you think this client expressed concern to Deussen?

The nature of the public relations field opens up opportunities for women—from owning their own firm or consultancy to leading the communications arm of a global organization.

Text Credits

Credits are listed in order of appearance.

Reprinted by permission of Rebecca Knight.

Photo Credits

Credits are listed in order of appearance.

National Photo Company Collection/Library of Congress Prints and Photographs Division [npcc.30738]; Alexandre Marchi/NCY/Photopqr/L'EST REPUBLICAIN/Newscom; Phoenix79/Shutterstock; Bettmann/Corbis;

(tr) Handout/Getty Images News/Getty Images; (bc) Bain Collection/Library of Congress Prints and Photographs Division[LC-DIG-ggbain-05640]; B Holmes/Shutterstock; Metropolitan Transportation Authority; Bettmann/Corbis;

Bettmann/Corbis; (br) Schiller/F1online digitale Bildagentur GmbH/Alamy; (tc) AP Photo/File; ARENA Creative/Shutterstock; Samuel Borges/Shutterstock; Julie Campbell/Shutterstock; Greg Gard/Alamy

Tactics image: Petr Z/Shutterstock
Tablet image: Falconia/Shutterstock

Careers in Public Relations

From Chapter 2 of *Think Public Relations*, 2013 Edition. Dennis L. Wilcox, Glen T. Cameron, Bryan H. Reber, Jae-Hwa Shin.
Copyright © 2013 by Pearson Education, Inc. Published by Pearson. All rights reserved.

Careers in Public Relations

"Robust" and Increasingly Integrated

The job market in public relations outlook went from "bleak to cautiously optimistic to positively robust" in the years 2009, 2010, and 2011, according to *PRWeek*. This positive trajectory is good news for the communications industry, which includes public relations, advertising, and marketing. But the PR landscape is complicated and ever-changing. A number of game-changing shifts have occurred in recent years, including the ascendancy of ad agencies that are increasingly offering their clients public relations counsel. On the global stage, it was an advertising agency that won the PR Grand Prix at the Cannes Lions International Festival of Creativity in 2010 and 2011. But it's not as simple as suggesting that advertising is elbowing its way into traditional public relations' space. It's more accurate to suggest that public relations firms and advertising agencies are, with increasing frequency, combining efforts to offer integrated communications solutions. Global public relations firm Fleishman-Hillard CEO Dave Senay told *PRWeek*, "We have more than 100 collaborations underway right now with non-PR agencies.... We are also increasingly pitching as part of integrated teams, often with ad agencies in the mix."

What does all this mean for new public relations practitioners? It means that strategic integration of communications campaigns is increasingly important. It means that opportunities are strong for novice practitioners. It means that public relations professionals should expect to work with advertising and marketing colleagues and must, therefore, speak their language.

Now back to the topic of the "positively robust" nature of public relations. Both internal departments and public relations firms have been going on hiring sprees lately. For example, Edelman told the trade publication that it added 274 full-time employees in the first half of 2011. And the agency's chief recruiter said that during that time frame, Edelman always had at least 125 openings. Entry-level pay is creeping up and rapid promotion is the norm. According to *PRWeek*'s annual salary survey, for public relations practitioners ages 21 to 25, the median salary in 2011 was $38,000, up a little over $1,000 from the previous year. For practitioners in the next age bracket (26 to 30 years old), the median salary increased to $56,000, and then to $85,000 for those 31 to 35 years old.

1 What does it mean that the communications function is increasingly "integrated"?

2 Why is social media know-how a must in today's hiring environment?

3 What evidence can you cite that supports the statement that public relations is a robust profession?

> How Is the Field of Public Relations Changing?

> Which Personal Qualifications, Attitudes, and Abilities Help Professionals Succeed in Public Relations?

> What are the Different Job Levels and Roles in Public Relations Practice?

> How Much Do Public Relations Professionals Earn?

A CHANGING Focus
IN PUBLIC RELATIONS

A person entering the field of public relations has the opportunity to develop a career that encompasses numerous areas of an increasingly diverse profession. A wide variety of personal traits and skills contribute to success in this arena. Certain abilities, such as writing well, are necessary for all areas, but many public relations practitioners also go on to develop specialized skills in particular practice areas, such as investor relations, governmental affairs, or brand management.

Competition and conflict management are more essential than ever to organizations in a complex world where public acceptance and support are key to the success of a company or a nonprofit group.

Now more than ever, this competition takes place on the global stage. Certainly, the daily news coverage of conflicts arising from heated competition or from clashing ideologies and worldviews showcases the importance of public relations skills.

Traditionally, it was widely believed that public relations practitioners should begin their careers as newspaper reporters or wire service correspondents to polish their writing skills and to learn firsthand how the media function. Many of the leading pioneers in public relations were, in fact, originally journalists. This, however, is no longer the case, for several reasons.

First, the field of public relations has broadened far beyond the concept of "media relations" and placing publicity in the mass media. Today, much writing in public relations is done for controlled media, such as company publications, direct mail campaigns to key audiences, speech writing, brochures, and material posted on an organization's website. With this approach, no media savvy or contacts are necessary. Writing skill and knowledge of the media are still vital, but so is training in management, logistics, event management, coalition building, budgeting, and supervision of personnel.

According to a report by the International Communications Consultancy Organization, some specialty areas of public relations are projected to be growth areas, including corporate communications, public affairs,

The Occupy Wall Street movement with its rallying cry of "We are the 99%!" illustrates the role that conflict plays in current issues.

Careers in Public Relations

56

and crisis management. The industries cited as areas of growth for PR professionals are health care, consumer goods, financial services, and technology.

think What sort of experiences and coursework are the best training for success in public relations?

Another expanding area of public relations practice is crisis communication counseling. This key role strengthens the influence of public relations in organizations and requires considerable professional experience. Crisis management, which takes place within the larger context of strategic management of conflict, is where many practitioners find their greatest satisfaction as professionals; they have an impact on their organization and add enormous value to the viability of their department.

Women and men entering public relations find employment in a variety of settings, including public relations firms; corporations; nonprofit organizations; entertainment, sports, and travel; government and politics; education; and international public relations. Of these, corporations employ the largest numbers. The second largest employer group is public relations firms, which handle a variety of tasks for any number of clients.

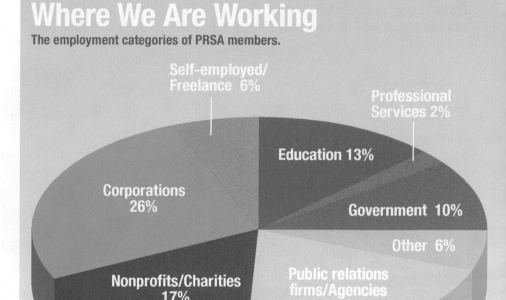

Where We Are Working
The employment categories of PRSA members.

- Self-employed/Freelance 6%
- Professional Services 2%
- Education 13%
- Government 10%
- Other 6%
- Public relations firms/Agencies 20%
- Nonprofits/Charities 17%
- Corporations 26%

b t w ...

Increasingly, universities have established joint public relations/advertising programs, in part because of the growing trend toward integrated marketing communications. The Public Relations Student Society of America (PRSSA) now has more than 320 chapters and a membership exceeding 10,000 students. The Commission on Public Relations Education, which includes public relations educators and representatives from all of the major professional organizations, has set the standard for an ideal curriculum. In its most recent report, the commission recommended that undergraduates sign up for the following six basic courses (in addition to a supervised public relations internship): (1) introduction to public relations; (2) case studies in public relations; (3) public relations research, measurement, and evaluation; (4) public relations law and ethics; (5) public relations writing and production; and (6) public relations planning and management.

Careers in Public Relations

Fortunately, the number of public relations jobs continues to increase as the field expands. The Bureau of Labor Statistics predicts a 24 percent increase in employment through 2018.

"Because of the changes in communications, every constituency is hearing all your messages. You used to be able to have discreet communications. Employees hear what you're saying to investors. It's a much more strategic conversation."

Dan Bartlett, U.S. president and CEO of Hill and Knowlton, in *PRWeek*

Personal QUALIFICATIONS AND ATTITUDES

Any attempt to define a single public relations type of personality is pointless: the field is so diverse that it needs people of differing personalities. Some practitioners deal with clients and the public in person on a frequent basis; others work primarily at their desks, planning, writing, and researching. Many do both. Whether in a creative position, in a resident journalist slot pitching stories to the media, in a job requiring lots of people skills and socializing, or in a top executive post shaping policy and direction for an employer in the external communication environment, the focus is always on helping meet the organization's goals and objectives—that is, on managing competition and conflict.

"The ability to take on multiple projects and clients along with being knowledgeable about multiple disciplines are becoming the expectation for those on the job market."

Karen Freberg, in the PRSA blog, *ComPRehension*

Six Essential Abilities

Individuals who plan careers in public relations should develop knowledge and ability in six basic areas, no matter which type of work they ultimately engage in.

1 **Writing Skills** The ability to convey information and ideas in written documents and online communications quickly, clearly, and concisely is essential. Good grammar and correct spelling are vital.

2 **Research Ability** Arguments must be supported by facts rather than generalities. A person must have the persistence and ability to gather information from a variety of sources as well as be able to conduct original research

by designing and implementing opinion polls or audits. Skillful use of the Internet and computer databases is an important element of research work. Reading newspapers and magazines is also important.

3 Planning Expertise
Communication tools and activities are most effective when they are carefully developed and coordinated. A person needs to be a good planner to make certain that materials are distributed in a timely manner, events occur without problems, and budgets are not exceeded. Public relations people must be highly organized and detail oriented, yet still able to see the "big picture."

4 Problem-Solving Ability
Innovative ideas and fresh approaches solve complex problems and make a public relations program unique and memorable. Higher salaries and more

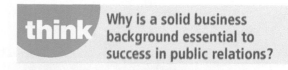

think Why is a solid business background essential to success in public relations?

frequent promotions go to those individuals who show top management they can solve problems creatively.

5 Business/Economics Competence
The increasing emphasis on public relations as a management function calls for public relations students to learn the "nuts and bolts" of business and economics. More than half (52 percent) of the corporate practitioners responding to *PRWeek's* corporate communications survey said they always had a place at the decision-making table. Students preparing for careers in public relations should obtain a solid grounding by taking elective courses in economics, marketing, and especially management.

6 Expertise in Social Media
Employers still value expertise in mainstream media relations, but it's now just as important to have social media savvy. Three important skills today are social networking, blogging, and tweeting. In addition, employers prefer job applicants who know about podcasting, search engine optimization (SEO), web content management, and social bookmarking. According to MarketingVox, "These social media skills will likely increase in importance as PR professionals continue to take the lead in managing most organizations' social media communication channels."

Of course, not every job in public relations requires all six essential abilities in equal proportion. The right mix often depends on your specific job responsibilities and assignments.

"I firmly believe in being versatile as a communicator. These are those who can do it all—write well, handle a crisis, and approach marketing communications with almost a sales mentality. I also do employee communications, so it's important to have those skills and obviously all the digital skills. A well-rounded candidate is who companies will increasingly want because the companies are leaner. They want people who can move around."

Andy Katell, communications SVP at GE Energy Financial Services, to PRWeek

My Summer as a New York Fashion Intern

I'M EXCITED. Several of my friends studying public relations have plum internships—the British Consulate-General in Boston, the TOUR golf championship sponsored by Coca-Cola, ESPN in Bristol, CT, and the National Geographic Society in Washington, D.C. But I think I've got the best internship of all. I'm working in the editorial department of fashion house Dolce & Gabbana in New York.

Week 1

I arrived at the New York office for my first day of work. The office has interns in both the editorial and entertainment public relations (EPR) departments. After a short orientation, another intern and I are put to work collecting press clippings from print and online media. Everything down to the type font and size must be recorded precisely. Each day's clippings are sent to the Milan office. If the information isn't recorded correctly, the Milan office won't know how to read the report and everyone will get into trouble, especially the interns.

Week 2

This week I worked with the send-outs and returns from various publications. A magazine doing a shoot will request a "look" from the Dolce & Gabbana collection. The editorial manager reviews and approves or rejects these requests. Once the look request is approved, it must be packaged, checked out, and sent via messenger to the magazine or photo-shoot site. After the shoot, the look is returned. It's my responsibility to check in the pieces and return them to their proper home according to the collection. It's confusing, and it took me a few mistakes to learn how important it is to know the collections. All items must be logged in so they're easy to retrieve for future press requests.

Week 3

My supervisor left for Milan for the week, so I had many new responsibilities. Besides responding to requests for looks from editors, I found myself pulling looks to send to the various publications. I couldn't believe I was being allowed to decide what to send to *Vogue, InStyle, WWD* (*Women's Wear Daily*), etc. This level of responsibility inspired me to work even harder to show my employers that they hadn't made a mistake by trusting me.

Week 4

The men's resort show took place in Milan this week, so lots of people were out of the office. While in Italy, my supervisor went to shows thinking about what publication editors might like and what was going to be "in" this season. She also received a request from Dolce & Gabbana designers for a report of all the credits we'd received for the past six months in various publications. We compiled reports and sent them on a wiki so the designers could make their own notes. The New York office has to keep track of the U.S. publications because the Milan office doesn't receive them. I think I proved that I was catching on and could work quickly. I also realized the importance of not getting behind on keeping press records.

Week 5

Everyone returned from Milan this week. I have to admit, it was a bit of a letdown. My workload lightened considerably. I found myself reorganizing the showroom, making sure everything is in its place—a boring task. But it did give me a chance to show that I can find work on my own. Nobody likes an intern who must be told every move to make or who just sits there, counting the hours before he or she can leave the office.

Later this week, I was taken aside by my supervisor and asked to do magazine editorial reports. You might think that looking at magazines all day is fun, but in this case we were under such a tight deadline that there was no relaxing with the magazines. While I was playing catch-up with the editorial reports, the other intern was updating the press list—making cold calls to see if reporters or editors are at the same publications and in the same jobs. I guess the biggest lesson this summer is that working in fashion PR, or in PR in general, you absolutely must be able to jump in and figure things out for yourself.

Week 6

My last day was more fun than work. All the interns were taken to a café around the corner instead of ordering in food and working through lunch, like usual. To my surprise, my supervisors asked me when I was graduating. I've only got one semester left, so they said they'd like to have the first chance at hiring me when I graduate. What a great end to a great internship!

I walked away from this internship with a broad knowledge of what it takes to succeed in the fashion PR world. Too many people think that fashion is glamorous and all fun: they forget that there's a business side to things, which is what public relations is ultimately all about. Not everyone is cut out for PR. You must be able to think for yourself and integrate all parts of your life and knowledge to be successful. You have to be able to work with all publics in order to make your client happy. And you have to be prepared for the good and bad and have an open mind at all times.

Source: Adapted from the internship journal of Hannah Thomas, a senior majoring in public relations at the University of Georgia.

1 What did this intern learn about public relations in general and fashion PR in particular in her six-week internship?

2 Does this student's experience give you new insights into PR? Explain your answer.

3 Describe your ideal public relations internship. In which company, organization, and industry would you most like to work? Why?

Cultural Literacy

THE IMPORTANCE OF BREADTH AND DEPTH OF KNOWLEDGE

In addition to writing skills, strategic thinking, and media savvy, employers say PR pros need to be culturally literate. So what is cultural literacy, and why in the world is it important in public relations?

Public relations programs at most colleges and universities require a substantial foundation of arts, humanities, and natural science education. This is because having a strong knowledge of the industry in which you practice public relations is essential, but it's not enough.

Cultural literacy refers to a knowledge of history and practices within a culture as well as cultural norms and popular trends. Curiosity and sincere interest in a broad range of subjects, traditions, and people serves public relations practitioners well.

English language scholar E. D. Hirsch has promoted the idea of cultural literacy in several books. He defines cultural literacy as shared knowledge that allows people to communicate effectively.

In fact, Hirsch and his colleagues developed *The Dictionary of Cultural Literacy* in 1988 and updated it twice, most recently in 2002. The dictionary suggests that a culturally literate American needs knowledge of everything from biblical proverbs to world geography. Public relations professionals are charged with understanding and representing the interests, needs, and preferences of a broad array of publics. How can you do that without a broad understanding of diverse cultural issues?

And how do you develop cultural literacy? Rather than memorizing Hirsch's dictionary, it is probably better to take a broad range of college classes; consume a variety of media—newspapers (pick up your campus newspaper for starters), magazines, television, books, online blogs and news sites; travel as widely as possible (take a study abroad course); and interact with people from different backgrounds, whether that be social strata or ethnic or country origins.

Ask yourself whether you can hold your own when discussions turn to American history, biology, or funding for space travel. How does today's political behavior compare to that of early twentieth-century politicians or to colonial political leaders? What are the religious traditions in the United States? In India? In Brazil? How do they affect the behavior of citizens in those countries?

Which countries are the global economic engines now, and why? What are the areas of greatest business growth? Who has more Facebook fans—Lady Gaga or Barack Obama? Curiosity feeds conversation and can be useful when you're developing campaigns targeted at 20-somethings or 40-somethings or 60-somethings. Knowledge, interests, and needs are different for each age bracket and vary by ethnicity and socioeconomic status as well.

In your preparation to be an excellent public relations professional, brush up on your cultural literacy. You might find it fun and addicting.

WHAT EMPLOYERS WANT: 10 QUALITIES

Media Savvy

Media convergence means that there are now multiple platforms for disseminating the organization's message—social media, print media, webcasts, Internet news sites, radio and television, and so on. Each platform has different deadlines, formats, and needs. Understanding their unique characteristics and being able to work with editors in each domain is essential.

Contacts

Positive relationships with people in media, government, industry groups, and nonprofit organizations, as well as with colleagues in other companies, will serve you well. The ability to pick up the phone and get crucial information or make things happen is essential.

PR Tactics, the monthly publication of the Public Relations Society of America (PRSA), asked job-placement experts which set of skills and experience was needed in today's employment market. Belinda Hulin compiled the following list based on the top responses:

Good Writing

Excellent writing skills are more necessary now than ever before.

Intelligence

Although the descriptions vary ("bright," "clever," and "quick-witted"), placement executives agree that public relations isn't a refuge for people with mediocre minds and lackluster personalities.

Cultural Literacy

Employers want individuals who are well rounded and well educated about the arts, humanities, and current events. According to *PR Tactics*, "You can't expect management to take your advice if you have no shared frame of reference."

The Ability to Recognize a Good Story When You See One

The ability to manage your organization's image—in both large and small ways—starts with the identification and management of good stories that give the organization visibility, build brand recognition, and enhance the organization's reputation.

Good Business Sense

The best companies weave public relations into their overall business strategy. To work at that level, however, public relations practitioners need to have a firm understanding of how the business operates in general and how an employer's industry works in particular. This includes the need to link public relations outcomes to the organization's ROI (return on investment).

Broad Communications Experience

To succeed, a PR professional must be familiar with all aspects of communications, from in-house newsletters to media and investor relations' documents. A working knowledge of social media platforms is essential, as is an understanding of video production processes and online distribution.

Specialized Experience

After getting some general experience, individuals should consider developing a specialty. Health care, finance, and technology are some of the most promising areas today.

Fresh Perspective

Avoid career clichés. If your only reason for getting into the PR business is because you "like people" and enjoy organizing events, you should think about another field. Employers are looking for broad-based individuals with multiple communication and problem-solving skills.

ORGANIZATIONAL Roles

Systematic research has shown that there is a hierarchy of roles in public relations practice. Professors Glen Broom and David Dozier of San Diego State University were among the first researchers to identify organizational roles ranging from the communication technician to the communication manager.

Practitioners in the technician role, for example, are primarily responsible for producing communication products and implementing decisions made by others. They take photographs, write brochures, prepare news releases, and organize events. These individuals function primarily at the "tactical" level of public relations work; they do not participate in policy decision making, nor are they responsible for outcomes. Many entry-level positions in public relations are at the technician level, but there are also many experienced practitioners whose specialty is tactical duties, such as writing and editing newsletters, maintaining information on the company's intranet or website, or even working primarily with the media in the placement of publicity.

At the other end of the employment spectrum is the communication manager. Practitioners playing this role are perceived by others as the organization's public relations experts. They make communication policy decisions and are held accountable by others and themselves for the success

Job Levels in Public Relations

EXECUTIVE
Organizational leadership and management, including developing the organizational vision, corporate mission, strategic objectives, annual goals, businesses, broad strategies, policies, and systems

DIRECTOR
Constituency and issue-trend analysis; communication and operational planning at departmental level, including planning, organizing, leading, controlling, evaluating, and problem solving

MANAGER
Constituency and issue-trend analysis; departmental management, including organizing, budgeting, leading, controlling, evaluating, and problem solving

SUPERVISOR
Project supervision, including planning, scheduling, budgeting, organizing, leading, controlling, and problem solving

ENTRY-LEVEL TECHNICIAN
Use of technical "craft" skills to disseminate information, persuade, gather data, or solicit feedback

Source: Adapted from the *Public Relations Professional Career Guide.* Public Relations Society of America, 33 Maiden Lane, New York, NY 10038.

or failure of communication programs. Managers counsel senior management, oversee multiple communication strategies, and supervise a number of employees who are responsible for tactical implementation.

Other research conducted since Broom and Dozier's study indicates that the differences between managers and technicians aren't that clear-cut. In smaller operations, a public relations professional may perform daily activities at both manager and technician levels.

The Value of INTERNSHIPS

Internships are extremely popular in the communications industry, and a student whose résumé includes practical work experience along with a good academic record has an important advantage when seeking permanent employment. The Commission on Public Relations Education believes that the internship is so important that it's one of the six recommended courses for any high-quality college or university public relations curriculum (see the btw feature in this chapter).

An internship is a win–win situation for the student and the organization. The student, in most cases, receives academic credit and gets firsthand knowledge of work in the professional world. This gives the student an advantage in getting that all-important first job after graduation. In many cases, employers hire recent graduates who worked as interns in their offices. As *PRWeek* reporter Sara Calabro says:

> Agencies and corporate communications departments are beginning to see interns as the future of their companies. While a few years ago it was typical for an intern to work for nothing, it is almost unheard of for an internship to be unpaid these days (see nearby btw feature). Examples of the essential work now entrusted to interns include tasks such as media

b t w ...

Although national and international firms routinely pay interns, this is often not the case at the local level. Many smaller companies claim that they cannot afford to pay an intern or that the opportunity to gain training and experience should be more than adequate compensation. Dave DeVries, a senior PR manager for the PCS Division of Sprint, disagrees. He wrote in PRSA's Tactics, "Unpaid internships severely limit the field of potential candidates" because, as he points out, the best and brightest students will always gravitate to employers who pay. Former Fortune 500 executive Tom Hagley also argued in Tactics that paying interns enables the students to focus their efforts and maintain high performance standards, resulting in an excellent return on any salary investment by the company.

In sum, students should make a concentrated effort to negotiate paid internships. These internships generally provide more meaningful experience, and the employers have higher expectations.

think Why are organizations more likely to favor a job candidate with internship experience?

monitoring, writing press releases, financial estimating, and compiling status reports. In many cases, interns are being included in all team and client meetings as well as in brainstorming sessions.

Calabro cites Jane Dolan, a senior account executive, who says that upper management is always impressed with the work that interns do for their final projects. "It is amazing to see them go from zero to a hundred in a matter of months," says Dolan.

Many major public relations firms have formal internship programs.

At Edelman Worldwide, for example, students enroll in "Edel-U," an internal training program that exposes them to all aspects of agency work. The summer internship program at Weber Shandwick in Boston is called "Weber University."

Hill & Knowlton also has an extensive internship training program in its New York office, taking about 40 interns each year from an applicant pool of 600 to 700 students. In its view, the internship program is "the cheapest and most effective recruiting tool available." Ketchum also places great emphasis on finding outstanding interns and making sure

they are actively involved in account work rather than spending most of their time running the photocopier or stuffing media kits.

Of course, it's not always possible for a student to do an internship in Chicago or New York. Thankfully, many opportunities are available at local public relations firms, businesses, and nonprofit agencies. It is important, however, that the organization have at least one experienced public relations professional who can mentor a student and ensure that he or she gets an opportunity to do a variety of tasks to maximize the learning experience.

Salaries IN PUBLIC RELATIONS

Public relations work pays relatively well compared to other communication professions. Many practitioners say they like the income and opportunities for steady advancement and enjoy the variety and fast pace that the field provides.

Entry-Level Salaries

Several surveys have attempted to pinpoint the national average salary for recent graduates in their first full-time job in the public relations field. Probably the most definitive survey is the one conducted by Lee Becker and his associates at the University of Georgia. They work with journalism and mass communications programs throughout the nation to compile a list of recent graduates who are then surveyed (www.grady.uga.edu/ annualsurveys/).

The latest data available (published in 2011 and based on previous-year data) show that the median annual salary for recent graduates working in public relations was $32,000. This is slightly higher than the median national average for all communication fields, which is $30,000.

Another survey, conducted by *PRWeek*, provided a more optimistic view on starting salaries in public relations. The 2011 survey found that the median salary for those with less than two years experience was $37,000.

Salaries for Experienced Professionals

While the national median salary for practitioners with 7 to 10 years of experience is approximately $85,000, the median salary for practitioners with more than 20 years of experience is considerably higher—$150,000.

Salaries, of course, depend on a number of factors, including geographic location, job title, the industry, and even the public relations specialty. Major metropolitan areas, for example, generally have higher salaries, but there are also some regional differences.

Job title also means a lot when it comes to determining salary. A senior vice president (SVP) receives a median salary of $180,000, whereas an account executive at a public relations firm gets $42,000. In terms of setting, individuals who work

think Why might people in PR earn more than their peers with similar experience working in other communication fields?

for a corporation make a median salary of $110,000, whereas those who work for a nonprofit net only $61,000 per year.

The *PRWeek* salary figures are based on a poll of just over 1,000 respondents. Due to the small size of that group, the salaries reported may or may not be indicative of the entire field. In the absence of more complete salary data, however, surveys by publications such as *PRWeek* have become the standard reference in the industry.

A good source for checking current salaries for public relations in major cities throughout the United States and around the world is PRSA's website (www.prsa.org/jobcenter). The site posts current openings and provides the salary ranges for various job classifications. For example, PRSA listed the national median salary for a corporate PR SVP in 2011 as $169,000; however, in the largest

Median Salaries for Communication Majors

Average median yearly salaries reported by recent graduates for communication fields.

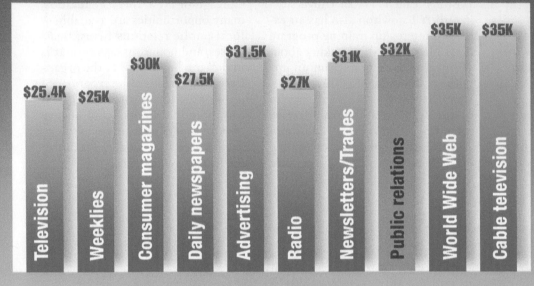

Television	$25.4K
Weeklies	$25K
Consumer magazines	$30K
Daily newspapers	$27.5K
Advertising	$31.5K
Radio	$27K
Newsletters/Trades	$31K
Public relations	$32K
World Wide Web	$35K
Cable television	$35K

Source: 2011 Annual Survey of Journalism and Mass Communication Enrollments, Grady College of Mass Communication and Journalism, University of Georgia.

markets (New York, Atlanta, Chicago, and Los Angeles), the average SVP earned $179,000. The median for a corporate public relations specialist in those cities, by comparison, was $80,000.

Salaries for Women: The Gender Gap

The *PRWeek* survey clearly shows an across-the-board gender gap in salaries.

The salary advantage that men enjoy over women is not unique to public relations; rather, it is widespread in the United States and throughout the world. The American Federation of Labor–Congress of Industrial Organizations (AFL–CIO) reports that women are paid about 80 cents for every dollar in salary men receive, a figure that has changed little over the past 10 years.

A number of studies have probed the pay differential between men and women in public relations.

The first studies in the 1980s simply noted the gap without taking into consideration the multiple factors that could lead to discrepancies. Some of these factors include (1) years of experience in the field, (2) technician duties versus managerial responsibilities, (3) the nature of the industry, (4) the size of the organization, and (5) women's attempts to balance work and family.

Some studies, for example, concluded that women were relatively new to the field and didn't have the experience yet to compete with men who had been in the field for some years. *PRWeek* points out that male respondents to its annual survey have been in the business for an average of 15 years, while the women respondents average only 11.7 years in the business.

Other studies have noted that women traditionally have been assigned low-paying "technician" roles

and have a tendency to work in areas of public relations that traditionally have low salaries, such as community relations, employee communications, or nonprofits. In contrast, a large percentage of practitioners in finance and investor relations—areas that pay well—are men.

Professors Linda Aldoory and Elizabeth Toth of the University of Maryland also explored salary discrepancies. They presented a number of factors, but essentially concluded:

The difference in the average salary of male respondents compared to female respondents was statistically significant. Regression analysis revealed that years of public relations experience accounted for much of the variance, but that gender and job interruptions also accounted for the salary difference. Age and education level were not found to be a significant influence on salary.

An Overview of Salaries in the Public Relations Field

PRWeek conducts an annual survey of salaries. The following tables are excerpted from its 2012 survey, which polled 1,007 practitioners in the field.

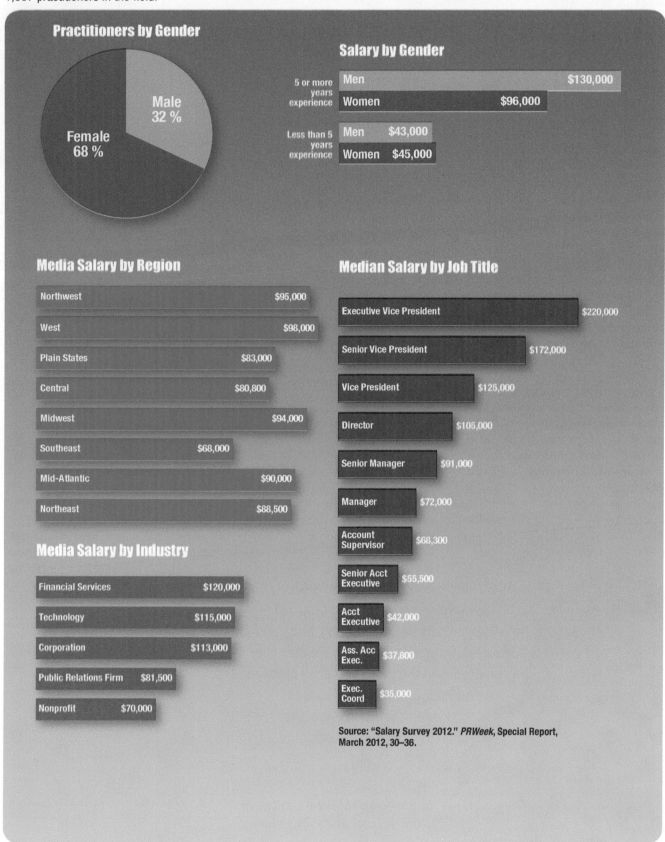

Practitioners by Gender

Male 32 %

Female 68 %

Salary by Gender

5 or more years experience	Men	$130,000
	Women	$96,000
Less than 5 years experience	Men	$43,000
	Women	$45,000

Media Salary by Region

Region	Salary
Northwest	$95,000
West	$98,000
Plain States	$83,000
Central	$80,800
Midwest	$94,000
Southeast	$68,000
Mid-Atlantic	$90,000
Northeast	$88,500

Media Salary by Industry

Industry	Salary
Financial Services	$120,000
Technology	$115,000
Corporation	$113,000
Public Relations Firm	$81,500
Nonprofit	$70,000

Median Salary by Job Title

Job Title	Salary
Executive Vice President	$220,000
Senior Vice President	$172,000
Vice President	$125,000
Director	$105,000
Senior Manager	$91,000
Manager	$72,000
Account Supervisor	$68,300
Senior Acct Executive	$55,500
Acct Executive	$42,000
Ass. Acc Exec.	$37,800
Exec. Coord	$35,000

Source: "Salary Survey 2012." *PRWeek*, Special Report, March 2012, 30–36.

The Value of PUBLIC RELATIONS

Today more than ever, the world needs not just information, but also savvy communicators and facilitators who can explain the goals and aspirations of individuals, organizations, and governments to others in a socially responsive manner.

Public relations provides businesses and society with a vital service. On a practical level, Laurence Moskowitz, chairman and CEO of Medialink, says that public relations is informative. "It's part of the news, the program, the article, the stuff readers and viewers want. It's relevant. Positive messaging through the news lifts other forms of marketing, too. Good PR increases the effectiveness of ads, direct mail, sponsorship, and all other forms of 'permission' marketing."

But the latest developments in public relations push the field beyond information dissemination. Today's practitioner must understand what effect information and communication efforts will have on the competitive position of the employer, whether that employer operates in the for-profit or nonprofit sector of the economy. By helping the modern organization manage competition and conflict, public relations professionals in this century bring added value to their employers and thereby earn a chance to exert greater influence over the destiny of the organizations where they practice public relations. That earned influence leads to greater respect and better rewards in everything from salary to personal satisfaction.

What Would You Do?

Job Hunting
A typical entry-level job posting at the PRSA.org job center is exemplified by this one from Starbucks:

Job Description: The corporate communications manager will contribute to Starbucks' success by leading communications programs across the company that focus on day-to-day incident, issues, and crisis management as well as proactive thought leadership projects and other key corporate initiatives. This role helps protect and enhance the company's reputation with strategic communication plans and materials and provides timely strategic communications counsel to all levels of the organization, including direct interaction with senior leadership of the company. The ideal candidate will have experience in issues and crisis management plus strong management skills in order to lead and/or influence teams of communicators and other cross-functional team members to execute and implement these communications strategies and plans.

Viewing job postings like this one can help you plan for your future job searches. How will you land your first job? What skill set do you believe you already have that will help you be successful in the profession? It is never too soon to be thinking along these lines. Create or update your own résumé and then draft an inquiry letter to this employer about yourself. Share the letter with a classmate and discuss ways you can make sure you are considered for an interview.

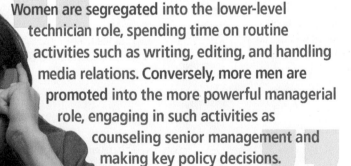

"Women are segregated into the lower-level technician role, spending time on routine activities such as writing, editing, and handling media relations. Conversely, more men are promoted into the more powerful managerial role, engaging in such activities as counseling senior management and making key policy decisions."

Julie O'Neil, professor at Texas Christian University, summarizing the conclusion of several studies, in the *Journal of Public Relations Research*

 Which vital service does public relations provide to modern organizations?

Careers in Public Relations

Beyond Facebook and Twitter QR Codes, CSCs, and StarStar Numbers

Do you get tired of organizations asking you to like, friend, follow, check in, or fan them? In *Public Relations Tactics*, Sarah Evans argues that we may be becoming oversaturated with the "social ask."

"If your social marketing consists of 'Like us on Facebook' or 'watch us on YouTube,' then this is an opportunity for you to improve," Evans writes. "You already embrace social networks, so now it's time to move away from the 'ask.'"

Evans provides some suggestions for moving beyond the "social ask":

1. Use common short codes (CSCs) to engage stakeholders on their mobile devices. Encourage key publics to enter five- or six-digit numbers into their mobile devices to access information.

2. StarStar numbers allow people to enter a mobile number beginning with ** to request a text message that may send them to a website, a video, or a place to cast a vote or enter a contest.

3. Quick response or QR codes can be used to deliver content (video, audio, text, images) or to automatically allow your stakeholder to "like" your Facebook page without having to go to the page.

PRWeek notes that retailers such as Macy's are increasingly using QR codes to lead consumers to video tips from designers whose products are sold in the department stores; HBO uses QR codes to link to a trailer for an upcoming television series; and Best Buy uses QR codes to get consumers to its mobile shopping site.

Public Relations Tactics reports that a study by Burson-Marsteller and Proof Integrated Communications found that 62 percent of *Fortune* 50 companies are using mobile communications to reach their stakeholders. Twenty-two percent of those companies are using QR codes to drive key publics to information. Jason Kintzler, CEO of social media release firm PitchEngine, suggests using QR codes to provide journalists with content when they're on the go.

Museums use QR codes to provide additional information about special exhibitions.

Social media consultant and best-selling author Chris Brogan summed up the importance of mobile communication tactics in a recent interview with *Public Relations Tactics*. "Knowing about technology won't prove your influence or your reputation," he said. "Instead, you have to show that you can leverage the new tools to improve relationships. That's the goal. The tools are just that. We don't talk about hammers when we see a new house."

1. What are some of the uses employed by organizations for QR codes, CSCs, and StarStar numbers?

2. Do you think people have become saturated by the "social ask" from organizations? Why or why not?

3. The use of QR codes in retail and media relations settings is discussed above. How might you use this tactic in employee communications? In investor relations? In community relations?

summary

How Is the Field of Public Relations Changing?

- In the past, individuals entering the field of public relations were often former journalists; this is no longer the case, because public relations has evolved beyond publicity and media relations.

- Public relations is now widely recognized as its own distinct academic discipline in colleges and universities throughout the world.

- Competition and conflict management are more essential than ever to organizations in a complex world where public acceptance and support are key to a company's or a nonprofit group's success.

Which Personal Qualifications, Attitudes, and Abilities Help Professionals Succeed in Public Relations?

- Those who plan careers in public relations should have the following abilities: writing skills, research ability, planning expertise, problem-solving ability, traditional and social media savvy, and business/economic competence.

What are the Different Job Levels and Roles in Public Relations Practice?

- Public relations professionals are employed in a variety of fields: corporations, nonprofits, entertainment and sports, politics and government, education, and international organizations and businesses.

How Much Do Public Relations Professionals Earn?

- Entry-level salaries are higher in public relations than in many other communications fields.

- A person with one or two years of experience can earn a salary of approximately $37,000, whereas a more experienced professional can earn a six-figure salary.

- Although the gender gap has somewhat narrowed, in general, women working in PR earn less than men.

questions
FOR REVIEW AND DISCUSSION

1 Public relations practitioners work for a variety of organizations. Which type of organization do you think you will prefer if you pursue work in public relations?

2 The text mentions six essential qualities for working in public relations. On a scale of 1 to 10, how would you rate yourself on each ability? How can you improve on the qualities in which you rank yourself lowest?

3 Why is it important for a student to complete an internship in college? Do you think interns should be paid?

4 The text states that job-placement directors agree that employers typically look for 10 key qualities in applicants. Can you name at least 5 of the 10 qualities? Do you possess these qualities?

5 Do you think entry-level salaries in public relations are low, high, or about what you expected? What about the salaries for experienced professionals?

6 Is there still a gender gap in salaries in public relations? If so, do you think that it is caused by discrimination, or other factors?

7 What are some of the latest ways to use social media to reach publics discussed in this chapter's Social Media in Action feature?

MySearchLab®

Today's Practice: Departments and Firms

From Chapter 4 of *Think Public Relations*, 2013 Edition. Dennis L. Wilcox, Glen T. Cameron, Bryan H. Reber, Jae-Hwa Shin.

Today's Practice: Departments and Firms

Ask Yourself

Texting Program Reaches Out to Mothers

Seventy-seven infants die every day in the U.S. Many of these deaths are preventable if expectant mothers are informed of appropriate prenatal care. A coalition of organizations—Healthy Mothers Healthy Babies Coalition, technology company Voxiva, CTIA-The Wireless Foundation, and Johnson & Johnson—created "text4baby" to address this issue. An article in *Public Relations Strategist* describes "text4baby" as "a free service that texts medical information to new mothers and mothers-to-be based on their baby's due date or date of birth. These weekly text messages give women information about their child's development, when to visit the doctor, how to best care for their baby, and how to manage the different challenges of pregnancy and parenthood."

Hill and Knowlton developed an award-winning campaign to promote the program. The PR firm started with research to identify the appropriate publics. Although many mothers and mothers-to-be could benefit from such a service, the data pointed to young low-income women as the mothers whose infants are most at risk. These young women were targeted as the primary public. Focus group research also told the PR firm that the texts needed to be friendly, not mechanical or overly technical.

With a relatively nominal $150,000 allocated for the nationwide campaign, Hill and Knowlton turned to opinion leaders and sought out sponsors to stretch dollars and effectively distribute the message.

Hill and Knowlton leveraged their modest budget by offering an exclusive to the Associated Press, getting the program mentioned on the White House blog, and having text4baby featured in episodes of the MTV series *Teen Mom* and *16 and Pregnant*.

By the end of the initial campaign, 134,000 women had signed up for the program. Almost all (96 percent) said they would recommend it to a friend. The goal of Hill and Knowlton and its partners is to have 1 million women signed up by the end of 2012.

1 How did the Hill and Knowlton firm make the most of its budget for this campaign?

2 What research informed the campaign? Why was it important?

3 Can you think of some additional strategies that might help the campaign reach its goal of enrolling 1 million women?

> Which Factors Determine the Roles and Status of Public Relations Departments in an Organization?

> Which Levels of Influence Can Public Relations Departments Exercise in an Organization?

> Which Services Do Public Relations Firms Provide?

> What Are the Pros and Cons of Employing a Public Relations Firm?

PUBLIC RELATIONS Departments

For more than a century, public relations departments have served companies and organizations. Today, public relations is expanding from its traditional functions to exercise influence in the highest levels of management. Faced with the variety of pressures in a changing environment, executives increasingly see public relations not as simply publicity and one-way communication, but as a complex and dynamic process of negotiation and compromise with key publics.

James Grunig, head of a six-year IABC (International Association of Business Communicators) Foundation research study on excellence in public relations and communications management, calls the approach "building good relationships with strategic publics." This approach requires public relations executives to be "strategic communication managers rather than communication technicians."

Grunig continues:

> When public relations helps that organization build relationships, it saves the organization money by reducing the costs of litigation, regulation, legislation, pressure campaign boycotts, or lost revenue that result from bad relationships with publics—publics that become activist groups when relationships are bad. It also helps the organization make money by cultivating relationships with donors, customers, shareholders, and legislators.

Ideally, professional public relations people assist top management in developing policy and communicating with various groups. The IABC study emphasizes that CEOs

WEEKLY.   VOLUME XXXI, NO. 1581.

THE ALTERNATING SYSTEM.

Incandescent Electric Lighting from Central Stations made Universal, Economical, and Profitable, irrespective of distance.

The Westinghouse Electric Co.,
PITTSBURGH, PA.
Eastern Office, 17 CORTLANDT STREET, NEW YORK.

George Westinghouse reportedly created the first corporate public relations department in 1889 when he hired two men to publicize his pet project, alternating current (AC) electricity. Eventually Westinghouse's approach won out over Thomas A. Edison's direct current (DC) system, and AC electricity became the standard in the United States.

want communication that is strategic, is based on research, and involves two-way communication with key publics.

Organizational Factors Determine the Role of Public Relations

Research indicates that the role of public relations in an organization often depends on the type of organization, the perceptions of top management, and even the capabilities of the public relations executive. Studies conducted by Professor Emeritus Larissa Grunig at the University of Maryland and

Mark McElreath at Towson State University, among others, show that large, complex organizations have a greater tendency than smaller firms to include public relations in the policy-making process.

Companies such as IBM and General Motors, which operate in a highly competitive environment, are sensitive to policy issues and public attitudes and have a vested interest in establishing a solid corporate identity. Consequently, they place greater emphasis on news conferences, formal contact with the media, executive speeches, and counseling management about issues that could potentially affect the corporate bottom line. In such organizations, the authority and power of the public relations department are quite high; public relations is part of the "dominant coalition" and has a great deal of autonomy.

In contrast, a small-scale organization that offers a standardized product or service feels few public pressures and faces little governmental regulatory interest. It has

The results of the IABC study of 200 organizations showed that CEOs considered public relations operations to provide a 184 percent return on investment (ROI).

nominal public relations activity, and PR staff members may be relegated to technician roles such as producing the company newsletter and issuing routine news releases. Public relations in such organizations has little or no input into management decisions and policy formation.

However, research also indicates that the type of organization may be less significant in predicting the role of public relations than are the perceptions and expectations of its top management. In many organizations, top-level management perceives public relations as primarily a journalistic and technical function—that is, as media relations and publicity. In large-scale organizations of low complexity, there is also a tendency to think of public relations as merely a support function of the marketing department.

Such perceptions severely limit the role of the public relations department as well as its power to take part in management decision

> ## "PR departments that closely align their own goals with their companies' strategic business goals receive greater executive support, have larger budgets, and have a **higher perceived contribution** to their organizations' success."
>
> *PRWeek* summary of a study by the Strategic Communication and Public Relations Center at the University of Southern California's Annenberg Center and the Council of Public Relations Firms

making. In these types of organizations, public relations is relegated to a tactical function—preparing messages without input on message strategy. In many cases, however, in these organizations public relations personnel self-select technician roles because they lack a knowledge base in research, environmental scanning, problem solving, and managing total communication strategies or because they are more personally fulfilled by working tactically rather than strategically.

The most reputable *Fortune* 500 corporations tend to think of public relations as a strategic management tool. A study by the Strategic Communication and Public Relations Center at the University of Southern California's Annenberg Center and the Council of Public Relations Firms found that these companies dedicated a larger percentage of their gross revenues to public relations activities, extensively used outside public relations firms to supplement their own large staffs, and did not have their public relations staff report to the marketing department.

The primary indicator of a department's influence and power, however, is whether the top communication

officer has a seat at the management table. In fact, gaining and maintaining a seat at the management table should be an ongoing goal of public relations practitioners. Experts indicate that it is increasingly common for the top public relations practitioner in an organization to report to the CEO. But these PR pros must know how to contribute to maintain their place at the table, according to Tom Martin, former senior vice president of corporate relations for ITT industries.

In its 2012 GAP VII report based on a survey of 620 senior-level practitioners, the Strategic Communication and Public Relations Center at the University of Southern California's Annenberg Center found that almost 60 percent of all corporate respondents reported to either the CEO (chief executive officer) or the COO (chief operating officer).

> ## "In order for PR to be at its most effective, it simply has to report up to the CEO."
>
> Gil Schwartz, executive vice president and chief communication officer at CBS

The 2012 report also noted that 60 percent of the respondents strongly agreed that the public relations function is well received in the C-Suite and that members of the public relations/communications department are invited to attend senior-level strategy meetings. In a prior GAP report, the Center found that CEO's ranked public relations second only to marketing for its contribution to organizational success.

Whether they report to the C-suite or not, public relations personnel have influence. A 2011 survey of corporate

think Why does it contribute to organizational health when public relations are part of the managerial subsystem and contribute to the company's overall strategy?

---

b t w ...

Dudley H. Hafner, former executive vice president of the American Heart Association (AHA), asserts, "In the non-profit business sector, as well as in the for-profit business of America, leadership needs to pay close attention to what our audiences (supporters or customers as well as the general public) want, what they need, what their attitudes are, and what is happening in organizations similar to ours. Seeking, interpreting, and communicating this type of critical information is the role of the communications professional."

Julie O'Neil of Texas Christian University reported in a *Public Relations Review* article that the following factors determine whether corporate public relations practitioners have influence in the company:

1 Perception of value by top management
2 Practitioners taking on the managerial role
3 Reporting to the CEO
4 Years of professional experience

Bruce Berger of the University of Alabama and Bryan Reber of the University of Georgia interviewed 162 public relations professionals and found five major sources of influence among those practitioners:

1 Relationships with others
2 Professional experience
3 Performance record
4 Persuasive skills with top executives
5 Professional expertise

communicators by *PRWeek* found that 94 percent of respondents said they have a seat at the decision-making table at the earliest stages of discussions that will eventually require internal or external communications.

How Public Relations Departments Are Organized

The head executive of a public relations or similarly named department typically has one of three titles: manager, director, or vice president. A vice president of corporate communications may have direct responsibility for the additional activities of advertising and marketing communications.

A department is usually divided into specialized sections that have a coordinator or manager. Common divisions found in large corporations include media relations, investor relations, consumer affairs, governmental relations, community relations, marketing communications, and employee communications.

Many large global corporations such as IBM and General Electric have a substantial communications function. Communications at IBM, for example, is led by a senior vice president (SVP) of marketing, communications, and citizenship. Directly beneath the SVP in the organizational structure are 13 vice presidents overseeing areas including external relations, marketing, corporate affairs, executive communications, and employee

communications. The range of job titles runs from general manager for public relations at Porsche, North America, to managing director, head of communications and public affairs at Deutsche Bank USA.

Companies like GE are the exceptions, however. The USC study found that among the largest companies, the average public relations staff size is 60 employees. And 15 percent of these companies experienced hiring even in a down economy. Sixty-two percent experienced no change in staffing during the recent economic downturn. Another study by the Conference Board of other large U.S. corporations found that the typical public relations department had nine professionals. The USC study found that the average annual budget across all categories, from corporate to nonprofit, was $4.7 million. Reported average budgets ranged from $900,000 for government departments and small companies to $8.2 million for the largest companies. Of course, thousands of even smaller companies employ only one or two public relations practitioners.

Public relations personnel may be so dispersed throughout an organization that an observer can have difficulty ascertaining the true extent of public relations activity. Some staff may focus on marketing communications in the marketing department. Others may be assigned to the personnel department as communication specialists

producing newsletters and brochures. Still others may be in marketing, working exclusively on product publicity.

In addition to operating in different departments and fulfilling the functions listed in the nearby feature "Who Is Doing What?," public relations practitioners report that recently they have had to take on new responsibilities. In a 2011 survey by *PRWeek*, 47 percent of corporate

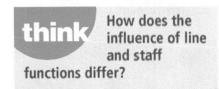
think How does the influence of line and staff functions differ?

communicators said they have added social networks and applications to their list of responsibilities; 30 percent have added blogger relations; 20 percent have added online tracking; and 15 percent each have added search marketing or digital creative/website development. We discuss decentralization of the public relations function and the frictions it causes later in this chapter.

Line and Staff Functions

Traditional management theory divides an organization into line and staff functions. A line manager, such as a vice president of manufacturing, can delegate authority, set production goals, hire employees, and directly influence the work of others. Staff people, in contrast, have

Who Is Doing What?

The Functions of Corporate Public Relations/ Communication Departments

Function	Percentage
Media relations	97%
Crisis/issues management	96%
Executive communications	93%
Social networks and applications	89%
Online tracking	85%
Blogger relations	84%
Community relations	84%
Employee communications	82%
Promotions	75%
Cause-related marketing	74%
Public affairs/government relations	69%
Investor/financial relations	57%
Annual reports/quarterly reports	55%
Issues advertising	54%
Marketing research and analytics	49%
Product/brand advertising	48%
Direct marketing	46%
Corporate reputation management	39%
Other	14%

The percentages of corporate departments that said they were ultimately responsible for various activities in response to a 2010 survey by *PRWeek*.

Source: Corporate Survey, *PRWeek*, October 2010.

little or no direct authority. Instead, they indirectly influence the work of others through suggestions, recommendations, and advice.

According to accepted management theory, public relations is a staff function. Public relations professionals are experts in communication; line managers, including the CEO, rely on them to use their skills in preparing and processing data, making recommendations, and executing communication programs to meet organizational objectives.

Public relations staff members, for example, may find through a community survey that people have only a vague understanding of what their company manufactures. To improve community comprehension and create greater rapport, the public relations department may recommend to top management that a community open house be held, featuring product demonstrations, tours, and entertainment.

Notice that in this example, the PR department simply recommends this action. It has no direct authority to decide on its own to hold an open house or to order various departments within the company to cooperate. If top management approves the proposal, the PR department may take responsibility for organizing the event. Top management, as line managers, has the authority to direct all departments to cooperate in the activity. Although public relations departments can function only with the approval of top management, they may exert varying levels of influence over the organization and its direction. These levels will be discussed shortly.

The power and influence of a public relations department usually result from access to top management, which uses advice and recommendations from the remainder of the organization to formulate policy. That is why public relations, like some other staff functions, is located high in the organizational chart and is called on by top management to make reports and recommendations on issues affecting the entire company. In today's environment, public acceptance or nonacceptance of a proposed policy is an important factor in decision making.

Levels of Influence

Management experts state that staff functions in an organization operate at various levels of influence and authority. At the lowest level, the staff function may be simply advisory: line management has no obligation to take recommendations or even request them.

When the public relations department serves in a purely advisory role, it often is not effective. The Susan G. Komen for the Cure foundation, the nation's leading breast cancer advocacy group, learned this lesson in 2012 the hard way. It created a storm of protest when word got out that its board of directors had decided to stop giving grants to Planned Parenthood to provide poor women with breast cancer screenings.

The decision immediately energized the pro-choice community who perceived it as a "political" decision by the foundation to appease anti-abortion advocates who were opposed to Planned Parenthood because it also provided abortion counseling to women among its many other health services. Adding credence to this perception was Komen's senior vice president of public policy, Karen Handel, who described herself as "staunchly and unequivocally pro-life."

The advice and counsel of Komen's public relations staff seems to have been minimal in terms of how the public and the media would respond to Komen's decision to enter the fray of partisan debate on abortion. In fact, the organization didn't even issue a news release about its decision, nor did it inform its affiliates and employees of the decision, which inflamed even more criticism among thousands of "pro-choice" women who had given time and money to the organization.

The fall-out was immediate. The volume of online chatter about Komen's decision went up 80 percent in just a day, and almost 70 percent of the posts were negative about the decision. In addition, 26 U.S. senators sent a letter of protest and pro-choice activists around the country called for a boycott of Komen's corporate sponsors. Mainstream media also editorialized about the decision. The *San Jose (CA) Mercury News*, for example, said "Cutting off funds for breast cancer screenings by Planned Parenthood could be the most cowardly act by a health foundation in U.S. history."

By the end of the week, the Komen Foundation reversed its decision and said it would continue to fund Planned Parenthood's cancer screening program. A week later, Karen Handel resigned as the foundation sought to rebuild its credibility and reputation.

Johnson & Johnson, in contrast, accords its public relations staff function higher status. The Tylenol crisis in the 1980s, in which seven

The Challenge of Being a Spokesperson

ethics in ACTION

One duty of a public relations practitioner is to serve as an organization's official spokesperson. What a spokesperson tells the media is not considered a personal opinion, but rather management's official response or stance to a situation or event. Lauren Fernandez, a public relations professional and blogger, says, "As PR professionals, we represent a client, brand, and organization."

The challenge comes when a spokesperson may personally disagree with what he or she is asked to say on behalf of the organization. Or, in some cases, a public relations professional may be asked to give information to the media that he or she knows is untrue or deliberately misleading. Consider these examples:

- The spokesman for Anthony Weiner, former representative to Congress from New York, told the media that Weiner's Facebook and Twitter accounts had been hacked. The spokesman blamed Weiner's political enemies. "This is intended to be a distraction, and we're not going to let it become one. Anthony's accounts were obviously hacked. He doesn't know the person named by the hacker, and we will be consulting on what steps to take next." All of the denials were ultimately proven false—Weiner posted the photo, knew the woman, and his accounts were not hacked by political enemies.

- When nuclear reactors were compromised following a tsunami in Japan, the industry was accused not only of providing erratic and contradictory information about safety during the crisis, it was also accused of having perpetuated a "safety myth" through

public relations efforts before the crisis occurred. For example, exhibitions that extolled the virtues of nuclear power had been promoted as virtual tourist attractions in Japan, some even featuring animated robots of characters from *Alice in Wonderland.* After the accident, the Japanese minister of economy, trade, and industry said in a press conference, "In Japan, we have something called the 'safety myth.' It's a fact that there was an unreasonable overconfidence in the technology of Japan's nuclear power generation."

These examples raise important ethical issues. Should a spokesperson just tell the media what the organization wants communicated, or should the individual also be guided by what he or she thinks is truthful and accurate?

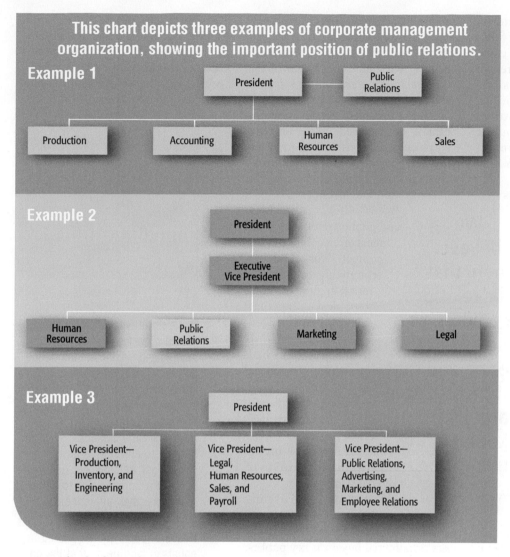

This chart depicts three examples of corporate management organization, showing the important position of public relations.

Example 1

President — Public Relations

Production | Accounting | Human Resources | Sales

Example 2

President

Executive Vice President

Human Resources | Public Relations | Marketing | Legal

Example 3

President

Vice President—Production, Inventory, and Engineering | Vice President—Legal, Human Resources, Sales, and Payroll | Vice President—Public Relations, Advertising, Marketing, and Employee Relations

persons died after taking capsules that had been tampered with and contained cyanide, is a classic case that clearly shows how the company based much of its reaction and quick recall of the product on the advice of public relations staff. In this case, public relations occupied a *compulsory-advisory* position. Under a *compulsory-advisory* setup, organizational policy requires that line managers (top management) at least listen to the appropriate staff experts before deciding on a strategy.

Another level of advisory relationship within an organization is *concurring authority*. In this type of organization for example, an operating division wishing to publish a brochure cannot do so unless the public relations department approves the copy and layout. If differences arise, the parties must

agree before work can proceed. Many firms use this mode to prevent departments and divisions from disseminating materials that do not conform with established company standards.

Concurring authority may limit the freedom of the public relations department as well. For example, some companies have a policy that all employee-created magazine articles and external news releases must be reviewed by the legal staff before publication. Material cannot be disseminated until legal and public relations personnel have agreed on the content. The situation is even more restrictive for public relations when the legal department has *command authority* to change a news release with or without the consent of public relations. This

is one reason that some news releases are so filled with "legalese" as to be almost unreadable.

Sometimes legal counsel and public relations practitioners work collaboratively. When Norfolk Southern railroad embarked on a bid to buy Conrail, Norfolk Southern's public relations executive Robert Fort recalled that in-house representatives of public relations and law met daily. "We had to be very careful what we said and how we said it and also to get it reported to the Securities and Exchange Commission on a daily basis," said one of Norfolk Southern's in-house lawyers. Fort noted that legal and public relations personnel were on equal footing. "In the past ... eventually, if there is a point of contention between PR and law, law usually wins," he explained. "In this case, the law department was not only asking us for our advice, but then used it when we gave it to them. I think they recognized that this was an historic event about to take place and that as it unfolded it was going to have to be won on the basis of public opinion."

Logic dictates that an organization needs a coordinated and integrated approach to communications strategy. Indeed, one survey found that 65 percent of corporate managers are now spending more time on developing integrated communication programs than they had in the past.

Sources of Friction

Ideally, public relations is part of the managerial subsystem and contributes to organizational strategy. Public relations is, say professors James and Larissa Grunig, "the management of communication between an organization and its publics." Of course, other staff functions are also involved in the communication process with internal and external publics. In addition, internal friction can occur. Internal friction often involves the relationship between public relations and legal, human resources, advertising, and marketing departments.

Legal. Legal staff members are always concerned about the possible effect of any public statement on current or potential litigation. Consequently, lawyers often frustrate public relations personnel by taking the attitude that any public statement can potentially be used against the organization in a lawsuit. Conflicts over which information to release and when often have a paralyzing effect, causing the organization to seem unresponsive to public concerns. This is particularly true in a crisis, when the public demands immediate release of information.

Human Resources. Turf battles can erupt between human resources

and public relations over who is responsible for employee communications. Human resources personnel believe that they should control the flow of information; public relations administrators counter by stating that satisfactory external communications cannot be achieved unless effective employee relations are conducted simultaneously. Layoffs, for example, affect not only employees but also the community and investors.

Advertising. Advertising and public relations departments often collide as they compete for funds to communicate with external audiences. Philosophical differences may also arise. Advertising's approach to communications may be, "Will it increase sales?" while public relations might ask, "Will it make friends?" These different orientations can cause breakdowns in coordination of overall strategy.

Marketing. Marketing personnel, like advertising staff, tend to think exclusively of customers or potential buyers as key publics. In contrast, public relations practitioners define *publics* in a broader sense—as any group that can affect

the operations of the organization. These publics include governmental agencies, environmental groups, neighborhood clubs, and a host of other groups that marketing would not consider customers.

> "We believe, then, that public relations must emerge as a discipline distinct from marketing and that it must be practiced separately from marketing in the organization."
>
> James Grunig

Achieving the Goal of Developing Integrated Communication Programs

- Representatives of departments should serve together on key committees and exchange information on how collaboration among departments with shared interests in communication issues can help achieve organization-wide business goals. If representatives from human resources, public relations, legal, and investor relations present a united front to senior managers, their influence can increase exponentially.

- Heads of departments should be equals in job title so that the autonomy of one department is not subverted by another.

- All department heads should report to the same superior, so that all viewpoints are considered before an appropriate strategy is formulated.

- Informal, regular contact between representatives of other departments should be encouraged to help dispel competitive mind-sets and foster understanding and respect.

- Written policies should spell out the responsibilities of each department. Such policies are helpful in settling disputes over which department has authority to communicate with employees or manage the organization's social media platforms.

Organizational Alignment Between Public Relations and Marketing

35% say alignment is a big issue but their department is making satisfactory progress in that direction

3% do not consider alignment a priority

49% are satisfied with the level of alignment

13% say alignment is a big issue and they are not satisfied with the level of alignment

Source: Corporate Survey, *PRWeek*, October 2010.

The Trend Toward OUTSOURCING

A major trend among U.S. corporations has been the outsourcing of services ranging from telecommunications, accounting, customer service, software engineering, to even legal services. Similarly, organizations have sought to outsource their communication activities to public relations firms and outside contractors in recent years. Indeed, the 2012 USC study found that corporations now spend 18 percent of their public relations budgets on outside firms. More than 90 percent of the large companies in the 2012 survey use outside counsel in varying degrees.

The trend toward outsourcing of the public relations function, say many experts, follows what has occurred in advertising. It currently appears that public relations firms will be the major beneficiaries of this trend. Instead of relying exclusively on an in-house department or using just one firm, today's major corporations now use multiple firms for various projects.

Top Ten Reasons for Working with Agencies

Below are the top reasons that organizations give for working with agencies and the percentage of respondents who cited each reason.

1 They provide additional "arms and legs" 6.0%
2 They provide a unique perspective 5.7%
3 They provide market insight 5.6%
4 They offer a strategic point of view 5.3%
5 They extend the geographic reach 4.5%
6 They help quantify results 4.4%
7 They provide expertise in digital/social media 4.3%
8 We have a limit on internal "head count" 4.2%
9 They are cheaper 4.1%

From the 2012 GAP VII Study by USC's Annenberg Center.

Most Frequently Outsourced Activities

1. Writing and communications

2. Media relations

3. Publicity

4. Strategy and planning

5. Event planning

Source: Bisbee & Co. and Leone Marketing Research.

An Annenberg study found that *Fortune 500* companies now typically work with three or four different agencies to "cherry-pick" the best agency for a particular situation.

PUBLIC RELATIONS Firms

There are public relations firms in every industrialized nation and in most countries in the developing world. Firms range in size from one- or two-person operations to global giants such as Edelman, which employs almost 3,700 professionals in 15 U.S. offices and 57 offices around the world. The scope of services that PR firms provide to clients varies, although some common denominators do exist. Large or small, each firm gives counsel and performs technical services to carry out an agreed-upon program. A firm may operate as an adjunct to an organization's public relations department or, if no in-house department exists, conduct the entire effort.

The United States is home to most of the world's public relations firms and generates the most fee income because of its large population and economic base. In fact, the international committee of the Public Relations Consultancies Association reported in a worldwide study that the fee income of U.S. firms "plainly dwarfs those in all other regions."

In 2011, the five largest independent firms (Edelman, Fleishman-Hillard, Waggener Edstrom Worldwide, Ruder Finn, and APCO Worldwide) generated $937,075,658 in revenues in the United States alone. (Some of the largest firms, such as Burson-Marsteller and Ketchum, are part of conglomerate holding companies that don't release separate financial data for each of their companies.)

American public relations firms have proliferated in proportion to the growth of the global economy. As U.S. companies expanded after World War II into booming domestic and worldwide markets, many corporations felt a need for public relations firms that could provide them with professional expertise.

think — Why does the United States have more public relations firms than all other nations combined?

Increased urbanization, expansion of government bureaucracy and regulation, more sophisticated mass media systems, the rise of consumerism, international trade, and the demand for more information have also stimulated the growth of public relations firms. Executives of public relations firms predict healthy future growth for the industry as more countries adopt free-market economies and more international media outlets are established. In addition, the skyrocketing use of the Internet has expanded the global reach of public relations firms. In a 2011 survey, *PRWeek* reported that 58 percent of marketing practitioners said they expected social media to have an increasing impact on generating sales and revenue.

Public relations firms are beginning to discard the term *public relations* as part of their official names. For example, it's "Burson-Marsteller," not "Burson-Marsteller Public Relations." Other firms use the term *communications* to describe their business. For example, Fenton Communications describes itself as a "public interest communications firm."

Increasingly, public relations firms are emphasizing the counseling aspect of their services, although most of their revenues come from implementing tactical aspects, such as writing news releases and organizing special events or media tours.

FedEx turned to global public relations firm Ketchum to help promote goodwill between the U.S. and China and raise awareness of the air cargo company's Asian routes and its logistical expertise with sensitive cargo. The FedEx Panda Express was promoted by the return of two giant pandas from U.S. zoos to a preserve in China.

Today's Practice: Departments and Firms

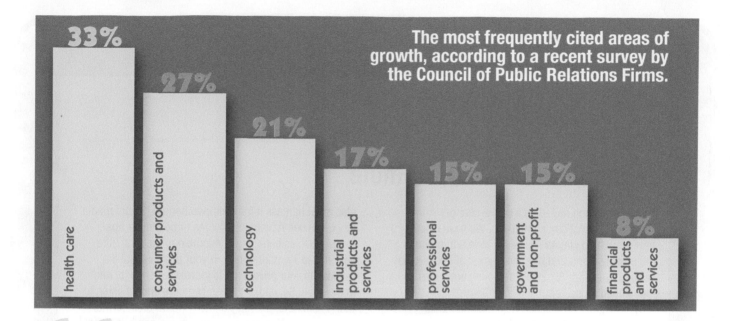

33% health care

27% consumer products and services

21% technology

17% industrial products and services

15% professional services

15% government and non-profit

8% financial products and services

The most frequently cited areas of growth, according to a recent survey by the Council of Public Relations Firms.

"In the beginning, top management used to say to us, 'Here's the message; deliver it.' Then it became, 'What should we say?' Now, in smart organizations, it's 'What should we do?'"

Harold Burson, chairman of Burson-Marsteller

Services Provided by Public Relations Firms

- **Marketing Communications.** Promote products and services through such tools as news releases, feature stories, special events, brochures, and media tours.
- **Executive Speech Training.** Coach top executives on public affairs activities, including personal appearances.
- **Research and Evaluation.** Conduct scientific surveys to measure public attitudes and perceptions.
- **Crisis Communication.** Counsel management on what to say and do in the event of an emergency, such as an oil spill or a product recall.
- **Media Analysis.** Examine appropriate media in order to target specific messages to key audiences.
- **Community Relations.** Counsel management on achieving official and public support for projects such as new building construction or factory expansion.
- **Events Management.** Plan and conduct news conferences, anniversary celebrations, rallies, symposia, and national conferences.
- **Public Affairs.** Prepare materials and testimony for government hearings and regulatory bodies; prepare background briefings.

- **Branding and Corporate Reputation.** Provide advice on programs that establish company brands and promote reputation.
- **Financial Relations.** Counsel management to communicate effectively with stockholders, security analysts, and institutional investors and avoid takeover by other firms.
- **Specialty services.** Firms such as Edelman have formed **digital media** practices that concentrate on online and social media. Ketchum offers expertise in crisis management. Burson-Marsteller set up a specialty area in grassroots outreach. Addressing new realities for both businesses and government entities, Fleishman-Hillard set up a practice in global **security** and promotes the services of its International Advisory Board of former federal and military experts in terrorism and security. Other firms offer specialty services in such areas as **litigation public relations** to help organizations give their side of the story when major lawsuits are filed.

SocialMediaInAction

Firms Tweet to Self-Promote

Twitter has been hailed as a game-changer within many public relations campaigns. We have discussed how firms help clients use social media to promote the organizations that hire the firms, but here we ask another question: Are public relations firms also using microblogging systems to self-promote?

Research by U.K.-based ActiMedia, a media directory organization, identified trends in the use of Twitter by public relations firms. Although only 528 of the 10,911 public relations firms listed by ActiMedia were using Twitter in 2011, the use of Twitter in self-promotion is a trend that will likely grow and that is worth monitoring.

There are substantial differences between countries in the adoption of Twitter by PR agencies. The country with the highest proportion of agencies that tweet is China, at 71 percent. That is, 71 percent of the Chinese agencies listed in the ActiMedia database use Twitter. Italy came in second, with 33 percent of its agencies tweeting. Twenty-one percent of Canadian agencies used Twitter. But only 5 percent of U.S. agencies and 7 percent of U.K. agencies were found to tweet.

Globally, the trend among PR firms of creating Twitter accounts started in 2007 and peaked in 2009, with 259 in that year. In 2011, only 73 firms created accounts.

As you know, tweeters are measured by the company they keep. Just as Facebook fans are the lifeblood of Facebook pages, Twitter followers are the ultimate goal of tweeters. The most popular PR tweeter according to the ActiMedia report was based at Edelman PR Germany and generated 56,581 tweets to 7,559 followers beginning in 2007. The most-followed agency was Ink Foundry PR, with 21,766 followers. ICPAR DEHLI garnered nearly as many (20,242) followers.

Public relations firms not only need to know how to advise their clients on employing social media, they also must harness it for their own benefit. Social media blogger Helen Alfvegren provides three simple tips for businesses engaging in microblogging. First, she writes, use Twitter not only in your professional life, but also in your private life to increase credibility and knowledge. Second, business tweeters should listen to their customers, and they should embed their Twitter feeds on their homepages to encourage consumers to follow the feeds. Finally, she suggested that it's useful to learn from others. Follow the tweets of people and organizations you admire and that are involved in your business sector.

1 Should public relations firms or practitioners engage in tweeting? Why or why not?

2 Do you rely on Twitter as a means to learn about organizations or individuals?

Because of the counseling role played by many PR organizations, we use the phrase "public relations *firm*" instead of "public relations *agency*" throughout this book. Advertising firms, in contrast, are properly called agencies because they serve as agents, buying time or space on behalf of a client.

A good source of information about public relations counseling is the Council of Public Relations Firms, which has approximately 100 member firms. This group provides information on its website (www.prfirms.org) about trends in the industry and offers advice on how to select a public relations firm, as well as a variety of other materials. In addition, the Council of Public Relations Firms operates a career center and posts résumés on its website for individuals looking for employment with a public relations firm.

Global Reach

Public relations firms, large and small, are usually located in metropolitan areas. On an international level, firms and their offices or affiliates can be found in most of the world's major cities and capitals. Fleishman-Hillard, for example, has employees in 70 countries. Ogilvy Public Relations has 1,950 employees in 9 U.S. offices and 72 offices worldwide.

The importance of being an international presence is reflected in the fact that most of the major public relations firms generate substantial revenues from international operations. Edelman, for example, had $530 million in revenues in 2010, but one-third of this revenue came from its international offices. Burson-Marsteller, with 68 offices globally, generates one-half to two-thirds of its revenues from its international operations.

International work is not reserved only for large firms. Small- and medium-sized firms around the world have formed working partnerships with one another so that they can serve their clients' needs more effectively. One prominent group in this regard is Worldcom Public Relations Group, with 107 firms in 91 cities on six continents. Other groups include Pinnacle Worldwide, with 46 firms in 28 nations, and Iprex, with 68 firms with 90 offices in 30 nations.

When working as part of a global affiliation, firms cooperate with one another to service clients with international public relations needs. For example, a firm in India may call its affiliate in Los Angeles to handle the details of news coverage for a visiting trade delegation from India.

> **"One of the reasons we started in the first place was to provide clients with a need for reach beyond their own markets."**
>
> Bob Oltmanns, head of Iprex, in *PRWeek*

The Rise of Communication Conglomerates

Until the 1970s, the largest public relations firms were independently owned by their founders or, in some cases, by employee stockholders. A significant change began in 1973, when Carl Byoir & Associates, then the largest U.S. public relations firm, was purchased by the advertising firm of Foote, Cone & Belding. In short order, other large public relations firms were purchased by major advertising agencies.

Today, both public relations firms and advertising agencies have become part of large, diversified holding companies with global reach. Interpublic Group (IPG) not only owns Foote, Cone & Belding (now called Draftfcb) and other advertising agencies, but also 11 public relations firms. These firms include Weber Shandwick, Golin-Harris, Carmichael Lynch Spong,

DeVries Public Relations, and Tierney Communications.

IPG, despite total 2010 revenues of $6.5 billion, is only the fourth-largest holding company. London-based WPP, the largest with $14.4 billion in revenues, generates almost 60 percent of its revenues outside of advertising. Like the other communication conglomerates, it owns a host of companies specializing in such areas as advertising, marketing, billboards, direct mail, special event promotion, graphic design, survey research, and public relations. For example, WPP owns 10 major public relations firms, including Burson-Marsteller, Cohn and Wolfe, Hill and Knowlton, and Ogilvy PR.

Large conglomerates acquire public relations firms for several reasons. One is the natural evolutionary step of integrating various communication disciplines into "total communication networks." Supporters of integration assert that no single-function agency or firm is equipped with the personnel or resources to handle complex, global, integrated marketing functions efficiently. In addition, joint efforts by public relations and advertising professionals can offer prospective clients greater communications impact, generate more business, and expand the number of geographical locations served around the world.

think What advantages can a global conglomerate offer a corporate client?

A second reason to acquire PR firms is purely economic. Holding companies find public relations firms to be attractive investments. According to *PRWeek*, revenues from advertising clients have remained somewhat static over the years, whereas revenues of public relations firms often experience double-digit growth.

Efforts to create total communication networks for clients have met with success. Considerable new

What are the
disadvantages
of going with a
large conglomerate?

Global campaigns still need to take local customs into account.

business is also generated when units of the same conglomerate refer customers to each other. As communication campaigns become more integrated, even more synergy will become commonplace.

Holding companies originally started out primarily as a stable of advertising agencies under one umbrella, but they have evolved beyond that. London-based WPP, for example, now employs 146,000 people (including associates) in more than 100 nations. Martin Sorrell, chairman of WPP (London), told a *Wall Street Journal* interviewer, "If you want to upset me, call me an advertising agency. The strategic objective is for two-thirds of our revenue to come from nontraditional advertising in 5 to 10 years. Instead of focusing on network television, we have to look at public relations and radio and outdoor and mobile

messaging and satellite. Media planning becomes more important."

Sorrell also makes the point that "one size doesn't fit all" when it comes to global communications strategies and campaigns. Campaigns still have to be tailored

to local customs, ethnic groups, and religious preferences. For example, Muslims are projected to constitute 26 percent of the world's population by 2030. By the same year, two-thirds of the world's population will be Asian.

Major Public Relations Firms Owned by CONGLOMERATES

An estimated 60 percent of the global business in public relations is conducted by firms that are owned by communication conglomerates that also own advertising agencies, marketing firms, billboard companies, direct mail firms, and event planning specialty shops.

The following pie charts identify the major holding companies based on their 2010 total revenues, including the percentage of their revenues that came from nonadvertising sources. The pie slices shown in white are the percentages of revenues that come from public relations.

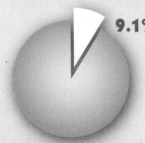

9.1%

9%

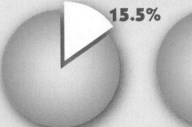

15.5%

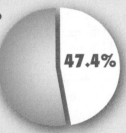

47.4%

OMNICOM
Total revenues: $12.5 billion
Percentage of revenues from public relations: 9.1 percent, or about $1.1 billion
Owns these public relations firms, among others: Porter Novelli, Fleishman-Hillard, and Ketchum

WPP
Total revenues: $14.4 billion
Percentage of revenues from public relations: 9 percent, or about $1.38 billion
Owns these public relations firms, among others: Hill and Knowlton, Burson-Marsteller, and Ogilvy Public Relations

INTERPUBLIC GROUP
Total revenues: $6.53 billion
Percentage of revenues from public relations: 15.5 percent, or about $1.01 billion
Owns these public relations firms, among others: Weber Shandwick and GolinHarris

PUBLICIS GROUPE
Total revenues: $7.4 billion
Percentage of revenues from public relations: 47.4 percent
Owns this public relations firm, among others: MSLGroup

Source: "Agency Business Report 2011." *PRWeek*, May 2011, 76–79.

Structure of a Counseling Firm

A small public relations firm may consist only of the owner (president) and an assistant (vice president) who are supported by an administrative assistant. As you might expect, larger firms generally have a more extended hierarchy.

The organization of Ketchum's San Francisco operation is fairly typical. The president is based in Ketchum's New York office, so the executive vice president is the on-site director in San Francisco. A senior vice president is the associate director of operations. Next in line are several vice presidents who primarily do account supervision or special projects.

Each account supervisor is in charge of one major account or several smaller ones. Each account executive reports to an account supervisor and is in direct contact with the client and handles most of the day-to-day activity involving that account. At the bottom of the pecking order are the assistant account executives, who do routine maintenance work such as compiling media lists, gathering information, and writing rough drafts of news releases.

Recent college graduates usually start as assistant account executives. Once they learn the firm's procedures and show ability, promotion to account executive may occur within 6 to 18 months. After two or three years, it is not uncommon for an account executive to become an account supervisor.

Executives at the vice-president level and above are typically heavily involved in selling their firm's services. To prosper, a firm must continually seek new business and sell additional services to current clients. To that end, the upper management of the firm calls on prospective clients, prepares proposals, and makes new business presentations. In this very competitive field, a firm that is not adept at selling itself does not succeed and prosper.

Firms frequently organize account teams, especially to serve a client whose program is multifaceted. One member of the team may set up a nationwide media tour in which an organization representative is booked on television talk shows. Another may supervise all materials for the print media, including news stories, feature articles, background kits, and artwork. A third may concentrate on the trade press or arrange special events.

Pros and Cons of Using a Public Relations Firm

Because public relations is a service industry, a firm's major asset is its people. Potential clients thinking about hiring a public relations firm usually base their decisions on the quality of the staff at the firm, according to a survey of *Fortune* 500 corporate communication vice presidents.

Thomas L. Harris, a consultant who conducted a survey of corporate communication directors, found that clients believe that meeting deadlines and keeping promises are the most important criteria in evaluating firms. Other important considerations are, in descending order, client services; honest, accurate billing; creativity; and knowledge of the client's industry.

Advantages. Public relations firms offer several advantages for the organizations that hire them when compared to doing the work in-house:

- *Objectivity.* The firm can analyze a client's needs or problems from a new perspective and offer fresh insights.
- *A Variety of Skills and Expertise.* A firm has specialists, whether in speech writing, trade magazine placement, or helping with investor relations.
- *Extensive Resources.* A firm has abundant media contacts and works regularly with numerous suppliers of products and services. It has research materials, including

data information banks. International jobs, such as handling the corporate sponsorship issues that arise in conjunction with the Olympics, benefit from the extensive resources of a firm.

- *Offices Throughout the Country.* A national public relations program requires coordination in major cities. Large firms have on-site staffs or affiliate firms in many cities and even around the world.
- *Special Problem-Solving Skills.* A firm may have extensive experience and a solid reputation in desired areas. For example, Burson-Marsteller has specialty practices in crisis communications, health and medical issues, and financial communication.
- *Credibility.* A successful public relations firm has a solid reputation for professional, ethical work. A client who is represented by such a firm is likely to get more attention from opinion leaders in mass media, government, and the financial community.

Disadvantages. There are also drawbacks to using public relations firms:

- *Superficial Grasp of the Client's Unique Problems.* Although objectivity is gained from an outsider's perspective, there is often a disadvantage in that the public relations firm may not thoroughly understand the client's business or needs.
- *Lack of Full-Time Commitment.* A public relations firm has many clients. No single client can monopolize its personnel and other resources.
- *Need for Prolonged Briefing Period.* Some companies become frustrated because a public relations firm needs time and money to research the organization and make recommendations. Consequently, the actual launch of a public relations program may take weeks or months.
- *Resentment by Internal Staff.* The public relations staff members of a client organization may resent

Ogilvy and LG Team Up to Raise Technology Awareness Through a Texting Championship

IN THE LAST HALF OF 2006, according to global PR agency Ogilvy, almost 94 billion text messages were sent. By 2011, the number had reached 8 trillion. To celebrate texting and raise awareness of LG products, in 2006 Ogilvy and its client LG Electronics created the LG National Texting Championship—the first national text-messaging contest. Thousands competed in the first competition, and Ogilvy gained remarkable media coverage for LG. According to Ogilvy, the agency secured "more than 700 hits from key trade, business and consumer media." Among those "hits" were *The Today Show, Good Morning America, The Early Show, Time,* and the *Los Angeles Times.*

More than 15,000 entrants competed in the second contest. Twenty-year-old Nathan Schwartz took home $50,000 in prize money with his winning phrase, which he had texted in 60 seconds: "Does everybody here know the alphabet? Let's text. Here it goes ... AbcDeFghiJKlm-NoPQrStuvWXy & Z! Now I know my A-B-C's, next time won't you text with me?"

By 2011, the contest had truly become a phenomenon. MTV produced and aired a documentary, *Thumbs,* which, according to the *MTV Movies Blog,* claimed to go "below the surface of the trend and try to crack the secret world of texting." The documentary followed six teens during the 2010 LG National Texting Championship. Academy Award–winning director and filmmaker Bill Couturie told MTV that he became interested in the project after noticing his own 14-year-old son's texting prowess. He described the movie as being "about kids having a good time, but there's also a little bit of a moral in there that texting can be addictive."

LG celebrated the documentary's debut by treating audiences in New York and Los Angeles to a sneak peek. "LG is proud of its texting legacy and has worked to become a pioneer in the space with its QWERTY devices and ongoing programs, such as the annual LG National Texting Championship," said LG marketing executive Carl Brown.

Brown told *PRWeek,* "We feel like we brought texting to the masses. Our goal is to keep a close connection with our consumer base, especially those who are very passionate about texting and staying connected with their social circles."

While the event started as a "small grassroots program," in 2011 LG expected "more than 1 million game plays, which is how people test their texting skills and enter the contest," *PRWeek* reported. In 2011, LG and Ogilvy embraced Facebook as a means to raise awareness of the competition. The competition was touted on the LG Texter Facebook page.

The 2011 competition was based on a new LG product "hero," which was the texting device used during the competition. In addition to following the number of "hero" products sold after the competition, LG and Ogilvy measured success of the fifth annual event through the number of game plays, Facebook fans, and PR value.

1 How does the texting contest engage potential consumers of LG products?

2 What PR value does the contest generate? What PR value did the movie *Thumbs* provide?

3 How might you alter or add to the competition to embrace new technologies or social media?

the use of outside counsel because they think it implies that they lack the ability to do the job.

- *Strong Direction by Top Management Required.* High-level executives must take the time to brief outside counsel on the specific objectives to be fulfilled.
- *Need for Full Information and Confidence.* A client must be willing to share its information—including skeletons in the closet—with outside counsel. Cooperation between the public relations firm and the client is essential.

- *High Costs.* Outside counsel is expensive. In many situations, routine public relations work can be handled at lower cost by internal staff.

Fees and Charges

The three most common methods that public relations firms use to charge clients, which are also used by law firms and management consultants, are (1) a basic hourly fee, plus out-of-pocket expenses; (2) a retainer fee; and (3) a fixed project fee. A fourth strategy—

pay for placement—is used less often.

- *Basic Hourly Fee, Plus Out-of-Pocket Expenses.* The number of hours spent on a client's account is tabulated each month and billed to the client. Work by personnel in the counseling firm is billed at various hourly rates. Out-of-pocket expenses, such as cab fares, car rentals, airline tickets, and meals, are also billed to the client.
- *Retainer Fee.* A basic monthly charge billed to the client covers ordinary administrative and overhead expenses for maintaining the account and being "on call" for advice and strategic counseling. This approach might be the preferred choice of clients who have in-house PR departments but who still need specialized expertise. Many retainer fees specify the number of hours the firm will spend on an account each month. Any additional work is billed at normal hourly rates. Out-of-pocket expenses are usually billed separately.
- *Fixed Project Fee.* The public relations firm agrees to do a specific project, such as an annual report, a newsletter, or a special event, for a fixed fee. For example, a counseling firm may write and produce a quarterly newsletter for $30,000 annually. The fixed fee is the least popular payment option among public relations firms because it is difficult to predict all work and expenses in advance. Many clients, however, like fixed fees for a specific project because it is easier to budget and there are no "surprises."
- *Pay for Placement.* With this payment method, which is not widely used, clients don't pay for hours worked but rather for actual placements of articles in the print media and broadcast mentions. Placement fees for a major story can range anywhere from hundreds to thousands

---

A Job at a Corporation or a PR Firm?

Recent college graduates often ponder the pros and cons of joining a corporate department or working for a public relations firm.

Corporate PR: Depth of Experience	PR Firm: Breadth of Experience
• Jobs more difficult to find without experience; duties more narrowly focused.	• Experience gained quickly. (Tip: Find a mentor you can learn from.)
• Sometimes little variety at entry level.	• Variety. Usually work with several clients and on several projects at same time. Opportunity for rapid advancement.
• Growth can be limited unless you are willing to switch employers.	• Fast-paced, exciting.
• May be slower paced.	• Seldom see the impact of your work for a client; removed from "action."
• Heavy involvement with executive staff; see the impact of your work almost instantly. You are an important component in the "big picture."	• Abilities get honed and polished. (This is where a mentor really helps.)
• Strength in all areas expected. Not a lot of time for coaching by peers.	• Networking with other professionals leads to better job opportunities.
• Sometimes so involved in your work that you don't have time for networking.	• Learn other skills, such as how to do presentations and budgets and establish deadlines.
• Same "client" all the time. Advantage: Get to know organization really well. Disadvantage: Can become boring.	• Intense daily pressure on billable hours, high productivity. Some firms are real "sweatshops."
• Less intense daily pressure; more emphasis on accomplishing long-term results.	• Somewhat high employment turnover.
• Less turnover.	• Budgets and resources can be limited.
• More resources usually available.	• Salary traditionally low at entry level.
• Salaries tend to be higher.	• Insurance, medical benefits can be minimal.
• Benefits usually good.	• Little opportunity for profit sharing, stock options.
• Can be more managerial and involved in strategic planning.	• High emphasis on tactical skills, production of materials.

of dollars depending on the prestige, circulation, or audience size of the media outlet that uses a story proposed by a pay-for-placement firm. The vast majority of public relations firms don't use this business model for several reasons: It reduces public relations to media relations and media placement, when it is in reality a much broader field; it presents cash-flow problems because payment isn't made until a placement is made; and media gatekeepers ultimately decide what to use and what not to use, so placement is never guaranteed despite the number of hours firm staff members devote to "pitching" a story.

The primary basis of the most common methods that a public relations firm charges for its services—the basic hourly fee, the retainer fee, and the fixed project fee—is to estimate the number of hours that a particular project will take to plan, execute, and evaluate. The first method—the basic hourly fee—is the most flexible and most widely used among large firms. It is preferred by public relations people because they are paid for the exact number of hours spent on a project.

A number of variables are considered when a public relations firm estimates the cost of a program. These factors include the size and duration of the project, the geographical locations involved, the number of personnel assigned to the project, and the type of client. A major variable, of course, is billing for the use of the firm's personnel to a client at the proper hourly rate.

An account executive may earn approximately $65,000 per year. Benefits (health insurance, pension plan, and so on) may cost the firm an additional $23,000. Thus the annual cost of the employee to the firm totals $88,000. Assuming there are 1,600 billable hours in a year (after deducting vacation time and holidays), the account executive makes $55 per hour.

The standard industry practice is to bill clients at least three times a person's salary. This allows the firm to pay for office space, equipment, insurance, and supplies, and try to operate at a profit level of 10 to 20 percent before taxes. Thus, the billing rate of the account executive (3 × $55) is rounded to $165 per hour.

The primary income of a public relations firm comes from the sale of staff time, but some additional income results from markups on photocopying, telephone, fax, and artwork that the firm supervises. The standard markup in the trade is between 15 and 20 percent.

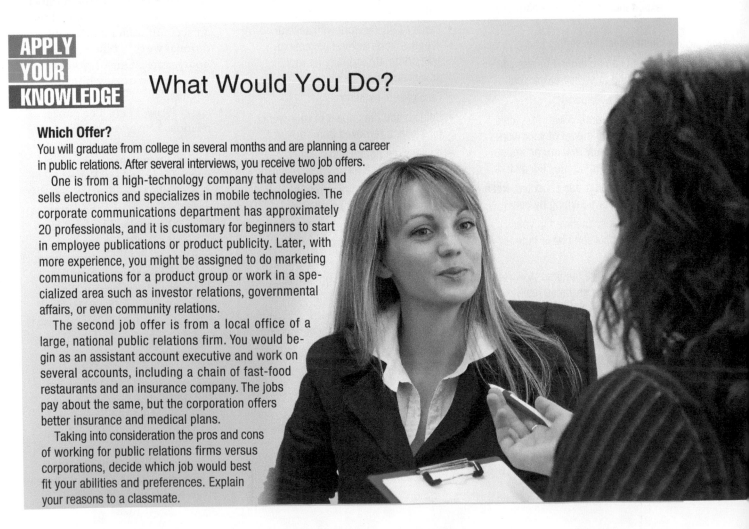

APPLY YOUR KNOWLEDGE

What Would You Do?

Which Offer?

You will graduate from college in several months and are planning a career in public relations. After several interviews, you receive two job offers.

One is from a high-technology company that develops and sells electronics and specializes in mobile technologies. The corporate communications department has approximately 20 professionals, and it is customary for beginners to start in employee publications or product publicity. Later, with more experience, you might be assigned to do marketing communications for a product group or work in a specialized area such as investor relations, governmental affairs, or even community relations.

The second job offer is from a local office of a large, national public relations firm. You would begin as an assistant account executive and work on several accounts, including a chain of fast-food restaurants and an insurance company. The jobs pay about the same, but the corporation offers better insurance and medical plans.

Taking into consideration the pros and cons of working for public relations firms versus corporations, decide which job would best fit your abilities and preferences. Explain your reasons to a classmate.

summary

Which Factors Determine the Roles and Status of Public Relations Departments in an Organization?

- The role of public relations in an organization depends on the type of organization, the perceptions of top management, and the capabilities of the public relations executive and staff.

Which Levels of Influence Can Public Relations Departments Exercise in an Organization?

- Public relations is a staff function rather than a line function.
- Public relations professionals often serve at the tactical and technician levels, but others are counselors to the top executive and have a role in policy making.
- Public relations is expanding from its traditional functions to exercise influence in the highest levels of management.

Which Services Do Public Relations Firms Provide?

- Public relations firms come in all sizes and are found worldwide, providing myriad services.
- In recent decades, many public relations firms have either merged with advertising agencies or become subsidiaries of diversified holding companies.

What Are the Pros and Cons of Employing a Public Relations Firm?

- Advantages of using outside firms include versatility and extensive resources, among other considerations.
- Disadvantages associated with employing outside public relations firms are that they may lack the full-time commitment of an in-house department, need a lot of direction, and are often more expensive.

questions
FOR REVIEW AND DISCUSSION

1 In what ways do the structure and culture of an organization affect the role and influence of the public relations department?

2 Which kinds of knowledge does a manager of a public relations department need to succeed in today's organizational cultures?

3 What is the difference between a line function and a staff function? To which function does public relations belong, and why?

4 Why is a compulsory-advisory role within an organization a good one for a public relations department to have?

5 Which four areas of an organization are the most likely to develop friction with public relations? Explain.

6 Name at least seven services that a public relations firm offers clients.

7 How important is international business to U.S. public relations firms?

8 Twitter has been hailed a game-changer within many public relations campaigns. How would you defend this statement?

Text Credits

Credits are listed in order of appearance.

Courtesy of Jon Iwata.

Photo Credits

Credits are listed in order of appearance.

LWA/Dann Tardif/Blend Images/Alamy;
Bettmann/Corbis;
g_studio/iStockphoto;
Dobresum/Shutterstock;

Fotokostic/Shutterstock;
ZUMA Press/Newscom;
(cr) Barry Lewis/Alamy;
Geraint Lewis/Alamy;

(tr) Lisa S./Shutterstock;
Monkey Business Images/Shutterstock;
Little_Desire/Shutterstock

Tablet image: Falconia/Shutterstock

Research
and Campaign
Planning

From Chapter 5 of *Think Public Relations*, 2013 Edition. Dennis L. Wilcox, Glen T. Cameron, Bryan H. Reber, Jae-Hwa Shin.
Copyright © 2013 by Pearson Education, Inc. Published by Pearson. All rights reserved.

Research and Campaign Planning

Tapping Into Research Helps Ensure Success

Research is essential to campaign planning.

Using impressive research skills, five students at the University of Georgia developed an award-winning campaign for the U.S. Census Bureau titled iCount. Research included online and oral surveys. Surveys were produced in both English- and Spanish-language versions. Three hundred University of Georgia students filled out surveys online; 113 surveys were completed by nonstudent community members. The surveys measured respondents' knowledge of the U.S. Census, perception of its benefits, and intent to participate.

Interviews with campus and community opinion leaders were also conducted. The student team was especially interested in talking with members of the mayor-appointed Athens Complete Count Committee and Latino opinion leaders. In addition to the surveys and the interviews, focus groups were conducted with three groups: Greek life campus representatives, students living off-campus, and customers at a restaurant catering to Spanish-speakers. The focus groups were used to pretest messages, slogans, and themes. Finally, the students conducted content analysis of news stories and editorials focusing on the U.S. Census that had appeared in the local media in the 10 years since the last census.

With knowledge in hand from the research, the student team set three broad goals, to increase: (1) knowledge about the U.S. Census; (2) support for the census, and (3) intent to participate by target publics.

After the extensive campaign, post-campaign surveys were conducted and compared to the precampaign data. The comparison showed that knowledge of the census increased by 12 percent. To evaluate support, the team measured outreach tactics. They found that local media placements about the census reached 700,000 people. In addition, 167,400 people were reached through events and speaking engagements. The last goal was measured by the pre- and post-campaign surveys that showed that there was an 8 percent increase in the number of people who said they were likely to participate in the census.

This research-driven campaign won both the national Public Relations Society of America (PRSA) Bateman case competition and the top award given by PRSA, the Silver Anvil.

1 Which types of research did the University of Georgia team employ?

2 Why was it important for the team to research media placements in their post-campaign evaluation?

Ask Yourself

> What Are the Four Essential Steps of Effective Public Relations?

> How Is Research Used in Public Relations?

> How Is Research Conducted in Public Relations?

> What Role Does Planning Play in Effective Public Relations?

> What Are the Eight Elements of a Program Plan?

THE Four Essential Steps OF EFFECTIVE PUBLIC RELATIONS

Effective public relations is a process with four essential steps: (1) research, (2) planning, (3) communication, and (4) measurement. *Research* provides the information required to understand the needs of publics and to develop powerful messages. *Planning* is referred to as the central function of management; it is the process of setting goals and objectives and determining ways to meet them. *Communication* is related to message strategy—making a message appealing and persuasive to the public. *Measurement* (or evaluation) is becoming increasingly important in public relations. Executives justifiably demand accountability from public relations practitioners. Measurement techniques provide a means for demonstrating to management that public relations is achieving objectives and contributing in a meaningful way to the organization.

This chapter describes the first two of these four steps—research and planning—and examines the role they play in an effective public relations program.

Research: THE FIRST STEP

The crucial first step in the public relations process is research. Research is an integral part of the planning, program development, and measurement process. Effective public relations professionals conduct formative research (research carried out prior to the campaign to lay a foundation or to inform the campaign) and evaluative research (research done during and after the campaign to determine—evaluate—whether tactics are working to meet objectives). In basic terms, research is a form of listening.

Before public relations professionals can develop a program, they must collect and interpret data. Research is essential. It informs top managers as they make policy decisions and map out strategies for effective communication programs. Research also provides a way to evaluate and measure a program once it has been completed.

In addition to winning numerous awards, the research-rich campaign discussed in the chapter opening vignette had a genuine impact on the state: Georgia was awarded one more seat in the House of Representatives, bringing its total count to 14.

> **Research is essential to any public relations activity or campaign. As evidenced in many public relations models, research is the beginning of a process that seeks to bring about a specific objective.**
>
> –Don W. Stacks, author of *Primer of Public Relations Research.*

Different types of research can accomplish an organization's objectives and meet its information needs. The choice of research type really depends on the particular subject and situation. As always, time and budget are major considerations, as is the perceived importance of the situation.

Many questions should be asked before formulating a research design:

▶ What is the problem?

▶ Which kind of information is needed?

▶ How will the research results be used?

▶ Which specific public (or publics) should be researched?

▶ Should the organization do the research in-house or hire an outside consultant?

▶ How will research data be analyzed, reported, or applied?

▶ How soon are the results needed?

▶ How much will the research cost?

Asking key questions helps public relations professionals determine the extent and nature of the research needed. Sometimes, only

Top management in many organizations is increasingly isolated from the concerns of employees, customers, and other important publics. Research helps bridge the gap by periodically surveying key publics about problems and concerns. This feedback serves as a "reality check" for executives and often leads to better policies and communication strategies.

informal research is pursued because of budget constraints or the need for immediate information. At other times, a random scientific survey is appropriate, despite its high cost and time investment, because more precise data are needed. We discuss the pros and cons of various research methods later in this chapter.

Research is a key part of virtually every phase of a communications program. Studies show that public relations departments typically spend 3 to 5 percent of their budgets on research; however, some experts argue that this share should be as much as 10 percent. In the 2011 fiscal year, companies with less than $500 million in revenues devoted 5.2 percent of their public relations budgets to measurement. In companies with more than $500 million in revenues the number was 6.2 percent, according to *PRWeek*. The University of Southern California found that the amount of public relations budget dedicated to evaluation ranges from 2.2 to 6.6 percent.

Meaningful measurement can lead to greater accountability and credibility with upper management.

Public relations professionals use research in a number of ways.

Achieving Credibility with Management

Executives want facts, not guesses and hunches. One criticism of public relations practitioners is that they too often don't link communications issues to business outcomes. Research paves the way for such linkages.

> "We recommend that between 5 and 10% of your budget should be spent on measurement. Doesn't it make sense to spend that much to find out if the other 90-95% is doing anything for you?"
>
> –Katie Paine, CEO of KD Paine and Partners.

Research and Campaign Planning

Defining Audiences and Segmenting Publics

Gathering detailed information about demographics, lifestyles, characteristics, and consumption patterns helps to ensure that messages reach the proper audiences. A successful children's immunization information campaign in California, for example, was based on state health department statistics showing that past immunization programs had not reached rural children and that Hispanic and Vietnamese children were not being immunized at the same rates as children in other ethnic groups.

 think How does research help determine what to say and whom to say it to in a public relations campaign?

Formulating Strategy

Too much money can be spent pursuing the wrong strategies. Consider what happened when officials of the New Hampshire paper industry, given bad press about logging and waterway pollution, thought a campaign was needed to tell the public what it was doing to reduce pollution. However, an opinion survey of 800 state residents by a public relations firm indicated that the public was already generally satisfied with the industry's efforts. Consequently, the new strategy focused on reinforcing positive themes such as worker safety, employment, and environmental responsibility. Research was extremely critical in appraising whether a threat existed and served to inform the paper industry's strategy. Ultimately it helped officials focus communication resources where they would do the organization the most good.

> "Research gives a context in which to talk about the product."
>
> –Lisa Eggerton, SVP and head of consumer practice, RSCG Magnet.

Testing Messages

Research can determine which message is most salient to a target audience. According to one focus group study for a campaign to encourage carpooling, the message that resonated the most with commuters was saving time and money, not improving air quality or saving the environment. As a result, the campaign emphasized how many minutes could be cut from an average commute by using carpool lanes and the annual savings to be had by reducing gasoline, insurance, and car maintenance expenditures.

> We have all seen a Tweet and/or Facebook comment or traditional news story explode onto the world stage in a matter of minutes. With [real-time media monitoring], we can ensure that our clients are rapidly prepared and ready to blunt any challenges to their reputations.
>
> **Brad MacAfee, senior partner, managing director of Porter Novelli, Atlanta**

Measuring Social Media

Evaluative research often requires measuring social media. The rules for measuring social media are no different than those for measuring traditional media.

Virginia Miracle, SVP and senior digital influence strategy head at Ogilvy PR, argues that social media metrics need to track with business metrics. She wrote in her Ogilvy blog, "No CEO is banging on the table looking for more tweets, he's looking for shareholder value—sales, market share, preference, purchase intent and a legion of other measures that cannot be ripped off the back of Facebook insights."

Miracle offers tips for meaningful social media measurement. She contends that objectives must be focused on business outcomes, and they must be measurable. She writes: "TEST: Can it be measured? If the answer is no, it isn't an objective." She also asserts that public relations practitioners must plan to measure. If you don't plan to measure from the outset—even before the campaign—then your measurements won't have much meaning. If you plan, then you can benchmark knowledge or attitudes before the campaign. Finally, she says that in social media it's key to find where members of your target public are interacting on a relevant topic. That's where you should be and what you should measure.

Steve Shannon, VP of sales and marketing for Critical Mention, also offers tips for measuring social media. In *PRWeek* he advised:

- Use an audit of social media to see where your organization is most discussed. Don't just stick to obvious social media like Twitter. YouTube forums are often overlooked, for example.

- It's not enough to count mentions on social media. "Identifying the positive and negative mentions is often indicative of where we need to focus

our energy in crisis or what platforms present the most opportunity."

- Share of voice or how much is being said about your organization compared to others, "demonstrates how social media efforts move the overall needle for an organization." Determine what your organization's share of voice is for a specific keyword or phrase compared to your competition. "If it's increasing, you're on the right path."

Miracle finally reminds public relation practitioners, "The baseline [measure] is going to be the key to your 'winning' metric such as 'increased purchase consideration by 45%.' That is the type of metric that CEOs do care about and that will keep your social media efforts on strategy and in budget the following year."

1 What are benchmark or baseline measures and why do they matter?

2 How can measuring "share of voice" in social media help an organization?

3 What is a social media audit? How can it inform strategy?

Preventing Crises

An estimated 90 percent of organizational crises are caused by internal operational problems rather than by unexpected natural disasters or external issues. The Institute for Crisis Management says that 61 percent of crises are "smoldering" rather than sudden. Research can often uncover trouble spots and public concerns *before* they become news. Analyzing complaints made to a toll-free number or monitoring blogs and tweets, for example, might tip off an organization that it should act before a problem attracts media attention. Professionals can prevent a conflict or crisis through environmental scanning and other research tactics.

Monitoring the Competition

Savvy organizations keep track of what the competition is doing. Research on the competition can be done with surveys that ask consumers to comment on competing products, content analysis of the competition's media coverage, and reviews of industry reports in trade journals. Monitoring can be made much easier by setting up alerts that are fed directly to an e-mail inbox.

Google Alerts, for example, allows a user to choose a list of search terms; once the alert request is set up, news information that mentions the selected terms is delivered via e-mail. Google Alerts is promoted as being useful in "monitoring a developing news story" or "keeping current on a competitor or industry." Similarly, RSS (Really Simple Syndication) feeds can be set up from key websites. For more sophisticated and targeted monitoring, commercial Internet monitoring services are also available from companies such as Dow Jones and BurrellesLuce. Computer programs such as those offered by Radian6 also help with social media monitoring. Such research helps an organization shape its marketing and communication strategies to counter a competitor's strengths and capitalize on its weaknesses. These are all useful in issues and crisis management, too.

Generating Publicity

Polls and surveys can generate publicity for an organization. Indeed, many surveys seem to be designed with publicity in mind. Cottonelle toilet tissue drew attention when it held an online poll at CottonelleRollPoll.com asking the age-old question: Do you roll your toilet paper over or under? Cottonelle garnered 250,000,000 media impressions, had 600,000 votes at its website, and generated 685,000 social media interactions. Similarly, Simmons Bedding Company once received publicity when it polled people to find out if they slept in the nude, as did Norelco Phillips for its Bodygroom shaver by citing a telephone survey that found more than half of female respondents preferred boyfriends with a hairless back.

Measuring Success

The bottom line of any public relations program is whether the time and money spent accomplished the stated objective.

Research METHODS

When the term *research* is used, people tend to think exclusively of scientific surveys and complex statistics. In public relations, however, other research techniques are used to gather data and information as well.

Literature searches—the most often used informal research method in public relations—can tap an estimated 1,500 electronic databases that store an enormous amount of current and historical information.

Research Techniques

In fact, a survey of practitioners by Walter K. Lindenmann, former senior vice president and director of research for Ketchum, found that three-fourths of the respondents described their research techniques as casual and informal rather than scientific and precise. The technique cited most often was literature searches/database information retrieval. This technique is called secondary research, because it uses existing information in books, magazine articles, electronic databases, and so on. In contrast, in primary research, new and original information is generated to answer a specific question. Examples of primary research include in-depth interviews, focus groups, surveys, and polls.

In addition to categorizing research as primary or secondary, we can distinguish between qualitative and quantitative research. In general, qualitative research affords researchers rich insights and understanding of situations or target publics. It also provides "red flags," or warnings, when strong or adverse responses occur. These responses may not be easy to extrapolate to a larger population and, therefore, are often referred to as "soft" data, but they can provide practitioners with early warnings of potential problems. In contrast, quantitative research is often more expensive and complicated, but it allows for greater extrapolation to large populations. For this reason, its findings are sometimes known as "hard" data. If enormous amounts of money are to be spent on a national campaign, it may be best to make an investment in quantitative research.

Organizational Materials. Robert Kendall, in his book *Public Relations Campaign Strategies*, terms the process of researching organizational materials *archival research.* Such materials may include an organization's policy statements, speeches by key executives, past issues of employee newsletters and magazines, reports on past public relations and marketing efforts, and news clippings. Marketing statistics, in particular, often provide baseline data for public relations firms that are hired to launch a new product or boost awareness and sales of an existing product or service. Archival research also is a major component in audits that are intended to determine how an organization communicates to its internal and external publics.

Library and Online Database Methods. Reference books, academic journals, and trade publications can be found in every library. Online databases such as Proquest, Factiva, and LexisNexis contain abstracts or full-text of thousands—or even millions—of articles.

Some common reference sources used by public relations professionals include the *Statistical Abstract of the United States* (http://www.census.gov/statab), which summarizes census information; the Gallup Poll (http://poll.gallup.com/), which provides an index of public opinion on a variety of issues; and *Simmons Study Media and Markets,* an extensive annual survey of households on product usage by brand and exposure to various media.

Public relations practitioners need to follow current events and public affairs issues so that they can provide thoughtful counsel in their organizations. Reading newspapers and watching television news programs is a habit that young professionals should embrace.

Information delivery systems now seem to be virtually limitless in number and form. Web-based magazines (zinio.com) or newspapers (pressdisplay.com and newsstand.com) provide products that are formatted like their print counterparts, but also include online links and video. Smart phones and tablet readers feature free or moderately priced applications that allow access to quality news sources, such as the *New York Times*, *USA Today*, CNN Mobile, World News Feed,

Qualitative Research **VS** Quantitative Research

Qualitative Research	Quantitative Research
"Soft" data	"Hard" data
Usually uses open-ended questions, unstructured	Usually uses closed-ended questions, requires forced choices, highly structured
Exploratory in nature; probing, "fishing expedition" type of research	Descriptive or explanatory type of research
Usually valid, but not reliable	Usually valid and reliable
Rarely projectable to larger audiences	Usually projectable to larger audiences
Typically uses nonrandom samples	Typically uses random samples
Examples: Focus groups; one-on-one, in-depth interviews; observation; participation; role-playing studies; convenience polling	Examples: Telephone polls; mail surveys; mall-intercept studies; face-to-face interviews; shared cost, or omnibus, studies; panel studies

A wide array of information resources enables public relations practitioners to stay current and be knowledgeable about their own organization and its place in the larger world.

BBC, and many others. These services make the work of monitoring news and trends easier for on-the-go professionals. Aggregators such as Flipboard combine the power of RSS, news, Twitter, and Facebook feeds to create an individualized magazine of online content. Services such as Audible.com deliver audio to MP3 players, including content from newspapers, books, television and radio broadcasts, and podcasts, thereby enabling commuters to multitask. Some newspapers also provide interactive versions of their daily editions that are read to car commuters through satellite radio; users can then save or forward stories to colleagues. Listeners of National Public Radio (NPR) can forward stories or order transcripts or broadcasts.

The Internet. The Internet is a powerful research tool for the public relations practitioner. Any number of corporations, nonprofit organizations, trade groups, special-interest groups, foundations, universities, think tanks, and government agencies post reams of data on the Internet.

think How can Internet search engines help inform public relations campaign development?

Online search engines are essential for finding information on the Internet. Researchers can use specialized search engines or search tools to locate audio and video content or content of topical interest, such as sports or business news.

Reviews and directories of search engines are available at searchenginewatch.com. Public relations professionals should visit such sites frequently to stay up-to-date on search capabilities as well as to monitor changes in search engines' policies, such as fees required for high placement in search results.

Researchers can use profession-specific social media such as PROpenMic.org, which is a clearinghouse for PR-specific blogs, forums, and other online resources; and HelpAReporterOut.com, which is a social media site to connect reporters and news sources; and several Yahoo!-based PR discussion groups, such as YoungPRPros. Professional organizations such as the Public Relations Society of America and the International Association of Business Communicators (IABC) support members-only, special interest discussion groups. Blogs, including briansolis.com, examine PR business trends. IABC has blogs addressing branding, employee communications, measurement, and media relations compiled in the IABC Exchange (http://x.iabc.com/available-exchange-sites/).

Google was by far the most popular search engine worldwide in late 2011, with 91 percent of mobile/tablet searches, according to www.marketshare.hitslink.com.

Content Analysis. Content analysis is the systematic and objective counting or categorizing of content. In public relations, content often is selected from media coverage of a topic or organization. This research method can be relatively informal or quite scientific in terms of random sampling and establishing specific subject categories.

Don Stacks, University of Miami professor and author of *Primer of Public Relations Research*, writes that content analysis "is particularly appropriate for the analysis of documents, speeches, media releases, video content and scripts, interviews, and focus groups. The key to content analysis is that it is done objectively ... content is treated systematically ... [and] messages are transformed from qualitative statements to numbers, data that can be quantified and compared against other data."

At a basic level, for example, a researcher can assemble news clips in a scrapbook and count the number of column inches. A good

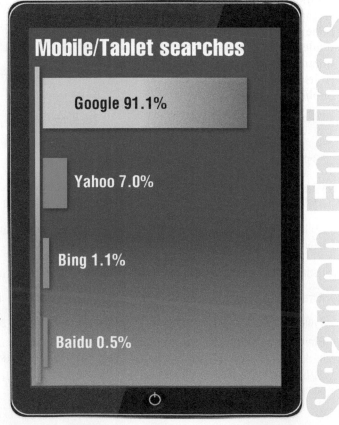

Mobile/Tablet searches

Google 91.1%

Yahoo 7.0%

Bing 1.1%

Baidu 0.5%

Search Engines

example of content analysis is the way one company evaluated press coverage of its publicity campaign to celebrate its one-hundredth anniversary. Staff measured the campaign's success with a low-budget content analysis of 427 references to the client and its product in newspapers, magazines, radio, and television. The content analysis revealed that the client's themes and copy points were included in the media coverage.

Content analysis can help determine the quality of media coverage. For instance, when Kimberly-Clarke wanted to gain media coverage for its Cottonelle toilet tissue, it hosted an online poll to determine whether most people roll the toilet paper over or under the roll. An evaluative content analysis showed that almost 90 percent of media mentions were positive in tone, 86 percent of media coverage included at least three key messages, more than 60 percent of placements included a quote, and 43 percent included an image.

Content analysis also can be applied to letters, phone calls, and Internet postings, which often provide good feedback about problems with an organization's policies and services. A pattern of letters and phone calls or postings pointing out a problem is evidence that something should be done.

Interviews. Like content analysis, interviews can be conducted in several different ways. Almost everyone in public relations talks to colleagues on a daily basis and calls other organizations to gather information. In fact, personnel faced with solving a particular problem often "interview" other public relations professionals for ideas and suggestions.

If information is needed on public opinion and attitudes, many public relations firms will conduct short interviews with people in a shopping mall or other public place. This kind of interview is called an *intercept interview*, because people are literally intercepted in public places and asked their opinions.

Although the intercept interview does not use a generalizable sampling method (i.e., the survey results cannot be applied to the general population), it does give an organization a sense of current thinking or exposure to certain messages. Intercept interviews typically last only two to five minutes.

Sometimes, the best approach is to conduct more in-depth interviews in an effort to obtain more comprehensive information. A major fund-raising project by charitable groups, for example, may require in-depth interviews of community and business opinion leaders to ascertain support levels for the campaign. The success of any major fund drive depends on the support of key leaders and wealthy individuals. This more in-depth approach is called *purposive interviewing*, because interviewees are carefully selected based on their expertise, influence, or leadership in the community.

Focus Groups. A good alternative to individual interviews is the focus group. The focus group technique is widely used in advertising, marketing, and public relations to help identify the attitudes and motivations of important publics. Another purpose of focus groups is to formulate or pretest message themes and communication strategies before launching a full campaign. Focus groups usually consist of 8 to 12 people who possess the characteristics of the larger target audience, such as employees, consumers, or community residents.

Surveys of public opinion, which are often conducted by researchers on the street or in shopping malls, help public relations practitioners target audiences they wish to reach and to shape their messages.

It is now common practice to conduct and record focus groups at various points around the country or the globe and then upload these recordings to a secure server for the client to view via password on the web. Time and location are becoming less relevant to conducting focus groups, increasing their utility.

During a focus group, a trained facilitator uses nondirective interviewing techniques that encourage group members to talk freely about a topic or give candid reactions to suggested message themes. The setting is usually a conference room, and the discussion is informal. A focus group may last one or two hours, depending on the subject matter.

A focus group, by definition, is an informal research procedure that develops qualitative information rather than hard data. Results obtained through this research technique cannot be summarized by percentages or even projected to an entire population. Nevertheless, focus groups are useful in identifying the range of attitudes and opinions among participants. Such insights can help an organization structure its messages or, on another level, formulate hypotheses and questions to be covered by a quantitative research survey.

Increasingly, focus groups are being conducted online. With this approach, the technique can be as simple as posing a question to an online chat or interest group. Researchers can use more formal selection processes to invite far-flung participants to meet in a prearranged virtual space. In the coming years, techniques and services will be further developed for cost-effective, online focus group research.

Copy Testing. All too often, organizations fail to communicate effectively because they produce and distribute materials that a target audience can't understand. In many cases, the material is written above the educational level of the audience. To avoid this problem, representatives of the target audience should be asked to read or view the material in draft form before it is mass-produced and distributed. This type of copy testing can be done on a one-on-one basis or in a small-group setting.

In some cases, executives and lawyers who must approve the copy may understand the material, but a worker with a high school education might find the material difficult to follow.

Another approach to determine the degree of difficulty of material is to apply a readability formula to the draft copy. Fog, Flesch, and other similar techniques relate the number of words and syllables per sentence or passage with reading level. Highly complex sentences and multisyllabic words are typically better suited to college-educated audiences.

Two ways to test copy using the Internet are web surveys and wikis. Web survey systems such as Survey Artisan (www.surveyartisan. com) allow attachment of video or photo files that can be critiqued by a target audience across many locations. A less sophisticated but equally effective way to test copy is simply to attach the copy to an e-mail and provide a link to an online survey. Similarly, photos or videos can be tested through secure Flickr or YouTube sharing communities. A wiki is a website that allows users to easily edit content; these sites provide a way for clients or audience members to critique and correct copy, essentially turning audience members into copy collaborators.

A brochure about employee medical benefits or pension plans should be pretested with rank-and-file employees for readability and comprehension.

Scientific Sampling Methods

The research techniques we discussed in the previous section can provide public relations personnel with good insights and help them formulate effective programs. Increasingly, however, public relations professionals need to conduct polls and surveys, as well as more rigorous content analyses, using highly precise scientific sampling methods. Such sampling is based on two important factors: randomness and a large number of respondents.

think Why is it important to use a random sample if possible when conducting research?

Random Sampling. Effective polls and surveys require a *random sample*. In statistics, this means that everyone in the targeted audience (as defined by the researcher) has an equal or known chance of being selected for the survey. A group selected in this manner is also called a *probability sample*. In contrast, a *nonprobability sample* is not randomly selected at all—an important consideration because improper sampling can lead to misleading results.

The most precise random sample is generated from a list that contains the name of every person in the target audience. Selection of such a sample is a simple matter if you're conducting a random survey of an organization's employees or members, because the researcher can randomly select, for example, every twenty-fifth name on a list. However, care must be taken to avoid patterns in the lists based on rank or employee category. It is always advisable to choose large intervals between selected names so that the researcher makes numerous passes through the list. Computerized lists allow for random selection of names.

Another way to ensure appropriate representation is to draw a random sample that matches the statistical characteristics of the audience. This practice is called quota sampling. Human resources departments usually have breakdowns of employees by job classification, and it is relatively easy to proportion a sample accordingly. For example, if 42 percent of employees work on the assembly line, then 42 percent of the sample should consist of assembly-line workers. A quota sample can be drawn based on any number of demographic factors—age, sex, religion, race, income, etc.—depending on the purpose of the survey.

Random sampling becomes more difficult when comprehensive lists are not available. In those cases, researchers surveying the general population may use telephone directories or customer lists to select respondents at random. The prevalence of cellular telephones without recorded numbers makes using directories a challenge. A more rigorous technique employs random computerized generation of telephone numbers; this process ensures that new, unlisted, and mobile numbers are included in the sample.

Sample Size. In any probability study, sample size is an important factor. In public relations, the primary purpose of poll data is to get indications of attitudes and opinions, not to predict elections. Therefore, it is not usually necessary or practical to do a scientific sampling of 1,500 people.

8:00 am

4:00 pm

8:00 pm

A number of factors can influence who is interviewed using the MALL-INTERCEPT METHOD, such as the time of day or location of the intercept interviews.

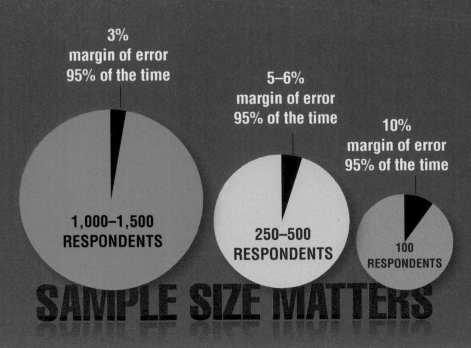

National polling firms usually sample 1,000 to 1,500 people and get a highly accurate idea of what the U.S. adult population is thinking. A sample of 1,500 people provides a margin of error within 3 percentage points 95 percent of the time. That means that when the same questionnaire is administered, the results should be within the same 3 percentage points and reflect the whole population fairly accurately. A sample of 250 to 500 people provides relatively accurate data—with a 5 or 6 percent margin of error—that will help to determine general public attitudes and opinions. A sample of approximately 100 people, accurately drawn according to probability guidelines, will have a 10 percent margin of error.

3% margin of error 95% of the time

1,000–1,500 RESPONDENTS

5–6% margin of error 95% of the time

250–500 RESPONDENTS

10% margin of error 95% of the time

100 RESPONDENTS

SAMPLE SIZE MATTERS

A 10 percent error would be acceptable if a public relations person, for example, asked employees what they want to read in the company magazine. Sixty percent may indicate that they would like to see more news about opportunities for promotion. If only 100 employees were properly surveyed, it really doesn't matter if the actual percentage is 50 or 70 percent. Such a percentage, in either case, would be sufficient to justify an increase in news stories about advancement opportunities.

Reaching Respondents

Once a sample has been identified and a questionnaire has been developed, it must be delivered to prospective respondents. There are pros and cons to each of the primary methods of delivery—(1) mail questionnaires; (2) telephone surveys; (3) personal interviews; (4) piggyback, or omnibus, surveys; and (5) web and e-mail surveys. We address the pros and cons of each method in the material that follows.

Mail Questionnaires. Questionnaires may be used in a variety of settings. For different reasons, survey questionnaires are often mailed to respondents. However, mail

Questionnaire Guidelines

- ☐ Determine the type of information that is needed and in what detail.
- ☐ State the objectives of the survey in writing.
- ☐ Decide which group(s) will receive the questionnaire.
- ☐ Determine the optimal sample size.
- ☐ State the purpose of the survey and guarantee anonymity to respondents.
- ☐ Use closed-ended (multiple-choice) answers as often as possible. Respondents find it easier and less time-consuming to select answers than to compose their own.
- ☐ Design the questionnaire in such a way that answers can be easily coded for statistical analysis.
- ☐ Strive to make the questionnaire contain no more than 25 questions. Long questionnaires put people off and reduce the number of responses, particularly in print questionnaires, because it is easy to see how long the survey will take to complete.
- ☐ Use categories when asking questions about education, age, and income. People are more willing to answer when a category or range is used. For example, choose the category that best describes your age: (a) younger than 25; (b) 25 to 40; and so on.
- ☐ Use simple, familiar words. Readability should be appropriate for the group being sampled. At the same time, don't talk down to respondents. Avoid ambiguous words and phrases that may confuse respondents.
- ☐ Edit out leading questions that suggest a specific correct response or bias an answer.
- ☐ Remember to consider the context and placement of questions. Keep in mind that questions can influence responses to subsequent questions.
- ☐ Provide space at the end of the questionnaire for respondents' comments and observations. This area allows them to provide additional information or elaboration that may not have been covered in the main body of the questionnaire.
- ☐ Pretest the questions for understanding and possible bias. Arrange for representatives of the proposed sampling group to read the questionnaire and provide feedback as to how it can be improved.

questionnaires do have some disadvantages—most notably, a low response rate. The more closely people identify with the organization and the questions, the better the response.

You can increase the response rate to a mail questionnaire, experts say, if you follow the guidelines of questionnaire construction shown on the preceding page. In addition, researchers should keep the following suggestions in mind:

- Include a stamped, self-addressed return envelope and a personally signed letter explaining the importance of participating in the survey.
- Provide an incentive. Commercial firms often encourage people to fill out questionnaires by including a token amount of money or a discount coupon. Other researchers promise to share the results of the survey with the respondents.
- Mail questionnaires by first-class mail. Some research shows that placing special-issue stamps on the envelope attracts greater interest than using a postage meter.
- Mail a reminder postcard three or four days after the questionnaire has been sent.
- Do a second mailing (either to nonrespondents or to the entire sample) two or three weeks after the first mailing. Again, enclose a stamped, self-addressed return envelope and a cover letter explaining the crucial need for participation.

Telephone Surveys. Surveys by telephone, particularly those that are locally based, are used extensively by research firms. The major disadvantage of telephone surveys is the difficulty in getting access to telephone numbers. In many urban areas, as many as one-third to one-half of all numbers are unlisted. Although researchers can let a computer program pick numbers through random dialing, this method is not as effective as actually knowing who is being called. The dominance of cell phones whose numbers are not listed is another increasingly difficult hurdle for telephone surveys. Because phone numbers are portable, it is difficult to know whether the 212 prefix you dialed belongs to a current or former resident of New York City or someone who simply wants to appear to be from New York. Another barrier is convincing respondents that a legitimate poll or survey is being taken. Far too many salespeople attempt to sell goods by posing as researchers.

Personal Interviews. The personal interview is the most expensive form of research because it requires trained staff and travel. Even if only travel within a city is involved, a trained interviewer may be able to interview just 8 or 10 people per day, and salaries and transportation costs make this technique quite expensive. Considerable advance work is required to arrange interviews and appointments and, as previously noted, residents are reluctant to admit strangers into their homes.

Nevertheless, in some instances personal interviews can be cost-effective. Most notably, they can generate a wealth of information if the setting is controlled. Many research firms conduct personal interviews at national conventions or trade shows, where there is a concentration of people with similar interests.

Piggyback Surveys. An alternative method of reaching respondents is the piggyback survey, also known as the omnibus survey. In basic terms, an organization "buys" a question in a national survey conducted by a survey organization such as Gallup or Harris. For example, General Mills may place one or two questions in a national poll that ask respondents which professional athletes they most admire as a way to find new spokespeople for its breakfast foods. In the same survey, the American Cancer Society may place a question asking how the public feels about new government guidelines regarding cancer screening examination frequency.

This research method is attractive to public relations people for two reasons. The first reason is cost: an organization pays much less to participate in a piggyback poll than to conduct its own survey. A second reason is expertise: firms such as Gallup or Harris have the skill and organization to conduct surveys properly and efficiently.

Piggyback surveys, however, do have limitations. An organization can get only a small snapshot of public opinion with one or two

A telephone survey has several advantages

- > The response (or nonresponse) is immediate. A researcher doesn't have to wait several weeks for responses to arrive (or not arrive) by mail.
- > A telephone call is personal. It is effective communication and much less expensive than a personal interview.
- > A telephone call is less intrusive than going door-to-door and interviewing people. Surveys have

found that many people are willing to talk on the phone for as long as 45 minutes, but they will not stand at a door for more than 5 or 10 minutes and are unwilling to admit strangers to their homes.

- > The response rate, if the survey is properly composed and the phone interviewers trained, can reach 80 to 90 percent.

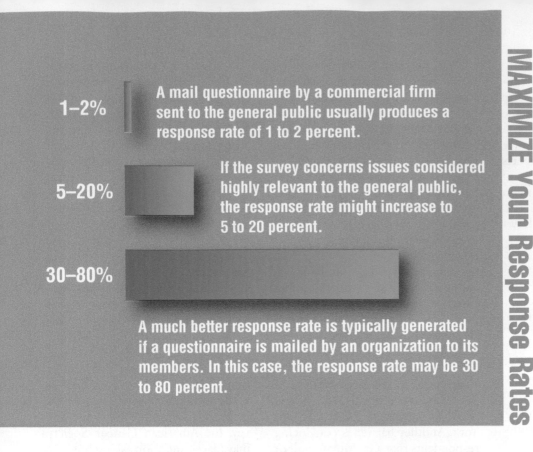

1–2%

A mail questionnaire by a commercial firm sent to the general public usually produces a response rate of 1 to 2 percent.

5–20%

If the survey concerns issues considered highly relevant to the general public, the response rate might increase to 5 to 20 percent.

30–80%

A much better response rate is typically generated if a questionnaire is mailed by an organization to its members. In this case, the response rate may be 30 to 80 percent.

characteristics of the respondents, because a website is accessible to virtually anyone with a computer and an Internet connection. It is also very important to prevent repeated participation by the same respondent by identifying the unique identifying number of each computer (the IP address) and allowing only one submission from each address. One of the biggest problems for online surveys is the low response rate due to the impersonal nature of the survey and the ease of exiting the survey's website with a single mouse click. For this reason, many online surveys begin with the most crucial questions.

questions, and the subject matter must be relevant to the general public.

Web and E-Mail Surveys. The most common way to reach respondents is through electronic communications. One such method is to post a questionnaire on an organization's website and ask visitors to complete it online. One advantage of this approach is that responses are immediately available and results are added to the running tabulation.

Researchers use several methods to attract respondents to a website, including (1) banner ads announcing the survey on other websites or online networks, (2) sending e-mail invitations to members of the target audience, (3) telephoning individuals with an invitation to participate, or (4) sending postcards.

The major disadvantage of web surveys is that it is difficult to control the exact

Posting a questionnaire on an organization's website and asking visitors to complete it online can be a good strategy. An undergraduate campaign team sought to test messages about the National Wildlife Foundation's travel program, which was targeted at persons older than age 50. The students sampled from an e-mail list of university alumni by year of graduation so that they reached the appropriate age group. They invited the alumni to visit a website and rate several of the travel program's message strategies.

Research and Campaign Planning

If reaching a specific audience is important, an e-mail survey may be sent to a list of known respondents. Organizations can compile e-mail lists of clients or customers or purchase e-mail address lists from a variety of sources. Full-service web survey companies target populations, collect responses, and deliver data to the client. The costs of such surveys can be low if an online survey service such as freeonlinesurveys.com—more of a do-it-yourself service—is used. Zoomerang (info. zoomerang.com) and Harris Interactive recruit and maintain pools of respondents to fit profiles that clients want to survey. Gender, income, and political persuasion are examples of characteristics that can be selected for web survey purposes.

Planning: THE SECOND STEP

The second step of the public relations process, following research, is program planning. Before professionals implement any public relations activity, they must give considerable thought to which actions should be taken in which order to accomplish an organization's objectives.

A good public relations program supports an organization's business, marketing, and communications objectives and is strategic. A practitioner must think about a situation, analyze what can be done about it, creatively conceptualize the appropriate strategies and tactics, and determine how the results will be measured. Planning involves the coordination of multiple methods—news releases, special events, webpages, social media sites, press kits, CD-ROM distribution, news conferences, media interviews, brochures, newsletters, speeches, and

A blueprint of what is to be done and how it will be executed makes programs more effective and public relations more valuable to the organization.

so on. Systematic planning prevents haphazard, ineffective communication.

Approaches to Planning

Planning is like putting together a jigsaw puzzle. Research provides the various pieces. Then it is necessary to arrange the pieces so that a coherent design, or picture, emerges. The best planning is systematic—gathering information, analyzing it, and creatively applying it for the specific purpose of attaining an objective.

think How is asking the right questions key to strategic planning?

In the two approaches to planning discussed in this section of the book, the emphasis is on asking and answering questions to generate a road map for success. One popular approach to planning is a process called "management by objective" (MBO). MBO provides focus and direction to strategy formulation and allows organizations to achieve specific objectives.

In their book *Public Relations Management by Objectives*, Norman R. Nager and T. Harrell Allen discuss nine basic MBO steps that can help

a practitioner conceptualize everything from a simple news release to a multifaceted communications program (see the nearby feature, The 9 Basic MBO Steps). The steps serve as a planning checklist that provides the basis for strategic planning.

By working through the checklist adapted from Nager and Allen's book, a practitioner has in place the general building blocks for assembling a public relations plan. These building blocks serve as background to create a specific plan. Ketchum, a global public relations firm, offers more pointed questions in its "Strategic Planning Model for Public Relations." Ketchum's organizational model (see the nearby feature *Ketchum's Strategic Planning Model*) makes sense to professionals and clients alike, moving both parties toward a clear situation analysis needed to make planning relevant to the client's overall objectives.

These two approaches to planning, MBO and Ketchum's model, lead to the next important step—writing a strategic public relations plan. The elements of an effective strategic public relations plan are explained in the following section.

The Eight Elements of a Program Plan

A public relations program plan identifies what is to be done, why, and how to accomplish it.

The 9 Basic Management By Objective (MBO) Steps

1. Client/Employer Objectives. What is the purpose of the communication, and how does it promote or achieve the objectives of the organization? Specific objectives such as "to make consumers aware of the product's high quality" are more meaningful than "to make people aware of the product."

2. Audience/Publics. Who exactly should be reached with the message, and how

can that audience help achieve the organization's objectives? What are the characteristics of the audience, and how can demographic information be used to structure the message? For example, the primary audience for a campaign to encourage carpooling consists of people who regularly drive to work, not the general public.

3. Audience Objectives. What is it that the audience wants to know, and how can the message be tailored to audience self-interest? Consumers are more interested in the color and clarity of a flat-screen television than in the technological differences among plasma, LCD, and LED models.

4. Media Channels. What is the appropriate channel for reaching the audience, and how can multiple channels (e.g., news media, blogs, brochures) reinforce the message? An ad may be best for making consumers aware of a new product, but a news release may be better for conveying consumer information about the product.

5. Media Channel Objectives. What is the media gatekeeper looking for in a news angle, and why would a particular publication be interested in the information?

6. Sources and Questions. Which primary and secondary sources of information are required to provide a factual base for the message? Which experts should be interviewed? Which databases should be used to conduct research? A quote from a project engineer about a new technology is better than a quote from the marketing vice president.

7. Communication Strategies. Which factors will affect the dissemination and acceptance of the message? Are there other events or pieces of information that negate or reinforce the message? A campaign to conserve water is more salient if there has been a recent drought.

8. Essence of the Message. What is the planned communication impact on the audience? Is the message designed merely to inform, or is it designed to change attitudes and behavior? Informing people about the values of physical fitness is different from instructing them about how to achieve it.

9. Nonverbal Support. How can photographs, graphs, videos, and artwork clarify and visually enhance the written message? Bar graphs or pie charts are easier to understand than columns of numbers.

KETCHUM'S STRATEGIC PLANNING MODEL encourages professionals to ask and determine answers to key questions about facts, goals, and audiences when planning public relations efforts.

FACTS

- *Category Facts.* What are recent industry trends?
- *Product/Service Issues.* What are the significant characteristics of the product, service, or issue?
- *Competitive Facts.* Who are the competitors, and what are their competitive strengths, similarities, and differences?
- *Customer Facts.* Who uses the product and why?

GOALS

- *Business Objectives.* What are the company's business objectives? What is the time frame?
- *Role of Public Relations.* How does public relations fit into the marketing mix?
- *Sources of New Business.* Which sectors will produce growth?

AUDIENCE

- *Target Audiences.* Who are the target audiences? What are their "hot buttons"?
- *Current Mind-Set.* How do audiences feel about the product, service, or issue?
- *Desired Mind-Set.* How do we want them to feel?

KEY MESSAGE

- *Main Point.* What one key message must be conveyed to change or reinforce mind-sets?

By preparing such a plan, either as a brief outline or as a more extensive document, the practitioner makes certain that all elements have been properly considered and that everyone involved understands the "big picture."

It is common practice for public relations firms to prepare a program plan for client approval and possible modification before implementing a public relations campaign. In crafting the plan, both the public relations firm and the client reach a mutual understanding of the campaign's objectives and the means to be used to accomplish them. Public relations departments within organizations also map out particular campaigns or show the departments' plans for the coming year.

Kids Kicking Cancer used research and planning to identify celebrities Gerard Butler, Demi Moore, and Miley Cyrus as appropriate spokespersons to bring attention to a mobile app called "Breath Break" that teaches kids with cancer pain-reducing techniques such as meditation and deep breathing.

Although there can be some variation, public relations plans include **eight basic elements:**

1. **Situation**
2. **Objectives**
3. **Audience**
4. **Strategy**
5. **Tactics**
6. **Calendar/timetable**
7. **Budget**
8. **Measurement**

1 SITUATION. Public relations professionals cannot set valid objectives without a clear understanding of the situation that led to the conclusion that there was a need for a public relations program. Three situations often prompt a public relations program: the organization must conduct a remedial program to overcome a problem or negative situation; the organization needs to conduct a specific one-time project; or the organization wants to reinforce an ongoing effort to preserve its reputation and public support.

• Loss of market share and declining sales often require a remedial program. For example, Atkins Nutritionals—linked with the low-carb Atkins Diet—found itself in a highly competitive arena of diet programs such as Nutrisystem and Weight Watchers. Atkins engaged celebrity chefs to create budget-friendly, great tasting low-carb fare. The recipes were promoted via Atkins ChefRecipes.com, appearances on morning shows, and YouTube chef demo videos, leading to what *PRWeek* called "sales success." Other organizations may launch such campaigns to change public perceptions.

• Specific one-time events often lead to public relations programs. The introduction of Apple's iPad was a one-time event; it required a program plan that included invitations to key journalists to come to Apple's Cupertino, California, headquarters to try out the iPad before its official introduction to the public and led to stories like Stephen Fry's in *Time* magazine titled, "The iPad Launch: Can Steve Jobs Do It Again?"

• Program plans are also initiated to preserve and develop customer or public support. Department 56, a leading designer and manufacturer of miniature lighted village collectibles, already had a successful business, but it wanted new customers. To accomplish this goal, its public relations program included distribution of brochures on home decoration for the Christmas holidays and participation by its dealers in local efforts to decorate Ronald McDonald houses.

• It's a good idea to include relevant research as part of the situation in a program plan. In the case of Department 56, consumer market analysis revealed a strong link between consumers interested in home decorating and those involved in collecting. Such research provides the foundation for setting program objectives and shaping other elements of the program plan.

• The program plan is informed by proactive research. Issues should be tracked to assess potential competition or threats. The greater the threat, the more important the strategizing, planning, and development of objectives.

2 OBJECTIVES. Once the situation or problem is understood, the next step is to establish objectives for the program. Evaluate a proposed objective by asking three questions: Does it really address the situation? Is it realistic and achievable? Can success be measured in meaningful terms?

• State an objective in terms of program outcomes rather than inputs. Objectives should not be the "means" but the "end." A poor objective, for example, is to "generate publicity for a new product." Publicity is not an "end" in itself; the actual objective is to "create consumer awareness about a new product."

• It is particularly important that public relations objectives complement and reinforce the organization's objectives. Basically, objectives are either informational or motivational.

• Many public relations plans are designed primarily to expose audiences to information and to increase awareness of an issue, an event, or a product; these are referred to as informational objectives. The following are examples of informational objectives:

– Travelocity: "Increase consumers' overall awareness and excitement for the brand."
– National Association of Manufacturers (NAM): "Educate target audiences on the fundamental importance of manufacturing to our nation's current competitiveness and future prosperity."

• One difficulty with informational objectives is measuring how well a particular objective has been achieved. Public awareness and the extent to which education takes place are somewhat abstract and difficult to quantify. Survey research can be informative, but many organizations infer "awareness" by counting the number of media placements. In reality, however, message exposure doesn't necessarily mean increased public awareness.

• Although changing attitudes and influencing behavior are difficult to accomplish in a public relations campaign, motivational objectives are easier to measure. That's because they are bottom-line oriented and are based on clearly measurable results that can be quantified. This is true whether the goal is increased product sales, a sellout crowd for a theatrical performance, or more donations to a charitable

agency. The following are examples of motivational objectives:

– Absolut Vodka: "Deplete 15–20K cases of ABSOLUT BROOKLYN in three months and exceed sales of ABSOLUT BOSTON."
– Asthma and Allergy Foundation of America: "Drive Hispanic patients to engage their physicians in conversations about asthma triggers and asthma control."
– Caribou Coffee: "Outperform Amy's Blend sales over last year and raise a campaign high for Susan G. Komen for the Cure."

• A public relations program will often have both informational and motivational objectives. A good

> "As practitioners move away from seat-of-the-pants practices, as they abandon the notion that communication is an end in itself, they must consider realistically the kinds of effects programs can achieve."
>
> David Dozier, San Diego State University, co-author of *Manager's Guide to Excellence in Public Relations and Communication Management.*

example is the Fighting Hunger in Wisconsin campaign. Its objectives were to increase public awareness of hunger in Wisconsin, enlist additional volunteers, and raise more money than in the previous year to support hunger relief programs around the state.

3 **AUDIENCE.** Public relations programs should be directed toward specific and defined audiences or publics. Although some campaigns are directed to the general public, such instances are the exception. When FedEx developed its Panda Express campaign to return pandas to China from the U.S., among the target publics were U.S. and Chinese government officials. Planners also identified FedEx employees worldwide as a public to be reached by aspects of the campaign.

The Asthma and Allergy Foundation of America's campaign objective is to "Drive Hispanic patients to engage their physicians in conversations about asthma triggers and asthma control."

- Public relations practitioners typically target specific publics within the general public through market research that identifies key publics based on such demographic factors as age, income, social strata, education, existing ownership or consumption of specific products, and residence. For example, a water conservation campaign defines its target audience by geography—people living in a particular city or area.

- In many cases, common sense is all that is needed to adequately define a specific public. Take, for example, the Ohio vaccination program for children younger than the age of two. The primary audience for the message is parents with young children. Other audiences are pregnant women and medical professionals who treat young children. Perhaps a more complex situation involves a company that wants to increase the sale of a home improvement app for do-it-yourselfers. Again, the primary audience is not the general public, but rather those people who have a tablet device and enjoy working around the house. Such criteria would exclude a large percentage of the U.S. population.

- The following are examples of how some of the organizations already mentioned have defined target audiences:

  – ABSOLUT Vodka: "'Ambitious socials': educated, professional men and women, ages 21–29, living in metropolitan areas"
  – Asthma and Allergy Foundation of America: Puerto Rican "adult patients with asthma … caregivers of children with asthma, particularly mothers"
  – Caribou Coffee: "Women 25 to 54, college-educated, $35,000+ HHI [household income]; urban and suburban"

- A thorough understanding of publics is key to accomplishing a program's objectives. Such

Some organizations identify the media as a "public." On occasion, in programs that seek media endorsements or try to change how the media report on an organization or an issue, editors and reporters can become a legitimate "public." In general, however, mass media outlets fall in the category of a "means to an end." In other words, they represent channels to reach defined audiences that need to be informed, persuaded, and motivated.

knowledge also provides guidance on the selection of appropriate strategies and tactics to reach defined audiences.

4 STRATEGY. A strategy statement describes how, in concept, a campaign will achieve objectives; it provides guidelines and themes for the overall program. Strategy statements provide a rationale for planned actions and program components. Professionals can outline one general strategy or several strategies, depending on the objectives and the audience.

- In the Caribou Coffee campaign strategies were to: "Expand the 15th year of the program to heighten campaign awareness via the power of connection by leveraging Caribou's personal story"; and "Increase Caribou's share of voice among key stakeholders and consumers, and subsequently, create a groundswell of support to create the largest company donation to date."

- The strategy element of a program plan determines key themes and messages to reiterate throughout the campaign on all publicity materials. The Ohio juvenile immunization program "was based on the concept that parents love their children and want them to be healthy." The theme of the campaign was "Project L.O.V.E.," with the subhead "Love Our Kids Vaccination Project."

5 TACTICS. Tactics are the nuts-and-bolts part of the plan. They describe, in sequence, the specific activities that put strategies into operation and achieve the stated objectives. Tactics use the tools of communication to reach audiences with key messages.

6 CALENDAR/TIMETABLE. The three aspects of timing in a program plan are deciding when a campaign should be conducted, determining the proper sequence of activities, and compiling a list of steps that must be completed to produce a finished product. All three aspects are important to achieving maximum effectiveness.

> Cost is a driving factor; spending large sums to reach members of the general public on matters in which they have no stake or interest is nonproductive and a waste of money.

7 BUDGET. No program plan is complete without a budget. Both clients and employers inevitably ask, "How much will this program cost?" In many cases, the reverse approach is taken. That is, organizations may establish an amount they can afford and then ask the public relations staff or firm to write a program plan that fits the budget.

- A budget can be divided into two categories: staff time and out-of-pocket (OOP) expenses.

Zumba and Komen Party in Pink to Support Breast Cancer Research

One easy way to think about the steps of a public relations campaign is by following the acronym RACE (research, action, communication, and evaluation). Formative research begins the process, identifying key publics, goals and objectives, and strategies. Then comes the plan of action and the communication or program. Finally, the success of the campaign is evaluated.

Zumba Fitness urges people to party themselves into shape. The company's slogan is "Ditch the workout, join the party." When Zumba wanted a philanthropy with which to partner, it went to Susan G. Komen for the Cure. Together they developed the "Party in Pink" movement.

Research

A search for philanthropic partners requires purposeful steps. Zumba monitored its message boards to see what themes arose that might help direct them to the right partner. The company learned that women afflicted with breast cancer praised Zumba's sexy Latin dance moves. The dancing helped them overcome emotional trauma, they said. And the group nature of Zumba provided a built-in support system.

Armed with this information, Zumba considered Komen for the Cure as a partner. But Zumba was worried about competing with Komen's trademark Race for the Cure events. So the company piloted a concept Zumbathon for charity in Pittsburgh. Seven hundred people turned out; many were breast cancer survivors. Positive response on Zumba message boards and in the press validated the idea.

Zumba discovered that 69 percent of media coverage during Breast Cancer Awareness Month was focused on Komen. Furthermore, 80 percent of respondents to a survey associated the Komen name with leadership in breast cancer research support.

Action

Zumba's strategy was to partner with Komen to create a Zumba Fitness fundraising and awareness program. Zumba instructors played a key role in hosting local events and Zumbathons provided a fresh way to support breast cancer research.

Publics addressed in the campaign were existing and new Zumba instructors and participants as well as U.S. consumer mass media.

Zumba developed three objectives: (1) increase class attendance by 20 percent and Zumba instructor training registrations by 10 percent, (2) sell $135,000 in Zumbawear and donate $40,000 to Komen, and (3) secure 10 million media impressions (the potential number of people exposed to the message).

Communication

Tactics in the campaign included a new slogan, "Party in Pink," a logo, and a website, PartyinPink.com. The website was a place for both communicating about events and for sharing among "Party in Pink" participants. "Party in Pink" Zumbawear was also developed and sold, with 30 percent of proceeds going to Komen for the Cure.

The Zumba team created template promotional materials and a web-based planning document so events in different communities would be uniform. An informational e-mail was sent to instructors with details about how to schedule and promote an event.

The media campaign included development of a press kit. The kit included standard press materials, Zumbathon posters, and "Party in Pink" apparel. A medical oncologist was selected as campaign spokesperson.

Evaluation

All objectives were met and surpassed: (1) there was an increase of 61 percent in class attendance and 22 percent in training workshops; (2) Zumba sold $280,000 in "Party in Pink" Zumbawear and donated $550,000 to Komen for the Cure; and (3) media impressions exceeded 22 million. Zumbathons were promoted on *The Today Show* and in *Newsday* and *The Washington Post*.

1. What role did research play in Zumba's choice of a philanthropic partner?

2. How did Zumba manage to differentiate its events from the popular Race for the Cure?

3. Was Komen a good philanthropic match for Zumba? Why or why not?

TIMING IN A PROGRAM PLAN

TIMING. Program planning should take into account the environmental context of the situation and the time when key messages are most meaningful to the intended audience. A campaign to encourage carpooling, for example, might be more successful if it follows on the heels of a major price increase in gasoline or a government report that traffic congestion has reached gridlock proportions.

Some subjects are seasonal. Department 56, the designer and manufacturer of miniature lighted village collectibles and other holiday giftware, timed the bulk of its campaign for November to take advantage of the Christmas holidays, when interest in its product lines peaked. Charitable agencies, such as the Wisconsin hunger project, also gear their campaigns toward the Christmas season.

SCHEDULING. Another aspect of timing is the scheduling and sequencing of various tactics or activities. A typical pattern is to concentrate the most effort at the beginning of a campaign, when a number of tactics are implemented. The launch phase of a campaign, much like that of a rocket, requires a burst of activity just to break the awareness barrier. By comparison, after the campaign has achieved orbit, less energy and fewer activities are required to maintain momentum. Public relations campaigns often are the first stage of an integrated marketing communications program. Once public relations has created awareness and customer anticipation of a new product or service, the second stage may be an advertising and direct mail campaign.

COMPILING A CALENDAR. An integral part of timing is advance planning. A video news release, a press kit, or a brochure often takes weeks or months to prepare. Arrangements for special events also take considerable time. Practitioners must take into account the deadlines of publications. Monthly periodicals, for example, frequently need to receive information at least six to eight weeks before publication. A popular talk show may book guests three or four months in advance.

The public relations professional must think ahead to make things happen in the right sequence, at the right time. One way to achieve this goal is to compile timelines and charts that list the necessary steps and their required completion dates. An excerpt from one day of the April calendar (left), where the initials in the left column indicate the person responsible for the activity. Gantt charts (below) are also used for planning purposes. Essentially, a Gantt chart is a column matrix that has two sides. The left side has a vertical list of activities that must be accomplished, and the top has a horizontal line of days, weeks, or months.

Wednesday, April 12

M	Begin development of invitation, RSVP, envelopes, tickets, program, nametags, placards, etc.
J/M	Review printing costs and options
T	Investigate possibility of having palette tasting trays
T	Reserve Stars' Grill Room for eve (asking Jess)
T	Determine RSVP voice mail #
ALL	2 p.m. Committee Meeting at SF Memorial and Performing Arts Ce

PR Timeline

	Sept.	Oct.	Nov.	Dec.	Jan.	Feb.	Mar.
Positioning							
VC Launch							
Editorial Calendars							
Tech./App. Articles							
Press Release Program							
Trade Show Support							
Guest Editorials							
YouTube videos							
Executive Round Table							
Primer Brochure							
Ongoing Services							

Staff and administrative time usually consumes the lion's share of any public relations budget. In a $100,000 campaign done by a public relations firm, for example, it is not unusual for 70 percent of the program cost to consist of salaries and administrative fees.

• One method of budgeting is to use two columns. The left column lists the staff cost for writing a pamphlet or compiling a press kit. The right column lists the actual OOP expense for having the pamphlet or press kit designed, printed, and delivered. Internal public relations staffs, whose members are on the payroll, often complete only the OOP expenses budget. It is good practice to allocate approximately 10 percent of the budget for contingencies or unexpected costs.

• In a program plan, professionals usually estimate budgets on the basis of experience and estimates from vendors. After the program is completed, the measurement process involves assessment of estimated expenses versus actual expenses.

think Why is it important to compare estimated cost to actuals after a program is completed?

8 MEASUREMENT. The evaluation element of a plan relates directly back to the stated objectives of the program. Objectives must be measurable in some way to show clients and employers that the program accomplished its purpose. Evaluation criteria should be realistic, credible, specific, and in line with client or employer expectations. The measurement section of a program plan should restate the objectives and list the measurement methods to be used.

• Measurement of an informational objective often entails a

APPLY YOUR KNOWLEDGE

What Would You Do?

Plan for Success

Sunshine Café, a chain of coffee houses, conducted market research and found that college students would be an excellent audience for its product and services. To this end, Sunshine Café has contacted your public relations firm and asked that you develop a comprehensive plan to do two things: (1) create brand awareness among college students and (2) increase walk-in business at its local stores in college towns.

Using the eight-element planning outline described in this chapter, write a public relations program for Sunshine Café. You should consider a variety of communication tools, including campus events. No money has been allocated for advertising.

compilation of news clips and an analysis of key message point appearance. Other methods include determining the number of brochures distributed or the estimated number of viewers who saw a video news release. Sales or market share increases often are used to measure and evaluate motivational objectives,

as are the number of people who called a toll-free number for more information or "like" a Facebook page, or benchmark surveys that measure people's perceptions before and after a campaign.

We have now covered the first two essential steps in effective public relations: research and planning.

summary

What Are the Four Essential Steps of Effective Public Relations?

- Effective public relations is a process with four essential steps: (1) research, (2) planning, (3) communication, and (4) measurement.

How Is Research Used in Public Relations?

- Research is the basic groundwork of any public relations program; it involves the gathering and interpretation of information and is used in every phase of a communications program.

How Is Research Conducted in Public Relations?

- Secondary research uses information from library and online and Internet sources. Primary research involves gathering new information through interviews or sampling procedures.
- The sampling method constrains the extent to which the findings can be analyzed in detail and extrapolated to a larger population. Probability samples generate the best results, particularly when doing quantitative research.
- Survey respondents may be reached by mail, e-mail, telephone, the Internet, personal interviews, or piggyback (omnibus) surveys.

What Role Does Planning Play in Effective Public Relations?

- After research, the next step is strategic program planning.
- Two approaches to planning are management by objective (MBO) and Ketchum's Strategic Planning Model. Both involve asking and answering many questions.

What Are the Eight Elements of a Program Plan?

- Program plans usually include eight elements: situation, objectives, audience, strategy, tactics, a calendar or timetable, budget, and measurement.

questions
FOR REVIEW AND DISCUSSION

1 Which questions should a public relations professional ask before formulating a research design?

2 List and describe five ways that research is used in public relations.

3 How can survey research be used as a public relations tool?

4 What is the procedure for organizing and conducting a focus group?

5 Which guidelines should be followed when releasing the results of a survey to the media and the public?

6 Name the eight elements of a program plan.

7 Explain the difference between an informational objective and a motivational objective.

8 What is the difference between a strategy and an objective?

MySearchLab®

tactics

Master Class

Are Traditional Ways of Doing Research Still Valuable in the Age of Social Media?

With the advent of social media, the landscape of public relations research has changed, as have the ways that we analyze issues and strategies. A combination of traditional media research techniques and social media research methods are needed to tackle the new media environment.

Both traditional media research and social media conversation analysis can be used to find information about an organization, its public, and the situation. The important thing is that a team selects the appropriate method to address the given public relations problem.

From the June 01, 2011 Issue of *PRWeek*

The following is an excerpt from a Master Class panel discussion from *PRWeek*.

Annette Arno, research director, Cision Global Analysts: This isn't an either/or situation. Both traditional media research and social media conversation analysis are valuable for what they contribute to PR research efforts. Analyzing social media content is definitely newer than traditional methodologies such as surveys and focus groups, but there is a reason why the former has spread like wildfire: the results provide immediate and visceral insights into the public's reaction to issues as they arise, and can even contribute to the development of events.

Having a handle on this kind of immediacy is invaluable. Issues are constantly arising, and thus, social media content should be tracked on an ongoing basis. From the research perspective, social media input can answer a lot of the questions that would otherwise take up time and money, as it can be used to inform the design of traditional research. After all, knowing what issues to flesh out gets you into the meat of a survey faster.

This allows you to capitalize on the strengths of survey research: getting specific answers to specific questions - questions that probably aren't part of trending online conversations, but are the next logical questions that organizations want answers to. Traditional research methodologies also allow you to target specific audiences not clearly identifiable through self-reported social media demographics.

The basic research rules to follow are the same for new and old methodologies: what are your goals and do they match those of your organization? Who is your audience? What media combination best captures their attention?

Selecting the best-fitting research path to your answers is key. Social media input and tracking can allow traditional research methodologies to shine as if they were new.

Johna Burke, SVP of marketing, Burrelles-Luce: Far from reducing the importance of focus groups and surveys, the stunning growth of social media has, in fact, made traditional research tools even more valuable and necessary than ever before.

More valuable because the rising chorus of social media voices and the expanding boundaries of social media conversation provide increasing opportunities and incentives for communications professionals to obtain the kind of data that sets the course toward a winning campaign.

More necessary, because much of social media discussion produces loud background noise that can drown out the sounds that help give strategic meaning to all the overlapping conversations. Focus groups and surveys can filter out the clamor of social media and help make sense of the unrelenting chatter that, for better or worse, constitutes the essence of social media. Traditional research techniques can translate social media comments into usable commentary, and turn random information into coherent intelligence.

For instance, the nature of social media does not allow for a control group, but a survey can easily accommodate one. It is in such a way that PR pros can gain the clearest insight into - and exert the greatest influence on - the tone and tenor of the social media discussion that surrounds their company or client.

Just as communications pros have begun to realize there is room in their toolkits for both social and traditional media, they should recognize that social media and traditional research methods are complementary components in an effective, holistic approach to successful media relations.

Heidi D'Agostino, EVP of insights and research, Ogilvy PR: We're at another important transition in research, much like the move from paper surveys to telephone, and then online. That progression was necessitated by the desire to reach constituents and deliver on client needs within a valuable and actionable budget and time frame.

Technological advances have elevated the implementation of research to meet people where they are, showcase creative in various forms, and be more efficient.

I'm a huge advocate of using new research methods, particularly online focus groups, iPad online surveys, and digital usability testing, but research-tool selection should always be driven by the learnings and outcomes desired, as well as the audiences being studied.

Real world, "old school" methods can still provide an avenue to intelligence that cannot be garnered through online or social media research. Online methods might provide abundant commentary, but people speak in a broader language than they would ever type.

Recently, we were asked to consider technology usability research among an aging professional population who would be the key drivers of adoption. Initial thinking was technology equals online testing. However, after careful consideration of the research objectives and audiences, we realized that in-person, in-depth interviews where we could see keystrokes, facial expressions, and probe on confusion would provide the most valuable insights for informing development.

These are some examples of new research methods using digital technologies. The advantage of using these techniques is that they are good venues to explore public relations environments in social online era. Technologies can be used to facilitate research. They are often efficient, inexpensive and provide quick results.

Social media research can offer current, detailed information that traditional media research techniques miss, especially when you are targeting members of the social media generation. More and more organizations are adopting social media research tools and techniques in their public relations campaigns.

Traditional research techniques can be used to understand certain public relations phenomena whose results can be formative or evaluative research for a successful campaign. The key is how and how well the research process and the findings support the designs and implementation of a public relations campaign.

This is an example on how traditional research is still very valuable. Traditional research methods often produce in-depth information and accurate projections, following systematic procedure based on a given research goal and objectives.

Text Credits

Credits are listed in order of appearance.

Reprinted by permission of PRWeek.

Photo Credits

Credits are listed in order of appearance.

U.S. Census Bureau;
Hill Street Studios/Blend/Photolibrary/Getty Images;
Jim West/Alamy;
Porter Novelli;
wavebreakmedia td/Shutterstock;

Jeff Greenberg/PhotoEdit;
Thierry Berrod, Mona Lisa Production/ Science Source/Photo Researchers, Inc.;
(br) Beau Lark/Corbis; (tr) asiseeit/iStockphoto; (tr) Nadia Borowski Scott/Zuma Press;

Jeroen van den Broek/Shutterstock;
stefanolunardi/Shutterstock;
Newscom;
Rob Marmion/Shutterstock;
Stockbyte/Getty Images

Tactics image: Petr Z/Shutterstock
Tablet image: Falconia/Shutterstock

Communication and Measurement

From Chapter 6 of *Think Public Relations*, 2013 Edition. Dennis L. Wilcox, Glen T. Cameron, Bryan H. Reber, Jae-Hwa Shin.

Communication and Measurement

An Interesting Campaign for a "Most Interesting" Beer

A brand whose spokesperson is The Most Interesting Man in the World faces a challenge when it comes to living up to its Most Interesting reputation. Dos Equis Mexican beer employs novel public relations tactics to engage its Most Interesting fans. In one contest, shown here, Dos Equis challenged New Yorkers to break into the man ice sculpture to dig out prize cards frozen in its center using any "tools" they had in thier pockets.

Another popular approach involved the "Feast of the Brave" food truck. *PRWeek* highlighted Dos Equis and its agency of record (AOR), Hill and Knowlton, for their efforts on this campaign. Targeting 21- to 34-year-olds in Manhattan and Brooklyn, the company gave away exotic tacos from a branded food truck for the two weeks leading up to Cinco de Mayo. New York City news website gothamist.com announced the event with the headline: "Free Food Alert: Dos Equis Taco Truck Doles Out Tongue & Cricket Tacos." The website went on to report, "… bugs and brains … ostrich, cow tongue, veal brain, and cricket are the sole taco-filling offerings on the truck."

"Feast of the Brave was an extension of the brand proposition [of leading a more interesting life]," Paul Smailes, senior brand director for Dos Equis and Sol, told *PRWeek*. "We leveraged that on a street level and amplified it through PR and social media to reach a much wider audience." The truck parked at lunch locations where the target public and members of the media would be likely to find it. At night, the truck parked near popular bars and restaurants that served Dos Equis.

The locations were announced on the Dos Equis Facebook page and via the campaign's @FeastoftheBrave Twitter handle. Brand ambassadors also posted photos and updates on Facebook and Twitter. Key food bloggers and reporters were sent six-packs, bottle openers, and invitations to visit the truck. "The notion of being brave enough [to try the tacos] is something people can brag about," Hill and Knowlton SVP Ben Trounson told *PRWeek*. "It generates far more chatter online."

Over the course of the campaign, 3,000 tacos were given away, 2,500 new Facebook likes were generated, and 2,500 tweets were sent. The Twitter handle had 587 followers, which was impressive given the relatively short duration of the campaign. Forty stories appeared in the media, accounting for about 9 million media impressions.

Dos Equis's other novel campaigns include The Most Interesting Show in the World (a traveling circus-like show that performs at bars and restaurants) and Flash Parties.

1 Why did campaign planners believe that the Dos Equis food truck would generate online chatter?

2 How did Dos Equis and Hill and Knowlton use social and online media to promote the campaign?

3 Do you think that giving away exotic tacos was an effective link to the Dos Equis brand? Why or why not?

Ask Yourself

> What Are the Goals of Public Relations Communication?

> Which Factors Influence Message Reception, Comprehension, Retention, Credibility, and Adoption?

> Why Is Measurement of Public Relations Program Effectiveness Important?

> Which Methods Are Used to Measure the Effectiveness of Public Relations Programs?

Communication: THE THIRD STEP

he four essential steps of effective public relations are research, planning, communication, and measurement. In this chapter, we discuss the third and fourth steps of this process—communication and measurement.

The third step in the public relations process, after research and planning, is communication. Communication is also sometimes referred to as execution. In a public relations program, communication is the process and the means by which objectives are achieved. A program's strategies and tactics may take the form of news releases, news conferences, special events, brochures, viral marketing, speeches, dedicated Twitter, Facebook or YouTube accounts, bumper stickers, newsletters, webcasts, blogs, rallies, posters, and the like.

Kirk Hallahan of Colorado State University makes the point that today's communication revolution has given public relations professionals a full range of communication tools and media, and the traditional approach of simply obtaining publicity through the mass media—newspapers, magazines, radio, and television—is no longer sufficient, if it ever was:

> PR program planners need to reexamine their traditional approaches to the practice and think about media broadly and strategically. PR media planners must now address some of the same questions that confront advertisers. What media best

meet a program's objectives? How can media be combined to enhance program effectiveness? What media are most efficient to reach key audiences?

The Goals of Communication

The goals of communication are to inform, persuade, motivate, or achieve mutual understanding.

When planning a message on behalf of an employer or client, public relations professionals must

---

To be an effective communicator, you must understand three factors:

1 WHAT constitutes communication and how people receive messages

2 HOW people process information and change their perceptions

3 WHICH kinds of media and communication tools are most appropriate for a particular message

consider a number of variables. In addition to examining proposed content, a successful communicator determines exactly which objective is being targeted through the communication. James Grunig, emeritus professor of public relations at the University of Maryland, cites five key objectives for communication:

1 **Message Exposure.** Public relations personnel provide materials to the mass media and disseminate other messages through controlled media such as newsletters and brochures. Intended audiences are exposed to the message in various forms.

2 **Accurate Dissemination of the Message.** The basic information, often filtered by media gatekeepers, remains intact as it is transmitted through various media.

3 **Acceptance of the Message.** Based on its view of reality, the audience not only retains the message, but also accepts it as valid.

4 **Attitude Change.** The audience not only believes the message, but also makes a verbal or mental commitment to change behavior as a result of the message.

5 **Change in Overt Behavior.** Members of the audience actually change their current behavior or purchase the product and use it.

An Integrated Public Relations Media Model

The variety and scope of media and communication tools available to public relations professionals runs the gamut from mass media (public media) to one-on-one communication (interpersonal communication). Here, in chart form, is a concept developed by Professor Kirk Hallahan at Colorado State University.

← **MASS COMMUNICATION**
High Tech
Perceptually Based
Low Social Presence
Asynchronous

PERSONALIZED COMMUNICATION →
Low Tech
Experientially Based
High Social Presence
Synchronous

Public Media	Controlled Media	Interactive Media	Events	One-on-One
Key Uses in a Communication Program				
Build awareness; Enhance credibility	Promotion; Provide detailed information	Respond to queries; Exchange information; Engage users	Motivate participants; Reinforce existing beliefs, attitudes	Obtain commitments; Negotiation; Resolution of problems
Principal Examples of Media				
Publicity/advertising/ advertorials/product placements in: Newspapers Magazines Radio Television *Paid advertising* Transit media Out-of-home media (Billboards, posters, electronic displays) Directories Venue signage Movie theater trailers, advertising	Brochures Newsletters Sponsored magazines Annual reports Books Direct mail Exhibits and displays Point-of-purchase support DVDs/Video brochures Statement inserts Other collateral or printed ephemera Advertising specialties	E-mail, instant, text and microblog messages E-newsletters, e-zines Automated telephone call systems Web sites, blogs Vodcasts/podcasts Games Web conferences, Webinars, webcasts Information kiosks Internets and extranets Social networking sites Forums (chats, groups) Media-sharing sites Paid text/display click-through advertising	Meetings/conferences Speeches/presentations Government or judicial testimony Trade shows, exhibitions Demonstrations/rallies Sponsored events Observances/anniversaries Contests/sweepstakes Recognition award programs (Often supported with multimedia presentations)	Personal visits/lobbying Correspondence Telephone calls

> ## "To be successful, a message must be received by the intended individual or audience. It must get the audience's attention. It must be understood. It must be believed. It must be remembered. And ultimately, in some fashion, it must be acted upon. Failure to accomplish any of these tasks means the entire message fails."
>
> **David Therkelsen, executive director of Crisis Connection in St. Paul, Minnesota**

Most public relations experts usually aim to achieve the first two objectives: exposure to the message and accurate dissemination of that message. The first two objectives are easier to accomplish than attitude change. Achieving the last three objectives depends in large part on a mix of variables—predisposition to the message, peer reinforcement, feasibility of the suggested action, and environmental context, to name a few.

Although the communicator cannot always control the outcome of a message, effective dissemination is the beginning of a process that leads to opinion change and adoption of products or services. For these reasons, it is important to review all components of the communication process.

Making Sure the Audience Receives the Message

Several communication models explain how a message moves from sender to recipient. Some are quite complex, attempting to incorporate an almost infinite number of events, ideas, objects, and people that interact among the message, channel, and receiver. Most communication models, however, focus on only four basic elements. David K. Berlo's classic model is an example. It features a sender/source (encoder), a message, a channel, and a receiver (decoder). A fifth element—feedback from the receiver to the sender—is incorporated into modern models of communication.

One-way communication, from sender to receiver, simply disseminates information. This kind of monologue is less effective than two-way communication, which establishes a dialogue between the sender and the receiver. Grunig postulates that the ideal public relations model consists of two-way symmetric communication. In other words, communication should be balanced between the sender and the receiver. In reality, research shows that most organizations have mixed motives when they engage in two-way communication with audiences.

Feedback can also be thought of as two-way communication.

> **think** What are the five primary objectives of an effective public relations campaign?

Models of communication emphasize the importance of feedback as an integral component of the process. As they implement communication strategies, successful public relations personnel pay careful and constant attention to feedback.

The practice of public relations is dynamic. During any campaign, motives and strategic goals may change depending on a variety of factors. For example, as a public relations practitioner, you may advocate providing a new benefit for employees. In doing so, your motives are mixed: Employees will be pleased with the new benefit, but your real objective is to save the organization money by limiting employee turnover.

The most effective type of two-way communication, of course, is interpersonal or face-to-face communication between two people. Likewise, small-group discussion is very effective. In both forms, the message is fortified by gestures, facial expressions, intimacy, tone of voice, and immediate feedback. If a listener asks a question or appears puzzled, the speaker has an instant cue and can rephrase the information or amplify a point.

Barriers to communication multiply in large-group meetings and, ultimately, in the mass media. Via mass media outlets, organizational materials can reach thousands and even millions of people, but the psychological and physical distance between sender and receiver in these types of campaigns is considerable. Communication is less effective because the audience is no longer involved with the source. No immediate feedback is possible, and the message may become distorted as it passes through the various mass media gatekeepers.

> "In the symmetric model, understanding is the principal objective of public relations, rather than persuasion."
>
> **James Grunig**

SCHRAMM'S ORIGINAL MODEL

Source → **Encoder** → **Signal** → **Decoder** → **Destination**

Mass media researcher Wilbur Schramm started with a simple communication model (see figure above), but he later expanded the process to include the concept of shared fields of experience (see figure below).

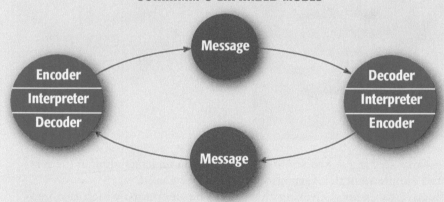

FIELD OF EXPERIENCE   FIELD OF EXPERIENCE

Source | Encoder → Signal → Decoder | Destination

Shared experience refers to the concept that little or no communication happens unless the sender and the receiver share a common language and an overlapping cultural or educational background. The importance of shared experience is apparent if you think of a highly technical news release about a new computer system that causes a local business editor to shake his or her head in bewilderment. Effective communication can only take place within a sphere of "shared experience" according to Schramm.

SCHRAMM'S EXPANDED MODEL

Encoder / Interpreter / Decoder — Message → Decoder / Interpreter / Encoder — Message →

Schramm's third model (see above) incorporates the idea of continuous feedback. Both the sender and the receiver continually encode, interpret, decode, transmit, and receive information. Communication to internal and external audiences produces feedback that is taken into consideration during research (the first step of the public relations process) and measurement (the fourth step). In this way, messages are continuously refined.

Making Sure the Audience Pays Attention to the Message

Although in public relations, we emphasize the formation and dissemination of messages, this effort is wasted if the audience pays no attention. It is important to remember the axiom of Walt Seifert, a pioneer public relations educator at Ohio State University: "Dissemination does not equal publication, and publication does not equal absorption and action." In other words, "All who receive your message won't publish it, and all who read or hear your message won't understand or act upon it."

Strategy should be based on more than common sense or rote routines. The management of competition and conflict requires a sophisticated understanding of the climate in which an organization operates and the dispositions of its publics on a variety of matters.

Sociologist Harold Lasswell defined the act of communication as "Who says what, in which channel, to whom, with what effect?"

The basic premise of the media uses and gratification theory of communication is that the communication process is interactive. The communicator wants to inform and even persuade; the recipient wants to be entertained, informed, or alerted to opportunities that can fulfill individual needs. This theory assumes that people make highly intelligent choices about which messages require their attention and fulfill their needs. If this is true—and research indicates it is—the public relations communicator must tailor messages that focus on grabbing the audience's attention.

One approach for achieving this goal is to understand the mental state of the intended audience. In *Managing Public Relations*, James Grunig and Todd Hunt suggest that communication strategies be designed to attract the attention of two kinds of audiences: those who actively seek information and those who passively process information.

Passive audiences may initially pay attention to a message only because it is entertaining and offers a diversion. They can be made aware of the message through brief encounters: a billboard glimpsed on the way to work, a radio announcement heard in the car, a television advertisement broadcast before a show begins, or an informational flyer picked up in a doctor's waiting room.

People use mass media for a variety of purposes. They use it for surveillance of the environment to find out what is happening, locally or even globally, that has some impact on them; entertainment and diversion; reinforcement of their opinions and predispositions; and to gain information in order to make decisions about buying products or services.

Active audiences seek out information.

Passive audiences use communication channels that can be accessed while they are doing something else.

At any given time, an intended audience contains both **passive** and **active** information seekers. For this reason, **multiple** messages and a **variety** of communication tools should be used in a full-fledged information campaign.

Passive audiences need messages that are stylish and creative. Photos, illustrations, and catchy slogans lure this type of audience into processing the information. Press agentry, dramatic images, celebrity pitches, radio and television announcements, and events featuring entertainment can make passive audiences aware of a message. The objectives of these types of communications are simply exposure to, and accurate dissemination of, messages. In most public relations campaigns, communications are designed to reach primarily passive audiences.

In contrast, a communicator employs a different approach with audiences that actively seek information. These people are already interested in the message and are typically seeking more sophisticated supplemental information. Effective tools for delivering this content may include links to more detailed information on an organization's website, brochures, in-depth newspaper and magazine articles, slide presentations, video presentations, symposiums and conferences, major speeches before key groups, and demonstrations at trade shows.

Making Sure the Message Is Understood

Communication is the act of transmitting information, ideas, and attitudes from one person to another. Communication can take place only if the sender and the receiver have a common understanding of the symbols being used.

The degree to which two people understand each other depends heavily on their common comprehension of words. Anyone who has traveled abroad can readily attest that only limited communication can occur between two people who speak different languages. And even if the sender and the receiver speak the same language and live in the same country, the effectiveness of communication depends on a variety of key factors, such as education, social economic class, regional differences, nationality, and cultural background.

Employee communication specialists are keenly aware of these differences, as multicultural workforces have become the norm for most organizations. The globalization of the economy has resulted in organizations with operations and employees in many countries as well as the increasingly diverse composition of the American workforce. In light of these trends, communicators need to be informed

Audience background and literacy level are important considerations for any communicator.

about cultural differences and conflicting values so that they can establish common ground and build bridges among various groups. The key is to produce messages that appeal, in content and structure, to the characteristics of the audience. One approach is to copy-test all public relations materials on a target audience. This step can help convince management—and communicators—that what they like isn't necessarily what the audience wants, needs, or under-

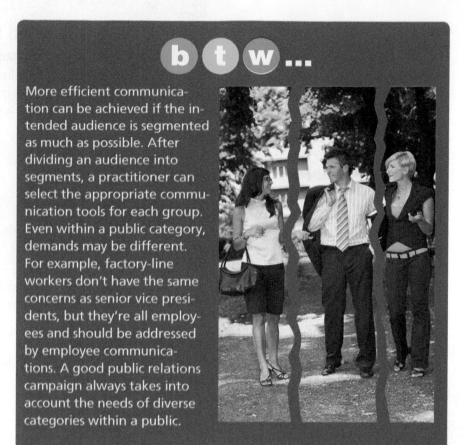

More efficient communication can be achieved if the intended audience is segmented as much as possible. After dividing an audience into segments, a practitioner can select the appropriate communication tools for each group. Even within a public category, demands may be different. For example, factory-line workers don't have the same concerns as senior vice presidents, but they're all employees and should be addressed by employee communications. A good public relations campaign always takes into account the needs of diverse categories within a public.

The Flesch readability formula assesses average sentence length and the number of one-syllable words per 100 words. If a randomly selected sample of 100 words contains 4.2 sentences and 142 syllables, it is ranked at about the ninth-grade level, which is a common level for mass distributed material.

In the Cloze procedure, copy is tested for comprehension and redundancy by having people read passages in which every fifth or ninth word is removed. Their ability to fill in the missing words determines whether the pattern of words is familiar, which in turn determines where the message is understandable.

stands. Another strategy is to apply readability and comprehension formulas to materials before they are produced and disseminated. Learning theory asserts that the simpler the piece of writing, the easier it will be for audiences to understand the message.

Making the Message Credible

Credibility is one key variable in the communication process. Members of the audience must perceive a source as knowledgeable and expert on the subject as well as honest and objective. Audiences, for example, ascribe lower credibility to statements in an advertisement than to the same information

think Why is it important for a communicator to understand the cultural background of an audience?

in a newsarticle, because news articles are selected by media gatekeepers and are perceived as more objective.

Source credibility is a problem for any organizational spokesperson, because the public already has a bias based on the person's relationship to the organization. The problem of source credibility is the main reason that organizations, whenever possible, use respected outside experts or celebrities as representatives to convey their messages.

Another variable is the context of the message. Action (performance) speaks louder than a stack of news releases. A bank may spend thousands of dollars on a promotion campaign with the slogan, "Your Friendly Bank—Where Service Counts," but the effort is wasted if employees are not trained to be friendly and courteous. Incompatible rhetoric and actions can even be amusing at times. At a press briefing about the importance of "buying American," the U.S. Chamber of Commerce passed out commemorative coffee mugs marked in small print on the bottom, "Made in China."

Involvement is another important factor that influences how messages are processed by audience members. Involvement can be described in simple terms as interest in or concern about an issue or a product. Those with higher involvement often process persuasive messages with greater attention to detail and to logic, whereas those with low involvement in a topic are impressed more by cues, such as

think Is it unusual for members of an audience to change their mind about source credibility?

In a study conducted for the GCI Group,

Opinion Research Corporation found that **MORE THAN HALF** of those surveyed were likely to believe that a large company is probably guilty of wrongdoing if it is being investigated by a government agency or if a major lawsuit is filed against the company.

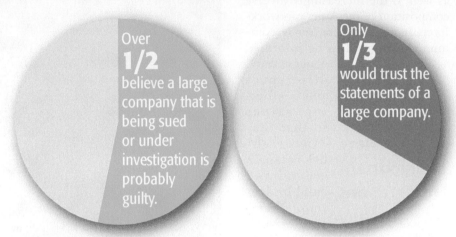

Over **1/2** believe a large company that is being sued or under investigation is probably guilty.

Only **1/3** would trust the statements of a large company.

an attractive spokesperson, humor, or the sheer number of arguments given. Public relations professionals can capitalize on the involvement concept by devising messages that focus more on "what is said" for high-involvement audiences and that pay more attention to "who says it" for low-involvement audiences.

Making the Message Memorable

Communicators often build repetition into a message. Key points are mentioned at the beginning and then summarized at the end. If the source is asking the receiver to call for more information or write for a brochure, the telephone number or address is

REPETITION
REPETITION
REPETITION
REPETITION
REPETITION
REPETITION
REPETITION
REPETITION
REPETITION

- Is **NECESSARY** because all members of a target audience don't see or hear the message at the same time. Not everyone reads the newspaper on a particular day or watches the same television news program.
- **REMINDS** the audience, so there is less chance of failure to remember the message. If a source has high credibility, repetition prevents erosion of opinion change.
- Helps the audience **REMEMBER** the message. Studies have shown that advertising is quickly forgotten if not repeated constantly.
- Can lead to **IMPROVED LEARNING** and increase the chance of penetrating audience indifference or resistance.
- **OFFSETS THE "NOISE"** surrounding a message. People often hear or see messages in an environment filled with distractions—a baby crying, the conversations of family members or office staff, a barking dog—or even while daydreaming or thinking of other things.
- Contributes to **CREDIBILITY**. A study funded by public relations firm Edelman Worldwide found that 60 percent of the respondents had to hear a message about a company three to five times before they believed it.

Increase Audience Understanding and Comprehension

Use Symbols, Acronyms, and Slogans

Message clarity and simplicity are enhanced by the use of symbols, acronyms, and slogans. These forms of shorthand conceptualize an idea so it can travel through extended lines of communication.

Avoid Jargon

One source of blocked communication is technical and bureaucratic jargon. Social scientists call it semantic noise when such language is delivered to a general audience. Jargon interferes with the message and impedes the receiver's ability to understand it. A news release may be perfectly appropriate for an engineering publication serving a particular industry, but the same information must be written in simpler terms for the readers of a daily newspaper.

Avoid Clichés and Hype Words

Highly charged words can pose problems, and overuse of clichés and hype words can seriously undermine the credibility of a message. Author and viral marketing specialist David Meerman Scott analyzed more than 700,000 news releases to determine the most commonly overused words and phrases. The top 15, in descending order, were: innovate, pleased to, unique, focused on, leading provider, commitment, partnership, new and improved, leverage, 120 percent, cost-effective, next generation, 110 percent, flexible, and world class.

Avoid Euphemisms

Public relations personnel should use positive, favorable words to convey a message, but they have an ethical responsibility not to use euphemisms—

Advertising Age listed the top five slogans of the twentieth century as "Diamonds Are Forever" (De Beers), "Just Do It" (Nike), "The Pause That Refreshes" (Coca-Cola), "Tastes Great, Less Filling" (Miller Lite), and "We Try Harder" (Avis).

Corporate symbols such as the Mercedes Benz star, the Nike swoosh, and the apple of Apple Computer are known throughout the world. Corporations invest time and money to make their names and logos synonymous with quality and service—a process referred to as branding. A corporate symbol should be unique, memorable, widely recognized, and appropriate. Organizations seek unique symbols that convey the essence of what they are or what they hope to be.

that is, words that hide information or mislead readers. Little danger exists in substituting positive words, such as saying a person has a disability rather than using the adjective *handicapped*. More dangerous are euphemisms that actually alter the meaning or impact of a word or concept. Writers call this practice doublespeak—words that pretend to communicate but really do not. Corporations often use euphemisms and doublespeak to hide unfavorable news. Reducing the number of employees, for example, may be called "right-sizing."

Avoid Discriminatory Language

In today's world, effective communication also means nondiscriminatory communication. Public relations personnel should double-check every message to eliminate undesirable gender, racial, and ethnic connotations.

repeated several times. Such precautions also fight entropy, which is the information disintegration that occurs as media channels and people process the message and pass it on to others.

The key to effective communication and message retention is conveying information in a variety of ways via multiple communication channels. This "shotgun approach" helps people remember the message as they receive it through different media and extends the message to both passive and active audiences.

Making Sure the Audience Acts on the Message

The ultimate purpose of any message is to affect the recipient. Public relations personnel communicate messages on behalf of organizations to change perceptions, attitudes, opinions, or behavior in some way.

The communicator should be aware of the various factors that affect persuasion in the adoption process and attempt to implement communication strategies that will overcome as many objections as possible. Repeating a message in various ways, reducing its complexity, taking into account compet-

A number of factors affect persuasion in the adoption process. Everett Rogers, author of *Diffusion of Innovations*, lists at least five.

1. Relative Advantage— the degree to which an innovation is perceived as better than the idea it replaces

2. Compatibility— the degree to which an innovation is perceived as being consistent with the existing values, experiences, and needs of potential adopters

3. Complexity—the degree to which an innovation is perceived as difficult to understand and use

4. Trialability—the degree to which an innovation may be experienced on a limited basis

5. Observability— the degree to which the results of an innovation are visible to others

ing messages, and structuring the message to meet the needs of the audience are ways to achieve this goal.

Another aspect to consider is the amount of time needed to adopt a new idea or product. Depending on the individual and situation, the entire adoption process may take place almost instantly if it is of minor consequence or it requires only low-level commitment. Buying a new brand of soft drink or a bar of soap is relatively inexpensive and is often done on impulse. In contrast, deciding to buy a new car or vote for a particular candidate may involve an adoption process that takes several weeks or months.

Everett Rogers's research shows that people approach innovation in different ways, depending on their personality traits and the risk involved. "Innovators" are venturesome individuals who are eager to try new ideas, whereas "laggards" are traditionalists who are the last to adopt anything. Between the two extremes are "early adopters," who are opinion leaders; "early majority" members, who take a deliberate approach; and "late majority" members, who are often skeptical but bow to peer pressure. Communicators often segment audiences and target their messages toward those who

One study about employee communications found that rank-and-file workers got only

20 percent of a message

that had passed through four levels of managers.

Communication and Measurement

have "innovator" or "early adopter" characteristics and would be predisposed to adopting new ideas.

Of particular interest to public relations practitioners is the primary source of information at each step in the five-stage adoption process (see nearby figure). Mass media vehicles such as advertising, short news articles, feature stories, and radio and television news announcements are most influential at the awareness stage of the adoption process. For example, a news article or a television announcement makes people aware of an idea, event, or new product. They may also first become aware of the message through such vehicles as direct mail, office memos, and simple brochures.

Individuals at the interest stage also rely on mass media vehicles, but at this point are actively seeking information and pay attention to longer, in-depth articles. They rely more on detailed brochures, specialized publications, and reviews posted by consumers on the Internet to provide details.

At the evaluation, trial, and adoption stages, group norms and opinions are the most influential. Feedback—negative or positive—from friends and peers may determine the likelihood of adoption. If a person's friends generally disapprove of a candidate, a movie, or an automobile brand, it is unlikely that the individual will complete the adoption process even if he or she is highly sold on the idea. If a person does make a commitment, mass media vehicles become reinforcing mechanisms.

The complexities of the adoption process show that public relations communicators need to think about the entire communication process—from the formulation of the message to the ways in which receivers ultimately process the information and make decisions. By doing so, communicators can form more effective message strategies and develop realistic objectives for what can actually be accomplished.

THE FIVE-STAGE ADOPTION PROCESS

Getting people to act on a message is not a simple process. Research shows that it can be a somewhat lengthy and complex procedure that depends on a number of intervening influences. One key to understanding how people accept new ideas or products is to analyze the adoption process.

1 **AWARENESS.** A person becomes aware of an idea or a new product, often by means of an advertisement or a news story.

2 **INTEREST.** The individual seeks more information about the idea or the product, perhaps by ordering a brochure, picking up a pamphlet, or reading an in-depth article in a newspaper or magazine.

3 **EVALUATION.** The potential consumer evaluates the idea or the product on the basis of how it meets specific needs and wants. Feedback from friends and family is part of this process.

4 **TRIAL.** The person tries the product or the idea on an experimental basis, by using a sample, witnessing a demonstration, or making qualifying statements such as "I read…"

5 **ADOPTION.** The individual begins to use the product on a regular basis or integrates the idea into his or her belief system. "I read…" becomes "I think…"

Every person does not necessarily go through all five stages with any given idea or product. The process may end after any step. In fact, the process is like a large funnel; although many people are made aware of an idea or a product, only a few will ultimately adopt it.

SocialMediaInAction

Facebook Friends = Brain Power?

Researchers at University College London have linked Facebook friends and brain power. In a scientific article published in the journal *Proceedings of the Royal Society B*, neuroscientists reported an experiment that showed the brains of people with lots of Facebook friends are different from the brains of people with fewer online friends.

"The researchers at University College London found that users with the greatest number of friends on the social networking site had more grey matter in brain regions linked to social skills. The finding suggests that either social networking changes these brain regions, or that people born with these kinds of brains behave differently on websites like Facebook," reported *The Guardian*, a British newspaper.

The neuroscientists conducted magnetic resonance imaging (MRI) brain scans on more than 100 study participants. The volunteer participants also answered questions about the number of Facebook and "real-world" friends they had. Three areas of the brain that are associated with our ability to extract social cues from facial expressions and remember faces and names were denser in those study participants who claimed the most Facebook friends.

"What we've shown is an association between the number of friends on Facebook and certain areas of the brain and the structure of those areas," said Dr. Geraint Rees, the lead researcher on the project, at a press conference, according to *USA Today*. But Rees cautioned that it is still not known if "people have a large number of friends on Facebook simply because the structure of these brain regions is larger" or whether it's the other way around.

What this study tells public relations practitioners is that Facebook users with lots of friends are likely to be opinion leaders and highly sociable beyond the online world. These may be the sought-after "early adopters" who can help a campaign reach its maximum audience. Many corporate Facebook pages also rely on users with high numbers of Facebook friends to identify trends in consumer attitudes and preferences and reach out to their target audiences. For example, according to the *Wall Street Journal*, Coca-Cola uses its Facebook page for brand building and promotion. Starbucks looks to its Facebook community for customer feedback. A New Delhi restaurant uses its Facebook fan page to generate customer leads and reserve tables. Ching's Secret, an Indian consumer food brand, told the *Wall Street Journal* it considers the Facebook community to be its "most effective customer relationship management tool."

Women with lots of Facebook friends may be particularly valuable to engage. Women use social networks like Facebook to shape an external persona based on brands they choose to "like," according to a report in the U.K. edition of *PRWeek*. Magazine editor Lucie Cave told *PRWeek* that female Facebook users "are gentle and genuinely seem to want advice," making them a logical community for corporate Facebookers to court.

All this research suggests having lots of Facebook friends may affect your brain and friends with lots of friends may positively affect your organization's communication strategy.

1 Why should public relations practitioners care about the biological characteristics of social media users?

2 Do you think spending lots of time on Facebook might change your brain? Why or why not?

3 How can corporate Facebook strategists take advantage of research like this?

Communication and Measurement

136

Measurement: THE FOURTH STEP

The fourth step of the public relations process is measurement—the evaluation of results against agreed-upon objectives that are established during planning.

> "The literature of communication contains several models of evaluation. They basically all evaluate success along three standards. The first is success that justifies the budget expenditure. The second is effectiveness of the program itself. The third is whether the objectives were met."

–Laurie Wilson and Joseph Ogden, authors of *Strategic Communication Planning*.

The desire to do a better job next time is a major reason for evaluating public relations efforts, but another, equally important driving force is the widespread adoption of the "management by objectives" system by clients and employers. People want to know if the money, time, and effort expended on public relations are well spent and how those efforts contribute to the realization of an organizational objective. Furthermore, evaluation or monitoring throughout a campaign may suggest that tactics or organizational stances should change. Measurement helps practitioners make appropriate adjustments in the dynamic, ever-changing reality that is public relations practice.

 think How does evaluation improve the public relations process?

Objectives: A Prerequisite for Measurement

Before any public relations program can be properly evaluated, it is important to have a clearly established set of measurable objectives. These should be part of the program plan.

Public relations personnel and management need to agree on the criteria that will be used to measure success. Also, don't wait until the end of the public relations program to determine how it will be evaluated. Albert L. Schweitzer of Fleishman-Hillard makes the point that "evaluating impact/results starts in the planning stage. You break down the problem into measurable goals and objectives; then after implementing the program, you measure the results against goals."

If an objective is informational, measurement techniques must show how successfully information was communicated to target audiences. Such techniques measure "message dissemination" and "audience exposure," but they do not measure the effect on attitudes or overt behavior and action. Motivational objectives are more difficult to accomplish. If the objective is to increase sales or market share, it is important to show that the public relations efforts caused the increase, rather than advertising or marketing strategies. Or, if the objective is to change attitudes or opinions, research should be done both before and after the public relations activity to measure the percentage of change.

> "Write the most precise, most results-oriented objectives you can that are realistic, credible, measurable, and compatible with the client's demands on public relations."
>
> Ketchum monograph

Although campaign objectives vary, every practitioner should ask the following

BASIC MEASUREMENT QUESTIONS:

- Was the activity or program adequately planned?
- Did the recipients of the message understand it?
- How could the program strategy have been more effective?
- Were all primary and secondary audiences reached?
- Was the desired organizational objective achieved?
- Did any unforeseen circumstances affect the success of the program or activity?
- Did the program or activity fall within its budget?
- Which steps might be taken to improve the success of similar future activities?

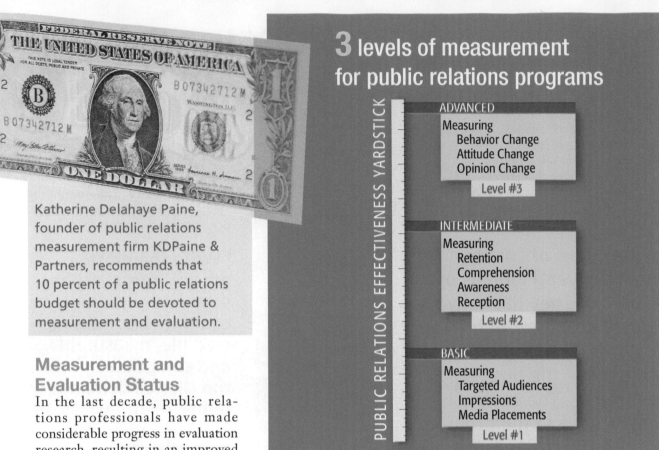

Katherine Delahaye Paine, founder of public relations measurement firm KDPaine & Partners, recommends that 10 percent of a public relations budget should be devoted to measurement and evaluation.

3 levels of measurement for public relations programs

PUBLIC RELATIONS EFFECTIVENESS YARDSTICK

ADVANCED
Measuring
Behavior Change
Attitude Change
Opinion Change
Level #3

INTERMEDIATE
Measuring
Retention
Comprehension
Awareness
Reception
Level #2

BASIC
Measuring
Targeted Audiences
Impressions
Media Placements
Level #1

Measurement and Evaluation Status

In the last decade, public relations professionals have made considerable progress in evaluation research, resulting in an improved ability to tell clients and employers exactly what has been accomplished. Sophisticated techniques are used, including computerized news clip analysis, survey sampling, quasi-experimental designs in which the audience is divided into groups that see different aspects of a public relations campaign, and attempts to correlate efforts directly with sales.

Today, the trend toward more systematic measurement is well established. One reason for this emphasis on measurement: there is increasing pressure on all parts of the organization—including public relations—to prove their value to the "bottom line."

Walter K. Lindenmann, a former senior vice president and director of research at Ketchum, in *Public Relations Quarterly* suggests that public relations personnel use a mix of measurement techniques, many borrowed from advertising and marketing, to provide more complete evaluation. In addition, he notes that at least three levels of measurement and evaluation exist. On the most basic level are compilations of message distribution and media placement. The second level, which requires more sophisticated techniques, deals with the measurement of audience awareness, comprehension, and retention of the message. The most advanced level is the measurement of changes in attitudes, opinions, and behavior.

MEASUREMENT OF
Message Exposure

The most widely practiced form of public relations program evaluation is the compilation of print stories and radio or television mentions. Local public relations firms and company departments often have staff members scan and clip area newspapers for relevant articles. Large companies with regional, national, or even international outreach typically hire clipping services to scan large numbers of publications. Electronic clipping services can monitor and tape major radio and television programs on a contractual basis. To track message exposure in online media, public relations practitioners may simply count hits on a website or

One elementary form of evaluation is simply counting how many news releases, feature stories, photos, letters, and the like are produced in a given period of time. This kind of evaluation, referred to as measurement of production, is intended to give management an idea of a staff's productivity and output. Public relations professionals, however, do not believe that this kind of evaluation is very meaningful because it emphasizes quantity instead of quality. It may actually be more cost-effective to write fewer news releases and spend more time on the few that really are newsworthy and are more likely to be picked up by leading publications.

Another production measurement approach involves specifying the amount of media coverage. For example, a client may want to evaluate a campaign based on the number of feature stories that run in the top newspapers in the region or the number of news releases picked up by local media outlets. Such evaluation criteria not only are unrealistic, but are almost impossible to guarantee, because media gatekeepers—not the public relations person—make these decisions.

visits to a blog; they may also count posted comments on a blog, which would suggest a higher level of exposure and involvement. Google Analytics is also a simple tool to track website and social media traffic in a more sophisticated manner. Social media such as Facebook can be platforms for messaging as well. Beyond monitoring traffic, exposure might be measured by the number of "fans" an organization or cause accumulates.

Effectiveness of Measurement Tools

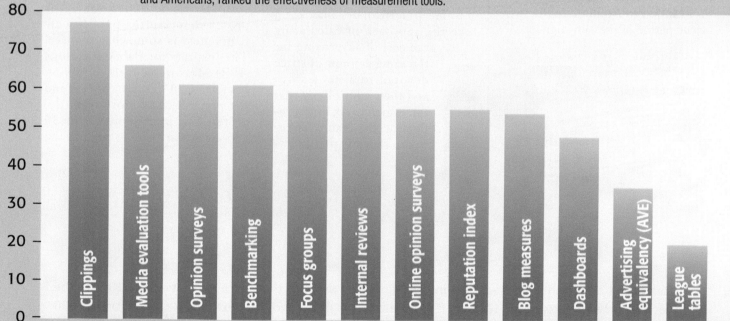

BenchPoint, a measurement firm, conducted a global survey of public relations and communications professionals for the First European Measurement Summit in Berlin. Respondents, primarily Europeans and Americans, ranked the effectiveness of measurement tools.

Percentage of Practitioners Who View This Tool as Effective

(Bar chart, left to right: Clippings ~77, Media evaluation tools ~66, Opinion surveys ~61, Benchmarking ~61, Focus groups ~58, Internal reviews ~58, Online opinion surveys ~54, Reputation index ~54, Blog measures ~53, Dashboards ~47, Advertising equivalency (AVE) ~34, League tables ~19)

Communication and Measurement

Media Impressions

In addition to the number of media placements, public relations departments and firms report how many people may have been exposed to the message. These numbers are described as *media impressions*, or the potential audience reached by a periodical or a broadcast program.

A regional or national news story can generate millions of impressions by simple multiplication of each placement by the circulation or audience of each medium.

Old Spice's Smell Like a Man, Man campaign reported more than 2 billion media impressions resulting from more than 1,000 placements including Oprah Winfrey, Ellen DeGeneres, and Jay Leno.

Similarly popular was a 7-Eleven campaign conceived following a comment by President Barack Obama that political rivals were just sitting around sipping Slurpees. Convenience store 7-Eleven developed a campaign poking fun at a prospective Slurpee Summit featuring a "Purple for the People" Slurpee and a Slurpee Unity Tour. The Slurpee story landed on every major broadcast media outlet. The campaign generated 1.7 billion media impressions from almost 2,000 media stories. Fans of the Slurpee Facebook page grew from 1.5 million to 2 million in the two-week period of the campaign.

Media impressions are commonly used in advertising to document the breadth of penetration of a particular message. Such figures give a rough estimate of how many people are exposed to a message. Unfortunately, they do not disclose how many people actually read or heard the stories or, more important, how many absorbed or acted on the information. Other techniques are needed for this kind of evaluation.

Internet Hits

A cyberspace version of media impressions involves counting the number of people reached via an organization's website or through social media posts. Each instance of a person accessing a site is regarded as a hit or a visit.

Advertising Equivalency

Another evaluation approach involves calculation of the value of message exposure, referred to as advertising equivalency (AVE). This methodology involves converting the value of stories in the regular news columns or on the air into their equivalent advertising costs. For example, a five-inch article in a trade magazine that charges $100 per column inch for advertising would be worth $500 in publicity value. The 7-Eleven Slurpee campaign claims to have generated coverage equivalent to $5.5 million in advertising.

Some practitioners may even take the approach of calculating the cost of advertising for the same amount of space devoted to a news story and then multiplying that total three to six times, reflecting the results of research showing that a news story has greater credibility than an advertisement.

Although such dollar amounts may impress some executives, calculating advertising equivalency is really comparing apples with oranges. One reason why publicity and advertising can't be compared is the fundamental difference between them. Advertising copy is directly controlled by the organization and can be oriented to specific objectives. The organization dictates the content, size, placement and timing of the message. News mentions, by comparison, are determined by media gatekeepers and can be negative, neutral, or positive. In addition, a news release can be edited to the point that key corporate messages are deleted. In other words, public relations can't control the size, placement, timing, or content of such items.

Ultimately, the utility of the AVE approach becomes a question of what is being measured. Should an article be counted as equivalent to advertising space if it is negative? Is a 15-inch article that mentions the organization only once among six other organizations comparable to 15 column inches of advertising space? Also, the numbers game doesn't take into account that a 4-inch article in the *Wall Street Journal* may be more valuable in reaching key publics than a 20-inch article in a local daily.

In short, the dollar-value approach to measuring publicity effectiveness is somewhat suspect. The Institute for Public Relations (IPR) Measurement Commission has rejected AVEs, the concept and the practice. And more recently, professional practitioners from 30 nations met in Spain to endorse the

X   circulation of 130,000   =   130,000 media impressions

If a story about an organization appears in a local daily newspaper that has a circulation of 130,000, the number of media impressions is 130,000. If another story is published the next day, it counts for 130,000 more impressions. Estimated audiences for radio and television programs, certified by auditing organizations, also are used to compile media impressions.

Justin Bieber is second only to Lady Gaga in the number of Twitter followers. He has almost 15 million followers; she has just over 16 million. Bieber also has almost 29 million Facebook fans. After his first single and album were released, his YouTube video received 100 million views.

When tween singing idol Bieber (a.k.a. the Bieb), lost the Best New Artist Grammy to jazz artist Esperanza Spalding, his fans (a.k.a. Bieliebers) took to social media—a medium that the Bieb uses quite effectively for promotional purposes—to belittle Spalding and her talent. But, the very fact that Bieber had lost the Grammy race suggests social media fans and followers don't necessarily translate into success in every aspect of business.

Because of Bieber's popularity on social media compared to Spalding, his fans thought he was more deserving of the Grammy. The HuffPost Celebrity blog reported, "Bieber fans seemed vaguely confused about how one goes about winning a Grammy. Isn't it based on how popular you are on Twitter? They seemed lost that someone like Spalding, who has much fewer followers on the networking site, could have been given the award. 'So the Esperanza Spalding has only 8 thousand followers on twitter and how many does justin bieber has?' one fan tweeted and many agreed."

Overall, Bieber's social media strategy shows real sophistication. But it also shows that evaluation in social media is multifaceted and requires a bit of measurement savvy to achieve useful data.

"Unlike other marketing communications disciplines, public relations practitioners have consistently failed to achieve consensus on what the basic evaluative measures are or how to conduct the underlying research for evaluating and measuring public relations performance."

David Michaelson and Don W. Stacks, in *Public Relations Journal*

Barcelona Principles that included the condemnation of AVEs as a form of legitimate measurement. The practice of equating publicity with advertising rates for comparable space also does not engender good media relations, because it reinforces the opinion of many media gatekeepers that all news releases are just attempts to get free advertising.

Systematic Tracking

As noted earlier, message exposure was traditionally measured by sheer volume of mentions. Technological advances make it possible to track media placements in a more sophisticated way.

Computer databases can be used to analyze the content of media placements based on such variables as market penetration, type of publication, tone of coverage, sources quoted, and mention of key copy points. Ketchum, for example, can build as many as 40 variables into its computer program, including the tracking of reporter bylines to determine if a journalist is predisposed negatively or positively toward the client's key messages. Other firms, such as Carma International and Cision, do extensive database analysis for clients.

The value of systematic tracking is manifold. Continuing, regular feedback during a campaign can identify whether an organization's publicity efforts are paying off in terms of placements and mention of key messages. Tracking coverage and comparing it over a period of time is called *benchmarking*.

Communication and Measurement

An example of benchmarking is the campaign that Capitoline/MS&L public relations conducted on behalf of the Turkish government to make Americans more aware of Turkey as a travel destination. By comparing the number of stories before and after the campaign was launched, Carma International found that articles with Turkey as the primary destination increased 400 percent. Favorable articles on Turkey increased 90 percent from the previous year.

Another form of analysis is comparing the number of news releases sent with the number actually published and in which media. Such analysis often helps a public relations department determine which kinds of publicity are most effective and earn the most return on investment (ROI).

Information Requests
Counting the number of requests for more information generated by a public relations effort is yet another form of media exposure evaluation. A story in a newspaper or on a blog or an appearance by a company spokesperson on a broadcast often provides information about where people can get more information about a subject. In many cases, a toll-free number, e-mail address, or website is provided.

An information program by the U.S. Centers for Disease Control and Prevention on an influenza outbreak earned the CDC 45,000 followers on one of its Twitter accounts, CDCemergency. The CDC developed dozens of podcasts, video public service announcements (PSAs), brochures, flyers, and FAQs and made them available in PDF format for download. During the beginning days of the outbreak, the CDC received 300 media requests for information from its website each day.

Cost per Person
Message exposure can also be monitored by determining the cost of reaching each member of the audience. This technique is commonly used in advertising to place costs in perspective. Although a 30-second commercial during the 2012 Super Bowl telecast cost $3.5 million, advertisers believed it was well worth the price because an audience of more than 111 million would be reached for just over three cents each. This was a relative bargain, even if several million viewers visited the refrigerator while the commercial played.

Cost-effectiveness, as this technique is known, is often also used to evaluate public relations campaigns.

Specifically, cost per thousand (CPM) is calculated by taking the cost of the publicity program and dividing it by the total number of media impressions.

Audience Attendance
Measuring attendance at events is an additional, simple way of evaluating the effectiveness of pre-event publicity. The Wheat Foods Council attracted about 8,000 to its three-day Urban Wheat Field event in New York City. The object of the event was to promote the farm-to-fork movement through experiential activities based at a live one-quarter acre wheat field planted near New York's South Street Seaport. In addition to the wheat field, interested individuals and groups also saw a full-sized combine, functioning mills, a bread-baking demonstration, and a nutrition lab.

Conversely, poor attendance at a meeting or event can indicate inadequate publicity and promotion. Another major cause of lackluster attendance is apathy (lack of public interest), even when people are aware that a meeting or event is taking place. Low attendance usually results in considerable finger-pointing; thus an objective evaluation of exactly what happened—or didn't happen—is a good policy.

MEASUREMENT OF Audience Awareness, Attitudes, and Action

Measuring message dissemination and audience exposure is one thing. An even higher level of evaluation is involved in determining whether the audience actually became aware of the message and understood it. Once an audience is made aware, it is important that its attitude is altered by the message and it goes on to take action.

Audience Awareness
PR measurement expert Walter Lindenmann calls audience awareness the second level of public relations evaluation. He notes:

At this level, public relations practitioners measure whether target audience groups actually received the messages directed at them: whether they paid attention to those messages, whether they un-

 think What can survey research tools tell public relations professionals about the effectiveness of public relations campaigns?

derstood the messages, and whether they have retained those messages in any shape or form.

The tools of survey research answer such questions. Members of the target audience are asked about the message and what they remember about it. Public awareness of which organization sponsors an event also is important. The Southern California Mountain Area Safety Task Force (MAST) needed to inform homeowners of the importance of removing dead and dying trees to relieve the potential for forest fires. MAST found that only 15 percent of homeowners knew the proper definition of a healthy forest and only 56 percent knew the proper spacing of trees. Following an extensive campaign that employed media relations, a speaker's bureau, newsletters, brochures, websites and more, the awareness of the correct definition of a healthy forest soared to 80 percent, and 76 percent were able to cite the proper spacing of trees.

Another way of measuring audience awareness and comprehension is day-after recall. With this method, participants are asked to view a

> "How then does the PR function prove its worth? … A clearly defined program of communication helps establish that proof, beginning with a baseline against which to measure success or failure, and moving through benchmarked points where certain objectives are evaluated.
>
> Don W. Stacks and Shannon A. Bowen, *Public Relations Tactics*

specific television program or read a particular news story. The next day they are interviewed to learn which messages they remembered.

Audience Attitude

Closely related to audience awareness and understanding of a message are changes in an audience's perceptions and attitudes that result from internalization of the message. A major technique to determine such changes is the *baseline study*, which entails measurements of audience attitudes and opinions before, during, and after a public relations campaign. Baseline studies, also called benchmark studies, measure the percentage difference in attitudes and opinions as a result of increased information and publicity. A number of intervening variables may account for changes in attitude, of course, but statistical analysis of variance can help pinpoint how much of the change is attributable to public relations efforts.

The insurance company Prudential Financial regularly conducts baseline studies. When it implemented a corporate social responsibility (CSR) program that provided matching grants to volunteer medical service squads so they could purchase portable cardiac arrest equipment to treat heart attack victims before they reach the hospital, baseline research found that its favorable corporate reputation rating among survey respondents increased from 48 percent to 77 percent over a two-year period.

Audience Action

The ultimate objective of any public relations effort, as has been pointed out repeatedly, is to accomplish organizational objectives. The objective of an amateur theater

think **What is the ultimate goal of any public relations activity?**

group is not to get media publicity, but to sell tickets. The objective of an environmental organization such as Greenpeace is not to get editorials written in favor of whales, but rather to motivate the public (1) to write to elected officials, (2) to send donations to fund preservation efforts, and (3) to get legislation passed. The objective of a company is to sell its products and services, not to get 200 million media impressions. In all cases, the tools and activities of public relations are a means, not an end. Thus public relations efforts ultimately are evaluated on how well they help an organization achieve its objectives.

AT&T, its public relations firm, Fleishman-Hillard, and advertising firm BBDO, employed a variety of research methods, most notably focus groups, when developing a campaign aimed at curtailing the practice of texting and driving. The campaign used the theme: "Txting and Drivng: It Can Wait," which arose out of focus groups.

Employers and clients increasingly have their eyes on the bottom line of public relations campaigns. This scrutiny and attention to accountability shape the emphasis on measurement in public relations. The public relations process is driven by the interaction among research, strategic planning and measurable objectives, creative tactics and messaging, and credible measurement techniques.

> "The outcome of a successful public relations program is not a hefty stack of news stories… Communication is important only in the effects it achieves among publics."
>
> David Dozier, San Diego State University

"Don't Be That Guy" Campaign Fights Binge Drinking

IMAGINE YOUR GOAL is to address binge drinking among enlisted U.S. servicemen, ages 18 to 24. How do you reach such a public with a topic they probably don't want to hear about? The U.S. Department of Defense teamed up with Fleishman-Hillard to develop the "That Guy" campaign, described on thatguy.com as "a multimedia campaign that uses online and offline communication with the goal of reducing excessive drinking among young servicemen." The campaign uses humor and provides viral tools to deliver a serious message.

The website includes an interactive comedy club where the visitor can drag a microphone from patron to patron for a series of "You might be That Guy if…" one-liners. A "Facts" page offers drinking facts, links to alcohol treatment programs, and what to do if your friend is That Guy.

According to *PRWeek*, "The 'Don't Be That Guy' message was delivered to reach the audience where they live, work, and play, with a multimedia-enabled website, campaign materials, and targeted offline/online advertising delivering the message and driving people to the website." Before launching the campaign globally, the Department of Defense pilot tested it on four bases. To raise awareness and drive people to the website, it ran newspaper ads in military installations and in community newspapers, used "That Guy" tray liners in military food courts, and video and radio public service announcements (PSAs) were broadcast on military media and in communities with high military presence.

The campaign was honored for best use of research/measurement by *PRWeek*. "That Guy" was developed following a formative research phase. Benchmark surveys were used to evaluate success of the campaign; they identified 44 percent awareness of the campaign and a drop in binge drinking among the target public from 45 percent who binge to 39 percent. Evaluation measures also showed that there was 38 percent binge drinking on bases participating in the program compared to 49 percent binging on nonparticipating bases. More than 1 million viewers visited thatguy.com.

1 How was the target public driven to the campaign website to increase audience awareness?

2 What audience action was the desired end of the campaign?

3 How was measurement used to evaluate the success of the "That Guy" campaign?

What Would You Do?

Getting Blood from a Stone?

Your student public relations agency has received a $2,000 grant from the American Red Cross to create and pilot test a campaign on your campus to inform students about the importance of participating in community blood drives.

According to the Red Cross website, you should give blood because (1) it makes you feel good, (2) you can spare blood, (3) you can help make sure there is blood available when it is needed, (4) it will make you someone's hero, and (5) you get juice and cookies.

Your agency needs to develop an information campaign on campus that will use a variety of communication tactics to reach all students and encourage them to participate in a blood drive. You should think about ways to effectively use campus media, conduct outreach to various student groups, and stage activities (events) that would attract student attention. What would you suggest? Prepare a memo that (1) states the objective of your information campaign, (2) lists your primary and secondary audiences on campus, (3) outlines your key strategy, (4) gives specific details about which tactics will be used, and (5) describes how your team will measure (evaluate) the success of your campaign.

summary

questions
FOR REVIEW AND DISCUSSION

What Are the Goals of Public Relations Communication?

- Five possible objectives of communication are message exposure, accurate dissemination of the message, acceptance of the message, attitude change, and change in overt behavior.

Which Factors Influence Message Reception, Comprehension, Retention, Credibility, and Adoption?

- Successful communication involves interaction, or shared experience, because the message must be both sent and received.
- The most basic element necessary for understanding between communicator and audience is a common language. Public relations practitioners must consider their audiences and style their language appropriately, taking into consideration literacy levels, clarity and simplicity of language, and avoidance of discriminatory language.
- Key variables in message believability include source credibility, context, and the audience's predispositions, especially members' level of involvement.
- Five steps in acceptance of new ideas or products are awareness, interest, evaluation, trial, and adoption.

Why Is Measurement of Public Relations Program Effectiveness Important?

- Evaluation is the measurement of results against objectives; it can enhance future performance and establish whether the goals of management by objective have been met.
- Criteria must be set to evaluate the level of success in attaining the established objectives.

Which Methods Are Used to Measure the Effectiveness of Public Relations Programs?

- On the most basic level, practitioners can measure message distribution and media placements. A second level would entail measurement of audience awareness, comprehension, and retention. The most advanced level is the measurement of changes in attitudes, opinions, and behaviors.
- Changes in audience attitudes can be evaluated through a baseline or benchmark study, which focuses on measuring awareness and opinions before, during, and after a public relations campaign.
- Ultimately, public relations campaigns are evaluated based on how they help an organization achieve its objectives through changing audience behavior, whether it involves sales, fund-raising, or the election of a candidate.

1 Why is two-way communication (feedback) an important aspect of effective communication?

2 Which kinds of messages and communication channels would you use for a passive audience? For an active information-seeking audience?

3 Why is it necessary to use a variety of messages and communication channels in a public relations program?

4 Explain the five steps of the adoption process. What are some of the factors that affect the adoption of an idea or product?

5 What is the role of stated objectives in evaluating public relations programs?

6 List four ways that publicity activity is evaluated. What, if any, are the drawbacks of each evaluation method?

7 How does measurement of message exposure differ from measurement of audience comprehension of the message?

8 Which measurement methods can be used to evaluate the effectiveness of a company newsletter or magazine?

MySearchLab®

Photo Credits

Credits are listed in order of appearance.

Tablet image:

Public Opinion and Persuasion

Public Opinion and Persuasion

Going Green: Everybody's Doing It

In an effort to win goodwill among publics who care about the environment, companies are climbing on the green bandwagon. Examples are too numerous to count; many large companies have made a public commitment to environmental accountability by creating divisions of environmental sustainability. Overall, green initiatives typically have been focused in two directions: first, cutting energy consumption through conservation, and second, using technology to reduce reliance on nonrenewable energy sources. There have been some notable success stories of companies (such as Apple, Mattel, Google, Intel, Philips Lighting, and Frito-Lay) that aim for net-zero energy consumption. eBay and Google, for example, generate the power they need (and then some) from solar and other renewable sources. On a smaller scale, health care provider North Shore–LIJ Health System set out to reduce the amount of paper used by transitioning to electronic messaging systems. In doing so, the organization reaped genuine savings and helped improve internal communications in a single stroke. Although comparatively modest in scale, the result of the campaign was impressive enough to win the North Shore–LIJ Health Systems' PR team a 2011 Silver Anvil Award from the PRSA.

Green is often in the eye of the beholder. Toyota heads the top 50 of Interbrand's Best Global Green Brands of 2011. Based on data from Thomson Reuter's ASSET4, the scores compare public perception of environmental accountability with actual performance data. But of course public perception is not always accurate. The Yale Center for Environmental Law and Politics (http://envirocenter.yale.edu/) is one of many centers devoted to accurately assessing corporate environmental accountability. Rather than relying on polls alone, it used meta-data to develop the Environmental Performance Index (http://www.epi.yale.edu/).

Communicating a message about a company's commitment to environmental stewardship is laudable—as long as the company's actions back up the rhetoric. Watchdog groups such as the Sierra Club and Nature Conservancy, as well as bloggers and other independents, keep an eye out for organizations that engage in efforts to "greenwash" their images. BP is one corporation whose actions have undermined its attempts to present an environmentally-friendly image. Polls by Gallup, CBS News, and *The Washington Post*–ABC News found between 70 and 81 percent of Americans rated BP's response to the disastrous 2010 Gulf Oil Spill as "poor."

1 Why do corporations engage in greenwashing?

2 Can a company change public opinion without taking action?

3 Does public opinion ever fly in the face of actual data or accurate information?

Ask Yourself

> What Is Public Opinion?

> Who Are Opinion Leaders?

> What Role Do the Mass Media Play in Shaping Public Opinion?

> How Does Conflict Affect Public Discourse?

> What Makes Communication Persuasive?

> What Are the Limitations of Persuasion?

What Is PUBLIC OPINION?

Editorial cartoonists humanize public opinion in the form of John or Jane Q. Public, characters who have come to symbolize the way people think about any given issue. The reality is that public opinion is somewhat elusive and extremely difficult to measure at any given moment.

Public Opinion Is a Moving Target

People constantly form and revise their opinions about public figures such as the Kardashian sisters, Michelle Obama, or Alex Rodriguez, often in response to recent television appearances or Internet gossip. The court of public opinion is fickle and variable. Yesterday's superstars may be tomorrow's has-beens, until they release a ghost-written tell-all biography and are again thrust into the public spotlight. Accurately predicting the future direction of public opinion is extremely difficult because of the number of contingent variables involved.

In fact, few issues inspire unanimity of thought, and public opinion is usually split in several directions that may be in conflict with one another. Even when members of an identifiable group share common beliefs and interests, the opinions of individuals or subgroups within the larger group may vary widely. For example, the issue of Israeli–Palestinian relations in the

Public opinion is an important topic for politicians and public officials.

United States arouses a variety of responses among Christian groups. Fundamentalists tend to support Israeli policy unequivocally, linking current events to biblical prophecy, whereas liberal Christians are likely to express some sympathy for

According to Irving Crespi, a prolific public opinion researcher, public opinion can be an almost tangible force that affects all kinds of people, altering their beliefs or attitudes about controversial issues.

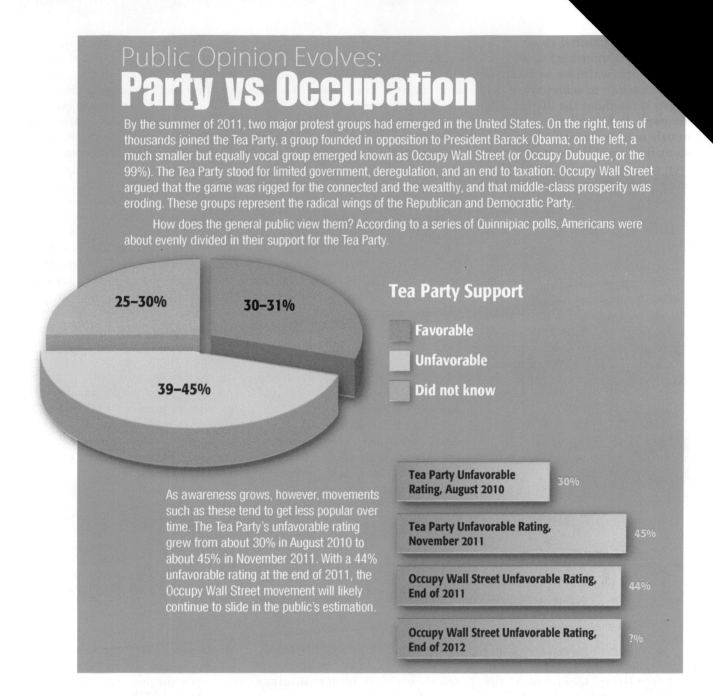

Public Opinion Evolves:
Party vs Occupation

By the summer of 2011, two major protest groups had emerged in the United States. On the right, tens of thousands joined the Tea Party, a group founded in opposition to President Barack Obama; on the left, a much smaller but equally vocal group emerged known as Occupy Wall Street (or Occupy Dubuque, or the 99%). The Tea Party stood for limited government, deregulation, and an end to taxation. Occupy Wall Street argued that the game was rigged for the connected and the wealthy, and that middle-class prosperity was eroding. These groups represent the radical wings of the Republican and Democratic Party.

How does the general public view them? According to a series of Quinnipiac polls, Americans were about evenly divided in their support for the Tea Party.

25–30%

30–31%

39–45%

Tea Party Support

- Favorable
- Unfavorable
- Did not know

As awareness grows, however, movements such as these tend to get less popular over time. The Tea Party's unfavorable rating grew from about 30% in August 2010 to about 45% in November 2011. With a 44% unfavorable rating at the end of 2011, the Occupy Wall Street movement will likely continue to slide in the public's estimation.

Tea Party Unfavorable Rating, August 2010 — 30%

Tea Party Unfavorable Rating, November 2011 — 45%

Occupy Wall Street Unfavorable Rating, End of 2011 — 44%

Occupy Wall Street Unfavorable Rating, End of 2012 — ?%

the concept of Palestinian sovereignty. Likewise, there will always be various conflicting public opinions about hot-button issues such as abortion, same-sex marriage, taxes, and war.

Typically, only a small number of people at any given time participate in public opinion formation on specific issues. However, once people and the press begin to refer to public opinion on an issue as an accepted fact, it can take on its own momentum.

Three reasons explain the profound influence of vocal segments of society and public opinion momentum:

1 **SOCIETY IS PASSIVE.**
Psychologists have found that the public by and large tends to be passive.

2 **SOCIETY IS SEGMENTED.** One issue may engage the attention of a part of the population with a particular vested interest, whereas another issue arouses the interest of another segment.

3 **SOCIETY IS DIVIDED.**
People have some opinions that may conflict or compete with others' opinions about the same issue. People also sometimes hold contradictory opinions or attitudes.

Understanding and assessing the dynamics of competing or conflicting opinions is a crucial dimension of public relations work. The formation of public opinion is a constantly evolving process, and should not be regarded as static by public relations professionals. The public

...out an is-
...o address
...d beliefs
...their in-
...cycle of
...is profes-
...nd track
...ons, and
...oost these
opinions, to affect public relations
outcomes.

Public Opinion Is Powerful

Public opinion plays a role in moving a group of people to action in relation to an issue. Awareness and discussion leads to crystallization of opinions and consensus building among the public. As awareness grows, the issue becomes a matter of public discussion and debate, of-

ten garnering extensive media coverage. Through media coverage, the issue is placed on the public agenda and even more people become aware of it.

Suppose, for example, activist and special-interest groups organize a protest against scenic areas being threatened by logging or strip mining. Although these groups may have no formal power, they could serve as "agenda stimuli" for the media, which crave controversy and conflict. Opportunities for vivid television coverage would arise when activists stage rallies and demonstrations. As is often the case, the issue may become simplified by the media into an "us-versus-them" stance. Opinion leaders might then begin to discuss the issue, perhaps viewing it as being symbolic of broader environmental and societal issues.

Public relations professionals often identify key audiences or publics through analysis of public opinion, thereby resolving the issue from

their standpoint. For example, polls about global warming reveal a wide variance. A Gallup Poll taken in the summer of 2011 suggests that only 19 percent of Americans believe that human activity has no bearing on global warming. On the other hand, a series of monthly Rasmussen polls showed that more than 40 percent of Americans believe that global warming is not caused by humans.

How can there be such wide variance in public opinion polls? Rasmussen in particular is known for its conservative slant, and thus the sample group polled may display traditional beliefs, just as one might expect National Public Radio (NPR) listeners as a sample group to be more educated and liberal or progressive than the average American. Still, polling results provide useful fodder for interest groups to advance their agenda. Organizations can and do "cherry pick" surveys with results that support their position, dismissing as flawed those that do not.

OPINION LEADERS AS Catalysts

According to research in *Roper Reports*, 10 to 12 percent of the population, identified by the magazine as "influentials," drive public opinion and consumer trends. Knowledgeable experts who articulate opinions about specific issues in public discussion are called *opinion leaders* or *power leaders*.

Sociologists Elihu Katz and Paul Lazarsfeld define opinion leaders as people who, because of their interest in and knowledge of a subject, become experts and inform others either formally as spokespeople or informally through daily interaction with family members, colleagues, and peers. Opinion

leaders are not necessarily highly visible in the community, nor are they always leaders in other regards—it is as common to find an opinion leader among a group of coal miners or housewives as it is among a group of politicians or *Fortune* 500 company executives. Opinion leaders are evenly distributed among the social, economic, and educational strata within their community. They help frame and define issues that often have their roots in individuals' self-interests. It is through the influence of opinion leaders that public opinion often crystallizes into a measurable entity. Public relations

professionals attempt to influence these leaders just as they seek to influence the public at large.

Many public relations campaigns, and particularly those in the public affairs arena, concentrate on identifying and reaching key opinion leaders who are pivotal to the success or failure of an idea or project. In 1948, sociologists Paul Lazarsfeld, Bernard Berelson, and Hazel Gaudet published a paper titled "The People's Choice" that analyzed how people choose candidates in an election. They found that the mass media had minimal influence on electoral choices, but voters did rely on

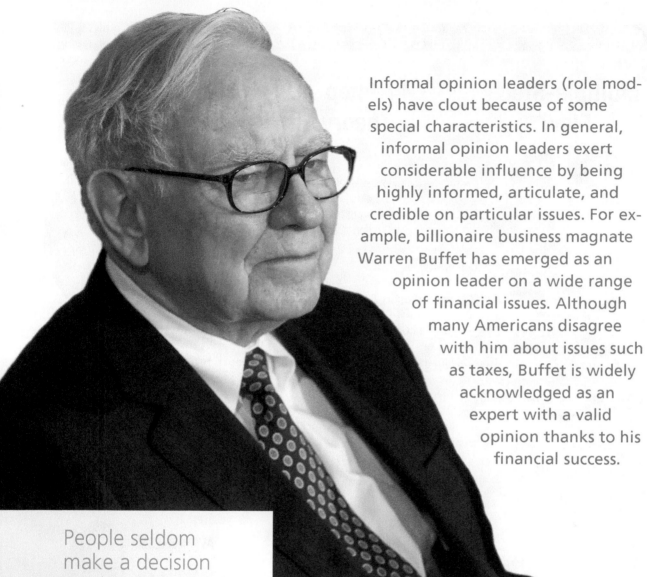

Informal opinion leaders (role models) have clout because of some special characteristics. In general, informal opinion leaders exert considerable influence by being highly informed, articulate, and credible on particular issues. For example, billionaire business magnate Warren Buffet has emerged as an opinion leader on a wide range of financial issues. Although many Americans disagree with him about issues such as taxes, Buffet is widely acknowledged as an expert with a valid opinion thanks to his financial success.

People seldom make a decision on their own. They are influenced by friends, **parents**, educators, **supervisors**, church leaders, **physicians**, public officials, **celebrities**, and the media in general when deciding to vote for a president or mayor, or to purchase a car or even toothpaste.

person-to-person communication with formal and informal opinion leaders.

These findings, refined by Lazarsfeld and Katz, became known as the *two-step flow theory of communication*. Although later research confirmed that multiple steps were involved, the basic concept remains valid. Public opinion is generally formed around the views of people who have taken the time to sift information, evaluate it, and form an opinion that they express to others. Information is disseminated through the media (print, radio, and television) to opinion leaders, who then interact with other less informed members of the public.

Multiple-step flow theory indicates that some people eventually become interested in, or at least aware of, an issue through a chain of two-step flow processes. At the heart of the multiple-step flow model are "opinion makers." They derive large amounts of information from the mass media and other sources and then share that information with people, who are labeled the "attentive public." Attentive publics are interested in the issue but rely on opinion leaders to synthesize and interpret information. The "inattentive public" are unaware of or uninterested in the issue and remain outside the opinion-formation process.

the FLOW of OPINION

Multiple-Step Flow

OPINION MAKERS derive large amounts of information from the mass media and other sources and share that information with people.

The **ATTENTIVE PUBLIC** is interested in the issue but rely on opinion leaders to synthesize and interpret information.

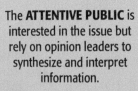

The **INATTENTIVE PUBLIC** are unaware of or uninterested in the issue and remain outside the opinion-formation process.

N-step Theory

N-step theory states that individuals are seldom influenced by only one opinion leader but actually interact with different leaders.

Diffusion Theory

Individuals adopt new ideas or products in five stages: awareness, interest, trial, evaluation, and adoption. Individuals are influenced by media in the first two steps and by friends and family members in the third and fourth steps. Each individual is a decision maker who adopts a new idea or product when they reach the final step.

Step 1
AWARENESS

Step 2
INTEREST

Step 3
TRIAL

Step 4
EVALUATION

Step 5
ADOPTION

Another variation of the two-step model is N-step theory. Individuals are seldom influenced by only one opinion leader but interact with different leaders around an issue.

The final theory we discuss in this section is diffusion theory. Diffusion theory explains that individuals adopt new ideas or products through five stages: awareness, interest, trial, evaluation, and adoption.

The multiple-step flow model, N-step theory, and diffusion theory are graphically illustrated in the nearby figure.

THE ROLE OF Mass Media

Public relations personnel often use opinion leaders to influence key publics. They can also reach targeted publics directly via mass media such as radio, television, newspapers, blogs, and magazines. *Mass media*, as the term implies, means that information from a source can be efficiently and rapidly disseminated to masses of people, sometimes literally millions. The mass media inform and influence people daily. Thus it is important to understand who controls the media and sets the media agenda.

Oscar H. Gandy, Jr. of the University of Pennsylvania and other theorists have concluded that public relations professionals are major players in forming public opinion because they are often the first to provide mass media with information. Although journalists argue that they rarely use public relations materials, one simply has to look at the daily newspaper to see this type of material—for example, a quote from the press officer at the sheriff's department, an article on a new computer product, statistics from the local real estate board, or even a postgame interview with the winning quarterback. In almost all cases, a public relations source provided the information or arranged the interview. Indeed, Gandy estimates that as much as 50 percent of what the media carry comes from public relations sources in the form of "information subsidies."

Media can also have a negative effect on public opinion. In a series of investigative reports, Donald L. Barlett and James B. Steele argued that political leaders, corporate executives, and the media exacerbated the recent financial crisis in the U.S., at least in the short term, by providing counterproductive information. Fox News, MSNBC Business News, and the Wall Street Journal were singled out as framing public opinion in the interest of the so-called "productive class," the wealthiest 1 percent of Americans.

From a public relations standpoint, even getting a subject on the media agenda is an accomplishment that advances organizational goals. In a striking example, sales of Apple's iPad rose as the media reported on its success and the public became increasingly aware of this "hot" item.

To better understand how public relations practitioners inform the public and shape public opinion via the mass media, let's review briefly some theories about mass media effects.

Agenda Setting

One early theory, pioneered by mass communications researchers Max McCombs and Don Shaw, contends that media content sets the agenda for public discussion. People tend to talk about what they see or hear on the television news programs or read on the front pages of newspapers. According to this theory, the media, by selecting stories and headlines, tell the public what to think about, albeit not necessarily what to think. The global financial crisis, for example, has ranked high on the media agenda in recent years, but public opinion polls indicate a variety of viewpoints on the subject. Social scientist Joseph Klapper calls this the limited-effects model of mass media. He postulates, "Mass media ordinarily does not serve as a necessary and sufficient cause for audience effects, but rather functions among and through a nexus of mediating factors and influence." Such factors include the way that opinion leaders analyze and interpret the information provided by the mass media.

More recently, Wayne Wanta of Oklahoma State University and other scholars of agenda-setting theory have found evidence that the media not only set agendas but also convey a set of attributes about the various subjects in the news. These positive or negative attributes are internalized and, in turn, color public opinion. Research is ongoing regarding how public relations efforts can build the media agenda, and thus affect public opinion.

Framing

Media content is influenced by a broad array of forces, ranging from the professionalism of individual journalists to corporate ownership of media outlets to cultural and ideological factors, according to Pamela J. Shoemaker at Syracuse University and Steve Reeves at the University of Texas–Austin. Traditionally, framing theory was related to how journalists selected certain facts, themes, treatments, and even words to "frame," or shape, a story. This effort goes beyond journalists' simple selection of potential news stories in their role as gatekeepers and involves their interpretation of issues or creation of subtle nuances. For example, how media frame the debate over health care and the role of health maintenance organizations often plays a major role in public perceptions of the issues involved.

Increasingly, scholars and professionals apply framing theory to public relations efforts. In a paper titled "PR Goes to War: The Effects of Public Relations Campaigns on Media Framing of the Kuwait and Bosnian Crises," James Tankard and Bill Israel noted that the governments involved in these conflicts used public relations professionals to help frame the issues involved. The issues, as framed by the professionals, were then reflected in press coverage and, in turn, influenced the public's opinion about the crises. Tankard and Israel point out that the media dependency of most Americans—who often have little direct knowledge of such faraway places or the complex issues involved in international conflicts—means that they accept the media's version of reality, which originally came from what the two researchers describe as "special interest groups or other groups with particular causes."

Dietram Scheufele at the University of Wisconsin–Madison suggests that two types of framing exist: media framing and audience framing. He argues that framing is a continuous process and that the behavioral, attitudinal, cognitive, and affective statuses of individuals influence how they interpret issues. For example, voters in Florida may be less likely to respond favorably to a story about increased school funding, because a large number of Floridians are older than the age of 65 (16.7 percent) and have already raised their children. Conversely,

Internet Censorship in China

ethics in ACTION

Entry into a global market poses public relations opportunities and challenges because of the different and often conflicting cultures, values, norms, rules, and laws that companies inevitably encounter when venturing outside their domestic market. Companies can hardly succeed in a foreign market unless they can win the court of public opinion at home.

The market for Internet service in China holds enormous profit potential for U.S. computer software and support corporations. With an estimated 28.8 percent of the country's 1.4 billion people using the Internet, the potential for growth in China is staggering. Thus it is comes as little surprise that Google, together with rivals Yahoo!, Microsoft, and local Chinese company Baidu and Alibaba, was eager to sign deals with the Chinese government to provide Internet service and support. However, that decision has come at a notable cost.

At the crux of the issue is the Chinese government's insistence that all online activity be subject to scrutiny by the Golden Shield Project, which is thought to employ approximately 30,000 "Internet police." The Golden Shield (also known as "The Great Firewall of China") censors content it considers obscene or offensive. It has also restricted political speech, blocking search terms related to such topics as Falun Gong, Tiananmen Square, Tibet and the Dalai Lama, freedom of the press, and the Taiwanese government. Oddly enough, the Golden Shield also blocks search terms related to Karl Marx and communism. Google initially agreed to abide by this censorship practice in order to do business in China and faced widespread criticism for doing so.

In March 2010, Google suddenly reversed course. It stopped censoring Internet searches, closed google.cn, and began routing traffic through Hong Kong. It used a mirror site, elgooG, which at least for a time managed to evade censorship.

Meanwhile, the struggle for Internet freedom in China continued. In May 2011, the State Internet Information Office was established to continue the work of state censorship. Sina Weibo, a messaging service often used for social media, has been a target of censorship. However, in the wake of a train accident in Wenzhou in July 2011, citizens were able to use Sina to provide information, especially related to government corruption or misinformation.

Many Chinese citizens have challenged censorship, but it does seem to be an entrenched aspect of Chinese Internet use for the foreseeable future. Because they do not know whether the government is watching, many Chinese citizens engage in a degree of self-censorship for political concerns or to keep social harmony. While we take it for granted that the Internet should be free and uncensored, the situation in China shows that there are limits to this freedom. And Google's role may stray from the commercial to the ethical as the company decides how best to respond to the Chinese government's actions.

voters in Georgia, a state with fewer people older than age 65 (9.2 percent), might react more favorably to school funding increases. However, a range of variables, beliefs, and attitudes simultaneously affect how individuals interpret an issue.

Political science professors Shanto Iyengar and Donald Kinder focus on the media's power to prime people in a more subtle but significant form of persuasive effect. They note how public relations professionals working for political campaigns seek to emphasize considerations that will help voters decide in their favor, often enlisting the expertise of a popular leader in service of this objective, and to downplay those considerations that will hurt their cause or candidate. Ultimately, the goal is to encourage voters to change the basis on which they make decisions about voting rather than simply change their choices about a given candidate or issue.

 think What role does the media play in forming the public opinion of you and your peers?

THE ROLE OF Conflict

The process of public discourse is often rooted in conflict. Social scientists and legal scholars define conflict as any situation in which two or more individuals, groups, organizations, or communities perceive a divergence of interests. Conflict theory offers insight into differences among individuals or groups and explains conflicting interests, goals, values, or desires. Public opinion reflects differing views, attitudes, and behaviors.

According to conflict resolution scholars Morton Deutsch and Peter Colman, conflict in the public arena does not necessarily yield negative outcomes, but rather creates a constructive process that builds toward consensus. Conflict or consensus regulate and help ensure social stability and peaceful change within a democratic society.

Controversies often serve to shape public opinion intensively and extensively. Public relations professionals frequently have the challenging role of trying to minimize or resolve controversy in conflict situations.

At other times, public relations practitioners may generate or promote controversy to engender positive or supportive public opinion. In October 2011, presidential candidate Herman Cain released a campaign advertisement on YouTube featuring Mark Block, his campaign manager, smoking a cigarette during a testimonial. Straightforward representation of the socially-maligned habit of smoking may have been included to suggest the authenticity of Cain's message or his maverick identity. The spot did generate buzz. No less an authority on politics and media than Henry Kissinger pronounced it "brilliant."

Mass media play a role in the unfolding of a conflict and serve to promote public debate by engaging widespread public involvement, a process known as *escalation*.

Media players may also mediate among parties and de-escalate the conflict. Often, increasing direct communication between parties does more harm than good, as the same arguments tend to repeat in a destructive way and nonnegotiable positions become more entrenched. Mediated communication and shuttle diplomacy can be an effective means of resolving conflict, particularly at the early stages of a dispute. The role of the media is to interpret the issue, deliver the position of the opposing party, and even suggest avenues for resolution. Conflict is inherent in how a reporter frames an issue, because the reporter's story on a conflict can be the sole information available to an audience. For example, a news story by an investigative reporter with special access to information about a controversial secret program at the Pentagon may represent the only perspective seen by the public. How that reporter

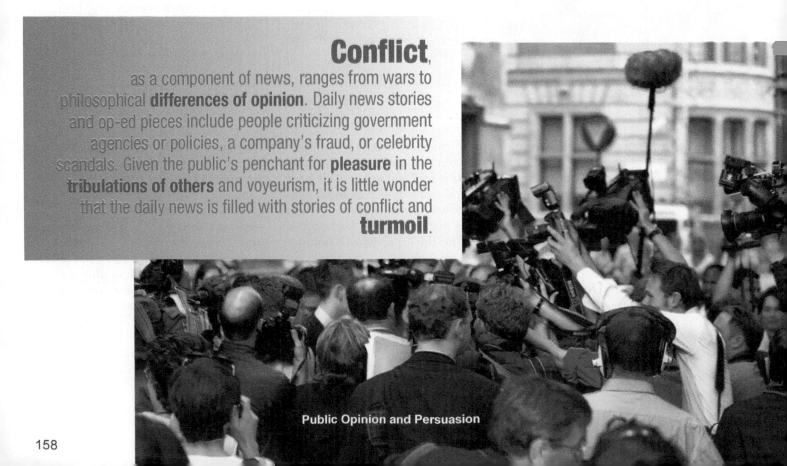

Conflict, as a component of news, ranges from wars to philosophical **differences of opinion**. Daily news stories and op-ed pieces include people criticizing government agencies or policies, a company's fraud, or celebrity scandals. Given the public's penchant for **pleasure** in the **tribulations of others** and voyeurism, it is little wonder that the daily news is filled with stories of conflict and **turmoil**.

Public Opinion and Persuasion

Handguns in America

OF THE 12,996 MURDERS COMMITTED in the U.S. in 2010, 8,775 were caused by firearms. Most of these (6,009) involved a handgun. Gun ownership, a right guaranteed by the Second Amendment to the U.S. Constitution, is vigorously defended by the National Rifle Association (NRA). The NRA includes over 20 million members, making it one of the largest advocacy organizations in the county. The NRA's public relations messages emphasize gun ownerships as a direct and significant connection to our revolutionary past—and invoke images of free men collectively defending their property.

The U.S. has more guns than registered voters. According to the NRA, Americans feel proud, free, and powerful when they hold guns. While not all members of the NRA champion absolute deregulation of firearms—which would include the sale of "cop-killer bullets" or extending the right to bear arms to convicted criminals and the mentally ill—most believe that *any* new restrictions on handguns will create a slippery slope leading ultimately to confiscation of all guns. In defense of gun rights, the NRA has fought for such things as the right to possess a gun in a bar, on a train, and in elementary and preschools.

The NRA disseminates its position through aggressive public relations and government relations efforts. Its website (http://home.nra.org) is sophisticated, easily navigated, and impressive—linking blogs, Twitter, Facebook, podcasts, video, and other interactive social media with traditional press releases and commentary.

Though a dominant force on gun issues—the NRA does face some challengers. One of the most visible of these is the Brady Campaign to Stop Gun Violence. This group was founded by Jim Brady, who suffered a traumatic brain injury after being shot during an assassination attempt on President Ronald Reagan. The Brady Campaign website, while clearly less well funded than the NRA's, features a running total of gunshot victims in the U.S and a daily tally that are both continually updated. The Brady Campaign seems to have strong public opinion on its side. Consider the following examples from the Brady website:

Criminal background checks for purchase of a handgun: opposed by NRA; supported by 94% of police chiefs

Dealers must stop selling if license has been revoked: opposed by NRA; supported by 80% of Americans

Limit individuals to purchasing one handgun per month, opposed by NRA; supported by 65% of Americans

Limit sales of assault weapons: opposed by NRA; supported by 82% of Americans

For the most part, the two sides in the war on guns in America are at loggerheads and are working as foils to each other, each attempting to outdo the other in shock value. Each organization uses statistics, anecdotes, and testimonials to build a case and persuade the public of its position. The NRA does not have to worry about a mass confiscation of firearms, at least any time soon, and the Brady campaign is situated to sadly await the next shooting tragedy in a school or shopping mall to bring its message to the forefront. From a public relations perspective on both websites, however, it is interesting to note how many of their tactics to win public opinion are similar.

1. How does the handgun control debate demonstrate the polarization of public opinion in America?

2. If you were assigned the task of bringing these two opposing groups into a meaningful dialogue, how could you evoke shared goals to further negotiations?

3. Do you think polarized public opinion regarding issues such as handgun control can be changed over time? What factors could bring about that change?

frames the conflict can bias the public in favor of one party, or one solution, over another. Because the media are so crucial not only to presenting and explaining conflicts but also to keeping them from escalating, it is necessary for the parties involved in the conflict as well as the public relations practitioners to know how to work effectively with the media. Similarly, the media play a central role when public relations professionals want a conflict to escalate, thereby bringing the issue to the fore.

All too often conflict is regarded as more newsworthy than its resolution. Details about a volatile political election or corporate malfeasance are far more interesting to the public than the reporting of an amicable settlement or an acquittal.

> [P]ublic relations professionals are influential rhetors. They design, place, and repeat messages on behalf of sponsors on an array of topics that shape views of government, charitable organizations, institutions of public education, products and consumerism, capitalism, labor, health, and leisure. These professionals speak, write, and use visual images to discuss topics and take stances on public policies at the local, state, and federal levels.
>
> Robert Heath, University of Houston

 think Why do mass media news broadcasts emphasize conflict?

The media's inclination to focus on tribulation posing as human interest often creates a dilemma for their sources. To maintain their credibility as objective judges of information, journalists are primed for conflict as part of their strategic approach to dealing with sources. However, public relations practitioners, as advocates for favorable coverage, have a tendency to be accommodative or cooperative with reporters, according to researchers Jae-Hwa Shin and Glen T. Cameron (two of the coauthors of this text). Public relations professionals should understand journalists' orientation to escalate conflict as a means of maintaining balance and independence. These practitioners should also try to transform conflicts in constructive ways. The public interest can best be served by healthy competition among public relations sources and media, as opposed to reporting from the perspective of a dominant power, such as governments, and delivering a unified or consistent ideology expressed as an alignment of political power and media conglomerates. From this perspective, public relations can serve as a challenge or a corrective, and as an influential social force in the ongoing creation of news and news trends or agendas.

Persuasion IN PUBLIC OPINION

Persuasion has been around since the dawn of human history. More than 2,500 years ago, the Greeks formalized the concept of persuasion by instituting rhetoric, the art of using language effectively and persuasively, as a central part of their educational system. Aristotle was the first to set down the ideas of ethos, logos, and pathos, which roughly translate as "source credibility," "logical argument," and "emotional appeal," respectively. Richard Perloff, author of *The Dynamics of Persuasion*, offers an updated definition of persuasion: "Persuasion is an activity or process in which a communicator attempts to induce a change in the belief, attitude, or behavior of another person or group of persons through the transmission of a message in a context in which the persuadee has some degree of free choice."

Most public relations efforts are persuasive communication management and ultimately seek to change the attitudes and behavior of people. For example, public relations professionals disseminate information about their products or services to potential customers in an effort to persuade them to recognize or buy those products or services. They also try to persuade legislators and other politicians in seeking favorable tax or regulatory actions. Politicians, for their part, use public relations to attract votes or raise money. Nonprofit organizations such as Greenpeace or the Red Cross persuade people to become aware of social or environmental issues, take actions, and donate money.

The dominant view of public relations is one of persuasive communication actions performed on behalf of clients, according to professors Dean Kruckeberg at the University of North Carolina–Charlotte and Ken Starck at the University of Iowa. Oscar Gandy, Jr. adds that "the primary role of public relations is one of purposeful, self-interested communications." Edward L. Bernays described public relations as the "engineering" of consent to create "a favorable and positive climate of opinion toward the individual, product, institution, or idea which is represented."

The Uses of Persuasion

Persuasion is used to (1) change or neutralize hostile opinions, (2) crystallize latent opinions and positive attitudes, and (3) maintain favorable opinions.

The most difficult persuasive task is to turn hostile opinions into favorable ones. There is much truth to the old adage, "Don't confuse me with the facts; my mind is made up." Once people have decided, for instance, that oil companies are making excessive profits, they tend to ignore or disbelieve any information that contradicts this view. The public may overlook information pointing to geopolitical factors or increased demand from countries such as China and India as affecting the price of oil, and instead believe that executives at ExxonMobil and the Shell Group are conspiring to gouge consumers. People generalize from personal experience, what they read in the newspaper or see on television, and what peers tell them. For example, if a person has an encounter with a rude clerk, the inclination is to generalize that the entire department store chain is not very good.

Persuasion becomes much easier when the message is compatible

with a person's ⬚
toward a subjec⬚
person tends to ⬚
a company with ⬚
he or she may e⬚
by purchasing o⬚
call can adversel⬚
opinion quickly, however. Organizations strive to have a good reputation—it translates into sales and donations.

Persuasion and Negotiation

Persuasion is comparable to negotiation. Negotiation is the process by which two or more parties attempt to settle disputes, reach agreement about courses of action, and bargain for individual or collective advantage. Negotiation is sometimes used in lieu of a lawsuit as a means of alternative dispute resolution (ADR), whereas persuasion conspicuously occurs in the marketplace as a form of communicative action, according to professor Jae-Hwa Shin at the University of Southern Mississippi. In nearly all cases, some degree of conflict exists between parties, both in persuasion and in negotiation. Like negotiators, a persuader and the persuadee intentionally or

A Major Persuasion Concept:
EVERYONE IS DOING IT

Research by behaviorists, for example, points out that the messages should remain simple and relay the impression that "everyone is doing it."

Robert Cialdini, author of the popular book *Influence*, tells Michael Grunwald of *Time* magazine, "People want to do what they think others will do." Cialdini and other behaviorists say getting people to alter their behavior is difficult, but they suggest the following strategies may be effective.

Make It Clear
Better information and more lucid material, from sources such as websites that explain the situation, can help people make better choices. "Public outreach and celebrity spokespersons can help; strict rules requiring disclosure can clarity and help more."

Make It Easy
Individuals are lazy. Enrolling people for a service or program is better than asking them to sign up themselves. That's why magazines automatically extend

subscriptions, and a person has to take action to opt out. In most cases, people don't opt out because it takes more effort. "We'll do almost anything—even things that are not good for us—to avoid extra paperwork."

Make It Popular
According to Grunwald, "Nothing drives behavior more than the power of conformity. Research shows that homeowners are most likely to save energy, weatherize, or recycle when they think everyone else is doing it."

Persuading Citizens to Join the U.S. Army

Persuading young people to consider a career in the U.S. Army has become more of a challenge in recent years. Protracted wars, with waning public support, has led to declining enlistment. Potential soldiers, and their family members, it appeared, were weighing their options more carefully than they were in the immediate wake of 9/11, when quick victory seemed assured. The public relations firm Weber Shandwick won a contract with the U.S. Army Accessions Command (the group responsible for recruiting soldiers) to help get the message out about what it means to serve a country and to help potential recruits learn about opportunities offered by the army for education and career advancement. The firm was also charged with addressing negative perceptions about military service. Its target audiences were high school students as well as opinion leaders—educators, coaches, media, and influential people within the community. The campaign targeted young Hispanic and African Americans as well as fans of NASCAR and college football.

After research indicated the importance of building grassroots support, Weber Shandwick launched Army Strong Stories. The goal was to present a positive yet unscripted portrayal of military service through the voices of solders. To engage the target audience of young adults (17–26) the firm used social media communication channels, such as Twitter and Facebook. More importantly, it also recruited an army of its own—600 soldier bloggers sharing their experiences on Army Strong Stories.

Measuring the effect of communications designed to persuade is often complex. In this case, however, the campaign clearly exceeded expectations by more than 40 percent; over 1.3 billion media impressions were documented in 2010. And the results are clear—the army has met its recruiting goals since the campaign began. To

further hammer home the campaign's effectiveness, Weber Shandwick broke its results down into a series of useful metrics, including social contagion and influencer engagement scores, quality media scores and impressions, and cost per engagement. The campaign appears to have succeeded by gaining high influencer engagement and social media contagion scores. Anecdotal reports suggest that the campaign has been effective at "building trust" between potential recruits and soldier bloggers by facilitating a "transparent, authentic" online experience. A model of effective, targeted persuasion, Army Strong Stories won a PRSA Silver Anvil Award of Excellence in 2011.

1 How does social media fit in with the army's overall strategy to communicate with recruits?

2 What tactics does the army use to make the social media communication experience more authentic?

3 If you were part of this public relations team, what types of controversy would you anticipate arising in relation to social media use, and how would you advise the army to handle it?

unconsciously bargain according to their interests, values, or needs and, ideally, are willing to compromise on the differences. There is always some degree of resistance on the part of the persuadee based on his or her inclination to accept or reject the persuader's message and terms.

How parties position themselves before negotiations begin can be crucial to how the give-and-take unfolds. Public relations can play a major role in this positioning. As a consequence, persuasion is an

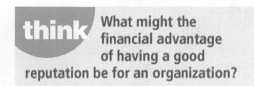

think What might the financial advantage of having a good reputation be for an organization?

integral component of the public relations effort to bring parties into ultimate agreement. For example, using persuasion to put your organization on an equal footing with a competitor could lead to the realization that the two parties need

to talk. In other words, public relations can be used as a tool leading to the ADR process. ADR takes place outside the traditional courtroom and has gained acceptance among public relations professionals, the legal profession, and the public at large. It is typically much less expensive, and often much more efficient, than a traditional lawsuit.

Factors IN PERSUASIVE COMMUNICATION

A number of factors are involved in persuasive communication, and public relations practitioners should be knowledgeable about each component embedded in the communication process: sender, message, channel, and receiver. In this section of the chapter, we present a brief discussion of each of the 10 factors related to persuasive communication: (1) audience analysis, (2) appeals to self-interest, (3) audience participation (4) suggestions for action, (5) source credibility, (6) clarity of message, (7) content and structure of messages, (8) channels, (9) timing and context, and (10) reinforcement.

Audience Analysis
Knowledge of audience characteristics such as beliefs, attitudes, values, concerns, and lifestyles is an

Demographics for Key Groups

Baby Boomers:
- Born between the 1946 and 1964
- Have established their careers and are planning for impending retirement
- Primary concerns include their health status and financial security
- Politically active and heavy consumers of print media and television

Generation X:
- Born between the mid-1960s and the early 1980s
- Heavy users of new media
- Tend to make purchases based on technological appeal

Millenials:
- Born after 1981
- Under intense pressure from parents and peers to achieve
- Tend to follow structure, be team-oriented, and accept social mores

Because of their predisposition to novel, technological innovation, Generation Xers may be more likely to be interested in purchasing a revolutionary automobile during the first model year than boomers or millenials.

PROPAGANDA

No discussion of persuasion would be complete without mentioning propaganda and the techniques associated with it. Its roots stretch back to the seventeenth century, when the Roman Catholic Church set up the *Congregatio de Propaganda Fide* ("congregation for propagating the faith"). Today, propaganda connotes falsehood, lies, deceit, disinformation, and duplicity—practices that opposing groups and governments accuse one another of employing. Advertising and public relations messages for commercial purposes often use several techniques commonly associated with propaganda:

- **Plain Folks.** An approach often used by individuals to show humble beginnings and empathy with the average citizen. Political candidates, in particular, are quite fond of recounting their "humble" beginnings.
- **Testimonial.** A frequently used device to achieve source credibility. A well-known expert, popular celebrity, or average citizen gives testimony about the value of a product or the wisdom of a decision.
- **Bandwagon.** The implication or direct statement that everyone wants the product or that the idea has overwhelming support encourages people to agree with the idea; for example, "Come see why everyone is buzzing about ClearVision Optical."
- **Card Stacking.** The selection of facts and data to build an overwhelming case on one side of the issue, while concealing the other side. This technique is particularly effective because what is presented is often factually accurate, but misleads by omitting crucial aspects that allow the audience to make an informed decision.
- **Transfer.** The technique of associating the person, product, or organization with something that has high status, visibility, or credibility. This approach is often used in advertising and political campaigns. For example, many car dealerships display enormous American flags, an unsubtle attempt to suggest that buying a new car is a patriotic act.
- **Glittering Generalities.** The technique of linking a cause, product, or idea with favorable abstractions such as freedom, justice, democracy, and the American way.

Presidential candidates often offer to bring the country back to prosperity. Congresswoman and once Republican presidential hopeful Michele Bachman, for example, earned wide support for "leading the way in cutting spending, reducing taxes and deep-sixing our 3.8-million-word Internal Revenue Code" without providing a specific plan to accomplish this lofty goal.

Public relations professionals should be aware of these techniques and make certain that they don't intentionally use them to deceive and mislead the public. Ethical responsibilities exist in every form of persuasive communication.

essential part of persuasion. It helps communicators tailor messages that are salient, answer a perceived need, and provide a logical course of action. Understanding such audience characteristics is critical to creating messages.

Basic *demographic* information, which is readily available through census data, can help determine an audience's age, gender, ethnicity, income, education, and geographic residence groupings. Other data that are often gathered by marketing

departments include information on a group's buying habits, disposable income, and ways of spending leisure time. Polls and surveys may tap a target audience's attitudes, opinions, and concerns. Such research can reveal much about the public's resistance to some ideas, as well as its predisposition to support others.

Another audience-analysis tool is *psychographics*. This method attempts to classify people based on their lifestyle, attitudes, values,

and beliefs. The Values and Lifestyle Program, known as VALS, was developed by SRI International, a research organization in Menlo Park, California. VALS is routinely used in public relations to help communicators structure persuasive messages to different elements of the population. A good illustration is the way Burson-Marsteller used VALS in preparing a public relations campaign for the National Turkey Foundation. The client's problem

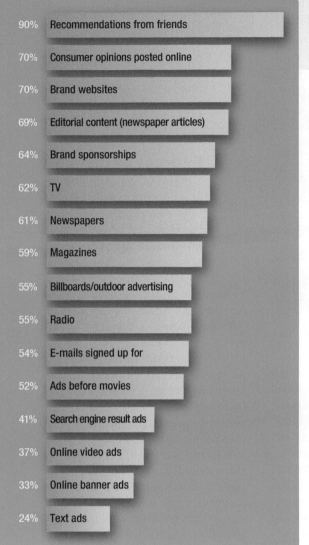

A Friend's Recommendation Is MOST Trusted

90%	Recommendations from friends
70%	Consumer opinions posted online
70%	Brand websites
69%	Editorial content (newspaper articles)
64%	Brand sponsorships
62%	TV
61%	Newspapers
59%	Magazines
55%	Billboards/outdoor advertising
55%	Radio
54%	E-mails signed up for
52%	Ads before movies
41%	Search engine result ads
37%	Online video ads
33%	Online banner ads
24%	Text ads

The Nielsen Global Online Consumer Survey of more than 25,000 Internet consumers in 50 nations found that recommendations from personal friends or opinions posted by consumers online are the most trusted form of source credibility. Advertisers and public relations personnel should be encouraged to learn that company websites are also trusted by 70 percent of consumers.

Source: Nielsen Global Online Consumer Survey, April 2009.

more innovative and willing to try new foods.

Burson-Marsteller tailored a strategy for each group. This segmentation of the consumer market into various VALS lifestyles enabled the company to select appropriate media for pitching specific story ideas. An article placed in *True Experience*, a publication reaching a population with the demographic characteristics of survivors and sustainers, was headlined "A Terrific Budget-Stretching Meal." Articles in *Better Homes and Gardens* with such titles as "Streamlined Summer Classics" and stories about barbecued turkey on the Fourth of July were used to reach belongers. Articles for achievers in *Food and Wine* and *Gourmet* magazines included recipes for turkey salad and turkey tetrazzini.

Appeals to Self-Interest

People become involved in issues or pay attention to messages that appeal to their psychological, economic, or situational needs. For example, if a cosmetics company wants to emphasize the antiaging effects of a new face cream, its messages might include testimonials from a well-known actress, such as Meryl Streep, who may appeal to an older demographic group. If it wishes to market the product to younger women, it may seek to employ Kristen Stewart of *Twilight* movie fame.

Appeals to self-interest are also used by charitable organizations to increase donations. While charities don't sell products, they do need volunteers and donations. Charities can increase the effectiveness of their appeals by carefully structuring their messages to highlight what volunteers or donors might receive in return. This is not to say that altruism is dead. Thousands of people give freely of their time and money to charitable organizations, but they do receive something in return. The "something in return" may be self-esteem, ego gratification, recognition from peers and the community, a sense of belonging, the opportunity to make a contribution to society, or even a tax deduction. Public relations people understand these psychological needs and rewards, which explains why there is always recognition of volunteers in newsletters and at award banquets.

Twentieth-century American sociologist Harold Lasswell asserted that people are motivated by eight basic appeals: to power, respect, well-being, affection, wealth, skill, enlightenment, and physical and mental vitality. Psychologist Abraham Maslow, in his renowned psychological theory, asserted that any appeal to self-interest must be based on a five-level hierarchy of needs:

- The first (and lowest) level involves basic needs such as food, water, shelter, and even such things as transportation to and from work.
- The second level involves "security" needs; people need to feel secure in their jobs, safe in their homes, and confident about their retirement.

was simple: how to encourage turkey consumption throughout the year, not just at Thanksgiving and Christmas.

One element of the public was called "sustainers and survivors"; VALS identified members of this group as low-income, poorly educated, often elderly people who ate at erratic hours, consumed inexpensive foods, and seldom ate out. Another element was known as the "belongers," who were highly family-oriented and served foods in traditional ways. The "achievers" were those who were

- The third level includes "belonging" needs—people seek association with others. This need explains why individuals join organizations or communities.
- The fourth level consists of "love" needs; humans have a need to be wanted and loved.
- At the fifth and highest level in Maslow's hierarchy are "self-actualization" needs.

Once the needs in the first four levels have been met, Maslow says that people are free to achieve maximum personal potential—for example, through traveling extensively or becoming a recognized expert on a particular topic.

Maslow's hierarchy helps explain why some public information campaigns have difficulty getting their messages across to people classified in the VALS categories as "survivors" and "sustainers." An example of this problem is efforts to inform low-income groups about AIDS. For these groups, the potential danger of AIDS may be less arresting in comparison to the day-to-day problems of poverty and their pursuit of basic needs such as daily food and shelter.

The challenge for public relations personnel, as creators of persuasive messages, is to tailor information to create, fill, or reduce a need. According to social scientists, success in persuasion largely depends on accurate assessment of audience needs and their self-interests.

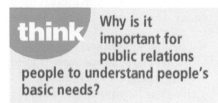
think Why is it important for public relations people to understand people's basic needs?

Audience Participation

Attitude or beliefs are changed or enhanced by audience involvement and participation.

> Activist groups use participation as a way of helping people actualize their beliefs. Not only do rallies and demonstrations give people a sense of belonging, but the act of participation also reinforces beliefs. Asking people to do something, such as conserve energy, collect donations, or picket, activates a form of self-actualization and commitment.

Nineteenth-century showman P. T. Barnum clearly recognized the power of audience participation. He observed that many people were willing to pay admission to see obvious hoaxes, such as the "Feejee mermaid" (a stuffed monkey sewn to the tail of a fish), because they enjoyed the process of exposing the "humbuggery" to their presumably less sophisticated companions.

Today, audience participation can take many forms. For example, an organization may have employees discuss productivity in a quality-control circle. Management may already have figured out what is needed, but if workers are involved in the problem solving, they are more committed to making the solution work because they participated in the decision-making process. Sample distributions—companies letting consumers try a product without expense—are also a means to encourage audience participation.

Suggestions for Action

A key principle of persuasion is that people endorse ideas and take actions only if they are accompanied by a proposed action from the sponsor. Recommendations for action must be clear to follow. Public relations practitioners not only must ask people to conserve energy, for instance, but must also furnish detailed data and ideas about how to do it.

Source Credibility

A message is more believable to an intended audience if the source has credibility with that audience. Source credibility is based on three factors.

The first factor is *expertise*. Does the audience perceive the person as an expert on the subject? The California Strawberry Advisory Board, for example, arranged for a home economist to appear on television talk shows to discuss nutrition and to demonstrate easy-to-follow strawberry recipes. The viewers, primarily homemakers, identified with the representative and found her highly credible. By the same token, a manufacturer of sunscreen lotion used a professor of pharmacology and a past president of the State Pharmacy Board to discuss the scientific merits of its sunscreen versus other lotions.

The second component is *sincerity*. Does the person come across as believing what he or she is saying? The third component, which is even more elusive, is *charisma*. Is the individual attractive, self-assured, and articulate, projecting an image of competence and leadership? Martin Luther King is an excellent historic example. His polished, inspiring public speaking made him a charismatic figure. King had the aura of a person possessed of high intellect and was able to communicate empathy with a broad range of people.

Many actors, such as George Clooney and Angelina Jolie,

become spokespersons for political or social causes. Using celebrities has its problems, however. One is sheer number of celebrity endorsements, to the point that the public sometimes can't remember who endorses what. A second problem can be overexposure of a celebrity, such as Jennifer Lopez, who in addition to a music career and numerous movie and television roles, earns millions of dollars annually from endorsing products.

The third problem occurs when an endorser's actions undercut the product or service. For example, Tiger Woods, once a sought-after product spokesperson, placed his career in jeopardy with indiscretions and a very public divorce.

"Anytime an advertiser pins its image to a star, whether an athlete or an actor, it takes a chance that reality won't live up to the storyboard," says Christina White, a reporter for the *Wall Street Journal*.

Studies show that the impact of a persuasive message will generally tend to decrease over time. The "sleeper effect" predicts that a message from a low-credibility source will actually increase in persuasiveness under the right circumstances. Low credibility may be caused by a "discounting cue," such as when a government official predicts improving economic conditions, because he or she is presumed to be biased. However, the message may gain credibility when dissociated from its source.

What are the pros and cons of using celebrities for product endorsements?

Clarity of Message

Many messages fail because the audience finds them unnecessarily complex in content or language. The most persuasive messages are direct, are simply expressed, and contain only one primary idea.

Public relations personnel should always ask two questions: (1) Will the audience understand the message? and (2) What do I want the audience to do with the message? Although persuasion theory says that people retain information better and form stronger opinions when they are asked to draw their own conclusions, this factor doesn't negate the importance of explicitly stating which action an audience should take. Is it to buy the product, visit a showroom, write a member of Congress, or make a $10 donation? If an explicit request for action is not part of the message, members of the audience may not understand what is expected of them.

Channels

Different media with different features can be used for diverse public relations purposes. Television is visual, sensational, and entertaining. Newspapers offer a lot of in-depth information and discuss conflicting views. Radio is flexible or adaptable in format and content, and is accessible to people at almost any place and at any time. Radio also reaches target audiences quickly, making it an effective means of communication in crisis situations. Newer forms of communication, such as texting or tweets, provide companies and organizations with the means to reach thousands or millions of followers with instant, targeted messages. Likewise, social networking sites such as Facebook and Google+ are immediate channels of communication about an emerging event or crisis.

Ultimately, however, face-to-face communication has benefits that cannot be matched by mass media channels. According to communication scholar Steve H. Chaffee, people seek information from available sources, and interpersonal sources often are effective ways to reach people, even through word of mouth. For example, a company president speaking with employees who are threatening to strike may encourage a compromise through a personal appeal, whereas a mass-media message could make the employees angrier via interrupted messages, confused interpretation, or the impersonal nature of the statements.

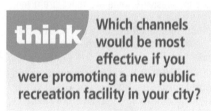

Which channels would be most effective if you were promoting a new public recreation facility in your city?

Timing and Context

A message tends to be more persuasive if environmental factors support the message or if the message is received within the context of other messages and situations with which the individual is familiar. These factors are called *timing* and *context*, respectively. For example, information from a utility on how to conserve energy will be more salient if the consumer has just received a January heating bill. A pamphlet on a new stock offering will be more effective if it accompanies an investor's dividend check. A citizens' group lobbying for a stoplight will receive more attention if a major accident has just occurred at the intersection in question.

> "An innovation, to be effective, has to be simple and it has to be focused. It should do only one thing, otherwise it confuses."
>
> Peter Drucker, management expert

Content and Structure of Messages....................

A number of techniques can make a message more persuasive. Expert communicators employ many different devices, including drama, surveys and polls, statistics, examples, mass media endorsements, and emotional appeals.

DRAMA AND STORIES. The first task of a communicator is to get the audience's attention. This objective is often accomplished by graphically illustrating an event or situation. Relief organizations, in particular, attempt to galvanize public concern and donations through stark black-and-white photographs and emotionally charged descriptions of suffering and disease.

SURVEYS AND POLLS. Airlines and auto manufacturers use the results of surveys and polls to show that they are first in "customer satisfaction," "service," and even "leg room" or "cargo space."

STATISTICS. Numbers convey objectivity, size, and importance in a credible way that can influence public opinion. A company might cite how many reams of paper its new electronic communication initiative is saving, for example.

EXAMPLES. A statement of opinion is often more persuasive if some examples are given. For instance, a school board may solicit support for a bond issue by citing examples of how present facilities are inadequate for student needs.

ENDORSEMENTS. In addition to endorsements by paid celebrities, products and services may benefit from favorable statements by experts in the form of a third-party endorsement.

A well-known medical specialist may publicly state that a particular brand of exercise equipment is best for general conditioning. The media also produce news stories about new products and services that, because of the media's perceived objectivity, are considered a form of third-party endorsement.

CAUSES AND RATIONALES. People tend to accept social ideas, norms, or practices engaged in by a group or society, thereby forging a psychological connection to the community. Public relations professionals must assess and understand the social norms of a target audience to provide messages that emphasize tangible social benefits. By advocating a cause that taps into social norms and one that an audience is passionate about, public relations personnel effectively reach the audience and generate goodwill. For example, by sponsoring a breast cancer awareness event such as a walkathon, an athletic footwear company builds good faith with potential consumers whose norms support better health.

EMOTIONAL APPEALS. Fund-raising letters from nonprofit groups, in particular, often use emotional appeals as a persuasive device. Such pleas can do much to

galvanize the public into action—but they also can backfire. A description of suffering makes many people uncomfortable. As a result, they may tune out the message rather than take action. Research indicates, however, that moderate fear appeal, accompanied by a relatively easy solution, is effective. Allstate Insurance, for example, has run print ads warning about the dangers of texting while driving. The ad leads with the statistic that 5,000 teenagers will die as a result of texting at the wheel. Humor appeals are also effective at enhancing attention, message comprehension, and recall.

Political candidates are aware of public concerns and avidly read polls to learn which issues are most important to voters. For example, if polls indicate that taxation and immigration are key issues, the candidate will refer to these issues—and offer his or her proposals to resolve them—in the campaign.

Timing and context also play an important role in achieving publicity in the mass media. Public relations personnel should read newspapers and watch television news programs to find out which topics the media gatekeepers consider newsworthy. A manufacturer of a locking device for computer files got extensive media coverage

about its product simply because its release followed a rash of news stories about thieves' gaining access to bank accounts through computers. Public relations professionals aim to disseminate information at the time when it is most highly valued.

Reinforcement

People tend to ignore or react negatively to messages that conflict with their value or belief systems. A public relations campaign that is out of sync with an audience's core beliefs is unlikely to be successful. For this reason, it is important for public relations professionals to have a firm understanding of the public's core values so they can

be taken into consideration when designing a message aimed at that particular audience.

People seek and support messages that support their currently held beliefs and avoid those that challenge these attitudes. Beliefs and attitudes that are not fully formed can be affected by persuasive messages; in contrast, long-established

For purposes of discussion, the limitations on effective persuasive messages can be listed as lack of message penetration, competing messages, self-selection, and self-perception.

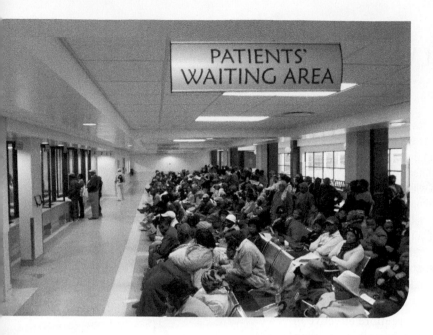

PATIENTS' WAITING AREA

Opponents to health care reform capitalized on the core values of many citizens who believed that the government should not be involved in administering health care plans.

values are highly resistant to change. In addition, attitudes that have been tested are more resistant to change. Public relations professionals can use such inoculated attitudes to create resistance to potentially opposing arguments or negative publicity. In a crisis situation, inoculation accompanied by tested beliefs can help a public figure or a company get through a crisis and maintain its prior reputation.

The Limits OF PERSUASION

In reality, the effectiveness of persuasive techniques is greatly exaggerated. Persuasion is not an exact science, and no surefire way exists to predict that people or media gatekeepers will be persuaded to believe a message or act on it. If persuasive techniques were as refined as the critics say, everyone would be driving the same make of automobile, using the same soap, and voting for the same political candidate. In practice, the ability to persuade is contingent on a complex set of factors as opposed to persuasive messages that translate directly into behavior. Conflicting and competing messages frequently interrupt or cancel one another through a course of ongoing communication, given the freedom of receivers to be selective or even apathetic regarding particular messages.

Lack of Message Penetration

Despite modern communication technologies, the diffusion of messages is not pervasive. Not everyone, of course, watches the same television programs or reads the same newspapers and magazines. Not everyone views the same websites or reads the same blogs. Not everyone follows the same Twitter feeds or attends the same meetings. Not everyone the communicator wants to reach will be in the eventual audience. Despite advances in audience-segmentation techniques, communicators cannot ensure that 100 percent of their intended audiences will be reached.

There is also the problem of message distortion as messages pass through media gatekeepers such as reporters, editors, and bloggers. Key message points often are left out, buried among less relevant information or placed in ineffective contexts, or even delivered in an unintended or negative way.

Competing or Conflicting Messages

Today, communication experts realize that no message is received in a vacuum. Messages are filtered through social structures and belief systems. Nationality, race, religion, gender, cultural patterns, family, and friends are among the variables that screen out and dilute persuasive messages. According to social scientists, a person usually conforms to the standards of his or her family and friends; most people do not believe or act on messages that are contrary to the norms of their peer group.

Self-Selection

The people most sought after in an audience are often the least likely to be there. Vehement supporters or loyalists frequently ignore information from the other side. They do so by being selective about messages that they listen to, reading books, newspaper editorials, blogs, and magazine articles and viewing television programs that support their predispositions. This tendency explains why social scientists say that the media are more effective in reinforcing existing attitudes than in changing them.

Self-Perception

Self-perception is the channel through which messages are interpreted. Different people will perceive the same information differently, depending on their predispositions and preexisting opinions.

Depending on a person's views, an action by an organization may be considered a "great contribution to the community" or a "self-serving gimmick." Social judgment theory suggests that internal factors such as beliefs, attitudes, and values will limit the extent to which an individual accepts or rejects a persuasive message.

 How might a PR campaign reach a person who does not watch TV or listen to radio?

Persuasion Don'ts

ethics in ACTION

Public relations professionals, by definition, are advocates for their clients and employers. They use persuasive communication to influence a particular public in some way. At the same time, public relations practitioners must conduct their activities in an ethical manner.

Persuasive messages require truth, honesty, and candor for two practical reasons. First, as noted by Robert Heath, a professor at the University of Texas–Houston, a message is already suspect because it is advanced on behalf of a client or organization. Second, half-truths and misleading information do not serve the best interests of the public or the organization.

The use of persuasive techniques, therefore, calls for some additional guidelines. Professor Richard L. Johannesen of Northern Illinois University, writing in *Persuasion: Reception and Responsibility,* a text by Charles Larson, lists the following ethical criteria

for using persuasive devices that should be kept in mind by every public relations professional:

- **DON'T** use false, fabricated, misrepresented, distorted, or irrelevant evidence to support arguments or claims.
- **DON'T** intentionally use specious, unsupported, or illogical reasoning.
- **DON'T** represent yourself as informed or as an "expert" on a subject when you are not.
- **DON'T** use irrelevant appeals to divert attention or scrutiny from the issue at hand. Among the appeals that commonly serve such a purpose are smear attacks on an opponent's character and appeals to hatred and bigotry or innuendo.
- **DON'T** ask your audience to link your idea or proposal to emotion-laden values, motives, or goals to which it actually is not related.

- **DON'T** deceive your audience by concealing your real purpose, your self-interest, the group you represent, or your position as an advocate of a viewpoint.
- **DON'T** distort, hide, or misrepresent the number, scope, intensity, or undesirable features of consequences.
- **DON'T** use emotional appeals that lack a supporting basis of evidence or reasoning or that would not be accepted if the audience had time and opportunity to examine the subject itself.
- **DON'T** oversimplify complex situations into simplistic either–or choices.
- **DON'T** pretend certainty when tentativeness and degrees of probability would be more accurate.
- **DON'T** advocate something in which you do not believe yourself.

summary

What Is Public Opinion?

- Public opinion can be difficult to measure; there are few, if any, issues on which the public (which is, in fact, many publics) can be said to have a unanimous opinion. In reality, only a small number of people will have opinions on any given issue.

Who Are Opinion Leaders?

- People who are knowledgeable and articulate on specific issues can be either formal opinion leaders (power leaders) or informal opinion leaders (role models).

What Role Do the Mass Media Play in Shaping Public Opinion?

- Information from public relations sources reaches the public through mass media.
- The mass media frame issues; editor and journalists select certain facts and disregard others.
- Journalists and public relations professionals frequently use the agenda-setting process in public discourse and act as gatekeepers, affecting how the public interprets issues.

How Does Conflict Affect Public Discourse?

- In public relations, conflict theory offers insight into the differences among individuals and groups and analyzes conflicts of interest, goals, desires, and values.
- The media play a role in unfolding conflicts and can promote public debate regarding the issue.

What Makes Communication Persuasive?

- Persuasion can be used to change or neutralize hostile opinions, crystallize latent opinions and positive attitudes, and reinforce favorable opinions.
- Factors involved in persuasion include audience analysis, audience participation, suggestions for action, source credibility, appeal to self-interest, message clarity, content and structure of messages, timing and context, and channels.

What Are the Limitations of Persuasion?

- The limitations on effective persuasive messages include lack of message penetration, competing messages, self-selection, and self-perception.

questions
FOR REVIEW AND DISCUSSION

1 What is the role of opinion leaders in the formation of public opinion?

2 What is the role of media in the formation of public opinion?

3 Public opinion is highly influenced by self-interest and events. Explain this statement.

4 List the three uses of persuasion in public relations work. Which objective is the most difficult to accomplish?

5 Name and describe the nine factors involved in persuasive communication.

6 List the three factors involved in source credibility.

7 Which techniques can be used to write persuasive messages?

8 Name several propaganda techniques and list ways they might be employed by public relations practitioners.

MySearchLab®

tactics

Three lessons all tech companies should learn from Apple's latest audit

By Chris O'Brien

Mercury News Columnist, Posted: 04/02/2012 06:05:45 PM PDT, Updated: 04/03/2012 11:45:18 AM PDT

The audit of facilities that manufacture Apple products, released by the Fair Labor Association last week, revealed nothing that wasn't already known. And despite immediate promises to end overtime abuses, activists are justified in remaining vigilant to make sure that happens.

But whatever its shortcomings, the report offers much for the rest of the tech industry. I spent some time examining the supply chain disclosures of 10 of the largest tech companies and found they fall all over the map. While some come close to matching Apple, others leave us almost completely in the dark.

The bar has been raised (even if there is a debate about how much), and every tech company ought to find a way to match it. This will require a steeper climb for some than others.

Here are three things the industry can do right now:

MORE TRANSPARENCY: What other tech companies tell us about their supply chains and manufacturing is too inconsistent.

At one end, for instance, is Oracle, which discloses pretty much nothing when it comes to this topic. The company acquired Sun Microsystems a couple of years ago, getting into the hardware business. On Oracle's website, it does have a copy of its supplier code of conduct, and notes that it does conduct audits. But as far as what those audits find, we're told nothing.

An Oracle spokesperson said the company had no comment.

At the other end are companies such as Hewlett-Packard and Intel.

Each publishes an annual corporate sustainability report that provides information about the number and types of violations found and metrics about the progress being made to resolve them.

Intel also publishes a list of its 75 largest suppliers that account for about 90 percent of its supply chain. HP lists almost all of them. According to a statement from an HP spokesperson:

"HP takes seriously the challenge of raising social and environmental responsibility (SER) standards in its supply chain. HP was the first electronics company to publish its list of suppliers in 2008 and has published an aggregate table of audit results annually since 2006."

Activist groups with a broad perspective argue against unconscionable work days. The electronics industry, and even a segment of the workers in Apple factories, favor long work days for increased profits and larger paychecks. This give-and-take in the marketplace of ideas is central to the contingency theory of conflict.

For this response, Oracle earns a failing grade in Public Relations 101. Some response to reporters improves media relations and prevents the public from harboring the suspicion that the company is hiding something.

Reports like this are an example of an effective response to criticism from detractors. Crisis communication specialists call it "corrective action."

HP employed the bandwagon technique by implying the company is a leader simply for providing what everyone wants—in this case, transparent disclosure of social and environmental information. The adoption of green practices is timely and widely admired.

Public Opinion and Persuasion

172

Publishing the results of audits and full lists of suppliers should become the norm. Currently, most tech companies (including Apple) have developed their monitoring through a trade industry group called the Electronics Industry Citizenship Coalition, or EICC. But the EICC doesn't mandate such disclosures. As a group, these companies should realize the game has changed and so should their rules.

TARGETING VIOLATIONS: Part of those changes should also extend to not just naming suppliers, but detailing where violations occur. One genuine step forward Apple took with the report last week was that it specifically talked about the conditions at a major manufacturer, Foxconn. The FLA will next audit the second- and third-largest manufacturers of Apple products and release reports on them as well.

Members of the EICC have in the past discussed and rejected this so-called "naming and shaming" approach to dealing with suppliers, arguing it would be counterproductive to publicly humiliate important partners. When I called the EICC last week to discuss their approaches, spokesperson Wendy Dittmer said the organization allowed for a wide range of approaches within certain frameworks.

The thing to remember is that everyone is trying to improve conditions," Dittmer said. "We're not at odds in terms of the goal."

But the effect that the spotlight on Foxconn has had—promises to end overtime abuses and raise pay—makes me think the EICC should make naming supplier violations standard for members.

GREATER INDEPENDENT OVERSIGHT: Apple trumpeted its decision to become a member of the FLA, a third-party organization whose members primarily include apparel-makers and universities. The nonprofit was established in the wake of the sweatshop controversies of the 1990s.

The company noted that in asking the FLA to conduct inspections, these would be the first "independent" audits of its suppliers' facilities.

"We believe that workers everywhere have the right to a safe and fair work environment, which is why we've asked the FLA to independently assess the performance of our largest suppliers," said Tim Cook, Apple's CEO, in a news release at the time. "The inspections now underway are unprecedented in the electronics industry, both in scale and scope, and we appreciate the FLA agreeing to take the unusual step of identifying the factories in their reports."

The problem is that many human and labor rights activist view the FLA with skepticism because it receives the bulk of its funding from members, making it only slightly more credible than the EICC in their eyes.

"If the FLA doesn't have any teeth, it's fair to say the EICC doesn't have gums," said Scott Nova, executive director of the Workers Rights Consortium.

The FLA did not respond to a request for comments. But it has previously said that it has checks in place to make sure that its monitoring groups are not influenced by members' fees. And certainly, its detailed report on Foxconn has gotten good reviews.

Still, appearances matter, and the FLA should rethink its funding. When the organization first started, it got the bulk of its funding from government grants, but shifted over time to membership fees. This topic is critical enough to U.S. industry and consumers that the federal government (and some foreign governments) ought to be able to scrape together the $3.7 million to replace the member fees it received in 2010.

The money spent to enhance the credibility of the U.S. tech industry and home and abroad would be worth every penny.

Text Credits

Credits are listed in order of appearance.

Photo Credits

Credits are listed in order of appearance.

Managing Competition and Conflict

From Chapter 8 of *Think Public Relations*, 2013 Edition. Dennis L. Wilcox, Glen T. Cameron, Bryan H. Reber, Jae-Hwa Shin.

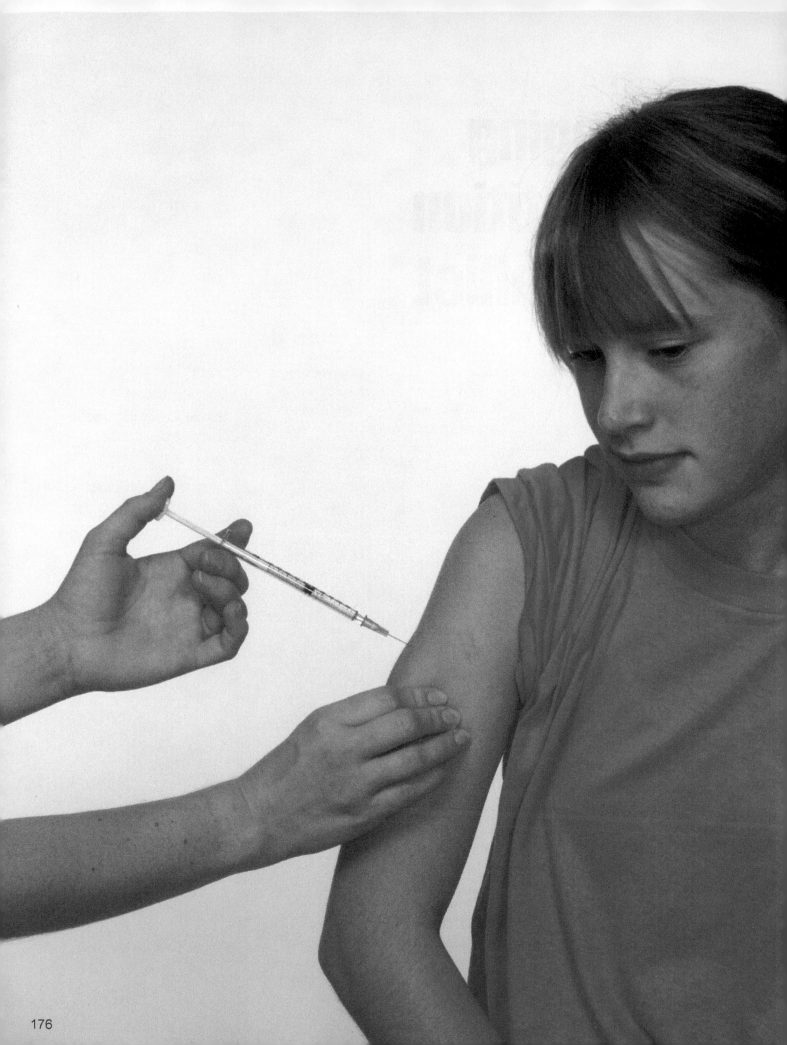

Managing Competition and Conflict

Good Intentions Go Further with Smart PR

An old adage states that "the road to hell is paved with good intentions." For Merck, the maker of a vaccine to prevent cervical cancer, that saying may prove to be all too true. The company's anticancer vaccine has faced criticism, attacks, and a political maelstrom in a free society where clashing views are heard. Merck's Gardasil is a vaccine against the human papillomavirus (HPV). HPV causes painful recurring genital warts and is a major risk factor for cervical cancer. HPV has also been identified as a risk factor for penile cancer.

Those unaware of the central role of conflict in news and public relations might imagine that inventing a vaccine against a pernicious virus would be a guaranteed ticket to fame and fortune for the scientists, companies, and politicians involved. But Gardasil has had a conflict-ridden and crisis-plagued journey since its 2006 FDA approval, even playing a show-stealing role in the 2011 debates among Republican presidential hopefuls.

In one debate, socially conservative Minnesota Senator Michele Bachmann sharply criticized Texas Governor Rick Perry for issuing an executive order in his state requiring that sixth-grade girls be vaccinated against HPV.

The crisis for the Perry campaign brought Gardasil to center stage, where other voices took up the public discourse about vaccines. Diverse groups who joined the chorus against the vaccine included:

- Public health professionals who expressed concern that females would become complacent about protected sex and omit regular pap smears
- Anti-vaccine groups who argued that Merck was greedily profiting from "risky" vaccinations
- Social activists who worried that offering access to Gardasil for lower-income families at public health clinics was a form of racial profiling
- Advocates of sexual abstinence before marriage

Merck stayed above the fray, offering a short statement affirming the efficacy and safety of Gardasil and pointing out that millions of girls were being vaccinated without incident each year. A Merck spokesperson said, "Despite much media attention and strong opinions from many quarters, vaccines remain one of the greatest tools in the public health arsenal."

1 Gardasil has become a platform for social action and political groups to further their own positions by fomenting conflict. Do you think this conflict escalation strategy is ethical?

2 What role should the public relations team at Merck play in the very public debate about Gardasil?

> What Role Do Competition and Conflict Play in Public Relations?

> What Factors Affect the Stance that an Organization Takes During Conflict Management?

> What Are the Phases of the Conflict Management Life Cycle?

> How Can Public Relations Professionals Best Manage the Conflict Management Life Cycle?

A NEW WAY OF THINKING:
Conflict & Competition

As the chapter-opening story about the Gardasil vaccine illustrates, the road to heaven or hell—or even just good health policy—is rife with conflict and crisis. Because so much is at stake, health public relations is one of the most polemical and highly charged specialties in public relations. Skill and understanding of how public discourse and strategic conflict management interact in a free society provide perspective for communicators striving to improve human health and wellbeing as well as address other important topics.

Public relations can be defined as the *strategic management* of conflict and competition in the best interests of an organization and, when possible, also in the interests of key publics. The paramount concern of public relations professionals is managing communication in the interests of their employers and clients to enhance their competitive position and handle conflict effectively, provided the objectives of their employers are worthy and ethical.

This definition is more assertive than definitions that emphasize building mutually beneficial relationships between an organization and its various stakeholders. Building relationships is a key objective, but it is only part of the larger role that public relations plays in ensuring an organization's success.

Public relations enables both for-profit and nonprofit organizations to compete for limited resources (e.g., customers, volunteers, employees, donations, grants) and to engage in healthy, honest conflict with those who hold different views

of what is best and right for society. Achieving these sorts of objectives increases the value of public relations to an organization. It is also how public relations professionals earn the influence that leads to greater recognition by top management, increased respect in the field, and, ultimately, better-paying, more

secure positions for public relations professionals in general.

Most public relations activities and programs deal with competition between organizations for sales and customers. Conflict, in contrast, usually involves confrontations between organizations and various stakeholders or publics.

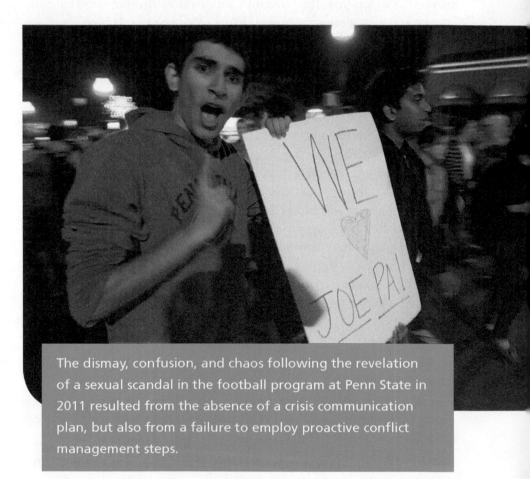

The dismay, confusion, and chaos following the revelation of a sexual scandal in the football program at Penn State in 2011 resulted from the absence of a crisis communication plan, but also from a failure to employ proactive conflict management steps.

Penn State students took to the streets to protest the firing of legendary coach Joe Paterno, the university's handling of sex abuse allegations against a former coach, and the media's coverage of the case. Some of the protests turned violent, as a television news van and several light posts were toppled.

> " I believe that many of the well-known crisis communication management techniques were overlooked or inappropriately implemented. The adage to 'tell the truth and tell it quickly' surely was ignored when one considers the timeline of the alleged events. "

Dr. Robert Baukus, head of the Department of Advertising/ Public Relations at Penn State

More than 10,000 Penn State students show their support for the victims of the sex abuse scandal at a peaceful gathering on November 11, 2011.

COMPETITION and CONFLICT

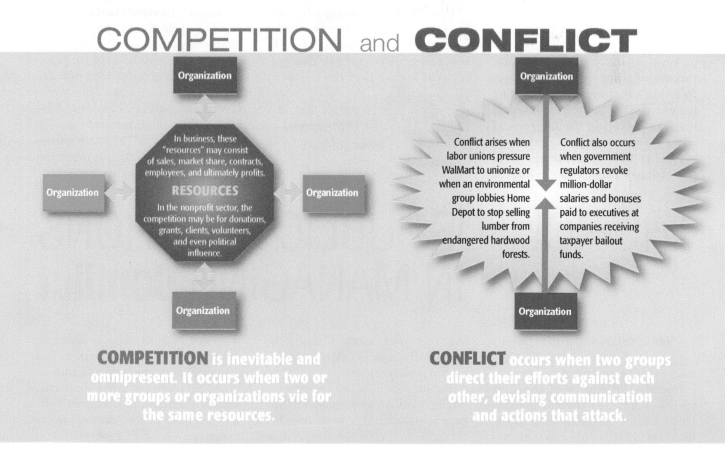

Organization

Organization

In business, these "resources" may consist of sales, market share, contracts, employees, and ultimately profits.

RESOURCES

In the nonprofit sector, the competition may be for donations, grants, clients, volunteers, and even political influence.

Organization

Organization

Organization

Conflict arises when labor unions pressure WalMart to unionize or when an environmental group lobbies Home Depot to stop selling lumber from endangered hardwood forests.

Conflict also occurs when government regulators revoke million-dollar salaries and bonuses paid to executives at companies receiving taxpayer bailout funds.

Organization

COMPETITION is inevitable and omnipresent. It occurs when two or more groups or organizations vie for the same resources.

CONFLICT occurs when two groups direct their efforts against each other, devising communication and actions that attack.

Admittedly, the distinction between competition and conflict is partly a matter of degree, but it is also a matter of focus. In competition, everyone's eyes are on the prize—such as sales or political support, for example. With conflict, all eyes are on the opposition—that is, on dealing with or initiating threats of some sort or another. In either case, striving for mutual benefit is extremely important. It involves balancing the interests of an employer or client with those of a number of stakeholders. Often, professionals can accommodate the interests of both the organization and its various publics. But sometimes organizations may not be able to please all of their publics because there are differences in worldviews.

Wal-Mart may please labor unions by paying more employee benefits, but consumers who like low prices may object to that policy if it means that the company will charge more for its goods. To compound conflict management challenges, a powerful third public is the stock investor who provides essential capital to corporations. Environmentalists may want to close a coal plant, but the company's employees and the local community may be avid supporters of keeping the plant open despite any environmental concerns. Given competing agendas and issues, public relations professionals must look first to the needs of the organization, and then manage the inevitable conflicts that arise.

 think To whom does a PR professional owe primary allegiance?

THE ROLE OF PUBLIC RELATIONS IN MANAGING **Conflict**

Public relations professionals must develop communication strategies and processes to influence the course of conflicts to the benefit of their organizations and, when possible, to the benefit of the organizations' many constituents. This deliberate influence is called *strategic conflict management*.

Public relations can involve reducing conflict, as is frequently the case in crisis management. At other times, conflict is escalated for activist purposes, such as when antiabortion advocates picket health clinics and assault clients, doctors, and nurses. Some strategies are less dramatic, such as when industry advocates lobby to open parts of the Alaskan wilderness to exploration for oil, striving to win approval from the public—and ultimately, from Congress.

Conflict management often occurs when a business or industry contends with government regulators or activist groups that seem determined to curtail operations through what the industry considers excessive safety or environmental standards. Industries

think Is conflict always bad for organizations?

will often organize as coalitions or trade groups to fight back. For example, the American Coalition for Clean Coal Electricity (cleancoalusa.

org) spends tens of millions of dollars annually on public relations, including advocacy ads on television claiming that industry innovations have turned coal into a clean, abundant source of energy. Speeches and news releases from this organization also warn against excessive regulation that would curtail the role of

Moral Conflicts Pose Special Challenges

ethics in ACTION

When organizations clash over a heated issue or a moral conflict such as embryonic stem cell research or capital punishment, charges leveled at the opposition often aim at impugning the ethics of the opponent. Often, such charges can be paraphrased as "*We* are just trying to tell the truth, but *they* are lying and twisting facts." Sometimes this "truth telling" is contrasted with the "spin" practiced by the other side—even though both sides use the same tactics in addition to a full range of persuasive public relations strategies. When proponents embrace

absolute moral values in this way, they fail to reach out to, or understand, the other side.

Most news conferences begin with an opening statement by the organization holding the news conference. Write an opening statement for a press conference on a current moral conflict somewhere in the world. You might take the role of a WikiLeaks spokesperson making an appeal for support of its mission to expose secret documents and practices to the light of day. Or perhaps you prefer to serve as a Pentagon spokesperson decrying the

threat to the safety of American troops in sensitive operations being compromised by WikiLeaks disclosures. Outline your statement for the side that you support most strongly, and then try to understand the worldview of the other side and sketch an opening statement for that group.

Does this exercise prove that it is foolish for public relations people to stand for something they believe in when there is no absolute right or wrong? Or does the classic adage, "You've got to stand for something or you'll fall for anything" ring more true in your ears?

coal in America's energy future. On the other side, environmental groups such as the Sierra Club lobby Congress and regulatory agencies for restrictions in coal burning, claiming that the concept of "clean" coal is a myth. Solar energy enthusiasts, in an effort to capitalize on the clean coal controversy, have employed an interesting approach. One such group hosts a website that uses the words "clean coal" in its URL; only when visitors reach the website do they learn that the site actually touts solar technology, not clean coal. The creation of such anti-sites are a popular guerrilla tactic for activist groups with small budgets.

Sometimes an organization is able to catch a conflict at an early stage and reduce damage to the organization by employing a strategy that crisis management experts term "stealing thunder." In other cases, an issue may smolder for some time before turning into a major fire. For example, lavish executive salary packages had periodically emerged as a point of contention over the past decade. Nevertheless, it wasn't until the 2009 economic collapse in the United States, which was precipitated largely by rampant speculation perpetrated by high-salaried managers in banking and insurance, that a broad groundswell of resentment found its voice in the Occupy Wall Street movement. Although the tactics, the anarchistic philosophy, and even the appearance of some of the Occupiers may not sit well with conformist middle-class Americans, the call for justice and equity does.

Unfortunately, most conflict situations do not have a clear-cut, ideal solution. In many cases, public relations professionals will not be able to accommodate the concerns of an activist group or a particular public because of many factors, including those related to the continued viability of the organization. In such cases, public relations professionals must make tough calls and advocate on behalf of their organizations.

think Which factors determine how a public relations professional reacts to conflict?

The regime that ruled Egypt for decades faced mobilized and determined physical presence in Tahrir Square that was motivated and organized through **effective strategic communication.** The Mubarak government gradually moved toward **greater and greater accommodation** of the demands for democratic representation, **ultimately capitulating** to the will of the people.

Managing Competition and Conflict

It Depends: FACTORS THAT AFFECT CONFLICT MANAGEMENT

Working with management, a public relations professional or team must determine the stance the organization will take toward each stakeholder involved in a conflict situation. This stance determines the strategy employed—what will be done and why. The stance-driven approach to public relations began with the discovery that virtually all practitioners share an unstated, informal approach to managing conflict and competition: "it depends." In essence, the stance taken "depends" on many factors, and it changes in response to changing circumstances. One approach to determining how to react in a conflict is the *threat appraisal model* and another is *contingency theory*. In this section of the chapter, we discuss them both briefly.

The Threat Appraisal Model

A good public relations practitioner monitors the external communication environments, such as news, social media, and the blogosphere, for threats, assesses them, arrives at a stance for the organization, and begins communication efforts from that stance. Practitioners face a complex set of forces to monitor and consider. A threat to an organization requires an assessment of the demands that the threat makes on the organization as well as an assessment of the resources available to address the threat. Once a threat is identified the public relations professional must consider a variety of factors. Are the knowledge, time, finances, and management commitment available to combat the threat? What is the best method to assess the severity of the danger? Is it a situation with the potential for

a long duration, or is it a relatively simple matter that can be resolved fairly quickly?

After carefully assessing the threat, professionals sometimes decide to ignore an issue or a pressure group, thereby saving themselves and their clients time, energy, and trouble. Letting an issue or a group "die on the vine" may appear to be accommodative or even humane, but is often considered an affront, even an insult. It should be done only after ethical deliberation.

Contingency Theory

Two fundamental principles underlie the definition of public relations as strategic management of competition and conflict. The first principle is that many factors determine the stance or position of an organization when it comes to dealing with conflict and perceived threats. The second principle is that the public relations stance for dealing with a particular audience or public must be dynamic. The stance must change as events unfold; there is a continuum of stances ranging from pure

advocacy to pure accommodation. These two principles form the basis of *contingency theory*.

Contingency factors. The public relations approach that is used is "contingent" on many factors that professionals must take into account.

In a survey of 1,000 members of the Public Relations Society of America (PRSA), most practitioners reported that the expertise and experience of the public relations professional play a major role in formulating the proper strategy for dealing with a conflict or issue. Organizational-level variables, however, are also important. Likewise, the values and attitudes of top management clearly have a great influence on how an organization responds to conflict and threats.

The contingency continuum. Depending on circumstances, factors such as the attitudes of top management and the judgment of public relations professionals may move the organization either toward or away from accommodation of a public. The range of response forms a continuum from pure advocacy to pure accommodation.

> "Christi McNeill, who oversees social media communication at Southwest, told *PR Daily* on Wednesday that social media is a key component of the airlines' crisis plan. 'As soon as we get some facts, we share it with our customers,' McNeill said. 'We want our customers to find out about it from us, before it hits the evening news.' So much for the 'not commenting until the incident has been reviewed by the FAA and NTSB' response that some other airlines fall back on."
>
> Blogger Gil Rudawsky

Free Silva

FOR SILVA HAROTONIAN, a pleasant afternoon drinking tea with friends ended at Iran's notorious Evin prison. Seven months later, a deceptive legal process resulted in her three-year conviction for "attempting to overthrow the Iranian government." International outcry followed against the allegation that an Iranian citizen of Armenian heritage working on maternal and child health initiatives for IREX was a genuine threat to Iran's theocratic dictatorship. After all, IREX is simply a Washington DC-based international nonprofit organization that administers the Fulbright scholarship and many other U.S. State Department programs. The charges against Harotonian, which claimed she was plotting a "soft revolution" as a U.S. "spy," may have arisen from the role she had played in facilitating visits to Iran by child health experts.

To reverse this travesty of justice, IREX hired public relations firm Edelman to mount a communication campaign and obtain her release. The international firm executed a global program designed to:

- raise international awareness of the case;
- build leverage that could be used as part of diplomatic negotiations;
- develop relationships with key influencers; and
- minimize anything that might link Silva to the U.S. as a "spy."

With the help of this program, IREX and Harotonian's family and lawyers ultimately gained the leverage they needed to successfully negotiate her release.

Crucial components of the award-winning campaign included research and planning. Edelman conducted extensive research of other detainments to find patterns in media coverage and diplomacy that could be emulated. Planning focused on identifying specific influentials who could impact Harotonian's situation, particularly the Ayatollah, the president of Iran, religious clerics, U.S. diplomats, and governmental officials around the world. Concerns expressed through the campaign gave Harotonian a voice. The highest profile advocate was Harotonian's former cellmate, journalist Roxana Saberi, who had endured a similarly unjust incarceration.

Tactics of the strategic plan included:

- An advocacy website as the core platform for Harotonian's "voice," with tracking tools to show massive global support
- Targeted international media, which demonstrated widespread support for Harotonian while maintaining a respectful tone toward Iran and downplaying U.S. connections
- Assisting in public and private diplomatic efforts to make personal appeals for Silva's release

Edelman's staff identified key Iranian and Armenian holidays and significant historical dates to time program pushes accordingly. The firm engaged and mobilized respected human rights advocates and organized a press conference and symbolic event at the Human Rights Esplanade in Paris in June 2009 to commemorate the one-year anniversary of Harotonian's detention.

Results from the pointed tactics were impressive. Many influential appeals were made to Iranian leaders against a backdrop of media coverage from top-tier outlets that included the Associated Press, Reuters, *USA Today,* CNN, and Fox News. Coverage of the Paris event was aired in Tehran, a media market known for its heavy censorship of anything thought critical of the regime. The website was such a successful advocacy tool that Iranian officials stipulated its removal as a condition of Harotonian's freedom. After three months of private negotiations and 11 months into her three-year sentence, Harotonian was paroled from Evin prison. In March 2010, she was allowed to leave Iran.

1 Edelman opted for the more accommodative stance of negotiation and compromise. How did this stance shape the strategy of the campaign?

2 Would you have taken a stronger advocacy approach if you were leading this campaign?

Competing
Litigation
Public Relations
Arguing
Competition
Contending
Compromising
Avoiding
Cooperation
Collaborating
Negotiation
Compromise
Capitulation
Apology and Restitution

CONTINGENCY CONTINUUM

ADVOCACY

ACCOMMODATION

When it was claimed that used syringes were found in cans of Pepsi, the company took the stance that such claims were a hoax and stood 100 percent behind its product, resisting suggestions that a product recall was needed.

When videos of its kitchen workers stuffing shredded cheese up their noses went viral on the web, Dominos faced damage to its 50-year-old brand as a Twitter storm ensued. Using the same social media channels its employees had used to besmirch its good name, Dominos swiftly apologized and took corrective actions that restored its solid reputation.

Pure advocacy is a hard-nosed stance of completely disagreeing with or refuting the arguments, claims, or threats of a competitor or a group concerned about an issue. The other extreme on this continuum is pure accommodation. In accommodation, the organization agrees with its critics, changes its policies, makes restitution, and even makes a full public apology for its actions. Of course, there are other stances in between these two extremes. The continuum shows the dynamism of strategic conflict management. In many cases, an organization initially adopts a pure advocacy stance, but as the situation changes, new information comes to light, and public opinion shifts, the stance changes toward more accommodation, provided such a move does not violate deeply held principles.

THE CONFLICT MANAGEMENT
Life Cycle

Successful public relations professionals serve as more than communication technicians carrying out the tactics of organizing events, writing news releases, handling news conferences, and pitching stories to journalists. They also take on the responsibility within the organization for managing conflict and weathering the crisis situations inevitably faced by all organizations at one time or another.

The conflict management life cycle illustrates the "big picture" of how to manage a conflict. Strategic conflict management can be divided into four general phases, but bear in mind that the lines between the phases are not absolute, and that some techniques overlap in actual practice. Furthermore, in the exciting world of public relations, busy practitioners may be actively managing different competitive situations as well as conflicts in each of the four phases simultaneously.

Proactive Phase
The proactive phase of the conflict management life cycle includes activities and thought processes that

The CONFLICT MANAGEMENT LIFE CYCLE

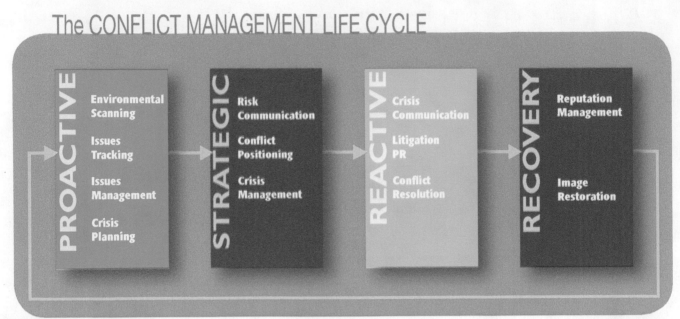

This figure shows the four phases of the conflict management life cycle and numerous techniques that public relations people use to deal with conflict. Typically, events move through time from left to right along the life cycle. At the end of the cycle, the process begins all over again.

can prevent a conflict from arising or from getting out of hand. The first step in the proactive phase is *environmental scanning*—the constant reading, listening, and watching of current affairs with an eye toward the organization's interests. As new issues emerge, *issues tracking* becomes more focused and systematic through processes such as blog monitoring and daily news story scanning. *Issues management* occurs when the organization makes behavioral changes or creates strategic plans to address emerging issues. In the proactive phase, well-run organizations also develop a general *crisis plan* as a first step in preparing for the worst—an issue or an event that escalates to crisis proportions.

Strategic Phase

In the strategic phase of the life cycle, an emerging conflict is identified as meriting action by the public relations professional. Three broad strategies are undertaken in the strategic phase. Through *risk communication*, dangers or threats to people or organizations are conveyed to forestall personal injury,

health problems, and environmental damage. *Conflict positioning* strategies enable the organization to situate itself favorably in anticipation of actions such as litigation, boycott, adverse legislation, elections, or similar events that will play out in "the court of public opinion." To be prepared for the worst outcome—that is, an issue that resists risk communication efforts and becomes a conflict of crisis proportions—a specific *crisis management* plan is developed.

Reactive Phase

Once the issue or imminent conflict reaches a critical level of impact on the organization, the public relations professional must react to events as they unfold in the external communication environment. *Crisis communication* includes the implementation of the crisis management plan as well as 24/7 efforts to meet the needs of publics such as disaster victims, employees, government officials, and the media. When conflict has emerged but is not careening out of control, *conflict resolution* techniques are used

to bring a heated conflict—such as collapsed salary negotiations—to a favorable resolution. Often, the most intractable conflicts end up in the courts. *Litigation public relations* employs communication strategies and publicity efforts in support of legal actions or trials.

think Is the job of public relations finished once a conflict has been resolved?

Recovery Phase

In the aftermath of a crisis or a high-profile, heated conflict with a public, an organization employs strategies to bolster or repair its reputation. *Reputation management* includes conducting systematic research to learn the state of the organization's reputation and then taking steps to improve it. When the damage is extreme, *image restoration* strategies can help, provided the organization is willing to undergo genuine change.

MANAGING THE Life Cycle
OF A CONFLICT

Although challenging, conflict management is not impossible. Four systematic processes that correspond to the four phases of the conflict management life cycle provide guidance and structure for this highly rewarding role played by public relations professionals: (1) *issues management* in the proactive phase, (2) *strategic positioning and risk communication* in the strategic phase, (3) *crisis communication* in the reactive phase, and (4) *reputation management* in the recovery phase.

think How can early issue identification help prevent a crisis?

Issues Management

Identifying and dealing with issues in a timely manner is one of the more important functions of the proactive phase of the conflict management life cycle. Issues management is a systematic approach to predicting problems, anticipating threats, minimizing surprises, resolving issues, and preventing crises.

Issues management is proactive planning. Writing in *Public Relations Review*, Philip Gaunt and Jeff Ollenburger say, "Issues management is proactive in that it tries to identify issues and influence decisions regarding them before they have a detrimental effect on a corporation." Gaunt and Ollenburger contrast the issues management approach with crisis management, which is essentially reactive in nature. They note, "Crisis management tends to be more reactive, dealing with an issue after it becomes public knowledge and affects the company." Active planning and prevention through

issues management often mean the difference between a noncrisis and a crisis—or, as one practitioner put it, the difference between little or no news coverage and a front-page headline. This point is particularly relevant because studies have shown that the majority of organizational crises are self-inflicted, in that management ignored early warning signs.

With appropriate handling, issues and situations can be managed or even forestalled by public relations professionals before they become crises, or before they lead to significant losses for the organization, such as a diminished reputation, alienation of key stakeholders, and financial damage to the organization.

Strategic Positioning and Risk Communication

Strategic positioning is any verbal or written exchange that attempts to communicate information to position the organization favorably regarding competition or an anticipated conflict. Ideally, the public relations professional communicates in a way that not only positions the organization favorably in the face of competition and imminent conflict, but also favorably influences the actual behavior of the organization. For example, a handful of state governments have mounted challenges to President Obama's health care mandate, arguing that the legislation co-opts states' rights. Both political parties have staked out positions in the health care debate, and health care providers/insurance companies have also strategically positioned themselves in anticipation of Supreme Court decisions that could trigger major public debate or even outrage.

Often public relations professionals can communicate in ways that

> **Effective issues management requires two-way communications, formal environmental scanning, and active sense-making strategies.**
>
> Martha Lauzen, San Diego State University

reduce risks for affected publics and for their employers. Communicating about risks to public health and safety and the environment is a particularly important role for public relations professionals in the strategic phase.

Organizations, including large corporations, are increasingly engaging in risk communication to inform the public of risks such as those associated with food products, chemical spills, radioactive waste disposal, or the placement of drug abuse treatment centers or halfway houses in neighborhoods. These issues deserve public notice in fairness to the general populace. In addition, expensive lawsuits, restrictive

think Is it an organization's responsibility to warn consumers of risks that may occur naturally, such as beach undertows and riptides near a hotel beach?

legislation, consumer boycotts, and public debate may result if organizations fail to disclose potential hazards. As is often the case, doing the right thing in conflict management often proves the least disruptive tactic in the long run. When risk communication fails, however, an organization may face a true crisis.

Crisis Communication

In public relations, high-profile events such as accidents, terrorist attacks, disease pandemics, and natural disasters can dwarf the effectiveness of even the best strategic positioning and risk management strategies. This is when crisis management takes over. The conflict management process, which includes ongoing issues management and risk communication efforts, is severely tested during crisis situations when a high degree of uncertainty exists. Unfortunately, even the most thoughtfully designed conflict management process cannot prepare an organization to deal with certain crises, such as planes flying into the World Trade Center. And sometimes, even when risk communication is employed to prevent an issue from evolving into a major problem, that issue will grow into a crisis. At such times, verifiable information about what is happening or has happened may be lacking.

Uncertainty causes people to become more active seekers of information and, research suggests, more dependent on the media for information to satisfy the human desire for closure. A crisis situation, in other words, puts a great deal of pressure on organizations to respond with complete and accurate information as quickly as possible.

Smoldering Crises. Crises are not always unexpected. One study by the Institute for Crisis Management found that only 14 percent of business crises were unexpected. The remaining 86 percent were what the institute called "smoldering crises," in which an organization was aware of a potential business disruption long before the public found out about it. The study

SUGGESTIONS
FOR COMMUNICATORS

Suzanne Zoda, writing on risk communication in *Communication World,* gives the following suggestions to communicators:

- **Begin early and initiate a dialogue.**

  Do not wait until the opposition marshals its forces. Early contact with anyone who may be concerned or affected is vital to establishing trust.

- **Actively solicit and identify concerns.**

  Informal discussions, surveys, interviews, and focus groups are effective in evaluating issues and identifying outrage factors.

- **Recognize the public as a legitimate partner in the process.**

  Engage interested groups in two-way communication and involve key opinion leaders.

- **Address issues of concern, even if they do not directly pertain to the situation.**

- **Anticipate and prepare for hostility.**

  To defuse a situation, use a conflict resolution approach. Identify areas of agreement and work toward common ground.

- **Understand the needs of the news media.**

  Provide accurate, timely information and respond promptly to requests.

- **Always be honest, even when it hurts.**

How an organization responds in the first 24 hours, experts say, often determines whether the situation remains an "incident" or becomes a full-blown crisis.

also found that management—or in some cases, mismanagement—caused 78 percent of the crises.

"Most organizations have a crisis plan to deal with sudden crises, like accidents," says Robert B. Irvine, president of the Institute. "However, our data indicates many businesses are denying or ducking serious problems that eventually will ignite and cost them millions of dollars and lost management time."

Echoing Irvine's thought, another study by Steven Fink found that 89 percent of the chief executive officers of *Fortune* 500 companies reported that a business crisis was almost inevitable; however, 50 percent admitted that they did not have a crisis management plan. This situation has prompted crisis consultant Kenneth Myers to write, "If economics is the dismal science, then contingency planning is the abysmal science." With proper issues management and conflict planning, many smoldering crises could potentially be prevented from bursting into flames.

How various organizations respond to crises. Recent research has shown that organizations don't all respond to crises in the same way. W. Timothy Coombs of Eastern Illinois University lists the following crisis communication strategies that organizations may use:

- *Attack the Accuser*—The party that claims a crisis exists is confronted and its logic and facts

> **"When people believe that because nothing has gone wrong, nothing will go wrong, they court disaster. There is noise in every system and every design. If this fact is ignored, nature soon reminds us of our folly."**
> Donald Chisholm and Martin Landry

are faulted; sometimes the organization threatens a lawsuit.

- *Denial*—The organization explains that there is no crisis.
- *Excuse*—The organization minimizes its responsibility for the crisis by denying any intention to do harm and saying that it had no control over the events that led to the crisis. This strategy is often used when a natural disaster or product tampering occurs.
- *Justification*—The crisis is minimized with a statement that no serious damage or injuries resulted. Sometimes, the blame is shifted to the victims. This is often done when a consumer misuses a product or when an industrial accident occurs.
- *Ingratiation*—The organization acts to appease the public involved. Consumers who

b t w ...
What Is a Crisis?

Kathleen Fearn-Banks, in her book *Crisis Communications: A Casebook Approach,* defines a crisis as a "major occurrence with a potentially negative outcome affecting the organization, company, or industry as well as its publics, products, services, or good name." In other words, an organizational crisis can constitute any number of situations. A *PRWeek* article included "a product recall; a plane crash; a very public sexual harassment suit; a gunman holding hostages in your office; an *E. coli* bacteria contamination scare; a market crash, along with the worth of your company stock; a labor union strike; [and] a hospital mal-practice suit" in its list of crisis scenarios.

Cantaloupes from Colorado were condemned as the source of a New Mexico listeriosis outbreak in 2011.

complain are given coupons or the organization makes a donation to a charitable organization.

- *Corrective Action*—The organization takes steps to repair the damage from the crisis and to prevent it from happening again.
- *Full Apology*—The organization takes responsibility and asks forgiveness. Some compensation of money or aid is often included.

The Coombs typology gives options for crisis communication management depending on the situation and the stance taken by the organization. As Coombs notes, organizations do have to consider more accommodative strategies (ingratiation, corrective action, full apology) if defensive strategies (attack accuser, denial, excuse) are not effective. The more accommodative strategies not only meet immediate crisis communication demands but can also help to subsequently repair an organization's reputation or restore previous sales levels.

Often, however, an organization doesn't adopt an accommodative strategy because of corporate culture and other constraints included in the contingency theory of conflict management matrix. Organizations do not, and sometimes cannot, engage in two-way communication and accommodative strategies when confronted with a crisis or conflict with a given public. In some cases, the contingency theory contends that the ideal of mutual understanding and accommodation doesn't occur because both sides have staked out highly rigid positions and are not willing to compromise their strong moral positions. Taking such an inflexible stance can be a foolish strategy and a sign of lack of professionalism.

At other times, conflict is a natural state between competing interests, such as oil interests seeking to open Alaskan wildlife refuges to oil exploration and environmental groups seeking to block that exploration. Frequently, one's stance and strategies for conflict management entail assessment and balancing of many factors.

Reputation Management

Reputation is the collective representation of an organization's past performance that describes the firm's ability to deliver valued outcomes to multiple stakeholders. Put in plain terms, reputation is the track record of an organization in the public's mind.

The three foundations of reputation. Reputation scholars describe the three foundations of reputation as (1) economic performance, (2) social responsiveness, and (3) the ability to deliver valuable outcomes to stakeholders. Public relations plays a role in all three, but professionals who manage conflict effectively will especially enhance the latter two. The social responsiveness of an organization results from careful issues tracking and effective positioning of the organization. Social responsiveness is further enhanced when risk communication is compelling and persuasive. The ability to make valuable contributions to stakeholders who depend on the organization results in part from the organization's ability to fend off threats that might impair its mission.

In addition to tracking and dealing proactively with issues, conveying risks to publics, and managing crises as they arise, public relations practitioners need to apologize at those times when all

 think Which factors determine how effective an apology is?

Public relations scholar Lisa Lyon makes the point that **reputation,** unlike corporate image, **is owned by the public.** Reputation isn't formed by packaging or slogans. A good reputation is created and destroyed by everything an organization does, from the way it manages employees to the way it handles conflicts with outside constituents.

efforts to manage conflict have fallen short. The future trust and credibility of the organization are at stake, based on how well this recovery phase of conflict management is handled.

The frequent platitude in post-crisis communication is that practitioners should acknowledge failings, apologize, and then put the events in the past as quickly as possible. In reality, public relations scholar Lisa Lyon has found that apology is not always effective because of the hypocrisy factor. When an organization has a questionable track record (i.e., a bad reputation), the apology may be viewed as insincere and

"I'm honored that @MicheleBachmann was on our show yesterday and I'm so sorry about the intro mess. I really hope she comes back," a Tweet from late night talk show host Jimmy Fallon after his house band played Fishbone's "Lyin' *ss Bit**" as presidential hopeful Michele Bachmann took the stage. Despite political and feminist furor, the apology forestalled crisis. The band was "grounded" by Fallon.

Social Media and the BP Oil Spill Crisis

The explosion aboard BP's Deepwater Horizon drilling rig in the Gulf of Mexico in April 2010 set off a chain reaction that resulted in the deaths of 11 workers, the largest ocean oil spill in history, and threats to the environmental and economic viability of the American Gulf Coast region. Needless to say, the spill dominated U.S. news coverage for several months. Everything that BP said and did mattered; especially since this was just the most recent transgression in a line of BP safety violations.

While BP was heavily criticized for how it managed its public relations problems in general, its use of social media received strong public relations industry praise for communicating a central narrative that BP cares, explaining its commitment to the Gulf coast region, communicating remorse for the damage, and defending its efforts to respond to the spill.

Researchers at Marist College and Nanyang Technological University reviewed all of BP's online press releases, Facebook posts, and Twitter tweets throughout the five-month crisis. They concluded that BP's public relations response in social media was coordinated and positive, although it was still found wanting in some ways.

BP used different social media tools to strategically address different aspects of the company's central narrative touting BP's positive response to the disaster. Typical Facebook posts highlighted people, programs, and events. Twitter was employed differently. Though still emphasizing a positive identity, typically BP tweets emphasized status updates on the leak and cleanup efforts and defended criticisms of its leaders and actions. BP's social media response was synchronized, but the company used different social media to communicate different parts of the story.

BP's response also demonstrated another challenge in bridging the gap between social media and public opinion—if the messages do not go viral, the social media effort is not likely to have a strong positive impact on public opinion. Though BP seemed to have communicated all of the "right" messages in its social media effort, Pew Research found that the spill story generated considerably less attention on blogs, Twitter, and YouTube than it needed to go viral.

BP pressed all the right social media buttons but did not evoke an e-wom, or electronic word-of-mouth, spread of its messages. Perhaps netizens did not "buy" the BP narrative. Or perhaps if the BP postings had been edgier or more moving, the narrative would have moved spontaneously to vast audiences. What do *you* think?

Source: Audra Diers (Marist College), Augustine Pang (Nanyang Technological University, Singapore), Jennie Donohue (Marist College).

Examples of Typical BP Facebook Posts

From June 30, 2010
The health and safety of those involved with the cleanup efforts is a top priority. BP has been working with the U.S. Department of Labor's Occupational Safety and Health Administration (OSHA) in distributing thousands of safety guides and fact sheets to employees involved with the oil spill cleanup.

From July 12, 2010
Wildlife rescue leader Ken Rice returned from brief retirement to oversee efforts to rescue and rehabilitate animals. After a career lasting three decades, Rice moved to Alabama but didn't settle long, joining the relief effort as a branch director in three Gulf states. Despite uncertainty in the region, Rice is steadfast: "I know we are going to recover from this."

From July 12, 2010
Want to know more about BP's claims process? Watch as BP's Darryl Willis provides more information about the process, the improvements that will be made in the future, and what BP is doing to "get money out the door as quickly as possible, especially for businesses" in the video below. For more information on the claims process, please visit: http://www.bp.com/claims.

Examples of Typical BP Tweets

From August 23, 2010:
Alert: The last 862 square miles of fishing waters in Louisiana have reopened to recreational fishing.

From June 4, 2010
BP takes full responsibility for responding to #oilspill and will compensate for all legitimate claims.

From May 25, 2010
BP is committed to openness and transparency in our response to the #oilspill in the Gulf of Mexico.

hypocritical. Coombs suggests a relational approach, which assumes that crises are episodes within a larger stakeholder–organizational relationship. Determining how stakeholders perceive the situation can help communicators determine which strategy is best to rebuild the stakeholder–organization relationship and restore the organization's reputation.

Image restoration. Reputation repair and maintenance is a long-term process, but one of the first steps in the recovery process is the final one in the conflict management life cycle. The image restoration strategy that an organization chooses depends a great deal on the situation, or what has already been described as the "it depends" concept. If an organization is truly innocent, a simple denial is a good strategy. Not many situations are that black and white, however. Consequently, a more common strategy is acknowledging the issue, but making it clear that the situation was an accident or the result of a decision with unintentional consequences. Professor William Benoit of Ohio State University calls this approach the strategy of "evading" responsibility.

Another strategy for restoring an organization's reputation relies on reducing offensiveness. Ultimately, the most accommodative response is a profuse apology by the organization to the public and its various stakeholders.

Despite the public relations practitioner's best efforts, the chosen strategy or combination of strategies may not necessarily restore the organization's reputation. A great deal depends on the perceptions of the public and other stakeholders. Do they find the explanation credible? Do they believe the organization is telling the truth? Do they think the organization is acting in the public interest? In many cases, an organization may start out with a defensive strategy only to find that the situation ultimately demands corrective action or an apology.

What Would You Do?

Adversarial or Accommodative?

This chapter points out that public relations professionals can influence the larger goals of an organization through litigation public relations by addressing the marketplace of ideas that revolves around lawsuits and court proceedings. Sometimes the litigation hinges on momentous questions facing society. For example, controversies exist about the legal rights surrounding the patenting of life forms developed in labs. These life forms can be specialized plants or biopharmaceuticals—or potentially in the future, nano-creatures that will carry out medical procedures inside the human body.

The *Fortune* 500 company Monsanto is alternately demonized or glorified for its agricultural breakthroughs in patenting plant seeds that increase production, tolerate drought, or resist herbicides. Monsanto has invested enormous amounts in developing a soybean plant that enables farmers to kill weeds (using a pesticide from Monsanto called Roundup) without harming the food plant itself. Less tilling is required and harvests are higher—but of course, there is a catch.

Traditionally, farmers have kept some of their crop to serve as seed for the coming year. This practice is a violation of Monsanto's patent requiring new seed to be purchased each season. To protect its patent, the company has filed suit against small farmers and businesses that reseed with its Roundup-Ready soybeans rather than purchasing new seed. (The fascinating documentary film *Food Inc.* puts a very human face on this litigation.)

Monsanto's decision to sue—undoubtedly a difficult one for a corporate giant that operates globally and claims to be a key player in the battle to end worldwide hunger—has served as a lightning rod for media coverage and contentious discussion. The company is taking an advocacy stance in the courts in defense of its right to protect its (expensively developed) intellectual property. Naturally, the publisher of this textbook would not want a small bookstore to buy one copy, photocopy it, and sell the copies to hundreds of students each semester. But does the same hold for copying (growing) a plant?

In what ways does the adversarial stance taken by Monsanto shape its communication strategies? Draft a proposal for a campaign to address the issues that the company's stance necessitates. Discuss with your classmates how a movement on the continuum toward a more accommodative stance might cause you to revise your campaign.

Déjà Vu—All Over Again

To paraphrase Yogi Berra, conflict management is like déjà vu all over again. After a crisis, the best organizations, led by the best public relations professionals, will strive to improve performance by starting once again at the beginning of the conflict management life cycle, with tasks such as environmental scanning and issues tracking. Issues that are deemed important receive attention for crisis planning and risk communication. When preventive measures fail, the crisis must be handled with the best interests of all parties considered in a delicate balance. Then restoration and burnishing of the organization's reputation must be given due attention. At all times, the goal is to change organizational behavior in ways that minimize damaging conflict, not only for the sake of the organization, but also for its many stakeholders.

summary

What Role Do Competition and Conflict Play in Public Relations?

- Public relations can be defined as strategic management of competition and conflict.

- Some of the most crucial roles played by public relations professionals involve the strategic management of conflict.

What Factors Affect the Stance That an Organization Takes During Conflict Management?

- The outstanding practitioner monitors for threats, assesses those threats, arrives at a desirable stance for the organization, and then begins communication efforts from that stance.

What Are the Phases of the Conflict Management Life Cycle?

- Strategic conflict management is broadly divided into four phases. Specific techniques and functions are part of each phase: the proactive phase, the strategic phase, the reactive phase, and the recovery phase.

How Can Public Relations Professionals Best Manage the Conflict Management Life Cycle?

- Issues management is a proactive and systematic approach to predicting problems, anticipating threats, minimizing surprises, resolving issues, and preventing crises.

- Risk communication attempts to convey information regarding concerns about public health and safety and the environment.

- One of an organization's most valuable assets is its reputation, which is influenced by how the organization deals with conflict, and particularly crises that generate significant media attention.

questions
FOR REVIEW AND DISCUSSION

1 Do you accept the proposition that conflict management is one of the most important functions of public relations? Why or why not?

2 How can effective issues management prevent organizational crises?

3 How would you apply what you have learned in this chapter about the contingency theory of conflict management (the continuum from accommodation to advocacy) in advising management on a rising conflict situation?

4 Do you think that image restoration is merely a superficial fix or a substantive solution to adverse events? Support your view with some examples from current news stories.

5 What are the phases of the conflict management life cycle?

6 Why are the first 24 hours after a crisis so crucial in public relations?

7 Consider the Monsanto case discussed in the *Apply Your Knowledge* feature in this chapter. Why would lawyers benefit from working closely with public relations counsel? For litigation? For dispute resolution through effective negotiation?

Photo Credits

Credits are listed in order of appearance.

DK Images;
Michael R. Sisak/Icon SMI 254/Newscom;
Archie Carpenter/UPI/Newscom;
Paul Buck/AFP/Newscom;

ZUMA Wire Service/Alamy;
(cr) Nelson Hancock/DK Images; (cl) Alex Staroseltsev/Shutterstock;
Wostok Press/MAXPPP/Newscom;

AP Photo/Carolyn Kaster;
Digitalreflections/Shutterstock;
Jim McKinley/Alamy;
qingqing/Shutterstock

Tablet image: Falconia/Shutterstock

Ethics and
the Law

From Chapter 9 of *Think Public Relations*, 2013 Edition. Dennis L. Wilcox, Glen T. Cameron, Bryan H. Reber, Jae-Hwa Shin.

Ethics and the Law

Helping a Tyrant Burnish his Image

After the late Libyan leader Muammar Gaddafi renounced terrorism and expressed a desire to rejoin the international community in the mid-2000s, there was cautious optimism in the international community that this tyrant was changing. It was in this context that Monitor Group, a Boston-based consulting group with offices in 26 cities worldwide, engaged in a relationship with Gaddafi and the Libyan government. In 2011, Monitor described its work for the Libyan government between 2006 and 2008 as focusing on "economic development [and] the training of hundreds of high-potential leaders ... to enable processes of reform."

Some thought this behind-the-scenes work was lobbying. For example, Libya paid Monitor Group $250,000 a month to, among other things, identify and introduce "thought leaders" to Muammar Gaddafi. Some of these thought leaders then returned to the U.S. and wrote opinion pieces praising Gaddafi and Libya that were published in several U.S. newspapers and magazines.

While Monitor Group eventually registered as a lobbying firm in 2011 (lobbying groups are required to register with the U.S. government according to FARA, the Foreign Agent Registration Act), the *Boston Globe* reported that the group's original failure to register reflected "a deeper problem: The company was not transparent about the fact that it was engaged in a calculated effort to burnish Gaddafi's reputation, even to professors recruited in the effort."

A lawyer for Monitor Group argued that the firm did not see its work for Libya and Gaddafi as public relations, but as management consulting. The intention of the "Project to Enhance the Profile of Libya and Muammar Gaddafi" was to introduce Gaddafi to famous intellectuals to "enhance understanding and appreciation for Libya" and portray Gaddafi "as a thinker and intellectual." The *New York Times* reported a related story about the Libyan leader's family and the London School of Economics after reports surfaced that Seif al-Islam Gaddafi, son of the dictator, may have plagiarized the doctoral dissertation he wrote at the school. Monitor Group eventually acknowledged that part of its $250,000 monthly retainer included helping Seif al-Islam Gaddafi with his dissertation.

Lionel Beehner wrote in *USA Today*, "Nation-branding, of course, is a big business. Each year, countries dole out billions of dollars to tidy up their images abroad .... [I]t should come as no surprise that many of them with cash lying around employ lobbyists, PR flacks and even academics to manipulate public opinion and burnish their democratic credentials."

1 What ethical and legal issues can you identify in this case?

2 Is it right or wrong to "manipulate public opinion"? Is that what public relations does when it raises awareness about a product or service?

Ask Yourself

> Why Is Ethics a Relevant Issue for Public Relations Practitioners?

> What Do Public Relations Professionals Need to Know About Defamation, Employee and Privacy Rights, Copyright, and Trademark Laws?

> Which Guidelines and Government Agencies Govern the Commercial Speech Used by Public Relations Professionals?

> How Can Public Relations Professionals Facilitate Good Working Relationships with Lawyers?

WHAT IS **Ethics?**

Today's public relations practitioners are faced with myriad ethical dilemmas and legal issues. A well-prepared professional must be ready to deal effectively with these issues. In this chapter, we examine some of the ethical concerns and legal issues facing public relations practitioners.

A person's conduct is measured not only against his or her conscience, but also against some norm of acceptability that is determined by society, professional groups, or even a person's employer. The difficulty in ascertaining whether an act is ethical lies in the fact that individuals have different standards and perceptions of what is "right" or "wrong." Most ethical conflicts are not black-or-white issues, but rather fall into a gray area.

Because public relations practitioners serve as advocates for their organizations or clients and yet also must strive to represent the interests of various stakeholders in their organizations, difficult ethical issues are bound to arise. Students, as well as public relations critics, are often concerned about whether a public relations practitioner can ethically communicate at the same time he or she is serving as an advocate for a particular client or organization. To some, traditional ethics prohibits a person from assuming an advocacy role because in that role a person is "biased" and trying to "manipulate" people.

David L. Martinson of Florida International University makes the point, however, that the concept of

> "When public relations professionals fall short of the ideals of responsible advocacy, they threaten practitioner autonomy and may pave the way for heightened legal regulation of public relations work."
>
> Kathy Fitzpatrick and Carolyn Bronstein, in *Ethics in Public Relations: Responsible Advocacy*

When Worlds **Collide**

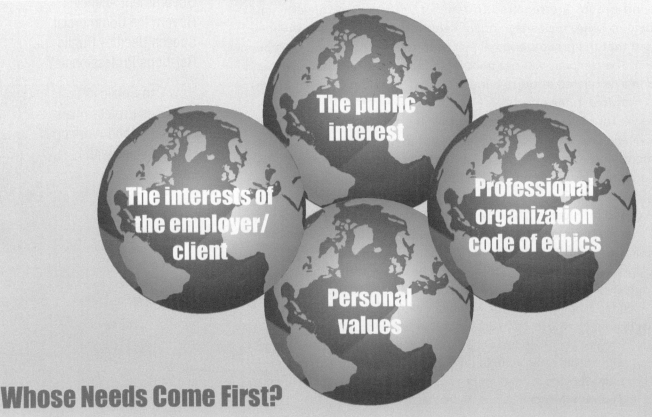

The public interest

The interests of the employer/ client

Personal values

Professional organization code of ethics

Whose Needs Come First?

role differentiation is important. Society, in general, expects public relations people to be advocates, just as they expect advertising copywriters to make a product sound attractive, journalists to be objective, and attorneys to defend someone in court. Because of such expectations, Martinson believes that "Public relations practitioners are justified in disseminating persuasive information so long as objective and reasonable persons would view those persuasive efforts as truthful." Some public relations theorists have argued that pure advocacy—that is, unwavering support for the organization's or client's position—is unethical. They suggest that the most ethical way to practice public relations is to consider accommodating the needs of both organizations and their publics.

Contingency theory takes a more nuanced view. From this perspective, public relations practitioners sometimes face a categorical imperative, or moral obligation, to advocate purely for the organization's position. For example, what would the ethical advocate representing the cattle industry do when faced with demands from People for the Ethical Treatment of Animals (PETA) to stop producing beef products? Would the ethical advocate—a person who works for the cattle industry because he or she believes in modern agriculture's role

think When is it the moral obligation of a public relations professional to advocate purely for a client's position, even in the face of opposition?

WHAT WOULD YOU DO if you were asked to keep news about a planned layoff from your coworkers?

WHAT IF YOUR SUPERVISOR asked you to defend your company's questionable environmental practices?

WHAT IF YOUR CLIENT asked you to make positive, but unsubstantiated, claims about a new product?

Ethics and the Law

in feeding the world—attempt to find ways to accommodate PETA's demands? Or would he or she continue to purely advocate for cattle-raising clients? Instances frequently arise when conflict between an organization and its publics is unavoidable due to a clash of worldviews. To accommodate the demands of a public, such as PETA, would be unethical when a categorical moral imperative to advocate for your organization or client drives your professional decisions.

Professional GUIDELINES

Professional organizations such as the Public Relations Society of America (PRSA) and the International Association of Business Communicators (IABC) have standards for ethical, professional public relations practice and have worked to help society understand the role of public relations. Practitioners and public relations scholars alike suggest that professional organizations can play a key and powerful role in advancing ethical practice.

Codes of Conduct

Nearly every national public relations organization has developed a code of ethics, and the codes of such organizations as the Canadian Public Relations Society (CPRS), the Public Relations Institute of Southern Africa (PRISA), and the Public Relations Institute of Australia (PRIA) are very similar to the PRSA code (see box below). Most national organizations place heavy emphasis on educating their members on professional standards rather

HOW TO SAY "NO" AND KEEP YOUR JOB

The Plank Center for Leadership in Public Relations hosted a panel of PR ethics experts to discuss teaching ethics. Bruce Berger, a professor at the University of Alabama, home of The Plank Center, summarized the experts' suggestions in *PRWeek*.

He cited six ways to "say 'no' to a boss or executive who asks you to do something unethical and still keep your job":

► Use and cite the Public Relations Society of America code of ethics as a framework for responding to unethical requests.

► Point to your organization's own stated values.

► Let your boss know what the headlines might say if the unethical behavior is discovered.

► Use the point of view of the affected public to make a rational or emotional appeal.

► Get others in your organization to join you in saying "no."

► Note cases in which other organizations behaved similarly and highlight any negative outcomes.

► Public relations professionals are often faced with ethical dilemmas. They should be prepared to check their personal moral compass and professional ethics code when they're asked to misbehave.

PRSA CODE OF ETHICS

The Public Relations Society of America (PRSA) has a fairly comprehensive code of ethics for its members. The group believes that "professional values are vital to the integrity of the profession as a whole." Its six core values are as follows:

1 ADVOCACY: Serving the public interest by acting as responsible advocates for clients or employers.

2 HONESTY: Adhering to the highest standards of accuracy and truth in advancing the interests of clients and employers.

3 EXPERTISE: Advancing the profession through continued professional development, research, and education.

4 INDEPENDENCE: Providing objective counsel and being accountable for individual actions.

5 LOYALTY: Being faithful to clients and employers, but also honoring an obligation to serve the public interest.

6 FAIRNESS: Respecting all opinions and supporting the right of free expression.

Specific provisions within the code call for the following: maintaining a free flow of information; being honest when critiquing competitors; disclosing important information to key publics as soon as possible; maintaining client confidences; acknowledging and avoiding potential conflicts of interest; and enhancing the profession by providing trustworthy information.

Ethics begins with the individual. To what extent, if any, would you compromise your personal beliefs in the course of doing your job?

conducts workshops on ethics, and encourages chapters to include discussions of ethics in their local programs.

Critics complain that such codes of ethics "have no teeth" because there's really no punishment for being unethical and unprofessional. Even if a practitioner is expelled from the organization, he or she can continue to work in the public relations field.

Problems with code enforcement are not unique to public relations groups, of course. Professional organizations, including the Society for Professional Journalists, are voluntary organizations, and they lack the legal authority to ban members from the field because no license is required to practice. Such organizations run a high risk of being sued for defamation or restricting the First Amendment guarantee of free speech if they try to expel members or restrict their occupations.

Consequently, most professional groups believe that the primary purpose of establishing codes of ethics is not enforcement, but rather education and information. They seek to enunciate standards of conduct that will guide members in their professional lives. This approach seems to work. Several studies have shown that the members of PRSA and other organizations have a much higher awareness of ethics and professional standards than nonmembers.

Ethics in Individual Practice

Even in light of codes of professional practice and formalized accreditation, ethics in public relations can boil down to deeply troubling questions for the individual practitioner: Would I lie for my employer? Would I rig a door-prize drawing so that a favorite client can win? Would I deceive someone to gain information about another agency's clients? Would I issue a news release presenting only half the truth? Would

than having a highly structured grievance process in place. They do exercise the right, however, to censure or expel members who violate the organization's code or who are convicted of a crime in a court of law.

The IABC's code is based on the principle that professional communication should be not only legal and ethical, but also in good taste and sensitive to cultural values and beliefs. Members are encouraged to be truthful, accurate, and fair in all of their communications.

The code is published in several languages, and IABC bylaws require that articles on ethics and professional conduct be published in the

 If a profession does not license its members, can it enforce ethical standards?

organization's monthly publication, *Communication World.* In addition, the organization includes sessions on ethics at its annual meeting,

I quit my job rather than cooperate in a questionable activity?

These and similar questions plague the lives of many public relations professionals. If employers make a suggestion that involves questionable ethics, the public relations person often can talk them out of the idea by citing the possible consequences of such an action—adverse media publicity, for example.

Adherence to professional standards of conduct is the chief measure of a public relations professional. Faced with such personal demands as mortgages to pay and children to educate, practitioners may be strongly tempted to become sycophants and decline to express their views forcefully to an employer, or to resign. But ethics in public relations really begins with the individual—and is directly related to his or her own value system as well as to the good of society. Although it is important to show loyalty to an employer, practitioners must never allow a client or an employer to rob them of their self-esteem.

DEALING WITH THE News Media

The most practical consideration facing a public relations specialist in his or her dealings with the news media is that anything less than total honesty will destroy credibility and, with it, the practitioner's usefulness to an employer.

Achieving trust is the aim of all practitioners, and trust can be earned only through highly professional and ethical behavior. Public relations practitioners should not undermine their relationship with members of the media by providing junkets of questionable merit, invitations to extravagant parties,

In the summer of 2011, investigators learned that *News of the World* reporters had hacked into the phone of a dead teenager, and had even deleted messages, which led the teen's parents and police to have hope that the girl was alive. There was also evidence suggesting that reporters or private investigators with whom they were working had hacked into the phones of relatives of British soldiers killed in Afghanistan and Iraq. All this was rumored to be done with the implicit permission of the newspaper's management.

Legal **HOT** Water

The law and its many ramifications can be somewhat abstract to the average person. Many people may have difficulty imagining exactly how public relations personnel can run afoul of the law or generate a lawsuit simply by communicating information. What follows is a sampling of recent government regulatory agency cases and lawsuits that involved public relations materials and the work of practitioners:

- Koch Industries filed a lawsuit when Internet pranksters affiliated with Youth for Climate Truth issued a news release attributed to the conglomerate suggesting that Koch Industries had changed its support of climate change research and advocacy. Koch sued for "damages for the cost of responding to the fake release, trademark infringement, cybersquatting and legal expenses in pursuing the pranksters," according to *Suffolk Media Law* journal.

- The U.S. Justice Department investigated Merck & Co., a global pharmaceutical company, to determine whether Merck had engaged in criminal activity in the promotion and marketing of three of its drugs.

- ICU Medical sent a cease and desist order to TransMedia and its client RyMed Technologies, alleging that in promoting RyMed products, the PR firm was infringing on ICU Medical patents.

- Two interns who worked on the Oscar-nominated film *Black Swan* filed a class action lawsuit against Fox Searchlight Pictures. The lawsuit claimed that Fox improperly classified many employees as unpaid interns, thereby violating federal and state employment laws. The lawsuit sought millions of dollars in unpaid wages and overtime.

- A former employee of MSLGROUP and Publicis Groupe filed a $100 million class action lawsuit against her former employer for discrimination against female public relations employees. The lawsuit claimed, "Publicis's glass ceiling might as well be a cement wall. Gender discrimination permeates Publicis's entire PR practice."

Many of these charges were eventually dismissed or settled out of court, but the organizations likely paid dearly for the adverse publicity and the expense of defending themselves.

---

expensive gifts, or personal favors to media representatives. Gifts of any kind, according to PRSA, can contaminate the free flow of accurate and truthful information to the public.

Although it may be presumed that public relations representatives would benefit from being able to influence journalists with gifts or offers of paid advertising, this is not the case. A major selling point of public relations work is the third-party credibility of reporters and editors. The public trusts journalists to be objective and to be basically impartial in the dissemination of information. If the public loses that trust because they believe the media can be "bought," the information provided by public relations sources also becomes less trusted.

Transparency is another issue. Should a celebrity who mentions a product on a television talk show reveal that he or she is being paid by the company to endorse its product? Should tax dollars be spent on public relations? Should you reveal when you find your

organization has done something wrong? These questions often lie at the heart of real-world situations.

For example, when the management of the once venerable British newspaper *News of the World* was faced with allegations of cell phone and e-mail hacking in order to break news, it initially vociferously denied the charges.

The 168-year-old newspaper was one of the premier media properties owned by Rupert Murdoch's News Corporation, which also owns Fox Broadcasting, the *Wall Street Journal*, the *New York Post*, and the *Times* of London.

As early as 2006 there were accusations that reporters with the tabloid had hired private investigators to hack into the cell phones of members of the British monarchy. The arrests of an editor and a private investigator followed.

In July 2009, according to a report in the British newspaper *The Daily Telegraph*, "News of the World reporters, with the knowledge of senior staff, illegally accessed messages from the mobile phones of celebrities and politicians . . . from 2003 to 2007." *The Daily Telegraph* also reported that Murdoch newspapers paid out in excess of £1 million to settle cases in which journalists were accused of phone hacking.

Rupert Murdoch eventually intervened to first appoint a new managing editor and then to quickly announce the closing of the newspaper.

Managing editor of *PRWeek* Steve Barrett wrote: "And the whole drama was played out on Twitter, as advertisers communicated their decisions [to quit advertising with *News of the World*] to their publics and the rolling news story developed... As everyone in PR already knows, the lesson for media outlets is that trust and brand reputation is a fragile thing. In this age of conversation and interaction a lack of transparency is simply untenable."

 think How can gift giving undermine the credibility of a public relations professional?

PUBLIC RELATIONS AND **the Law**

Just as public relations practitioners deal with ethical quandaries on a regular basis, so, too, do they face issues that can get themselves or their clients into legal trouble. And oftentimes ethical and legal dilemmas go hand-in-hand. Depending on the field of practice, regulatory and legal demands can be a part of everyday life for a public relations professional. Globalization adds to the complexity of dealing with these demands. And in all fields of practice, public relations professionals often find themselves dealing with legal questions regarding copyright, privacy, liability, and other related issues.

On more than one occasion, the courts have ruled that public relations firms cannot hide behind the defense of "The client told me to do it." Public relations firms have a legal responsibility to practice "due diligence" in the type of information and documentation supplied by a client. Regulatory agencies such as the Federal Trade Commission have power under the Lanham Act to file charges against public relations firms that distribute false and misleading information.

Defamation

Public relations professionals must be thoroughly familiar with the concepts of libel and slander. Such knowledge is crucial if an organization's internal and external communications are to meet legal and regulatory standards with a minimum of legal complications.

Traditionally, *libel* was the term used for a printed falsehood and

think Why are corporations considered "public figures" by the courts in cases involving defamation?

slander was the term used for an oral statement that was false. Today, as a practical matter, there is little difference in the two, and the courts often use *defamation* as a collective term for these types of offenses. Essentially, defamation is making a false statement about a person (or organization) that creates public hatred, contempt, or ridicule, or inflicts injury on reputation.

Private citizens usually have more success winning defamation suits than do public figures or corporations. With public figures—government officials, entertainers, political candidates, and other newsworthy personalities—there is the extra test of whether the libelous statements were made with actual malice (*New York Times v. Sullivan*). *Actual malice* has been defined by the U.S. Supreme Court as making a libelous statement while knowing the information is false or

Twitter can lead to lawsuits. Rocker Courtney Love ranted about a fashion designer on Twitter, was sued, and settled out of court for $500,000. A Portland, Oregon, blogger critiqued a local physician. After her critique was linked to one tweet, the doctor filed a lawsuit against her for $1 million.

Ethics and the Law

Facebook Campaign Raises an Ethical Ruckus

THE HEADLINES IN THE *WALL STREET JOURNAL*, the *New York Times*, *USA Today* and countless online news websites said it all: "Facebook admits secret PR move to spawn bad press for Google," "Facebook waged stealth PR war on Google," and "Facebook unmasked as Burson-Marsteller's mystery client."

The stink was about Facebook hiring Burson-Marsteller (B-M), a major public relations firm, to plant articles and op-eds in the media that criticized the privacy policies of a new Google search feature, Social Circle. This assignment rapidly became an ethical quagmire when both the client and the public relations firm tried to hide the fact that Facebook was funding the campaign.

The so-called whisper campaign was launched by two B-M staffers who had been journalists. They contacted reporters at major publications and leading social network bloggers offering to provide (somewhat inaccurate) information and help them write opinion articles criticizing Google. When several suspicious bloggers asked them the name of their client, they refused to answer. It didn't take long for *USA Today* and the *Daily Beast* to figure out that B-M was engaging in a stealth campaign on behalf of Facebook.

The fallout was immediate. Many publications picked up the story, and it went viral. Facebook was severely criticized by leading tech bloggers for lack of transparency. Fraser Seitel, a public relations counselor in New York, told *Ragan's PR Daily*, "If Facebook has problems with Google, then it should have the confidence and decency to express the reasons why, from the mouth of a Facebook executive."

The public relations community also slammed B-M for agreeing to hide the fact that Facebook was its client. Rosanna Fiske, chair of the Public Relations Society of America (PRSA) wrote, "Under the PRSA code, B-M would be obligated to reveal its client and to disclose the client's intentions, which appear to mount to an attack on Google's practices." Steve Barrett, editor of *PRWeek* opined, "In not disclosing Facebook as its client, Burson engaged in activity that contravenes industry guidelines and is considered unethical."

Both Facebook and Burson-Marsteller sought to minimize the negative coverage by issuing statements. Facebook denied that the company had engaged in a "smear campaign" and said it was simply trying to bring what it believed was a problem with the Google product to the attention of reporters and privacy advocates. Burson-Marsteller executives issued a statement saying that it no longer represented Facebook and that the campaign "was not at all standard operating procedure and is against our policies." The statement continued, "We have talked through our policies and procedures with each individual involved in the program and have made it clear this cannot happen again." The firm also said it was redistributing its code of ethics to all employees.

PRSA chair Fiske best sums up the profession's black eye caused by the Facebook/B-M fiasco: "It's not that ethical public relations equals good public relations; it is, however, that those who do not practice ethical public relations affect all of us, regardless of the environment in which we work, and the causes we represent."

1. In what way did Burson-Marsteller violate the ethics of the profession?

2. What is a whisper campaign? Is it ethical? Is it legal?

3. Do you agree that incidents like these give the entire public relations profession a black eye?

---

publishing the information with "reckless disregard" as to whether it is false.

Corporations, to some degree, are also considered "public figures" by the courts for three reasons:

1. They engage in advertising and promotion offering products and services to the public.

2. They are often involved in matters of public controversy and public policy.

3. They have some degree of access to the media—through regular advertising and news releases—that enables them to respond and rebut defamatory charges made against them.

This is not to say that corporations cannot win lawsuits regarding defamation. In what is now an almost classic example, General Motors (GM) filed a multimillion-dollar defamation suit against NBC after the network's *Dateline* news program carried a story about gas tanks on GM pickup trucks exploding in side-impact collisions. In a news conference, GM's general counsel meticulously provided evidence that NBC had inserted toy rocket "igniters" in the gas tanks, understated the vehicle speed at the moment of impact, and wrongly claimed that the fuel tanks could be easily ruptured. Within 24 hours after the suit was filed, NBC caved in. It agreed to air a nine-minute apology on the news program and pay GM $2 million to cover the cost of its investigation.

Increasingly, corporations are also filing defamation suits against bloggers and even individuals who tweet about their businesses. A woman in Chicago, for example, was slapped with a $50,000 defamation suit after tweeting that a real estate company didn't do anything about her moldy apartment. The company claimed that the woman "maliciously and wrongfully

Prove It!

A person filing a libel suit usually must prove four things:

1. The false statement was communicated to others through print, broadcast, or electronic means.

2. The person claiming to be libeled was identified or identifiable.

3. There was actual injury in the form of money losses, loss of reputation, or mental suffering.

4. The person making the statement was malicious or negligent.

published the false and defamatory tweet on Twitter, thereby allowing the tweet to be distributed throughout the world."

Avoiding Libel Suits

Libel suits can be filed against organizational officials who make libelous accusations during a media interview, send out news releases that make false statements, or injure someone's reputation. For example, some executives have lived to regret that they lost control during a news conference and called the leaders of a labor union "a bunch of crooks and compulsive liars" and a news reporter "a pimp for all environmental groups."

Such language, although highly quotable and colorful, can provoke legal retaliation. Accurate information, and a delicate choice of words, must be used in all news releases. That's why it's common for a news release to state that an executive has left the company for "personal reasons" even if he or she may have been fired for incompetence or violation of company policies.

Another potentially dangerous practice is making unflattering comments about the competition's products. Although comparative advertising is the norm in the United States, companies walk a thin line between comparison and "trade libel," or "product disparagement." Statements should be truthful, with factual evidence and scientific data available to substantiate them. Companies often charge competitors with overstepping the boundary between "puffery" and "factual representation."

Employee COMMUNICATIONS

Public relations staff must be particularly sensitive to the issue of employee privacy and have a good understanding of employee rights and responsibilities as these topics relate to a number of legal and ethical issues.

For example, it is no longer true, if it ever was, that an organization has an unlimited right to publicize the activities of its employees in employee newsletters. In fact, according to Morton J. Simon, a

Philadelphia lawyer and author of *Public Relations Law*, "It should not be assumed that a person's status as an employee waives his right to privacy." Simon correctly points out that a company newsletter or magazine does not enjoy the same First Amendment protection as the news media enjoy when they claim "newsworthiness" and "public interest." A number of court cases, he says, show that company newsletters are considered

commercial tools of the trade. This distinction does not impede the effectiveness of newsletters, but it does indicate editors should try to keep employee stories organization oriented.

Product Publicity and Advertising

An organization must have a signed release on file if it wants to use photographs or comments of its employees and other individuals in

Written permission for use of the image should be obtained if the employee's photograph will appear in sales brochures or even in the corporate annual report. The same rule applies to other situations. A graduate of Lafayette College **sued the college** for using a photo of his mother and him at graduation ceremonies, **without their permission**, in a financial aid brochure.

product publicity, sales brochures, and advertising. An added precaution is to give some financial compensation to make a more binding contract.

Chemical Bank of New York unfortunately learned this lesson the hard way. The bank used pictures of 39 employees in various advertisements designed to "humanize" the bank's image, but the employees maintained that no one had requested permission to use their photos in advertisements. Another problem was that the pictures had been taken as long as five years before they began appearing in the series of advertisements.

An attorney for the employees, who sued for $600,000 in damages, said, "The bank took the individuality of these employees and used that individuality to make a profit." The judge agreed, ruling that the bank had violated New York's privacy law. The action is called misappropriation of personality, discussed later in this chapter.

Employee Free Speech

A modern, progressive organization encourages employee comments and even criticisms. Indeed, many employee newspapers carry letters to the editor because they breed a healthy atmosphere of two-way

communication and make company publications more credible.

At the same time, recent developments have indicated that not all is well for employee freedom of expression. An employee of Google, for example, was fired for using a Google-sponsored blog to post a personal chronicle of his first week on the job for friends and family. In another case, a Delta Airlines flight attendant sued the airline claiming she was fired for photos she placed on her personal blog, "Diary of a Flight Attendant."

Although employee privacy remains an important consideration, the trend is toward increased monitoring of employee e-mail by employers. Employers are concerned about being held liable if an employee posts a racial slur, engages in sexual harassment online, and even transmits sexually explicit jokes that might cause another employee to perceive the workplace as a "hostile" environment. In other words, everyone should assume that any e-mails they write at work are subject to monitoring and that they can be fired if they violate company policy. Further complicating this issue is the fact that government employees may have their e-mails made public if some

interested party files a Freedom of Information Act (FOIA) request. E-mails produced by a public employee on a government-owned computer are considered requestable documents under the FOIA.

Other important—and sometimes controversial—aspects of employee free speech include whistle-blowing and protection of an organization's

Don Sneed, Tim Wulfemeyer, and Harry Stonecipher, in a *Public Relations Review* article, say that a news release should be written to identify clearly statements of opinion versus statements of fact. They suggest that (1) opinion statements be accompanied by the facts on which the opinions are based, (2) statements of opinion be clearly labeled as such, and (3) the context of the language surrounding the expression of opinion be reviewed for possible legal implications.

#SocialMediainAction

Challenges Arise in Social Media Regulation

The nature of social media makes it a difficult medium for professional communicators to manage. In a highly regulated business such as finance or pharmaceuticals, employees have to be careful what they communicate online. And something posted by a third party on a company's Facebook page or website can raise legal issues.

The Securities and Exchange Commission (SEC) regulates publicly traded companies. The Food and Drug Administration (FDA) regulates pharmaceuticals. (See the section later in the chapter on government agencies for more on the SEC and the FDA.) Both agencies monitor social media, but have been slow to provide guidance to these industries. Because these federal regulatory agencies have the power to levy stiff fines, communicators in health and finance are understandably reluctant to wade too deeply into social media. This leads to frustration by both public relations professionals and consumers.

"Given that 8 out of 10 Internet users are looking online for health information, according to the Pew Internet & American Life Project, it is imperative that the FDA find a solution to its ongoing battle to provide timely and relevant guidelines for pharmaceutical social-media communications and marketing," Leigh Fazzina, of PR-SA's Health Academy, wrote on the organization's blog.

Among the challenges is knowing whether comments posted by a consumer on a drug company's website or Facebook page is considered company communication. Some companies worry they will be held responsible when a consumer recommends an unapproved use for a drug in discussions on the company's website. As of late 2011, the FDA had not provided the industry with guidelines.

In the area of finance, the Financial Industry Regulatory Authority (FINRA), an independent securities regulator, developed guidelines in 2010. These guidelines addressed blogs, e-mail, and social networking sites (such as Facebook, LinkedIn, and Twitter). Among FINRA's recommendations was: "As a best practice, firms should consider prohibiting all interactive electronic communications that recommend a specific investment product" unless that communication has been approved by leadership of the firm. The investment industry has paid close attention to FINRA's suggestions in the absence of SEC guidelines.

> **I'd love to start tweeting to the general public once they can clearly tell me what I can and can't do. However, putting yourself out there without specific guidelines is just not worth the risk.**
>
> Doug Flynn, a capital management advisor, in *Investment News*

The primary takeaway is that, while social media are incredibly useful public relations tools, you must handle them with care in regulated industries if you're going to stay out of trouble.

1. Why is social media use different in financial and pharmaceutical industries?

2. How might social media posts from consumers put at risk companies on whose social media sites the posts appear?

3. What other industries might need to be especially careful in their employment of social media tools?

trade secrets. State and federal laws generally protect the right of employees to "blow the whistle" if an organization is guilty of illegal activity. Whistle-blowing can occur in corporate, nonprofit, and government organizations. For example, an employee might blow the whistle on his or her organization by reporting to the Environmental Protection Agency the illegal release of a toxic substance from a manufacturing plant.

Copyright LAW

Should a news release be copyrighted? How about a corporate annual report? Can you include a *New Yorker* cartoon in the company magazine without permission? What if you reprint an article from *Fortune* magazine and distribute it to the company's sales staff? Are government reports copyrighted? What constitutes copyright infringement?

These are questions that a public relations professional should be able to answer. In very simple terms, *copyright* means protection of a creative work from unauthorized use. Knowledge of copyright law is important from two perspectives: (1) which organizational materials should be copyrighted, and (2) how the copyrighted materials of others may be used correctly.

The shield of copyright protection was weakened somewhat in 1991, when the U.S. Supreme Court ruled unanimously that directories, computer databases, and other compilations of facts may be copied and republished unless they display "some minimum degree of creativity." The court stated, "Raw facts may be copied at will."

A copyright does not protect ideas, but only the specific ways in which those ideas are expressed. An idea for promoting a product, for example, cannot be copyrighted— but brochures, drawings, news features, animated cartoons, display booths, photographs, recordings, videotapes, corporate symbols, slogans, and the like that express a particular idea can be copyrighted.

Because much money, effort, time, and creative talent are spent on developing organizational materials, obtaining copyright protection for them is important. By copyrighting materials, a company can prevent its competitors from capitalizing on its creative work or producing a facsimile brochure that may mislead the public.

The law presumes that material produced in some tangible form is copyrighted from the moment it is created. This presumption of copyright is often sufficient to discourage unauthorized use, and the writer or

> Registration is not a condition of copyright protection, but it is a prerequisite to an infringement action against unauthorized use by others.

creator of the material has some legal protection if he or she can prove that the material was created before another person claims it.

A more formal step, providing full legal protection, is official registration of the copyrighted work within three months after its creation. This process consists of depositing two copies of the manuscript (it is not necessary that it has been published), recording, or artwork with the Copyright Office of the Library of Congress.

The Copyright Term Extension Act, passed in 1998 and reaffirmed by the U.S. Supreme Court (*Eldred v. Ashcroft*) in 2003, protects original material for the life of the creator plus 70 years for individual works and 95 years from publication for copyrights held by corporations.

Fair Use VERSUS Infringement

Public relations people are in the business of gathering information from a variety of sources, so it is important to know where fair use ends and infringement begins. *Fair use* means that part of a copyrighted article may be quoted directly, but the quoted material must be brief in relation to the length of the original work. It may be, for example, only one paragraph in a 750-word article, but as long as a 300-word passage in a long article or book chapter. Complete attribution of the source must be given regardless of the length of the quotation. If the passage is quoted verbatim, quote marks must be used.

The concept of fair use has distinct limitations if part of the copyrighted material is to be used in advertisements and promotional brochures. In this case, permission

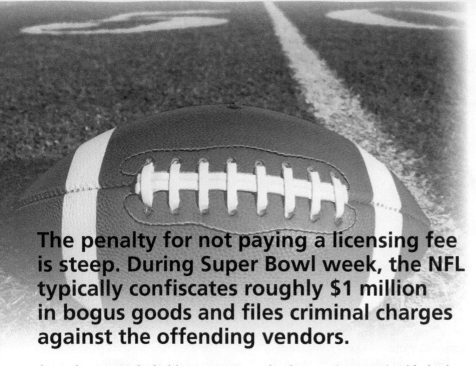

The penalty for not paying a licensing fee is steep. During Super Bowl week, the NFL typically confiscates roughly $1 million in bogus goods and files criminal charges against the offending vendors.

from the copyright holder to reuse the original material is required. It also is important for the original source to approve the context in which the quote is used. A quote taken out of context often runs into legal trouble if it implies endorsement of a product or service.

The Rights of Photographers and Artists

The copyright law makes it clear that freelance and commercial photographers retain ownership of their work. In other words, a customer who buys a copyrighted photo owns the photo itself, but not the right to make additional copies of the photo. That right remains with the photographer, unless it is explicitly transferred in writing.

This interpretation was established in a 1990 U.S. Federal District Court case in which the Professional Photographers of America (PP of A) sued a nationwide photofinishing firm for ignoring copyright notices on pictures sent for additional copies.

Freelance photographers generally charge for a picture on the basis of its use. If it is used only once, for an employee newsletter, for example, the fee is low. In contrast, if the company wants to use the picture in a widely distributed corporate annual report or on the company calendar,

the fee may be considerably higher. Arrangements and fees then may be determined for one-time use, unlimited use, or the payment of royalties every time the picture is used.

Computer manipulation of original artwork can also violate

copyright provisions. Slightly changing a copyrighted photo or a piece of artwork can also be considered a violation of copyright if the intent is to capitalize on widespread recognition of the original art. This was the case when the estate of the children's author Dr. Seuss (Theodor Geisel) won a $1.5 million judgment against a Los Angeles T-shirt maker for infringement of copyright. The manufacturer had portrayed a parody of Dr. Seuss's Cat in the Hat character smoking marijuana and giving the peace sign.

Similarly, sports logos are registered trademarks, and a licensing fee must be paid before anyone can use logos for commercial products and promotions. The sports retail industry earns about $11.5 billion in sales of licensed merchandise. Licensed video

 think Why is the concept of fair use applied differently when it comes to advertising and promotional materials?

Copyright Issues on the Internet

The Internet has raised new issues about the protection of intellectual property.

DOWNLOADING MATERIAL. In general, the same rules apply to cyberspace as to more long-standing methods of disseminating ideas. Original materials in digital form are still protected by copyright. The fair use limits for materials found on the Internet are essentially the same as those for materials disseminated by any other means.

Related to this issue is the use of news articles and features that are sent via e-mail or the web to the clients of clipping services. An organization may use such clips to track its publicity efforts, but it cannot distribute the article on its own website or intranet without obtaining permission and paying a royalty to the publication in which the article appeared. National clipping services like Burrelle's have agreements with hundreds of newspapers that allow its customers to pay a small royalty fee in exchange for being able to photocopy clippings and make greater use of them.

UPLOADING MATERIAL. In many cases, owners of copyrighted material have uploaded various kinds of information with the intention of making it freely available. Examples of these items include software, games, and even the entire text of *The Hitchhiker's Guide to the Galaxy*. The problem comes, however, when third parties upload copyrighted material without permission.

Copyright holders are increasingly patrolling the Internet to stop the unauthorized use of material.

Ethics and the Law

games earn another $1 billion. The sale of college and university trademarked goods adds to that mark.

The Rights of Freelance Writers

Although the rights of freelance photographers have been established for some years, it was more recently that freelance writers gained more control over the ownership of their work. In the case of *Community for Creative Non-Violence v. Reid*, the U.S. Supreme Court in 1989 ruled that writers retained ownership of their work and that purchasers of it simply gained a "license" to reproduce the copyrighted work. Under this interpretation of the copyright law, ownership of a writer's work is subject to negotiation and contractual agreement. Writers may agree to assign all copyright rights to the work they have been hired to do or they may give permission only for a specific one-time use. In a related matter, freelance writers won a major victory in 2001 when the Supreme Court (*New York Times v. Tasini*) ruled that publishers, by making articles accessible through electronic databases, infringed on the copyrights of freelance contributors.

Public relations firms and corporate public relations departments are responsible for ensuring compliance with the copyright law. This means that all agreements with a freelance writer must be documented in writing, and the use of the material must be clearly stated. Ideally, public relations personnel should negotiate multiple rights and even complete ownership of the copyright.

Trademark LAW

What do the names Coca-Cola, Marlboro, and IBM; the Olympic rings; and the logo of the Dallas Cowboys have in common? They are all registered trademarks protected by law.

A *trademark* is a word, symbol, or slogan, used singly or in combination, that identifies a product's origin. Research indicates, for example, that 53 percent of Americans say brand quality takes precedence over price considerations. Consequently, branding is important to companies and organizations.

The Protection of Trademarks

Trademarks are always capitalized and are never used as nouns. They are always used as adjectives modifying nouns. For example, the proper terms are "Kleenex tissues," "Xerox copies," and "Rollerblade skates."

Organizations adamantly insist on the proper use of trademarks to avoid the problem of having a name or slogan become generic. Put another way, a brand name becomes a common noun through general public use. Some trade names that have become generic include *aspirin, thermos, cornflakes, nylon, cellophane,* and *yo-yo.* This means that any company can now use these names to describe a product.

Trademark Infringement

Today, in a marketplace populated with thousands of businesses and organizations, finding a trademark not already in use is extremely difficult.

> "[Trademark] also serves as an indicator of quality, a kind of shorthand for consumers to use in recognizing goods in a complex marketplace.

Susan L. Cohen, in *Editor & Publisher*'s annual trademark supplement

всё будет *Coca-Cola* Присоединяйся!

There has been a proliferation of trademarks and service marks in modern society. Coca-Cola may be the world's most recognized trademark, according to some studies, but it is only one of almost 1 million active trademarks registered with the federal Patent and Trademark Office.

Ethics and the Law

What is the downside for a corporation whose trademark becomes too commonly used?

The task becomes even more frustrating when competing organizations claim similar slogans or trademarks. The complexity of finding a new name, coupled with the attempts of many to capitalize on an already known trade name, has spawned a number of lawsuits claiming trademark infringement. Consider the following examples:

- *Entrepreneur* magazine was awarded $337,000 in court damages after filing a trademark infringement lawsuit against a public relations firm that changed its name to "EntrepreneurPR."
- The widow of the man who said, "Let's roll," when he and others tried to overpower the hijackers of Flight 93 over Pennsylvania on September 11, 2001, petitioned the federal government to trademark the phrase. She wanted to license the phrase to fund a foundation to assist children who had lost a parent.

- Phi Beta Kappa, the academic honor society, filed a $5 million trademark infringement suit against Compaq Computer Corp. after the company launched a "Phi Beta Compaq" promotion targeted at college students.
- A jury awarded Adidas $304.6 million against Payless Shoesource. The discount shoe retailer was found to have taken advantage of Adidas's familiar three-stripe trademark logo by putting two and four parallel stripes on the store brand athletic shoes.

In these cases and many others, organizations claimed that their registered trademarks were being improperly exploited for commercial or organizational purposes.

Misappropriation of Personality

A form of trademark infringement also can result from the unauthorized use of well-known entertainers, professional athletes, and other public figures in an organization's publicity and advertising materials. A photo of Ryan Gosling may make a company's advertising campaign more interesting, but the courts would call it "misappropriation of

Telltale Signs of Trademark Infringement

Some guidelines used by courts to determine if trademark infringement has occurred include the following:

- Has the defendant used a name as a way of capitalizing on the reputation of another organization's trademark—and does the defendant benefit from the original organization's investment in popularizing its trademark?
- Is there intent (real or otherwise) to create confusion in the public mind? Is there intent to imply a connection between the defendant's product and the item identified by trademark?
- How similar are the two organizations? Are they providing the same kinds of products or services?
- Has the original organization actively protected the trademark by publicizing it and by actually continuing to use it in connection with its products or services?
- Is the trademark unique? A company with a trademark that simply describes a common product might be vulnerable.

Energy drink Red Bull won a trademark infringement case against a competing product, Bullfighter. The court found that Bullfighter intentionally appropriated part of the identity of Red Bull to capitalize on its reputation.

Ethics and the Law

212

Cavern Club, in Liverpool, England, birthplace of the Beatles, hit Hard Rock Café International with a trademark infringement lawsuit when a Las Vegas Hard Rock Café opened a special events room and labeled it "The Cavern Club." The UK Cavern Club owns the trademark in the United Kingdom and 25 other countries, but not in the United States. Hard Rock and Cavern Club have clashed before because Hard Rock has Cavern Clubs in other U.S. cities.

personality" if permission and licensing fees have not been negotiated.

Deceased celebrities are also protected from exploitation by others. To use a likeness or actual photo of a personality such as Elvis Presley, Marilyn Monroe, or Michael Jackson, the user must pay a licensing fee to an agent representing the family, studio, or estate of the deceased. The estate of Peanuts comic strip creator Charles Schulz licenses Peanuts characters in 40 countries, driving $1 billion annually in retail product sales.

The legal doctrine is the right of publicity, which gives entertainers, athletes, and other celebrities the sole ability to cash in on their fame. This legal right is loosely akin to a trademark or copyright, and many states have made it a commercial asset that can be inherited by a celebrity's descendents.

Regulations by
GOVERNMENT AGENCIES

The promotion of products and services, whether through advertising, product publicity, or other techniques, is not protected by the First Amendment. Instead, the courts have traditionally ruled that such activities fall under the doctrine of commercial speech. As a consequence, messages can be regulated by the state in the interest of public health, safety, and consumer protection.

Both the states and the federal government have passed legislation that regulates commercial speech and even restricts it if standards of disclosure, truth, and accuracy are violated. One result of such legislation was the banning of cigarette advertising on television in the 1960s. Public relations personnel involved in product publicity and the distribution of financial information should be aware of any applicable guidelines established by government agencies.

The Federal Trade Commission

The Federal Trade Commission (FTC) has jurisdiction to determine if advertisements are deceptive or misleading. Public

How do government regulations on advertising protect consumers?

relations personnel should also know that the commission has jurisdiction over product news releases and other forms of product publicity, such as videos and brochures. In the eyes of the FTC, both advertisements and product publicity materials are vehicles of commercial trade—and, therefore, subject to regulation. In fact, Section 43(a) of the Lanham Act makes it clear that anyone, including public relations personnel, may be subject to liability claims if that person participates in the making or dissemination of a false and misleading representation in any advertising or promotional material. This legislation applies to advertising and public relations firms, which also can be held liable for writing, producing, and distributing product publicity materials on behalf of their clients.

An example of an FTC complaint is one filed against Campbell Soup Company for claiming that its soups were low in fat and cholesterol and, therefore, helpful in fighting heart disease. The FTC charged that the claim was deceptive because publicity and advertisements failed to disclose that the soups had a high sodium content, which increases the risk of heart disease.

The Campbell's case raises an important aspect of FTC guidelines. Although a publicized fact may be accurate in itself, FTC staff also consider the context or "net impression received by the consumers." In this case, advertising copywriters and publicists ignored the information about the high sodium level, which created an entirely new perspective on the health benefits of Campbell's soup.

Hollywood's abuse of endorsements and testimonials to publicize its films also has attracted the scrutiny of the FTC. Sony Pictures, for example, was found to have concocted quotes from a fictitious movie critic to publicize four of its films. And Twentieth Century Fox admitted that it had hired actors to appear in "man in the street" commercials to portray unpaid moviegoers.

FTC investigators are always on the lookout for unsubstantiated claims and various forms of misleading or deceptive information. Some of the terms in promotional materials that trigger FTC interest are *authentic, certified, cure, custom-made, germ-free, natural, unbreakable, perfect, first-class, exclusive,* and *reliable*. In recent years, the FTC also has established guidelines for "green" marketing and the use of the terms *low carb* and *organic* in advertisements and publicity materials for food products.

The FTC has ruled that anyone who endorses a product, including celebrities and bloggers, must make explicit the compensation received from companies. The FTC guidelines also state that businesses and reviewers (including bloggers) may be held liable for any false statements about a product.

Companies found in violation of FTC guidelines are usually given the opportunity to sign a consent decree. Under such an agreement, the company admits no wrongdoing but agrees to change its advertising and publicity claims. Companies may also be fined by the FTC or ordered to engage in corrective advertising and publicity.

The Securities and Exchange Commission

The SEC closely monitors the financial affairs of publicly traded companies and protects the interests of stockholders. The SEC guidelines on public disclosure and insider trading are particularly relevant to corporate public relations staff members who must meet these requirements. The distribution of misleading information or failure to make a timely disclosure of material information may be the basis of liability under the SEC code. A company may even be liable if, despite satisfying regulations by getting information out, it conveys crucial information in a vague way or buries it deep within the news release.

The SEC has volumes of regulations, but the three concepts most pertinent to public relations personnel are as follows:

1 Full information must be given on anything that might materially affect the company's stock.

2 Timely disclosure is essential.

3 Insider trading is illegal.

A court may examine all information released by a company, including news releases, to determine whether, taken as a whole, they create an "overall misleading" impression.

In 2000, the SEC issued another regulation related to fair disclosure, known as Reg FD. Although regulations already existed regarding "material disclosure" of information that could affect the price of stock, the new regulation expanded the concept by requiring publicly traded companies to broadly disseminate "material" information via a news release, webcast, or SEC filing. According to the SEC, Reg FD is intended to ensure that *all* investors—not just brokerage firms and analysts—receive financial information from a company at the same time.

Other Regulatory Agencies

Although the FTC and the SEC are the major federal agencies concerned with the content of advertising and publicity materials, other agencies have also established guidelines that can affect practitioners in these fields.

The Food and Drug Administration. The Food and Drug Administration (FDA) oversees the advertising and promotion of prescription drugs, over-the-counter medicines, cosmetics, and food. Under the federal Food, Drug, and Cosmetic Act, any "person" (which includes advertising and public relations firms) who "causes the misbranding" of products through the dissemination of false and misleading information may be held liable under provisions of the law.

Other federal agencies that occasionally get involved in distribution of public relations materials include the Bureau of Alcohol, Tobacco and Firearms and the Federal Communications Commission.

The Federal Trade Commission charged social networking site Facebook with deception, saying that it promised privacy settings and then continued to share private information. "Facebook is obligated to keep the promises about privacy that it makes to its hundreds of millions of users," said Jon Leibowitz, chairman of the FTC. "Facebook's innovation does not have to come at the expense of consumer privacy. The FTC action will ensure it will not." Facebook proposed solutions that settled the FTC charges.

The FDA has established specific guidelines for video, audio, and print news releases on healthcare topics. First, the release must provide "fair balance" by telling consumers about both the risks and the benefits of the drug or treatment. Second, the writer must be clear about the limitations of a particular drug or treatment—for example, that it may not help people with certain conditions. Third, a news release or media kit should be accompanied by supplementary product sheets or brochures that give full prescribing information.

Liability For SPONSORED EVENTS

Public relations personnel often focus on the planning and logistics of events. Consequently, they must also take steps to protect their organizations from liability and possible lawsuits associated with those activities.

Plant tours, open houses, and other events should not be undertaken lightly. They require detailed planning by the public relations staff to guarantee the safety and comfort of visitors. Consideration must be given to such factors as possible work disruptions as groups pass through the plant, safety, and amount of staffing required.

A well-marked tour route is essential; it is equally important to have trained escort staff and tour guides. Guides should be well versed in company history and operations, and their comments should be somewhat standardized to make sure that key facts are conveyed. In addition, guides

should be trained in first aid and thoroughly briefed on what to do in case of an accident. At the beginning of the tour, the guide should outline to the visitors what they will see, the amount of walking involved, the time required, and the number of stairs. This warning tells visitors what they can expect.

Many of the points about plant tours are also applicable to open houses. The added problem with open houses is having the presence of large numbers of people on the plant site at the same time. Such an event calls for special logistical planning by the public relations staff. Such precautions will generate goodwill and limit the company's liability. It should be noted, however, that a plaintiff can still collect if negligence on the part of the company can be proved.

Promotional events are planned primarily to promote product sales, increase organizational visibility, or

raise money for charitable causes. Events that attract crowds require the same kind of planning as open houses. Public relations personnel should be concerned about traffic flow, adequate restroom facilities, signage, and security.

Liability insurance is a necessity when any such events are planned. Any public event sponsored by an organization should be insured against accidents that might result in lawsuits charging negligence. Organizations can purchase comprehensive insurance to cover a variety of events or a specific event. The need for liability insurance also applies to charitable organizations if they sponsor a 10k run, a bicycle race, or a hot-air balloon race. Participants should sign a release form that protects the organization against liability in case of an accident. Promotional events that use public streets and parks also need permits from the appropriate city departments.

WORKING WITH Lawyers

This chapter has outlined a number of areas in which the release of information (or the lack of release) raises legal issues for an organization. Public relations personnel must be aware of legal pitfalls, but they are not lawyers. By the same token, lawyers aren't experts in public relations and often lack sufficient understanding of how important the court of public opinion is in determining the reputation and credibility of an organization.

In today's business environment, with its high potential for litigation, it is essential for public relations professionals and lawyers to have cooperative relationships.

Six Keys to WINNING in the Court of Law—and in the Court of Public Opinion

PRSA's monthly tabloid *Tactics* offers the following tips:

1. Make carefully planned public comments in the earliest stages of a crisis or legal issue.

2. Understand the perspective of lawyers and allow them to review statements when an organization is facing or involved in litigation.

3. Guard against providing information to the opposing side in a legal case.

4. Counsel and coach the legal team.

5. Build support from interested parties, such as industry associations or chambers of commerce.

6. Develop a litigation communication team before you need it.

The relationship between lawyers and public relations practitioners is such an important issue that both professions regularly deal with it in publications and seminars. In the public relations arena, *PR News* has an online newsletter, *Crisis and Legal PR Bulletin*, and provides publications and programming that address the intersection of law and public relations. On the other side, the University of Georgia School of Law has provided practicing lawyers with a daylong continuing education program titled "Winning in the Court of Public Opinion."

What Would You Do?

Ethics in Practice

A well-known professional baseball player is suspected of having used steroids and other performance-enhancing drugs. He has not been charged with any crime. His agent asks you to advise and assist him in handling the intense media interest in the case. The agent wants you to try to place favorable stories about the athlete in the media and create a positive environment for him. If the athlete is formally accused, it could mean irreparable damage to his baseball career.

You are not asked to do anything unethical. The money is quite good, and you know the publicity from working on the case will probably help your public relations consulting career, especially if the athlete is exonerated. Would you take the account?

The agent tells you confidentially that the athlete has admitted that he took some substance that was unknown to him but may have been steroids. Does this information affect your decision? What are the ethics of the situation as you see them? Write a brief essay defending your choice.

summary

Why Is Ethics a Relevant Issue for Public Relations Practitioners?

- Ethics refers to a person's value system and the means by which he or she determines right and wrong.

- When a person is an advocate for a particular organization or cause, the individual must always behave in an ethical manner.

- Groups such as PRSA, IABC, and IPRA play an important role in setting the standards and ethical behavior of the public relations profession. Most professional organizations have published codes of conduct and educational programs.

What Do Public Relations Professionals Need to Know About Defamation, Employee and Privacy Rights, Copyright, and Trademark Laws?

- The concept of defamation involves a false and malicious (or at least negligent) communication with an identifiable subject who is injured either financially or by loss of reputation or mental suffering.

- It is important to get written permission to publish photos or use employees in advertising materials, and to be cautious in releasing personal information about employees to the media.

- Employees are limited in expressing opinions within the corporate environment.

- Copyright is the protection of creative work from unauthorized use. It is assumed that published works are copyrighted, and permission must be obtained to reprint such material.

- New copyright issues have been raised by the popularity of the Internet and the ease of downloading, uploading, and disseminating images and information.

- A trademark is a word, symbol, or slogan that identifies a product's origin. It can be registered with the U.S. Patent and Trademark Office. Companies vigorously protect trademarks to prevent them from becoming common nouns.

Which Guidelines and Government Agencies Govern the Commercial Speech Used by Public Relations Professionals?

- Commercial speech is regulated by the government in the interest of public health, safety, and consumer protection.

- The agencies involved in this regulation include the Federal Trade Commission, the Securities and Exchange Commission, the Food and Drug Administration, and the Bureau of Alcohol, Tobacco, and Firearms.

How Can Public Relations Professionals Facilitate Good Working Relationships with Lawyers?

- Public relations practitioners should be aware of legal concepts and regulatory guidelines and receive briefings from the legal staff on impending developments.

questions
FOR REVIEW AND DISCUSSION

1 Define ethics in your own words. Why might two individuals disagree about what constitutes an ethical dilemma or concern?

2 Some critics say voluntary codes of ethics "have no teeth" because they cannot be enforced. Why do organizations develop and publish codes of ethics?

3 How can a public relations professional play the role of an "ethical advocate"?

4 Public relations practitioners often have conflicting loyalties. In your opinion, do they owe their first allegiance to their client or employer or to the standards of their professional organization, such as PRSA?

5 Why do public relations staff and firms need to know the legal aspects of creating and distributing messages?

6 Which steps can a public relations person take to avoid libel suits?

7 Which precautions can a public relations person take to avoid invasion of privacy lawsuits?

8 If an organization wants to use the photo or comments of an employee or a customer in an advertisement, which precautions should be taken?

9 Which basic guidelines of copyright law should public relations professionals know about?

MySearchLab®

The PR Hacks Behind Facebook's Google Smear

Dan Lyons | Daily Beast, May 13, 2011

Burson-Marsteller, a major public relations firm, failed to supervise its new employees working on the Facebook account. Facebook management demanded and received an underhanded media campaign to damage the reputation of Google without disclosing that Facebook was behind the smear tactics.

A code of ethics is a common management tool in large firms. However, to be effective in shaping employee behavior the mere existence of such a code is not enough. Staff need orientation and regular refresher courses.

The former reporters knew the news business but apparently lacked the moral compass expected of public relations professionals. Perhaps the cynical stereotypes in newsrooms of public relations practices led the new employees to believe deception and lack of transparency were acceptable stratagems.

PR agency Burson-Marsteller, caught up in a scandal for running a covert anti-Google smear campaign on behalf of Facebook, says it will not fire the two PR guys who ran the operation. Instead, Burson says it will give them extra training.

"We have talked through our policies and procedures with each individual involved in the program and made it clear this cannot happen again," Burson's USA President Pat Ford told *PR Week*. Ford told PR Week that Burson has a code of ethics and will redistribute it to all employees in the wake of the Facebook smear campaign scandal.

The two PR guys involved are new to Burson and new to PR. They are Jim Goldman, a former tech reporter for CNBC, and John Mercurio, a former political reporter. The pair were pitching anti-Google stories to newspapers, urging them to investigate claims that Google was invading people's privacy with a tool called Social Circle. Mercurio even offered to help a blogger write a Google-bashing op-ed, and promised to place the op-ed in the *Washington Post*, Huffington Post, and other publications.

Instead, the blogger turned the tables on Burson, posting Mercurio's embarrassing email pitch online. A few days later, *USA Today* broke a story saying Goldman had been trying to sell that newspaper on the same sleazy pitch. Nobody knew who had hired Burson to do this dirty work, and the agency wouldn't say. Fingers pointed at Apple and Microsoft. But on Wednesday, *The Daily Beast* revealed that the client was Facebook.

PR people in Silicon Valley said they weren't surprised to see Facebook spreading negative information about Google. But they were shocked—and delighted—by how clumsy the Burson guys were.

Burson put out a statement Thursday blaming the whole mess on Facebook. The statement said Facebook insisted on being kept anonymous, and that Burson should not have gone along with that request.

Questions remain, however. For example, who at Facebook initiated the campaign? Did Mark Zuckerberg, Facebook's CEO, know about it, and if so, when? Was it his idea? Nobody at Facebook will talk. Their idea seems to be to just brazen it out, and hope the storm blows over. Sadly, that will probably work.

Dan Lyons is technology editor at Newsweek and the creator of Fake Steve Jobs, the persona behind the notorious tech blog, The Secret Diary of Steve Jobs. Before joining Newsweek, Lyons spent 10 years at Forbes.

Ethics and the Law

Photo Credits

Credits are listed in order of appearance.

Benedicte Desrus/Alamy;
ZUMA Wire Service/Alamy;
Martin Novak/Shutterstock;
ZUMA Wire Service/Alamy;

Eric Carr/Alamy;
Hasan Shaheed/Shutterstock;
Susanna Price/DK Images;
David Lee/Shutterstock;

Alvaro Leiva/age fotostock/Getty Images;
DSPA/Shutterstock;
Imagebroker/Alamy;
Mkabakov/Shutterstock

Tactics image: Petr Z/Shutterstock
Tablet image: Falconia/Shutterstock

Reaching Diverse Audiences

From Chapter 10 of *Think Public Relations*, 2013 Edition. Dennis L. Wilcox, Glen T. Cameron, Bryan H. Reber, Jae-Hwa Shin.

Reaching Diverse Audiences

Engaging Ethnic Audiences

The Hispanic market represents the fastest-growing segment of the emerging multicultural market. People of Hispanic descent in the U.S., according to a 2011 Pew Hispanic Center study, currently number 50.5 million, approximately 16 percent of the population.

The African American population, now the second-largest minority group in the U.S., stands at 12 percent. Another significant group is Asian Americans, who now constitute about 5 percent of the population.

Although public relations professionals have, to a greater or lesser degree, engaged African American audiences for many years and products and services designed for ethnic consumers have long been part of the American experience, not until the late 1980s did most companies and organizations make sustained attempts to understand and target messages to a wider array of distinct audiences. Campaigns aimed at engaging Hispanics, Asians, or other racial groups as well as the LGBT (lesbian, gay, bisexual, transgender) group, which is estimated to be about 16 million adults, are a relatively new phenomenon.

Since 2003, Harley-Davidson has made a concerted effort to connect with Hispanic riders. Social media has been part of the Harley-Davidson strategy with Hispanics since 2009, when Harley developed an interactive section of its website dedicated to Hispanic riders. The company has also produced a film titled *Harlistas: An American Journey* celebrating the historic connection between the company and Latinos.

Ideally, understanding and engaging diverse audiences is based on regular, ongoing interaction with target audiences, with the goal of understanding the interests, attitudes, and behavior of distinct groups. Estée Lauder's "Every Woman Can Be Beautiful" campaign promoting makeup designed for various skin tones has targeted Hispanic, Asian, and Caucasian women with an integrated, but segmented, public relations campaign. In addition to using social media channels such as Facebook and Twitter, Estée Lauder created mobile ads and microsites to support distribution of 6 million product samples. With these efforts, the company has engaged thousands of customers, and collected surveys from 10,000 consumers in the U.S.—part of what Charisse Ford, SVP for global marketing, describes as "creative ways to sample in that social space."

1 Who are emerging publics in the multicultural marketplace?

2 What are important factors to consider when reaching out to diverse audiences?

Ask Yourself

> How Does the Diverse Nature of Audiences Affect Public Relations Practice?

> How Can Information About the General Characteristics of Key Demographic Groups Inform Effective Public Relations Efforts?

> Why Is It Important to Match Media Type to Audience?

THE Nature OF THE PUBLIC RELATIONS Audience

If the audience for public relations messages was a monolithic whole, the work of practitioners would be far easier—and far less stimulating. In reality, an audience is a complex intermingling of groups with diverse cultural, ethnic, religious, and socioeconomic attributes, whose interests coincide at times and conflict in other situations.

Dynamic and Segmented Audiences

A successful public relations campaign takes into account the shifting dynamics of audiences and targets those segments of an audience that are most desirable for its particular purpose. It also employs traditional and social media that would be most effective in reaching those segments.

Diversity is the most significant aspect of the mass audience, or general public, in the United States. Differences in geography, history, culture, and economy among the regions of this sprawling country are striking; ranchers in Montana have different attitudes than residents in heavily populated Eastern Seaboard cities. Yet people in the two areas often share national interests. Ethnicity, generational differences, and socioeconomic status also shape

the audience segments that public relations practitioners address. For example, the American Heart Association (AHA) provides specific resources aimed at African American populations, such as the Power to End Stroke campaign. Kmart, another brand with deep ties to the African American community, hosts events, such as the "Share the Word" celebration of Black History Month with comedian Steve Harvey, and "Dress for Success," a career development forum for women.

The international audience for public relations has expanded swiftly. Growth of global corporations and expanded foreign

marketing by smaller firms create new public relations challenges, however, as does increased foreign ownership of U.S. companies. For example, McDonald's has 33,000 restaurants in 119 countries. This company successfully tailors public relations campaigns along with its menus and décor to match the culture and values of each nation. For example, because eating beef is prohibited by the Hindu religion in India, McDonald's offers the Maharaja Mac made from chicken or lamb.

Technology can be used to segment a mass audience and compile valuable demographic information. Public relations professionals can employ search engines and

Some audience segments are easily identifiable and reachable as "prepackaged publics." For example, advocacy, civic, educational, and charitable organizations are generally well-organized groups whose members are bound by common interests; thus they constitute ready-made targets for public relations practitioners.

Reaching Diverse Audiences

International and multicultural audiences are a diverse and significant target for public relations campaigns.

digital databases to conduct both primary and secondary research to narrow in on desirable target audiences.

Geographic and social statistics from Census Bureau reports provide a rich foundation, which can be broken down by census tract and ZIP code. Data on automobile registrations, voter registrations, sales figures, mailing lists, and church and organization memberships also can be merged into computer databases.

The Internet provides an efficient and effective way to move beyond geographical limits in public relations messages, but it requires quicker responses to its swiftly changing audiences. In the twenty-first century, the enormous impact of television has increased visual orientation, and this has been compounded by many people now obtaining a good deal of their news online. At computer screens, consumers are exposed to dynamic multimedia content, including websites with streaming videos and Flash graphics, regularly updated blogs, instant messaging, and web forums.

The swift pace of presentation may lead to viewers' shortened attention spans. In recognition of this trend, political leaders now reach the public largely in 10-second "sound bites." Television and the Internet also serve as a potent communicator of manners, mores, and aspirations. *American Idol* and reality shows, for example, have made the dream of becoming famous seem tangible—if only, as artist Andy Warhol predicted in 1968, for 15 minutes.

"Understanding the preferences of diverse consumers has other benefits. According to McDonald's U.S. marketing director, Robert Jackson, "In many cases ethnic consumers are bellwethers to a trend that ultimately winds up in the broader market."

Audiences sometimes coalesce around single issues. Some individuals become so zealously involved in promoting or opposing a single issue that they lose the social and political balance so necessary to support a democracy. Animal

McDonald's had been a leader in merging corporate and local cultural values at its more than 33,000 restaurants worldwide.

rights and right-to-life activists frequently have been accused of going too far. For example, in November 2010 alleged animal rights activists mailed razor blades, said to have been tainted by the AIDS virus, to J. David Jentsch, an animal researcher studying the effect of methamphetamines on monkeys at the University of California, Los Angeles.

Society places a heavy emphasis on personality and celebrity. Sports stars, television and movie actors, and musical performers are virtually worshipped. When stars embrace causes, people often take note of those causes. Increasingly, celebrities are used as spokespersons and fund-raisers, even though their expertise as performers does not necessarily qualify them as experts or opinion leaders.

Celebrities tweet about products for a price. Reality TV star Khloe Kardashian, for example, charged $8,000 to tweet about a brand of jeans that make "your butt look scary good."

Another modern development with implications for public relations practice is the strong distrust of authority and suspicion of conspiracy that have arisen from sensationalistic investigative reporting. For example, the unethical and illegal hacking of celebrity e-mail and phone lines by Rupert Murdoch's News Corporation in the UK and the business practices of executives at Enron, Tyco, WorldCom, Countrywide Mortgage, and other large corporations have generated a recent atmosphere of general distrust toward corporations. Legal (but highly suspect) practices such as questionable manipulation of stock trades and the slicing-and-dicing of derivatives by banks and insurance companies such as JP Morgan and AIG were largely responsible for the 2008 economic recession.

One marketing research organization, Claritas, has divided the Chicago metropolitan area into **62 lifestyle clusters** and assigned a name to each cluster. For example, the buying habits of "Boomers & Babies," Claritas says, include "rent more than five videos a month, buy children frozen dinners, read parenting magazines."

Adding to this sense of unease, the highly publicized—and highly illegal—Ponzi schemes perpetuated by Bernie Madoff have made investors and people in general skeptical about the motives and honesty of financial managers and Wall Street as a whole. The "Occupy Wall Street" movement, which began as a peaceful protest mounted by the Canadian Adbusters on July 13, 2011, represents a protest against the power of large corporations to affect the democratic process. Following in the footsteps of the "Arab Spring" revolutions, Occupy Wall Street is an expression of the frustration many people are feeling about the financial crisis, lack of opportunity, and vast inequities in wealth distribution.

People are so bombarded with exaggerated political promises, see so much financial chicanery, and are exposed to so much misleading or even contradictory information that many of them now

 think How has television shaped the characteristics of modern American audiences?

distrust what they read and hear in the news. Many consumers suspect evil motives of anyone trying to sell them anything. The need for public relations programs to develop an atmosphere of justifiable, rational trust is obvious.

Occupy Oakland, originally organized on October 10, 2011, was one of the more confrontational protests in recent years. The movement offered dramatic evidence of a new lack of trust in established institutions.

Strategic Public Relations Targets Key Audiences

Public relations has, by necessity, become more strategic in practice; audiences are targeted very precisely and in some instances messages are even customized at the individual level. In health care settings, for example, e-mail messages are tailored to the individual patient based on his or her most recent examination. Not only can the public relations professional target a precise public, but in many cases the practitioner can actually bypass the mass media and communicate directly with the preselected audience through customized mailings or other direct means such as personalized e-mails or broadcast faxes. The use of communication channels that directly reach an audience is called controlled media. Examples of controlled media include sponsored films or videos and events, such as *Harlistas*, the Harley-Davidson film discussed in the chapter-opening example.

As the demographic makeup of the United States continues to change dramatically, some major target audiences have emerged that deserve special attention. One is senior citizens, also known simply as "seniors." This group frequently is defined as men and women 65 years or older, although some sociologists, marketing experts, and organizations such as AARP (formerly the American Association of Retired Persons) include everyone older than age 50. Comparable groups include the so-called tween market, which consists of youths aged 7 to 12; the well-defined teenage demographic group; and baby boomers, people born between 1946 and 1964.

Other emerging audiences with unique profiles include gender and lifestyle groups such as those made up of women, members of religious groups, or the LGBT community as well as groups formed by racial and ethnic minorities, particularly audiences of African American and Hispanic descent. Beyond the diversity of ethnic markets in the United States, similar trends have become evident in an international context as a result of globalization.

Age Group AUDIENCES

Members of the same age group, while not monolithic groups, often do share some distinct characteristics. It is important for public relations professionals to understand the key interests and aspirations of age group audiences to be able to communicate with them effectively.

Youth

The current youth market has been labeled as *Generation Y* (Gen Y), a term used for those born between 1981 and 2003. Another popular name for this age group is the Millennial Generation. They succeed *Generation X* (Gen X), which was born between 1965 and 1980—a demographic group that is frequently defined as independent, tech savvy, and resourceful.

Because they are such voracious consumers of electronic media, some pundits have labeled Generation Y "the E-Generation." The Fortino Group (Pittsburgh) projects that typical members of Generation Y will spend about a quarter of their lifetime online.

The youth audience poses many opportunities and challenges for public relations professionals. Members of this audience have in-

 **think** How is the youth market of today distinct from their parents and grandparents?

creasing buying power, and are establishing attitudes toward brands and causes during these formative years. Public relations professionals have long recognized the importance of the youth market. Children and teenagers influence their parents' buying decisions, have purchasing power of their own, and ultimately mature into adult consumers.

Today's children have greater autonomy and decision-making power within the family than their predecessors in previous generations. Children often pester or nag their parents into purchasing items they would not otherwise buy. *Kidfluence*, a marketing publication, notes that pestering can be divided into two categories—"persistence" and "importance." Persistence nagging (a plea that is repeated over and over again) is less sophisticated than importance nagging, which appeals to parents' desire to provide the best for their children. Like every new generation before them, this generation of children causes adults to fret about their character but shows signs that they, too, will rise to the challenges that come with maturity.

According to consumer market research company Packaged Facts, today's youth market (15- to 24-year-olds) has more than

Some General Characteristics of **Youth**

Spending one-third of their lives online will have interesting effects on Gen Y members:

- They will spend as much time interacting with friends online as in person.
- Initial interaction online will precede most dating and marriages.
- They will spend 10 times more time online than in interaction with parents.
  - They will be more reserved in social skills.
  - They will be savvy and skeptical about online identities, such as chat participants.

- They will not tolerate print forms, slow application processes, and archaic systems.

Generation Y values relationships and trust. In a survey of 1,200 teens worldwide, Ketchum's Global Brand Marketing Practice found that:

- Parents still rule when it comes to advice about careers and some lifestyle choices and have a strong influence on product decisions.
- Trust in information is derived from relationships.
- The top five sources of advice are parents, doctors, clergy, friends, and teachers.
- As avid and skilled Internet users, Gen Y is savvy about unfiltered and unpoliced content.

- Teens recognize the credibility of editorial content compared to ads and even public service announcements, with television being the most trusted medium for them.
- Publicity for products and issues will influence members of Gen Y, whether those messages are directed at them or at those to whom they look for advice.

> **Youth of today have spending power and they also have loyalty to brands. Some of this comes from their parents, but they also make their own decisions.**

Regina A. Corso, senior vice president for youth and education research at Harris Interactive

$500 billion of purchasing power. However, as economic uncertainty continues, a corresponding increase has been noted in the number of "boomerang" children, so named because they return after leaving home. Whether unable to find jobs or aiming to save money, the number of young adults who have opted to remain in their parent's home has increased from 11.8 percent in 2007 to 14.2 percent in 2011, according to an article published November 17, 2011, in the *New York Times*. Given that only 74 percent of people ages 25 to 34 were employed at the time, young peoples' reluctance to move away from their parents can be seen as an effective (if not entirely healthy) defensive strategy.

Baby Boomers

The term *baby boomer* refers to people born between 1946 and 1964. This period was characterized by a high birth rate and general prosperity in the United States following World War II. Unlike their parents, baby boomers did not suffer through prolonged economic depression and enjoyed many advantages as the international stature of the United States grew. As a consequence, they are more willing to spend disposable income on consumer goods and luxury items. However, the outlook of baby boomers varies widely depending on when they were born during the 1946–1964 span. Those born in the late 1940s and early 1950s faced the turmoil of the Vietnam era. Those born later, who did not experience the war as directly, share many of the characteristics of Generation X. People born between 1956 and 1964 are sometimes referred to as "shadow baby boomers."

Baby boomers were the first generation to come of age during the advent of television. As such, their buying habits and lifestyle are heavily influenced by visual advertising. At the same time, they tend as a group to be more skeptical and discerning than their parents' generation.

The first baby boomers turned 65 in 2011. By 2030, approximately one-fifth of the U.S. population, or 71.5 million people, will be 65 or older. Advances in medical science and a concern for health among baby boomers mean that they most likely will be the longest-lived generation. Boomers control 70 percent of total household worth, and have an estimated annual buying power of $40 billion, making them the largest and most economically advantaged group in the United States. The aging of the baby boomers will bolster the ranks of the already powerful AARP, which lobbies for legislation on health care and other political issues.

Seniors

Medical advances and better living conditions have improved life expectancy to the point that today, about 40 million Americans, or 13 percent of the U.S. population, are age 65 or older, according to the 2010 U.S. Census data. According to Census Bureau projections, 72 million Americans will be 65 or older by 2030. After 2030, however, the percentage of aged population in the U.S. is projected to remain fairly stable.

Older citizens form an important opinion group and a consumer market with special interests. As is the case with other demographic groups, they are not a monolithic audience, but rather display many variations in personality, interest, financial status, health concerns, and lifestyles. Nevertheless, public relations professionals should not overlook the general characteristics of the senior audience.

By 2015, it is estimated that 94 percent of Americans will be online. At a projected 50.6 percent penetration, seniors will continue to lag behind other groups in Internet use. However, senior women are among the fastest-growing segment of Facebook users. Unsurprisingly, seniors also lead as consumers of daytime television, magazines, books, and newspapers.

Some General Characteristics of Baby Boomers

- Baby boomers tend to define themselves according to their profession.
- Baby boomers are, as a group, well educated and take pride in accomplishment.
- Baby boomers often question authority and are likely to take a strong position on social issues.
- Baby boomers are competitive, particularly when it comes to their careers.
- Baby boomers have great appreciation for leisure time, which they believe is well earned.
- Baby boomers may retire later than their parents due to improved health as well as financial uncertainty.

Some General Characteristics of Seniors

- With the perspective of long experience, seniors often are less easily convinced than young adults, demand value in the things they buy, and pay little attention to fads.
- They vote in greater numbers than their juniors and are more intense readers of newspapers and magazines. Retirees also watch television more frequently than younger persons.
- Seniors represent an excellent source of volunteers for social, health, and cultural organizations because they have time and often are looking for something to do.
- They are extremely health conscious, out of self-interest, and want to know about medical developments. A Census Bureau study showed that most people older than age 65 say they are in good health; not until their mid-80s do they frequently need assistance in daily living.
- Despite their historic wealth and buying power, many seniors have seen their savings erode in recent years. An estimated 450,000 American seniors, who are older than 65 but still looking for work, are unemployed. The median net worth for seniors aged 55–64 has declined from $273,000 to $254,000 since the advent of the recent economic crisis in 2008.

Reaching Emerging Youth and Male Audiences

YOUNG MEN AGED 16 to 27 make up a modest but significant audience segment. For both men and women, the period between late teen and early adult years is when attitudes toward brands and causes tend to become fixed. A recent spate of campaigns target young men using hypermasculine spokesmen, who are at the same time often "metrosexual" in some respects. To reach this demographic, companies such as Old Spice, Heineken, Dos Equis, at least one tequila brand, and Dairy Queen employ essentially the same character—though in different racial and ethnic guises—in their oddly similar campaigns. In each case, the character (or a narrator) speaks in a deep baritone voice explaining some aspect of the character's exploits in relation to the product. Usually, the combination of the character's or narrator's direct confrontation of the camera as he boasts about outlandish exploit, establishes a humorous, ironic, or preposterous situation. All the while, the protagonist maintains a steely, if self-depreciating resolve.

Depiction of such consistent characters, especially when witnessed across media and campaigns, points to its establishment as a cultural *meme. A meme* is an idea that tends to get reproduced with constant and recognizable attributes. Examples of these hypermasculine, though slightly effete and detached, men include characters in television shows such as *Mad Men* as well as roles created by actors such as Zac Efron and Ryan Gosling.

These campaigns can be seen to embody new characteristics of youth, especially in America—where young people are seen to be increasingly disengaged and less optimistic than in the past. A recent of survey of the attitudes of 9,240 people aged 20 to 29 in 21 countries by the marketing research firm YouGovStone indicate that young people in the U.S. lag far behind their global counterparts on several questions regarding ambition and long-term outlook for the future. When asked if they agree with the statement, "I feel very positive about my country's future," only 29 percent of Americans agreed with the statement, compared to 45 percent globally. Only 38 percent of young Americans aspire to run their own business, compared to 68 percent of global youth. And only 42 percent of the Americans asked believe that climate change is a matter of concern, in contrast to 69 percent of their peers.

A conflicting view is offered by John D. Miller, a researcher with the Longitudinal Study of American Youth at the University of Michigan. In a 2009–2010 survey, when Generation X young adults were asked "Thinking about all aspects of your life, how happy are you now?," the mean score was 7.5 on a scale of 1 to 10, and the median was 8. Less than 10 percent answered lower than 5. Thus, while American youth seem to hold little optimism for the long-term prospects, they seem to be essentially happy with their lives at present. This suggests that American youth are accustomed to more immediate gratification and living in the moment, compared to their Asian and European counterparts.

On one hand, the boasting Old Spice character, or Dos Equis's "World's Most Interesting Man" may be a reflection of American youth's confidence in their own abilities. On the other, the preposterous, surreal aspect of the campaigns may reflect young Americans' lack of engagement with the difficult problems of the future.

1 What are some distinguishing characteristics of young audiences in the U.S.?

2 How can public relations professionals co-opt the characteristics of young audiences for a successful public relations campaign?

3 How can public relations professionals deal with competing perspectives of young audiences who are reported to hold little optimism about long term prospects, but are essentially happy with their lives at present?

Gender/Lifestyle AUDIENCES

Emerging audiences, such as women, members of religious groups, and the LGBT community, have characteristics that public relations professionals should make themselves more aware of, so that they may communicate effectively with these growing demographic groups.

Women

Women constitute an enormous and diverse demographic group that has always been an important and distinct target audience from marketing and public relations standpoints. Women now account for 61 percent of the U.S. workforce, have more undergraduate degrees than men in the 25 to 34 age group, and even attend graduate school in greater numbers than men. In many global settings, women are beginning to exercise the kind of political and social power that they attained in the United States, Europe, and parts of Asia during the last century.

In addition to their impressive purchasing power, women are more likely than men to exercise influence as opinion leaders. Research suggests

> **Today's women hold an overwhelming share of consumer purchasing influence,** making more than 80 **percent of household purchase decisions, and spending over $3.3 trillion annually.**
>
> Kelley Skoloda, director of global brand marketing, Ketchum

that women have a larger network of friends and tend to maintain more regular contact with the circle of friends and acquaintances than men. They tend to value the opinions of friends, experts, and media as opposed to marketing messages. Public relations giant Ketchum has established a division named Women 25 to 54 to meet the needs of companies and organizations seeking to reach this demographic group. Because of time pressures and competition for their attention, women are thought to receive and absorb information in smaller chunks.

The LGBT (Lesbian, Gay, Bisexual, and Transgender) Community

The gay community shows impressive growth as an emerging demographic. "PR professionals neglect

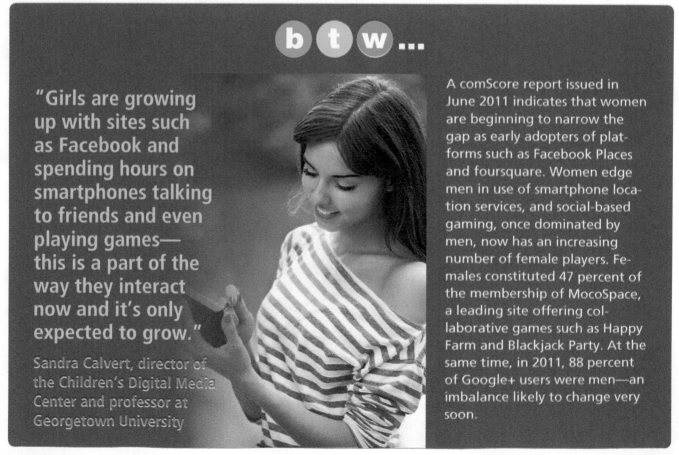

b t w ...

"Girls are growing up with sites such as Facebook and spending hours on smartphones talking to friends and even playing games—this is a part of the way they interact now and it's only expected to grow."

Sandra Calvert, director of the Children's Digital Media Center and professor at Georgetown University

A comScore report issued in June 2011 indicates that women are beginning to narrow the gap as early adopters of platforms such as Facebook Places and foursquare. Women edge men in use of smartphone location services, and social-based gaming, once dominated by men, now has an increasing number of female players. Females constituted 47 percent of the membership of MocoSpace, a leading site offering collaborative games such as Happy Farm and Blackjack Party. At the same time, in 2011, 88 percent of Google+ users were men—an imbalance likely to change very soon.

Reaching Diverse Audiences

a valuable opportunity if they don't reach out effectively to the nation's gay community," according to Fred Lameck and Bob Witeck writing in *Public Relations Tactics*.

Like many audiences and like members of the evangelical

Twenty-nine percent of gay households have median incomes exceeding $90,000 per year. Witeck-Combs communication and Packaged Facts estimate that the estimated 16 million LGBT adults in the U.S. wield buying power of about $743 billion per year.

Christian demographic group (discussed later in this chapter), LGBT consumers tend to support companies and brands that reflect and support their views. To that end, Human Rights Campaign launched the "Buying for Equality 2010" initiative to help identify companies sympathetic to LGBT issues.

According to Garber, a dating website, the gay community has high brand loyalty, purchasing products that target advertisements to gay consumers and support gay issues. Subaru pioneered "gay-specific" advertising in 1996 with a campaign specifically targeting lesbian consumers using gay tennis star Martina Navratilova as a spokesperson. The Internet travel site Orbitz, McDonald's, Virgin Mobile, Disney, Wells Fargo, and Bud Lite have also made efforts to appeal directly to gay audiences. OutNewsWire.com provides relevant news and entertainment content to LGBT news channels.

Although emerging LGBT audiences have a great deal of appeal to marketers, public relations professionals should be careful about the messages they release. The LGBT community may be offended by conventional or normative principles that conflict with their values and lifestyles. As with any target audience, public relations professionals need to thoughtfully consider the nuanced identities of these audience members and ensure that public relations messages are a nonstereotypical reflection of the gay community.

Lameck and Witeck, in their *Public Relations Tactics* article, suggest several tips. One is to connect your event or news announcement with festive occasions, such as Halloween or St. Valentine's Day, that resonate with LGBT households. It's also good to remember

that LGBT same-sex couples are families too, and as such respond to authentic family images.

Religious Groups

As society changes, new audiences continually emerge. Public relations professionals must be aware of this dynamic and pay attention to such audiences. For example, Catholic and evangelical Christian religious groups are growing in size and sometimes bonding together in new constellations. For example, many members of the Tea Party express conservative or evangelical Christian views.

The U.S. religious publishing and products (RPP) market rose to about $6 billion in 2008, though it has fallen slightly since. As of 2011, the religious market accounts for about 10 percent of all books sold in the U.S. From a marketing/public relations point of view, it is clear that products and services structured around religious themes sell. The RPP market has achieved mainstream status and continues to grow at a steady rate. In a global setting, it competes with other religious traditions.

Halloween and St. Valentine's Day are festive occasions that may resonate with many LGBT households.

A Comfortable Discussion or Too Much Information?

When the first ad for Kotex feminine napkins appeared in *Ladies' Home Journal* in January 1921, it created something of a scandal. Public discussion of matters related to hygiene, especially of such a personal nature, was taboo. The campaign connected the product to Kotex's bandages used during World War I, and featured nurses. Because of the delicate nature of the subject, Kotex enlisted a woman, a nurse, to write the copy. In the end, the Kotex campaign changed the way Americans viewed intimate aspects of personal health. Many scholars cite the Kotex advertisements as an important catalyst leading to the gradual acceptance of women's issues as an appropriate topic of discussion in the public sphere.

And progress marches on. "People are just becoming more comfortable talking about sex," according to Alan Cheung, the senior brand manager of Durex, the company that owns Trojan, a popular brand of condom. Supporting this perspective is the steady stream of news stories about politicians and athletes engaged in online sexual behavior and the rising popularity of social media applications that feature sexual content or interaction.

In this context, Durex launched its Triphoria vibrator, supported by a campaign with a slogan asserting that "Vibrators carry the conversation." Because the Internet allows privacy and anonymity—and because vibrators are still not a common topic of discussion—Durex focused on social media in the campaign, using Facebook, Twitter, and other platforms to engage audiences in a more comfortable setting. Durex also used sly, allusive television spots to generate discussion. The company is betting that Americans agree with Brian Weiss, VP of Trojan subsidiary Church & Dwight, that "when it comes to vibrators, people are very open to saying this is something that's good for sexual health."

In addition to the titillating aspect of the conversation, the Durex campaign has a serious side, aspiring to help couples "balance physical, emotional, and sociological factors" related to sexual health. To that end, the "Durex Community" offers support in the form of expert advice and interaction with others via an online forum.

1 What factors led to the success of the groundbreaking 1921 Kotex campaign?

2 Why are social media of particular importance in the context of the Durex campaign and others like it?

Ethnically Diverse AUDIENCES

Historically, the United States has welcomed millions of immigrants and assimilated them into the cultural mainstream. Immigrants have given the United States an eclectic mixture of personal values, habits, lifestyles, and perceptions that have been absorbed slowly, sometimes reluctantly.

Recently, ethnic groups—primarily Hispanics, African Americans, Asian Americans, and Native Americans—as a whole have been growing five times faster than the general population. Nonwhite ethnic groups now account for the majority in some states such as California, with 22.5 million out of 37.5 million residents claiming minority status. According to the latest census data. the combined Asian (13 percent) and Hispanic (37.6 percent) populations of California outnumber Caucasians. The U.S. Census Bureau also announced that more than 50 percent of the population in Texas claimed minority ethnic background in 2010. This is also the case in such cities as New York, San Diego, Las Vegas, and Memphis.

A basic point for public relations professionals to remember is that these populations form many target audiences, not massive homogeneous groups whose members have identical interests. Hispanics in Miami may have different cultures and concerns than Hispanics

think Why is it never safe to assume that all native Spanish speakers share similar values?

living in Texas or Arizona. To be more precise, even the common terms for minority groups, such as Asian American, misrepresent the cultural diversity among racial groups. For example, the lifestyles, values, and interests of fourth-generation Japanese Americans in Los Angeles are dramatically different from those prevalent among recent immigrants from Vietnam living in the suburbs of Denver. A public relations professional must

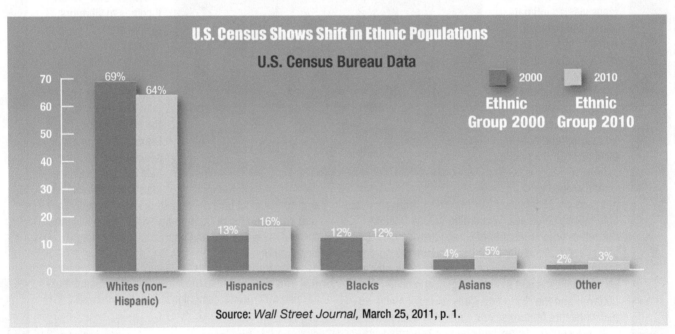

U.S. Census Shows Shift in Ethnic Populations

U.S. Census Bureau Data

Ethnic Group 2000 (2000) Ethnic Group 2010 (2010)

- Whites (non-Hispanic): 69%, 64%
- Hispanics: 13%, 16%
- Blacks: 12%, 12%
- Asians: 4%, 5%
- Other: 2%, 3%

Source: *Wall Street Journal*, March 25, 2011, p. 1.

The white (non-Hispanic) population accounted for 64 percent of the U.S. population in 2010, down from 69 percent in 2000. According to the Census Bureau, even greater changes will occur by 2040. The non-Hispanic white population is predicted to drop to 50.8 percent of the population—and then drop to 46.3 percent of the population by 2050. Notably, Latinos will increase in numbers because they now account for one in four people under age 18. The *Wall Street Journal* notes that this "holds the potential to shift the political dynamics across the country." In fact, this shift has already affected messaging in 22 of the country's 100 largest urban areas where non-Hispanic whites are now the minority. In Washington, D.C., for example, the city prints brochures about home foreclosures not only in English and Spanish, but also in Mandarin, Vietnamese, and Amharic—a language spoken in Ethiopia.

identify and define an audience with particular care and sensitivity, not only taking race into account but also considering the cultural and ethnic self-identity of target audience segments.

Diversity Media

The number and reach of minority media channels has increased, just as the number of their constituents has expanded. In the last 20 years, newspaper revenues in general have declined by 48.8 percent. At the same time, Hispanic papers have increased from a mere handful to 832 in 2010, and circulation has been increasing steadily at an annual rate of 17 percent. Spanish-language and African American radio stations also have increased in number. Two principal Spanish-language TV networks, Univision and Telemundo, serve millions of viewers.

The Black Entertainment Television Network (BET) has a large national audience, augmented recently with the success of *The Game*, a hit reality show that portrays the lives of professional football players. An average of 7.7 million viewers tuned into *The Game* in January 2011.

KTSF's weeknight news, targeted at Chinese viewers, rose 44 percent in 2010. Serving the San Francisco region, the KTSF news broadcast placed third but was ahead of both Fox and NBC, with 110,000 average weekly viewers.

Many cable and satellite providers offer special packages in a variety of native languages. A substantial number of outlets exist for public relations messages, provided news releases and story pitches are translated and culturally appropriate. Business Wire, a major distributor of public relations messages, recognizes this diversity of interest among racial and ethnic minority groups and operates separate Hispanic, African American, and Asian American media circuits within the United States.

Public relations practitioners should be aware of mixed-race individuals whose representation in the media is perhaps more complex than traditional ethnic group categorization. Barack Obama, the first U.S. president of acknowledged mixed race, is often portrayed simply as an African American in media representations—celebrated as the first "black president." For example, Peggy Noonan wrote in the Wall Street Journal that Obama was a "brilliant young black man" prior to his election. To describe or represent a complex ancestry, it would seem, requires a great deal of effort and finesse, and it is difficult to find a clear consensus on just how to do it sensitively.

One in seven new marriages is interracial or interethnic.

Hispanics

The expansion of the Hispanic population represents a challenge for public relations practitioners. Merely translating messages into Spanish is not enough to ensure that they reach this population in the intended fashion. Instead, public relations practitioners must proactively shape communications to be responsive to Hispanic culture. According to New America Strategies Group and DemoGraph Corporation, Hispanic culture traditionally places great emphasis on family and children and spends three times more on health care and entertainment than comparable

non-Hispanic households. Hispanic spending on consumer goods has so far outpaced that of other ethnic groups in the United States.

Radio is an especially important way to reach this ethnic group. *Arbitron Hispanic Radio Today 2010* revealed that 97 percent of Hispanic men aged 45 to 54 and 96 percent of women age 25 to 44 listen to the radio. Hispanic station KLVE-FM has the largest audience in Los Angeles, more than any English-language station.

> "The rapid growth of the Hispanic market has generated a number of headlines since the Census numbers were revealed, but the increase of Asian households should not be overlooked."
>
> Pat McDonough, Nielsen senior vice president, insights and analysis

Television also has a large, rapidly expanding Hispanic audience. According to the Nielsen rating service, the number of Hispanic households with televisions rose by an estimated 4.6 percent in the 2011–2012 TV season. This rate of increase has been steady. Univision, the predominant Spanish-language TV network, claims to reach 75 percent of Hispanic viewers. Univision consistently has ranked fourth or fifth among all broadcast networks in the 18- to 34-year-old demographic, according to Nielsen's National Television Index. The Spanish-language TV network Telemundo is also making impressive market share gains.

The Nielsen Company conducted extensive research on the media habits of various ethnic groups and issued a summary of its findings in June 2011. The following are highlights of its report compiled by Cheryl Pearson-McNeil, SVP of community relations and public affairs, and Todd Hale, SVP of consumer and shopper insights.

AFRICAN AMERICANS are the heaviest TV consumers, watching 6 hours and 54 minutes a day versus the 5 hours and 11 minutes average for all U.S. households. More than 30 percent of African American households have four or five televisions, and heavily subscribe to subscription or premium cable services. On their mobile phones, this group uses more voice minutes than other groups (1,261 minutes per month).

HISPANICS are very active on smartphones, texting the most out of all ethnic groups (943 texts per month), and take advantage of a variety of mobile activities such as mobile banking. Smartphone penetration among Hispanics has reached 45 percent, matching only Asian American usage in popularity.

ASIAN/PACIFIC ISLANDERS are the most active PC and Internet users, spending almost 80 hours on PCs (the national average is about 55 hours). They also consume more Internet content than any other group, visiting 3,600 web pages in an average month. Although they watch the least amount of TV (3 hours and 14 minutes per day), they stream the most online video, averaging more than 10 hours in an average month—more than double the overall mean of 4 hours and 20 minutes.

Reaching Out to Hispanics

Despite a slightly lower immigration rate for Hispanics in recent years, the U.S. Hispanic market has continued to expand at a pace that surpasses the growth rates for other demographic groups in the country. In 2010, Hispanic populations in the U.S. made up approximately 16 percent of the total population. Between 2000 and 2010, the Hispanic population grew by 15.3 million, or about 43 percent. This was four times the national average of 9.7 percent growth. Given these numbers, it is no surprise that many organizations and corporations have made efforts to target Hispanic constituents and consumers.

As this group grows, efforts to reach out to them through campaigns are moving out of the shadows into the spotlight. For example, Walmart recently announced that it was going to "blow up" its multicultural marketing budget, according to Tony Rogers, senior vice president for brand marketing and advertising. He argued for integration: "The first level of 'getting it,' he said, "is not doing anything." The second level is recognizing its importance, but keeping efforts pretty siloed, like spending some money during Black History Month and Hispanic

Heritage Month and considering the multicultural box to be ticked off. "The next step is where we are—making multicultural part of everything we do," said Rogers. To tailor communication messages, Walmart employs leading multicultural agencies: Lopez Negrete Communications handles the Hispanic Market, GlobalHue the African American market, and IW Group specializes in Asian communications. Walmart is following the example of Proctor & Gamble, a pioneer in reaching out to multicultural audiences.

Hispanic consumers have been prime consumers of media, but the economic downturn has taken its toll on Hispanic print outlets. While print sales languish among Hispanics, this group is increasingly viewed as an emerging online audience. After a slower start, the use of social marketing and networks among Latinos has expanded in recent years. According to a 2011 survey conducted by TeleNoticias-LatinoWire and the Hispanic Public Relations Society, Latino social media traditionally has enjoyed about half as many users as there are users in the U.S. population as a whole. And while 92 percent of companies surveyed indicated that

they had social media initiatives, only 45 percent said those efforts targeted Latino audiences. However, 69 percent of respondents claimed that they viewed Hispanic social media programs as important within their overall communication strategy. Said Tom Mulgrew, vice president of Latino Wire, "What can be derived from the survey is that social media is still very much in the formative state at most companies and hasn't yet become a part of the strategic communications plan." He added, "I think we can expect that to change in the coming years."

> **Too often, companies don't realize the inherent differences of our community, are not aware of the market size impact, and have not optimized efforts to develop messages beyond those that coincide with Black History Month.**
>
> Cloves Campbell, president of the National Newspaper Publishers Association

More impressive are the gains made among Asian households during the 2011–2012 season—9.6%. Asian homes in 2011 constituted 4.6 percent of the Nielsen sample.

African Americans

Historically the most readily identifiable racial group in the United States, African Americans are far from a monolithic group sharing a common heritage or goals. On November 10, 2011, the Huffington Post announced that African American buying power was projected to reach $1.1 trillion by 2015.

In recent years, affluent members of the African American community have been responsible for many of these purchases. Specialized magazines, such as *Uptown*, and websites catering to affluent African American professionals have seen a marked increase in readership. "The world is now a different place for the affluent African American demographic," said Len Burnett, cofounder of *Uptown*. "Luxury brands understand the importance of niche shoppers with disposable income and *Uptown* delivers them efficiently." Business Wire's "Black PR Wire" includes listings for more than 1,200 black-owned publications, including both newspapers and magazines.

The urban market is often associated with African Americans, although it is not necessarily exclusively urban or restricted to people of African descent. The 2010 Census revealed that the African American population declined in major urban areas as increasing numbers moved to the suburbs or more dispersed settlements, especially in the South. The percentage of African Americans in Atlanta contracted from 61 percent in 2000 to 53 percent in 2010. At the same time, the percentage of African Americans living in the countless suburbs surrounding that city increased by 40 percent. The African American community of metropolitan Atlanta stands at 1.7 million.

In addition, the urban market is defined by fashion trends set by hip-hop music stars, and it extends principally to members of Generation X and Y of all ethnic backgrounds. Like all Americans, African Americans have faced harsh economic times in recent years.

Public relations has come a long way in the last decade in Russia and other former Soviet countries, mirroring in many instances the best practices in the U.S., Europe, and Asia. For example, when McDonald's opened its first restaurant in Russia immediately after the breakup of the Soviet Union in 1991, the press embraced the fast-food restaurant as a symbol of all that was positive about Western culture in contrast to Soviet culture. As the novelty of Western-style capitalism wore thin, however, public relations systems in Russia often reanimated old-style Soviet propaganda tools. In the early 1990s, so-called public relations "technologists" funneled millions of dollars into journalists' hands in exchange for favorable press coverage. Overloading the press with rumor and hearsay about rival politicians or corporations—a technique known as "black public relations"—was also a frequent strategy.

With the dawn of the new millennium, Russian public relations professionals began to recognize the benefit of modern public relations approaches. In 2010, for instance, Ketchum acquired the Moscow-based firm Maslov PR, with whom they had enjoyed a 15-year relationship. John Higgins, a Ketchum senior partner and CEO, International, noted that, "Russia is an increasingly important region for our clients, and Maslov PR has time and again proven itself an exemplary and impressive partner."

Global AUDIENCES

Audiences in places such as Russia, China, India, Latin America, and Europe are drawing the attention of public relations professionals as trade (and, correspondingly, public relations) expands globally. Public relations professionals must overcome language barriers and consider social differences if they are to practice culturally appropriate and locally acceptable public relations. Differences in lifestyles, customs, values, and cultures are not the only challenges. Unique aspects of the local political, economic, and industrial structures also affect the strategic planning and execution of public relations campaigns.

China is one growing market undergoing revolutionary political, social, and industrial changes. Since

think **What are some of the challenges to reaching global audiences with cultural, social, economic, and political differences?**

it reopened to Western markets in 1978, the growth of business opportunities in China has been phenomenal. Despite the dark shadow of corruption and government regulation as ongoing concerns, American and European companies have embraced the Chinese market. Awareness of local customs and business practices is critical in pursuing these opportunities, however. "There are cultural differences that you have to become attuned to," said Cynthia He, an investment relations manager with the search engine company

Baidu in China, in an interview with *Time* magazine Asia edition reporter Bill Powell. "I've been at meetings when I've been very blunt in pointing something out, and there will be an awkward second or two of silence, and then someone will politely say, 'Well, that's a very American way of looking at it,' which is another way of saying, 'Hey, will you tone it down a bit!'" In China, personal influence is important in every aspect of the business, social, and media systems. For example, if public relations practitioners want to send out news releases, they may need to get to know the reporters personally as part of the process.

MATCHING THE Audience WITH THE Media

Given the broad array of print, audio, visual, and new media outlets available, public relations practitioners must make wise choices to use their time and budgets efficiently and effectively to produce desired outcomes. Some general guidelines can be given for matching audiences with the media. In this section, we quickly introduce the different types of media.

Print

Print media are the most effective choice for delivering a message that requires absorption of details and contemplation by receivers. Printed matter can be read repeatedly and kept for reference. Although newspapers are comparatively quick to

disseminate information, they face increasing competition from online content delivery systems such as the iPad, Kindle, and Nook. Magazines, although slower to disseminate topical information, are better for reaching special-interest audiences. Books take even longer to publish and subsequently digest, but can generate strong impact over time. However, publish-on-demand services and texts designed for the iPad or other tablet platforms may see a reduction in the time elapsed between writing, publishing, and distributing. Traditional print media still remain popular among both older and more highly educated audiences.

Newspapers are aimed at an audience of varying educational and

economic levels and are designed for family reading. They attempt to include something of interest to men, women, and children. Newspaper editors cast a wide net to capture the reading interests of as many people as possible. Newspapers have a broad appeal among adults and are effective at handling complex or in-depth material that television cannot adequately cover. While hard copies of newspapers such as the *New York Times*, *Washington Post*, or *Wall Street Journal* reach older public opinion leaders, young people turn to print newspapers less often, favoring online media instead.

Magazines differ markedly from newspapers in terms of content, time frame, and methods of operation. Thus, they present different opportunities and problems to public relations practitioners. In contrast to daily newspapers, which have tight deadlines, magazines are published weekly, monthly, or sometimes quarterly. Because these publications usually deal with subjects in greater depth than newspapers do, magazine editors may allot months for the development of an article. Public relations professionals who seek to supply subject ideas or ready-to-publish material to magazines must plan much further ahead than is necessary with newspapers.

Magazine subscriptions were down 1.5 percent in 2010. *Reader's Digest* lost an astonishing 22 percent. On the other hand, *Game Informer Magazine* gained an impressive 33.3 percent. Only one other magazine, *Parenting*, gained more than 2 percent.

At least in the U.K., the promise on online subscriptions—supplying digital editions—has not lived up to expectations. Only two of the online magazines that responded to a 2011 ABC survey sold more than 1,000 copies, *HELLO!* and *Men's Health*. *Condé Nast Traveller* managed to sell only 182 copies.

Because their writing and publication is a time-consuming process, often involving years from the conception of an idea until the appearance of the printed volume, books are not popularly recognized as public relations tools. Yet they can be. A book, especially a hardcover one, has stature in the minds of readers. As channels of communication, books reach thoughtful audiences, including opinion leaders, who are willing to devote time to their study. Publication of a book often starts a trend or focuses national discussion on an issue. In addition, e-books represent an emerging market. The Kindle, marketed by Amazon, has emerged as an early leader among the many e-readers available. Sony and Samsung readers, now popular in Asia, are also gaining strides.

Radio and Video

Radio's greatest advantages are its flexibility and ability to reach specific target audiences. Messages can be prepared for and broadcast on radio more rapidly than on television, and at a much lower cost. Because there are nine times as many radio stations as TV stations in the United States, audience exposure is easier to obtain. However, radio lacks the visual impact of television.

Speed and mobility are the special attributes that make radio unique among the major media, although Internet communications such as blogs and podcasts are threatening to unseat radio from this unique position. If urgency justifies such action, messages can be placed on the air almost instantly upon their receipt at a radio station. Because radio programming is more loosely structured than television programming, interruption of a program for an urgent announcement can be done with less internal decision making.

Television

Television has the strongest emotional impact of any type of mass media. The vividness and personality of the TV communicator creates an influence that print media cannot match. Although the issue is complicated by the profusion of cable, on-demand services, and content providers such as Netflix and Hulu, television currently has the largest and broadest audience.

The visual element differentiates television from other media and gives it such pervasive cultural impact. Producers of entertainment shows, newscasts, and commercials regard movement on the screen as essential. Something must happen to hold the viewer's attention. The single "talking head" set against a simple backdrop once common to television news programs has evolved into bold graphics, running headlines, sports scores, and stock quotes—sometimes to the detriment of the central message.

think How is the Internet changing the role that radio and TV play in public relations campaigns?

Video is another important public relations tool. Both corporations and nonprofit organizations use films and videos for internal purposes as part of audiovisual programs to train and inform their employees or to inform and influence the public. Facebook and YouTube have emerged as the most popular platforms for sharing multimedia content. Social media is more cost-effective than television and print ads, and allows for direct interaction with the target audience. Many companies, such as Pepsi Cola and Southwest Airlines, employ social media to conduct contests, provide feedback, and encourage followers to submit their own photographs and videos.

Online and Social Media

Not so long ago, online media were thought of as just a supplemental method of reaching a generally well-educated, relatively affluent audience. Their role has since expanded exponentially. Currently, a little more than 80 percent of U.S. households own a computer and nearly 95 percent of those who own a computer have Internet access. E-mail, text, VoIP, cloud computing, and electronic drop boxes dominate modern communication. The traditional letter is almost an extinct species.

The personal computer represents a significant and swiftly expanding tool for public relations practitioners. With e-mails, tweets, listservs, and Facebook analytics, public relations practitioners can deliver specially tailored information about clients' projects, establish contacts with reporters, and exchange ideas. Social media has drastically altered the intellectual and entertainment landscape in the brief span of 20 years. It is surprising to recall that e-mail was not widely used before the early 1990s

Reaching Diverse Audiences

and that the first World Wide Web page appeared in 1991.

The Internet offers unusual opportunities to deliver messages to audiences in the exact form that public relations practitioners conceive them. Millions of companies, nonprofit organizations, and individuals maintain websites to explain their companies and brands, promote their products and services, and sell merchandise directly to consumers. By participating in online discussion groups, chat rooms, and similar online interchanges, public relations people reach opinion leaders in specific fields with facts and opinions favorable to their cause. They directly reach target consumers, investors, community members, and employees without having to pass through any media gatekeepers. With tweets, e-mails, and listservs, public relations practitioners deliver specially tailored messages to precisely targeted audiences.

Public relations professionals especially depend on online media for communicating with Generations X and Y. Members of Gen X and Gen Y spend an inordinate amount of time in front of computers, posting on social media sites, searching the web, chatting with their friends, playing videogames, or shopping. The virtual environment allows them opportunities to multitask, perhaps doing research for a paper while also making friends whom they may never meet face-to-face, and in the most extreme instances, even dating and marrying someone from the other side of the world.

Today, there are 311 million people in the U.S., with 164 million PCs and 293 million mobile phones. Social network users number 142 million. With these numbers in mind, public relations professionals will do well to remember that multicultural audiences are among the most enthusiastic and voracious consumers of social media. Many companies and organizations have made strides in exploiting this channel. Story Worldwide's "2010 U.S. Hispanic Social Media and Marketing Overview" identified a number of successful campaigns. For example, Pepsi attracted 6,830 fans to its "Yo Sumo" (I Count) site between February and May of 2010.

"Mujeres Como Tú" (Women Like You), a social media campaign for Proctor and Gamble's Pantene shampoo, designed by Fleishman Hilliard, was "liked" by 10,200 people, with many followers taking advantage of the tab customized for Spanish speakers, "Lo Nuevo."

Of course, many challenges must be overcome when using social media for public relations applications. Chief among them is the need to develop tactics to ensure cultural relevancy, avoid clichés, and move beyond standardized approaches.

According to research conducted by the Florida State University Center for Hispanic Marketing Communications and the Captura Group, older English-speaking Hispanic users (defined as 36 or older) were **more than twice as likely** to use social media than their non-Hispanic counterparts.

What Would You Do?

Finding Your Place in the Sun

Spray-on sunscreen is sold in canisters, which emit a clear mist that completely coats the skin without damaging the ozone layer. Dermatologists claim that spray-on sunscreens offer the same protection as lotions. They also have the advantage of being easy to apply, which means that individuals will be more likely to coat every part of the body rather than just dabbing a little lotion on their arms, nose, or shoulders.

Banana Boat brand markets its UltraMist sunblock to compete with other major brand offerings such as Coppertone Continuous Spray and Neutrogena Fresh Cooling Body Mist Sunblock. Target and Walmart market their own brands of spray-on sunscreens.

Market research indicates that a major demographic group for spray-on sunscreens is college students, who, whenever they can, spend time tanning and going to the beach. Indeed, spring break finds thousands of college students crowding the beaches of Florida, Texas, California, and Mexico.

Banana Boat has retained your public relations firm to develop a product publicity program for UltraMist sunblock aimed directly at the college audience. One suggestion for making Banana Boat the market leader is to position the company as the leading authority on sunscreens and ways to use them effectively, including educating the public about SPF ratings, among other things.

Plan a public relations campaign that would reach college students through traditional media (i.e., newspapers, magazines, radio, or television) as well as online media and social media. Don't forget to explain which kinds of special events or promotions you would plan to effectively reach the target audience.

Reaching Diverse Audiences

summary

How Does the Diverse Nature of Audiences Affect Public Relations Practice?

- The public relations practitioner must reach a diverse and constantly changing audience. One of the most important aspects of this job is identifying the target audience so as to appropriately and effectively customize communications and public relations efforts.

How Can Information About the General Characteristics of Key Demographic Groups Inform Effective Public Relations Efforts?

- The senior group has grown in number as life span has increased. Young people represent another growing audience with a changing face. Their values, lifestyle, interests, and consumption patterns are conspicuously different from those of other demographic groups. In the United States, baby boomers are an economically advantaged group with great purchasing power.

- Women have significant purchasing power and exercise great influence as opinion leaders in general. The lesbian, gay, bisexual, and transgender (LGBT) community is a demographic and lifestyle group that travels, consumes luxury goods, and tends to support companies that are sympathetic to gay and lesbian issues. Religious groups such as Catholic and evangelical religious groups are growing in market and political power.

- The ethnic-minority population is increasing at about five times the rate of the general population in the United States, though such groups comprise many different target audiences. When addressing these publics, the public relations practitioner must be sensitive to the special issues, concerns, or interests of specific national and ethnic audiences.

Why Is It Important to Match Media Type to Audience?

- Public relations practitioners should consider the appropriate media (or, sometimes, a single medium) for each public relations campaign so as to speak effectively to target audiences.

questions
FOR REVIEW AND DISCUSSION

1 Which key characteristics of the youth market have been identified as relevant to public relations practice? What are the media-use habits of this public?

2 How can women's roles as opinion leaders be leveraged from a public relations standpoint?

3 What are some effective ways for public relations professionals to reach different gender and lifestyle audiences, such as LGBT and religious groups?

4 How do you think the various changes in the racial and ethnic makeup of the United States will affect the practice of public relations in the future?

5 What are some challenges facing public relations professionals in dealing with global audiences?

6 What are some attractive features of social media in terms of reaching audiences? What are some possibilities for the public relations specialist to take advantage of the growth of sites like Facebook and Twitter?

Photo Credits

MySearchLab®

The Mass Media

From Chapter 11 of *Think Public Relations*, 2013 Edition. Dennis L. Wilcox, Glen T. Cameron, Bryan H. Reber, Jae-Hwa Shin.

The Mass Media

A Varied Campaign Helps Slurpee Unite America

It all started at a presidential press conference. During midterm elections, President Barack Obama criticized Republicans by saying that Democrats were doing all the heavy legislative lifting while Republicans sat around "sipping Slurpees." After congressional Democrats took what Obama called a "shellacking" in those elections, the president was asked at a press conference whether he might get the new Republican and Democratic leadership together for a Slurpee Summit. He replied, "Slurpees are delicious drinks." Moments after the press conference had ended, "Slurpee Summit" began trending high on Twitter. Convenience store 7-Eleven, the home of the Slurpee, saw this as an opportunity too good to miss and put together a campaign of varied public relations tactics.

Margaret Chabris, a spokeswoman for 7-Eleven, told *USA Today*, "This is a rare opportunity for a brand. We don't want to be opportunistic, but nothing has ever been this big for Slurpee." 7-Eleven and its public relations firm, New Partners, quickly contacted the White House to offer to host a summit.

The catered Summit never happened, but a fast and varied public relations campaign did. Together with public relations firm FreshWorks/Ketchum, 7-Eleven put together a 3,000-mile, multi-city "Slurpee Unity Tour," its own "Slurpee Summit" in Washington, D.C., and "Purple Friday," an event held on the Friday after Thanksgiving (popularly referred to as Black Friday) during which free purple Slurpees were offered to 7-Eleven customers. To get the free drink, customers had to go to Slurpee's Facebook page and print a coupon. This campaign tactic added 500,000 Facebook fans to Slurpee's page.

The Slurpee Unity Tour began in Dallas, Texas, headquarters to 7-Eleven, and took a two-week route through 13 cities, ending in Washington, D.C. In Washington, 7-Eleven hosted a public concert featuring live music and entertainment and gave away free "Purple Slurpees for the People."

Media relations tactics generated spectacular news coverage. Every major broadcast network referenced President Obama's meeting with congressional leadership as the "Slurpee Summit." The campaign also earned mention in *Vanity Fair*, *The Washington Post*, National Public Radio, the *New York Daily News*, the *Los Angeles Times* and many other national media.

1 Identify the public relations tactics used in this case.

2 Why do you think this campaign was so successful at capturing media attention?

Ask Yourself

> Why Are News Releases the Most Commonly Used Public Relations Tactic?

> How Are Media Advisories, Fact Sheets, Media Kits, and Pitch Letters Used in Public Relations Campaigns?

> Which Public Relations Tactics Are Best for Reaching Television and Radio Audiences?

> How Can Product Placements Be Leveraged to Promote Products and Services?

News RELEASES

Public relations professionals rely on a toolbox full of varied tactics. News releases, public service announcements, media conferences, and special events are just some of the best-known and time-honored methods. In this chapter, we introduce you to these tactics and others.

The news release, also called a press release, is the most commonly used public relations tactic. The primary purpose of this simple document is the dissemination of information from public relations sources to mass media such as newspapers, broadcast stations, and magazines. A great deal of the information in weekly and daily newspapers originates from news releases prepared by publicists and public relations practitioners on behalf of their clients and employers.

Newsrooms have had to cut staff dramatically in recent years, and this gives PR practitioners a tremendous opportunity to deliver worthwhile content to news media.

A study by Arketi Group found that to generate story ideas, 77 percent of journalists use press releases and 80 percent use public relations sources.

Is It Time for a News Release?

Before writing a news release, a public relations professional should ask and answer a number of questions:

- *What is the key message?* This answer should be expressed in one sentence.

think Why do some editors refer to public relations professionals as "unpaid reporters"?

- *Who is the primary audience?* Is it consumers who may buy a product or service? Or is it purchasing agents in other companies? The answer to this question determines whether the release is sent to a daily community newspaper or to a trade magazine.
- *What does the target audience gain from the product or service?* What are the potential benefits and rewards?
- *What objective does the release serve?* Is it to increase product sales, to enhance the organization's reputation, or to increase attendance at an event?

After the key public relations questions are addressed, the next step is to think like a journalist and write a well-crafted news story that includes the traditional five W's and H: who, what, when, where, why, and how.

Although the traditional news release is still mailed primarily to weekly newspapers in small towns across the nation, the vast majority of news releases today are prepared for distribution by e-mail or via electronic distribution services such as BusinessWire.

PRNewswire claims that its multimedia news releases get almost 80 percent more views than the standard e-mail release and that readers are 3.5 times more likely to share the multimedia release with friends.

News releases distributed online are only effective if the writer carefully uses what is known as search engine optimization (SEO) techniques. Essentially, SEO is the process of selecting keywords for the news release that make the content easily retrievable if a journalist or even a consumer conducts a search on Google, Bing, or Yahoo!. You should also use one or two keywords within the first 65–70 characters of the headline and in the first two paragraphs of your news release because search engines, like us, read from top to bottom.

So how do you know what keywords would generate the most search results for you? Fortunately, Google has some tools that give you guidance. One tool is *Google AdWords*, which gives you insight into what phrases are searched most frequently. The *Google External Keyword* tool is also helpful because it lists the other words associated with a major keyword and how much the related terms are searched. And *Google Trends* provides information about when certain terms are searched, so you can more precisely time your online release.

SEO also plays a major role in the multimedia news release, which is often referred to as a *social media release* (SMR). These releases, pioneered by the major electronic distribution services, such as BusinessWire, PR Newswire, PRWeb, and Marketwire, make it possible to embed a news release with high-resolution photos/graphics, video, and audio components. Electronic distribution services have teamed up with search engines such as Google, Yahoo!, and MSN to promote maximum exposure of the news release.

An SMR, for example, will include social media tags so the content can be circulated through Digg, Technorati, del.icio.us and other social bookmarking sites to increase search engine rankings of the release and to drive targeted traffic to the organization's website. Other links will be to blogs, an organization's online newsroom, and even a space where readers can post comments about the news release. In this way, the SMR has expanded the audience beyond just the traditional media outlets.

Multimedia news releases, of course, are touted as being much more effective than the less sophisticated e-mail release that only has text and perhaps one embedded photo. The SMR also fulfills the prediction of Manny Ruiz, president of Hispanic PR Wire, that "the press release of the last century is dead." He enthusiastically adds, "In its place is a dynamic service that is more of an interactive marketing tool, more relevant and compelling for journalists; the difference is it's not only for journalists."

Crafting a NEWS RELEASE

The Standard News Release

Standard news releases adhere to a common format. Consider the following tips when crafting your own news releases:

- Identify the sender (contact) in the upper-left corner of the page and provide the sender's name, address, telephone number, fax number, and e-mail address.
- Provide a boldface headline that gives the key message of the release so the editor knows exactly what the release is about at a glance.
- Provide a dateline—for example, "Minneapolis, MN: June 21, 2012"—to indicate where the news release originated.
- Start the text with a clearly stated summary that contains the most important message you want to convey to the reader. Lead paragraphs should be a maximum of three to five lines.
- Use a 10- or 12-point standard type, such as Times Roman or Courier.
- Never split a paragraph from one page to the next. Place the word "more" at the bottom of each page of the news release (except on the last page, of course).
- Place an identifying slug line (a short phrase or title used to indicate the story content) and page number at the top of each page after the first one.
- Use Associated Press (AP) style. Most newspapers and broadcast stations use this stylebook.
- Be concise. Remove "puff" words, technical jargon, clichés and over-used phrases. Few news releases need to be more than two pages long.
- Double-check all information. Be absolutely certain that every fact and title in the release is correct.
- Eliminate boldface and words in all capital letters.
- Include a short paragraph at the end of the news release that provides a thumbnail sketch of what the organization does, how many employees it has, and so on. This is called a "boilerplate."
- Localize whenever possible. Most studies show that news releases with a local angle get published more often than generic news releases giving a regional or national perspective.

The Online News Release

The basic components of the traditional news release are the same for an online release, but an e-mail release has

(continued)

several differences when it comes to format. Note the following formatting differences when creating an online release:

- Copy should be single-spaced instead of double-spaced.
- The ideal length is 200 to 250 words instead of up to 400 words.
- The emphasis is on brevity so journalists can view most of the release without scrolling.
- The subject line in the e-mail becomes the headline that determines whether a recipient clicks "open" or "delete."
- Contact information is often given at the bottom of the e-mail release instead of at the top.
- A quote in larger type is often highlighted in the body of the news release.
- A photo or logo is often embedded in the release for possible use with the story.

> ## "Social media releases are generally formatted so information is easy to scan, utilizing bullets and lists of ready-made quotes instead of dense text."
>
> Paolina Milana, vice president for Marketwire

The Multimedia News Release

The multimedia news release, is also referred to as a *social media release* (SMR). This release includes high-resolution photos/graphics, video, and audio components. The following are some tips for preparing SMRs:

- Include links to pages where multiple instances of your keywords/key phrases reinforce your message.
- Place keywords in headlines and first paragraphs.
- Distribute a release through a service that carries hyperlinks to sites such as Yahoo!, Google, Digg, Facebook, and Twitter.
- Be judicious with links. Too many links will confuse journalists and draw focus away from key messaging.
- Use high-resolution multimedia that can be easily downloaded.
- Be selective about photos and videos; make sure they complement the key message.

It's still worth remembering that the vast majority of news releases, even those carried by the electronic distribution services, are still basic releases about mundane activities that don't require photos, videos, or audio components. There's also some evidence that SMRs are not that popular with most journalists. One survey, conducted via Twitter, found that almost 75 percent of the respondents actually preferred a news release as text in an e-mail. Consequently, public relations staff often prepare an e-mail text version and a multimedia version of the same news release.

The Content of a News Release

A news release is like a news story. The lead paragraph is an integral and important part of the text, because it forms the apex of the journalistic "inverted pyramid" approach to writing. With this approach, the first paragraph succinctly summarizes the most important part of the story, and succeeding paragraphs fill

Press releases are often accompanied by a photo relating to the release. A McCormick Grill Mates release was accompanied by a photo of a juicy hamburger.

in the details in descending order of importance. The inverted pyramid structure also applies to multimedia news releases.

Publicity Photos

News releases are often accompanied by photos. Studies show that more people "read" photographs than read articles. The Advertising Research Foundation found that three to four times as many people notice the average one-column photograph as read the average news story. In another study, Wayne Wanta of the University of Florida found that articles accompanied by photographs are perceived as significantly more important than those without photographs.

Like news releases, publicity photos are not published unless they appeal to media gatekeepers. Although professional photographers should always be hired to take the photos, public relations practitioners should supervise their work and select which photos are best suited for media use.

THE INVERTED PYRAMID

Three reasons to use the inverted pyramid structure.

1. If the editor or reporter doesn't find anything interesting in the first three or four lines of the news release, it will be discarded.
2. Editors cut stories from the bottom. *Business Wire News* estimates that more than 90 percent of news releases are rewritten in much shorter form than the original text. If the main details of the story appear at the beginning, the release will still be understandable and informative even if most of the original text has been deleted.
3. Readers don't always read the full story. Statistics show that the average reader spends less than 30 minutes per day reading a metropolitan daily newspaper. Readers look at a lot of headlines and first paragraphs—but not much else.

Six Tips for GREAT PHOTOS

1 Photos must have good contrast and sharp detail so that they can be reproduced in a variety of formats.

2 The best photos are uncluttered. Use tight shots with minimum background and an emphasis on detail, not whole scenes, and limit wasted space by reducing gaps between individuals or objects.

3 Sometimes context may be important. Environmental portraits show the subject of the photo in his or her normal surroundings—for example, a research scientist in a lab.

4 Action gives a photo interest. It's better to show people doing something—talking, gesturing, laughing, running, or operating a machine.

5 Emphasize scale. Amazon, for example, might illustrate its newest Kindle by showing a person holding the device while surrounded by a large stack of print books, demonstrating how many titles it can store.

6 Most websites use images at a resolution of 72 dpi (dots per inch) to ensure fast downloads, but newspapers and magazines need a minimum of 300 dpi for reproduction purposes. Consequently, organizations usually have an online newsroom that provides high-resolution JPEG-format photos for journalists.

Media Advisories,
FACT SHEETS, MEDIA KITS, AND PITCH LETTERS

On occasion, public relations staff will send a note to reporters and editors about a news conference or upcoming event. In public relations parlance, these notes are referred to as media advisories or media alerts. Advisories can also let the media know about an interview opportunity with a visiting expert or alert them that a local person will be featured on a network television program. Alerts may be sent either alone or with an accompanying news release.

The most common format for media advisories is short, bulleted lists rather than long paragraphs. A typical one-page advisory might contain the following elements: a one-line headline, a brief paragraph outlining the story idea, answers to some of journalism's five W's and H questions, and a short paragraph telling the reporter whom to contact for more information or to make arrangements.

Fact sheets are often distributed as part of a media kit or with a news release to give additional background information about the product, person, service, or event. A variation on the fact sheet is the FAQ (frequently asked questions).

Fact sheets are usually one to two pages in length and serve as a "crib sheet" for journalists when they write a story. A fact sheet about an organization may use headings that provide the following items: (1) the organization's full name, (2) the products or services offered, (3) annual revenues, (4) the number of employees, (5) the names and one-paragraph biographies of top executives, (6) markets served, (7) the company's position in the industry, and (8) any other pertinent details.

A media kit is usually prepared for major events and new product launches. It provides editors and reporters with a variety of information and resources to make it easier to report about the topic. The basic elements of a media kit are (1) the main news release; (2) a news feature about the development of the product or something similar; (3) fact sheets on the product, organization, or event; (4) background information; (5) photos and drawings with captions; (6) biographical material on the spokesperson or chief executives; and (7) basic contact information such as e-mail addresses, phone numbers, and website URLs.

Another public relations tactic is to write short letters or e-mails to editors that will grab their attention. In the public relations industry, this practice is called a *pitch*. In many cases, the correspondence will be accompanied by a sample of the product. Public relations people also use pitches—either mailed, e-mailed, phoned, or tweeted—to ask editors to assign a reporter to a particular event, to pursue a feature angle on an issue or trend, or even to book a spokesperson on a forthcoming show.

A pitch lets the editor know, in brief form, about the contents of the media kit. It also outlines why a periodical or broadcast outlet should consider the information as a news article, photograph, or video feature. Pitching is a fine art that requires great skill. Before undertaking such an effort, public relations personnel must first do some basic research about the publication or broadcast show that they want to contact. It's important to be familiar with the kinds of stories that a publication usually prints or the kinds of guests who typically appear on a particular talk show. Knowing a journalist's beat and the types of stories he or she has written in the past is also helpful. In addition, because the media tend to express great interest in trends, it's a good idea to relate a particular product or service to something that is already identified as part of a particular fashion or lifestyle.

Media kits—also commonly called press kits—are usually in digital format. Providing a CD or posting a media kit online is economical and enables access to multimedia content such as photos, short videos, and links to more information. Flash drives are even more portable and cost-efficient than CDs, so a number of companies, such as Hewlett-Packard (HP), now use this platform for media kits. The HP approach is to embed the flash drive in a package about the size and thickness of a business card.

Saving the Arctic with Iconic Brand Mascots

HERE WE CONSIDER CORPORATE SOCIAL RESPONSIBILITY and its related public relations tactics.

In October 2011, the public voted the Coca-Cola polar bears onto the Madison Avenue Advertising Walk of Fame. While it was a 1993 ad campaign that catapulted the polar bear mascots onto the Walk of Fame, Coca-Cola has been using polar bears to advertise their brand since 1922. So it was logical that the global beverage maker would link a CSR effort to saving the habitat of endangered polar bears.

Coca-Cola partnered with the World Wildlife Fund in a campaign titled, "Arctic Home." To kick off the campaign in November 2011, Coca-Cola changed the color of its soft drink cans from the iconic red to white. The company pledged $3 million to the World Wildlife Fund's polar bear conservation efforts. Fans of the beverage were also invited to text a $1 donation to the cause.

Coca-Cola partnered with 7-Eleven to create an app-based contest to raise money and awareness for the polar bear cause. The Snowball Effect app could be downloaded free of charge to iPhones, iPads, and iPod Touches. Players with Facebook pages could earn points and challenge friends by having virtual snowball fights, checking in at 7-Eleven stores, and entering codes from 7-Eleven and Coca-Cola product containers, thereby spreading the word of the plight of the polar bear and the Arctic Home campaign.

> "[W]e're using one of our greatest assets—our flagship brand, Coca-Cola—to raise awareness for this important cause. And by partnering with WWF, we can truly make a positive difference for these majestic animals," said Muhtar Kent, chairman and CEO of The Coca-Cola Company, in a company press release."

The online home of the campaign was ArcticHome.com, where local Arctic time and temperature were reported. An interactive map showed the location of polar bears who wore tracking devices. The website also described the efforts of both Coca-Cola and World Wildlife Fund on behalf of the Arctic environment. And there was more: a trailer on the website announced a new 3-D IMAX film, *To the Arctic 3D*; a link to WWF field work introduced the scientific team and announced live online events; and video tours educated online guests about the Arctic home, polar bears, and the Arctic environment.

The case stands as a fine example of corporate entities using their resources to do good. Research shows that such programs engender loyalty among existing customers and employees and can serve as a recruiting tool for new customers. The link between Coca-Cola and the Arctic is a natural fit, thanks to the brand's lovable polar bear mascots.

1 Why is CSR considered a public relations tool? How do you see CSR used by other companies?

2 What tactics did Coke and 7-Eleven leverage in this campaign?

3 Is the World Wildlife Fund a logical partner for Coca-Cola?

Interviews WITH JOURNALISTS AND News CONFERENCES

A common request fielded by public relations practitioners is to arrange for a journalist to talk with an expert or newsmaker. These interviews are key sources of information for journalists and important uncontrolled media tactics for PR pros.

News conferences, on the other hand, are used to introduce news or newsmakers to journalists. While they are still uncontrolled tactics, it is the public relations practitioner, not the journalist, who initiates the interaction in a news conference.

Interviews

An interview with a newspaper reporter may last about an hour, perhaps taking place at lunch or over coffee in an informal setting. This person-to-person talk will typically result in a published story of perhaps 400 to 600 words, in which the interviewer weaves bits from the conversation together in direct and indirect quotation form, works in background material, and perhaps injects personal observations about the interviewee. Neither the person being interviewed nor a public relations representative should ask to approve an interview story before it is published. Such requests are rebuffed automatically as a form of censorship.

News Conferences

At a news conference, communication is two-way. The person speaking for a company or a cause submits to questioning by reporters, usually after making a brief opening statement. A news conference makes possible quick, widespread dissemination of information and opinions through the news media. It avoids the time-consuming task of presenting the information to news outlets individually and ensures that the intensely competitive newspapers and electronic media hear the news simultaneously. From a public relations point of view, these are the principal advantages of the news conference. These important pluses must be weighed against the fact that the person holding the conference opens himself or herself up to direct and potentially antagonistic questioning.

In terms of public relations strategy, the news conference can be either an offensive measure or a defensive device, depending on the client's need. Most news conferences—or *press conferences*, as they frequently are called—are positive in intent; they are affirmative actions intended to project the host's plans or point of view. For example, a corporation may hold a news conference to unveil a new product whose manufacture will create many new jobs, or a civic leader may do so to reveal the goals and plans for a countywide charity fund drive that she or he will head. Such

An interview subject has no control over what is published, although he or she can exercise self-control in answering the questions.

Magazine interviews usually explore a subject in greater depth than interviews published in newspapers, because the writer may have more space available. Most magazine interviews have the same format as those in newspapers; others appear in question-and-answer form. These kinds of interviews require prolonged taped questioning of the interviewee by one or more writers and editors.

news conferences should be carefully planned and scheduled well in advance.

If a business firm, an association, or a politician becomes embroiled in some kind of difficulty that is at best embarrassing, or at worst possibly incriminating, the media and public will demand an explanation. A bare-bones printed statement is not enough to satisfy

the clamor and may draw greater media scrutiny if the organization appears to be stonewalling. A well-prepared spokesperson may be able to achieve a measure of understanding and sympathy by reading from a carefully composed statement when the news conference opens.

No matter how trying the circumstances, the person holding the news conference should create an atmosphere of cooperation and project a sincere intent to be helpful. The worst thing to do is to appear angry or resentful of the questioning. A good posture is to admit that a situation is bad and that the organization is doing everything in its power to correct it—an approach described by Professor Timothy Coombs at the University of Central Florida as the "mortification" strategy.

There are two other types of news conferences of note. One occurs spontaneously, arising out of a news event: a winner of the Nobel Prize meets the media to explain his or her award-winning

work, or a runner who has just set a world record breathlessly describes his or her feelings. The other type is the regularly scheduled conference held by a public official at stated times, even when there is nothing special to announce. Usually this type of event is called a *briefing*—the daily U.S. State Department briefing is one example of such a news conference.

 When is a printed statement enough? When is it necessary to hold a news conference?

Planning and Conducting a News Conference

First ask the question, "Should we hold a news conference?" Frequently, the answer should be "No!" Reporters and camera crews should not be summoned to a press conference to hear propaganda

The Mass Media

If a business firm, an association, or a politician becomes embroiled in some kind of difficulty that is at best embarrassing, or at worst possibly incriminating, the media and public will demand an explanation.

(instead of news) or information of minor interest to a limited group. When this happens, their valuable time has been wasted—and it *is* valuable. If the material involved fails to meet the criteria of significant news, a wise public relations representative will simply distribute it through a press release.

Every news outlet that might be interested in the material should be invited to a news conference. An ignored media outlet may become an enemy, like a person who isn't asked to a party. The invitation should describe the nature of the material to be discussed so that an editor will know which type of reporter to assign to the event.

At a news conference, public relations representatives resemble producers of a movie or television show. They are responsible for briefing the spokesperson, making arrangements, and ensuring that the conference runs smoothly. They stay in the background during the actual event, however.

THE Media Party AND THE MEDIA TOUR

In the typical news conference, the purpose is to transmit information and opinions from the organization to the news media in a businesslike, time-efficient manner. Often, however, a corporation, an association, or a political figure wishes to deliver a message or build rapport with the media on a more personal basis. In these circumstances, a social setting such as a press or media party or a media trip is desirable.

A press party may be a luncheon, a dinner, or a reception. Whatever form it takes, standard practice is for the host to rise at the end of the socializing period and make the

think Why do reporters attend media parties?

"pitch." This may be a hard-news announcement, a brief policy statement followed by a question-and-answer period, or merely a soft-sell thank-you to the guests for coming and giving the host an opportunity to get to know them better. Guests usually are provided with press packets of information, either when they arrive or as they leave.

The host who expects that food and drink will buy favorable media

coverage may receive an unpleasant surprise, however. Conscientious reporters and editors will not be swayed by this kind of "wining and dining." In their view, they have already given something to the host by setting aside a part of their day for the party. They accept invitations to media parties because they wish to develop potential news contacts within the host's organization and to learn more about its officials.

Of the three kinds of media tours, the most common is a trip, often called a *junket*, during which editors and reporters are invited to inspect a company's manufacturing facilities in several cities, ride an inaugural flight of a new air route, or watch previews of the television network programs for the fall season, for example. The host usually picks up the tab for transporting, feeding, and housing the reporters.

A second variation of the media tour is the *familiarization trip*. "Fam trips," as they are called, are

Press parties may give the media an opportunity to preview an art exhibit or a new headquarters building, for example.

offered to travel writers and editors by the tourism industry. Convention and visitors bureaus, as well as major resorts, pay all expenses in the hope that the writers will report favorably on their experiences. Travel articles in magazines and newspapers usually result from a reporter's fam trip.

In the third kind of media tour, the organization's executives travel to key cities to talk with selected editors. For example, Motorola executives might tour the East Coast to talk with key magazine editors and demonstrate the capabilities of the company's newest Droid smartphone. Depending on editors' preferences, the executives may visit a publication and give a background briefing to key editors, or a hotel conference room may be set up so that the traveling executives can talk with editors from several publications at the same time.

THE REACH OF Radio AND Television

Broadcasting and its various forms, including webcasting, are important because they reach the vast majority of the U.S. public on a daily basis. Each week, it is estimated that radio reaches 92 percent of Americans ages 12 and older, with a total audience of 234 million. Fifty-one percent of U.S. adults said they got local news from radio at least once a week, according to the Pew Research Center. With the average American now commuting nearly 50 minutes each workday, a large percentage of this audience is reached in their cars. Writing and preparing materials for broadcast and digital media require a special perspective. Instead of writing for the eye, a practitioner has to shift gears and think about adding audio and visual elements to the story.

Radio

News releases prepared for radio differ in several ways from releases prepared for print media. Although the basic identifying information is the same (letterhead, contact, subject), the standard practice is to write a radio release using all uppercase letters in a double-spaced format.

The length of the printed radio news release needs to be indicated. Radio announcements should take 30 or 60 seconds to read. Broadcasters

---

Who Pays for What?

ethics in ACTION

The policies of major dailies forbid employees from accepting any gifts, housing, or transportation; the newspapers pay all costs associated with a media tour on which a staff member is sent. In contrast, some smaller dailies, weeklies, and trade magazines with more modest budgets accept offers for expense-paid trips. Rules also may differ by department. Reporters in the hard-news area, for example, cannot accept gifts or travel, but such policies may not be enforced for reporters who write soft news for the sports, travel, and lifestyle sections.

Given the mixed and often confusing policies of various media, public relations professionals must use common sense and discretion when offering "freebies" to reporters.

Don't violate the PRSA code of ethics, which forbids gifts and free trips that have nothing to do with covering a legitimate news event.

Be sensitive to the policies of news outlets and design events to stay within those parameters. For example, offer reporters the option of reimbursing the company for travel and hotel expenses.

Who should pick up the tab when a travel writer visits a resort?

must fit their messages into a rigid time frame that is measured down to the second.

Radio news releases, like releases for print and online media, must be newsworthy and not too commercial. Unlike the case with regular news releases, however, radio demands that the story be told in 60 seconds (about 125 words).

A news release for a newspaper or website uses standard English grammar and punctuation. Sentences often contain dependent and independent clauses. In a radio release, a more conversational style is used, and the emphasis is on strong, short sentences. This format allows the announcer to breathe between thoughts and the listener to follow what is being said. An average sentence length of about 10 words is a good goal.

think How does writing for radio differ from writing for print or online sources?

Audio News Releases Although broadcast-style news releases can be sent to radio stations for announcers to read, the most common and effective approach is to send the radio station a recording of the news announcement.

An audio news release, commonly called an *ANR*, can take two forms. One simple approach is for someone with a good radio voice to read the entire announcement; the person doing the reading is typically not identified by name. This type of ANR is called an *actuality*. In a second approach, an announcer reads the release, but a quote called a *sound bite* is also included from a satisfied customer or a company spokesperson. This approach is better than a straight announcement because the message comes from a "real person" rather than a nameless announcer. This type of announcement is also more acceptable to stations, because the radio station's staff can elect either to use the whole recorded announcement or to use just the sound bite.

Television **News**
Reaches a Mass Audience

24.5 million Americans watch national news on NBC, ABC, or CBS, according to Nielsen Media Research. Eighty-nine percent of Americans said they rely on local television for weather information, and 80 percent said they look to local television first for local breaking news, according to the Pew Research Center.

The average American watches 34 hours and 39 minutes of TV per week, according to Nielsen Media Research.

The preferred length for an ANR is one minute, although shorter ones can be used. The audio recording, usually delivered as an MP3 file, should also be accompanied by a copy of the script, which enables the news director to judge the value of the audio without having to listen to it.

Public Service Announcements Public relations personnel working for nonprofit organizations often prepare public service announcements (PSAs) for radio stations. A PSA is an unpaid announcement that promotes the programs of government or voluntary agencies or that serves the public interest. As part of their responsibility to serve the public interest, radio and TV stations provide airtime to charitable and civic organizations to inform the public about such topics as heart disease, mental illness, and AIDS.

Radio PSAs, like radio news releases, are written in uppercase and double-spaced format. Their length can be 60, 30, 20, 15, or 10 seconds. Unlike radio news releases, the standard practice is to submit multiple PSAs on the same subject in various lengths, allowing the station flexibility in using a PSA of a particular length to fill a specific time slot. A PSA is usually delivered as an MP3 file to stations along with an electronic copy of the script.

60-Second Public Service Announcement

The following is an example of a 60-second announcement distributed by the Guide Dogs for the Blind:

"As a blind person, how fortunate I've been. I've traveled with Guide Dogs for over 38 years, each in their own way irreplaceable. Bobby, who went to high school with me; Kenny, who so calmly guided me from class to class in college; Bev, who was there when I got married; Jalisa, who helped me start my business; Krista, without whom I wouldn't be here today; and now Primrose, my companion in retirement. For every milestone in my life, there are memories of a Guide Dog beside me. It's a bond unlike any you can have with a human being. These dogs come into our lives and grab a piece of our hearts."

Diane Phelps is from Napa, California. Bobby, Kenny, Bev, Jalisa, Krista and Primrose all came from Guide Dogs for the Blind with the help and support of people like you. Call 1-888-884-Dogs, or visit guidedogs.com.

Almost any topic or issue can be the subject of a PSA, although stations seem to be more receptive to particular topics. A survey of radio station public affairs directors by West-Glen Communications, a producer of PSAs, found that local community issues and events were most likely to receive airtime, followed by children's issues. The respondents also expressed a preference for PSAs involving health and safety, service organizations, breast cancer, and other cancers.

Many national organizations, such as the American Cancer Society and the American Red Cross, make their nationally distributed PSAs more interesting by incorporating music, sound bites, and other sounds in the script.

Radio Media Tours Another public relations tactic for radio is the radio media tour (RMT). In an RMT, a spokesperson conducts a series of one-on-one interviews from a central location with radio announcers across the country or a region. A public relations practitioner (often called a publicist in such a situation) books telephone interviews with DJs, news directors, or talk show hosts at various stations, and the personality gives interviews over the phone that can be broadcast live or recorded for later use. A selling point for the RMT is its relatively low cost and the convenience of giving numerous short interviews from one central location.

Television

There are four approaches for getting your organization's news and viewpoints on local television. The first approach is to simply send the same news release that the local print and online media receive. If the news director thinks the topic is newsworthy, the item may earn

---

How Long Is Your Message?

Most announcers read at a rate of 150 to 160 words per minute. Of course, word lengths vary, so it's not feasible to set the timing based on the number of words in a message. Instead, the general practice is to use an approximate line count.

With word processing software set for 60 spaces per line, the following standard can be applied:

2 lines = 10 seconds (about 25 words)

5 lines = 20 seconds (about 45 words)

8 lines = 30 seconds (about 75 words)

16 lines = 60 seconds (about 125 words)

---

a brief 10-second mention by the announcer on a news program. A news release may also prompt the assignment editor to consider visual treatment of the subject and assign the topic to a reporter and a camera crew for follow-up.

A second approach is to send a media alert or advisory (discussed earlier in the chapter), which informs the assignment editor about a particular event or occasion that would lend itself to video coverage. The third approach is to phone, text, or e-mail the assignment editor and make a pitch to have the station do a particular story. The secret to successfully pitching a television news editor is to emphasize the visual aspects of the story.

The fourth approach is to produce a video news release (VNR) that, like an ANR, is formatted for immediate use and requires a minimum effort on the part of station personnel. The VNR can be used by numerous stations on a regional, national, or even global basis.

Video News Releases An estimated 5,000 VNRs are produced annually in the United States, primarily by large organizations seeking enhanced recognition for their names, products, services, and causes.

A typical 90-second VNR may cost a minimum of $20,000 to $50,000 for production and distribution. Costs vary, however, depending on the number of location shots, special effects, the use of celebrities, and the number of staff required to produce a high-quality tape that meets broadcast standards. The production costs of VNRs are more easily justified if there is potential for national distribution and multiple pickups by television stations and cable systems.

Public relations departments or firms must carefully analyze the news potential of the information and consider whether the topic lends itself to a fast-paced, action-oriented visual presentation. A VNR should not be produced if it contains nothing but "talking heads," charts, and graphs. Another aspect to consider is whether the topic will still be current by the time the video is produced. On average, it takes four to six weeks to script, produce, and distribute a high-quality VNR. In a crisis situation or for a fast-breaking news event, however, a VNR can be produced in a matter of hours or days.

Because of the specialized knowledge that is required, public relations departments and firms usually outsource production to a firm specializing in scripting and producing VNRs.

The VNR package should include two or three minutes of B-roll. B-roll is video only, without narration, giving a television station maximum flexibility to add its own narration or use just a portion of the video as part of a news segment. This allows TV news producers to repackage the story. Typical B-roll includes additional interviews, sound bites, and file footage. A Nielsen Media Research survey of 130 TV news directors, for example, found that

Writing a script for a VNR is a bit more complicated than writing one for an ANR because the writer has to visualize the scene, much like a playwright or screenwriter. Adam Shell, in *Public Relations Tactics*, describes the required skills:

Producing a VNR requires expert interviewing skills, speedy video editing, a creative eye for visuals, and political savvy. The job of the VNR producer is not unlike that of a broadcast journalist. The instincts are the same. Engaging sound bites are a result of clever questioning. Good pictures come from creative camera work. A concise, newsworthy VNR comes from good writing and editing. Deadlines have to be met, too. And then there are all the tiny details and decisions that have to be made on the spot. Not to mention figuring out subtle ways to make sure that the client's signage appears on the video without turning off the news directors.

 What is B-roll and why is it important in a VNR?

70 percent preferred VNRs with B-roll attached. In fact, evidence shows that television news directors generally prefer B-roll packages instead of fully scripted VNRs. Even the term "video news release" seems to have fallen into disfavor according to Brian Schwartz, a former executive of Medialink, a producer of such material. Video production firms have increasingly moved to just producing B-roll packages on behalf of clients.

An advisory should accompany the VNR package or be sent to news directors before the actual satellite transmission of the video to the station. The advisory contains the key elements of the story, background and description of the visuals, editorial and technical contacts, satellite coordinates, and the date and time of the transmission.

While most VNRs are distributed via satellite transmissions, they often reach an even larger audience than is possible with local television through YouTube. Most organizations, with

VNRs, while effective, are somewhat controversial because televisions stations often use them without attributing the source. In 2011, the Federal Communications Commission (FCC) levied a fine of $4,000 against a Fox television affiliate in Minneapolis for airing a VNR without attribution.

Broadcast and Cable reported, "The FCC said that the station should have identified the GM VNR, in a story about new cars, and that failure to do so violated its sponsorship violation rules."

Such issues reinforce the need for public relations professionals to clearly identify the source of VNRs both in accompanying material and on the VNR itself.

YouTube Video Challenges Stereotype: Community Crafts Its Own PSA

Grand Rapids, Michigan, had a bone to pick with *Newsweek*. The magazine reported data from Mainstreet.com that labeled Grand Rapids a "dying city." Not so fast, city leaders said. "I took great exception to *Newsweek's* characterization of a dying city," Grand Rapids Mayor George Heartwell told ABC News. "We're a city that's young, that's vibrant, that's alive, that's growing. It's a fun place to be."

Rob Bliss, a Grand Rapids native and events organizer, joined forces with friend Scott Erickson and came up with the idea of creating a video that vividly demonstrated Grand Rapids' vibrance. More than 25 organizations in the community raised the $40,000 it took to shoot a 10-minute video lip-dub of Don McLean's *American Pie*. Five thousand townspeople were seen in the video. It featured "thousands of town residents touring the streets of the city, playing football, cheerleading, and lip synching the McLean song as they went along," reported *PRWeek*. In addition to cheerleaders and football players, there are fire trucks, police cars, news vans, a helicopter, politicians, a wedding, a concert, and a marching band.

Mayor Heartwell told ABC News, "We said, 'Rob, what do you need? We'll close the streets, we'll turn out the fire engines, the mayor will sing, whatever you need.' And in fact, he needed all that.... The mayor has certain prerogatives and I exercised all the prerogatives in this case ... pulled out all the stops and the result was I believe well worth it."

"The result" was a video that was posted to YouTube and that quickly went viral. The video was uploaded to YouTube on May 26, 2011, and by the end of the year, it had more than 4.3 million views. Film critic Roger Ebert tweeted that the Grand Rapids video was "the greatest music video ever made." Lindsey Smith of National Public Radio opined, "But as much as it's a pure treat to watch, it's also quite moving, and very effective as a response to a list of cities that are allegedly dying." And *PRWeek* gave the tactic its highest "PR Play Rating" of "Ingenious."

1. What do you think it takes to make a video that will go viral on YouTube?

2. What YouTube viral videos have you seen that you believe are effective public relations tools?

3. Do you think this video effectively countered the "dying city" label? Why or why not?

a few technical adjustments, regularly upload their VNRs to their YouTube channel and even their corporate websites.

Satellite Media Tours The television equivalent of the radio media tour is the satellite media tour (SMT). An SMT is a series of prebooked, one-on-one interviews from a fixed location (usually a television studio) via satellite with a series of television journalists or talk show hosts.

The most efficient way to conduct an SMT is to make the organization's spokesperson available for an interview at a designated time. Celebrities are always popular, but an organization also can use articulate experts. In general, the spokesperson sits in a chair or at a desk in front of a television camera. Another popular approach to SMTs is to get out of the television studio and do the interviews on location. When the National Pork Producers Council wanted to promote pork and tailgating, they turned to Football Hall of Famer, three-time Super Bowl champion, and *Dancing with the Stars* winner Emmitt Smith. Smith, with his wife, Pat, participated in a national satellite media tour during which they conducted 25 interviews in broadcast markets from Atlanta to San Diego.

Personal Appearances

Radio and television stations increasingly operate on round-the-clock schedules, and require vast amounts of programming to fill the time available. When your goal is to get spokespersons on talk and magazine shows, your contact is the directors and producers of such programs. The most valuable communication tools in reaching these people are the telephone and the persuasive pitch via e-mail, text, or Twitter.

Before pitching directors and producers, it is necessary for the public relations staff to do their homework. They must be completely familiar with a show's format and content, as well as the type

It's important to be honest about the experience and personality of the spokesperson, so the booker isn't disappointed and your credibility remains intact.

of audience that it reaches. A public relations professional should watch the program and study the format. This research will help determine whether a particular show is appropriate for your spokesperson and suggest how to tailor a pitch letter to achieve maximum results.

Talk Shows and Magazine Shows Radio and television talk shows have been a broadcast staple for many years. KABC in Los Angeles started the trend in 1960, when it became the first radio station in the country to convert to an all-news-and-talk format. Since then 2,056 radio stations across the country have adopted this format. Stations that play music also may include talk shows as part of their programming. About 48 million Americans listen to talk radio each week, according to the Pew Project for Excellence in Journalism.

The same growth applies to television. Phil Donahue began his seminal talk show in 1967. Today, there are dozens of nationally syndicated talk shows and a number of locally produced talk shows. For many years, the number one syndicated daytime talk show was the *Oprah Winfrey Show*, whose May 2011 finale attracted more than 16 million viewers. With the end of the *Oprah Winfrey Show*, *Dr. Phil* and *Live with Kelly* vied for the top spot. At the end of 2011, each of those talk shows was averaging nearly 4 million viewers a day. Selection of talk show may also depend on the public you are trying

to reach. For example, in late 2011, *Maury* was the number one syndicated talk show among women ages 18 to 49. On the network level, three shows are the Holy Grail for publicists: NBC's *Today*, ABC's *Good Morning America*, and CBS's *Early Show*. Collectively, these three shows draw more than 13 million viewers between 7 and 9 A.M. every weekday.

The advantage of talk shows is the opportunity to have viewers see and hear the organization's spokesperson without the filter of journalists and editors interpreting and deciding what is newsworthy. Another advantage is the opportunity to be on air longer than the traditional 30-second sound bite in a news program.

Booking a Guest The contact for a talk show may be the executive producer or assistant producer of the show. If it is a network or nationally syndicated show, the contact person may have the title of talent coordinator or talent executive. Whatever the title, these people are known in the broadcasting industry as *bookers* because they are responsible for booking a constant supply of timely guests for the show.

One way to place a guest on a talk show is to contact the booker to briefly outline the qualifications of the proposed speaker and explain why this person would be a timely guest. Publicists may call or send a brief note, text, or e-mail about the story angle, explaining why it is relevant to the show's audience and why the proposed speaker is qualified to talk on the subject. In many cases, the booker will ask for video clips of the spokesperson's appearances on previous TV shows or newspaper clips of media interviews.

In general, talk shows book guests three to four weeks in advance. Unless a topic or a person is

think Which characteristics does a good talk show guest have?

A talk show is an effective way to get information out about an event, product, service, or issue. The gatekeeper filter is more modest and a spokesperson has several minutes (compared to seconds in a news program) to engage the audience and get his or her point across.

Broadcast**Interviews**

The popularity of talk shows, both on local stations and syndicated satellite networks, provides many opportunities for on-air appearances. A successful radio, television, or online interview appearance has three principal requirements:

- *Preparation.* Guests should know what they want to say.
- *Concise speech.* Guests should answer questions and make statements precisely and briefly without excessive detail or extraneous material. Responses should be kept to 30 seconds or less, because the interviewer must conduct the program under strict time restrictions.
- *Relaxation.* "Mic fright" is a common ailment for which no automatic cure exists. It will diminish if the guest concentrates on talking to the interviewer in a casual, person-to-person manner. Guests should speak up firmly; the control room can reduce volume, if necessary.

A public relations adviser can help an interview guest on these points. Answers to anticipated questions may be worked out and polished during a mock interview in which the practitioner plays the role of broadcaster.

All too often, talk show hosts know little about their guests for the day's broadcast. The public relations adviser can overcome this difficulty by sending the host in advance a fact sheet summarizing the important information and listing questions the broadcaster might wish to ask. On network shows and major metro stations, support staffs often do the preliminary work with guests. Interviewers on hundreds of smaller local television and radio stations, however, lack such staff resources. Hosts at these stations may go on the air almost "cold" unless public relations practitioners provide them with volunteered information.

extremely timely or controversial, it is rare for a person to be booked on one or two days' notice. Public relations strategists must keep this time frame in mind as part of the overall planning of a public relations campaign.

Product Placements

Television's drama and comedy shows, and theatrical films as well, are often good vehicles for promoting a company's products and services. It is not a coincidence that the hero of a detective series drives a Lexus or that the heroine is seen boarding a Delta Airlines flight.

Such product placements, sometimes called *plugs*, are often negotiated by product publicists and talent agencies. This practice is really nothing new. Product placements, however, truly came of age with the movie *ET* in the early 1980s. The story goes that M&M's Candies made a classic marketing mistake by not allowing the film to use M&M's as the prominently displayed trail of candy that the young hero used to lure his big-eyed friend home. Instead, Hershey jumped at the chance to showcase Reese's Pieces in the blockbuster film, and the rest is history. Sales of Reese's Pieces skyrocketed. Even today, 30 years after the film's debut, the candy and the character remain forever linked in popular culture and the minds of a whole generation of *ET* fans.

Retailers are particularly active in seeking out product placements because studies show that today's youth gets many of their ideas about what products to buy from watching television shows. That's why *Modern Family's* Phil Dunphy was desperate to receive a just-released iPad for his birthday, Bella wears Manolo Blahnik pumps as she walks down the aisle in the *Twilight* series movie *Breaking Dawn*, *Project Runway* contestants use HP and Intel products in their design studio, *Biggest Loser*

 think Why do film producers agree to product placements?

contestants eat Subway sandwiches, and *New Year's Eve* revelers wear Nivea hats while they're waiting for the ball to drop in Times Square. According to Brandcameo, Apple products appeared in 30 percent of the number one movies in 2010.

Another opportunity for product exposure on television is on game shows. *The Price Is Right* and *Wheel of Fortune*, for example, use a variety of products as prizes for contestants.

> "In the early 1900's, Henry Ford had an affinity for Hollywood and perhaps it is no coincidence that his Model T's were the predominant vehicle appearing in the first motion pictures of the era.
> IPRA *Frontline*"

According to the Nielsen Company, during a recent ratings period, *American Idol* logged the most product placements on television at 208, followed by the *Celebrity Apprentice* at 127; *America's Next Top Model* and *The Biggest Loser* each had 88 product placements, and *The Amazing Race* had 69.

In this photo, the judges on *The X Factor* are seen enjoying prominently placed Pepsi products

APPLY YOUR KNOWLEDGE

What Would You Do?

A Grand Opening

A new university library will open next month. The $100 million building is an eight-story wonder of glass and steel beams designed by a famous architectural firm, Skinner and Associates. The library has more than 125 commissioned artworks, 2,500 plug-ins for student laptops, numerous multiuse computer labs, and the most up-to-date meeting facilities for students and faculty. In a special coup, author J. K. Rowling of *Harry Potter* fame has agreed to cut the ribbon at the official opening.

You are charged with creating a media (press) kit for the library's grand opening. First, write a memo outlining which materials you will include in the media kit. Second, draft a persuasive pitch to television news directors about why they should cover the grand opening. Third, write 60-, 30-, and 10-second PSAs for local radio stations informing the public about the grand opening and inviting them to attend the ribbon-cutting ceremony. Finally, write a 140-character tweet to the university's Twitter followers.

summary

questions

What Is the Role of News Releases in Public Relations?

- The news release is the most commonly used public relations tactic. These releases are key sources for a large percentage of newspaper and online articles.
- News releases must be accurate, informative, and written in journalistic style.

How Are Media Advisories, Fact Sheets, Media Kits, and Pitch Letters Used in Public Relations Campaigns?

- Advisories (also known as alerts) let journalists know about an upcoming event such as a news conference or photo or interview opportunities.
- Fact sheets provide the five W's and H of an event in outline form.
- A media kit (press kit) is typically a print or electronic folder containing news releases, photos, fact sheets, and features about a new product, an event, or other newsworthy project undertaken by an organization.
- Public relations personnel pitches can take the form of letters, e-mails, tweets, texts, or even telephone calls.

Which Public Relations Tactics Are Best for Reaching Television and Radio Audiences?

- News conferences should be held only when there is news that requires elaboration and clarification.
- Radio news releases, unlike releases for print media, must be written for the ear. A popular format is the audio news release (ANR) that includes an announcer and a quote (sound bite) from a spokesperson.
- Both radio and television stations accept public service announcements (PSAs) from nonprofit organizations that wish to inform and educate the public about health issues or upcoming civic events.
- Radio media tours (RMTs) and television satellite media tours (SMTs) involve an organization's spokesperson being interviewed from a central location by journalists across the country.
- The video news release (VNR) is produced in a format that television stations can easily use or edit based on their needs. VNRs are relatively expensive to produce but have great potential for reaching large audiences.

How Can Product Placements Be Leveraged to Promote Products and Services?

- Producers are increasingly making deals with companies to feature their products on television shows or movies.

1 How should a news release be formatted? Why is the inverted pyramid structure used in news releases?

2 What are some differences between a standard, social media, and multimedia news release?

3 Before pitching an item to a journalist or editor, why is it a good idea to do some basic research on the individual, the publication, or the talk show?

4 Various methods can be used to deliver publicity materials to the media. Name four methods and compare their relative strengths and weaknesses. Some experts believe that e-mail is the ultimate distribution channel. Do you agree or disagree?

5 How does an audio news release differ from a standard radio news release?

6 What are the advantages of a radio media tour (RMT) or a satellite media tour (SMT) for an organization and for journalists? Are there any disadvantages?

7 What is the difference between a VNR and B-roll?

8 Companies increasingly are working with television programs and film studios to get their products featured as part of a program or movie. What do you think of this trend?

MySearchLab®

Text Credits

Credits are listed in order of appearance.

Reprinted by permission of Guide Dogs for the Blind;

Courtesy of Guide Dogs for the Blind (www.guidedogs.com).;

© 2011 New York University.

Photo Credits

Credits are listed in order of appearance.

AP Photo/Stephanie Oberlander;
Noam Armonn/Shutterstock;
Oleksiy Maksymenko Photography/Alamy;
(cr) Hewlett-Packard Company (Cupertino);
(tr) Kristoffer Tripplaar/Alamy; (bl) Iakov

Filimonov/Shutterstock;
(tl) Clynt Garnham Publishing/Alamy;
(br) Scott J. Ferrell/Congressional Quarterly/
Alamy;
haveseen/Shutterstock;

American Red Cross;
Rob Bliss;
NBC/Getty Images;
Ray Mickshaw/Fox/Everett Collection

Tablet image: Falconia/Shutterstock

The Internet
and Social
Media

From Chapter 12 of *Think Public Relations*, 2013 Edition. Dennis L. Wilcox, Glen T. Cameron, Bryan H. Reber, Jae-Hwa Shin.

The Internet and Social Media

Tweeting the Revolution

Social media is a major force in organizing protests, demonstrations, and even revolutions. Its power to crystallize citizen discontent and help organize massive demonstrations was clearly evident in the Arab Spring of 2011, when activists were able to circumvent the state-controlled media of autocratic regimes and reach millions of citizens via social media. One Egyptian activist put it succinctly: "We use Facebook to schedule the protests, Twitter to coordinate, and YouTube to tell the world."

Facebook, in particular, played a major role in Egypt. An anonymous human rights activist created the page "We Are All Khaled Said" after security police beat Said, an innocent man, to death, and 130,000 joined the page to exchange updates. In addition, Egypt's almost 500,000 Facebook users helped coordinate demonstrations throughout the country.

In the United States, the organizers of the Occupy Wall Street protests took inspiration from the Arab Spring.

At the height of the protests in November 2011, Twitter reported that about 330,000 Occupy-related hashtags were being tweeted every day. Individual protestors became "citizen journalists," uploading their own reports and images to blogs and platforms such as YouTube, Livestream, Tumblr, and major online news sites. The *Economist* called it "America's first true social media uprising."

One protestor told the San Jose (CA) *Mercury News*, "If it were not for Facebook, Twitter, YouTube, and e-mail, this movement wouldn't have gone national and global. It can't be slowed by big corporate media."

"We'll never again see a mass movement that doesn't make extensive use of the state-of-the-art social media and communications," asserted Kirk Hanson, executive director of the Markkula Center for Applied Ethics at Santa Clara University, in an interview with the *San Jose Mercury News*.

1 What are the strengths of social media to organize and publicize a social or political movement? What are its limitations?

2 Some pundits say that the power of social media to ferment societal change is somewhat exaggerated. What additional factors must be involved for a mass movement to actually cause social or economic change?

Ask Yourself

> How Did the Internet Cause a Communications Revolution?

> Which Characteristics of the Internet Make It a Powerful Public Relations Tool?

> How Are Webcasts and Podcasts Used in Effective Public Relations?

> Which Social Media Tactics Are Now Used by Public Relations Professionals?

THE Internet

Today's students have grown up with the Internet and carry their smartphones everywhere they go, so much so that it is difficult to imagine life without them. Even many of your parents fail to understand that the Internet is a revolutionary concept that has transformed a media system dating back to Gutenberg's invention of the printing press in the 1400s.

Mass media, in one form or another, has dominated the world's landscape for 500 years. Mass media was characterized by being (1) centralized/top-down, (2) costly to publish, (3) controlled by professional gatekeepers known as editors and publishers, and (4) primarily one-way communication with limited feedback channels. Thanks to the Internet, that situation has changed dramatically.

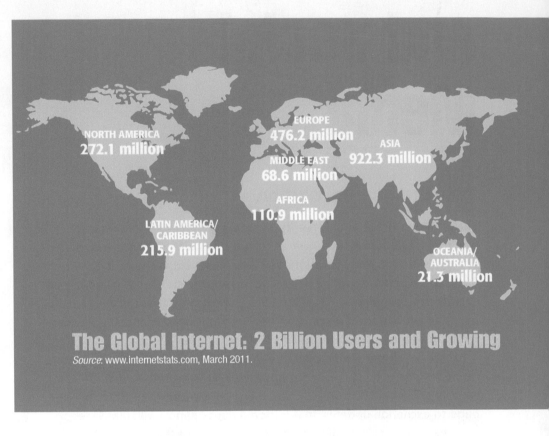

NORTH AMERICA
272.1 million

EUROPE
476.2 million

ASIA
922.3 million

MIDDLE EAST
68.6 million

AFRICA
110.9 million

LATIN AMERICA/
CARIBBEAN
215.9 million

OCEANIA/
AUSTRALIA
21.3 million

The Global Internet: 2 Billion Users and Growing
Source: www.internetstats.com, March 2011.

think In the age of social media, is there still a role for traditional, mainstream media in creating public awareness and fostering societal change?

The new media system, in a noted departure from traditional mass media, features (1) widespread broadband; (2) cheap or free, easy-to-use online publishing tools; (3) new distribution channels; (4) mobile devices, such as camera phones and tablet computers; and (5) new advertising paradigms. The Internet has compelled the democratization of information around the world for the first time in history as the chapter-opening essay described.

The Internet, which was originally created as a tool for academic researchers in the 1960s, came into widespread public use in the 1990s. Its first popular application was e-mail, which continues to be widely used today. In 2011, it was estimated by ccLoop.com that 2.8 million e-mails were sent every second.

It's worth noting, however, that the growth of the Internet and the World Wide Web continue at an astounding rate, and any figures are probably out of date by the time they are compiled and published.

think How has the Internet made media more democratic?

"Whereas it took nearly 40 years before there were 50 million listeners of radio and 13 years until television reached an audience of 50 million, a mere 4 years passed [after it became widely available] before 50 million users were logging on to the Internet."

Marc Newman, general manager of Medialink, Dallas

LEVERAGING THE
Power OF THE Internet

The exponential growth of the World Wide Web is due, in large part, to browsers such as Internet Explorer, search engines such as Google and Bing that have made the web accessible to literally billions of people, and the meteoric rise of social media sites such as Facebook and LinkedIn that connect people across the globe. The latest mobile devices like smartphones and tablets make all these sites even easier to access and enjoy.

The web has some highly attractive characteristics that enable public relations people to do a better job of distributing a variety of messages:

- Content producers can update information quickly, without having to reprint materials. This is an important consideration when it comes to major news events and dealing with a crisis.

- The web allows for interactivity; viewers can ask questions about products or services, download information of value to them, and let an organization know what they think.
- Online readers can dig deeper into subjects that interest them by linking to information provided on other sites, other articles, and sources.
- A great amount of material can be posted online. There is no space or time limitation.
- The web is a cost-effective method of disseminating information on a global basis to the public and journalists.
- Organizations can reach niche markets and audiences on a direct basis without messages being filtered through traditional mass media gatekeepers (editors).

- The media and other users can access details about an organization on a 24/7 basis from anywhere in the world.

A website, from a public relations standpoint, is literally a distribution system in cyberspace. Almost every company has a website to sell products and services, and online shopping by consumers is increasingly popular—showing major growth by the month. Besides offering shopping access, other pages and links in a website often provide information about an organization, its market share, its daily stock price, and the location of its stores or manufacturing plants. Journalists extensively mine company websites to retrieve current news releases, media kits, and photographs. One

> "A website that never changes is a cobweb."
>
> **John Gerstner, of IntranetInsider .com**

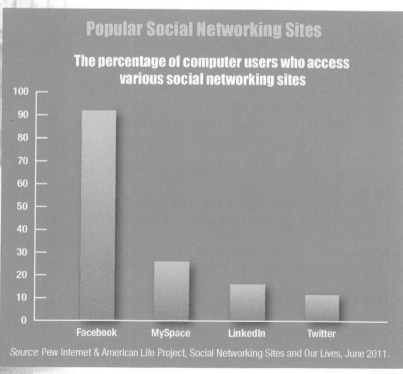

Popular Social Networking Sites

The percentage of computer users who access various social networking sites

Source: Pew Internet & American Life Project, Social Networking Sites and Our Lives, June 2011.

The Internet and Social Media

Keep Them Coming BACK for MORE

1 High quality content		**3** Quick to download	
2 Easy to navigate		**4** Frequently updated	

Four main reasons why visitors return to a website according to Forrester Research.

study by Arketi Group, for example, found that 81 percent of business journalists turn to corporate websites and webinars when looking for story ideas, breaking news, and contacting a corporate spokesperson. Consequently, most organizations also have an online newsroom as part of their websites.

Vocus, a supplier of public relations software, says an online newsroom should have the following five key components:

1 **Contact information.** The names, e-mail addresses, and phone numbers of public relations personnel.

2 **Corporate background.** History of company, executive profiles, and product descriptions.

3 **News releases and media kits.** Posted on frequent basis in reverse chronological order.

4 **Multimedia gallery.** Executive and product photos, charts, graphs, in high resolution and downloadable.

5 **Search capability.** A search function for journalists and consumers to easily find information.

Interactivity

A unique characteristic of the Internet, which traditional mass media do not offer, is interactivity between the sender and the receiver. One key aspect of interactivity is the "pull" concept. On the web, users actively search for ("pull") sites. At the website itself, visitors also actively "pull" information from the various links that are provided. Consumers are constantly interacting with a site and "pulling" the information most relevant to them. Users have total control over which information they call up and how deeply they want to delve into a subject. In contrast, under

> **Improved navigation ranks first on nearly every site's priority list. The goal: Fewer required clicks for users to access information because your site loses users at each step in your navigation.**
>
> Web Content Report

the "push" concept, information is delivered to the consumer without active participation. Traditional mass media—radio, TV, newspapers, magazines—are illustrative of the "push" concept, as are news releases that are automatically sent to media.

Another aspect of interactivity is the ability of a person to engage

Virtual Public Relations

Organizations leverage their websites in different ways:

- Boeing has adopted what has been called "branded journalism" by presenting newsy feature stories on its website about its various activities and projects. One video feature highlighted the testing of its new 787 airplane in the world's largest refrigerated hanger.
- Rutherford Hill Winery in California offers an online video tour of the winery.
- L.L. Bean's website presents a history of the company and even provides visitors with a list of attractions at 900 state and national parks.
- IBM has areas of its website devoted to its activities on various continents. One series of videos highlights its operations in Africa.
- Mayo Clinic has three major websites. One is a source of information on research and educational opportunities. A second one is a general consumer health education site, and the third one is a site for patients seeking treatment information and in-depth background on the clinic's physicians.

A virtual tour of an interesting locale, such as a winery, can lure the casual surfer deeper into a website.

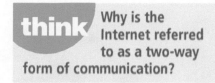
in a dialogue with an organization. Many websites, for example, encourage questions and feedback by providing an e-mail address that the user can click to send a message or hosting online dialogues and forums with users.

Cost-Effectiveness

Websites require staffing and budget but they are typically well worth the investment and contribute to the "bottom line" when calculated in terms of return on investment (ROI). Cisco Systems, for example, says news release distribution via its website, NEWS@ Cisco, saves it about $125,000 annually in distribution wire costs. Substantial savings are also realized by many companies by eliminating the print version of a company newsletter and posting everything on the organization's intranet instead.

Amy Jackson, director of interactive communications at Middleberg Associates, says calculating ROI on your website is one of the best ways to evaluate your online success: "Companies [that] invest in developing comprehensive, well-managed online media rooms can save thousands of dollars on printing and faxing costs if the media can readily find what they are looking for on the Web."

WEBCASTS, PODCASTS, and WIKIS

A website may often be enhanced and supplemented with webcasts. Webcasting has become more common as bandwidth has increased and technology has evolved. In fact, one survey found that more than 90 percent of public companies use webcasts, also commonly referred to as webinars, for everything from employee training to briefings for financial analysts and news conferences to launch new products. One big advantage associated with webcasts is that they save

time and money by eliminating the need for participants to travel.

Thomson Financial defines a webcast as "any event, live or archived, which involves the transmission of information from a person or organization to a larger audience over the Internet. Webcasts can be as simple as an audio-only address from a CEO or as elaborate

b t w ...

Live video streaming got a big boost in usage and popularity thanks to the Occupy Wall Street movement. Protestors, using their smartphones and iPads, constantly uploaded live video feeds to Ustream and Livestream to document their activities and record the efforts of police to remove protestors from encampments. A live chat window ran beside the video player on both Ustream and Livestream to give users an opportunity to not only watch events as they unfolded, but to also comment on them.

As a result, traffic to Livestream soared and viewing time went from 270 million minutes in July, 2011, to 411 million minutes in October. Occupy participants showed that almost anyone could broadcast news online by just using a mobile phone.

Brad Hunstable, founder of Ustream, told the *New York Times,* "Something is changing when a person with a cell phone video camera can command an audience around the world."

PODCASTS & PUBLIC RELATIONS

Organizations use podcasts for a variety of purposes—to share news about the company, make available in-depth interviews with executives and other experts, provide consumer tips about use of products and services, or offer training materials for employees. Consider the following two diverse examples:

• The University of Pennsylvania's Wharton School of Business produces podcasts that feature insights from professors regarding various trends and issues.

• Purina, the maker of pet food, has a podcast series that gives advice to pet owners. Its introduction of the series on its website shares the essence of the content: "Is it unusual for a cat to use the toilet? Is your dog bored out of its skull? Can cats and dogs suffer from heart attacks? Get answers to these questions and more in season two of *Animal Advice,* where veterinarians field questions from pet lovers like you."

as an audio/video Webcast with a PowerPoint slide show presented from multiple locations with follow-up questions from the audience."

In another application, Clarkson University uses webcasts to stream campus events in real time to its alumni and other supporters. One such event was a lecture by a Nobel Laureate, Dr. Paul Crutzen, who was visiting the campus to talk about global warming; another was a "Night at the Opera."

A variation of the webcast is a podcast. A podcast is a digital media file, or a series of such files, distributed over the Internet for playback on portable media players and personal computers. Most podcasts are audio only, but video podcasts have also found a home on smart phones, websites, YouTube, and other social networking sites.

The three major advantages of podcasts for distributing messages

are cost-effectiveness, the ability of users to access material on a 24/7 basis, and portability. A person can listen to an audio podcast while driving to work or view one on his or her smartphone while enjoying a cup of coffee at a cafe.

Creating a podcast that is interesting and relevant to the target audience can be challenging. A podcast is not an infomercial or even an executive reading a speech. Like radio programs, a podcast

Wikis: Paperless Editing

Interaction between individuals working together on a particular project is facilitated by wikis. Essentially, wikis are webpages that can be opened and edited by anyone. They are often used by organizations to keep employees and clients up-to-date on schedules and plans. Wikis can also be used in public relations campaigns and employee relations.

General Motors, for example, created a wiki site for its employees and customers as part of its centennial celebration. It encouraged individuals to contribute first-person experiences relating to the company's history via stories, images, video, and

audio. The advantage of the wiki format was that individuals could comment on other contributions, correct inaccurate information, and even add supplemental information regarding their experiences and viewpoints. GM originally considered publishing the standard "coffee table book" outlining the company's history. In the end, as company spokesperson Scot Keller told *MediaPost,* "We felt that a more social, more inclusive approach was appropriate, and the story is best told not by the corporation or media but by men and women who were there."

must be informal and conversational. The following are some tips about podcast content:

1 Keep it short. The ideal length is 10 to 20 minutes.

2 Use several stories or segments of about three or four minutes each.

3 Don't use a script. The tone should be informal and conversational.

4 Select an announcer or interviewer with a strong, animated voice.

5 Select a podcast title that matches the content. People search for a podcast on the basis of topic, not brand name.

SOCIAL Media

According to Wikipedia, "Social media describes the online technologies and practices that people use to share opinions, insights, experiences, and perspectives with each other." David Bowen of the *Financial Times* puts it more succinctly, "Social networks are all about a shift from vertical to horizontal communications on the Web." In other words, social media conversation is not organized, not controlled, and not on message. Instead, the conversation is vibrant, emergent, fun, compelling, and full of chance insights. This major shift, from scripted to spontaneous has, by any standard, made social media one of the most dramatic revolutions in history.

The rapid rise of social networking sites has also dramatically changed the landscape of public relations. Today, public relations needs to be focused on listening and engaging in a dialogue with citizens and consumers in a world where organizations must now operate in a totally transparent manner.

Markovsky Company puts it even more bluntly: "Collectively, the social media—including blogs, social networks, RSS feeds, podcasts, wikis, reviews, bulletin boards, and newsgroups—have the power to support or destroy a brand or reputation. Transparency is the key; but it's risky business and required a new mindset and toolkit."

Several categories of social media exist. We cover each of the following in more detail in the rest of this chapter. Blogs are now a mainstream application, and social networks such as, Facebook, Twitter, LinkedIn, and YouTube have become a major presence. And new social network sites such as Foursquare, Tumblr, and Livestream are created almost daily.

It is estimated that about 70 percent of all digital information in the world is now created by consumers.

think In what ways can social media help a public relations professional conduct research on audience attitudes and opinions more effectively?

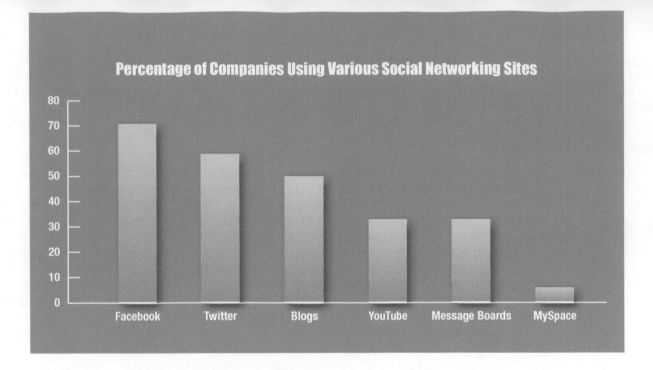

Percentage of Companies Using Various Social Networking Sites

All share the same goal: to facilitate conversation among people around the world.

Blogs

The first widespread application of social media was blogs, which first came on the scene in 1998. In the beginning, they were called weblogs, reflecting their roots as websites maintained by individuals who wanted to post their commentary and opinions on various topics. The abbreviated term "blog" is now commonly used for these free-form sites, most of which also include comments from their followers.

Although the majority of blogs are still primarily the province of individuals who post their personal opinions, blogging is widely recognized by public relations personnel as an extremely cost-effective way to reach large numbers of people.

There were an estimated 450 million English-language blogs in 2011. The vast majority don't have vast readership, but select few have gained a large following because their postings have a reputation for credibility. Some blogs even break news stories, which are then picked up by the traditional media. Indeed, surveys have shown that the majority of journalists regularly read blogs for story ideas and that blogs heavily influence today's news coverage.

Tumblr is a more recent frontier in blogging. Its format allows for easy sharing of text, photos, quotes, links, music, and videos. The *New York Times* declared that "Tumblr makes blogging blissfully easy." Tumblr was extensively used by participants in the Occupy Wall Street movement.

> In its best incarnation, corporations will use blogs to become more transparent to their customers, partners, and internally. By encouraging employees to speak their minds, companies will be able to demonstrate their heart and character. Not an easy trick for a faceless entity. This will facilitate stronger relationships and act as 'grease in the gears' of a business operation.

Larry Genkin, publisher of *Blogger and Podcaster* magazine

The Internet and Social Media

Public relations writers are usually involved in three kinds of blogs: corporate or organizational blogs, employee blogs, and third-party blogs.

Corporate or Organizational Blogs A corporate blog is usually written by an executive and represents the official voice of the organization. In many cases, someone in the public relations department actually writes the blog for the executive. Some corporate blogs are outsourced to public relations firms, although critics say this practice is a guaranteed way to ensure that the blog is artificial and full of "execu-babble."

Although all corporate blogs should provide an opportunity for the public to post comments, it's also important to provide useful and informative information that the audience can use. That was the aim of Ford & Harrison, a national labor and employment law firm, when it started a blog to address workplace issues from its uniquely legal perspective. The blog, called "That's What She Said," uses graphics and humor to explore workplace issues in terms of how much the behavior of the blog's main character would cost a company if the company were forced to defend his actions in a court of law. This tactic effectively showcases the firm's legal expertise in a user-friendly way. *PRWeek* noted, "This is pop culture meeting the conservative

"**57 percent of people talk to people more online than they do in real life.**"

www.digitalbuzzblog.com

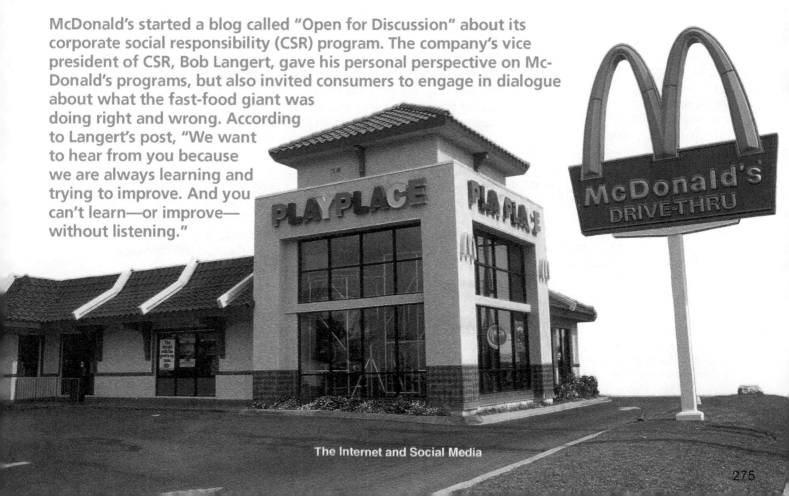

McDonald's started a blog called "Open for Discussion" about its corporate social responsibility (CSR) program. The company's vice president of CSR, Bob Langert, gave his personal perspective on McDonald's programs, but also invited consumers to engage in dialogue about what the fast-food giant was doing right and wrong. According to Langert's post, "We want to hear from you because we are always learning and trying to improve. And you can't learn—or improve—without listening."

The Internet and Social Media

Tomorrow's Workers: Tech Freedom Before Salary?

The millennial generation, born in the 1990s, seem to have different job requirements than previous generations. Instead of seeking jobs with good salaries and more vacation time, the new generation is more interested in workplace connectivity.

Cisco Systems conducted a survey of 2,800 college students in 14 nations. Some findings follow:

- One in three survey respondents said social media freedom and workplace mobility were more important than salary.

- More than 50 percent said they would not accept a job offer from a company that banned access to social media during work hours.

- Almost 75 percent of respondents said there should be no difference between using "personal" devices and company-issued devices because there is a blending of personal and work communications in their daily lifestyle.

- And 70 percent say they want to be out of the office regularly, working remotely.

---

think What are the potential upsides and downsides for individuals or organizations that blog?

world of law in a way that sets the blogosphere on fire."

Employee Blogs Many organizations encourage their employees to blog. Sun Microsystems, for example, has more than 4,000 employee blogs, but more than half of them, according to the company, are "super-technical" and "project oriented," appealing only to fellow computer programmers and engineers. Others, such as those written by the CEO as well as by managers in human resources and marketing, are more general in subject matter.

Most companies typically establish at least some guidelines for employee blogs. Cisco, for example, tells employees, "If you comment on any aspect of the company's business ... you must clearly identify yourself as a Cisco employee in your postings and include a disclaimer that the views are your own and not those of Cisco." Dell

also expects its employees to identify themselves if they do any sort of blogging, social networking, or other online activities related to the company. Other companies have policies warning employees to refrain from making any comments that disparage other employees.

Third-Party Blogs In addition to operating their own blogs and providing guidelines for employee blogs, organizations today must monitor and respond to the postings on external blog sites. The products and services of organizations are particularly vulnerable to attack and criticism by bloggers, and an unfavorable mention is often multiplied by links to other blogs and search engine indexing.

For example, Dell experienced the wrath of bloggers when it faced harsh criticism about its customer service, which ultimately caused the company's sales to decline. Today,

---

think How should bloggers be effectively included in the public relations relationship with the media?

according to the *New York Times*, "It's nearly impossible to find a story or blog entry about Dell that isn't accompanied by a comment from the company."

"You should also establish relationships with the most relevant and influential bloggers who are talking about your company," Rick Wion, interactive media director of Golin Harris, told Susan Walton in *Public Relations Tactics*.

A good example of this tactic is Weber Shandwick's work with about 20 influential food bloggers on behalf of its food industry clients. The public relations firm regularly monitors posts to find out what bloggers are saying and which "hot button" issues are being discussed. This type of engagement allows the firm to build relationships with the bloggers and, in turn, offer information that they can use in their blogs.

Facebook

Facebook, by any standard, is the most pervasive and popular social networking site on the planet. About a third of the world's two billion Internet users are on Facebook, and this fact has not escaped the notice of marketing, advertising, and public relations professionals. They see their client and employer Facebook pages as an excellent opportunity to gain consumer insights, build brand awareness, and create customer loyalty.

Establishing connections, however, takes a great deal of thought and creativity because organizations must shape messages that are relevant and interesting to their "friends." Achieving this goal often requires an emphasis on humor, short video clips, music, contests, and audience participation.

Audience engagement through contests is a popular way to build a fan base. Coors, for example, sponsored a contest on its Facebook page in which consumers could create video clips about drinking Coors and submit them to other networking sites to win prizes. Sharpie pens also sponsored a contest asking teenage girls to submit their Sharpie product creations on the brand's Facebook page. This ploy helped the company reach a total of 2 million fans.

Other organizations seek consumer involvement in other ways. Kraft, for example, asked Facebook users to submit smiling photos of themselves to show their loyalty to Kraft's popular Macaroni & Cheese product. Entergy, the local electric utility in New Orleans, cooperates with Second Harvest Food Bank: one way to fight hunger was posted on the Facebook pages of the utility and the nonprofit each day in September. Entergy donated 10 meals to Second Harvest for every "like" on its Facebook page. As a result, more than 10,000 meals were donated.

A holiday can also be the subject of a Facebook page. Spice maker McCormick Company established a turkey page for Thanksgiving to provide cooking tips and encourage fans to share their recipes and photos. If consumers "liked" the page, they were given additional access to recipes (which featured McCormick spices, of course) and the chance to have a recipe they created included in a "friend-sourced" cookbook to be produced by the company.

An organization's Facebook page, however, is an open forum and not a particularly good place for a controversy. Lowe's discovered this when it posted a statement on its Facebook page that it was dropping its advertising from a TLC channel program, *All American Muslim*, primarily because a conservative Christian group in Florida objected to the program. Lowe's announcement generated an avalanche of reader comments, both from individuals who criticized the decision and those who supported it. Many of the in-favor comments fell in the realm of hate speech, but Lowe's did nothing to delete the anti-Muslim tirades. This lack of action generated even more criticism, this time from civil rights groups who started to call for a boycott of Lowe's. An article about the controversy is annotated later in the chapter.

How Many Millions of Friends Do You Have?

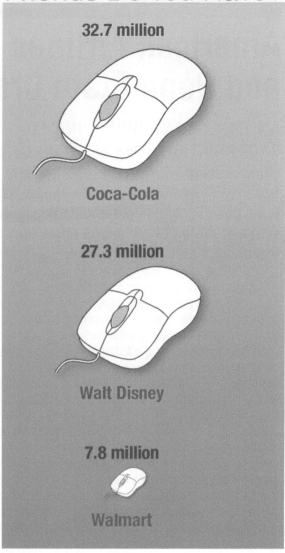

32.7 million
Coca-Cola

27.3 million
Walt Disney

7.8 million
Walmart

American Airlines Soars and Penn State Crashes

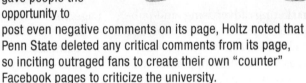

AN IMPORTANT GUIDELINE FOR ANY ORGANIZATION using social media is to communicate with candor and honesty. The truth won't necessarily make people happy, but a good Facebook page will allow them to vent and let the organization know how they feel about a particular situation.

Not all organizations, however, effectively use their Facebook page in such a way. According to Shel Holtz, an expert on social media and author of his own blog, American Airlines got it right when it lost Jack, a traveler's cat. In contrast, Holtz gives Penn State University a failing grade for how it handled the crisis involving allegations that former football defense coordinator Jerry Sandusky molested young boys while university officials, including head coach Joe Paterno, failed to take action.

American Airlines won praise for using its Facebook page to provide updates on the search for Jack the Cat after national media had picked up the story and many pet lovers had showed interest in the updates. Jack's story has a sad ending: he was found 61 days later, but was in such poor health that Jack's owner made the difficult decision to have him euthanized.

However, American handled the sad news honestly and openly. The airline reported Jack's passing and expressed its sympathy. It even tweeted the following note: "Jack the Cat was euthanized today. We are deeply saddened by his loss & offer sincere sympathy to his owner, Ms. Pascoe." Pet lovers posted comments criticizing American for losing the cat in the first place, but many also complimented the airline for communicating openly about the situation and for taking responsibility.

In contrast, the Penn State University home page somewhat buried its response to the sex scandal, even though the national news media and social media sites were filled with speculation about the revelations and the public was clamoring for information. According to Holtz, "On the Penn State news page, you have to scroll to the bottom to find any reference to the situation. Even then, you have to guess that 'Statement from President Spanier' is a reference to the controversy that is consuming the campus. One learns about ticket availability to the Nebraska game and Lady Antebellum before

there's a word from the Prez."

The University's Facebook page contained even less information. While American Airlines gave people the opportunity to post even negative comments on its page, Holtz noted that Penn State deleted any critical comments from its page, so inciting outraged fans to create their own "counter" Facebook pages to criticize the university.

Holtz concludes his blog post with this: "Ultimately, saying as little as possible and hoping for the best is not a crisis communication strategy. When the crisis is of your own making—as was the case in both these situations—your goal is to minimize the damage and put it behind you as quickly as possible. By inviting the conversation, American has ensured it will do just that, while Penn's evasion guaranteed that the story will linger long after the guilty have been punished."

1. American Airlines's crisis was the death of a cat, while Penn State was dealing with much more serious allegations. Should this make a difference on how they responded on Facebook?

2. Guidelines for online social media are candor and honesty. Why do Penn State and many other organizations seem to ignore these guidelines?

3. Penn State deleted critical comments from its Facebook page. Was this a good idea? What would be a better way to handle a scandal of this magnitude and gravity on public social media sites?

FACEBOOK by the NUMBERS (2011)

- **750 million users worldwide, or about one in every nine people on the planet.**
- **More than 75 percent of users now reside outside the United States.**
- Available in more than 70 languages.
- People spend 700 billion minutes a month on the site.
- Users spend an average of 15.5 hours a month on the site.
- An average of 250 million photos are uploaded each day.
- About 30 billion pieces of content is shared each month.
- More than 350 million people access the site on mobile devices.
- More than 2 million apps and websites are integrated on the site.
- Almost 50 percent of 18- to 34-year-olds check Facebook right after they wake up in the morning.

Source: Facebook.com/press/info, www.digitalblog.com, and www.jeffbullas.com.

Twitter

The second most popular social media network is Twitter. In a five-year period from its start in 2006 to 2011, it rapidly gained 300 million users, who are estimated to send about that many tweets a day. The microblogging site allows users (known as "twits") to post messages of up to 140 characters in length from computers and mobile phones to individuals who have signed up to "follow"

 think How can a public relations staff use Tweets to both promote a brand and an organization's activities?

an individual or a brand. Google is the most-followed brand with 3 million followers; Southwest Airlines has just over 1 million followers.

Public relations professionals often use Twitter as a distribution platform for late-breaking news, to refute a viral rumor, or to provide updates on a developing situation that has high news interest, such as an industrial accident or a major merger. In most cases, web links are embedded so that the public and journalists can easily access more details.

Organizations also use Twitter for marketing and promotion. Many brands regularly tweet their followers to promote products and even offer discounts. Major league teams have Twitter feeds to keep fans constantly informed about games, players, and other news about the team. Individual players also have their own Twitter accounts, which is a mixed blessing. Player tweets can extend the team fan base, but it can be embarrassing when a player decides to post his or her personal opinion about a politician or a particular ethnic group.

Celebrities, in particular, use Twitter as a publicity tactic to build a fan base. One Lady Gaga tweet to her almost 10 million followers

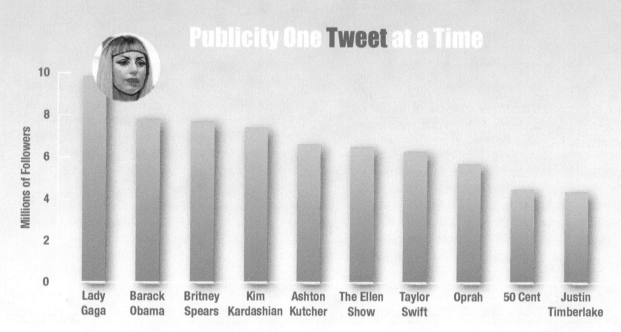

Publicity One Tweet at a Time

Source: wefollow.com/twitter/celebrity/followers.

The Internet and Social Media

The use of humor in tweeted promotions can sometimes backfire. Kenneth Cole shoes, for example, received a barrage of criticism for insensitivity when it posted the following Tweet during the Egyptian revolution: "Millions are in uproar in #Cairo. Rumor is they heard our new spring collection is now available online at http://bit.ly/KCairo-KC."

read: "Today's cancelled Paris show is rescheduled for Tuesday, 2mo-ro's show will happen as planned. I promise to give you the night of ure life."

The following examples illustrate how several organizations and their public relations staffs use Twitter:

- Intuit used Twitter to launch its mobile payment app, GoPayment, during Austin's South by Southwest event.
- The Los Angeles Fire Department used Twitter to communicate updates about California wildfires.
- Amtrak promotes its services, train schedules, and answers customer queries on its Twitter account.
- Planned Parenthood has two Twitter accounts to answer queries and to provide basic information about contraception.

YouTube

Video clips are an extremely popular medium of communication. In fact, one in four Americans watches a video online every day. And Cisco Systems predicts that online videos will account for 90 percent of the Internet traffic in the next three years, up from 51 percent in 2011. YouTube is currently the major video sharing site, with about 500 million visitors a month generating more than 90 billion page views. That amounts to about 2.9 billion hours per month, or about 326,294 years, according to blogger Jeff Bullas, who specializes in tracking social media stats.

Although many videos are posted by individuals, many organizations also create and post online videos on their own YouTube channels as part of their marketing and public relations outreach to online communities.

Harley-Davidson's YouTube channel, for example, posted a video that detailed the brand devotion of the Latino bikers, who called themselves "Harlistas." Even the U.S. Navy has a channel that contains video clips of various naval operations. One popular video shows how you can tone your body using the Navy SEAL workout.

YouTube houses Intel's almost 3,000 videos on a platform where

b t w ...

Looking for a job in public relations? A place to start is LinkedIn, which has become the world's leading professional social network with 135 million users in about 200 nations. LinkedIn's major focus is to help individuals build a network of professional contacts in order to locate jobs and other business opportunities.

Job-seekers use LinkedIn to post their résumés, research potential employers, and even apply online for various positions.

Users can easily access lists of jobs by specialization and even location. LinkedIn compiles lists of vacancies by industry and even location. Major companies such as Amazon.com, eBay, Cisco, and Campbell's maintain LinkedIn pages that provide background information about available jobs

The networking feature of LinkedIn is useful, as members can determine if anyone in their list of "connections" knows someone at an organization. Public relations personnel, both those who are employed and those looking for a job, can also join various interest groups on LinkedIn to discuss career issues and share information.

Currently, LinkedIn has almost a million such groups, including a number related to the communications and public relations field.

One note of warning: because potential employers use LinkedIn to search for possible job candidates, be sure to cross-check your profile with other social networking sites and make sure your information is accurate. In one study, about a third of employers reported that candidates had lied about their qualifications on their LinkedIn resumes.

think Do you go to YouTube for serious endeavors as well entertainment?

The advantage of YouTube, for better or worse, is that videos are often picked up by individuals and bloggers who re-post them to their friends and followers. In such a way, even a video that doesn't initially get many views on YouTube has a new life and may even be picked up by traditional media outlets.

customers and others can search for interesting footage. One video, for example, shows how Intel technology helps people, such as Chinese wedding photographers. According to Becky Brown, Intel's director of social media, "We've really transitioned to the branded journalistic approach where we've got really great stories that we're producing ourselves."

Most organizations try to produce YouTube videos that are informative and also entertaining. Disney Parks, for example, produced a video showing a visit by Darth Vader, who rides a teacup, stops by Cinderella's castle, and vents over his inability to get into a *Star Wars* ride. Hyundai, on the other hand, produced a video that would appeal to younger buyers

of its cars. One Hyundai video is about some "dudes" who find a magic wand and conjure up a car for a wild night on the town. Companies also use their YouTube channels for contests. Smirnoff teamed up with Madonna to generate submissions of a 60-second audition for the chance to be part of Madonna's tour and meet the superstar.

Political candidates have also employed YouTube. President Obama has a YouTube channel that posts clips of his speeches and White House events. Other politicians, such as Rick Perry of Texas, a Republican contender in the 2012 primaries, have also used YouTube with mixed success. Perry, for example, got a barrage of criticism (98 percent of the viewers disliked it) in 2011 when he stated in a video that there was "something wrong with the country" when gay members of the military serve openly, but schoolchildren cannot "openly celebrate Christmas or pray in school."

FLICKR: THE WORLD'S PHOTO GALLERY

Flickr hosts more than 6 billion photos, and it's estimated that people upload about 3,500 photos to the popular site every second. Most of the uploaded photos are posted by individuals who want to share their vacation, their children's first steps, or their twenty-first birthday celebration.

Public relations personnel, however, also find creative ways to use the social networking aspect of Flickr to build awareness of an organization or brand. Some common uses are the posting of (1) executive headshots, (2) images of corporate artifacts and history, (3) product shots, (4) infographics, and (5) photos of company events and celebrations. The following examples illustrate how various groups are using Flickr for public relations outreach:

The Monterey Aquarium encourages visitors to post photos taken at the facility. The aquarium's public relations staff monitor blogs, and if someone posts a good photo of an exhibit, staff ask the individual to post it on the Flickr site.

The Nature Conservancy also invites photographers to submit their photos to the organization's Flickr group. Outstanding nature photos are also posted on the organization's website. The Nature Conservancy's Flickr site now houses about 300,000 images.

Rotary International has a "Family of Rotary" Flickr feed that allows Rotarians worldwide to share photos of local clubs' activity. A story in the organization's magazine reported, "Using Flickr is a great way for Rotarians to promote Rotary's commitment to action-oriented service."

These examples make the point that social media sites such as Flickr can be used for public relations purposes only if the focus is on generating participation and involvement on the part of consumers and the general public. In these programs, the organization essentially acts as a facilitator for people connecting to people.

The Rising Tide of
MOBILE-ENABLED CONTENT

The widespread adoption of smartphones, tablets, and other mobile devices has now become a tsunami. The magnitude of the rising tide is outlined in a 2011 Microsoft mobile marketing report:

- By 2014, mobile internet should overtake desktop Internet use.
- One-half of all local searches are performed on mobile devices.
- 86 percent of mobile Internet users are using their devices while watching TV.
- 200 million YouTube views occur on mobile devices every day.
- 50 percent of Twitter's users take advantage of Twitter mobile.
- 1 billion people will access financial/banking services via mobile by 2015.

All this is possible because mobile phones have become the most widely adopted communications device on the planet. Research company Gartner forecasts that there will be 7.4 billion mobile connections by 2015, which is quite impressive since the earth's population is expected to be only 7.2 billion.

Indeed, the new generation of mobile phones and tablets are the new portable computers. Handheld devices call up stored online videos, photos, and PowerPoint presentations. Other popular features include complete map navigation in 3-D format for any location on the planet and interaction with social networks such as Facebook, allowing users to tell friends exactly where they are at any given moment. Access to a world of information and social interaction is as close as your pocket.

The mobile tsunami has deeply affected how public relations professionals distribute messages to the public. Websites and other digitally prepared materials must be optimized for viewing on mobile devices. McCormick & Company, for example, reformats its major news releases and recipes into short, narrow columns that will fit a smartphone screen. Organizations are also actively producing apps, which we discuss later in this section of the chapter.

Texting

The first widespread use of mobile phones—besides people actually talking to each other in real time—was texting. Texting continues to be the king of mobile messaging, and trillions of text messages are sent worldwide every year. Teenagers contribute a large percentage of these text messages. According to Nielsen, the average U.S. teenager sends about 3,000 text messages a month.

Texting is also employed by organizations and public relations staffs to reach employees, customers, and key publics. Shel Holtz, a social media expert, told Ragan.com that there are three levels of texting for organizations. The first level is the broadcast text, which companies often use to send a brief message to all employees at the same time. Such a message may be as mundane as reminding people to sign up for the company picnic, or it may play a more serious role in updating employees about a crisis situation. A second level of texting is subscription based, in which users sign up to receive text messages from groups or organizations in much the same way as they sign up for RSS feeds to their computers. A reporter, for example, may sign up to receive text messages from a company that he or she covers on a regular basis. The third method, says Holtz, is the "one-off," wherein a cell phone user sends a text message to a source to get an answer to a question. For example, an employee may text human resources personnel to get a short answer to a health benefits question.

Apps Everywhere

The widespread use of smartphones has created an explosion in apps. By January 2011, the Apple App Store had more than 400,000 apps, and the Android market was offering an additional 250,000.

In December 2011, the *New York Times* reported that "a developer pushed a button and the one millionth mobile app went on the market." By 2014, Gartner estimates

> "Every week about 100 movies get released worldwide, along with about 250 books. That compares to the release of around 15,000 apps per week."
>
> Anindya Datta, founder and chair of Mobilewalla, in the *New York Times*

> By mid-2011, almost two-thirds of U.S. adults aged 25 to 34 owned a smartphone, according to Nielsen research.

think Why are more and more U.S. states considering legislation banning the use of smartphones while driving?

On Campus and in the Kitchen

Organizations and their public relations staffs are creating a number of creative, innovative apps that provide valuable information to users. Consider the following two examples:

Texas Tech University

Texas Tech (TTU) has developed its own app for students, faculty, and visitors. With a few clicks on a home screen, users can visit specific modules that provide information on everything from the hours of the dining commons, to the course catalog, to instructor contacts. There's also a campus map that displays user location, a search function to find buildings, a plug-in to find the nearest shuttle stop, and a timer to show the length of the trip.

A help module also gives students quick access to the university's phone operator as well as the financial aid and student counseling offices. A 24-hour help line is also available, and students are invited to give feedback about the various modules. One new module displays TTU's main Facebook and Twitter feeds and enables users to post to Facebook, Twitter, or Foursquare through the app itself.

Bertolli Olive Oil

A celebrity chef who gives tips about how to use olive oil in various recipes is the focus of an HD-format iPad app offered by Bertolli. The app's primary goal is to educate consumers about the company's three different olive oils and how each of them can be used on salads, pasta, and other foods.

The app offers more than five hours of content, including celebrity chef Fabio Viviani's step-by-step

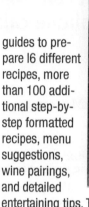

guides to prepare 16 different recipes, more than 100 additional step-by-step formatted recipes, menu suggestions, wine pairings, and detailed entertaining tips. There are also links so individuals can share content through Facebook and Twitter.

The Bertolli HD-iPad app sells for $2.99 at Apple's App Store, but consumers can also purchase an iPhone version for $1.99. "Our goal is to realize the broadest possible reach for the app," says Maria Hernandez Procaccini, brand manager for Bertolli, "and attaching a minimal price to it, as opposed to making it a free download, should achieve that objective...."

The Bertolli app will be publicized via other social media platforms. As Chef Viviani travels throughout the country to participate in various culinary events, he will post comments about the app and the various events on his personal Facebook and Twitter accounts. In conjunction with the app's release, Bertolli has also increased its Facebook and Twitter presence.

> **"We try to put Texas Tech in the palm of your hand."**
>
> Joshua Bucy, manager of TTU's app, in an interview with the *Ragan Report*

1. If your school had an app like Texas Tech, would you use it?

2. How many apps do you have on your smartphone? Which ones do you use most often?

3. What kind of app would be good for a medical center? Or a fitness center?

think Why are apps good communications tools for organizations?

> "QR codes have the advantage over text messages. Scan a code and you get a video, a website, a contact card, map directions; it can even initiate a phone call.

Shel Holtz

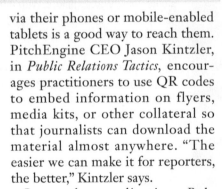

Sonoma County Airport Express
www.airportexpressmobile.co
Text BUS to 36638 to receive back a lir
to the Airport Express mobile website

that 70 billion apps will have been downloaded worldwide.

Organizations are rapidly embracing apps as an integral part of their digital communications strategy because they are simple, cheap, and don't require an Internet connection. With a few clicks on an iPhone, iPad, or other smartphone, an individual can access detailed information on almost any subject.

The following are examples of how organizations are using apps:

- A Coca-Cola app offers an interactive replication of its new Freestyle vending machine, enabling consumers to figure out how to use the new machines.
- Kids Kicking Cancer developed an app to raise awareness about cancer in children in order to increase financial support for the organization's work.
- The Association for Education in Journalism and Mass Communications (AEJMC) developed an app for its national conference that provided attendees with information about the conference schedule, meeting room details, maps of the hotel/ exhibit area and allowed visitors to set reminders for upcoming sessions.

- McCormick & Company launched two holiday Facebook apps—one with cookie recipes and another with tips for holiday menus.
- Spectrum Health, a group of hospitals in Michigan, has an app that allows patients to peruse their medical records, make appointments, and check out their lab results.

QR Codes: Just a Scan Away

Quick response codes, popularly known as QR, are now widely used in mobile messaging. The two-dimensional matrix bar codes can allow smartphone users to scan the matrix and immediately be connected to websites and any number of apps.

Many journalists are constantly on the go, so a QR code that gives them company or event information

think What do you think will be the next big thing in communication technology?

via their phones or mobile-enabled tablets is a good way to reach them. PitchEngine CEO Jason Kintzler, in *Public Relations Tactics*, encourages practitioners to use QR codes to embed information on flyers, media kits, or other collateral so that journalists can download the material almost anywhere. "The easier we can make it for reporters, the better," Kintzler says.

In another application, *Public Relations Tactics* displayed a QR code in a story about the president of the Public Relations Society of America (PRSA) that allowed readers to watch a video of the interview. Organizations also add QR codes to their advertising in newspapers, magazines, and brochures as well as on packaging.

What Would You Do?

Adding Friends and Followers

Brew House, a chain of pubs that features 100 different beers on tap, already has a website, a Facebook page, a Twitter feed, and a YouTube channel. Unfortunately, the adage that "if you build it, they will come" doesn't always apply; traffic is below the organization's expectations. Brew House wants to increase the number of visitors to its website and YouTube channel and generate more "friends" and "followers" on its Facebook page and Twitter feed. Your public relations firm is retained to accomplish these objectives. What strategies and tactics would you recommend to increase the traffic and visibility of Brew House on these sites? What kind of app should Brew House launch?

summary

How Did the Internet Cause a Communications Revolution?

- The Internet is the first medium that allows almost anyone to send messages to a mass audience without the message being filtered by journalists and editors. Prior to its advent, mass media were costly to produce, centralized, and primarily one-way communication with limited feedback.

Which Characteristics of the Internet Make It a Powerful Public Relations Tool?

- New media have unique characteristics, including easy updating of material, instant distribution of information, an infinite amount of space for information, and ready interaction with the audience.

How Are Webcasts and Podcasts Used in Effective Public Relations?

- Webcasting—the streaming of audio and video in real time over a website—is now used by the majority of organizations for everything from news conferences to employee training. Podcasts are radio on steroids, and are now also available in the form of videos that can be readily accessed by smartphones.

Which Social Media Tactics Are Used by Public Relations Professionals?

- Social media venues provide public relations professionals with the opportunity to participate in conversations, solicit feedback, and build relationships.
- Blogs are omnipresent in terms of both their numbers and their influence.
- Organizations are a presence on social networking sites. To successfully engage the audience in this venue, public relations materials need to be low-key and creative.
- YouTube is the premier social networking site for posting and viewing videos. To garner attention, clips must be innovative, interesting, and somewhat humorous.
- Texting, Twitter, and wikis are extensively used in public relations work.
- Apps have expanded the capability of smartphones to tap into information that consumers can use in their daily life. QR codes enable smartphone users to easily access a variety of websites and apps.

questions

FOR REVIEW AND DISCUSSION

1 What are some characteristics of the Internet that make it possible for public relations people to do a better job of distributing information?

2 Why is it important for an organization to have a well-developed online newsroom?

3 One aspect of web interactivity is the distinction made between "pull" versus "push." Describe the difference between these two concepts.

4 How can a website generate revenue and save money for an organization?

5 Which factors should an organization consider if it is thinking about producing a YouTube video?

6 List some ways organizations are effectively using Facebook, Twitter, LinkedIn, Flickr, YouTube, Apps, and QR codes to interact with publics.

7 How can you use LinkedIn to find a job in public relations?

MySearchLab®

Of Lowe's, *All-American Muslim,* and Facebook Home Page Improvement

Catherine P. Taylor, December 14, 2011

Social Media Insider (news@mediapost.com)

Here at the sumptuous offices of the Social Media Insider, there's nothing we love more than a corporate PR controversy and a chance to be a Monday morning (or, in this case, Wednesday afternoon) quarterback.

So in that spirit, let's talk about Lowe's!

For the uninitiated, here's the recap: a conservative Florida group, the Florida Family Association, got itself all up in arms this week over the advertisers in *All-American Muslim,* a show on TLC that shows the day-to-day life of a Muslim family in Dearborn, Michigan. To the FFA, the show misrepresents American Muslims, apparently because it is 100 percent jihadist-free. So Lowe's, one of the show's advertisers, pulled its advertising, hoping, it appears, to avoid controversy.

It turns out that pulling an ad from an inoffensive show—and trust me, having watched an episode, it is truly inoffensive—is a great way to court controversy. And of course, this being 2011, controversy went a-courtin' on Facebook. Lowe's posted a comment on its Facebook wall explaining its decision yesterday, saying that it pulled its ad because the show had become "a lightning rod." The post then became a lightning rod of its own, and a much bigger one than the FFA could ever hope to harness. Its original post garnered upwards of 20,000 comments, while, per AdFreak, Lowe's sat back and did nothing as the hate-filled language piled up on the page.

So what was Lowe's social media error? Treating Facebook like a broadcast channel, no matter how hard it tried to explain its way out of its conduct afterward. The company was smart enough to use Facebook to explain its decision (even if the decision itself was dumb), but not smart enough to have a strategy for what would happen when people actually started to comment. So what else did Lowe's do in the aftermath? It deleted the original post, sort of like pulling an ad schedule from a TV show.

Side annotations:

Activist groups, on the left and on the right, often pressure advertisers to drop sponsorship of TV programs.

A company must consider the views of activist groups, but also ascertain their influence and whether other major groups with more influence and numbers will react in turn. In this case, mainstream civil rights groups and the American-Muslim community called for a boycott of Lowe's to protest its decision.

Public relations staff must carefully assess the possibility of negative publicity that could result if an organization is perceived as caving into a highly vocal, but perhaps small, group of "extremists."

In crisis and conflict theory, a decision like this one, to pull ads from the show, is called "ingratiation" because the company decided to appease the publics involved. The tactic, however, failed because it only pleased the FFA and its supporters; it generated hostile comment from the Muslim-American community and various civil rights groups.

Facebook, by definition, is a two-way dialogue. Any statement by the company automatically will generate both favorable and unfavorable comments.

Yes, Lowe's is attempting what is essentially a social media mulligan, even though the trajectory of the initial wall posting has been rampantly posted in bits and pieces all over the Internet for all to see. Social media mulligans don't really exist. In a new post explaining what happened with the old post, the company explains that "out of respect for the transparency of social media," it had let the comments to the old post continue, even as the language became more hateful.

But that logic seems specious. It seems really unlikely that Lowe's could watch some of these comments flow by, as they were happening, and not interject. The media did interject. Google the phrase "Lowe's Facebook Muslim" and you'll discover more than 1,700 news stories. It seems far more likely that Lowe's realized how awful some of the comments were only once the media got hold of the story.

So how could this have played differently? For one, of course, Lowe's could have stood by the show. In retrospect, it seems silly to cave into a small group's demands, particularly when the content of the show itself doesn't merit rethinking the ad plan. That's particularly true in a media environment increasingly fueled by social media.

Second, it could remember that, while social media is a great place to issue corporate verbatim without the filter of the media, what happens next needs to be closely watched, and acted upon. It's a conversation, people.

Controversies can go viral within hours and attract the attention of the mainstream media, further damaging corporate reputation.

All communication is strategic. The decision to advertise on a particular TV show should be made based on whether the show reflects the organization's core values and helps accomplish a business objective. The cancellation of advertising calls into question Lowe's professed commitment to diversity and inclusiveness.

Organizations should have clear policies about the civil discourse on its own pages and make it clear that "hate speech" will not be tolerated. Lowe's, belatedly, decided to remove all 28,000 comments made about its decision.

Lowe's made no further comment after its official statement. Was this a good strategy in the age of social media?

Public relations staff are responsible for monitoring social media sites, assessing the possible implications, and responding in an appropriate manner.

TACTICS

Text Credits

Credits are listed in order of appearance.

Courtesy of Shel Holtz, Digital Communication Consultant.;

© 2011 MediaPost Communications, Social Media Insider. Used with permission.

Photo Credits

Credits are listed in order of appearance.

Jim West/Alamy;
Richard Scalzo/Shutterstock;
chaoss/Shutterstock;
(tr) Elizabeth A. Miller/Photoshot/Newscom;

Nikolai Pozdeev/Shutterstock;
Cox & Forkum;
Tony Freeman/PhotoEdit;
Steve Shott/DK Images;

Aflo Foto Agency/Alamy;
Goodluz/Shutterstock;
Monkey Business Images/Shutterstock;
abeadev/Shutterstock

Tactics image: Petr Z/Shutterstock
Tablet image: Falconia/Shutterstock

Corporate Public Relations

From Chapter 15 of *Think Public Relations*, 2013 Edition. Dennis L. Wilcox, Glen T. Cameron, Bryan H. Reber, Jae-Hwa Shin.
Copyright © 2013 by Pearson Education, Inc. Published by Pearson. All rights reserved.

Corporate Public Relations

Netflix Announcements Draw Consumer Ire

Corporate public relations practitioners face the constant potential of consumer discontent. For example, when mail-order DVD provider Netflix announced it would hike its subscription fees and separate its mail-order DVD and streaming video businesses, naming the mail-order business "Qwikster," consumers canceled their subscriptions in droves.

In July 2011, Netflix proposed separating its DVD-by-mail and streaming video businesses, which had been combined and offered at a monthly subscription price of $9.99. The company wanted to charge $7.99 for each service per month. Translation: the new DVD and streaming package would cost consumers $15.98 each month. In September 2011, Netflix CEO and Co-Founder Reed Hastings, who had only the year before appeared on the cover of *Fortune* as businessperson of the year, apologized to consumers in a blog posting on the Netflix website.

Hastings wrote: "It is clear from the feedback over the past two months that many members felt we lacked respect and humility in the way we announced the separation of DVD and streaming, and the price changes. That was certainly not our intent, and I offer my sincere apology."

In spite of the apology, Netflix did not immediately back away from the planned business separation and new pricing structure. By the end of October 2011, though, its plans had changed. In a quarterly conference call with investors, Hastings reported the first loss of subscribers in years. There were 800,000 fewer subscribers than there had been in July. The separation of services would not happen, Hasting declared. Qwikster was history. However, the new de facto $6 price increase would remain intact. Nonetheless, following the October announcement, Netflix stock prices rose.

Huffington Post blogger Jason Gilbert expressed the opinion of many consumers: "Qwikster was a dumb idea. Dumb, dumb, dumb. It should certainly be a first ballot entrant into the Bad Decision Hall of Fame."

"Consumers value the simplicity Netflix has always offered and we respect that," Hastings said in a press release announcing the end of Qwikster. "There is a difference between moving quickly—which Netflix has done very well for years—and moving too fast, which is what we did in this case."

1 **What could Netflix have done to better predict consumer response to these announcements?**

2 **What public relations tactics did Netflix use to address this problem?**

Ask Yourself

> What Role Can Public Relations Play in Rebuilding Public Trust in Business?

> How Do Media Relations, Customer Relations, Employee Relations, and Investor Relations Foster Corporate Health?

> What Is Integrated Marketing Communications?

> How Do Environmental Relations and Corporate Philanthropy Have a Positive Impact on the Public Image of a Corporation?

Managing corporate
REPUTATIONS

Giant corporations have operations and customers around the world. These companies deal with publics and governments at local, regional, national, and international levels. Their operations affect the environment, control the employment of thousands of people, and influence the financial and social well-being of millions of individuals.

The large size of corporations can distance them from stakeholders. A corporation has a "face"—the products, logo, and brand of any given corporation are often readily visible in advertising and billboards from Azerbaijan to Zimbabwe. Even so, the average consumer can't really comprehend

In a worldwide trust survey conducted by global public relations agency Edelman, 65 percent of respondents said that the ability to trust a corporation was the most important factor in corporate reputation.

the sheer size of organizations such as Walmart—the world's largest corporation, with $419 billion in worldwide sales—or Royal Dutch Shell, with $368 billion in global sales. These figures boggle the mind; in fact, they represent more than the combined gross national product (GNP) of many nations.

The public is often distrustful of the power, influence, and credibility of such giant corporations and business in general. This distrust of power was given voice in 2011 when activists "occupied" Wall Street and other cities worldwide. Specific corporate targets of consumer anger included Verizon when it announced that it would charge consumers $2 for the convenience of paying their bills online. Virulent subscriber reaction caused Verizon to backpedal on its

Consumers in the U.S. have a complicated relationship with huge corporations—complaining about corporate greed while they support organizations such as Walmart with their patronage.

AMERICAN OPINIONS about BIG BUSINESS

Forty-five percent of Americans believe that executives of large U.S. corporations are trustworthy, according to a recent Gallup survey.

By contrast, **79 percent** trust small business owners.

In its worldwide trust survey, public relations agency Edelman found that only 45 percent of Americans trust business to do what is right. Banks were singled out as especially untrustworthy: only 25 percent of respondents trusted banks to do what is right.

decision to charge consumers for paying their bills.

Major corporate financial scandals and the misdeeds of corporate executives also take their toll on corporate reputations. Public perceptions of greed and corporate misdeeds are reinforced by news stories. Hundreds of stories were written about the various misdeeds on Wall Street as protestors raised awareness of the wealth inequality between the vast majority of citizens – the "99 percent" – and the richest "1 percent," a label protestors linked to Wall Street. When much of the rest of the country was unemployed or underemployed,

financial institutions and corporations continued to dole out extravagant bonuses to executives, giving additional fuel to the activists' claims.

The extensive negative publicity about specific corporations and business in general over the past several years has made it imperative that companies regain their

> "We are the eyes and ears of an organization. The best way to be socially responsible is to have your eyes and ears trained on all the stakeholders, to know what they want and need from the company. These are classic public affairs issues and the idea that they should be handled by anyone else would show a lack of understanding."
>
> **Jack Bergen, vice president of corporate communications, Alcoa**

credibility and public trust. The concept of corporate social responsibility ranks high on the priority list of executives and public relations staffs that are charged with improving the reputation of their employers.

A number of strategies and tactics can be used to implement corporate social responsibility, which involves corporate performance as well as effective communications. Media relations, customer relations, employee relations, and investor relations can all contribute to corporate reputation, as do efforts made in the areas of marketing

> "At the beginning of the year we could feel something happening—and it was big. The young were more and more pissed off. They couldn't find jobs and their parents were losing their houses. Then suddenly there was the incredible Arab Spring, where young people with social media skills got millions into the streets."

Kalle Lasn, co-founder of *Adbusters* magazine, quoted in the *Toronto Star*

 What reasons does the public have to be mistrustful of large corporations?

communications, environmental relations, and corporate philanthropy. In the following sections, we talk about each of these key aspects of corporate public relations.

Corporations seek to achieve better reputations for a variety of reasons. First, responsible business practices ward off increased government regulation. Demonstrating what can happen when companies fail to police themselves, as a result of major financial scandals during the first decade of the century, the U.S. Congress passed new laws regarding accounting practices and disclosure. Second, there is the matter of employee morale: companies with good policies and good reputations tend to have less employee turnover. Corporate reputation also affects the bottom line.

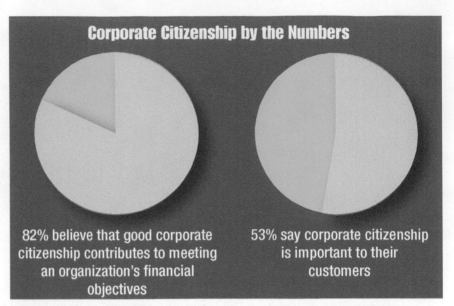

Corporate Citizenship by the Numbers

82% believe that good corporate citizenship contributes to meeting an organization's financial objectives

53% say corporate citizenship is important to their customers

Findings from a survey of executive attitudes conducted by the Center for Corporate Citizenship with the Hitachi Foundation.

4 KEY QUESTIONS About Corporate Citizenship

Being a good corporate citizen is an admirable goal, but corporations also face a number of pressures and counter pressures when making decisions and forming policies. General Electric once outlined four key factors that must be considered at all times when making a decision:

1. **POLITICAL:** How do government regulations and other pressures affect the decision?
2. **TECHNOLOGICAL:** Do we have the engineering knowledge to accomplish the goal?
3. **SOCIAL:** What is our responsibility to society?
4. **ECONOMIC:** Will we make a profit?

Media RELATIONS

The media are major sources of public information about business in general and individual companies in particular. In recent years, the news appearing in media outlets hasn't been especially favorable in regard to corporations.

Negative coverage can cause a corporation's reputation to plummet. Toyota fell from 18th to 139th place in one year on a corporate reputation list calculated by Prophet, a global marketing consultancy. The precipitous drop was blamed on negative news coverage surrounding product recalls. Given the potential for such a backlash, corporate executives are somewhat defensive about how journalists cover business; they often believe that too much emphasis is given to corporate misdeeds.

Many corporate executives have several ongoing complaints about media coverage: inaccuracy, incomplete coverage, inadequate research and preparation for interviews, and an antibusiness bias. Surveys routinely find that CEOs are dissatisfied with the business news and business reporters.

In their own defense, business editors and reporters state that often they cannot publish or broadcast thorough, evenhanded stories about business because many company executives, uncooperative and wary, erect barriers against them. Writers complain

Between 2009 and 2011, Toyota recalled several popular Toyota and Lexus models for issues ranging from braking to steering problems. Not surprisingly, the corporation's reputation took a huge hit.

> "I always thought that if you're getting a call from a PR agency or a call from Steve Jobs, which one is going to have the most impact? It was brilliant [of Jobs] to take the time to do that because most CEOs don't develop those relationships with reporters—and they also had access to him. He thought PR was so important that he spent a lot of his own time with the key media."

Fred Cook, CEO of GolinHarris, recalling in *PRWeek* how Steve Jobs sometimes pitched his own stories to journalists

b t w...

One survey by Hill & Knowlton found that Canadian CEOs believe that print and broadcast media criticism is the biggest threat to their company's reputation, even ranking ahead of such potential problems as disasters and allegations by the government about employee or product safety. At the same time, surveys show that media coverage is probably the most effective way for an organization to get its message across to its publics and to achieve business goals.

story involving unfavorable news about their company is negatively biased.

A survey of journalists conducted by TEKGROUP and *Bulldog Reporter* found that 45 percent of journalists agreed that public relations material is usually irrelevant to the journalist's work. Thirty-nine percent said they could not find necessary information on corporate websites. And one-third (34 percent) of journalists complained that public relations professionals did not provide access to corporate execs.

Public relations practitioners serving businesses stand in the middle of this tug-of-war. They must interpret their companies and clients to the media, while showing chief executives and other high officials how open, friendly media relations can serve their interests.

Savvy public relations professionals understand that business reporters often don't have adequate business preparation. For this reason, they spend a great deal of time and energy providing background and briefing reporters on the business operations of their clients and employers. It's one way of ensuring that coverage will be more accurate and thorough.

about their lack of direct access to decision-making executives and the proliferation of news releases that don't contain the information they need. Journalists assert, too, that some business leaders don't understand the concept of objectivity and assume that any

> "You [executives] should communicate factually, frequently, and consistently. Use this time wisely, say the journalists, to position yourself."

Don Middleberg,
PRWeek

Customer RELATIONS

In our society, sellers are expected to deliver goods and services of safe, acceptable quality on honest terms. Consumer rights are protected by the federal government, and federal and state agencies enforce those rights. In the United States, the Federal Trade Commission (FTC) regulates truth in advertising, the National Highway Traffic Safety Administration sets standards for automakers, and the Consumer Product Safety Commission examines the safety of other manufactured goods.

Customer service, in many respects, is the front line of public relations. A single incident, or a series of incidents, can severely damage a company's reputation and erode public trust in its products and services. Thanks to the Internet and blogs, a single dissatisfied customer is capable of informing thousands, or even millions, of people of his or her unhappiness in just one posting.

When animal rights activists posted an undercover video of employees abusing turkeys on ButterballAbuse.com and YouTube in December 2011, Butterball was slow to respond. It wasn't until six days later that Butterball posted a statement on its website citing a policy against mistreatment of the fowl. The government's reaction was less delayed. The single post resulted in a Butterball turkey farm being raided by law enforcement officials and news coverage on *ABC News*, and in the *Washington Post*, *USA Today*, and on Reuters, among others. However, the Butterball Twitter feed (with almost 5,500 followers) and Facebook page (with more than 47,000 fans) kept mum about the controversy, instead focusing on turkey handling and cooking tips for holiday meals.

Package delivery giant FedEx acted more quickly when a disgruntled consumer posted a security video of a FedEx delivery driver tossing a box clearly marked as carrying a computer monitor over a fence. The monitor was damaged, of course. The video received more than 5 million views in five days. *Ragan's PR Daily* reported that a FedEx executive embedded the video in a blog post and wrote: "I want you to know that I was upset, embarrassed, and very sorry for our customer's poor experience. This goes directly against everything we have always taught our people and expect of them. It was just very disappointing." According to *Ragan's PR Daily*, the blog entry described what FedEx did for the customer and how the video was now being used in employee training to avoid future episodes.

Traditionally, customer service has been kept separate from the communications or public relations function in a company. Bob Seltzer, a public relations consultant, told *PRWeek*, "I defy anyone to explain the wisdom of this. How a company talks to its customers is among, if not the, most critical communications it has."

> "One of the challenges a company will face is managing its reputation online. A more aggressive response strategy can help counteract some of the one-sided portrayal of the story in social media channels."
>
> Russ Williams, SVP of crisis and issues management at Cohn & Wolfe, in *PRWeek*

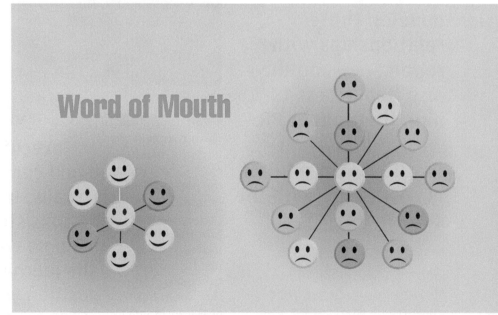

Word of Mouth

Consumer relations experts say that a dissatisfied customer will tell 9 to 15 people about a negative experience while a satisfied customer will tell only 4 to 6 people about positive experiences and share information on how their problems were resolved.

Corporate Public Relations

What Matters **MORE** Than Low Prices?

Public relations professionals also pay attention to consumer surveys. In particular, the American Customer Satisfaction Index is the definitive benchmark of how buyers feel about business practices. The index, which has been tracking customer satisfaction for 200 companies in 40 industries for more than a decade, has found that offering the lowest prices may not necessarily get a company the highest satisfaction rating. Walmart, for example, scores only 73 out of a possible 100 points.

While companies continue to use customer service call service centers, social media and the Internet have provided innovative ways for communication between companies and their customers. These media give consumers a voice and allow companies listening the opportunity to react and adjust quickly.

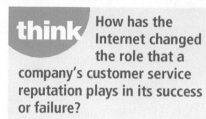

think How has the Internet changed the role that a company's customer service reputation plays in its success or failure?

Consumer Activism

Dissatisfied customers can often be mollified by prompt and courteous attention to their complaints or even an offer by a company to replace an item or provide discount coupons toward future purchases. Consumer activists who demand changes in corporate policies pose a more serious and complex threat to corporate reputation, and their efforts can ultimately affect sales.

Environmental activist group Greenpeace has urged consumers to support only tuna producers who require sustainable fishing methods. In its efforts to convince consumers to do so, it released a cartoon portraying the mascots for Bumblebee, Starkist, and

Increasingly, however, corporations are realizing that customer relations serves as a telltale public relations barometer. Many public relations departments regularly monitor customer feedback in a variety of ways to determine which policies and communications strategies need to be revised. One common method of doing so is to monitor customer queries on the organization's website. Another method comprises content analysis of phone calls to a company's customer service center.

It is important for public relations professionals to be involved in active listening to customer feedback so they can strategize the steps companies should take to ensure their good reputations.

Greenpeace's video cartoon criticizing the tuna industry features a character referred to as "Mr. Shadowy Multinational Corporation."

Corporate Public Relations

Controversial reality TV star Kim Kardashian has been the target of consumer anger.

to know." Bumblebee, Starkist, and Chicken of the Sea tuna brands sent Greenpeace a cease and desist order for trademark infringement related to the activist organization's critical cartoons.

Consumer Boycotts

The boycott—a refusal to buy the products or services of an offending company—has a long history and is a widely used consumer publicity tool. When Bank of America announced a new $5 monthly fee for debit card users, consumers objected. A post on financial blog *ZeroHedge.com* urged "any and all of our 5 million monthly readers to pull any funds they may have from Bank of America in retaliation." A "Boycott Bank of America" Facebook page appeared to address Bank of America's mortgage lending and foreclosure practices. The *Washington Post* reported: "It was a classic David-and-Goliath fight, fueled by the growing populist outrage against the nation's financial system. On Tuesday, the little guy won: Bank of America announced that it was abandoning the fee."

Celebrity endorsements can backfire when a boycott targets an individual. The website BoycottKim.com listed almost 50 brands that carried Kardashian-endorsed products and urged Kim Kardashian haters to boycott the brands. More than 600,000 signed

think How can a boycott be used as an effective negotiating tactic for a consumer group?

a petition and pledged: "We will refuse to shop at any retail store, both physical and online, which utilizes or hires Kim Kardashian as a spokesperson, or carries and sells Kim Kardashian products."

The efficacy of consumer boycotts is mixed. For example, a variety of activist groups have boycotted Procter & Gamble for years without making much headway because the company manufactures so many products under a variety of brand names that consumers can't keep track of the complete P&G product line. Perhaps because the boycott was focused, Bank of America abandoned its plans to change its debit card fees. On the other hand, Kim Kardashian's fortunes have remained strong.

A single product name can sometimes be more vulnerable to consumer activism than a large company that markets its goods and services under multiple brand names. BlackBerry customers were infuriated when Research In Motion (RIM) suffered service interruptions that lasted for days and affected BlackBerry users on five continents.

Chicken of the Sea as evil or bumbling pawns for food conglomerates. In La Jolla, California, home to Chicken of the Sea, Greenpeace also launched an airship with a cartoon mermaid on the side and the message "Tunasecrets.com: What the tuna industry doesn't want you

Dos and Don'ts of Working with Consumer Groups

At the strategic level, a company weighs the potential impact of the allegations on customers and the expected effect on sales before deciding on a course of action. Activist consumer groups are a major challenge to the public relations staff of an organization. Is it best to accommodate their demands? Is it better to stonewall them? Should the company change its policy? Douglas Quenqua, writing in *PRWeek*, offered some general guidelines on

how to take a proactive stance when working with consumer groups.

DO:

- Work with groups who are more interested in finding solutions than attracting publicity.
- Offer transparency. Activists who believe you are not being open with them are unlikely to keep dealing with you.

- Turn their suggestions into action. Activists want results.

DON'T:

- Get emotional when dealing with advocacy groups.
- Agree to work with anyone making threats.
- Expect immediate results. Working with adversaries takes patience—establishing trust takes time.

LinkedIn as a Public Relations Tactic?

Most job hunters or career-minded professionals know about LinkedIn, even if they don't have an account. The networking that LinkedIn allows is beneficial to career building, but the networks that develop on LinkedIn can also be beneficial to public relations practitioners.

In November 2011, there were 135 million LinkedIn users in 200 countries and territories worldwide, according to the company's own statistics. Fifty-nine percent of users were outside the United States. Every *Fortune* 500 company was represented on LinkedIn by at least one executive, and 2 million companies had LinkedIn Company Pages. Company Pages, according to LinkedIn "are a company's profile of record" and "present an opportunity to reveal the human side of your company."

Among the companies present on LinkedIn are Delta Air Lines, with 10,435 employees "LinkedIn"; ExxonMobil, with 13,997; Walmart, with 23,967; Target, with 24,615; and Microsoft, with 92,960. According to James L. Horton, public relations consultant, "LinkedIn presents a self-identified audience of employees and professional-level followers who are natural targets for company news and messages." He suggested that public relations practitioners consider using LinkedIn to post company news, foster a sense of employee community, and supplement the company's website. "LinkedIn is increasingly a social medium for reaching professionals," he continued.

Nada Arnot wrote in *PRWeek* that LinkedIn is an underused resource. She suggests five tips for organizations to ensure they are getting the most out of their LinkedIn Company Pages: 1) Present your page as a brochure, complete with discoverable keywords and pithy "elevator pitch" writing; 2) use the tabs that LinkedIn provides to "integrate images, videos, and callouts to special offers"; 3) ask customers to write recommendations and then post them to the appropriate product or service tab; 4) extend your message by contributing to LinkedIn Answers and Groups and by linking your Twitter feed to your page; and 5) use LinkedIn analytic tools to identify "follower growth and profiles, industry benchmarks, section page views, and visitor breakdowns."

1 How do the organizations you interact with use LinkedIn?

2 With what publics might LinkedIn company pages be more effective than Facebook pages?

3 How would you drive employees to the company page of a corporation you have worked for or hope to work for? How could you make employees want to be there?

Research In Motion apologized in a statement and a video. It also promised customers regular updates via social media channels.

Activists point out that a boycott doesn't have to be 100 percent effective to change corporate policies. Even a 5 percent drop in sales will often cause corporations to rethink their policies and modes of operation.

> "As we move ever closer to a world in which global publishing power lies in every person's pocket, the punishment for failing to listen, engage, anticipate and respond effectively will be severe; and the rewards for an organization that defines itself through communication will be rich indeed."
>
> Daniel Tisch, APR, Fellow CPRS, Chair, Global Alliance, and CEO, Argyle Communications

Employee RELATIONS

Like customers, employees are a primary public for any profit-making organization. In many ways, employees are the front line of any effective public relations program. A company's reputation may be enhanced or damaged by how rank-and-file employees feel about their employer. In its annual consumer trust survey, Edelman found that 63 percent of consumers in 23 countries said corporate reputation was highly affected by how well the corporation treats its employees.

Employees have been called an organization's "ambassadors" because they represent the company within a large circle of family, relatives, and friends. If morale is low or if employees believe the company is not treating them fairly, that unhappiness will likely be reflected in their comments to others. On the other hand, enthusiastic employees can do much to enhance an organization's reputation within a community as a good place to work. This factor, in turn, generates more job applicants and enhances employee-retention rates.

Maggie Fitzpatrick, COO of Cigna and president of the Cigna

> When people don't care about their jobs or employers, they don't show up consistently, they produce less, or their work quality suffers. On the other hand, when employees feel a sense of ownership and pride in a company's mission, it sparks a new level of commitment.
>
> Maggie Fitzpatrick, CCO of Cigna and president of the Cigna Foundation, in *PRWeek*

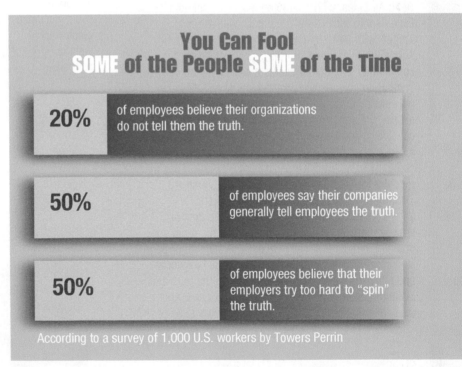

You Can Fool SOME of the People SOME of the Time

20%	of employees believe their organizations do not tell them the truth.
50%	of employees say their companies generally tell employees the truth.
50%	of employees believe that their employers try too hard to "spin" the truth.

According to a survey of 1,000 U.S. workers by Towers Perrin

Surveys indicate that the success of communication efforts varies widely among organizations. The value of credible and trustworthy communication with employees cannot be underestimated. Seasoned public relations professionals know that effective employee relations is more than just a string of well-written and informative messages.

Foundation, reports that her employees praised the company's support of the Martin Luther King, Jr. Memorial on the National Mall in Washington, D.C. She said employees believed it showed the company was sincere about diversity initiatives within as well as beyond the organization. Fitzpatrick told *PRWeek* that employees wrote blog posts about the company's support of the memorial and shared the following excerpts from employee posts: "It makes me so proud," "Thank you so much for doing this," and "I am doubly moved that you have honored the memory, contributions, and commitment of this great man."

The wise public relations department, often working with the human resources department, concentrates on communicating with employees just as vigorously as it does on delivering the corporate story to an external audience. Employees who respect management, have pride in their products, and believe they are being treated fairly are a key factor in corporate success.

One important legal and ethical workplace issue that affects both employees and management is sexual harassment. The U.S. Supreme Court ruled in *Meritor Savings Bank v. Vinson* (1986) that a company may be held liable in sexual harassment suits even if management is unaware of the problem and has a general policy condemning any form of verbal or nonverbal behavior that causes employees to feel "uncomfortable" or consider the workplace a "hostile environment." To protect themselves from liability and the unfavorable publicity associated with a lawsuit, organizations not only need to establish a policy on sexual harassment, but must also clearly communicate that policy to employees and conduct workshops to ensure that everyone thoroughly understands

> "The way in which a company handles job reductions can have a significant impact on its reputation, its share price, and its ongoing ability to recruit and maintain good staff. And that presents a major challenge for communication departments."
>
> Julia Hood, EVP of Haymarket Media

what might be considered sexual harassment.

Layoffs present a major public relations challenge to an organization. In the case of widespread layoffs, the expertise of the public relations department should be harnessed to ensure employee understanding and support. One cardinal rule is that layoffs should never be announced to the media before employees are informed. Another rule is that an employee should be informed of the furlough or termination in person by his or her immediate supervisor. Employees who are being retained should also be called in by their immediate supervisors to be informed of their status.

The rumor mill works overtime when there is uncertainty among employees about job security, so it's also important for the company to publicly announce layoffs and discuss their effects as quickly as possible. Companies should be forthright about layoffs; this is not the time to issue vague statements and "maybes."

Companies that are interested in their reputations and employee trust should make every effort to cushion the blows of a layoff by implementing various programs. The *New York Times*, for example, paid as much as two years' salary as severance to veteran employees who voluntarily separated from the media giant. Other companies offer outplacement services, the use of office space, and other support programs. Such programs do much to retain employee goodwill even as workers are being laid off.

Company decisions should be announced publicly before workplace gossip can fill the information vacuum and create a toxic environment.

Corporate Public Relations

Investor RELATIONS

Another major indicator of corporate health and wealth is good communication with current shareholders and prospective investors. Investor relations (IR) is at the heart of that process. Effective investor relations combines the disciplines of communications and finance to accurately portray a company's prospects from an investment standpoint. Key audiences for these efforts are financial analysts, individual and institutional investors, shareholders, prospective shareholders, and the financial media. Increasingly, employees are an important public, too, because they have stock options and 401(k) plans.

Individuals who specialize in investor or financial relations, according to salary surveys, are the highest-paid professionals in the public relations field. One reason for their high salaries is that they must be very knowledgeable about finance and the myriad regulations set down by the U.S. Securities and Exchange Commission (SEC) on initial public offerings (IPOs) of stock, mergers, accounting requirements, the contents of quarterly financial reports, and public disclosure of information. Government financial regulations are highly complex, and it is critical that they are followed to the letter. A company going public for the first time, for example, is required by the SEC to observe a "quiet time" when

think — Why are public relations professionals who specialize in investor relations so well compensated?

company executives are not allowed to talk about the offering to analysts or the financial press to avoid "hyping" the stock.

Investor relations expertise is key both to satisfying SEC rules and to keeping various publics informed. And the stakes are high. For example, investor relations could have been better, the experts say, when Google's IPO had to be delayed because cofounders Sergey Brin and Larry Page made some comments about the stock offering in a major magazine interview during the SEC's mandated "quiet period." The foul-up in this classic case gave Google a rocky start in terms of positioning the stock and building its reputation among Wall Street analysts.

Investor relations staff primarily communicate with institutional investors, individual investors, stockbrokers, and financial analysts. They also serve as sources of information for the financial press, such as the *Wall Street Journal*, *Barron's*, and the *Financial Times*. In their jobs, investor relations professionals make numerous presentations, conduct field trips for analysts and portfolio managers, analyze stockholder demographics, oversee corporate annual reports, and prepare materials for potential investors.

Marketing COMMUNICATIONS

Many companies use the tools and tactics of public relations to support the marketing and sales objectives of their business. This type of activity is called *marketing communications* or *marketing public relations*. Thomas L. Harris, author of *The Marketer's Guide to Public Relations*, defines marketing public relations (MPR) as the "process of planning, executing, and evaluating programs that encourage purchase and consumer satisfaction through credible communication of information and impressions that identify companies and their products with the needs, wants, concerns, and interests of consumers."

In many cases, marketing public relations is coordinated with a company's messages in advertising, marketing, direct mail, and promotion. In *integrated marketing communications* (*IMC*), companies manage all the sources of information about a product or service so as to ensure maximum message penetration. IMC is an important concept in modern public relations practice.

In an integrated program, public relations activities attempt to garner early awareness and credibility for

Special events can include publicity stunts. Nathan's Famous Frankfurters has hosted a Hot Dog Eating Contest every year since 1916. The event still generates media coverage. In an effort to keep the event fresh, in 2011 Nathan's separated the sexes and crowned both a men's and women's hot-dog-eating champion. The men's champion downed 62 hot dogs and buns during the 10-minute contest; the women's champ devoured 40.

a product. Publicity in the form of news stories is leveraged to secure credibility, excitement in the marketplace, and consumer anticipation. The early messages make audiences more receptive to advertising and promotions about the product in the later phases of the campaign. Indeed, a growing body of research asserts that public relations is the cornerstone of branding and positioning a product or service. The objectives of marketing communications, often called *marcom* in industry jargon, are accomplished in several ways, such as product publicity, cause-related marketing, viral marketing, and corporate sponsorship.

Product Publicity

As the cost and clutter of advertising have mounted dramatically, companies have found that creative product publicity is a cost-effective way to reach potential customers. Even mundane household products, if presented properly, can be newsworthy and capture media attention.

Nestlé, for example, generated numerous news articles and broadcast mentions for its Butterfinger candy bar by producing a film, *Butterfinger the 13th*, directed by Rob Lowe. The mock-horror short generated exclusive coverage on *Entertainment Tonight* and *The Insider*. Media impressions exceeded 500 million, with coverage on CNN and MTV.com and in *USA Today*.

Jaguar and Land Rover conducted a media campaign that included hosting 30 members of the press at the Los Angeles Auto Show, pre-show parties, a tour led by auto aficionado Jay Leno, and vehicle test drives. The campaign resulted in 500 TV appearances—reaching 22 million viewers on stations as diverse as MTV and the BBC and readers in the *New York Times* and *Wall Street Journal*.

A company can also generate product publicity by sponsoring a poll, even though the survey might be somewhat frivolous and the methodology unscientific. For example, *Glamour* magazine, in conjunction with Ralph Lauren Romance, conducted a survey and announced to the world that 90 percent of American adults believe in true love. It also found that the phone is the most preferred means of contact after a first date by both sexes. More breaking news: men like being complimented by being told they're funny (88 percent) while women prefer to be told they have a nice smile (93 percent). Surveys like this are often released near a relevant holiday or event. The *Glamour*/Lauren survey was released on February 8, right before Valentine's Day.

Product publicity can be generated in other ways. Nathan's Famous Frankfurters sponsors a hot dog eating contest. Briggs & Stratton, which makes lawnmowers, compiles an annual top 10 list of beautiful lawns; Hershey Foods set a Guinness Record by producing the world's largest Kiss—a chocolate candy that weighed several tons.

Product placement refers to the appearance of a product in a movie or television program, thereby helping promote the brand. The Mercedes-Benz that the characters in a movie drive to the airport, the

think How can public relations tactics effectively support the sales and marketing objectives of a business?

United Airlines flight that takes them to a destination, the Hilton where they stay, and the Grey Goose vodka martinis they drink in the bar are all examples of product placement.

Increasingly, product placements are the result of fees paid to film

think — How is cause-related marketing a win–win for a corporation and its community?

studios and television producers. Sometimes, there is a trade-off. For example, when American Eagle or Abercrombie & Fitch volunteers to provide the entire wardrobe for a television show, such a deal reduces the cost of production for the producer and at the same time gives the clothing firms high visibility.

Cause-Related Marketing

Companies in highly competitive fields, where there is little differentiation between products or services, often strive to stand

Cause-Related Marketing Tips

Selecting a charity or a cause to support involves strategic thinking. Here are some tips for conducting cause-related marketing:

- Look for a cause that is closely related to your products or services or one that exemplifies a product quality.
- Pick a cause that appeals to your primary customers.
- Choose a charity that doesn't already have multiple sponsors.
- Go with a local organization if the purpose is to build brand awareness for local franchises.
- Don't use cause-related efforts as a tactic to salvage your organization's image after a major scandal; such attempts usually backfire.
- Understand that association with a cause or nonprofit organization is a long-term commitment.
- Keep in mind that additional funds must be allocated to create public awareness and build brand recognition with the cause.

American Express was not the first company to engage in cause-related marketing, but its success in raising money to restore the aging Statue of Liberty and Ellis Island in 1984 set a new benchmark for effectiveness. The company spent $6 million publicizing the fact that one penny of every dollar spent on its credit cards would be donated to restoration efforts. American Express saw the use of its cards jump 28 percent, and applications for new cards increased 17 percent. In addition, the marketing campaign proved to be an excellent branding strategy—promoting an automatic association in the public's mind between American Express and an American icon.

GOOD DEEDS Are Expected and Rewarded

81 percent of respondents to a worldwide survey expect companies to play a positive active role in society.

20 percent of adults worldwide believe companies should support larger issues with donations and time.

30 percent believe companies should support larger issues with donations and time and advocate for change.

31 percent believe companies should change the way they operate to align with greater social and environmental needs.

94 percent said that when price and quality are the same, they were likely to switch brands to a company associated with a good cause.

Corporate Public Relations

Macy's Strives to Activate Millennials

IN A COLLABORATIVE CAUSE-RELATED MARKETING CAMPAIGN, nonprofit DoSomething.org and Macy's recently joined forces to both raise money and engage millennials and digital natives in social activism and volunteerism. Cause-related marketing is one aspect of corporate social responsibility (CSR). Like this one, CSR efforts are often based on partnerships between companies and nonprofits. Experts say such partnerships need to be sincere and relevant to succeed. "When this relevance exists, it has a natural positive impact on the business itself—on its bottom line, employee morale, and the brand's overall reputation," writes Emanate CEO Kim Sample, in *PRWeek*.

"Macy's has a long history of giving back, but this year we wanted to create something new and unique for our millennial customer," Holly Thomas, Macy's VP of media relations and cause marketing, told *PRWeek*. To do just that, Macy's partnered with DoSomething.org, a large, U.S.-based youth activism organization. DoSomething has a goal of 5 million active members by 2015. Its primary audience is "social changers 25 and under."

In its press release Macy's described the campaign: "this mobile campaign calls for young people to visit their local Macy's mystylelab departments (formerly juniors' and young men's) to take part in a scan-to-donate program that celebrates and rewards youth activism. In return for scanning the designated QR codes, Macy's will donate $1, up to a total of $250,000, to DoSomething.org. The scan will trigger the $1 donation and teens will have the opportunity to find out ways to take action locally around issues, such as bullying and the environment, in their community." Participants were also entered in a contest for shopping sprees.

In addition to the "Raise your phone" QR code aspect of the campaign, Macy's encouraged young consumers to "Raise your thumb and rock your cause," a reference to registering a thumbs-up "Like" on Macy's mystylelab Facebook page. Each Like generated an additional $1 toward the campaign donation goal.

Macy's produced a public service announcement for the collaboration with DoSomething.org featuring Nick Cannon, *America's Got Talent* host. Kelly Osbourne, celebrity singer, actress, and fashion designer, served as the in-store face of the campaign.

"We are excited to partner with DoSomething.org in an effort to mobilize youth around causes they care about," said Martine Reardon, Macy's EVP of marketing. "We've been so inspired by the amazing work of the DoSomething.org members, and we hope our program will bring added awareness and funding to the organization so it can engage and enable more kids to take meaningful action."

Responses on the blog *More4MomsBuck.com* suggested that Macy's had hit the mark. "It is great to see a company like Macy's be committed to giving back," wrote one blog reader. "I love the way Macy's is always trying to do something to go that extra mile for the community. Makes shopping there so worth the while!," gushed a second. A third replied, "I think giving back especially for a teen is a great way to show community involvement. It also makes your teen feel like they are contributing to something worthwhile. I think this sounds like a great idea."

1. Beyond the donations from Macy's, how did DoSomething.org benefit from the campaign?

2. Was this a logical pairing of corporation and cause? Why or why not?

3. Are there other social media tools that might have been useful for Macy's to employ in this campaign?

---

out and enhance their reputation for corporate social responsibility (CSR) by engaging in cause-related marketing. In this type of marketing, a profit-making company collaborates with a nonprofit organization to advance its cause and, at the same time, increase sales. Yoplait yogurt brand, for example, informs customers that 10 cents will be donated to support breast cancer research for each pink Yoplait lid they send in or register on Yoplait's website.

Corporate Sponsorships

One form of cause-related marketing is corporate sponsorship of activities and events such as concerts, art exhibits, races, and scientific expeditions. Companies spend approximately $48.7 billion annually

Shopping with a Conscience

In the last 12 months...

76% of consumers have bought a product with an environmental benefit.

65% have bought a product from a company associated with a cause.

56% have boycotted a company upon learning that it behaved irresponsibly.

worldwide sponsoring activities ranging from the FIFA World Cup and the Kentucky Derby to the Grammy Awards, PGA golf tournaments, and even the concert tours of Lady Antebellum or Rihanna. Many of these events, unlike causes, are money-making operations in their own right. Even so, a large part of the underwriting often comes from corporate sponsorship.

Corporate-sponsored events serve four purposes:

1 **They enhance** the reputation and image of the sponsoring company through association.

2 **They give** product brands high visibility among key purchasing publics.

3 **They provide** a focal point for marketing efforts and sales campaigns.

4 **They generate** publicity and media coverage.

Sponsorships can be more cost-effective than advertising. Visa International, for example, spends roughly $200,000 each year (approximately the price of a 30-second prime-time TV commercial) sponsoring the USA/Visa Decathlon Team. Speedo,

the swimwear manufacturer, sponsors swim teams from 14 countries, including the U.S. Olympic swim team, getting its name before millions of television viewers. At the London games, the majority of swimmers had flexible contracts, allowing them to wear Speedo gear even if they were sponsored by a rival—which in turn translated into brand dominance in terms of sales.

Local stadiums and concert halls almost everywhere now have corporate names. Citibank agreed to pay $400 million to have its name on the New York Mets's home stadium in Flushing, NY, for 20 years. Federal Express will pay $205 million over 27 years for naming rights to FedEx Field, home of the Washington Redskins. In Dallas, American Airlines will pay $195 million over 30 years for naming rights to American Airlines Center, home of the Dallas Mavericks.

The rationale behind naming rights is that a company will be identified as a major brand and will be better recognized by those attending events at the venue as well as the millions who watch major league ballgames at home on television. By the same logic, the online-only University of Phoenix enrolls more than 100,000 students

Warnaco CEO Joe Gromek presented Michael Phelps with a $1 million bonus check from Speedo at a broadcast of *The Today Show* in New York City after Phelps won a record eight gold medals in swimming at the Beijing Olympics. Phelps used the bonus to start the Michael Phelps Foundation. As part of Phelps's most recent Speedo deal, which extends through 2013, the brand will donate $10,000 to the Michael Phelps Foundation for every World Record that Phelps sets.

at 200 locations, and has no traditional main campus. It does, however, have the University of Phoenix stadium (for a mere $154 million over 20 years), home of the NFL's Arizona Cardinals.

Viral Marketing

Long before the rise of the Internet, professional communicators recognized the value of favorable recommendations and "buzz" about a product or service. For public relations programs, the primary objective has always been to enhance or maintain the reputation of a company or celebrity. Today, "word-of-mouth" is used to generate greater traffic to websites, where both marketing and public relations objectives can be met. The primary purpose of viral marketing is to stimulate impulse purchases or downloads, but pass-it-on techniques on the web are

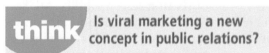

think Is viral marketing a new concept in public relations?

also intended to help public relations professionals meet goals for reputation management and message dissemination. Generating excitement about the release of a musician's latest recording and touting the opening of a movie are two common ways viral marketing is employed in the entertainment business.

Viral marketing has adopted terminology and some special techniques that take advantage of technology to stimulate the natural inclination of people to tell others about a good deal, a good service, or a good group. One classic example of viral marketing is Burger King's Subservient Chicken website (www.subservientchicken. com), which was launched in 2004. The site features a human in a chicken suit who responds to whatever command the web viewer types in. If a viewer tells the chicken to dance, it dances. If a viewer instructs it to jump, it

jumps. The connection to Burger King is twofold: it plays on the restaurant's long-time slogan "Have it your way," and it promotes the hamburger giant's chicken sandwich offerings.

When the site was launched, only 20 people—friends of employees in the agency that created the campaign—were told about the website. From those 20 people, use of the site exploded exponentially, to the point that the site garnered 46 million hits in its first week of operation—a truly viral event. The chicken is still taking orders and spreading virally through a "Tell a Friend" feature on the company's website.

Corporate websites are now rife with games far more sophisticated than the Subservient Chicken, but the chicken led the way. While the Burger King case illustrates how corporate website content can become viral, an ad developed by Dove beauty products and titled simply "Evolution" is a classic example of how viral advertising and public relations work hand in glove.

The "Evolution" ad is a time-lapsed illustration of the evolution of a rather normal looking woman into a glamorous model. Within a day of its posting, the 75-second YouTube clip received 44,000 views. By the end of the first month, it had more than 1.7 million views. As of this writing, the number of views has passed 14 million. The Dove ad generated discussion on *The View*, *Good Morning America*, and *The Ellen DeGeneres Show*, among others. The earned media exposure has been estimated to exceed $150 million.

Some viral marketing firms devise ways to stimulate the natural spread of recommendations through financial incentives called *cohort communication*. Going beyond the relatively organic spread of information via tactics like Burger King's "Tell a Friend" feature, viral marketing specialists

Business writer Paul Maccabee provided some tips and insights for developing a viral campaign: 1) Embrace the fact that viral content will result in user-generated responses. Because you are trying to engage the public, you will receive positive and negative feedback. 2) Accept that online video isn't free. Don't allow the CEO's clever teenager to produce the video. 3) Recognize that a YouTube video isn't guaranteed to "go viral." An online video is a communication channel, not a strategy. 4) Be willing to make fun of your own product or organization. It's okay to mock your product, tongue-in-cheek. 5) Remember that digital techniques don't replace traditional media. In fact, good viral campaigns use traditional media: Dove's "Evolution" campaign combined online video with traditional news and talk show coverage.

Maccabee also encouraged viral marketers to let campaigns evolve while remaining true to the brand heritage.

use more calculated tactics such as careful dissemination of favorable reviews. Software systems track referrals to a website or recommendations sent to friends, with senders chalking up cash or merchandise credits.

Detractors worry that viral marketing is too easily recognizable as commercial manipulation, except among hard-core enthusiasts. Smart Water took this complaint head-on when it produced a video commercial it hoped would go viral. In the ad, Jennifer Aniston and some research geeks tell viewers they are using all the tried-and-true techniques to make an ad go viral—dopey lip synching, babies doing antics, cute puppies, and Aniston flipping her locks in sexy slow motion. And it worked.

In early 2012, the commercial had more than 10 million views.

Viral marketing companies argue that the technique will work only when the idea, the movement, or the product earns genuine support from the marketplace. Public relations professionals need to make careful and ethical decisions to decide how best to use the web to spread messages.

Environmental RELATIONS

Another aspect of corporate responsibility is corporate concern for the environment and sustainable resources. The end of the twentieth century was witness to major clashes and confrontations between corporations and activist nongovernmental organizations (NGOs) about a host of environmental and human rights issues. The current trend, however, favors cooperation and partnerships among these former adversaries. Many companies, such as Shell, now issue annual sustainability reports and work with environmental groups to clean up the environment, preserve wilderness areas, and restore exploited natural resources.

Clothing company American Apparel has long been known for its activism. *Apparel* magazine named American Apparel as one of its first Sustainability All-Star Award winners. Among the environmentally friendly steps taken by the company is the development of a product line made entirely from the scraps of material that are a by-product of manufacturing. These scraps are made into headbands and belts rather than being sent to the landfill. The scraps are also made into underwear. This program recycles approximately 30,000 pounds of cotton per week.

American Apparel offers a sustainable edition of its clothing as well. The sustainable line is made of 100 percent organic and certified pesticide-free cotton. And the company does not stop there: it generates 20 to 30 percent of its energy from solar panels, and it recycles cardboard boxes and cell phones. Timers and motion sensors save electricity in unused rooms. Employees are encouraged to use company bicycles to pedal back and forth to work. They are also supplied with bus passes to limit their driving.

oo dles'
우들스
American Appa
American Apparel

Made in Downtown LA—Vertically Integrated Manufacturing

Corporate Social Responsibility Programs

A number of large corporations around the world forge alliances with various NGOs to preserve the environment, promote human rights, and provide social/medical services:

- Proctor and Gamble partners with nongovernmental organizations (NGOs) to provide puberty education, sanitary protection, and sanitary facilities for girls in developing countries. To date, the "Protecting Futures" campaign has worked with eight partner organizations to reach 80,000 girls in 17 countries.
- Beginning in 2009, Starbucks has held annual "Cup Summits" to bring government officials, suppliers, manufacturers, beverage businesses and competitors, recyclers, conservation groups, and academics together to discuss how to improve cup design, cup recycling and recycling infrastructure.
- In its Sustainability Report, Coca-Cola announced a project titled "Haiti Hope Project." Coca-Cola partnered with government and NGOs in Haiti to develop sustainable mango farming practices to double the income of farmers and improve the participation of women in mango production.
- Merck, the pharmaceutical giant, partnered with the Earth Institute at Columbia University to strengthen community health services for 400,000 people in rural communities in 10 African nations.

Corporate PHILANTHROPY

Another manifestation of organizational social responsibility is corporate philanthropy. This activity, in essence, consists of the donation of funds, products, and services to various causes, ranging from providing uniforms and equipment to a local Little League team to endowing a university with a multimillion-dollar gift to upgrade its science and engineering programs. In many cases, an organization's public relations department handles corporate charitable giving.

Corporations, of course, have long used philanthropy to

> **Never do it for publicity. Do it for building your business, your brand equity, and your stakeholder relations.**
>
> Research firm Cone/Roper

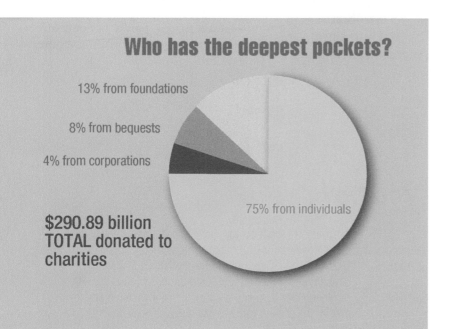

Who has the deepest pockets?

13% from foundations

8% from bequests

4% from corporations

75% from individuals

$290.89 billion TOTAL donated to charities

In 2010, U.S. corporations gave $15.29 billion to a variety of causes. Although there is a common perception that corporate philanthropy provides the lion's share of all donations, the actual percentage of charitable donations accounted for by corporations is very small. Of the $290 billion total given in 2010, only 4 percent came from corporations. The largest percentage of money given, 75 percent, was given by individuals.

In HomeBanc's case, funding Habitat for Humanity is a strategic decision to funnel contributions to a cause directly related to home ownership, which is the business of the mortgage company.

demonstrate community goodwill and to polish their reputations as good citizens. There's also evidence that corporate giving is good for gaining and retaining customers. In a Hill & Knowlton survey, 79 percent of Americans claim to take corporate citizenship into consideration when purchasing products. At the same time, 76 percent of the respondents believe that companies participate in philanthropic activities to get favorable publicity, and only 24 percent believe corporations are truly committed to the causes they support.

Getting good publicity, no doubt, is a factor in philanthropy, but it should not be a company's ultimate objective. Cone/Roper, a survey organization, says companies should be very careful about touting their good deeds so the public does not become skeptical about their motivation. Companies should concentrate on the people they help, and the programs they showcase should be more than "window dressing."

 **think** How can strategic corporate philanthropy help an organization achieve success?

A series of small grants to a wide variety of causes can dilute the impact of the contributions; sometimes a concentrated effort is more effective. HomeBanc Mortgage Corporation, for example, used to give $300,000 annually in small grants to a variety of causes, but it decided that the available funds could have more impact (and visibility) if they were directed to just one or two causes. Consequently, the company now directs most of its charitable funds to Habitat for Humanity, a nonprofit that builds homes for low-income families.

 **What Would You Do?**

Preparing to Work Abroad

You've just begun work with a global corporation. Its home offices are located in Chicago, but because of your Portuguese-language major and your two internships with Latin American companies, you've been hired to do public relations in the Sao Paulo office. How will you prepare for this assignment? What do you need to know about the company and its operations and relationship with key stakeholders in Brazil? What do you need to know about Brazilian media, consumers, and employee expectations? Make a to-do list for yourself to help you prepare for your new job effectively and hit the ground running when you relocate to Brazil.

summary

What Role Can Public Relations Play in Rebuilding Public Trust in Business?

- Corporations must make special efforts to win public credibility and trust. Public relations professionals are on the front line in this effort, counseling companies to be more transparent in their operations, to adopt ethical standards of conduct, and to improve corporate governance.

How Do Media Relations, Customer Relations, Employee Relations, and Investor Relations Foster Corporate Health?

- It is important for organizations to effectively tell their stories and establish rapport with business editors and reporters by being accessible, open, and honest about company operations and policies.

- Customer satisfaction is important for building loyalty, generating positive word of mouth for products, and maintaining the reputation of a company. Public relations professionals solicit customer feedback as often as possible and act to satisfy customers' needs for communication and service.

- Employees are the "ambassadors" of a company and serve as the primary source of information about the company for friends and relatives.

What Is Integrated Marketing Communications?

- Increasingly, companies are taking an integrated approach to campaigns. With this approach, public relations, marketing, and advertising staffs work together to complement one another's expertise.

- Product publicity and product placement are often part of marketing communications. Cause-related marketing involves partnerships with nonprofit organizations to promote a particular cause.

How Do Environmental Relations and Corporate Philanthropy Have a Positive Impact on the Public Image of a Corporation?

- Corporations and activist organizations sometimes engage in dialogue and collaborative efforts to change situations.

- In general, corporate philanthropy is part of an organization's commitment to social responsibility. Companies give approximately $15 billion per year to worthy causes in the United States.

questions
FOR REVIEW AND DISCUSSION

1 Why is there so much current public suspicion and distrust of corporate business entities?

2 Consumer activists are often very vocal about the misdeeds of corporations. How should a company react to charges and allegations from activist groups such as Greenpeace or PETA? As a public relations professional, which factors would go into your decision making if faced with this situation?

3 Why are employee relations efforts so important to a company's image and reputation?

4 List some examples of product publicity and product placement. How effective do you think these examples have been in promoting corporate images?

5 What is the concept of corporate social responsibility (CSR), and why is it important to today's corporations? What is the role of public relations professionals in CSR?

6 Why is corporate sponsorship of concerts, festivals, and even the Olympics considered a good marketing and public relations strategy?

7 Corporate philanthropy is now very strategic; companies support organizations and causes that have direct relationships to their businesses. Do you think this kind of linkage makes corporate philanthropy too self-serving? Why or why not?

MySearchLab®

Text Credits

Credits are listed in order of appearance.

Photo Credits

Events and Promotions

From Chapter 13 of *Think Public Relations*, 2013 Edition. Dennis L. Wilcox, Glen T. Cameron, Bryan H. Reber, Jae-Hwa Shin.

Events and Promotions

Mr. Bubble Turns 50 with a Splash

In 1961, Mr. Bubble bubble bath brought fun suds into children's bathtubs. The Village Company, LLC, owner of the Mr. Bubble brand, tapped Axiom Marketing Communications to help create a fiftieth birthday celebration worthy of an iconic character and the still-top-selling bubble bath.

Reminding consumers of Mr. Bubble's beloved slogan, "Making Getting Clean Almost as Fun as Getting Dirty!" and focusing on "fun," Axiom put together a record-setting world's largest bubble bath at the Water Park of America in Bloomington, Minnesota. The press release for the event announced: "The event will feature a 2,800-square foot bubble bath play area, highlighted with an 8-foot high, 20-foot wide bathtub. The party will also include birthday cake, a bubble beard contest and a chance to get your picture taken with Mr. Bubble."

At the event, a Mr. Bubble character joined participants on an indoor family raft ride and surfed on the Flow Rider Surf Simulator. Attendees enjoyed chocolate cupcakes with Mr. Bubble pink icing and were given T-shirts that read, "I Was There! World's Largest Bubble Bath. Mr. Bubble 50th Birthday. June 11, 2011." In addition to the main event at the Mall of America, Mr. Bubble also visited New York City to raise awareness and reinvigorate the brand.

Axiom used the milestone birthday as an opportunity to bring the brand into the social media age, starting a Twitter account for Mr. Bubble and giving his Facebook page a "facelift." "Part of the program also includes developing relationships with key mom bloggers," Kathleen Hennessy, principal at Axiom Communications, told *PRWeek*. "We invited several mom bloggers and their families to the event, hosted a Twitter party with their input, and are conducting product giveaways on their websites."

Several sponsors made the trip possible for bloggers—Mr. Bubble was the host, Radisson provided lodging, T.G.I. Friday's provided meals, and Nickelodeon Universe offered admission to post-bubble-bath entertainment. These sponsors shared the event-generated spotlight in postings by mommy bloggers.

1   Why was it key to line up sponsors for Mr. Bubble's birthday bash?

2   Who were the opinion leaders who helped promote this event and the Mr. Bubble brand?

3   Was this an appropriate way in which to raise awareness of Mr. Bubble? Why or why not?

Ask Yourself

> Which Planning and Logistical Steps Ensure Successful Event Planning and Execution?

> Which Elements Must Be Taken into Consideration When Creating a Budget for a Meeting or an Event?

> Why Is the Investment in Meetings and Events Justified for Most Organizations?

> How Can Public Relations Professionals Harness Creativity to Plan and Implement Memorable and Effective Events?

A WORLD FILLED WITH
Meetings AND Events

Meetings and events are vital public relations tools; they provide an opportunity for an audience to gather face-to-face, in real time. In this era of digital communication and information overload, there is still a basic human need to convene, to socialize, and to participate in group activities.

Individuals attending a meeting or event use all five of their senses—hearing, sight, touch, smell, and taste—thereby becoming more emotionally involved in the process. Marketing and public relations

"Event planning is a high-pressure, around-the-clock job where planners juggle multiple tasks and work down to the wire against crushing deadlines and a mountain of obstacles. For smooth event implementation, and for business success, it is essential that planners manage their own time as expertly as they manage an event."

Judy Allen, author of *Event Planning: The Ultimate Guide to Successful Meetings, Corporate Events, Fundraising Galas, Conferences, Conventions, Incentives and Other Special Events*

Large events require extensive planning and logistics to ensure there is adequate space, security, liability insurance, and even portable potties. The Belgrade Beer Fest held every August attracts about 100,000 revelers each night from Serbia and neighboring nations. Attendees sample the products of more than 40 breweries while listening to some of Europe's leading rock bands on a large stage flanked with giant video monitors.

think How does attending a meeting in person differ from participating in an online focus group or visiting a chat room?

professionals can foster brand awareness and loyalty with these kinds of events.

Meetings and events come in all forms and sizes. A civic club committee meeting or an office staff meeting may include only four or five people. Corporate seminars may be presented to 50 to 250 people. At the other end of the scale are trade shows such as the annual International Consumer Electronics Show (CES) in Las Vegas, which typically attracts 150,000 attendees over a four-day period.

Effective meetings and events don't just happen. Detailed planning and logistics are essential to ensure that defined objectives are achieved, whether the event is a committee meeting or a national conference. This chapter discusses various types of meetings and events and the steps public relations professionals take to plan and execute them.

> The Las Vegas Convention and Visitors Authority reports that the meetings and convention industry spends nearly **$9 billion** each year in that city. In 2010, Las Vegas hosted more than 18,000 conventions that attracted 4.5 million attendees. Among the **150,000 attendees** at the International CES, almost 50,000 were exhibitors, nearly 6,000 were journalists, and 672 were bloggers.

Group MEETINGS

The size and purpose of a meeting dictate the specifics of its plan. Even so, every plan must address some common questions: How many people will attend? Who will attend? When and where will the event be held? How long will it last? Who will speak? Which topics will be covered? Which facilities will be needed? Who will run the meeting? What is its purpose? How do we get people to attend?

"TO DO" LIST
for Planning and Hosting a Successful Meeting

The following is a general "to do" list that can serve as a starting point for organizing an event—anything from a local weekly dinner meeting for a service club to the annual gathering of a professional association.

In Advance

- Determine the best date and time to ensure maximum attendance.
- Make a realistic estimate of how many people will attend.
- Select the restaurant or other facility at least four to six weeks in advance.
- Confirm in writing the date, time, menu, cocktails, seating plan, number of guaranteed reservations, and projected costs.
- Enlist one or more speakers four to six weeks in advance. If a speaker is in high demand, make the arrangements several months in advance. Agree on the nature of the talk, its length, and any audiovisual requirements.
- Publicize the meeting to the membership and other interested parties. This activity should be done a minimum of three weeks in advance.
- Organize a phone committee to call members 72 hours before the event if reservations are lagging.
- Prepare a timetable for the evening's events. Organizational leaders, as well as the serving staff, should be aware of this schedule.
- Decide on a seating plan for the head table, organize place cards. You can tell VIPs as they arrive where they will be sitting.

On the Meeting Day

- Get a final count on reservations, and make an educated guess as to how many people might arrive at the door without a reservation.
- Check the speaker's travel plans and handle any last-minute questions or requirements.
- Give the catering manager a revised final count for meal service. In many instances, this might have to be done 24 to 72 hours in advance of the meeting day.
- Check the room arrangements one to two hours in advance of the meeting. Have enough tables been set up? Are tables arranged correctly for the meeting? Does the microphone/projection system work?
- Set up a registration table just inside or outside the door.
- Designate three or four members of the organization to serve as a hospitality committee to meet and greet newcomers and guests.

After the Meeting

- Settle accounts with the restaurant, or indicate where an itemized bill should be mailed.
- Send thank-you notes to the speaker and any committee members who helped plan or host the meeting.
- Prepare a summary of the speaker's comments for the organization's blog and newsletter and, if appropriate, send a news release to local media.

Meeting Location

The meeting site must be the right size for the expected audience. If it is too large, the audience will feel that the meeting has failed to draw the expected attendance. If it is too small, the audience will be crowded and uncomfortable. Most hotels have a number of meeting rooms available, ranging in size from small to very large.

After selecting a room, a planner must make sure that the audience members can find it. The name of the meeting or group and the name of the room should be registered on the hotel or restaurant's schedule of events for a particular day.

Meeting Invitations

For clubs, an announcement on the web site, in the newsletter, a flyer, or an e-mail should be an adequate invitation. For external groups—people who are not required to attend but whose presence is desired—invitations must be sent in the mail or via

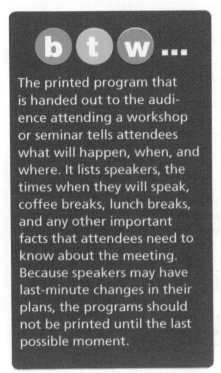

The printed program that is handed out to the audience attending a workshop or seminar tells attendees what will happen, when, and where. It lists speakers, the times when they will speak, coffee breaks, lunch breaks, and any other important facts that attendees need to know about the meeting. Because speakers may have last-minute changes in their plans, the programs should not be printed until the last possible moment.

MEETING FACILITIES

A small meeting may not need much in the way of facilities, whereas a large and formal gathering may require a considerable amount of equipment and furnishings. Questions to consider include the following:

- MEETING IDENTIFICATION. Is the name of the organization and meeting posted on the bulletin board near the building entrance?
- LIGHTING. Is it adequate? Can it be controlled? Where are the controls? Who will handle them?
- CHARTS. Are they readable? Is the easel adequate? Who will handle the charts?
- SCREEN OR MONITORS. Are they large enough for the size of the audience?
- PROJECTORS AND VIDEO EQUIPMENT. Are they hooked up and working? Who is the contact at the facility if you have technical difficulties?
- SEATING AND TABLES. Are there enough seats for the expected audience? Are they arranged properly?
- SPEAKER'S PODIUM. Is it positioned properly? What about a reading light? Is there a public address (PA) system? Is it working?
- AUDIENCE AND SPEAKER AIDS. Are there enough outlets for laptops? Is Wi-Fi available and, if so, how do audience members log on? Are there programs or agendas? Will there be notepaper, pencils, and handout materials?

e-mail. These invitations should go out early enough for people to fit the meeting into their schedules—three to six weeks is a typical lead time.

The invitation should include the time, day, date, place (including the name of the room), purpose, highlights of the program (including names of speakers), and a way for the person to accept or decline the invitation. The RSVP information may consist of a telephone number, an e-mail address, a reply card mailed back to the event's organizers, or an online registration service that may handle everything from making the reservation to processing the credit card information to pay for the event. It is also a good idea to provide a map with the location and parking information.

Getting the Meeting Started

If all of the attendees know one another, registration and identification can be highly informal. If the group is large however, it is customary to

set up a registration desk or table at the entrance. A representative of the sponsoring organization should be available at the entrance of the room. If the number of people attending is not too large, a personal welcome is in order. If hundreds of people are expected, this kind of greeting isn't possible; in such a case, the chairperson should greet the audience in his or her opening remarks.

Name tags are a good idea at almost any meeting. Label-making software can prepare name tags for everyone with advance reservations. Names should be printed in bold, large block letters so they can be read from a distance of four feet. If attendee affiliation is included on the name tags, this information can be presented in smaller bold letters. For people showing up without advance registration, have felt-tip pens available to make on-the-spot name tags.

Speakers

Speakers should be selected early—at least a month in advance, if possible. A speaker should be

Event invitations should grab attention like this one sent to members of the media to announce an opening night event for journalists at the San Jose (CA) Repertory Theater.

chosen because of his or her expertise, crowd-drawing capacity, and speaking ability. It is a good idea to listen to any prospective speaker before tendering an invitation, or at least to discuss the individual's speaking ability with an impartial person who has actually heard the speaker.

Meals

Club meetings and workshops often occur at a meal time. In fact, many meetings include breakfast, lunch, or dinner. Early-morning breakfast meetings have the advantage of attracting people who cannot take the time during the day to attend such functions.

Luncheons can be either sit-down affairs with a fixed menu or a buffet. A 30- to 45-minute cocktail period may precede a luncheon, usually as guests arrive and register. A good schedule for a typical luncheon is registration, 11:30 A.M.; lunch, noon; and adjournment, 1:30 P.M. In rare instances, the adjournment can be as late as 2 P.M., but it should never be later than that.

Dinner meetings are handled in much the same way as luncheons. A typical schedule is registration and cocktails, 6 P.M.; dinner, 7 P.M.; speaker, 8 P.M.; and adjournment, between 8:30 and 9 P.M. Speakers should talk for approximately 20 minutes.

An accurate count of people who will attend a meal function is essential. The hotel or restaurant facility will need a count at least 24 hours in advance to prepare the food and set up table service. The standard practice is for the organization to guarantee a certain number of meals, plus or minus 10 percent. If fewer people than expected show up, the organization still must pay for all the meals.

A Speaker NEEDS TO KNOW

Barbara Nichols, owner of a hospitality management firm in New York City, in conjunction with *Meeting News*, created this comprehensive checklist of things speakers need to know about a meeting:

- Information about the meeting sponsor and attendees
- Meeting purpose and objectives
- Presentation location, including meeting room, date, and hour
- Topic and length of presentation
- Anticipated size of the audience
- Session format, including length of time allowed for audience questions
- Names of those sharing the platform, if any, and their topics
- Name of person who will make the introductions
- Speaker fee or honorarium
- Travel and housing arrangements
- Meeting room setup and staging information
- A contact for audiovisual equipment requests
- Dress code (business attire, resort wear, black tie)
- Information about plans to tape or videotape the remarks (a release may be needed)
- Arrangements for spouse, if invited

Banquets

Banquets are fairly large and formal functions. They may be held to honor an individual, raise money for a charitable organization, or celebrate an event such as an organization's anniversary. A banquet or even a reception can have 100 or 1,000 people in attendance; for this reason, staging a successful one takes a great deal of planning. The budget, in particular, needs close attention.

Securing a well-known personality to speak at a banquet usually helps boost ticket sales, but is also a major expense item in a budget. Karen Kendig, president of the Speaker's Network, told *PR Tactics* that the going rate is $5,000 to $10,000 for "bread and butter" business-type talks, $15,000 or more for minor entertainment celebrities, and $100,000 or more for well-known politicians and celebrities.

Because such fees cannot be fully absorbed in the cost of an individual ticket, in addition to sending out individual invitations, a committee is typically formed that solicits corporations and other businesses to sponsor the event or "buy" tables for employees, clients, or friends. A corporate table for eight people, for example, may go for $25,000 or more, depending on the prestige and purpose of the event.

When organizing a banquet, contact the catering or banquet manager

 think How can planning ahead and being flexible help an organization save money when planning an event?

of the restaurant or hotel at least three or four months before your event. He or she will be prepared to discuss

Daytime talk show hosts Dr. Phil and **Ellen DeGeneres** command speaking fees in excess of $200,000. Former President **George W. Bush** reportedly charges between $100,000 and $150,000. Former Governor of Alaska Sarah Palin earns about $100,000 per speech, as do entertainment celebrities such as **Jon Stewart, Sarah Silverman, Conan O'Brien,** and **Steve Carell.** Reality television star **Kim Kardashian** reportedly earned $600,000 for hosting a 2012 New Year's Eve party and a few lesser events in Las Vegas. But for a mere **$50,000,** an organization may be able to book basketball player Charles Barkley, author and comedian **Chelsea Handler,** or tennis star Anna Kournikova. NASCAR racer **Al Unser, Jr.** is available for $20,000 to $30,000.

Creating a **BUDGET** for a Special Event

All events have two entries on both sides of the ledger: costs and revenues. Assorted expenses must be factored into the process of establishing the per-ticket cost of the event. Attendees are not paying $100 or more just for the traditional "rubber chicken" dinner, but are also footing the bill for the total cost of staging the event. If the purpose is to raise money for a worthy charitable organization or a political candidate, tickets might go for $150 to $350. The actual price depends on how fancy the banquet is and how much the organization is paying for its speaker.

It is important to prepare a detailed budget so an organization knows exactly how much an event will cost. This process will enable an organization to determine how much it will need to charge. Here are some items to consider:

Facilities
- Rental of meeting or reception rooms
- Setup of podiums, microphones, and presentation equipment

Food Service
- Number of meals to be served
- Cost per person
- Gratuities
- Bartenders for cocktail hours
- Wine, liquor, and soft drinks

Decorations
- Table decorations
- Direction signs

Design and Printing
- Invitations
- Programs
- Tickets
- Name tags

Postage
- Postage for invitations or publicity
- Mailing house charges

Recognition Items
- Awards, plaques, and trophies

Miscellaneous
- VIP travel and expenses
- Speaker fees
- Security

Transportation
- Buses
- Vans
- Parking

Entertainment
- Fees

Publicity
- Advertising
- News releases
- Banners

Office Expenses
- Phones
- Supplies
- Complimentary tickets
- Staff travel and expenses
- Data processing

Cars and Comedy Benefit Boys and Girls Clubs

FOR SEVERAL YEARS, the Boys and Girls Clubs of Broward County, Florida, has benefited from an unusual fundraising event—the Boca Raton Concours d'Elegance. The three-day event combines black-tie parties at the Boca Raton Resort and Club, a dinner auction, a hanger party at the Boca Raton Airport featuring luxury and exotic cars, motorcycles, boats, and vintage aircraft, and, in 2011, a performance by comedian and classic car lover Jay Leno.

> "You can't just ask people to simply step up and give money…. Give them a show."
>
> *Event creator Rick Case, in the Sun-Sentinel*

Zucker PR provided the public relations for the event pro bono. The event was conceived in 2007 by Rick Case, whose Florida automotive group operates 16 dealerships. Patterned after a similar upscale event that has been held for decades in Pebble Beach, California, the Boca Raton event draws hundreds of community and business leaders, celebrities, and motor industry notables.

The fifth annual event in 2011 celebrated the hundredth anniversary of the Indianapolis 500. Awards were presented to racing superstars A. J. Foyt, the Unser family, Roger Penske, Rick Mears, and Helio Castroneves. Attendees met and shook hands with racing hall of famers, bid on racing memorabilia, viewed race cars, and competed in an auction to be a guest of Roger Penske at the 2011 Indy 500.

Like Zucker PR, the committee and leadership of the fundraising event are all volunteers. "The hardest thing to give is time," Case said. "And when you can get people to do that, you've created passion. They're hooked."

The Zucker team helped recruit more than 40 sponsors in 2011, including Mercedes-Benz, Ferrari, and Comcast. About 20 media partners donated ads and coverage. Zucker PR created and distributed public service announcements and pitched the event to a variety of media outlets with emphasis on automotive, lifestyle, and philanthropy. Major automobile and motorcycle clubs in the U.S. were contacted either in person or by e-mail.

Zucker PR used Facebook, Twitter, and YouTube to distribute information about both Boys and Girls Clubs of Broward County and about the Concours d'Elegance. Jay Leno produced an 18-minute video for his Big Dog Garage website.

The public relations campaign helped the event garner $3 million, up from $750,000 the previous year, for Boys and Girls Clubs of Broward County. Attendance grew from 1,800 in 2010 to 7,000 in 2011. *PRWeek* reported, "More than 100 media outlets attended events. About 10 million media impressions were garnered in outlets including Univision, *AutoWeek*, and the *Miami Herald*."

Rick Case told *PRWeek*, "We surpassed expectations, and I attribute it to good PR."

Beyond benefiting the Boys and Girls Clubs, the Concours d'Elegance creates value for the community. Hotels, restaurants, and other hospitality services all benefit from the attendees. Additionally, sponsors garner exposure and sell their products, volunteers network, and attendees are entertained.

1. Name all the publics that this event attempts to reach.

2. What does it mean that Zucker PR worked "pro bono" on this campaign?

3. Put together a list of key decisions that were made in the planning of this event.

menus, room facilities, availability of space, and a host of other items.

Organizing a banquet requires considerable logistics, timing, and teamwork. Well conceived timelines are crucial. First, a timeline must be established for the entire process— from contacting catering managers to sending out invitations to lining up a speaker. Second, a detailed timeline must be drafted for the several days or day of the event to ensure that everything is in place. Third, a timeline for the event itself needs to be put in place, so that the event begins and ends at a reasonable time. In addition, organizers must work out the logistics to ensure that registration lines are kept to a minimum and everyone is assigned to a table.

Receptions AND COCKTAIL PARTIES

A short cocktail party can precede a club luncheon or dinner. It can also be part of a reception. The goal at this type of event is to encourage people to relax and socialize, but it is also a cost-effective way to celebrate an organization's or an individual's achievement, to introduce a new chief executive to the employees and the community, or to allow groups, such as college alumni, to get together.

Whatever the party's purpose, the focus is on interaction, not speeches. If there is a ceremony or speech, it should last a maximum of 5 to 10 minutes. A reception may last up to two hours, and the typical format is a large room where most people stand instead of sit. This arrangement facilitates social interaction and allows people to move freely around the room. Despite the informality, such gatherings, like

think Which special liability concerns should party planners take into account when planning a cocktail party?

any other event, require advance planning and logistics.

It is important, for example, that food be served in the form of appetizers, finger sandwiches, cheese trays, nuts, and chips. People get hungry, and food helps offset some effects of alcohol consumption. The bar is the centerpiece of any reception, but you should always make sure plenty of nonalcoholic beverages are offered, too. Such precautions will limit liability if someone drinks too much and has an accident on the way home. It can also limit liability to have a no-host bar, which means that guests buy their own drinks.

Most receptions, however, have a hosted bar, meaning that drinks are free. This setup is generally favored when a corporation is hosting the cocktail party or reception for journalists, customers, or community

A reception, like a meal function, requires coordination with the catering manager to order finger foods and decide how many bartenders are needed. As a rule of thumb, there should be one bartender per 75 people. For large events, bars should be situated in several locations around the room, so as to disperse the crowd and shorten lines.

leaders. In every case, it is important that bartenders be trained to spot individuals who appear to be under the influence of alcohol and politely suggest a nonalcoholic alternative.

As part of the planning process, the organizer of the cocktail party should find out how the facility will bill for beverages consumed. If the arrangement is by the bottle, it can lead to a problem with bartenders being very generous because more empty bottles mean higher profits for the caterer.

Starting a cocktail party is easy—just open the bar at the announced time. Stopping a party is not so easy, however. The only practical way to do so is to close the bar. The invitation may indicate a definite time for the reception to end, but don't rely on this method for shutting the party down. A vocal announcement typically does the job.

Open houses AND PLANT TOURS

Open houses and plant tours are conducted to develop favorable public opinion about an organization. Generally they are planned to show where the organization does its work and, in plant tours, how the work is done. For example, a factory might implement a plant tour to show how it turns raw materials into finished products, while a hospital open house

think Why do organizations welcome visitors to open house events?

could show its emergency facilities, diagnostic equipment, operating rooms, and patient rooms.

Open houses are customarily one-day affairs. If large numbers of people are likely to attend the event, however, it may be extended to more than one day. Attendance is usually by invitation, but in other instances, the event is announced in the general media, and anyone who chooses to attend may do so. If there is to be a community open house, think about entertainment and activities for the attendees.

Planning a SUCCESSFUL Open House
Things to Think About

Major factors to consider in planning an open house:

- **Day and hour.** The time must be convenient for both the organization and the guests.
- **Guests.** Invite families of employees, customers, representatives of the community, government officials, suppliers and competitors, reporters, or others whose goodwill is desirable.
- **Publicity and invitations.** Materials should be distributed at least a month before the event.

For any open house or plant tour, consider the following:

- **Vehicles.** Parking must be available, and the invitation should include a map showing how to get to the site and where to park.
- **Reception.** A representative of the organization should meet and greet all arriving guests.
- **Restrooms.** If a large crowd is expected, arrangements need to be made for portable toilets to supplement the regular facilities.
- **Safety.** Hazards should be conspicuously marked and well lighted. Barricades should be placed so as to prevent access to dangerous equipment.
- **Routing.** Routes should be well marked and logical (in a factory, the route should go from raw materials through production steps to the finished product).

- **Guides.** Tour leaders should be trained guides who have a thorough knowledge of the organization and can explain in detail what visitors are seeing on the tour.
- **Explanation.** Signs, charts, and diagrams may be necessary at any point to supplement the words of the guides. The guides must be coached to say exactly what the public should be told. Many experts cannot explain what they do, so a prepared explanation is necessary.
- **Housekeeping and attire.** The premises should be as clean as possible. Attire should be clean and appropriate.
- **Emergencies.** Accidents or illness may occur. All employees should know what to do and how to request appropriate medical assistance.

Many plants offer tours daily and regularly while the plant is in operation. These tours are most common among producers of consumer goods such as beer, wine, food products, clothing, and small appliances. These daily tours are geared to handle only a few people at any one time. By comparison, open houses generally have a large number of guests, so engaging in normal operations is not feasible during the tour.

Because the purpose of an open house or a plant tour is to create favorable opinion about the organization, it must be carefully planned, thoroughly explained, and smoothly conducted. Visitors need to understand what they are seeing. Achieving this goal requires careful routing, control to prevent congestion, signs, and guides. All employees should understand the purpose of the event and be thoroughly coached in their duties.

Conventions

A convention is a series of meetings, usually spread over two or more days. People attend conventions to exchange information, meet other people with similar interests, discuss and act on common problems, and enjoy recreation and social interchange.

Most conventions are held by national membership groups and trade associations. Because membership is widespread, a convention is nearly always "out of town" for many attendees, so convention arrangements must be made with this in mind.

When it comes to location and timing, know the convention audience and plan for audience members' convenience.

Las Vegas is one of the premier cities in the United States for large conventions—23 of the world's 35 largest hotels are located within a two-mile radius. The desert city's hotels and motels boast a combined total of 150,000 rooms.

Events and Promotions

Convention Planning

With conventions, it is essential to begin planning far in advance of the actual event. Planning for even the smallest convention should start months before the scheduled date; for large national conventions, it may begin several years ahead and require hundreds or thousands of

To get everything right, organizers need to know exactly what is to happen, who is going to participate, and when.

hours of work. The main components covered in planning a convention are (1) timing, (2) location, (3) facilities, (4) exhibits, (5) program, (6) recreation, (7) attendance, and (8) administration.

In terms of timing, you should avoid peak work periods when

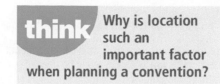

think Why is location such an important factor when planning a convention?

deciding on the date of the convention. Summer vacation is an appropriate time for educators, and after the harvest is a suitable schedule for farmers. Preholiday periods are bad for retailers, and mid-winter is a poor time in the northern states but may be very good in the South. Announcements and invitations should go out several months in advance, to allow attendees to make their individual arrangements.

As real estate agents say, a critical consideration for conventions is location, location, location. A national convention can be held anywhere in the country, but

Fairbanks, Alaska, is an unlikely venue, whereas Honolulu could be a great success because the glamour of the location might outweigh the cost and time of travel. Many organizations rotate their conventions from one part of the state, region, or country to another to equalize travel burdens.

Another factor in choosing a location is availability of accommodations. The site must have enough rooms to house the attendees and enough meeting rooms of the right size. Timing enters into this consideration, because many such accommodations are booked months or even years in advance. Once a tentative location has been selected, find out if the convention can be handled at the time chosen. Early action on this point can forestall later changes.

For every meeting to be held as part of the convention, it is necessary to have an appropriate room with necessary equipment. The convention might start with

b t w ...

Organizations attending conventions frequently want to show off their wares—which means that the convention manager must provide space suitable for that purpose. Most large convention centers have facilities that can accommodate anything from books to bulldozers. A charge is assessed for the use of these rooms, and the exhibitors pay for the space they use. The exhibit hall may be located in the hotel where the convention is being held, or it may reside in a separate building.

Recreation is a feature of practically all conventions; it can range from informal get-togethers to formal dances. Cocktail parties, golf tournaments, and sightseeing tours are among the many possibilities. Evening receptions and dinners at interesting venues such as an art gallery or museum are often planned for both attendees and their guests.

Events and Promotions

Increasing Event Attendance via Web Tools

While the standard direct mail invitations, press releases announcing an event, or paid advertisements in a trade publication are still tried and true means of promoting an event, event management companies are increasingly employing online and social media to increase attendance. For example, most event planners send invitations via the Internet and use social media tools to track response rates.

E-mail invitations, according to cvent (www.cvent.com), should incorporate eye-catching graphics, an effective subject line, and relevant content such as the five W's and H. Most individuals just concern themselves in generating a list of "yes," "no," and "maybe" answers in response to the online planning programs. Clubs and professional or trade groups, however, also need to link e-mail invitations with secure websites that enable attendees to pay their registration fees online. Online systems allow meeting planners to manage an entire event. Companies like cvent offer a variety of services—from gathering hotel bids to sending electronic invitations, tracking registrations online, and conducting post-event evaluation surveys.

Electronic tracking is helpful for figuring out exactly how many hotel rooms are needed; bad estimates, cancellations, and no-shows can add up to substantial hotel cancellation fees. Other management tools allow groups to track the flow of registrations. If registrations are lagging, another round of e-mails and direct mail can be sent out to bolster attendance. Session attendance can even be tracked once the meeting begins, with the data being used to inform decisions about future meetings. For example, if breakfast sessions aren't well attended, it might be wise to plan fewer early-morning meetings next year.

Social Media can help increase attendance. According to cvent, Twitter is good for connecting with industry leaders and marketers, promoting technology events, and indicating the size of your event by encouraging tweets from the event. LinkedIn is useful for promoting corporate events, marketing to other business professionals, and contacting workers in particular industries. Facebook is best to promote festivals, public fundraisers, sporting events, concerts, and parties. "YouTube can be a great channel to publish content for your event marketing and generate meaningful conversation across all of your other profiles, as well," according to cvent's e-book of tips.

Although e-mail invitations are economical and efficient, they are most appropriate for business-related meetings and events. It's still unusual to send an e-mail invitation to a wedding or to a major fundraising dinner for a community cause. In these instances, mailed invitations and replies remain the norm. However, if an invitation is mailed, an e-mail address or phone number can be provided for respondents in lieu of a reply card.

---

a general meeting in a large ballroom, where seating is theater fashion and the equipment consists of a public address system and a speaker's platform with large video monitors. After opening remarks, the convention might break into smaller groups that meet in different rooms with widely varying facilities. For example, one room may require a computer projector; another may need a whiteboard or an easel for charts; still another may need a DVD player and monitor.

Convention Programs

A convention program usually has a basic theme. Aside from transacting the necessary organizational business, most of the speeches and other sessions will be devoted to various aspects of that theme. Themes can range from the specific ("New Developments in AIDS Research") to the more general ("Quality Management and Productivity"). Some groups use an even broader theme, such as "Connections" or "At the Crossroads."

With a theme chosen, the developer of the program looks for prominent speakers who have something significant to say on a particular topic. In addition, there may be a need for discussions, workshops, and other sessions focusing on particular aspects of the general theme.

The printed program for the convention is a schedule. It identifies exactly when every session will take place, in which room it will be held, and who will speak on what subject. Large conventions often schedule different sessions at the same time, with attendees choosing which sessions they attend. Printing of the program should be delayed until the last possible moment. Last-minute changes and speaker defaults are common. Increasingly, convention planners are offering attendees the option of an electronic or printed version of the program in an effort to save costs … and trees.

Managing a convention is a strenuous job. The organization staff is likely to enjoy very little of the convention events and see, instead, a great many delegates with problems. Among the myriad tasks that must be handled are arranging for buses to convey delegates from the airport to the convention (if it is in a remote location) and to carry them on tours. Meeting speakers and getting them to the right place at the right time is another key task.

Getting people to attend a convention requires two basic things: (1) an appealing program and (2) a concerted effort to persuade members to attend.

Trade shows attract millions of people annually. They provide an opportunity to see new products from a number of companies, generate sales leads, and attract media coverage. For example, Verizon introduced its plans to "blanket the country with its 4G LTE network" at the 2011 Consumer Electronics Show (CES) in Las Vegas, which attracted 130,000 professionals from the electronics industry.

think How can advance preparations help public relations professionals stand out in the crowd of the pressroom at a trade show?

People arriving at the convention headquarters must be met, registered, and provided with all the essentials (name tags, programs, and any other needed materials). In addition, special arrangements should be made for the media. A small convention may interest only a few people from trade publications, whereas larger conventions may draw attention from the major media. In this case, a newsroom should be set up with telephones, fax machines, Wi-Fi, and computers.

TRADE Shows

Trade shows are the ultimate marketing event. There are thousands of trade shows held annually in the United States. They range in size from massive shows with more than 100,000 attendees to events geared toward very specialized industries that attract only several thousand people.

According to some estimates, nearly 65 million people attend trade shows on an annual basis.

The Consumer Electronics Show (CES), sponsored by the Consumer Electronics Association and held annually in Las Vegas, illustrates the power and influence of a trade show. At this show, which is only open to industry professionals, almost 3,000 companies show their new consumer products, taking up approximately 2 million square feet of exhibit space. At recent CES events, executives from Verizon, Samsung, Time Warner, Motorola, and Audi all took the dais to announce

TRADE SHOW CONSIDERATIONS

The following are some points to keep in mind if your company is considering trade show participation:

- Select the appropriate trade shows that have the best potential for developing contacts and generating future sales.
- Start planning and developing an exhibit 6 to 12 months in advance. Exhibit designers and builders need time to create a booth.
- Make the display or booth visually attractive. Use bright colors, large signs, and working models of products.
- Think about putting action in the display. Have a video or slide presentation running all the time.

- Involve visitors. Have a contest or raffle in which visitors can win a prize. Give people an opportunity to operate equipment or do something.
- Have knowledgeable, personable representatives on duty to answer questions and collect visitor contact information for follow-up.
- Offer useful souvenirs. A key chain, a tote bag, a USB memory stick, or even a luggage tag will attract traffic.
- Promote the exhibit in advance. Send announcements to potential customers and media kits to selected journalists four to six weeks before the trade show.

A survey by Access Communications found that more than 90 percent of journalists assigned to a trade show want to hear about the company and product news before the show even starts. Michael Young, senior vice president of Access, told *PRWeek*, "Journalists have limited bandwidth at the show. They can only do so much, so they want to know what the news is before getting there." In other words, media relations work starts before the show; it continues through the show and requires follow-up with reporters to provide additional information.

technological breakthroughs in their respective fields.

Exhibit Booths

Although food and entertainment costs are high at trade shows, the major expense at this kind of event is the exhibit booth. At national trade shows, it is not unusual for the cost of a basic booth to start at $50,000, including design, construction, transportation, and space rental fees. Larger, more elaborate booths can easily cost between $500,000 and $1 million.

 Why are organizations willing to spend so much and get so competitive when it comes to booth design?

All booths and exhibits should be designed for maximum visibility. Experts say an organization has about 10 seconds to attract a visitor as he or she walks down the aisle of exhibits. Consequently, companies try to out-dazzle one another in booth designs.

Most organizations believe that the large investment required to operate a booth at a trade show is worthwhile for two reasons. First, a trade show facilitates one-on-one communication

> "For people to pay attention at a trade show, you need real news."
>
> David Rich, senior vice president of George P. Johnson Marketing Company, as reported in *PRWeek*

with potential customers and helps generate sales leads. It also attracts many journalists, so it is easier and more efficient to provide press materials, arrange one-on-one interviews, and demonstrate what makes the product worth a story. Second, a booth allows an exhibitor to demonstrate how its products differ from the competition. This kind of hands-on demonstration for large numbers of people is more effective than just sending prospects a color brochure, and it is more cost-effective than making individual sales calls.

Hospitality suites are an adjunct to the **exhibit booth**. Organizations use them to entertain **key** prospects, give more **in-depth** presentations, and talk about **business deals**. Serious customers will stay in a hospitality suite long enough to hear an **entire presentation**, whereas they are likely to stop at an exhibit hall booth for only a few minutes. Although goodwill can be gained from free concerts and cocktail parties, the primary purpose of a hospitality suite is to generate leads that **ultimately result in product sales**.

Are You A Mayor?

Public relations practitioners continue to find innovative ways to employ location-based social media such as Foursquare in their campaigns. The geolocation app can be useful not only in retail settings, but is also increasingly popular among trade booth planners. Foursquare users check-in to locations using mobile devices. When a user has checked in at a venue more than anyone else during the last 60 days, he or she becomes the "mayor" of the venue. Similarly, the application allows a user to earn "badges," keep score, and become a "superuser." Foursquare was founded in March 2009. By December 2011, it boasted 15 million users worldwide, more than a billion check-ins, and 500,000 businesses employing the technology.

Businesses and brands both use Foursquare. For example, Intel had Foursquare create a special badge, which was awarded to followers who checked in at Intel's booth during an electronics trade show in Las Vegas. They also received the badge if they checked in at the show's keynote address, delivered by Intel's CEO.

Tradeshow Insight blogger Eric Lukazewski reflected on uses of Foursquare at tradeshows following Intel's much ballyhooed approach: "While you won't have the ability to create a custom badge unless you are able to partner with the Foursquare folks, you can still offer benefits to your attendees for checking in to various locations or functions at your event."

Beyond trade show and event uses for Foursquare, businesses engage Foursquare followers by providing discounts or specials when a follower checks in at the business. For example, Angelo and Maxie's Steakhouse in Midtown Manhattan used Foursquare to offer a free dessert to users with the purchase of an entrée when they checked in. And when Foursquare followers checked in to businesses *near* Angelo and Maxie's, they also received the information about the steakhouse offer.

Drugstore retailer Walgreens has about 70,000 Foursquare followers. Walgreens provides tips, alerts, and specials to Foursquare followers between the times shoppers check in and check out at a local Walgreens. Adam Kmiec, director of social media for Walgreens told *PRWeek*, "Location is a major part of our social strategy. Foursquare has been a great partner in helping us deliver on that aspect."

Credit card company American Express uses Foursquare to link the credit card and Foursquare accounts to give Foursquare users discounts when they use their Amex card and check in at select businesses. *PRWeek* reported, "Perhaps the most important aspect of utilizing Foursquare in a social media strategy is to make the experience easy and organic."

1. Imagine you're putting together a campaign for the local farmer's market. How could you use Foursquare to raise awareness about the market and about specific farmers?

2. How do special badges benefit a Foursquare-based public relations campaign?

3. Do you agree that making social media tactics easy and organic is important? Can you think of a social medium that suffers because it is not intuitive to use?

WORKING WITH THE MEDIA at Trade Shows

Sarah Skerik, director of trade show markets for *PR Newswire*, provides some tips for working with the media during a trade show:

- Plan major product announcements to coincide with the show.
- Include the name of the trade show in news releases, so journalists searching databases can log on using the show as a keyword.
- Include the booth number in all releases and announcements.
- Make it easy for journalists to track down key spokespeople and experts connected with the product by including cell phone numbers and e-mail addresses in press materials.
- Train spokespeople to make brief presentations and equip them with answers to the questions that are most likely to be asked.
- Consider using a looped video that runs in the booth, and make copies available to the media.
- Provide photos that show the product in use, in production, or in development.
- Provide online corporate logos, product photos, executive profiles, media kits, and PowerPoint presentations to those journalists who cannot attend or who prefer to lighten their suitcase by having everything in digital format.
- Have a few hard copies of news releases, fact sheets, and brochures available at the booth and in the press room.

> Keep media kits short and relevant, and offer newsworthy information. A common complaint of reporters at a trade show is that "media kits" are too thick and just a compilation of sales brochures.

Press Rooms and Media Relations

Trade shows such as CES and Macworld attract many journalists. Nearly a thousand reporters, for example, descend on Macworld every year. Consequently, every trade show has a press room where the various exhibitors distribute media kits and other information to journalists. Press rooms typically have phone, fax, and Wi-Fi that enable reporters to file stories with their employers.

The competition for reporters' time is intense, so public relations professionals need to be creative in pitching ideas and showing why their company's products or services merit a journalist's time when multiple other companies are also pitching them. As many preshow interviews and briefings should be arranged as possible.

Promotional EVENTS

Promotional events encourage sales, increase organizational visibility, make friends, and raise money for a charitable cause.

The one essential skill for organizing promotional events is creativity. Multiple "ho hum" events compete for media attention and even attendance in every city, so it behooves a public relations professional to come up with something "different" that creates buzz and interest.

Grand openings of stores or hotels, for example, can be pretty dull and generate a collective yawn from almost every journalist in town, let alone all the chamber of commerce types who attend such functions. So how do you come up with something new and different for the same old thing? First, you throw out the old idea of having a ribbon cutting. Second, you start thinking about a theme or idea that fits the situation and is out of the ordinary.

The opening of Swing Doctor, a baseball instruction school, featured an MBA star pitcher who threw the first baseball in the new business to a local high school star athlete.

> "The people who go want to engage with us and spend time with us, so having the opportunity to do that one-on-one, face-to-face in this really large setting is a unique opportunity."
>
> Deidre Mize, national account manager for Hallmark Cards, speaking of the 130,000 tech-savvy consumers who attend Comic-Con in San Diego

Nonprofit organizations often use events to raise money. The 2011 Susan G. Komen Global Race for the Cure attracted international press coverage as 34 diplomatic agencies and embassies fielded fundraising race teams at the Washington, D.C. event. Federal agencies within the U.S. government were represented by 36 teams. Forty-five congressional offices participated. The twenty-second annual global "race" involved almost 40,000 participants and raised more than $5 million. The charity has contributed more than $1.9 billion to breast cancer research worldwide since its inception in 1982.

Before Diggers Grill and Tap opened, the owners used the restaurant's Twitter account to engage followers in the restaurant's target demographic, encouraging them to sign up for a VIP invitation to the grand opening. The campaign lured 400 people to sign up for a VIP invitation; the restaurant decided to hold three grand opening events instead of one to accommodate consumer demand.

Corporate Sponsorships: Another Kind of Event

Many corporations, in an attempt to cut through the media clutter and establish brand identity, sponsor any number of events that are covered by the media. In North America alone, $18.2 billion is spent by corporations on sponsorship of various events. Globally, $48.7 billion is spent. According to Reuters, 68 percent of this total consists of sponsorship fees for sporting events.

The Olympics is one of the world's most prestigious corporate sponsorships. Coca-Cola, Acer, Atos, Dow, General Electric, McDonald's, Omega, Panasonic, Proctor & Gamble, Samsung, and Visa topped the list of official sponsors of the 2012 London Summer Olympics.

Coca-Cola has been an official sponsor since 1928 and marked its eightieth anniversary supporting the event at the Beijing Olympics in 2008. More than 40 percent of Olympic revenues are generated from corporate sponsorships.

Celebrity Appearances

Attendance can be increased at a promotional event with the appearance of a television or film personality. A public relations professional can exercise creativity in determining which "personality" fits the particular product or situation. For example, as Avon celebrated its 125 years in business, it enlisted actress Reese Witherspoon and singer Fergie to

Corporate Event Sponsorship Considerations

If an employer or client is thinking about sponsoring an event, consider the following questions:

- Can the company afford to fulfill its obligation? The sponsorship fee is just the starting point. Count on doubling it so that the company can construct an adequate marketing and public relations campaign to publicize the event.
- Is the event compatible with the company's values and mission statement?
- Does the event reach the organization's target audiences?
- Are the event organizers experienced and professional?
- Will the field representatives be able to use the event as a platform for increasing sales and/or revenue?

- Does the event give the organization a chance to develop new contracts and business opportunities?
- Can the organization make a multiple-year sponsorship contract that will reinforce its brand identity on a regular, consistent basis?
- Is there an opportunity to get employees involved in the event, thereby raising their morale?
- Is the event compatible with the personality of the organization or its products?
- Can trade-offs of products and in-kind services help defray the costs of the corporate sponsorship?

> "Security at public events is a significant aspect that should get as much attention as lighting, sound, or signage.

Matt Glass, managing partner at Eventage, as reported in *PRWeek*

draw crowds at events nationwide. Similarly, Kinect for Xbox 360 employed a surprise performance by Ne-Yo and Lady Sovereign to draw a crowd in New York's Times Square and promote the MTV game Dance Central. The Times Square dance party's reach was extended when participants posted YouTube videos.

A celebrity—or "personality," as these individuals are called in the trade—is not exactly the most creative solution to every situation. Nevertheless, hiring one is a time-honored way to increase the odds that the media will cover an event, because "prominence" is considered a basic news value. A personality, however, can be a major budget item. Stars such as Jessica Simpson, Chris Rock, and Katie Couric typically charge between $100,000 and $200,000 for an appearance.

Promotional Event Logistics

Events that attract large crowds require the same planning as open houses. Planners must be concerned about traffic flow, adequate restroom facilities, signage, and security. Professionally trained security personnel should be hired to handle crowd control, protect celebrities or government officials, and make sure no other disruptions occur that might mar the event.

Liability insurance is a necessity. Any public event sponsored by an organization should be insured, just in case an accident occurs and a lawsuit charges negligence. Charitable organizations also need liability insurance if they are running an event to raise money. This consideration is particularly relevant if an organization is sponsoring an event that requires physical exertion, such as a 10K run, a bicycle race, or even a hot-air balloon race.

The logistics of arranging cleanup, providing basic services such as water and medical aid, registering craft and food vendors, and posting signs must be addressed. Promotion of an event can often be accomplished by having a radio station or local newspaper co-sponsor the event.

What Would You Do?

Plan an Awards Banquet
The School of Business at your university has scheduled its annual awards banquet, which will be held six months from now. The event usually attracts about 500 alumni and members of the local business community. Traditionally, a speaker with a national reputation is asked to give the major address at the banquet. In addition, outstanding students will be recognized. Prepare a detailed outline of what must be done to plan the banquet, including a timeline or calendar stating what must be done by specific dates.

summary

questions
FOR REVIEW AND DISCUSSION

Which Planning and Logistical Steps Ensure Successful Meeting and Event Planning and Execution?

- Meeting and event organizers must consider a number of factors: meeting or event time, location, seating, facilities, invitations, name tags, menu, speakers, registration, and costs.
- In addition to the factors necessary for a club meeting, banquet planners must consider decorations, entertainment, audiovisual facilities, speaker fees, and seating charts.
- Open houses and plant tours require meticulous planning and routing, careful handling of visitors, and thorough training of all personnel who will come in contact with the visitors.
- Conventions require the skills of professional managers who can juggle multiple events and meetings over a period of several days.

Which Elements Must Be Taken into Consideration When Creating a Budget for a Meeting or an Event?

- Event planners must consider the characteristics of the audience to ensure that tickets are reasonably priced.
- The cost of facility rental, meals, speakers, invitations, programs, entertainment, and staffing must be considered.

Why Is the Investment in Meetings and Events Justified for Most Organizations?

- Meetings and events provide face-to-face social contact, which is better for building relationships instead of "virtual" communications.
- Attendance at events gets people involved and engaged through participation.

How Can Public Relations Professionals Harness Creativity to Plan and Implement Memorable and Effective Promotional Events?

- Planners should focus on those aspects or elements that make a product or service unique and determine how they can be highlighted through an event theme.

1 Develop an agenda and outline for a meeting for an organization to which you belong or with which you are acquainted. How can you make the meeting most effective?

2 Identify five key things a banquet coordinator should consider.

3 How can an open house serve as a public relations event?

4 How can journalists be encouraged to cover a trade show? How should they be accommodated at a trade show?

5 Why is "sponsorship" considered an event activity?

6 What key questions should be asked and answered when an employer or client is thinking about sponsoring a meeting or an event?

MySearchLab®

Text Credits

Credits are listed in order of appearance.

Invitation designed by PRx Inc. Original graphic designed by San Jose Repertory Theatre.

Photo Credits

Credits are listed in order of appearance.

Doug Meszler/Splash News/Newscom;
Dejan Grastic;
Golden Pixels LLC/Shutterstock;
sZUMA Press/Newscom;

AISPIX by Image Source/Shutterstock;
iofoto/Shutterstock;
ArrowStudio, LLC/Shutterstock;
Robyn Beck/AFP/Getty Images/Newscom;

Jim West/Alamy;
Maurice van der Velden/iStockphoto

Tablet image: Falconia/Shutterstock

Global Public Relations

From Chapter 14 of *Think Public Relations*, 2013 Edition. Dennis L. Wilcox, Glen T. Cameron, Bryan H. Reber, Jae-Hwa Shin.

Global Public Relations

Bono: "PR Man" for the World's Poor

Some people have a beef with Irish rock star Bono, not for his singing but oddly enough for his public relations efforts to help people who are desperately poor and ill around the globe. The legendary rocker and spokesperson for the world's downtrodden is not protected by his fame from vicious social media attacks, such as tweets like this one: "can't stand Bono ... self righteous, self promoting, self deluded ... thinks he's the savior ...."

Bono fares little better in the critical eye of traditional media. His fame serves not as a shield but as a magnet for reproach and investigative stories. Britain's *Daily Mail* took Bono to task because "his" foundation, called ONE, which operates around the world and draws on Bono's worldwide success as a performer, gives only about 1 percent of its funds to charity. This means that ONE plays a minimal role in the actual delivery of relief services to the needy; a glaring majority of its money goes to salaries as well as lavish events and press parties.

The ONE Foundation doesn't buy rice or medications; instead, it raises attention for tragic crises such as famine and death from infectious diseases, especially malaria and HIV AIDS. Essentially, the foundation focuses on cause-related public relations and consequently gets a bad rap. In its defense, a ONE spokesperson explains, "We don't provide programmes on the ground. We're an advocacy and campaigning organization." ONE argues that to focus resources and political will on the global problems of hunger and disease requires media attention, spurred by celebrity endorsement from stars like Bono and his cohorts.

The blogosphere begs to differ: "This is a typical caricature of [a] celebrity charity. They don't even pretend to be helping people. All their money goes to .... 'raising awareness' rather than actually helping the poor and starving on the ground," claims a posting on a discussion board at freerepublic.com.

Bono has remained above the fray and is widely admired by his legions of fans as well as world leaders of all political persuasions. For example, conservative talk-show host Mike Huckabee devoted a dozen valuable minutes of his prime-time program on Fox so that Bono could advocate for causes around the globe. On the show, Bono showed his mastery of the media. He was wisely nonpartisan, speaking passionately about the generosity of the American people under Republican and Democratic presidents alike.

1 Has the ONE Foundation been the victim of cheap shots, or the recipient of well-deserved and essential fiscal scrutiny?

2 Should Bono engage his detractors or is he wise to ignore them?

3 Are Bono's apparently heartfelt and often dramatic pleas in public, and even during his concerts, a good idea from a public relations angle?

Ask Yourself

> How Is Public Relations Practice Developing Around the World?

> What Challenges do Corporations Encounter When They Conduct Business Internationally?

> What Is Public Diplomacy?

> How Has the Role of NGOs in the Global Marketplace Evolved?

> What Career Opportunities Are Available in Global Public Relations?

WHAT IS global PUBLIC RELATIONS?

Global public relations, also called international public relations, comprises the planned and organized efforts of a company, institution, or government to establish and build relationships with the publics of other nations. These publics are the various groups of people who are affected by, or who can affect, the operations of a particular firm, institution, or government.

International public relations can also be viewed from the standpoint of its practice in individual countries. Although public relations is commonly regarded as a concept developed in the United States at the beginning of the twentieth century, some of its elements, such as countering unfavorable public attitudes through publicity and annual reports, were practiced by railroad companies in Germany as far back as the mid-nineteenth century, to cite just one example.

> **think** Why is public relations practice more likely to flourish in areas where there is an established industrial base and a large urban population?

Today, although some languages lack a term comparable to *public relations*, PR practice has spread to most countries, especially those with industrial bases and large urban populations. Even so, it is largely U.S. public relations techniques that have been adopted throughout the world, including in many totalitarian regimes. The broadening of the scope of public relations is primarily the result of worldwide technological, social, economic, and political changes and the growing understanding that public relations is an essential component of advertising, marketing, and public diplomacy.

> " The future of China lies in exporting Chinese brands to the world. PR has a vital role in building and maintaining brand value—and a nation which cannot master PR is at an enormous disadvantage. "
>
> Gyroscope consultancy report on public relations in China

International news events feature prominently in U.S. media, especially when American citizens are involved. Amanda Knox, the American college student convicted of murdering her roommate in Italy, burst into tears of relief after her verdict was overturned. A veteran public relations professional from her hometown worked tirelessly to reverse public perception of Knox throughout the four-year ordeal.

Global Public Relations

PUBLIC RELATIONS DEVELOPMENT IN other nations

Public relations as an occupation and a career has achieved its highest development in the industrialized nations of the world—the United States, Canada, the European Union (EU), and parts of Asia. It emerges more readily in nations that have multiparty political systems, considerable private ownership of business and industry, large-scale urbanization, and relatively high per-capita income levels, which also affect literacy and educational opportunities.

China has experienced explosive growth in public relations as it has become industrialized and has embraced a relatively free-market economy. Public relations revenues there have experienced double-digit gains over the past several years, and China is now the second largest market for public relations in Asia after Japan.

The United States and other European nations began exporting their public relations expertise to the People's Republic of China in the mid-1980s. Hill & Knowlton, which has been active in Asia for more than 30 years, began its Beijing operation in a hotel room with three U.S. professionals and a locally hired employee. Today, almost every global public relations firm has a Beijing office to represent U.S. and European companies in the Chinese market.

In addition, global public relations firms and advertising agencies are now buying stakes in, or affiliating themselves with, successful Chinese firms. Porter Novelli, for example, is affiliated with Blue Focus, one of the largest Chinese-owned firms, with about 200 employees. Fleishman-Hillard has an affiliation with Pegasus, another large Chinese agency.

Homegrown Chinese firms in advertising, public relations, and marketing have developed to the point that they are able to lure business away from large international firms. Chinese firms offer low cost and an extended reach. The more sophisticated Chinese public relations firms have advanced beyond product publicity and offer services in analysis, government, community relations, and even sports marketing.

Other nations and regions, to varying degrees, have also developed large and sophisticated public relations industries. Here are some thumbnail sketches from around the globe:

- **Thailand.** Thailand receives a great deal of foreign investment and has established itself as an assembly center for automobiles and computer hard drives. It's the primary hub in Southeast Asia for international tourism, and a number of public relations firms, advertising firms, and corporations have well-qualified staffs that are capable of handling media relations, product publicity, and special event promotion. The Thai tourism industry has faced several major crises that have deterred visitors. Antigovernment demonstrations in 2010 and major floods at the end of 2011 made world headlines.

- **Indonesia.** Home to about 230 million people, Indonesia is the fourth most populated country in the world. It is also a functioning democracy with a free media. Its public relations profession has grown rapidly in this environment, experiencing exponential growth. Corporations in Indonesia are now so committed to public relations that even products such as alcohol and cigarette brands, which are a major taboo in this predominantly Muslim country, seek media coverage and event management services from public relations firms. The nation, however, still suffers from a low postsecondary education rate of 4 percent, making for a small reading elite. Broadcast media fill the gap for the larger population, and social media shows remarkable penetration. Microsoft Indonesia claims the country ranks number one in Twitter activity and number two in Facebook users. A talent gap exists in public relations and is being addressed by major agencies such as Weber Shandwick, which leads a coalition called the Indonesian PR Practitioners Group to provide training to new hires. Business schools are offering degree programs that integrate marketing, advertising, and public relations. Indonesia is emblematic of the exponential growth of informed and interconnected populations in emerging economies.

> *India and China represent an opportunity to create top-line growth for companies. We have a lot more interest in those markets now than we've seen in the past two years.*
>
> Margery Kraus, CEO of APCO Worldwide, in *PRWeek*

There are now more than 2,000 PR firms in China, but most of them are one or two-person operations primarily dealing with publicity.

- **Japan.** Business and industry still perceive public relations as primarily media relations in Japan. Public relations firms and corporate communication departments work very closely with the 400-plus reporters' clubs that filter and process all information for more than 150 news-gathering organizations in Japan.
- **Australia, Singapore, and Hong Kong.** In these mature public relations markets, practitioners offer a variety of services ranging from financial relations to media relations and special event promotion. More attention is given to strategic planning and integrating communications for overall corporate objectives. A major growth area in Singapore is in the hospitality and service industry as this island nation adds new resorts and casinos.

- **Mexico.** Traditionally, small public relations firms dominated the Mexican market and provided primarily product publicity. Major growth in Mexican public relations practice is driven by multinational companies operating in the country with high expectations for the role and sophistication of campaigns. Highly visible drug cartel violence has dampened prospects for tourism public relations in recent years.
- **India.** India, with more than 1.2 billion people, is a major market for products, services, and public relations expertise. At least 1,000 large and small public relations firms serve the subcontinent, but training and educating qualified practitioners continues to be a major concern.
- **Brazil.** As the largest economy in South America, Brazil is home to approximately 1,000 public relations firms, most of which are located in the Sao Paulo area. To date, few global public relations firms have established a presence in this country, but this situation is changing rapidly, because the nation's booming economy makes it a major player in the world economy. To date, issues management, public affairs, internal communications, and marketing communications remain somewhat underdeveloped fields in the Brazilian public relations market. The public relations industries in Brazil's South American neighbor countries, Argentina and Chile, also are well developed.
- **The Russian Federation.** The rise of a market economy and private enterprise spurred the development of public relations activity in Russia after the Soviet Union's demise. The Russian public relations industry supports a broad spectrum of consumer products, but a weak judicial system and governmental restrictions on the media interfere with its ability

Brazil will host the 2016 Olympic Games, which will undoubtedly spur further development of its public relations industry. In this photo, Brazilians celebrate the news that they had been chosen as the site for the worlds largest venue for showcasing modern Brazil.

Global Public Relations

to thrive. Governmental transparency is also a problem, and Russians increasingly complain about corruption and cronyism among governmental officials and vote rigging in elections. At the beginning of 2012, opposition groups extensively used social media to organize massive demonstrations against Prime Minister Putin and the United Russia Party. Because the press and journalists are still very dependent on supplemental income, and news articles can be "bought" without much difficulty, confidence in the credibility of news stories has eroded. Ukraine, once part of the Soviet

> **"The way the [Russian] government's PR department managed the [financial] crisis was a remarkable example of a job well done, with little panic and timely government statements."**
>
> Arkady Matkovsky, director of public relations for Russian telecom giant TTK, in *PRWeek*

Union, now has a growing public relations industry, though it suffers from some of the same developmental problems as Russian firms do.

• *Middle East.* The Middle East comprises 22 nations and more than 300 million people. In general, the public relations industry here is relatively immature and unstructured and lacks trained personnel. Government-censored media and fear of transparent communications have hindered development of public relations in this region. Dubai, which is located in the United Arab Emirates, has positioned itself in recent years as a major business center and has attracted many international companies. Public relations

services will likely continue to expand in Dubai as the world's economy recovers from a major recession.

think How did the interconnectivity of the "global village" affect the impact of the recent financial crisis?

• *Africa.* South Africa is a mature market with a long tradition of public relations education, professional development for practitioners, and large corporations with international outreach. Nigeria, the most populous nation in Africa, has made strides in developing its public relations industry, in conjunction with its booming oil industry. Although Kenya has a relatively developed public relations industry owing to its tourism base, other nations in Africa are still relatively underserved in terms of public relations.

INTERNATIONAL corporate PUBLIC RELATIONS

For decades, hundreds of corporations based in the United States have been engaged in international business operations, including marketing, advertising, and public relations. All of these activities reached unprecedented heights over the past two decades in the climate of economic and cultural globalization. This climate is characterized by new communications technologies, development of 24-hour financial markets almost worldwide, lower trade barriers, sophisticated foreign competition in traditionally "American" markets, and shrinking cultural differences

thanks to extensive digital communication available everywhere humans live and work.

Globalization can be defined as increasingly connected international relationships that affect culture, people, and economic activity. Public relations, particularly marketing efforts, have facilitated extensive international distribution of goods and services by striving to open all markets to outside competitors. Globalization has contributed to economic growth in developed, and more notably in developing, countries as part of a larger transnational circulation of

ideas, languages, and popular culture. Public relations experts for NGOs and activist groups often alleged that globalization's benefits were overstated and its costs underestimated. And many thought those concerns were warranted when intertwined economic markets plummeted together in 2008 as a massive panic in banking spread almost instantaneously from continent to continent.

According to global public relations expert, Krishnamurthy Sriramesh at Massey University in New Zealand, the 21st century is typified by globalization, which has increased the importance of

Sin luchar, qué tendrás?

Overweening growth prior to the 2008 economic crisis in countries such as Ireland, Greece, and Italy partly resulted from liberal loan policies, but just as much from the exuberant communication about the new EU. In the wake of the crisis, governments and activists are using the same communication tactics to contend over the cause of the financial collapse and who should pay the cost of reckless policies.

international public relations. Globalization increased the need for cross-cultural communication experts for governments, multinational corporations, and a plethora of organizations working for social change. The public relations profession is being stretched to grow beyond the dominance of an American perspective and approach. Ethnocentricity in an increasingly globalized profession must be overcome by knowledge about the extreme diversity in culture, political economy, media systems, and activism that exists around the world.

Global public relations is fueled by new technologies that connect people worldwide as well as the social media applications operating on digital channels that build audiences, communities, and key publics for communication programs. Globalization, driven by a digital globe, has served to bring the "global village," as Marshall McLuhan once described it, ever closer to reality.

Today, almost one-third of all U.S. corporate profits are generated through international business. At the same time, overseas investors are moving into U.S. industries. It's not uncommon for 15 to 20 percent of a U.S. company's stock to be held abroad. In international bond

> "Today, global campaigns do not come from some NASA-like Mission Control center. Instead they originate from any corner of the world. And once originated, they have to find differing expressions to be effective in different markets.... Free-traveling, free-thinking ideas are the new lifeblood of global PR.
>
> Harris Diamond, CEO of Weber Shandwick

markets, the U.S. is a major debtor nation, with China alone holding 26 percent of total loan activity.

Like the U.S., other regions of the world also experience international connections. Although hampered by recession in recent years, public relations expenditures in the European Union (EU) region

have increased significantly. This increase has been generated in part by expansion of commercial television resulting from widespread privatization, the desire of viewers for more varied programming, satellite technology, and slowly developing EU business connections. Satellite TV, mobile broadband, and household broadband have all resisted the financial downturn, providing direct transmission of international programming and public affairs to homes that bypass conventional networks, local stations, and cable systems.

Although the EU has emphasized the phrase "a single Europe" to explain the benefits of its formation, corporations and public relations firms operating in this region still face the complex task of communicating effectively to 400 million people in 27 countries speaking multiple languages. Differences in language, laws, and cultural mores among countries pose a continuing challenge to culturally sensitive public relations practice. There also is a need for both managers and employees to learn to think and act in global terms as quickly as possible.

think Will Hofstede's five dimensions (see feature on the next page) be diminished by the homogenizing effects of global communication?

Five Cultural Dimensions

Geert Hofstede, a company psychologist for global giant IBM, came up with five basic cultural dimensions that are still useful 40 years later as we work to understand and appreciate various national cultures. As you read the following, think about this question: Do you believe that cultural dimensions are just style differences, or do they make a real difference in how international public relations is conducted?

1 POWER DISTANCE assesses people's tolerance for centralized power. Countries with a high acceptance of power distance include Mexico and France. Countries with a low acceptance include Austria and the United States.

2 INDIVIDUALISM/COLLECTIVISM contrasts loyalty to oneself versus loyalty to a larger group. Countries in Asia and Latin America gravitate toward collectivism, while the United States, Canada, and most European countries reward individualism.

3 MASCULINITY/FEMININITY differences focus on the contrast between competitiveness (traditionally considered masculine) and compassion/nurturing (traditionally feminine). Masculine nations include Australia, Germany, and Japan. Feminine nations include Sweden and Spain.

4 UNCERTAINTY AVOIDANCE describes how well a society tolerates ambiguity. Nations that have difficulty functioning in climates characterized by uncertainty include Japan, Belgium, Greece, and China. Nations that tolerate ambiguity include Great Britain, the United States, and Sweden.

5 LONG-TERM/SHORT-TERM ORIENTATION focuses on a society's willingness to consider the traditions of the past and carry them into the future. China and other East Asian nations tend to have long-term orientations. The United States has a short-term orientation.

Language and Cultural Differences

Companies operating in nations outside the United States are confronted with essentially the same public relations challenges as those serving the U.S. market. Their objectives are to compete successfully and to manage conflict effectively—but the task is more complex on an international and intercultural level.

Public relations practitioners need to recognize cultural differences, adapt to local customs, and understand the finer points of verbal and nonverbal communication in individual nations. Experts in intercultural communication point out that many cultures, particularly non-Western ones, are "high-context" communication societies. In these societies, the meaning of the spoken word may be implicit and based on the environmental context and personal relationships rather than on explicit, categorical statements. The communication styles of Asian and Arab nations, for example, are described as high context.

In contrast, European and American communication styles are considered low context. Great emphasis is placed on exact words, and receivers are expected to derive meaning primarily from the written or verbal statements, not from nonverbal behavior cues. For example, legal documents produced in the West are the ultimate in explicit wording.

Americans and others must learn the customs of the country in which they are working, relying on native professionals to guide them. When having media materials and advertising translated, the best approach is to employ native speakers who have extensive experience in translating ad copy and public relations materials.

think How is cultural insensitivity best overcome?

7-Eleven stores seem to be everywhere, often nestled into traditional street scenes as if they were old-fashioned tobacconists or bakeries. The chain's 39,000-plus stores peddle globally marketed products such as Cheetos and Slurpee drinks alongside local foods, newspapers, magazines, and sundries.

SocialMediaInAction

Making the Most of Social Networks Around the World

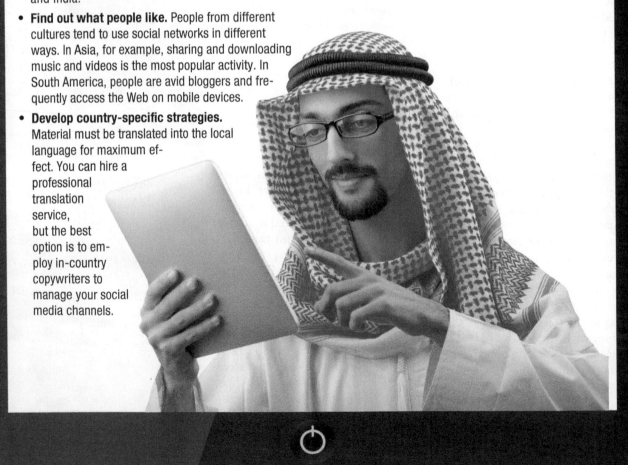

Many organizations must maintain a social media presence in multiple nations where they have retail stores and even manufacturing facilities. However, social media efforts must be localized for each market, which can be somewhat tricky.

Christian Arno, founder of the translation service Lingo24, offered the following tips in a *Ragan.com* article.

- **Choose the right social network for the market.** Facebook may be worldwide, but many nations also have their own social networking sites that are more popular. The biggest network in China, for example, is Qzone. Maxi is the largest network in Japan, and Orkut is the major player in Brazil and India.

- **Find out what people like.** People from different cultures tend to use social networks in different ways. In Asia, for example, sharing and downloading music and videos is the most popular activity. In South America, people are avid bloggers and frequently access the Web on mobile devices.

- **Develop country-specific strategies.** Material must be translated into the local language for maximum effect. You can hire a professional translation service, but the best option is to employ in-country copywriters to manage your social media channels.

- **Localize your content.** Translation is only the first level. You must also determine if the content is relevant to your audience and can be adjusted to audiences in different nations. A French context is a lot different than one for Brazilians. It's also important to take into account such factors as government sensitivity to some words (often the case in China) or even local current events that may render some messages inappropriate.

- **Interact.** The basic tenet of social media is to encourage interaction and engagement. *That's true in every nation.*

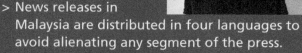

Cultural differences abound, no matter which country you may visit, as shown by the following examples:

> In China, tables at a banquet are never numbered. The Chinese think such table arrangements appear to rank guests and that certain numbers are unlucky. It's better to direct a guest to the "primrose" or "hollyhock" table.
> Americans are fond of using first names, but it's not proper business etiquette in Europe and Asia unless permission has been given.
> Early-morning breakfast meetings are not common in Latin America; by the same token, a dinner meeting in that part of the world might not start until 9 or 10 P.M.
> In Thailand, patting a child on the head is seen as a grave offense because the head is considered sacred. It's also a crime to make disrespectful remarks about the royal family, particularly the king.

> In Latin America, greetings may include physical contact, such as hugging individuals or grabbing them by the arm. Men and women commonly greet each other with a kiss on the cheek in Argentina and Chile.
> News releases in Malaysia are distributed in four languages to avoid alienating any segment of the press.
> Gift giving is common in Asian cultures. Executives, upon meeting for the first time, will exchange gifts as a way of building a social relationship.
> In conservative Muslim nations, particularly in the Middle East, men traditionally are encouraged not to stand near, touch, or stare at women.

Foreign Corporations in the United States

Corporations and industries in other countries frequently employ public relations and lobbying firms to advance their products, services, and political interests in the United States. The Center for Public Integrity (CPI) reported that in a six-year span, 1,150 companies with headquarters in about 100 nations engaged lobbyists to influence U.S. policy and budgets.

770 companies from around the world hired 2,340 lobbyists at a price tag of $90 million to represent climate change interests.

Even companies that don't operate in the United States may engage in lobbying. For example, with the politicization of global policies surrounding climate change, new players entered the U.S. lobbying arena. Countries and foreign corporations continually jockey for favorable positions on issues ranging from environmental regulation to new market opportunities for carbon-re-ducing technologies. After the Durban Climate Change Conference in December 2011 failed to achieve immediate, substantive commitments from member countries, carbon-based energy industries and rapidly growing economies such as India floated an adaptation argument. Adaptation proponents argue the global community cannot curtail carbon emissions, so nations should devote money and effort to dealing with predictable environmental changes, especially in poor regions with millions impacted by floods, drought, and storms. Corporate and environmental activist groups, as well as scientists and economists, will surely engage the best public relations talent available to contend over the question of just how inevitable climate change will be in coming decades.

Representing
U.S. CORPORATIONS
IN OTHER NATIONS

Many U.S. corporations are global in scope, with employees, products, manufacturing plants, and distribution centers around the world. The top six giant corporations (see graphic below), as well as hundreds of other U.S. companies, engage in extensive public relations and lobbying activities in other nations for virtually the same reasons that foreign countries lobby in the United States. The total amount expended on public relations and lobbying abroad is not known because the U.S. companies don't have to report such expenditures to the U.S. government.

Public relations professionals who work for corporate giants, as well as for a host of other smaller American companies, are considered to be participants in the field of international public relations, because their work involves many nations. Many multinational corporations also retain global public relations firms such as Burson-Marsteller and Hill & Knowlton to provide services from offices in major cities around the world.

American companies face a number of challenges abroad: competing with other large corporations headquartered in other nations; dealing with sustainable development; being

David Drobis outlined some of the challenges American companies face abroad in a speech before the International Communications Consultancy Organization (ICCO). Drobis declared that one major challenge is to better communicate the economic advantages of globalization to the world's people. These advantages must be communicated to three key groups:

> The first group comprises the companies themselves. Companies must realize that international capitalism has a negative connotation in many parts of the world. According to Drobis, most multinational firms have done little to correct this view, despite the efforts of a few highly responsible companies that have outstanding programs in this area.
> The second group that must be informed of the benefits of globalization consists of nongovernmental organizations (NGOs). Although many NGOs are outright hostile to all private enterprise, U.S. companies must realize that NGOs can become an important seal of approval and branding. Indeed, major mainstream NGOs, such as the World Wildlife Federation and Greenpeace, are working with corporations on sustainable development programs.
> The third group includes international institutions such as the World Trade Organization (WTO), the World Bank, the International Monetary Fund (IMF), and even the United Nations. Drobis says these organizations are unfairly criticized as being undemocratic, but fairly criticized for being nontransparent.

U.S.-BASED GLOBAL GIANTS

WalMart
$422 billion

ExxonMobil
$370 billion

Chevron
$205 billion

ConocoPhillips
$199 billion

General Electric
$150 billion

Global Public Relations

Happiness Ambassadors Lead Convergent Media Campaign for Coke

IMAGINE YOURSELF WITH THE FOLLOWING JOB TITLE: Happiness Ambassador for Coca-Cola. Your mission: to "seek out what makes young people happy in different cultures and document it all online, leveraging every facet of social media to generate an ongoing dialogue, while creating unique media relations and local market activation opportunities around the globe."

This dream job was a reality for three lucky young travelers who visited 206 countries where Coke does business over the course of 365 days in the Coca-Cola-sponsored event "Expedition 206." The goal of Expedition 206 was to link the Coke brand in the minds of young people with fun, adventure, and especially with happiness. The project was designed by Coke and the public relations firm Fast Horse to dovetail with Coca-Cola's broader worldwide marketing campaign, "Open Happiness."

Many companies with global reach attempt to develop integrated campaigns that cut across borders and cultural boundaries, but with little success. The award-winning genius of this particular Coke campaign was using social media to focus on the unity of humanity implicit in valuing the smaller things in life. Cutting-edge technology worked hand-in-hand with timeless public relations techniques of event planning and publicity as the three lucky travelers explored the world.

> "Throughout the entire trip, fans have been invited to interact with the team, offering or recommending places to stay, not-to-be-missed attractions, amazing places to eat, and more. The whole concept is pretty creative, inviting consumers to not just think about the product but about the message of unity that Coca-Cola can bring to the world. That's a difficult message to convey with traditional advertising.
>
> Mashable.com

The Expedition 206 campaign serves as a great example of thorough strategic planning combined with sensitivity to the lifestyle and interests of a youthful audience. Participation was high throughout the campaign, which kicked off with a worldwide vote to select the lucky happiness ambassadors. Information about the vote was disseminated to all leading media and blogger lists and an advance story was pitched to the Associated Press, garnering worldwide attention.

The execution was excellent, but advance research also got the campaign off to a great start. Careful analysis by other organizations as well as "brand love" research by Coca-Cola's Happiness Institute indicated that online teens regularly share and value artistic creations in social media. This sharing of artwork, photos, video, and stories often starts a virtual conversation, potentially leading to the viral spread of creative content. Coke's survey results also indicated that

> "Good for Coke, they totally get it! Building a brand is all about connecting with people's feelings and associating the product with the right image that resonates with their audience.
>
> Comment posted on Mashable.com

online programs dramatically boost consumer loyalty; a full 68 percent of respondents stated that online programs lead them to "exclusively love" Coke products.

The campaign generated a cavalcade of fascinating online content about everyday life and happiness in diverse cultures around the globe. All the social media creativity and sharing undoubtedly made Coca-Cola feel good about its work to make the planet smaller while at the same time increasing the brand love index for Coke.

1. Coke's campaign relied heavily on social media and new technologies to bring people around the globe closer to each other. Was social media essential to achieve this goal or could it have been done without the techie trimmings?

2. What is your response to closely associating a soft drink with the unity of humanity, happiness, and love? Is it a fun and creative marketing PR metaphor or an exploitation of timeless values to sell fizzy sugar water?

Source: PRSA Silver Anvil Awards, 2011

boycotted by nations that disagree with U.S. foreign policy; and striving to act as good corporate citizens at the local and national levels.

David Drobis, a former senior partner and chair of Ketchum, believes that public relations professionals are best suited to explain the benefits of globalization to global audiences. He asserts:

"Companies must take into consideration a broad group of stakeholders as they pursue their business goals globally. And by doing so, there are tangible and intangible business benefits. In this way, good corporate citizenship is not a cost of doing business, but rather a driver of business success. What's good for the soul is also good for business."

Drobis, in giving advice to U.S. companies doing business abroad, states that the era of "relationship building" is over. Instead, he claims, the twenty-first century should be a time of "confidence building" in the international arena so that various publics not only trust corporations to do the right thing, but also believe globalization will benefit hundreds of millions of poor people around the globe.

PUBLIC diplomacy

The U.S. government is the major disseminator of information around the world. The process of information dissemination is called *public diplomacy* and is primarily intended to present American society in all its complexity so citizens and governments of other nations can understand the context of U.S. actions and policies. An additional aim is to promote American concepts of democracy, free trade, and open communication around the world.

U.S. Public Diplomacy Efforts

The United States Information Agency (USIA) was created in 1953 by President Dwight Eisenhower to be the primary agency involved in shaping America's image abroad. USIA, in many ways, was the direct descendant of George Creel's Committee on Public Information (CPI), which was active during World War I, and Elmer Davis's Office of War Information, which was active during World War II. After World War II, a new threat was perceived—namely, the outbreak of the Cold War with the Soviet Union and the Communist bloc nations in Eastern Europe. The Cold War was a war of words on both sides to win the "hearts and minds" of governments and their citizens around the world.

 think Why is there typically an increased focus on public diplomacy in times of war?

At the height of the Cold War, USIA had a budget of approximately $900 million and 12,000 employees. When the Soviet Union imploded in the early 1990s, the fortunes of the USIA began to fall as Congress and other critics decided that the United States didn't need such a large public profile in the world. As a result, the agency was abolished in 1999 and most of its functions were transferred to the U.S. Department of State under an undersecretary of state for public affairs and diplomacy. The staff was cut 40 percent and funding for projects decreased sharply.

The September 11, 2001, terrorist attacks on the United States created a new impetus to "sell" America and the United States's decisions to invade Afghanistan and Iraq. Once again, the cry was to "win the hearts and minds" of the world's people and to gain public—as well as international—support for U.S. actions. According to *New York Times* reporters Eric Schmidt and Thom Shanker, immediate efforts were somewhat diffused and even amateurish because the Department of Defense and the White House spearheaded public diplomacy efforts rather than the State Department. In their book *Counterstrike*, the reporters document a 10-year process of increasingly masterful and effective communication by the United States, contrasting it with brutality, chauvinism, and inequity in the enemy camp.

The Obama administration placed increased emphasis on public diplomacy and cultural exchange. Today, the State Department particularly stresses the importance of youth exchanges and networking with exchange alumni to maintain

USIA Activities in the Cold War

In the past, USIA activities included (1) the stationing of public affairs officers (PAOs) at every American embassy to work with local media, (2) the publication of books and magazines, (3) the distribution of American films and TV programs, (4) the sponsorship of tours by American dance and musical groups, (5) art shows, (6) student and faculty exchange programs such as the Fulbright Program, and (7) the sponsorship of lecture tours by American authors and intellectuals.

long-term ties. As part of its $1.2 billion budget in 2010, the funding for the State Department included $520 million for worldwide public diplomacy and $633 million for educational and cultural exchange programs. Communication is clearly a crucial component in the mission and operations of the State Department.

Foreign Public Diplomacy Efforts

Virtually every country has one or more governmental departments devoted to communication with other nations. Much effort and millions of dollars are spent on the tourism industry, with the goal of attracting visitors whose expenditures will boost local economies. Even larger sums are devoted to lobbying efforts to obtain favorable legislation for a country's products; for example, Brazil's determined communication efforts over several years led to cuts in U.S. tariffs' severely limiting import to the U.S. of ethanol made from sugar cane. Foreign nations sometimes hire U.S. communi-

cation firms. Ten mammoth US public relations firms garnered most of the contracts from the

 think How can public relations help a foreign country improve its image in the United States?

top-spending countries. Interested parties ranged from oil-rich Dubai to tiny Bermuda, which wrangled free windows and doors for island residents living in Hurricane Alley. The hurricane relief also reduced claims to international insurance companies. Conflict and war also lead to public relations efforts. What do countries that woo the U.S. audience seek to accomplish? Burson-Marsteller's Carl Levin says that they pursue several goals:

- To advance political objectives
- To be counseled on the probable U.S. reaction to the client government's projected action
- To advance the country's commercial interests—for example, sales in the United States, increased U.S. private

investment, and tourism
- To assist in communications in English
- To counsel and help win understanding and support on a specific issue undermining the client's standing in the United States and the world community
- To help modify laws and regulations inhibiting the client's activities in the United States

Under the Foreign Agents Registration Act (FARA) of 1938, all legal, political, fund-raising, public relations, and lobbying consultants hired by foreign governments to work in the United States must register with the Department of Justice. They are required to file reports with the U.S. attorney general, listing all activities on behalf of a foreign principal, compensation received, and expenses incurred.

Normally hired by an embassy after open bidding for the account, public relations firms that act on behalf of non-U.S. governments first gather detailed information about the client country, including past media coverage. Attitudes toward

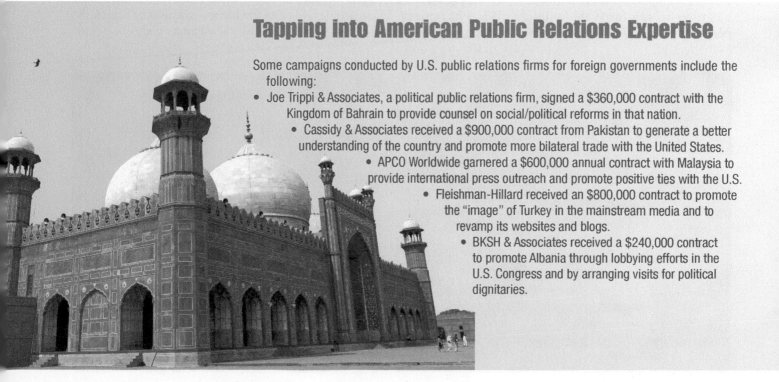

Tapping into American Public Relations Expertise

Some campaigns conducted by U.S. public relations firms for foreign governments include the following:
- Joe Trippi & Associates, a political public relations firm, signed a $360,000 contract with the Kingdom of Bahrain to provide counsel on social/political reforms in that nation.
- Cassidy & Associates received a $900,000 contract from Pakistan to generate a better understanding of the country and promote more bilateral trade with the United States.
- APCO Worldwide garnered a $600,000 annual contract with Malaysia to provide international press outreach and promote positive ties with the U.S.
- Fleishman-Hillard received an $800,000 contract to promote the "image" of Turkey in the mainstream media and to revamp its websites and blogs.
- BKSH & Associates received a $240,000 contract to promote Albania through lobbying efforts in the U.S. Congress and by arranging visits for political dignitaries.

Global Public Relations

On the Payroll of a Foreign Government

Public relations firms that work for foreign governments often confront some tough problems:

- Deciding whether to represent a country whose human rights violations may reflect adversely on the agency itself
- Persuading the governments of such nations to alter some of their practices so that the favorable public image sought may reflect reality
- Convincing officials of a client country, which may totally control the flow of news internally, that the American press is independent from government control and that they should never expect coverage that is 100 percent favorable
- Deciding whether to represent a nation whose government openly criticizes American policies

the country are ascertained both informally and through surveys.

The action program decided on will likely include the establishment of an information bureau to provide facts and published statements of favorable opinion about the country. In many cases, a nation may also use paid issue advertising in publications such as the *New York Times*, the *Washington Post*, the *Wall Street Journal*, and the *Financial Times* that reach a high percentage of opinion leaders and elected officials. The Republic of Kazakhstan, for example, placed full-page ads in major U.S. newspapers after its national elections to reinforce the public perception that it was a democracy.

The ad's headline: "Today, Kazakhstan has another asset besides oil, gas and minerals. Democracy." Regular paid messages on CNN World complement Kazakhstan's print ads with a focus on lavish modern architecture and hip western lifestyle in the emerging democracy.

Appointments also are secured with key media people and other influential individuals, including educators, business executives, and leaders of various public policy groups. In many cases, the primary audiences are key members of congressional committees, heads of various governmental agencies, and White House staff. These people are often invited to visit the client country on expense-paid trips, although some news-media people decline these invitations on ethical grounds.

Gradually, through expert and persistent methods of persuasion (including lobbying), public opinion about the client country may be changed, favorable trade legislation may be passed, foreign aid may be increased, or an influx of American tourists may visit the country.

Countries that have experienced image problems before global audiences have also hired professionals in attempts to address them. Taking on nations with patchy human rights records or politically repressive governments standing behind a façade of democratic institutions can be disastrous for public relations firms. The argument that all nations deserve communication counsel is borrowed from the legal profession, but does not hold when the accused faces no indictment.

London's *Guardian* newspaper claims that public relations firms in that city have earned the dubious accolade of reputation-laundering capital for the world's worst dictators and harsh governments. The paper rightly points out that some of the lucrative deals may breach the industry's voluntary code of conduct.

b t w ...

One nation that often seems to loom large in the minds of Americans is China. Christopher Millward, who has a decade of integrated communication and marketing experience, blogs about Chinese public relations at fire-brands.com. Chinese public relations offers a window into this vast and complex nation. Millward's recent commentaries note these hefty challenges for public relations communicators:

> Explaining the Chinese premier's fairly belligerent call to arms for public relations people to take the propaganda fight to Europe and America

> Defending the 2012 culture wars' crackdown on dating and reality TV shows that focus on sex and wealth at the expense of industriousness and modesty

> Asserting that renegade provinces such as Taiwan and Tibet should keep allegiances to the Beijing government

> Showcasing reforms in workplace conditions in the face of line worker suicides and mass protests

Repressive Governments Put PR Firms in an Uneasy Spot

Ask yourself these questions: If a repressive foreign government approached you with a lucrative PR contract, what would you say? What if your boss asked you to work on behalf of such a client?

Many international public relations firms and their staffs, as well as lobbying firms based in Washington, D.C., face these questions every day. And their answers are somewhat mixed. Qorvis Communications, for example, continued to represent the government of Bahrain even after a violent government crackdown on pro-democracy demonstrators caused multiple civilian deaths and injuries.

In somewhat of an understatement, Qorvis senior vice president Seth Thomas Pietras in the *New York Times* defended its involvement with Bahrain and several other Middle Eastern nations facing protests in the Arab Spring. He said,

"Our clients are facing some challenges now. But our long-term goals—to bridge the differences between our clients and the United States—haven't changed. We stand by them."

A Public relations firm, The Washington Media Group, made a different decision. It ended its $420,000 image-building contract with the government of Tunisia after the aggressive government crackdown on pro-democracy demonstrators before the Tunisian regime was toppled. Gregory L. Vistica, the firm's president, told the *New York Times,* "We basically decided on principle that we couldn't work for a country that was using snipers on rooftops to pick off its citizens."

Rosanna Fiske, chief executive of the Public Relations Society of America, has also weighed in on the ethical dilemma. In a letter to the *Financial Times* about U.S. public relations firms

representing Libyan dictator Muammar Gaddafi), she wrote, "We believe every person or organization has the right to have its voice heard in the global marketplace of ideas. But for PR firms to represent dictatorships that do not afford the same freedom to their own people is disingenuous towards the liberties of a democracy and to democratic societies' reputation in the marketplace for dissenting ideas."

Is there is anything defensible about working for a dictatorship or a repressive regime? What do you think of the argument that a PR firm can serve a useful function by counseling repressive governments to be more democratic and respect human rights? Does everyone, including dictators, have the right to be heard in the global marketplace of ideas?

THE RISE OF NGOs

Hundreds of nongovernmental organizations (NGOs) depend on international support for their programs and causes. Organizations such as Greenpeace, Amnesty International, Doctors Without Borders, Oxfam, and a large number of other groups have been effective in getting their messages out via the Internet, e-mail, and demonstrations.

NGOs continue to be more trusted than the news media, government, or corporations, according to Edelman Worldwide's 2011 survey of trust in more than 20 nations. Thought leaders, for example, indicate that they trust NGOs

more than government or corporations because they consider the NGOs' motivation to be based on "morals" rather than "profit."

There is some evidence that giant corporations are adopting a more accommodative stance by cooperating with activist NGOs to form more socially responsible policies. Citigroup, for example, adopted policies as early as 2004

think Why do some people find NGOs to be more credible than governments or corporations?

to reduce habitat loss and climate change after the Rainforest Action Network (RAN) urged customers to cut up their Citicards and plastered the Internet with nasty jibes against executives. However, even with such policies in place, the bank finances huge projects that inevitably have major impacts on the environment and communities. RAN's public relations team does not cut communicators for the bank any slack on current issues such as financing of TransCanada Corp's Keystone XL pipeline to bring Alberta tar sands oil to Gulf Coast refineries.

Opportunities
IN INTERNATIONAL WORK

Gavin Anderson, chairman of Gavin Anderson & Company, a pioneer in international public relations, penned the following observations some years ago—but his message remains relevant today:

The field needs practitioners with an interest in and knowledge of foreign cultures as well as top-notch public relations skills. They need a good sense of working environments, and while they may not have answers for every country, they should know what questions to ask and where to get the information needed.

The decision to seek a career in international public relations should be made early, so that a student who is interested in pursuing an international career has time to take courses in international relations, global marketing techniques,

strategic public relations planning, foreign languages, social and economic geography, and cross-cultural communication. Graduate study is an asset. Students should also study abroad for a semester or serve an internship with a company or organization in another nation as a desirable starting point. Students

 **think** In addition to studying a foreign language, what can students in U.S. schools do to prepare for a job in global public relations?

may want to apply to the Fulbright Program, which funds travel and study abroad. Rotary International offers students foreign study scholarships as well.

Students at U.S. schools should not assume they have an "inside" track on working for a U.S.-based

global corporation. Increasingly, global corporations are looking at a worldwide pool of young talent—including excellent international candidates who know several languages and are accustomed to intercultural communications. Hewlett-Packard is one example of an organization that casts a global net; it prefers to hire European- or American-trained Russians for its corporate communications efforts in Moscow and the Russian Federation.

Taking the U.S. Foreign Service Officers' examination is the first requirement for persons seeking international government careers. Foreign service work with federal agencies often requires a substantial period of government, mass media, or public relations service in the United States before international assignments are made.

APPLY YOUR KNOWLEDGE

What Would You Do?

Promoting Turkey

Turkey has a problem. The country was on track to become the fastest-growing tourist destination for Americans prior to September 11, 2001. That projection was derailed by the terrorist attacks and the subsequent invasions of Afghanistan and Iraq, which caused many Americans to think twice about visiting a Muslim nation—even one like Turkey, with a secular government and a strong European orientation.

Turkey is a virtual treasure house of art, culture, and cuisine that would appeal to seasoned travelers looking for a new experience and destination. To this end, the Turkish Culture and Tourism Office has retained your public relations firm to conduct a media relations program in the American press (and to some extent the European media).

Research and interviews with Turkish tourism authorities indicate that segmentation of various audiences would

be more fruitful than a general campaign. Travelers interested in food and wine, for example, might be reached through articles about the cuisine of Turkey. Music lovers might be interested in the new jazz sounds coming from Turkish musicians. Shoppers looking for vintage jewelry and exotic products such as carpets in the famous bazaars of Istanbul would be a good, specialized public. Then there are the history buffs who would be interested in visiting the sites of ancient civilizations.

Now that you know the possible interests of several target audiences, develop a public relations plan that will include appropriate social and mass media as well as events for these various audiences.

summary

How Is Public Relations Practice Developing Around the World?

- Public relations is a well-developed industry in many nations around the world. China, in particular, has a rapidly expanding industry that is becoming more sophisticated every year.

- In the new age of global marketing, public relations firms represent foreign interests in the United States as well as the interests of American corporations around the world.

What Challenges do Corporations Encounter When They Conduct Business Internationally?

- The international public relations practitioner must deal with issues related to language and cultural differences, including subtle differences in customs and etiquette and even ethical dilemmas.

What Is Public Diplomacy?

- The U.S. government refers to its international information efforts as "public diplomacy," meaning it attempts to enhance understanding of U.S. culture and promote U.S. foreign policy objectives.

How Has the Role of NGOs in the Global Marketplace Evolved?

- Nongovernmental organizations (which depend on international support for their causes) are widely believed to be more credible by the news media and the public on such issues as labor, health, and the environment, partly because they are perceived to lack the self-interest ascribed to governments and corporations.

- There is increasing evidence that giant corporations are adopting an accommodative stance by cooperating with activist NGOs to form more socially responsible policies.

Which Career Opportunities Are Available in Global Public Relations?

- Fluency in foreign language is a valued skill for global public relations. Also important is a background in international relations, global marketing techniques, social and economic geography, and cross-cultural communication.

questions
FOR REVIEW AND DISCUSSION

1 What is international public relations? What are some of the reasons for its growth in recent decades?

2 How can public relations facilitate the positive effects of globalization?

3 What are some of the difficulties that a corporation is likely to encounter when it conducts business in another country?

4 What are some of the objectives that foreign nations seek to accomplish by hiring U.S. public relations firms?

5 International surveys indicate that citizens of other nations have low approval ratings of the United States and its policies. Which "public diplomacy" efforts might the United States undertake to change these negative perceptions?

6 How can U.S. public relations practitioners in other countries adapt their practices to accommodate local values?

7 What is an NGO? How has new information technology enabled NGOs to expand their influence?

MySearchLab®

PR firms turn London into the Capital of reputation laundering

By Robert Booth The Guardian Weekly (UK) August 13, 2010

Many nations sign multi-million dollar contracts with PR firms to improve their images, advance tourism, and promote economic development.

Would you be willing to provide PR services to improve Bashir's image and defend Sudan against charges of genocide? What about defending the actions of Saudi Arabia, a nation that is a strong ally of the U.S., which has been repeatedly accused of human rights violations?

Public relations is not a licensed occupation or profession; one of the reasons for this is that the First Amendment guarantees "freedom of speech" for everyone.

Many former government officials and legislators find new careers in lobbying and public relations positions that allow them to capitalize on their "connections" and "influence."

It has a strong claim to be the world capital of everything from finance to design, but now London can add a more dubious distinction; it has become the reputation-laundering destination of choice for foreign heads of state whose controversial activities may have stained their countries' public images.

The capital's public relations groups are promoting foreign regimes with some of the world's worst human rights records, including Saudi Arabia, Rwanda, Kazakhstan, and Sri Lanka.

Even Omar al-Bashir, the president of Sudan, wanted by the international criminal court on suspicion of crimes against humanity relating to the Darfur genocide, has approached two London companies, via representatives, asking for their help.

"Autocratic governments are realizing they need to be more sophisticated in the way they act rather than just telling people how it is," said Francis Ingham, chief executive of the Public Relations Consultants Association. "There is great growth in the former communist blocs and in China."

Chime plc, headed by Lord Bell, Margaret Thatcher's former advisor, earned almost half of its 67 million pounds ($107 million) income last year from foreign contracts, up from 37% in 2008.

But some of the lucrative deals may breach the industry's voluntary code of conduct, which requires that "political consultants must advise clients where their activities may be illegal, unethical or contrary to professionals practice, and to refuse to act for a client in pursuance of any activity."

Portland PR, headed by Tim Allen, Tony Blair's former deputy press secretary, and Hill & Knowlton, among others, contested a recent contract to advise oil-rich Kazakhstan. Earlier this year, the regime was accused by Amnesty International of failing to address its human rights commitments under international law.

Bell Pottinger Sans Frontieres, the division of Chime that works most with foreign regimes, has not signed up to the industry code, although Portland and Hill & Knowlton have.

A spokesman for Portland said: "(We) certainly do not agree to any activities that are illegal, unethical, or contrary to professional practice, nor have we ever been asked to pursue any such activities by clients."

Paul Taaffe, chairman and chief executive of Hill & Knowlton, said his company "complies fully with locally applied rules and codes of conduct."

"More and more PR firms are moving from representing companies to representing countries, whatever their records," said MP Paul Farrelly, a member of the Commons culture, media, and sports select committee. "PR companies should take an ethical stance rather than the first shilling that is on offer. Any self-respecting professional should ask themselves if this is a regime they should be representing."

Bell Pottinger was one of the groups approached by Bashir to try to improve his reputation, but declined. The group is working for the Sri Lankan government after it allegedly bombed civilians and carried out executions during the final stages of its war against separatist Tamil rebels in 2009.

Chime has also represented the Zambian government, which in May was accused by human rights organizations of harbouring Rwandan genocide suspects. "I am not an international ethics body," Lord Bell said. "We do communications work. If people want to communicate their argument we take the view that they are allowed to do so."

The PRCA said its members must disclose every client and companies "who work with countries that people may take issue with must accept the risk to their own reputation."

> Many PR firms have their own codes of ethics about what kinds of clients and causes they will accept as clients.

> Most codes of ethics provide general guidelines about "truth" and "honesty," but few discuss what to do in specific situations.

> Would you agree that even unsavory regimes have the right to defend their actions in the marketplace of ideas?

> In the U.K., unlike in the U.S., firms are required to disclose their list of clients. However in the U.S., the Foreign Agent's Registration Act does require registered lobbyists to report contracts with foreign governments.

TACTICS

Text Credits

Credits are listed in order of appearance.

Photo Credits

Credits are listed in order of appearance.

Kazuhiro Nogi/AFP/Getty Images/Newscom;
Tiziana Fabi/AFP/Getty images/Newscom;
Khoo Si Lin/Shutterstock;
EFE/Antonio Lacerda/Newscom;

Madri/Xinhua/Photoshot/Newscom;
Franck Robichon/EPA/Newscom;
dboystudio/Shutterstock;
Elnur/Shutterstock;

Alex Segre/Alamy;
Naiyyer/Shutterstock;
Nigel Hicks/DK Images

Tactics image: Petr Z/Shutterstock
Tablet image: Falconia/Shutterstock

Government and Politics

From Chapter 17 of *Think Public Relations*, 2013 Edition. Dennis L. Wilcox, Glen T. Cameron, Bryan H. Reber, Jae-Hwa Shin.

Government and Politics

NuVal and Nutrition Keys vs. the Food and Drug Administration

Walmart, Michelle Obama, the Food Marketing Institute (FMI), and the Grocery Manufacturers Association (GMA) want you to embrace a new, simpler system of food labeling. NuVal, promoted as part of Michelle Obama's "Let's Move!" campaign to combat childhood obesity, assigns a numeric value from 1 to 100 depending on the healthfulness of the food (based on sodium, calories, saturated fats, sugar, etc.). The GMA has launched an aggressive campaign to promote NuVal, hiring three public relations firms—BBDO New York, Edelman, and FoodMinds—to oversee a $50 million campaign.

But the new system is not without its critics. Marion Nestle, professor of food science at New York University, worries that marketing concerns, rather than sound nutritional science, underlies industry initiatives like this. On her blog, www.foodpolitics.com, she asserts that these labels are an industry effort to protect profits, adding, "They have completely undermined the FDA." For its part, the Food and Drug Administration (FDA) is taking a wait-and-see approach. In a veiled criticism of NuVal, FDA press officer Siobhan DeLancey said, "Determining an optimal front-of-package system is a complicated endeavor."

This controversy illustrates the relationship between industry and regulation. The FDA is empowered to protect the consumer from harmful products (it is responsible for meat inspection and tobacco warning labels) as well as make recommendations about nutritional guidelines based on peer-reviewed research. Today, many rules and regulations are written by lobbyists and experts hired by industry. Government relations specialists work to promote industry interests, just as public affairs professionals working for the FDA advocate that organization's position. In many cases, roles overlap, with former public officials taking jobs in private industry, and state and federal agencies increasingly outsource communications to private firms.

1 **Identify some of the publics involved in the NuVal case and assess their interests.**

2 **What unique ethical issues are faced by government relations professionals working with private public relations firms?**

> What Are the Basic Purposes and Functions of Public Relations in Government Organizations?

> Which Public Relations Activities Do Government Organizations Engage in at the Federal, State, and Local Levels?

> What Are Public Affairs, Governmental Relations, and Lobbying?

> What Role Does Public Relations Play in Election Campaigns?

Government PUBLIC RELATIONS

National, state, and local governments around the world engage in similar public relations activities to succeed and thrive. In the United States, for example, government public information officers (PIOs) and public affairs officers (PAOs) engage in a variety of activities. These may include distribution of news releases, brochure and video preparation, speech writing, background briefings for legislators, and implementation of public information campaigns to improve the health and safety of citizens.

Ideally, the mission of government is public service; no one makes private profit directly from the operation of governments, and governments are noncommercial. In practice, there is widespread perception that government falls far short of these ideals. Nevertheless, the shortcomings of some government officials and employees should not blind citizens to the tangible benefits of the democratic system.

For federal, state, and local governments to function efficiently, each branch needs to communicate effectively with its constituents. From consumer information campaigns to military recruitment to floating a bond issue, the circulation of information—the core function of public relations—is an essential aspect of government administration. Skilled public relations professionals are required at every level of our government to ensure that information is disseminated clearly, efficiently, and to the largest number of people.

Aspiring public relations professionals should consider opportunities for employment in government. A related career path is work in governmental affairs for a corporation or a nonprofit. Many companies, trade groups, and nonprofits, for example, have public relations staff specializing in government relations. These staff members' primary responsibility is to inform the public, legislators, and governmental regulatory agencies about an organization's stance or position on current issues and pending legislation.

Closely linked to governmental affairs is lobbying. Lobbying groups are more directly involved in influencing proposed legislation that affect corporations, industries, or the activities of nonprofit groups. Lobbyists also get heavily involved in political campaigns to ensure that candidates favorable to their employers or clients are elected. The lobbying industry will be discussed later in this chapter.

think Which tactics do governments use to communicate with their publics?

In the United States, government public relations staff are active at the local, regional, and federal level.

Public INFORMATION AND PUBLIC AFFAIRS

Since the ancient Egyptians established the first unified state more than 5,000 years ago, governments have engaged in what is now known as public information and public affairs. There has always been a need for government communications, if for no other reason than to inform citizens of the services available and the manner in which they may be used.

> ## A nation of well-informed men who have been taught to know and prize the rights which God has given them cannot be enslaved. It is in the region of ignorance that tyranny begins.
>
> Benjamin Franklin

In a democracy, public information is crucial if citizens are to make intelligent judgments about policies and the activities of their elected representatives. Governments provide information in the hope that citizens will absorb the necessary background to participate fully in the formation of government policies.

Many people, including journalists, often criticize public information activities for simply producing reams of useless news releases promoting individual legislators or justifying questionable policies. Such abuse, coupled with snide news stories about the cost of maintaining government "public relations" experts, rankle dedicated public information officers (PIOs) at the various state and federal agencies who work very hard to keep the public informed with a daily diet of announcements and news stories. One PIO for a California agency said, "I'd like to see the press find out what's going on in state government without us."

Indeed, a major source of media hostility seems to stem from the fact that reporters are heavily dependent on news releases that are essentially information subsidies to the media. One study found that almost 90 percent of one state government's news releases were used by daily and weekly newspapers.

Public information efforts can be justified in terms of cost-efficiency. The U.S. Department of Agriculture public affairs office, for example, receives thousands of inquiries each year. Two-thirds of the requests can be answered by referring citizens to a simple pamphlet, a brochure, or a link on its website—all produced under the umbrella of public information.

Preventive public relations also saves money. The taxpayers of California spend an estimated $100 million annually to deal with the associated costs of teenage pregnancy, for example. Consequently, $5.7 million spent on a successful education campaign potentially could save the state a great deal of money in the form of reduced welfare costs. Cities also launch extensive public information campaigns to promote pet leash laws, recycling, and energy conservation. The City of Knoxville, Tennessee, for example, launched an information campaign to inform citizens about the availability of incentive grants to help residents install solar panels.

think How does public relations help citizens make more informed choices at the ballot box?

According to William Ragan, former director of public affairs for the U.S. Civil Service Commission, government information efforts have the following objectives:

- *Inform the public about the public's business.* Communicate the work of government agencies.
- *Improve the effectiveness of agency operations through appropriate public information techniques.* Explain agency programs so that citizens understand and can take actions necessary to benefit from them.
- *Provide feedback* to government administrators so that programs and policies can be modified, amended, or continued.
- *Advise management* on how best to communicate a decision or a program to the largest number of citizens.
- *Serve as ombudsmen.* Represent the public and listen to its representatives. Make sure that individual problems of taxpayers are satisfactorily solved.
- *Educate administrators* and bureaucrats about the role of the mass media and ways to work with media representatives.

The FEDERAL GOVERNMENT

The U.S. government is one of the world's leading collectors and disseminators of information. Advertising is a key governmental activity. Federal agencies spend several hundred million dollars each year on public service advertising, primarily to promote military recruitment, government health services, and the U.S. Postal Service.

The White House

At the apex of government public relations efforts is the White House—the president and his staff. The president receives more media attention than Congress and all the federal agencies combined. It is duly reported when the president visits a neighborhood school, tours a housing development, meets a head of state, or even takes his wife to New York City on a date.

All presidents have taken advantage of the intense media interest to implement public relations strategies to improve their popularity, generate support for programs, and explain embarrassing policy decisions. And each president has his own communication style.

> **Government agencies charged with emergency response have made a concerted push to build their social media capabilities. The Federal Emergency Management Administration (FEMA) has a blog, a Twitter account, a Facebook profile, and a YouTube account.**
>
> Erik Sass, writing in his blog, *The Social Graf*

Ronald Reagan was considered by many to be a master communicator. A former actor, he was extremely effective on television and could make his remarks seem spontaneous even when he was reading a teleprompter. He understood the importance of using symbolism and giving simple, down-to-earth speeches with memorable, personal appeal. Reagan's approach focused on the effective use of carefully packaged sound bites and staged events.

George H. W. Bush (senior) was no Ronald Reagan as a public speaker, but he did project enthusiasm for his job and had a friendly, but formal, working relationship with the White House press corps. Bill Clinton, by comparison, was more of a populist in his communication style. He was at home with information technology and made effective use of television talk shows. Clinton was most effective when he talked one-on-one with an interviewer or a member of the audience.

Terrance Hunt, an Associated Press reporter who covered the Reagan administration, says the former president's funeral in 2004 recalled the high style and stagecraft of his presidency. "Presidential appearances were arranged like movie scenes with Reagan in the starring role. There was a heavy emphasis on staging and lighting," says Hunt.

Government and Politics

President George W. Bush adopted Reagan's approach to stagecraft and symbolism. A team of television and video experts made sure every Bush appearance was masterfully choreographed for maximum visual effect. The Bush administration's concept of stagecraft manifested itself in tight control over information and limited media access. Bush, for example, gave substantially fewer press conferences, interviews, and other media events than either his father or Bill Clinton in their first two years in office.

When Barack Obama was campaigning, he was considered to be a master of the media. His campaign rallies were frequently compared to rock concerts. As president, some critics say his speeches became somewhat verbose and too "highbrow" for the average voter. Nevertheless, Obama is still considered a skilled orator with a compelling presence in the tradition of John F. Kennedy, Ronald Reagan, and Martin Luther King, Jr.

Congress

Members of the House of Representatives and the Senate regularly produce a barrage of news releases, brochures, radio and TV statements, e-mails, electronic newsletters, and videos (often uploaded to YouTube)—all designed to inform voters back home and keep the congressperson in the minds of voters. Most also have Facebook pages and Twitter accounts to keep their constituents informed on a daily basis.

Critics complain that most of these materials are self-promotional

> "Capitol Hill's press secretaries play a **significant role** in the shaping of America's messages and consequent public policies. In their role as **proxy** for individual members, the press secretaries act as **gatekeepers**, determining what information to share with, and hold from, the media; thus they have **command over news** shared with the citizenry."
>
> Edward Downes, Boston University

and have little value. In particular, the franking privilege (which provides free postage for members of Congress) is singled out for the most criticism. The late Senator John Heinz, a Republican from Pennsylvania, once distributed 15 million pieces of mail, financed by taxpayers, during a single election year. Each member of Congress employs a press secretary.

Federal Agencies

Public affairs officers (PAOs) and public information specialists engage in tasks that would be familiar to any member of the public relations department of a corporation. Specifically, they answer press and public inquiries, write news releases, work on newsletters, prepare speeches for top officials, oversee the production of brochures, and plan special events. Senior-level public affairs specialists counsel top management about communications strategies and recommend how the agency should respond to crisis situations.

One of the largest public affairs operations in the federal government is conducted by the U.S. Department of Defense (DOD)—the cabinet-level agency that oversees the armed forces. Its operations vary from the mundane to the exotic.

think In what ways is the job of a public affairs officer similar to that of a corporate public relations practitioner?

Headquarters of the Department of Defense, the Pentagon is a major employer of public affairs officers (PAOs) in Washington, D.C.

Military Pundits Get "Talking Points" from the Pentagon

Television news programs often interview retired military officers about U.S. strategy in war zones, but a Pentagon's program to provide "talking points" in support of the Bush administration's strategy in Afghanistan and Iraq raised ethical issues.

The Pentagon, under the direction of Donald Rumsfeld, began a program in 2002 to cultivate military analysts to help build public support for the war effort by giving analysts briefings and financing their trips to such places as Iraq and Guantánamo Bay, Cuba. The Pentagon also provided "talking points" to military analysts who were scheduled for various TV appearances.

The *New York Times* published a lengthy expose on the Pentagon program in 2008, which raised the question of whether the program was an effort to inform the public or an improper campaign of media manipulation. As a result, the Pentagon cancelled the program, and Congress asked the Pentagon's inspector general to investigate.

The inquiry found that Rumsfeld's staff hired a firm to track and analyze what the military analysts said during media appearances. At least four military analysts said they were ejected from the Pentagon's outreach program because they were critical of how the Pentagon was executing the war effort. Other analysts defended the program saying that its purpose was to merely inform and educate.

The inspector general's office issued a report in 2009 saying that it found no legal problems with the Pentagon program, but then retracted the entire report for inaccuracies and started a new inquiry. In December 2011, it issued another report stating that there was not conclusive evidence that the Pentagon violated regulations forbidding federal agencies to be advocates of administration policies.

What do you think? Was the Pentagon program merely a way to ensure that the public was adequately informed with the "facts" or was it an unethical manipulation of public opinion to support the Bush administration's military strategy?

A particularly exotic assignment for a military public affairs officer is giving background briefings and escorting the journalists who cover battlefield military operations. When the military initiated the policy of "embedding" journalists within military units during the 2003 invasion and occupation of Iraq, it assigned a large number of PAOs as escorts. The policy of "embedded" journalists has also been used with U.S. forces in Afghanistan. Journalists sometimes complain about restrictions on their freedom, however. For example, there has been criticism of the military's decision to forbid embedded journalists from photographing troops killed in action in Afghanistan.

The Pentagon (a nickname for the U.S. Department of Defense, derived from architecture of the agency's headquarters) also engages in recruitment drives. The U.S. Army recently released a campaign aimed at parents concerned about their son's or daughter's decision to join the military. "For Parents" is designed to "address your toughest questions and most pressing concerns. It delivers straight facts from the Army—and honest answers from parents like you." Questions may be submitted online, and the site offers hundreds of responses from Army public affairs specialists.

Another major operation of the Pentagon is assisting Hollywood with the production of movies.

One of the longest-running public relations efforts has been the preparation and distribution of "hometown" releases by the military. The Fleet Hometown News Center, established during World War II, sends approximately 1 million news releases annually about the promotions and transfers of U.S. Navy, Marine Corps, and Coast Guard personnel to their hometown media.

Government and Politics

Public information specialists work as liaisons with the film and television industries. They review scripts and proposals, advise producers on military procedures, and decide how much assistance, if any, a film or TV show portraying the military should receive. Movies portraying the military in a positive light, such *Transformers: Dark of the Moon* (2011) and *Iron Man 3* (2013) are more likely to receive assistance from the military than those with less flattering or ambiguous messages, such as *Stop Loss* (2008), *Redacted* (2007), and *The Messenger* (2009). For example, the Pentagon withdrew assistance for the filming of *Hurt Locker* (2009), because it didn't approve of some scenes in the script that were submitted for review. The film, however, went on to win the Academy Award for Best Picture, and many military personnel attested to reviewers about its authenticity.

Other federal agencies also conduct campaigns to inform citizens. In many cases, the agency selects a public relations firm through a bidding process. Ogilvy Public Relations Worldwide, for example, has done campaigns for the Centers for Disease Control and Prevention, the U.S. Department of Health and Human Services, and the Department of Veteran Affairs. Other major public relations firms, such as Ketchum and Edelman Worldwide, have received contracts to promote military recruiting, educate seniors about social security benefits, and increase the number of foreign tourists visiting the U.S.

Information campaigns are fairly common undertakings in most federal agencies. Sometimes public affairs staffs may find themselves on the front lines of a crisis or in the midst of a controversy that requires handling hundreds of press calls in a single day. An example of communication breakdowns between government agencies and the public was the dissemination of information to the public about the "Cash for Clunkers" program in 2009. Started on July 27 and ended abruptly on August 24, the program provided cash incentives for consumers to trade their older vehicles in for newer, more fuel efficient models. Lack of clear information about how long the program would last, which cars qualified for trade-in, and how dealers would be reimbursed with rebates led to widespread confusion and created frustration for both consumers and car dealers.

 Does government have the right to promote its programs with taxpayer money, even when partisan issues are involved?

State GOVERNMENTS

Like the federal government, the government of each of the 50 states disseminates information about its programs to various constituents. States develop campaigns to encourage tourism, educate the public about disease prevention, and promote economic development. In many cases, the state hires public relations firms to implement these campaigns.

Tourism, in particular, is heavily promoted because visitors are a major source of income for hotels, resorts, restaurants, convention centers, and a host of other related businesses that also produce more tax revenues.

Colorado, for example, spends about $12 million annually on marketing promotion. Arizona spends $7 million. New Mexico, in 2011, allocated about $3 million to upgrade its image as a tourist destination after deciding that the motto,

"Land of Enchantment" didn't quite cut it in the minds of potential tourists. A state survey found that many potential visitors had no image of New Mexico at all, except it was "close to Arizona." The 2010 BP oil spill in the Gulf of Mexico also generated a flurry of tourism marketing by the Gulf states to reassure potential visitors that beach resort areas were open for business.

Publicizing quality-of-life issues has emerged as a highly competitive arena, drawing on the resources of public relations professionals across many divisions or branches of state government. For example, the city of Colonie, New York, was pleased to promote itself as America's safest city after being so designated in 2010 by CQ press.

Every state provides an array of public information services. In California, the most populous state,

approximately 175 public information officers (PIOs) work in about 70 state agencies. On a daily basis, these PIOs provide routine information to the public and the press on the policies, programs, and activities of the various state agencies.

State agencies conduct a variety of public information and education campaigns, often with the assistance of public relations firms that have been selected via a bidding process. In a typical bidding process, a state agency will issue a request for proposal (RFP) and award a contract on the basis of presentations from competing firms.

One area that is often targeted by public relations campaigns is

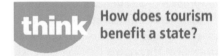

think How does tourism benefit a state?

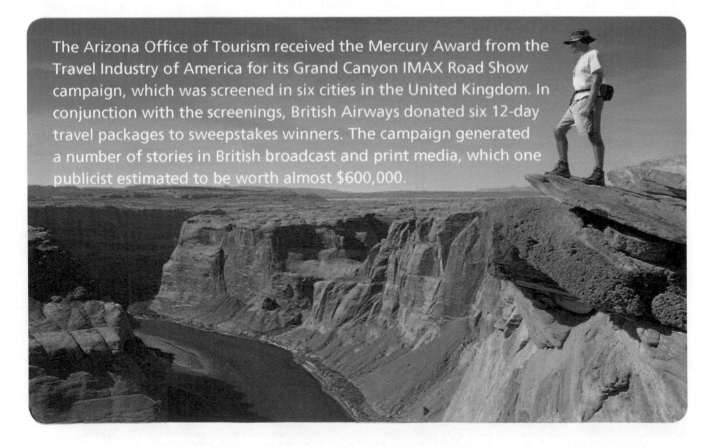

The Arizona Office of Tourism received the Mercury Award from the Travel Industry of America for its Grand Canyon IMAX Road Show campaign, which was screened in six cities in the United Kingdom. In conjunction with the screenings, British Airways donated six 12-day travel packages to sweepstakes winners. The campaign generated a number of stories in British broadcast and print media, which one publicist estimated to be worth almost $600,000.

health and safety. In recent years, most states have spent considerable money convincing people not to smoke. The funds, which typically come from the national tobacco settlement and state-imposed cigarette taxes, have provided somewhat of a windfall for public relations efforts. For instance, California generates approximately $120 million annually from tobacco taxes, 10 percent of which is devoted to antismoking advertising and public relations. Of course, as smoking decreases, so too does the amount of taxes collected on tobacco sales, leaving less money to support the campaigns.

The California Department of Health Services runs campaigns on a variety of health issues, such as childhood immunizations, breast cancer screening, and teen pregnancy prevention. The California Highway Patrol also conducts safety campaigns. A recent campaign alerted drivers that it was now illegal to use handheld cell phones while driving. The California Department of Health Services also runs campaigns on a variety of health issues, such as the Network for a Healthy California, the Worksite Program, Physical Activity Integration, and a number of other campaigns. One recent campaign entitled Children's Power Play! is designed to get children moving for at least 60 minutes a day.

States also promote tourism through advertising and public relations campaigns. Tourism and conventions are the second largest industry in Wisconsin, so its Department of Tourism concentrates on branding Wisconsin as a destination for cheese lovers (350 types of cheese are produced there) and beer drinkers ("Beer Capital of the U.S."). Tourism is also big business in Texas. Approximately 500,000 people are employed in the Lone Star State's tourism industry, which generates nearly $57 billion in spending on an annual basis. In a recent year, for example, the state spent almost $2 million on public relations and advertising in an effort to lure European travelers to Texas.

Local GOVERNMENTS

Cities employ information specialists to disseminate news and information from numerous municipal departments. Agencies include the airport, transit district,

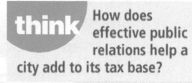

think How does effective public relations help a city add to its tax base?

redevelopment office, parks and recreation department, convention and visitors bureau, police and fire departments, city council, and the mayor's office.

Local governments hold meetings to inform and interact with concerned citizens.

The information flow occurs in many ways, but the objectives are always to inform citizens about, and help them take full advantage of, government services. The city council holds neighborhood meetings; the airport commission sets up an exhibit showing the growth needs of the airport; the recreation department promotes summer swimming lessons; and the city's human rights commission sponsors a festival promoting multiculturalism.

Cities also promote themselves to attract new business. Many cities pump millions of dollars into efforts to attract new business through a variety of communication tools, including elaborate brochures, placement of favorable "success" stories in the nation's press, direct mail, telemarketing, trade fairs, special events, and meetings with business executives.

Cities may promote themselves in an effort to increase tourism. As an example, consider the campaign by the Panama City (Florida) Convention and Visitors Bureau to position itself as a prime destination for college students during spring break. According to *PRWeek*, the bureau spent roughly $300,000 promoting the city through posters, news releases, brochures, advertising, and special events to let students know that they were welcome.

Cities often promote tourism by publicizing their cultural attractions and special events. Initiatives range from traditional tactics, such as issuing press releases, to more ambitious efforts at outreach, such as creating interactive media sites. The city of Boston operates a social media center (http://www.cityof-boston.gov/news/socialmedia.asp) with links to its Facebook, Twitter, YouTube, and LinkedIn sites. And states from Maryland to California have begun to embrace social networks as a means of engaging in two-way communication with their constituents.

> **The competition for cities and wider regions to attract businesses is as intense as ever, experts say, with an estimated 12,000 economic development organizations vying for the roughly 500 annual corporate moves/expansions that involve 250 or more jobs each.**
>
> PRWeek

Businesses monitor government in many ways. Probably the most active parties in Washington, D.C., and many state capitals are the trade associations that represent various industries.

Government RELATIONS BY CORPORATIONS

Government relations is a specialized component of corporate communications, closely related to lobbying (which we discuss in the next section of the chapter). This activity is so important that many companies, particularly in highly regulated industries, have separate departments of government relations. The reason is simple: The

 think | How do the actions of government agencies affect how businesses operate?

actions of governmental bodies at the local, state, and federal levels have a major influence on how businesses operate.

Government relations specialists, often called public affairs specialists, have a number of functions:

they gather and disseminate information, represent management's views, cooperate with government on projects of mutual benefit, and motivate employees to participate in the political process.

As the eyes and ears of a business or industry, practitioners in government relations positions spend considerable time gathering and processing information. They

A Short History of Government Efforts to Promote Nutrition

GOVERNMENT PUBLIC AFFAIRS officers have been involved in promoting healthy eating for more than 100 years. The first federal nutritional standards, dating from 1894, were issued by the newly established United States Department of Agriculture (USDA). Public affairs officers developed and promoted the concepts of "basic food groups" and "recommended dietary allowance" during World War II. During the 1960s, the ranks of public affairs officers swelled, and efforts continued to promote dietary guidelines to the American public through posters, reports, news subsidies, and public service announcements. The ongoing challenge has been to convey complex scientific information in a legible and relevant manner to the American public.

> **"Americans can visualize what they eat with MyPlate."**
>
> Patrick Delaney, communications director for the United Fresh Produce Association

Introduced in 1992, the USDA's Food Pyramid offered a simple, visual representation based on a food pyramid similar to the one used in Sweden. It was designed to allow consumers to make food selections at a glance: fruits and fiber at the bottom, and foods high in salt and fat at the top to indicate relative proportions. By 2009, it was clear that the Food Pyramid needed updating. Some nutritionists believed that the science was outdated, and "the pyramid was confusing," said Patrick Delaney, communications director for the United Fresh Produce Association. Young children in particular were found to have a hard time grasping the Food Pyramid and its 2005 update, MyPyramid.

In June 2011, the government tried again. Its MyPlate icon is a study in graphic simplicity. It's a circular plate divided into four sections—fruits, vegetables, grains, and protein—and a glass that represents dairy. The director for the Center for Science in the Public Interest says, "While no one graphic can communicate every nuance of healthy eating, this easy-to-understand illustration will help people remember what their own plate should look like." Citing its simplicity, Michelle Obama is also a supporter of MyPlate. "Kids are more visual than adults," said Amy Epstein, managing director of API Marketing and Public Relations.

The USDA is hoping that the food and restaurant industry will embrace MyPlate. A handful of food companies have offered endorsements. Jim Hodges, president of the American Meat Institute, is pleased that MyPlate "affirms the role that meat and poultry play in a healthy diet." The soft drink industry, on the other hand, is less than pleased.

A survey of American consumers conducted by the M Booth research firm in 2011 found that about half of Americans were aware of MyPlate, and about a quarter had considered following the program's dietary recommendations. On the other hand, a NPD market research Group National Eating Trends survey found that only 2 percent of Americans even come close to following MyPlate nutritional guidelines. Even though it may be off to a slow start, the campaign seems to be catching on in other quarters. Hill's Science Diet pet food company recently introduced the "MyBowl" labels to help guide canine nutritional selections.

1 What are the common themes in the U.S. government's campaigns to promote healthy eating over the last 100 years?

2 What issue is the MyPlate campaign targeted to address, and what audiences is it aimed at reaching?

3 What other public relations strategies and tactics would you suggest if you were a public relations professional working on the MyPlate campaign?

monitor the activities of many legislative bodies and regulatory agencies to keep track of issues coming up for debate and possible vote. This intelligence gathering enables a corporation or an industry to plan ahead and, if necessary, adjust its policies or provide information that may influence the nature of government decision making.

A Boston University survey showed that almost 70 percent of the responding companies monitored government activity in Washington, D.C., through their trade associations. The second monitoring effort cited on the list was frequent trips to the city by senior public affairs officers and corporate executives; 58 percent of the respondents said they engaged in this activity. Almost 45 percent of the responding firms reported that they had a company office in the nation's capital.

Government relations specialists also spend a great deal of time sharing information about their company's position to a variety of key publics. The tactics employed may include informal office visits to government officials or testimony at public hearings. In addition, public affairs people are often required to give or write speeches for senior executives. They may write letters and op-ed articles, prepare position papers, produce newsletters, and place advocacy advertising.

Although legislators are the primary audience for government relations efforts, the Foundation for Public Affairs reports that 9 out of 10 companies also communicate with employees on public policy issues. Another 40 percent communicate with retirees, customers, and other publics such as taxpayers and government employees.

Lobbying

The term *lobbyist* may have been coined by President Ulysses S. Grant, who often sought refuge from the White House by having a cigar and brandy in the Hotel Willard's lobby in Washington, D.C. Grant is said to have used the term to describe the people who sought favors from him when he was engaged in this kind of relaxation.

Today, lobbying is more formal than in Grant's era and is closely aligned with governmental relations or public affairs. In fact, the distinction between the two often blurs. In part, this overlap occurs because most campaigns to influence impending legislation have multiple levels. One level is informing and convincing the public about the correctness of an organization's viewpoint, which the public affairs specialist does. Lobbyist efforts are aimed at the defeat, passage, or amendment of legislation and regulatory agency policies.

Lobbyists work at the local, state, and federal levels of government. California has about 1,000 registered lobbyists, who represent about 2,000 special-interest groups. The interests represented in the state capital of Sacramento include large corporations, business and trade groups, unions, environmental groups, local governments, nonprofit groups, school districts, and members of various professional groups.

The number and variety of special interests increase exponentially at the federal level. According to the Center for Responsive Politics (CRP), there are now 1,900 firms that house more than 11,000 lobbyists registered to operate in Washington, D.C. In addition, there are hundreds of lobbyists directly employed by national trade groups, companies, and labor unions. In 2010, CRP calculated that $3.5 billion was spent on lobbying in Washington. As one critic quipped, "We have the best government that money can buy."

Lobbyists represent the interests of virtually the entire spectrum of

High-Tech Lobbying

Google has considerably expanded its Washington lobbying activities in recent years. It now has about 40 lawyers and policy advisors in its Washington office and about a dozen lobbying firms on retainer to ensure that government regulators don't file any antitrust suits due to its dominance of the search market. Google also wants to influence any legislation regarding online privacy. In 2011, Google spent $9.7 million on political persuasion, according to the *Washington Post*.

Facebook also has a Washington office, with high-profile lobbyists from both parties. Its main concern is also new legislation regarding privacy regulations, which could have a major effect on its operations.

U.S. business, educational, religious, local, national, and international pursuits. Lobbying is also conducted on behalf of foreign governments and interests. The American–Israel Public Affairs

Lobbyist's To-Do List

Professional fund-raisers recruit lobbyists to handle the following tasks:

- Hock tickets
- Decide whom to invite
- Design and mail invitations
- Employ people to make follow-up calls
- Rent the room and hire the caterer
- Make name tags
- Tell the candidate who came—and who didn't
- Hound attendees to make good on their pledges

> "Of the approximately 2,000 lobbyists working on financial reform, more than 1,400 had been congressional staffers or worked in the executive branch, and 73 had been members of Congress.
>
> A Center for Responsive Politics (CRP) report, quoted in *Time* magazine

Committee (AIPAC), for example, is a major player in Washington, D.C., because of its impressive resources. According to *The Economist*, "AIPAC has an annual budget of around $60 million, more than 275 employees, an endowment of over $130 million, and a new $80 million building on Capitol Hill.

Competing lobbying efforts often cancel each other out, which leaves legislators and regulatory personnel with the daunting chore of weighing the pros and cons of an issue before voting. Indeed, *Time* magazine notes that competition among lobbyists representing different sides of an issue does "serve

Comedian Stephen Colbert established his own super PAC in 2011 to mock the lack of restriction on campaign contributions. Colbert Super PAC SHH Institute funded satirical commercials that had a measurable effect on Republican primary elections. Colbert also offered the Republican party $500,000 to put a nonbinding referendum on the ballot asking voters to determine whether "corporations are people" or "people are people."

a useful purpose by showing busy legislators the virtues and pitfalls of complex legislation."

A perennial conflict that lobbyists weigh in on is the debate between saving jobs and improving the environment. A coalition of environmental groups constantly lobbies Congress for tougher legislation to clean up industrial pollution or protect endangered species. Simultaneously, local communities and politicians counter that the proposed legislation would result in the loss of jobs and economic chaos.

Most groups claim to be lobbying in the "public interest."

Pitfalls of Lobbying

Although a case can be made for lobbying as a legitimate activity, deep public suspicion exists about the motivations of former legislators and officials who capitalize on their connections and charge large fees for doing what is commonly described as "influence peddling." Indeed, the roster of registered lobbyists in Washington, D.C., includes a virtual who's who of former legislators and government officials. According to the watchdog group Center for Public Integrity, more than half of the 120 members of Congress who left in 2010 found employment as lobbyists (52 percent). For example, Chris Dodd (former Democrat–Connecticut) became the chief lobbyist for the Motion Picture Association of America.

The Ethics in Government Act forbids government officials from actively lobbying their former agencies for one year after leaving office. According to critics, this law has had little or no impact. Instances of people "cashing in" on connections give the press and public the uneasy feeling that influence ped-

think Why is it necessary to regulate lobbyists?

dling is alive and well in the nation's capitol. This practice also gives credence to the cliché, "It's not *what* you know, but *who* you know." The scandal involving lobbyist Jack Abramoff, for example, revealed just how closely legislators are tied to lobbyists. Abramoff's financial mismanagement and willingness to dispense illegal perks to legislators earned him a lengthy prison sentence. House Majority Leader Tom Delay (Republican–Texas) had to resign his leadership post, and Ohio congressman Bob Ney pleaded guilty to two counts of conspiracy and making false statements in the Abramoff scandal.

Grassroots Lobbying

Politicians in both parties have regularly decried the influence of lobbyists, but reform has taken a half century. At least 10 times since the first loophole-riddled lobbying regulations were passed in 1946, efforts to update the law have failed to get past the legislative obstacles. In 1995, Congress did pass a measure designed to reform lobbying, and President Clinton signed it. Part of the impetus behind this legislation was undoubtedly the impact of polls indicating that the public believed lobbyists had runaway influence over Congress.

One key provision was an expanded definition of who is considered to be a "lobbyist." The 1995 law defines a lobbyist as "someone hired to influence lawmakers, government officials or their aides, and who spends at least 20 percent of his or her time representing any client in a six-month period." Another key provision requires lobbyists to register with Congress and disclose their clients, the issue areas in which lobbying is being done, and roughly the amount they are paid for their services. Violators face civil fines of as much as $50,000.

One area exempted from the lobby reform bill is financial disclosures for so-called grassroots lobbying—the fastest-growing area in the political persuasion business. Grassroots lobbying is now an $800 million industry, according to *Campaigns and Elections*, a bimonthly magazine for "political professionals." What makes this area so attractive to various groups is that the lack of rules or regulations governing it. The tools of this sort of lobbying include advocacy advertising, toll-free phone lines, bulk faxing, websites, and computerized direct mail aimed at generating phone calls and letters from the public to Congress, the White House, and governmental regulatory agencies.

Grassroots lobbying also involves coalition building. The basic idea is to get individuals and groups with no financial interest in an issue to speak on the sponsor's behalf. The underlying premise is that letters and phone calls from private citizens are more influential than arguments from vested interests. Such campaigns make public interest groups wonder if they really shouldn't be called "Astroturf" campaigns, because the "grass" is often artificial. Michael Pertschuk, co-director of the Advocacy Institute in Washington, D.C., told *O'Dwyer's PR Services Report*, "Astroturf groups are usually founded with corporate seed money that is funneled through PR firms."

Election CAMPAIGNS

Public affairs activities and lobbying, either in the halls of Congress or at the grassroots level, are year-round activities. During election years, either congressional or presidential, an army of fund-raisers, political strategists, speech-writers, and communications consultants mobilize to help candidates win elections.

The high cost of running for office in the United States has made fund-raising virtually a full-time, year-round job for every incumbent and aspirant

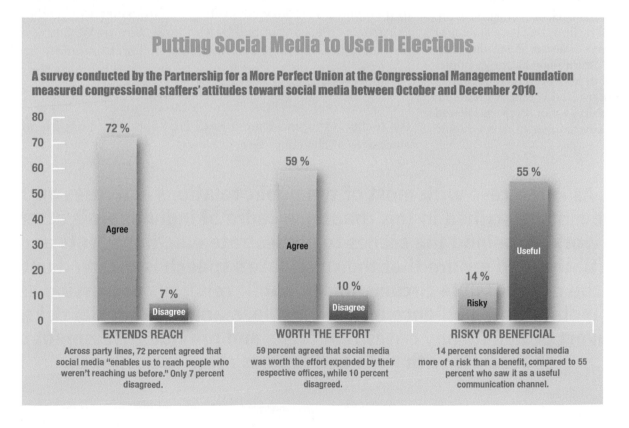

Putting Social Media to Use in Elections

A survey conducted by the Partnership for a More Perfect Union at the Congressional Management Foundation measured congressional staffers' attitudes toward social media between October and December 2010.

EXTENDS REACH — Across party lines, 72 percent agreed that social media "enables us to reach people who weren't reaching us before." Only 7 percent disagreed.

WORTH THE EFFORT — 59 percent agreed that social media was worth the effort expended by their respective offices, while 10 percent disagreed.

RISKY OR BENEFICIAL — 14 percent considered social media more of a risk than a benefit, compared to 55 percent who saw it as a useful communication channel.

to office. In fact, American-style campaigning is the most expensive in the world.

Candidates retain professionals to organize fund-raising activities. A standard activity in Washington, D.C., and other major cities across the country is the luncheon, reception, or dinner on behalf of a candidate. The *Wall Street Journal*, for example, once reported that 14 such events were held on a single day, raising $650,000 for Congressional incumbents. Individual donors and lobbyists for various organizations regularly attend these events. Although a chicken dinner or a cheese platter with crackers and champagne are not worth $2,000 per person in literal terms, the event shows support for the candidate and allows donors to have contact with him or her. No business is actually discussed, but the occasion gives both individuals and lobbyists for special interests an opportunity to show the "flag" and perhaps indirectly influence legislation or open the door for personal appointments at a later date after the election, if the candidate wins.

Some consultants specialize in direct mail and telemarketing. They are assisted by firms that have developed computer databases and mailing lists. Aristotle Publishers, for example, claims to have records on 128 million registered voters. A candidate can obtain a list of prospects tailored using any number of demographic

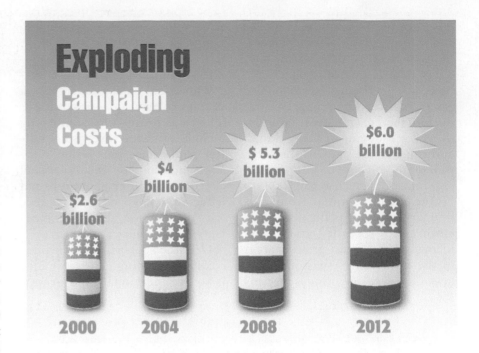

It is estimated that a colossal $6 billion will be spent on the 2012 elections for Congress and the presidency. According to the *Financial Times*, Barack Obama and his opponent, Mitt Romney, will probably spend about $2 billion in the presidential contest alone. According to Tom Daschle, a Democrat and former Senate majority leader, "Two billion could be conservative."

In addition to regular campaign spending, considerable amounts of money will also be spent by political action committees (PACS) that, thanks to a 2010 Supreme Court decision, can spend unlimited amounts of money advocating various issues and candidates. Crossroads GPS, co-founded by Karl Rove, George W. Bush's chief political advisor, planned to raise $240 million to promote issues, produce attack ads against Barack Obama, and promote the candidacy of Mitt Romney. By law, super PACs are not supposed to coordinate their activities with the campaigns of candidates, but the reality is that most super PACs are headed by close friends and associates of the candidate.

As is the case with most of the public relations activities and events described in this chapter, a cadre of individuals is often working behind the scenes to orchestrate election events and initiatives. To ensure that the candidate's speech is received under the best possible circumstances, public relations professionals mobilize the audience and the media, manage potential risks, avert or handle any crises that arise, and provide assessment of the results with polls and reports after each speech.

Seeing the Light: Social Media in Politics

By now, a politician using social media to drum up support, stay in touch with the public, and share news of evolving views of accomplishments is old news. Democrats such as Howard Dean in 2004 and Barack Obama in 2008 were early adopters. Said Dean in 2004: "Along comes this campaign to take back the country for ordinary human beings, and the best way you can do that is through the Net." Dean harnessed the power of two-way communication, and Obama followed his lead four years later, enlisting Mark Andreessen, founder of Netscape and a Facebook board member, to help devise his social media strategy. Said Andreessen, "He was the first politician I dealt with who understood that the technology was a given and that it could be used in new ways."

Bush's 2004 presidential run would be the last of its kind. Republican strategists have since learned that social media pay a greater return on the investment than stamps and phone banks. It also provides invaluable instant feedback, or as Dean said in 2004, "If I give a speech and the blog people don't like it, next time I change the speech." Social media were an essential and inevitable part of any candidate's election strategy. Democrats maintain a lead in cutting-edge communication channels such as

Google+ and iPhone apps—at least as far as the media are concerned. But Republicans are gaining ground fast. Said Patrick Ruffini, a political campaign strategist for 2012 presidential candidate Tim Pawlenty, "the notion that the Internet is owned by liberals, owned by the left, in the wake of the Obama victory, has proven false." Ruffini's contention was supported by a survey conducted by the Pew Research Center in 2011. Said Lee Rainie, director of Pew's Internet & American Life Project, "Lots more people—including Republicans, independents, supporters of the Tea Party—are just as active in this space as Democrats used to be." Republican presidential candidate Mitt Romney had about 1.3 million Facebook fans and about 200,000 Twitter followers as of December 2011. Newt Gingrich, whose campaign appeared to be over in mid-2011, rallied in November and added an average of 8,700 Facebook fans per day. At the state level, Republican Governor Jan Brewer leads with nearly 500,000 "likes." Among governors and congressmen, there is little disparity among Democrats and Republicans.

Still, gearing up for the presidential election, President Obama maintains a seemingly insurmountable lead. As 2011 ended, he had more than 24 million Facebook fans and more than 10 million Twitter followers. Obama's social media strategy has been criticized as a "blitzkrieg" approach for it lacks focus. But in one of his more successful efforts, he conducted an online town hall on Facebook on April 20, 2011—this time with the support of Facebook CEO and founder, Mark Zuckerberg.

1 If you were in charge of the social media initiatives for a political candidate, what are some of the strategies and tactics that you might use?

2 What are the potential benefits and risks of using social media in election campaigns?

3 What are some differences in terms of the application of social media tactics between government relations and corporate relations?

Meg Whitman at a rally.

variables, including party affiliation, voting record, contribution record, age, geographic location, and opinions on various issues.

Other firms handle mass mailings on behalf of candidates. Kiplinger Computer and Mailing Services is capable of running 10,000 envelopes per hour and printing personalized letters at a rate of 120 pages per minute. Although mailed campaign literature is on the wane—given the impact of the internet and social media—political candidates still depend on this traditional tactic.

A powerful tool for fund-raising and reaching supporters is the Internet. One use of the Internet is for research. The *Wall Street Journal*, for example, reported that an organization supporting the presidential candidacy of Senator John Kerry (Democrat–Massachusetts) in Concord, New Hampshire, was able to track down Democratic women voters, aged 18 to 30, who were interested in abortion rights. Within seconds, the computer was able to generate the names of 812 local women and provide a street map marking their addresses. Members of Planned Parenthood and other Kerry supporters followed up on this information by making door-to-door visits on behalf of the candidate.

Of course, there is a downside to reliance on the Internet and social media. Candidates must surrender some measure of control over the message and discussion. Any gaffes are instantly amplified through retweets and message boards. Constant vigilance is needed to rebut gossip and misinformation. Also, the opposition can create rogue websites that spoof or mimic the candidate's official site.

Careless use of social media has also been the undoing of politicians such as Congressman Anthony Weiner. Weiner was force to resign in early 2011 after tweeting photos of himself in his underwear to several of his college-age female followers. Despite these caveats, the Internet and social media have proven to be effective as both a public relations tactic and strategy.

What Would You Do?

Watching the Weather

One of the dilemmas faced by local, state, and federal governments when a natural disaster looms is how and when to warn residents of the danger. If government officials issue warnings too often or too early, or if they raise the alarm and nothing happens, residents may become desensitized and learn to disregard warnings. Conversely, officials will lose public trust if they fail to warn citizens in a timely manner.

Consider a scenario in which a Category 5 storm looms off the coast of North Carolina. National Oceanographic and Atmospheric Administration (NOAA) meteorologists predict that there is a 65 percent chance that the storm will hit the city in four days—but there is also a chance that it will miss entirely. If you were a public affairs specialist for North Carolina, which steps would you take immediately to inform the public? Which channels of communication would you use? How would you structure your message? Which steps would you recommend taking regarding communication with the public if the wrong decisions were made and the situation became a catastrophic disaster? Working with a small group, quickly brainstorm a communication plan.

summary

What Are the Basic Purposes and Functions of Public Relations in Government Organizations?

- Governments have always engaged in campaigns to educate, inform, motivate, and even persuade the public. In the United States, the emphasis is on "public information" efforts.

Which Public Relations Activities Do Government Organizations Engage in at the Federal, State, and Local Levels?

- Presidents throughout history have used media attention to lead the nation, convince the public to support administration policies, and get reelected.

- All agencies of the federal government employ public affairs officers and public information specialists. Members of Congress engage in extensive information-focused fforts to reach their constituents.

- All states employ public information officers to inform the public about the activities and policies of various agencies.

- All major cities employ public information specialists to tell citizens about city services and promote economic development.

What Are Public Affairs, Governmental Relations, and Lobbying?

- A major component of corporate communications is public affairs, which primarily deals with governmental relations at the local, state, national, and even international levels.

- Trade groups, which are typically based in state capitals or in Washington, D.C., have public affairs specialists representing various professions and industries who engage in governmental relations.

- A lobbyist directly works for the defeat, passage, or amendment of legislation and regulatory agency policies.

- Recent years, public concern.

What Role Does Public Relations Play in Election Campaigns?

- An army of specialists, including public relations experts, are retained by major candidates to organize and raise money for election campaigns.

questions
FOR REVIEW AND DISCUSSION

1 What are the basic purposes and functions of government relations?

2 What is the difference between someone who works in corporate public affairs (government relations) and a lobbyist?

3 Many lobbyists are former legislators and government officials. Do you think these players exercise undue influence in the shaping of legislation? Why or why not?

4 List some examples of public relations campaigns run by state or local governments.

5 How does public relations at the local level differ from public relations efforts at the state and federal levels? Which channels are typically used by federal and local officials to disseminate messages to the public?

6 How do grassroots groups use technology to disseminate their message? What are the benefits and risks of using social media to promote an agenda within the political arena?

MySearchLab®

Photo Credits

Credits are listed in order of appearance.

Kristoffer Tripplaar/Alamy;
Paul Franklin/DK Images;
AP Photo;
Ken Hammond/U.S.Department of Defense;
D.Myles Cullen/U.S.Department of Defense;

Christophe Testi/Shutterstock;
Marvin Nauman/FEMA;
USDA Center for Nutrition Policy and
Promotion (CNPP);
Kristoffer Tripplaar/Alamy;

Pete Souza/White House Photography;
ZUMA Wire Service/Alamy

Tablet image: Falconia/Shutterstock

Entertainment, Sports, and Tourism

From Chapter 16 of *Think Public Relations*, 2013 Edition. Dennis L. Wilcox, Glen T. Cameron, Bryan H. Reber, Jae-Hwa Shin.
Copyright © 2013 by Pearson Education, Inc. Published by Pearson. All rights reserved.

Entertainment, Sports, and Tourism

Internal and External Expectations Shape Tourism PR in Egypt

About 4 million of Egypt's 82 million citizens work in tourism. When political unrest rocked Egypt in early 2011, many tourists canceled planned visits to that country. Mounir Fakhry Abdel Nour, minister of tourism, reported that 32 percent fewer tourists came to Egypt in 2011 than in 2010. So to ensure that the numbers would not drop further, the Egypt Tourism Authority ratcheted up its "Egypt: Where It All Begins" promotional campaign.

Videos of bikini-clad vacationers on Egyptian beaches were posted to YouTube. Egypt Facebook pages included one labeled "Egypt. Tourism. Campaign." A two-page advertising spread in the *New York Times Sunday Magazine* included a crossword puzzle with Egypt-centric clues. Tourism officials conducted media relations. Abdel Nour noted that the great majority of tourists ("probably 90 percent ... maybe more") vacationed on Egyptian beaches in 2011.

And will those beaches be the same in the wake of the Arab Spring? Some conservative Islamic leaders have asserted that vacationers' expectations will have to change. The leader of a fundamentalist Islamic sect told the British Broadcasting Corporation (BBC), "Of course we have to prohibit selling alcohol. It's prohibited in the Koran, and it's my right as a Muslim to practice Sharia in my country, in my home and in my community. The lack of alcohol and bikinis won't stop open-minded progressive people [from] visiting."

Tourism officials argue that financial realities would ultimately drive policy. Hisham Zaazou, the senior assistant tourism minister, told National Public Radio (NPR) that tourists expect the Egyptian beach experience to mimic theirs at home. "To swim, you wear a bathing costume. To have dinner, part of the culture is to have a drink with the dinner," Zaazou told NPR. Those who are not in the tourism industry do not understand that tourists' expectations cannot be easily changed, Zaazou said.

1 **If you worked in the tourism ministry, how would you use public relations to educate Egyptian citizens of the importance of meeting tourists' expectations?**

2 **What would you do to assure international tourists that they would be secure in Egypt?**

Ask Yourself

> Which Elements Are Essential for an Effective Personality Campaign?

> How Can a Publicity Campaign Increase Event Attendance?

> What Role Does Public Relations Play in Sports Mania Around the World?

> What Role Does Public Relations Play in Attracting Visitors to Destinations and Keeping Them Happy Once They Arrive?

PUBLIC RELATIONS IN
Entertainment, Sports, AND Tourism

Public relations in business and industry is typically thought of as corporate work. A large percentage of public relations practitioners certainly do work for corporations, but there are other significant business segments of the public relations industry as well. In this chapter, we delve more deeply into some of the day-to-day issues that public relations practitioners face in the specialties of entertainment, sports, and tourism public relations.

Increasingly, public relations students express interest in careers in sports, entertainment, and tourism. Our society is characterized by a proliferation of major and minor league sports teams, university teams that rival professional clubs in terms of personnel and dollars, a growing cult of celebrity, and a strong convention and tourism sector. To many, jobs in these areas seem somewhat glamorous, and as a result these jobs can be much more competitive to land than other areas of public relations work.

Entertainment is big business. Public relations in the entertainment business can involve serving as a publicist for a celebrity or sports figure or working for an athletic team or a sports or entertainment venue. The field of entertainment public relations includes the travel industry, specific site or destination promotion, and specific travel businesses, such as a cruise line. These are just a few examples of public relations intersecting with the entertainment business.

Entertainment and sports are "entertainment," and both deal with the cult of celebrity. There's really no difference between Tom Brady and Nicki Minaj in terms of working as a publicist for them and the "branding" of them. Nor is there much difference between the hype for the Academy Awards or the Grammys and the Super Bowl.

In some cases, celebrity results from natural public curiosity about an individual's achievements or position in life. Frequently, however, it is carefully nurtured by publicists for commercial gain.

PROMOTING A PERSONALITY

A dominant aspect of today's mass media is the cult of celebrity. Sports heroes and television and movie personalities, in particular, along with radio talk-show hosts, members of the British royal family, high-profile criminals, and even some politicians, are written about, photographed, and discussed almost incessantly. The number and circulation of celebrity magazines continue to increase every year. *People*, the industry leader, has a circulation of more than 3.5 million copies per week for example.

The publicity buildup used to promote individuals lies outside the mainstream of public relations work, and some professional practitioners are embarrassed by the exaggerations and tactics employed by publicists for super star athletes and so-called beautiful people. Nevertheless, all students of public relations should know how the personal publicity trade operates.

Although a scandal often generates unwanted and unfavorable publicity for a celebrity, most public relations campaigns are initiated to generate public awareness of an individual who is intentionally seeking publicity. Such a campaign should be planned just as meticulously as any other public relations project. Practitioners conducting such campaigns typically follow a standard step-by-step process.

1 Interview the client for interesting and possibly newsworthy facts about the person's life, activities, and beliefs. Draw out details from clients and develop these facts as story angles.

DAMAGE CONTROL and Personal Publicity

Handling publicity for an individual involves special responsibilities. Clients may even turn to their publicists for personal advice, especially when trouble arises. A practitioner handling an individual client is responsible for both protecting the client from bad publicity and generating positive news. When the client appears in a bad light because of misbehavior or an irresponsible public statement, the publicist must try to minimize the harm done to the client's public image. The objective in such a case is damage control.

Personal misconduct by a client, or the appearance of misconduct, can strain a practitioner's ingenuity and at times his or her ethical principles. Some practitioners will lie outright to protect a client—a dishonest practice that only increases problems if the media expose the lie. On occasion, a practitioner acting in good faith may be victimized if his or her client has lied.

Issuing a prepared statement to explain the client's conduct, even though it may leave reporters and editors partially dissatisfied, is regarded as safer than having the client call a news conference, unless the client is a victim of circumstances and is best served by talking fully and openly. The decision about holding a news conference also is influenced by how articulate and self-controlled the client is. Unscripted, some celebrities may say something that only compounds a problem.

Music's "it" couple, Beyoncé and Jay-Z, became embroiled in controversy when their security detail was accused of taking over a floor in Lenox Hill Hospital, inconveniencing other maternity patients. Fuel was added to the fire when Beyoncé was quoted in a magazine saying, "Security was very tight, but not just for the sake of it, it was for the security of our daughter." Critics said the statement was insensitive to inconvenienced families. A publicist for Beyoncé allegedly said the statement was "completely made up" just to sell magazines.

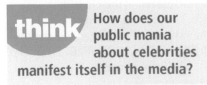

think How does our public mania about celebrities manifest itself in the media?

2 Prepare a basic four-page (or shorter) biography of the client. News and feature angles should be placed high in this "bio," so an editor or producer can find them quickly.

3 Assemble the biography, photos, videos, and personal background items in a media kit designed for extensive distribution via printed folders, DVDs, and website postings.

4 Determine precisely what is to be sold. Is the purpose solely to increase public awareness of the individual, or is it to publicize the client's team or product, such as a new television series, motion picture, or book?

5 Decide which audiences are the most important to reach.

6 Make telephone and e-mail pitches to editors and program directors to propose print and on-air interviews with the client. Every pitch should include a news or feature angle for the interviewer to develop.

An interview in an important magazine—a rising movie star in *Cosmopolitan* or *InStyle* or a young athlete in *Sports Illustrated* for example—has major impact among readers. Backstage maneuvering often takes place before such an interview appears. Agents for entertainers on their way up eagerly seek to obtain interviews. When a personality is "hot," however, publicists are in the enviable position of auctioning off exclusive photos and interviews to the highest bidder. People magazine, for example, paid $5 million for the first public pictures of Jennifer Lopez, Mark Anthony, and their newborn twins.

Photographs and video clips of the client should be submitted to traditional media, as well as websites as often as possible and justifiable. Media kits usually include the standard head-and-shoulders portrait, often called a "mug shot." Photographs of the client appearing at a newsworthy event such as an awards ceremony may be published with just a caption, without an accompanying story. The publicist and the photographer should be inventive, putting the client into unusual situations. If the client seeks national attention, material needs to be submitted to AP and Reuters for distribution to hundreds of newspapers and posted to online news sites.

> **Celebrities continue to embrace individual publicity because it feeds the same curiosity that has given rise to gossip websites and reality shows. But whereas bad publicity can initiate or rekindle interest in a celebrity, negative publicity is potentially more harmful to a company or brand.**
>
> Rosanna M. Fiske, chair and CEO, Public Relations Society of America

The entertainment business generates immense amounts of publicity for individuals and shows with the Oscar, Golden Globe, and Emmy awards. Winning a Golden Globe, an Emmy, or an Academy Award bolsters a performer's career.

think How can a probing interview with a client help a publicist promote the client more effectively and creatively?

Another way to intensify awareness of clients is to arrange for individuals to appear frequently in public places. Many organizations regularly pay for celebrities of various types to appear at a conference, a trade show, or even a store opening. When Avon celebrated its 125th anniversary with events in 16 cities, actresses Reese Witherspoon and Zoe Saldana and musician Fergie made appearances. Appearances like these benefit the sponsor by attracting crowds and help the entertainers and athletes stay in the public eye.

Clients who employ publicists want tangible results in return for their fees. To prove their worth, publicists need to compile and analyze the results of personality campaigns to determine the effectiveness of the various methods used. Tear sheets, photographs, copies of news releases, and video clips of their public appearances, and even stats on the number of followers on Twitter (Lady Gaga is the champ with 11.3 million followers) should be provided to clients. Monitoring services such as Cision and Vocus can help publicists assemble this material. At the end of campaigns, or at intervals in long-term programs, summaries of what has been accomplished should be submitted to clients.

SocialMediaInAction

Celebrities Thrive and Crash in 140 characters

Twitter, the microblogging phenomenon, has been both boon and bane for celebrities. Unknown comedy writers have found success by posting 140-character jokes. Superstars have promoted and damaged their reputations through their tweets. Politicians and executives have destroyed and rehabilitated their images.

Jen Statsky, for example, may not be a household name, but thanks to Twitter, her jokes are now delivered by Jimmy Fallon. Statsky originally applied as a writer for Fallon's late night show and didn't make the cut. After honing her one-liners through her Twitter account, however, Statsky got the late night gig. "It just got me in the practice of writing jokes every single day and being mindful of making them as punchy as possible," Statsky told the *New York Times*. Ashton Kutcher was so skilled at using social media that he became the first celebrity to draw 1 million followers; he even co-founded social media consulting company

Katalyst. But Kutcher caused an uproar when he tweeted, "How do you fire Jo Pa?" when Penn State football coach Joe Paterno was under fire for not adequately reporting sexual abuse allegations regarding a former assistant coach. After apologizing for being insensitive, Kutcher pledged to have Katalyst manage his Twitter account in the future.

New York Democratic congressman Anthony Weiner ended his career when he tweeted photos of himself in underwear to a college-aged woman. The tweets became public, and after initial denials and finger-pointing, Weiner admitted his gross error in judgment and resigned his post. Media mogul Rupert Murdoch was embattled when journalists at *News of the World* were accused of intercepting cell phone calls of British royals, among others. Part of his plan for redemption was to be more accessible and personable through a Twitter account. In a 2012 New Year's Eve tweet, he resolved to "try to maintain humility and always curiosity. And of course diet!"

"There was a time from 2008 to 2011 where Twitter was like, whatever was on your mind you tweeted about it—literally mindlessly," Cooper Lawrence, author of *The Cult of Celebrity*, told Portfolio.com. "Now you're going to see the other side of the bell curve, where people are more cautious."

> "A lot of people don't realize what Twitter is really about. It's very simple, really. It's about relationships. People who realize this tend to use it well.

Ben Johncock, social media expert and founder of the Twitter Consultancy

1. What are the best and worst uses of Twitter you've seen by celebrities?

2. How would you employ Twitter if you were developing a public relations campaign for a celebrity or politician?

3. Do you think people are being more cautious with Twitter, as Lawrence suggests? Why or why not?

PROMOTING AN
Entertainment Event

Attracting attendance at an event—anything from a theatrical performance to a fund-raising fashion show or a street carnival—requires a well-planned publicity campaign.

The primary goal of any campaign for an entertainment event is to sell tickets. An advance publicity buildup informs listeners, readers, and viewers that an event will occur and stimulates their desire to attend. Stories about a motion picture, rock concert, book signing, or similar commercial activity should focus on the personalities, styles, and popularity of the activities or products. Every time a product or show is mentioned, public awareness grows. Astute practitioners search for fresh news angles to generate as many stories as possible.

The "Drip-Drip-Drip" Technique

Motion picture studios, television production firms, and networks operate according to the principle of "drip-drip-drip" publicity when a show is being shot. In other words, a steady output of information is produced. For instance, a public relations specialist, called a unit man or woman, will be assigned to a film during production. That person turns out a series of stories for the general and trade press and plays host to media visitors to the set. In addition, television networks mail out daily news bulletins about their shows to media reviewers, cable TV channels such as TMZ, and popular bloggers who cover the entertainment industry. Both TV networks and film studios also invite reporters and reviewers to preview new programs and interview their stars. The heaviest barrage of publicity is released shortly before a show's opening.

For *The Twilight Series: Breaking Dawn*, the publicity arm of the film's production studio coordinated accommodations for the crowd of fans who camped out in downtown Los Angeles for up to five days preceding the movie's red carpet premiere. Media coverage of the accommodations and surrounding events provided preshow publicity fodder and a stream of stories for Hollywood reporters.

The *Twilight* public relations events included concerts featuring acts from the *Breaking Dawn* soundtrack as well as earlier films from the *Twilight* series playing on a giant screen outside the Nokia Theater each night. Beyond being first in line for the movie, the camping fans also vied for a prime location to watch the movie's stars arrive and walk the red carpet.

The pre-premiere vigil has become a tradition for *Twilight* fans. For the *Breaking Dawn* vigil, *Twilight* series author Stephanie Meyer showed up and handed out 600 autographed copies of *Breaking Dawn*, according to *USA Today*.

think — Why is this technique referred to as "drip-drip-drip" publicity?

A much-hailed publicity tactic is to have a star unveil his or her star on the Hollywood Walk of Fame just before the star's new film or show appears. When Boyz II Men was awarded the 2,456th star in January 2012, the R&B group was recognized for the 60 million records it had sold. Later the same month, Boyz II Men began a 17-city European concert tour followed by a U.S. tour to promote its new album, *Twenty*. Group member Shawn Stockman was also promoting *The Sing-Off*, an a capella group television show on which he is a judge. The day of the star ceremony, Boyz II Men tweeted: "We have sang [sic] for the Pope, Mandela, Presidents, Olympics, Super Bowls. But this today has us humbled like never before … twenty years ago, we shot [the] Motownphilly video, not sure what was going to happen. We are some blessed men!"

Was the timing of the star ceremonies and the release of the new album, concert tour, and singing show a coincidence, or was it part of a drip-drip-drip campaign aimed at selling more music and tickets?

One danger of excessive promotion of a celebrity is that audience expectations may become too high, so that the performance proves to be a disappointment. A skilled practitioner will stay away from "hype" that can lead to a sense of anticlimax.

Movies and Television

Motion picture public relations departments use market research, demographics, and psychographics

A study sponsored by a consortium of diverse interested parties, such as Microsoft, MovieTickets.com, and Facebook, among others, cites trends in information gathering that should shape public relations tactics for the promotion of both films and the celebrities who star in them.

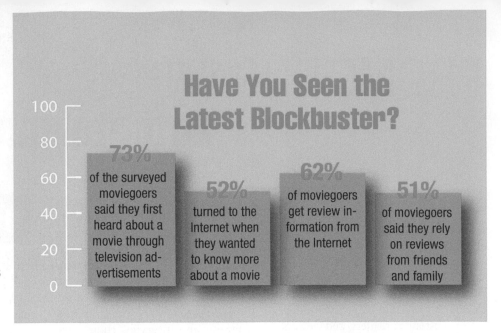

Have You Seen the Latest Blockbuster?

73% of the surveyed moviegoers said they first heard about a movie through television advertisements

52% turned to the Internet when they wanted to know more about a movie

62% of moviegoers get review information from the Internet

51% of moviegoers said they rely on reviews from friends and family

to define their target audiences. Most motion picture publicity is predominantly aimed at 12- to 24-year-olds, who make up the largest movie-going audience.

Professional entertainment publicity work is concentrated in New York and Los Angeles, the former as the nation's theatrical center and the latter as the motion picture center. American television production is also divided primarily between

these two cities, with the larger portion occurring in Los Angeles.

A typical Los Angeles–area public relations firm specializing in personalities and entertainment has two staffs: "planters," who deliver to media offices publicity stories about individual clients and projects, and "bookers," who place clients on talk shows and set up other public appearances. Some publicity stories are intended for general release; others are prepared

specifically for a single media outlet such as a syndicated Hollywood columnist or a major newspaper. The latter type is marked "exclusive," permitting the publication, station, or website that reports the item to claim credit for "breaking" the story.

Firms may provide tickets for a new movie to radio stations, where disc jockeys award them to listeners as prizes in on-air contests. In the process, these announcers mention

Television is a high-stakes business characterized by a great deal of uncertainty. The national television networks—ABC, CBS, NBC, Fox, and CW—offer dozens of pilot programs, most of which prove to lack staying power. Some pilots survive, but many others fail. *The Playboy Club* was axed by NBC after only three episodes. It was maligned by both women's rights groups and the Parents Television Council for objectifying women. Several advertisers dropped out in the second week. Despite being wildly popular in the 1970s, a remake of *Charlie's Angels* failed to satisfy either critics or its audience and was quickly chopped by ABC. On the positive side, *Revenge* was picked up for a full season and ABC ordered additional scripts for sitcom *Happy Endings.*

Entertainment, Sports, and Tourism

the name of the movie dozens of times. Occasionally firms invite media guests to glamorous premieres at distant locales, leveraging the luxury vacation to entice guests to speak highly of the show they attend. For such services to individual or corporate entertainment clients, major Hollywood publicists charge thousands of dollars a month. One informal study showed monthly retainers ranging from $1,500 to $4,000. Some publicists require a three-month minimum contract. The major studios and networks have their own public relations staffs.

Entertainment firms also may specialize in arranging product placements in movies and television programs. Usually movie or television producers trade visible placement of a product in a show or film in exchange for free use of the item.

The fast-food industry provides excellent opportunities for market-based public relations, involving giveaways of character figures with meals. Movies such as *Transformers: Dark of the Moon* received huge boosts in visibility and ticket sales from their relationships with fast-food purveyors. McDonald's had a variety of tie-ins worldwide. It offered six action figures (three

Movies like *Transformers* provide promoters an ideal venue for product placement.

autobots and three decepticons) in its Happy Meals. In Japanese Happy Meals, toy transformers popped out of toy hamburgers, shakes, and fries.

Worldwide and diverse product placement in *Transformers* is evidenced in the following press release excerpt from Ogilvy: "Tomorrow in the mainland China premiere of *Transformers: Dark of the Moon* moviegoers will be introduced to an exciting new character called Brains, an Autobot that camouflages in plain sight as a Lenovo Think-Pad Edge Plus laptop. The birth of Brains is the result of a 360 Degree integrated marketing effort by

Ogilvy Entertainment and Lenovo ThinkPad, in collaboration with acclaimed director Michael Bay."

The release also noted that, prior to China, the Lenovo campaign had reached moviegoers in the U.S., Russia, India, and Japan.

Transformers: Dark of the Moon reportedly had 68 products or brands placed throughout the movie. Among those, according to BrandChannel, were Apple, Mercedes-Benz, Ferrari, Nokia, Adidas, Nike, and Starbucks. Credits even noted that the movie was produced "In Association with [toymaker] Hasbro."

Sports PUBLICITY

The sports mania flourishing in the United States and around the world is stimulated by intense public relations efforts. Publicity programs at both the college and professional levels seek to arouse public interest in teams and players, sell tickets to games, and promote the corporate sponsors that subsidize events. Sports publicists also work with marketing specialists to drive sales of souvenirs and clothing, a lucrative sideline for many teams.

"For athletes, one minute you can be the flavor of the week, and the next you're on the chopping block.... As people in the limelight, athletes are easy prey, and once there is a crack in the armor, the story, true or not, will be out there for the world to see. It's important to know how to react to a problem, and the best medium to utilize to effectively communicate during a crisis.... The goal is to always be prepared to preserve and protect your brand."

Rich Nichols, legal crisis communications expert, in *PRO Sports Communications* blog

Entertainment, Sports, and Tourism

> ## Lacrosse's trend lines in every way we could measure were impressive and made us believe that this is a place where we could grow and be a part of something that would over time be very big.
>
> Michigan Athletic Director Dave Brandon, after announcing that the university would add both men's and women's lacrosse to its varsity sports

Sports public relations employs the elements of any public relations activity. Sports PR professionals need to be experts in relationship management, media relations, ethics and social responsibility, community relations, crisis communication, marketing communications, consumer (fan) relations, player relations and promotion, intercultural and international public relations, and more.

Sports publicists use the normal tools of public relations—media kits, statistics, interviews, television appearances, and the like—to distribute information about their clients. But conveying stats and facts is only part of their role—they also try to stir emotions. For college publicists, this goal means creating enthusiasm among alumni and making schools seem glamorous and exciting so that they can successfully recruit high school students to matriculate. Publicists for professional teams work to make them appear to be hometown representatives of civic pride, not merely athletes playing for high salaries.

Sometimes efforts succeed spectacularly, if a team wins. When a team is losing, however, the sports publicist's life turns grim. He or she must find ways to soothe public displeasure through methods such as having players conduct clinics at playgrounds and make sympathetic visits to hospitals.

In America, sports is big business, garnering $414 billion in gross annual revenues. Unfortunately, an unseemly side sometimes crops up in sports coverage. Public relations plays a critical role in these situations in sports, going far beyond the mere promotion of celebrities to provide sports crisis management. According to John Eckel, formerly of Hill & Knowlton's sports division, professional communicators must deal with the media focus

Athletes Who Tweet

While some sports franchises have clamped down on athletes' tweeting habits, the Professional Golf Association (PGA) has embraced the social medium. In 2012, the PGA had a PGA Tour Twitter account with more than 144,000 followers. The *New York Times* reported, "According to numbers compiled by the PGA Tour, 111 pros who are tour members or former members are part of the universe of 175 million registered Twitter users." Pro golfer Stewart Cink had more than 1.2 million followers, but that was modest compared to other athletes. The top 10 most-followed athletes on Twitter in 2012 were:

Kaká, midfielder, Real Madrid (Spain): 8,062,984 followers

Cristiano Ronaldo, winger, Real Madrid (Spain): 6,346,968 followers

Shaquille O'Neal, retired NBA center (Magic, Lakers, Heat, etc.): 4,844,036 followers

LeBron James, forward, Miami Heat: 3,324,671 followers

Lance Armstrong, professional cyclist: 3,228,411 followers

Chad Ochocinco (née Johnson), wide receiver, New England Patriots: 3,160,419 followers

Ronaldinho Gaúcho, midfielder, AC Milan (Italy): 2,897,364 followers

Dwight Howard, center, Orlando Magic: 2,890,860 followers

Neymar Júnior, striker, Santos (Brazil): 2,882,624 followers

Tony Hawk, professional skateboarder: 2,816,394 followers

on negatively charged issues ranging from player strikes to high ticket and concession costs to sex scandals to boorish athletes who deny that they are role models, even while they benefit from their visibility.

Sponsorship management is another key aspect of public relations in the sports world. The advertising agency DDB Worldwide studied the effectiveness of a very high-profile sponsorship—the Summer Olympics. The agency found that for a company to benefit in terms of sales and goodwill, the Olympic Games require a huge commitment of $100 million per sponsor, plus extensive costs in marketing that sponsorship.

Despite the estimated $45 billion annually spent worldwide on sponsoring sports events, tallying the benefits of these relationships is still a less-than-scientific endeavor. With that point in mind, Publicis Groupe developed an optical-resolution technology to scan sports broadcasts for brand names and images. According to the *Wall Street Journal*, "The scan tracks the percentage of the TV screen that is taken up by an individual corporate logo, as well as the logo's location on the screen and whether there are other brands on the screen at the same time. The data are then used to calculate the financial value of the screen time, based on a formula loosely tied to the cost of TV ad time." The Publicis Groupe program, for example, found that Honda was the highest-scoring brand in terms of exposure during the Indy 500 race broadcast on ABC. The data show that Honda received 1,400 seconds of broadcast exposure, estimated to be worth $1.33 million.

Sponsorships may also have an effect on a company's stock price. When University of Alabama professor Lance Kinney studied 61 sports event sponsorships, he found a significant increase in the stock prices of companies sponsoring Olympic events and baseball. Although no direct causal link can be proven, the relationship between sports sponsorships and corporate net worth is an interesting area of continuing research.

Because the public yearns for heroes, publicists focus on building up the images of star players, sometimes to excess.

Soccer is the world's most popular sport, and the World Cup is the most costly of all sports sponsorships. The 2010 FIFA World Cup, in South Africa, had a 48-game schedule. Attendance at the South Africa competition reached almost 3.2 million, with an average of 49,670 fans attending each match. The next World Cup will be hosted by Brazil in 2014. Every four years, these soccer matches are seen by billions of viewers around the world. Since 1970, Adidas has produced the official soccer balls for the World Cups. Soccer fans see the Adidas three-stripe logo on match balls, referee uniforms, outfits worn by volunteers, and billboards in and around the stadiums where the matches take place. Adidas also had exclusive rights to air advertisements during broadcasts of games in the United States by ABC and ESPN. Adidas paid $351 million to the World Cup's governing body, the Federation Internationale de Football (FIFA), for these sponsorship rights, which extend through 2014. In addition, the Adidas partnership gives it prominent marketing placement on FIFA's World Cup website, which organizers estimate attracts 4 billion visitors during the tournament alone. Nike, the archrival of Adidas, paid an estimated $144 million to be the official sponsor of the Brazilian team, which has won more World Cup championships than any other nation, until 2018.

Racing Sausages Win Fans' Hearts

In 1974, the San Diego Chicken made its debut at a Padres baseball game. The mascot has now grown beyond the San Diego Padres and is known as "The Famous Chicken." The chicken has made appearances at 8,500 ball games and 17,000 events, including parades, trade shows, conventions, and banquets. The chicken laid the foundation for what has become a nearly expected part of ball games at the professional, collegiate, and even high school level. Cartoon-like mascots are now commonplace.

According to a survey sponsored by *Forbes* magazine, the San Diego Chicken is the most well known mascot; the Milwaukee Brewers's Racing Sausages come in fourth. As evidence that sports promotion can be quantified, the *Forbes* survey found that awareness of the Racing Sausages was 10.6 percent, appeal was 71.2 percent, and affiliation recognition (among those aware of the mascot) was 78.6 percent. By comparison, the San Diego Chicken had 20.2 percent awareness, 78.7 percent appeal, and 92.4 percent affiliation recognition.

The Racing Sausages, sponsored by Klement's Sausages, first appeared at Brewers games in the mid-1990s. The first characters to race were Brett, the Bratwurst, Stosh, the Polish Sausage, and Guido, the Italian Sausage. They were later joined by Frankie Furter, the Hot Dog, and Cinco, the Chorizo. The five Racing Sausages now run at every Brewers home game.

The sausage races engage fans. The inning before the race, spectators are prompted by the scoreboard to text their choice for today's race's winner. "The sausages are so popular that they make public appearances, and the Brewers organized a five-kilometer run/walk for charity with five runners in the costumes," according to the *New York Times*. At Sunday games, the "adult" sausages do a mid-race hand-off to kids in similar costumes. Fans can follow the sausages on the "Klement's Official Racing Sausages" Facebook page and play a racing sausages video game at the sausages' online home at Klements.com.

But the sausages are not spokespersons, and the races are not fixed. Former racers admitted to the *Times* that they were instructed not to talk to anyone and to run a true race. "The sausages don't talk," Tyler Barnes, Brewers vice president for communications told the *New York Times*. "It's one of the basic rules of racing meat."

One example of the sausages' contribution to the community was an event in which area CEOs wore the costumes and raced to benefit the United Way. The Racine, WI, *Journal-Times* reported: "Attendees could purchase a hot dog lunch and/or bet on the winning sausages for the chance to win prizes." The Racing Sausages serve as an illustration of how a seemingly silly activity (famous athlete and sports commentator Joe Garagiola once complained that "baseball is being taken over by the Muppets") can serve a serious public relations purpose.

1 How, if at all, does your school use costumed mascots for public relations purposes?

2 What publics do sports public relations practitioners target?

3 What are other ways the Brewers could use the sausage races to actively engage fans?

Travel PROMOTION

As soon as people collect a bit of money in their pockets, they tend to want to go places and see things. Stimulating that desire and turning it into the purchase of tickets is the goal of the travel industry. The U.S. Travel Association reports that travel and tourism is a $759 billion industry and accounts for one out of every nine jobs in the U.S. Public relations plays an essential role in the travel and tourism industry—not only in attracting visitors to destinations, but also in keeping them happy once they arrive. Jobs range from working for destinations like theme parks or even countries to leading local or regional convention and visitors bureaus (CVB) to conducting public relations for a cruise line, and many more.

Traditionally, the practice of travel public relations has involved three steps:

1 Stimulating the public's desire to visit a place.

2 Arranging for the travelers to reach their destinations.

3 Making certain that visitors are comfortable, well treated, and entertained during their stay.

Interest in travel can be stimulated through articles in magazines and newspapers, alluring brochures distributed by travel agents and by direct mail, travel films and videos, and presentations on the World Wide Web. Locations also solicit associations and companies, encouraging them to hold conventions in particular locations to encourage group travel.

Some publications have their own travel writing staff; others hire freelance writers and photographers. Well-crafted articles by public relations practitioners about travel destinations often are published, too, as long as they are written in an informational manner without resorting to blatant salesmanship and purple prose.

Treating travelers well is critical in the travel and tourist industry. If a person spends a large sum on a trip, but then encounters poor accommodations, rude hotel clerks, misplaced luggage, and inferior sightseeing arrangements, he or she comes home angry. Even more ominously for the destination, unhappy travelers readily tell their friends how bad the trip was.

That said, even the best arrangements go awry at times. Planes are late, tour members miss the bus, and bad weather riles tempers. This is where the personal touch means so much. Careful training of travel personnel is essential. Many travelers, especially in foreign countries, are uneasy in strange surroundings and depend more on others than they would at home.

b t w ...

Diane Centeno, director of marketing for SeaWorld Parks and Entertainment, recently explained the workings of public relations in a theme park setting in a posting on a PRSA blog.

"I have been employed in the travel and tourism industry for the past 11 years, working for SeaWorld Parks & Entertainment. While I started my career in health care marketing and public relations—which was an incredibly satisfying experience—when a job opportunity at SeaWorld opened, I could not resist the idea of working for a top-notch theme park that had an amazing brand to proactively promote and communicate to moms and families. I have been able to build relationships with key broadcast, newsprint, and magazine outlets across the United States; dive into social media strategies; work with global communication agencies to promote our brands in key markets like the United Kingdom, Brazil, and South America; form partnerships with area convention and visitors bureaus in Virginia and Florida; travel for competitive research (it's always fun to visit another tourist attraction in the name of work); and host thousands of media personnel at our parks. While I have ridden roller coasters with reporters to show them our new attractions firsthand, given celebrities tours and publicized their visits to our parks, and traveled with animals for in-studio TV appearances, I have also been able to develop expertise in the areas of public affairs and employee communications in my ever-expanding roles."

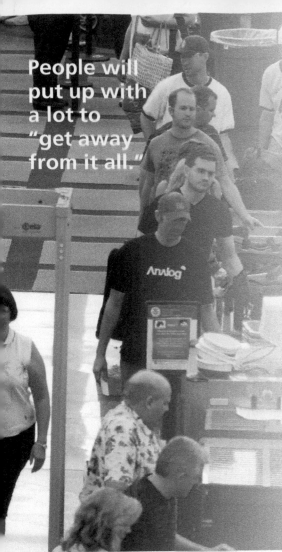

People will put up with a lot to "get away from it all."

Appeals to Target Audiences

Travel promoters identify target audiences, creating special appeals and trips for them. Great Britain's publicity in the United States is an example of a successful effort. It's an appealing invitation to visit the country's historic places and pageants. Promoters also highlight London theatrical tours, golf expeditions to famous courses in Scotland, genealogical research parties for those seeking family roots, and tours of famous cathedrals.

Packaging is a key word in travel public relations. Cruises for family reunions or school groups, family skiing vacations, archaeological expeditions, and even trips to remote Tibet are just a few of the so-called niche travel packages that are offered. A package usually consists of prepaid arrangements for transportation, housing, most meals, and entertainment, with a professional escort to handle the details. Supplementary side trips often are offered for extra fees.

The largest special travel audience is people older than age 40, and the 60-plus age cohort makes up a large

 think How do public relations professionals stimulate tourist interest in new locations?

percentage of cruise ship passengers. Many retirees have time to travel, and some have ample money to do so. Travelers born before 1946 take an average of 4.1 leisure trips a year. Business travelers in this category take an average of 6.7 business trips. Older boomers, those born from 1946 through 1954, take an average of 4.4 leisure trips a year, and business travelers in that age group take about 10.1 business trips. Hotels, motels, and airlines frequently offer discounts to attract these audiences. As a means of keeping old-school loyalties alive, many colleges conduct alumni tours, which are heavily

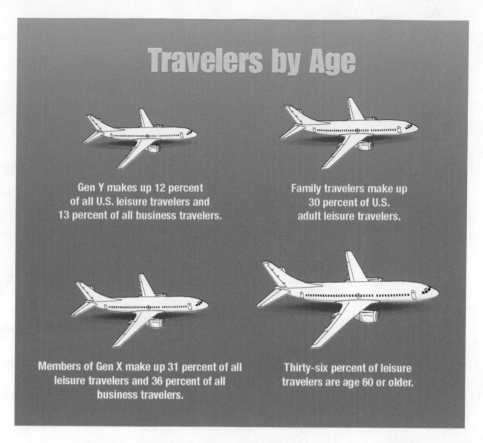

Travelers by Age

Gen Y makes up 12 percent of all U.S. leisure travelers and 13 percent of all business travelers.

Family travelers make up 30 percent of U.S. adult leisure travelers.

Members of Gen X make up 31 percent of all leisure travelers and 36 percent of all business travelers.

Thirty-six percent of leisure travelers are age 60 or older.

attended by senior citizens. A large percentage of cruise passengers, especially on longer voyages, are retirees. Alert travel promoters design trips with them in mind, including such niceties as pairing compatible widows to share cabins and arranging shore trips that require little walking.

Tourism in Times of Crisis

Crisis management is an important part of public relations in the travel industry, just as it is in corporate work. Crises come in many forms, from dangerous political crises to small but embarrassing blips.

Travel public relations professionals need to be prepared to deal with all sorts of crises. In 2012, the Costa Concordia, an Italian cruise liner run by the Costa cruise company, a subsidiary of Carnival Cruise lines, ran aground near Giglio, an island off the Tuscany coast.

Many of the 4,200 passengers complained that when the ship

initially lost power, cruise staff told passengers there was an electrical problem and they should return to their cabins until notified otherwise. It wasn't until the ship began to tilt that passengers were told the ship had hit a boulder that left a 160-foot gash in the ship's hull. Crew members were of no help, passengers complained, when evacuation began. In fact, the captain was accused of abandoning ship. Mayhem resulted, with passengers panicking and pushing their way to lifeboats, according to reports.

Within hours of the crisis, global PR firm Burson-Marsteller helped craft and release information regarding how many people were evacuated and the company's devotion to "provide all the needed assistance." Early communication from the cruise line included a spokesperson saying the captain "immediately understood the severity of the situation" and "performed a maneuver intended to protect both guests and crew," according to reports in the *New York Times*.

But, within three days of the crash, company officials began pointing fingers at the captain. At what the *Times* characterized as an "emotional" press conference, a company leader said that the correct route had been programmed into the $563 million ship's navigation computers. "The fact that it left from this course is due solely to a maneuver by the commander that was unapproved, unauthorized and unknown to [cruise company] Costa." Leaked transcripts of interrogation of the captain show him claiming that company officials had asked him to cruise near the island "for publicity."

Days after the wreck, shares of parent company Carnival Corporation dropped by 17 percent. Company officials predicted a loss of $95 million while the ship was out of service and at least $600 million in insurance costs.

Sometimes public relations crises move from bad to worse for companies. Only six weeks after the Costa Concordia accident, when international news coverage was beginning

to wane, a sister ship—the Costa Allegra—experienced a fire that left the ship without power in pirate-infested waters in the Indian Ocean. It took days for the ship to be towed to safety. Meanwhile, tourists onboard were sleeping on deck without electricity for lights or air conditioning, working toilets, or hot food.

The Costa Concordia tragedy illustrates the complexity of crises in the travel industry and the many players with whom public relations professionals must interact.

Among other areas of concern, travel firms need to make certain that they provide equal facilities and service to all. They also need to ensure that their facilities and practices are environmentally sound or risk negative publicity.

What Would You Do?

A Question of Ethics

Imagine that you are the public relations representative for a high-profile, major league athlete. You admire your client, perhaps even lionize him. You've been helping him fight charges that he used performance-enhancing drugs. One day, as you visit with him in the stadium locker room, you see a needle and drug bottle incompletely covered by some dirty socks. You begin to ask about it, but then decide to wait and think it over.

So what should you do? If you don't ask your client for more details, then you can continue to state that you know nothing about his drug use. Perhaps it was just a pain reliever, after all. If you do ask and find out that what you saw was, indeed, some form of performance-enhancing substance, do you continue your campaign to defend your client, do you quit representing him, or do you take some other step? If you continue representing him, do you talk to him about what you saw? Why or why not?

Write a short essay on how you would handle this situation. Be clear on why you would make your choices and how public relations should be used in the situation.

summary

Which Elements Are Essential for an Effective Personality Campaign?

- A public relations practitioner planning a campaign to generate awareness of an individual interviews the client, prepares a biography, plans a marketing strategy, and conducts the campaign through news releases, photographs, and public appearances.

How Can a Publicity Campaign Increase Event Attendance?

- Publicity campaigns include publicity to stimulate ticket sales. The "drip-drip-drip" technique involves a steady output of information as the event is being planned.

- The entertainment industry defines target audiences to promote motion pictures and television shows.

What Role Does Public Relations Play in the Sports Mania Flourishing Around the World?

- Sports publicists promote both college and professional teams. This effort becomes more difficult when a team isn't winning.

- Some publicity focuses on building images of star players.

What Role Does Public Relations Play in Attracting Visitors to Destinations and Keeping Them Happy Once They Arrive?

- Travel promotion involves increasing the public's desire to visit a place, arranging for travelers to reach it, making sure they enjoy their trips, and ensuring their safety.

questions
FOR REVIEW AND DISCUSSION

1 What is the first step in preparing a campaign to increase the public's awareness of an individual client?

2 Why do practitioners put emphasis on certain players on sports teams?

3 What are the basic phases of travel promotion?

4 What do demographic and technology changes mean for the future of promotion in the movie industry?

5 How are sports sponsorships leveraged by companies?

6 Why do you think Adidas pays such a premium for its sponsorship of the World Cup?

7 Why is it important for cruise ship companies and airlines to be well versed in crisis communication strategies?

MySearchLab®

Mexico Leans on PR to Lure Back Tourists

Alexandra Bruell | June 26, 2011

Advertising Age

Countries, like products, are considered "brands."

Tourism is big business and nations spend considerable amounts of money competing with each other to lure visitors. In Mexico, it's a $15 billion business.

Research indicates that public relations strategies are more effective for building brand and reputation than traditional advertising.

Research shows that individuals are more influenced by their friends, even virtual ones, than by traditional advertising.

Mexico's new branding campaign promotes atypical attractions, like underground rivers, swimming with whale sharks, and camping.

Mexico is undoubtedly a challenged brand. Drug cartels, violence, murder, and kidnappings have been grabbing headlines, thus deterring tourists who typically flock to the country for its beaches, Mayan archaeological sites, and tequila.

To turn things around, the Mexico Tourism Board is launching an offensive on two fronts: one, a positive branding campaign carrying the tagline, "The Place You Thought You Knew," and the other, a heightened PR effort to dismantle drug-and-violence-related U.S. press. While the first effort won't touch the second with a 10-foot-pole, both represent a shift in marketing investments to favor PR and digital, as well as an attempt to make people feel better about traveling to Mexico.

At the helm of the radical shift in marketing dollars is CMO Gerardo Lianes, who took on the role just four months ago. He plans to reallocate up to one-quarter of the Mexico Tourism Board's $100 million global marketing budget, much of which has been spent on traditional media buys in the past, to public relations and digital efforts. His approach will see PR spending double to $21 million, while traditional media spending will shrink from $21 million in 2010 to an expected $6 million next year.

"We believe word-of-mouth is getting to be a better tool for us right now, especially now that we're seeing some not-so-positive things in the media, especially in the U.S.," Mr. Lianes said.

Mr. Lianes has experience on both the agency and marketer sides of the business—he worked on the launch of Diet Coke in Mexico—but when the head marketing role at the Mexico Tourism Board opened up, he jumped at it. There's nothing quite as appealingly challenging as Mexico, he said. "Managing a country's brand is big," Mr. Lianes said.

"I knew what was being said and done outside of the country."

Much of the "not-so-positive" media has appeared in mainstream publications, with claims that cartel-related violence and murder, typically contained to the U.S.-Mexico border areas, has seeped into tourist destinations. Working with Ogilvy PR, Mr. Lianes has developed a public relations strategy. "We're reaching out to leader media outlets like Bloomberg, Newsweek, and CNN to help us tell our side of the story and get the facts straight," Mr. Lianes said. "We're not denying that there are some areas of the country that have problems, but we're saying if you hear something bad in Chicago, it wouldn't stop you from going to Los Angeles."

Despite reports of murder in tourist regions like Acapulco, Mr. Lianes is pushing the message that the crime index of 4 murders per 100,000 inhabitants in the entire country isn't much different from that of a city like New York or Houston, which he says have indexes of 16 and 14 respectively.

Still, thanks to press reports, not to mention an April travel warning from the U.S. Department of State, Mr. Lianes is battling a tourism perception problem despite the organization's reports of increases in visitor, hotel development, and occupancy rates. (It is worth stating, however, that those increases are year-over-year and compared to post H1N1 stats.) The *Wall Street Journal* recently reported that tour operators have experienced declines in business and a number of cruise lines have cancelled service to Acapulco. That's where the Mexico Tourism Board's new branding campaign, "The Place You Thought You Knew" comes into play.

The campaign, Mr. Lianes' first branding project, which will likely cost more than $1 million, aims to build awareness, via digital and social media platforms, of "the story people don't know about Mexico." The presence online via Twitter, new YouTube channels, a handful of new Facebook pages and targeted blogger and community engagement.

"There are a lot of Americans living in Mexico and traveling to Mexico," Mr. Lianes said of the group's new emphasis on social media. "It's better that an American talks to an American than having the Mexican government talk to an American."

"I'm trying to look at how do we create strategy to be more applicable in markets, more aggressive and more active in areas where traditionally we haven't been, like digital and social media, mainly because of the moment we're going through: the bad press and the development of social media," Mr. Lianes added. "We old guys are still in the TV and radio world. It's not like that anymore."

The organization's agency roster includes Havas Media and Vantage Strategies for online media, ZenithOptimedia for traditional media, Publicis for creative, Ogilvy PR for PR and social media, and Planet Hollywood for celebrity PR.

The strategy is to create a more interactive platform that can build engagement and even "buzz" for Mexico as an attractive tourism destination.

The Edelman Trust Barometer for 2012 found that for most people "people like myself" are more credible sources of information than company or government spokespersons.

It is extremely difficult to change a person's perceptions. One method is to create what is called cognitive dissonance - present facts and evidence that support a new view.

When individuals have no personal experience or knowledge of an issue or topic, the media is influential in shaping their perceptions of a nation as a tourist destination.

Mexico, in 2009, also suffered a major drop in tourism as the result of the H1NI (swine flu) pandemic that struck Mexico City.

Text Credits

Credits are listed in order of appearance.

Author: Diane Centeno, APR, Corporate Director, Advertising, Media & Brand at Sea-World Parks & Entertainment (2011), approx. 200 words. In "Intro to Travel and Tourism PR: Part One," from prnewpros.prsa.org, http://prnewpros.prsa.org/?p=703.; Reprinted by permission of Advertising Age.

Photo Credits

Credits are listed in order of appearance.

spfotocz/Shutterstock; Zuma/Zuma Wire Service/Alamy; ZUMA Wire Service/Alamy; Allstar Picture Library/Alamy; Allstar Picture Library/Alamy; AF archive/Alamy; Photos 12/Alamy; Shawn Pecor/Shutterstock; (tr) Allen Eyestone/The Palm Beach Post/ZUMA Wire Service/Alamy; Walter G. Arce AiWire/Walter G. Arce ASP/AiWire/Newscom; (cl) Peter Baxter/Shutterstock; Aurora Photos/Alamy; ZUMA Press, Inc./Alamy

Tactics image: Petr Z/Shutterstock
Tablet image: Falconia/Shutterstock

Nonprofit, Health, and Education

From Chapter 18 of *Think Public Relations*, 2013 Edition. Dennis L. Wilcox, Glen T. Cameron, Bryan H. Reber, Jae-Hwa Shin.

402

Nonprofit, Health, and Education

Faith-Based Advocacy Comes of Age

Faith-based organizations, one of the many types of nonprofit organizations, have taken an increasingly prominent role in social, political, and ethical debates in the last 30 years. From Jerry Falwell's Moral Majority of the early 1980s to Burns Strider's American Values Network, churches and religious leaders are sounding off about issues in ways not dreamed of by previous generations. Many faith-based organizations are not shy about sharing their views on hot-button issues such as climate change, gay marriage, or health care reform.

Well-organized and well-supported faith-based organizations have also enlisted the help of public relations and public affairs specialists. The U.S. Conference of Catholic Bishops maintains a media relations professional to promote its views on topics that churches have traditionally been involved in such as abortion as well as emerging issues such immigration reform. Faith in Public Life, a group founded by Mary Burns, who served as presidential candidate Hillary Clinton's faith advisor in 2008, has partnered with the Harvard University Hauser Center to advocate on behalf of the people of Vieques, an island off the coast of Puerto Rico devastated by U.S. Navy weapons testing.

The environment has also become a key talking point for some religious groups. Whereas conservative religious groups have traditionally sided with industry in opposing greater environmental regulation, the views of many religious groups and peoples are shifting. The U.S. Conference of Catholic Bishops now advocates responsible environmental stewardship; more surprising, so does the Baptist Student Association, a group known for its conservative views.

Nonprofit organizations often are more focused on causes than corporations are, and tend to emphasize advocacy in their efforts to motivate supporters.

1   What sorts of public relations activities do nonprofit organizations such as faith-based organizations engage in?

2   How do the public relations efforts of nonprofits differ from those of corporations?

> What Are the Basic Purposes and Functions of Public Relations in Nonprofit, Health, and Education Organizations?

> What Role Does Public Relations Play in the Fund-Raising Efforts of Nonprofit Organizations?

> Which Public Relations Goals and Tactics Do Nonprofit Advocacy Groups and Social Service Organizations Pursue?

> Which Public Relations Goals and Tactics Do Health and Education Organizations Employ?

The role OF PUBLIC RELATIONS IN NONPROFIT, HEALTH, AND EDUCATION ORGANIZATIONS

Nonprofit organizations, which are also referred to as *charities* or *not-for-profit organizations*, make up a broad area of public relations work. In the United States, there are 1.8 million such groups recognized by the Internal Revenue Service (IRS), according to GuideStar, an organization that compiles information on nonprofits. Approximately 7 million people work in the nonprofit sector. Volunteers contribute about 15 billion hours each year to nonprofit organizations, equivalent to nearly 3 billion dollars calculated at the average wage rate. The range of nonprofit institutions is astounding—from membership organizations, advocacy groups, and social service organizations, to educational organizations, hospitals and health agencies, small city historical societies, and global foundations

Guide Dog News
The quarterly publication of Guide Dogs for the Blind

What Your Support Means

GDB Alumna Holly McKnight of Arlington, Texas, is one of thousands of GDB graduates who extend their thanks to you. "*Pollyann* is my little girl; we'll do anything in the world for each other," she said. "Having a Guide Dog gives you more of a life...When they see a car or a bicycle coming toward you that you may not know is there and they see it and react—when they pull you back or push you back or get in front of you—you know they've literally just saved your life. I've cried on many a street corner, because, well, they're just amazing!"

Pictured, top right: Hugging his Guide Dog Bryson, Terry Blonier waves to the crowd from atop the Natural Balance Pet Food float during the Tournament of Roses Parade on New Year's Day. Bottom right: Holly McKnight and Pollyann.

Guide·Dogs FOR THE BLIND

California Campus: 350 Los Ranchitos Road, San Rafael, CA 94903 | Oregon Campus: 32901 S.E. Kelso Road, Boring, OR 97009

2011 · Volume 61 · No. 1   From the President's Desk   Does Your Dog Surf For Food?   Donor Honor Roll

> The defining characteristic of nonprofit organizations is that they are set up to serve the public good.

that disperse multimillion-dollar grants.

Nonprofit organizations are noncommercial entities whose main purpose is to serve the public interest. By definition, they do not distribute monies to shareholders or owners. This is not to say that nonprofit organizations cannot generate income or hold assets, but rather that a number of complicated restrictions regulate how their income may be generated and how their finances must be managed. From a public relations perspective, nonprofit organizations are often represented as fostering goodwill, and as beacons of social responsibility.

Nonprofits are tax exempt. The federal government grants them this status because these organizations enhance the well-being of their members, as is the case for trade associations, or enhance the human condition in some way, as is the case for environmental groups and medical research organizations. Many nonprofit organizations could not survive if they were taxed. Nonprofit organizations do not have shareholders who invest in the organizations and buy and sell stocks. As a result, they face the never-ending task of raising money to pay their expenses, finance their projects, and recruit both volunteer workers and paid employees.

At first glance, federal and state governments, state universities, and health and human services organizations or nonprofit hospitals might seem to have little in common with the Public Relations Society of America (PRSA), the National Academy of Songwriters, Mothers Against Drunk Driving (MADD), and the American Red Cross. Yet all of these groups engage in the same types of public relations tasks to succeed and thrive.

 think What are the key characteristics of a nonprofit organization?

> "We must be honest and ethical in all that we do. As the stewards of a public trust, we are accountable to the many stakeholders affected by the Foundations' work."
>
> From the "Our Values" document produced by the Doris Duke Charitable Foundation

According to their mission statement, the Maddox Jolie Pitt Foundation is "dedicated to eradicating extreme rural poverty, protecting natural resources and conserving wildlife. MJP promotes sustainable rural economies that directly contribute to the health and vitality of communities, wildlife and forests."

Because these organizations are not profit oriented, the practice of public relations on their behalf differs somewhat from public relations activities conducted in the business world. Traditionally, nonprofit social agencies have been seen as the "good guys" in our society—high-minded, compassionate organizations whose members work to help people achieve better lives.

All nonprofit organizations create communication campaigns and programs, including special events, brochures, radio and television appearances, and websites to stimulate public interest in organizational goals and invite further public involvement. Recruiting volunteers and keeping them enthusiastic are essential ends. Most of these organizations also establish fund-raising goals and formulate plans to raise money, although government agencies are funded primarily through taxes.

Competition, Conflict, and Cooperation

For many nonprofit organizations, partnerships are mutually beneficial. The United Way is a good case in point—many business and nonprofit organizations, ranging from the National Football League to the Advertising Council to numerous local organizations, partner with the United Way. This relationship maximizes donations to the United Way, which are distributed to hundreds of associated charities.

Unfortunately, however, the frustrating reality is that many nonprofits, instead of partnering, compete with one another for members, funds, and other resources. For example, universities or colleges within the same state compete for funding from their respective state governments, even as they enter into collaborative partnerships with one another to obtain federal funding. Hospitals compete for "customers," but need to work together to resolve shared concerns and issues. Government agencies struggle for budget allocations, but then must cooperate to serve the public.

Nonprofit organizations have a willingness to cooperate but must also compete for limited or scarce resources. Sometimes nonprofit groups enter into partnerships based on common interests, such as the United Way. In general, however, when advocating their individual interests, they are no different from business organizations that must struggle for market share.

Competition among nonprofit agencies for donations is intense. For many nonprofit groups, fund-raising, by necessity, is their most time-consuming activity. Without generous contributions from

think Why do the public relations efforts of advocacy groups sometimes clash with those of cultural and religious organizations?

companies and individuals, non-profit organizations could not exist. The scope of philanthropy in the United States and the amount of the money needed to keep voluntary service agencies operating are staggering. In 2010, American contributions to charity totaled $290.89 billion, according to the Giving Institute. This was down from a peak of $311 billion in 2007 before the economic recession, but charities were optimistic for increases in 2011 as the economy

rebounded somewhat. Andrew Watt, CEO of the Association of Fundraising Professionals, told the *Wall Street Journal* that year-end totals for various national groups were "healthier" than expected. In 2011, for example, the Salvation Army's "Red Kettle" campaign raised $147 million, up nearly 4 percent from 2010.

Other funds are donated to specialized nonprofit organizations that do not fall under the "charity" mantle, and still more are contributed by federal, state, and local governments.

Activist groups that espouse certain causes may sometimes come into conflict with other organizations that embrace different values, leading to high-profile disputes. For example, a number of religious organizations tussle with groups that advocate for secular values. The American Civil Liberties Union (ACLU), a nonprofit organization founded in 1920 "to defend and preserve the individual rights and liberties guaranteed to every person in this country by the Constitution and laws of the United States," often clashes with the American Center for Law and Justice, a conservative group founded by Pat Robertson to preserve "religious liberty, the sanctity of human life, and the two-parent, marriage-bound family." Although both organizations state that they are committed to preserving "liberty," their respective views of what constitutes "liberty" are often diametrically opposed.

Fund-raising

Finding ways to pay the bills is a critical challenge for virtually all nonprofit organizations, including those that receive government grants to finance part of their work. Fund-raising methods

are highly developed for nonprofit organizations.

Although the largest, most publicized donations are often made by corporations and foundations, individual contribution totals far

exceed combined corporate and foundation giving. In fact, individual contributions account for approximately 75 percent of annual U.S. philanthropic donations.

The Nature Conservancy — A Charity You Can Trust

Accountability and Transparency

As a charity, The Nature Conservancy holds itself accountable to its members, the public and all that have a stake in the preservation of the world's natural resources.

The Nature Conservancy consistently receives high marks from Charity Navigator and is a BBB Wise Giving Alliance Accredited Charity!

14% General & Administrative

10% Fund Raising & Membership

76% Program*

Source: 2010 Nature Conservancy Annual Report
*The Better Business Bureau and Charity Navigator both applaud Program efficiencies above 66%!

bbb.org/charity

CNP

Organizations such as the Nature Conservancy give donors a breakdown of where contributions are allocated in the interest of transparency.

Depending on their needs, voluntary organizations may try to catch minnows—hundreds of small contributions—or they may angle for the huge marlin—a large corporate gift. Some national organizations raise massive sums. In 2011, the American Red Cross raised approximately $3.3 billion and the Smithsonian Institution received just over $1 billion in contributions.

Charities often receive a flood of donations following well-publicized catastrophes, such as the January 2010 earthquake in Haiti or the Mississippi river floods in the summer of 2011.

Public relations professionals may participate directly in fund-raising by organizing and conducting solicitation programs; alternatively, they may serve as consultants to specialized development departments in their

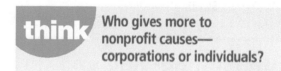

think Who gives more to nonprofit causes—corporations or individuals?

organizations. Some organizations employ professional firms to conduct their fund-raising campaigns on a fee basis. In those instances, the organizations' public relations professionals usually serve a liaison function.

Motivations for Giving

An understanding of what motivates individuals and companies to give money or volunteer their time is important to anyone involved in fund-raising. An intrinsic desire to share a portion of one's resources, however small, with others—an inherent generosity possessed in some degree by almost everyone—is a primary factor. Another urge—also very human, if less laudable—is ego satisfaction. The donor who makes

a large contribution has a building named for his or her family, and individuals have their names published in a list of contributors. Peer pressure—overt or subtle— is a third factor. Saying "no" to a direct request from a friend, neighbor, or co-worker is difficult. Despite the recent downturn in the economy and slight declines in charitable donations, volunteerism has continued to rise. Rob Mitchell, CEO of Atlas of Giving, explained, "2011 growth was fueled by strong stock market performance through July, low interest rates, an improving economy, modest inflation, and aggressive solicitation." He also noted that many nonprofits that depend on multiple small donations suffered.

Fund-raising involves risks as well as benefits. If an organization is to maintain public credibility, then both adherence to high ethical standards when soliciting contributions and close control of fund-raising costs, so that expenses constitute a reasonable percentage of the funds collected, are essential. Numerous groups

> **Almost three-quarters of giving is by individuals; the rest comes from foundations, bequests, and corporations.**
>
> *New York Times*

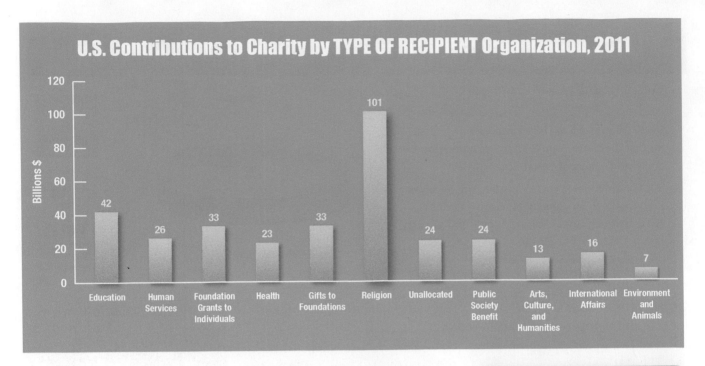

U.S. Contributions to Charity by TYPE OF RECIPIENT Organization, 2011

(Billions $)

- Education: 42
- Human Services: 26
- Foundation Grants to Individuals: 33
- Health: 23
- Gifts to Foundations: 33
- Religion: 101
- Unallocated: 24
- Public Society Benefit: 24
- Arts, Culture, and Humanities: 13
- International Affairs: 16
- Environment and Animals: 7

have had their reputations severely damaged by disclosures that only a small portion of the money they raise is actually applied to the causes they advocate, with the rest being consumed by solicitation expenses and administrative overhead.

Fund-Raising Methods

Public relations professionals generally implement different types of campaigns for fund-raising efforts depending on whom they are targeting, what tactics they are using, and what sorts of projects they are funding.

Organizations must regularly analyze the competition they face from other fund-raising efforts. The public becomes resentful and uncooperative if approached too frequently for contributions. This rationale explains why the United Way of America exists: to consolidate solicitations of numerous important local service agencies into a single unified annual campaign. The voluntary United Way management in a community, with professional guidance, announces a campaign goal. The money collected in the drive is distributed among participating agencies according to a percentage formula determined by the United Way budget committee.

Charitable Contributions: Ups and Downs

Charitable giving is a well-established U.S. institution. American contributions to charity totaled approximately $290 billion in 2010, according to the Giving Institute, up from $280 billion in 2009 but still down from $307 billion in 2007. About 40 percent of larger charities reported to the Nonprofit Research Center an increase in giving during 2010, though about 20 percent of smaller organizations reported that they were in danger of closing.

2007
$307 billion

2009
$280 billion

2010
$290 billion

Corporate and foundation donations. Organizations seeking donations from major corporations normally do so through the local corporate offices or sales outlets. Some corporations allow their local offices flexibility in making donations to local groups up to a certain amount. Even when the donation decisions

think Which strategies and tactics can public relations professionals use to incentivize giving?

are made at corporate headquarters, local recommendations are important. Requests to foundations generally should be made to the main office, which typically provide application forms.

Many corporations have established programs that match employee donations. Most commonly, matching is done on a dollar-for-dollar basis: if an employee gives $1 to a philanthropic cause, the employer does the same. Some corporations match donations at a two-to-one rate, or even higher. For example, Adobe, maker of Photoshop and Flash, matches up to $5,000 of an employee's charitable gifts each year. The company also donates $125 to charity for each 10 hours of volunteer work logged by an employee.

Structured capital campaigns. An effort to raise major amounts of money for a new wing of a hospital, for an engineering building on a campus, or for the reconstruction and renovation of San Francisco's famed cable car system is often called a *capital campaign*. In a capital campaign, emphasis is placed on obtaining substantial gifts from corporations and individuals.

Capital campaigns require considerable expertise and, for this reason, many organizations retain professional fund-raising counsel. A number of U.S. firms offer these services; the most reputable ones belong to the Giving Institute, founded in 1934. Donors often are recognized by the size of their gifts, and terms such as *patron* or *founder* are designated for those who give substantial amounts of money. Major donors may be given the opportunity to have rooms or public areas in the building named after them.

Direct mail. Although direct mail is expensive and ineffective, according to a recent report published in the *Chronicle of Philanthropy*, many organizations still use this communication channel. E-mail communication and social media is replacing direct mail in many cases. Still local, limited, direct mail campaigns are used to motivate recipients to donate. The classic direct mail format consists of a mailing envelope, letter, brochure, and response device, often with a postage-paid return envelope.

However, the *Chronicle of Philanthropy* has reported a sharp decline in direct mail contributions to several large national organizations, such as the Disabled American Veterans and Easter Seals. The publication asserts, "Americans have become increasingly fed up with direct-mail appeals from charities."

Event sponsorship. The range of events that a philanthropic organization can sponsor to raise funds is limited only by the imagination of its members. Participation contests are an especially popular method. Walk-athons and 5K races—notably those sponsored by the Susan G. Komen

Rather than depending entirely on contributions, some nonprofit organizations go into business on their own or develop tie-ins with commercial firms to earn a profit. This approach is increasingly popular, but, like any business venture, entails economic risks that must be carefully assessed. The following three types of commercial money-raising are the most common:

> Licensing use of an organization's name to endorse a product and receiving payment for each item sold, such as the American Heart Association's endorsement of lean beef.
> Sharing profits with a corporation from sales of a special product, such as when a television station agrees to donate a share of advertising revenues with a charitable foundation.
> Operating a business that generates revenue for the organization, such as the Metropolitan Museum of Art's gift shop.

Foundation, appeal to the American desire to exercise more. Staging parties, charity balls, concerts, exhibitions, and similar events in which tickets are sold is another widely used fund-raising approach. However, big parties often create more awareness than profit, with much of the money raised going to expenses such as catering, security, rental fees, printing, graphic design, and publicity—not to mention staff time. Other fund-raising methods include sponsorship of a motion picture premiere, a theater night, or a sporting event.

One key concept of a capital campaign is that 90 percent of the total amount raised will come from only 10 percent of the contributors. In a $10 million campaign to add a wing to an art museum, for example, it is not unusual that the lead gift will be at least $1 million or $2 million.

Continuous Interaction Among Donors Through Social Media

Nonprofits have been effective at using social media to accomplish organizational goals, such as outreach and fund-raising. Often strapped for operating expenses, and short on staff, nonprofits have successfully leveraged social media as principal and grassroots fund-raising and volunteer-recruiting strategies. "You can no longer do a major fund-raising event without the involvement of social media," said Patricia Goldman, VP of the March of Dimes—one of the oldest charities in the United States and a pioneer in raising funds via social media. On Facebook, 51,000 of the 71,000 March of Dimes friends downloaded the organization's fund-raising application. A good percentage, said Goldman, use the application to raise funds.

> ## Nonprofits need to remember that social media is, first and foremost ... social.
>
> Patricia Goldman, VP of the March of Dimes

The American Cancer Society has also had good success with its "Choose You" campaign targeted at women. Its strategy is to build enduring partnerships with publics. By soliciting a series of microdonations online, as opposed to a single payment, donors and supporters enjoy a continuous interaction through social media. Nonprofits, Goldman suggests, must make continuous effort to engage the audience in a meaningful way. "You can't languish," she adds.

The American Red Cross, another charity with a long history of successful campaigns, still relies on traditional methods such as identifying and cultivating ambassadors for personal appeals. However, the Red Cross was among the first charities to make effective use of Twitter to effectively raise funds after the Haitian earthquake crisis of 2010 and the tsunami in Japan in 2011. "All we had to do was tweet about it once," said Wendy Harmon, social media manager of the Red Cross.

While Harmon's statement may exaggerate how little work is required, social media has been shown to have a snowball effect. Not only have nonprofits used Facebook, Twitter, and other platforms as effective fund-raising tools—particularly to solicit small donations—but they have also used social media tools to engage, encourage, and inspire a new generation of socially-conscious individuals.

1. What are some ways nonprofit organizations are using social media?

2. How has the American Cancer Society or the American Red Cross fund-raised online? Were their methods effective? Why or why not?

3. What features of social media make it a good tool for nonprofit organizations to effectively fundraise?

Telephone solicitations. Solicitation of donations by telephone is a relatively inexpensive way to seek funds but is not always effective. Some people resent receiving telephone solicitations. If the recipient of the call is unfamiliar with the cause, it must be explained clearly and concisely—which is not always easy for a volunteer solicitor to do. In addition, there is a national Do Not Call Registry that prevents fund-raisers from randomly calling people, although legitimate charities are exempt from the regulation. Converting verbal telephone promises into confirmed written pledges is also problematic.

A number of political candidates and political action committees continue to use the notorious robocalls. Automated calls cost the candidate or organization only between 5 and 8 cents each. Even though messages are targeted to the potential voters most likely to support a candidate's message, many people have expressed objections to the impersonal nature of these calls. Even so, the practice persists.

Online and social media. Using the Internet to fund raise is cost-effective, compared with the cost of sending out thousands of pieces of mail. On the downside, most people remain wary of online solicitations. This skepticism likely explains why organizations such as the Salvation Army and Greenpeace, which are highly visible and trusted, have been more successful in soliciting donations online than other, lesser-known organizations. Nevertheless, some smaller groups have used the Internet successfully to raise money. The American Red Cross is among the most visited websites, but the comparatively small Heifer Project International, a hunger and environmental group with total assets of less than $150 million, topped the list of page views in early 2012.

In recent years, a variety of advocacy groups have used the Internet to raise funds, generate support, and galvanize constituents' attitudes. Social media such as blogs, Twitter, Facebook, LinkedIn, and YouTube are vital avenues that allow individuals to easily and interactively engage with causes that they support or oppose.

Membership ORGANIZATIONS

Membership organizations are composed of people who share common business or social interests. Their purpose is mutual help and self-improvement. Membership organizations often use the strength of their common bond to promote the professionalism of their members, endorse legislation, and support socially valuable causes.

Professional Associations

Members of a profession or skilled craft organize for mutual benefit. Examples include the Royal Institute of British Architects, the National Association of Professional Organizers, or the seemingly anachronistic Society of Gilders. In many ways, their goals resemble those of labor unions, in that they seek improved earning power, better working conditions, and public appreciation of their roles in society. Professional associations place their major emphasis on setting standards for professional performance, establishing codes of ethics, determining requirements for admission to a field, and encouraging members to upgrade their skills through continuing education. In some cases, they have quasi-legal power to license and censure members. In most cases, however, professional groups rely on peer pressure and persuasion to police their membership.

Public relations specialists for professional organizations use the same techniques as their colleagues in other branches of practice. Also like their counterparts in trade groups and labor unions, many professional associations maintain offices near the seat of government in Washington, D.C., and the various state capitals, and employ lobbyists to advocate for their positions.

Trade Associations

The membership of a trade association usually comprises manufacturers, wholesalers, retailers, or distributors in the same field. Memberships are held by corporate entities, not individuals. Examples of trade associations include the Electronic Industries Alliance, American Beverage Association, Property Casualty Insurers Association, and National Association of Home Builders. Approximately 7,600 trade

think What benefits do member organizations gain from belonging to trade associations?

and professional associations are active in the United States.

Because federal laws and regulations often affect the fortunes of an entire industry, about one-third of these groups are based in the Washington, D.C. area. There, association staff members can best monitor congressional activity, lobby for or against legislation, communicate late-breaking developments to the membership, and interact with government officials on a regular basis.

When a news situation develops involving a particular field, reporters frequently turn to the spokesperson of its association for comment. To promote their industry, many trade organizations create video news releases (VNRs) for broadcast on local and national news outlets. Some controversy surrounds this practice, however, because VNRs are often

In 2011, the governors of Ohio and Wisconsin attempted to pass legislation forbidding state workers such as teachers and civil servants from unionizing. Protestors poured into the streets of Madison, Wisconsin—and the halls of the state's capitol building—to protest Republican Governor Scott Walker's "budget repair bill" in February of 2011. The bill included a proposed rollback of collective-bargaining rights, and many perceived it as antiunion. Protesters managed to obstruct business as usual at the capitol for over a month.

presented by television stations as "straight news" without proper attribution and it is not always clear to the public that the material was underwritten or developed by a trade organization.

Labor Unions

Like trade associations, labor unions represent the interests of an entire industry. Whereas trade associations typically represent the interests of management, however, labor unions advocate on behalf of employees. As with other membership organizations, labor unions lobby for better working conditions, higher wages, increased safety regulations, better benefits, and education for their memberships. Since their apex in the late 1970s, labor unions have suffered serious membership losses in business and industry, but made gains in public employees, which now constitute more than half of America's union members. And despite drops in overall membership, unions are still are very much a part of the U.S. business scene, representing teachers, players in the National Basketball Association, UPS employees, and many other familiar groups.

Unions rely on public relations tools to assert their strength and influence. Unions employ public relations when communicating with their internal audiences in various companies or organizations. They must keep their memberships informed about the benefits that they receive in return for their dues, including recreational and social

> Labor unions are responsible for helping bring about many positive things that Americans today take for granted: the end of child labor, the 40-hour workweek, laws against discrimination in hiring and firing, workplace safety guidelines, the minimum wage, vacations, health insurance, and even the concept of the weekend.

programs and representation in communication and negotiations with company management. Labor unions may engage in conflict with management, which typically has the upper hand in negotiations in terms of both financial strength and political clout.

In every national political campaign, unions spend millions of dollars to support candidates whom they regard as friendly to their cause. Although some of this money goes directly to candidates, significant amounts are devoted to "issue ads" that do not explicitly endorse an individual. Despite rhetoric to

the contrary, this practice represents only a fraction of the money spent on issue ads supporting pro-business interests—it enables unions to provide support for candidates beyond the limits imposed on individual campaign contributions. And union spending on political races is expected to rise in the wake of the January 2010 Supreme Court decision that removed all limits on raising funds by individuals, businesses, unions, and trade groups to support political action committees (PACs).

Chambers of Commerce

A chamber of commerce is an association of business professionals who work to improve their city's commercial climate and to publicize its attractions. Above all, chambers of commerce serve as boosters of local business growth. State chambers of commerce and, on a national scale, the U.S. Chamber of Commerce, help guide local chambers and speak for business interests before state and federal government. According to the Center for Public Integrity, the U.S. Chamber of Commerce, one of the most powerful lobbying organizations in Washington, D.C., spent almost $530 million on lobbying activities between 1998 and 2009. (The American Medical Association, the second most aggressive spender, invested less than half of that amount in lobbying efforts.)

Advocacy GROUPS

A number of pressing issues affect communities to varying degrees—from social issues such as poverty, abortion, and racism, to threats such as epidemic diseases and environmental degradation. Organizations that fight for social causes can have significant effects on those issues, both positive and negative.

Advocacy groups include activist groups that adopt confrontational tactics such as Greenpeace and People for the Ethical Treatment of Animals (PETA), as well as social issue organizations, such as the National Rifle Association (NRA) and American Family Association (AFA). They promote their own causes, but may be perceived as lobbying for the good of the whole society. The positions such groups espouse often come in conflict with the views of other advocacy groups, however. For example, the AFA frequently expresses views that clash with those of the Gay and Lesbian Alliance Against Defamation (GLAAD).

New York was among a handful of states, including Iowa and Vermont, to legalize gay marriage. This issue has rallied advocacy groups on both sides and caused controversy and some uncomfortable moments for political candidates.

Advocacy Groups: Strategies and Tactics

Advocacy groups work in a variety of ways to achieve their goals.

LOBBYING. Much of this lobbying takes place at the state and local government levels.

LITIGATION. Organizations may file suits seeking court rulings favorable to their projects or attempting to block unfavorable projects.

MASS DEMONSTRATIONS. Designed to showcase public support for a cause and in some cases to harass the operators of projects to which the groups object, mass demonstrations require elaborate public relations machinations. Organizers must obtain permits, inform the media, and arrange transportation, housing, programs, and crowd control. The Occupy Wall Street movement, which spread to cities across the U.S. and other parts of the world, was together one of the largest mass demonstrations in recent history.

BOYCOTTS. Some boycotts achieve easily identifiable results. Others stay in effect for years with little evident success. One success story occurred when the Rainforest Action Network boycotted Burger King for buying Central American beef raised in cleared rainforests. The fast-food chain agreed to stop such purchases.

RECONCILIATION. Some environmental organizations have achieved good results by cooperating with corporations to solve pollution problems. The Environmental Defense Fund joined a task force with McDonald's to deal with the fast-food chain's solid-waste problem, leading to a company decision to phase out its polystyrene packaging.

FUND-RAISING. With so many groups in the field, competition for donations is intense. Some professional fund-raisers believe that as a whole, nonprofit groups depend too much on direct mail and should place more emphasis on face-to-face contacts.

Digital Grassroots Public Relations Campaigns

Water usage for yard maintenance is a crucial public issue in western states.

A NUMBER OF RECENT SUCCESSFUL nonprofit and public awareness campaigns are based on integration of existing Internet platforms, notably Facebook and Twitter, together with dedicated social media microsites developed specifically to accomplish organizational goals. For example, the Alliance for Climate Protection, an organization sponsored by Al Gore, has developed "Repower America," a video wall, which features brief interviews with ordinary Americans. Content and authenticity of individual voices are key components of a successful grassroots campaign. Tools such as streaming videos "allow the face of supporters to tell their stories to policymakers, as opposed to the less emotional value of a letter or petition," according to Jason Miner, MD, of the public affairs group at Glover Park Group. He adds that social media is a particularly effective means of "reaching legislators and other decision makers."

Giselle Barry, director of communications at Glover Park, points out how integrated campaigns connect website visitors "to other people who share the same interest." Interactive media allowed the Virginia Department of Social Science and its partners to gauge the level of public support for solutions such as food stamps and housing assistance. Similarly, the city of Santa Fe, with help from public relations firm Cook & Schmid, targeted homeowner's groups in an integrated campaign to reduce water usage, a crucial topic of concern in western and other U.S. states. Many individuals became "water ambassadors," volunteering to promote water conservation both online and in face-to-face interactions in a campaign that put a premium on "cultivating social relationships."

Enlisting voluntary support—finding people who agree with a cause enough to invest their time into promoting it without compensation—is the goal of a successful grassroots public relations campaign. For example, the Mommy Bloggers recruited by the National Association of Children's Hospitals were emotionally credible when they petitioned on behalf of member hospitals. However, not every grassroots campaign is so pure. The Federation for American Coal, Energy, and Security's website includes "Faces of Coal," a series of photographs of people described as "an alliance of people from all walks of life who are joining forces to educate legislators and the public about the importance of coal and coal mining to our local and national economies." Testimonials from Randy H., Tina S., and Jerry L., etc. feature statements such as, "Coal is the life-blood of Clay County. The loss of revenue generated by coal would devastate our county." What the site does not disclose is that the organization has been accused of paying individuals to express the view that the nation needs more coal mining. Whether or not the views of individuals or groups are accurately represented, it is unethical to compensate an individual for offering what is depicted as grassroots views. In public relations, this is known as "Astroturf," after the artificial grass.

1 What qualities characterize a successful grassroots public relations campaign?

2 Why are social media sites a natural fit for grassroots campaigns?

3 What is the difference between a grassroots campaign and an "Astroturf" campaign?

The principal ways in which advocacy groups work to achieve their goals are lobbying, litigation, mass demonstrations, boycotts, reconciliation, and public education. Some organizations work relatively quietly through lobbying or reconciliation. Others are stridently confrontational, using more hard-core tactics such as litigation or mass demonstrations to advance their goals.

Activist Groups

Greenpeace, an organization that operates in multiple countries including the United States, is perhaps the best known of the confrontational groups. With 2.8 million members, Greenpeace is second in size to the much less flamboyant National Wildlife Foundation among environmental groups.

Recently contributions to Greenpeace have declined; so has the group's political influence. However, the movement of which this group is a part remains vital.

Animal rights groups such as PETA at times resort to extremely confrontational tactics, such as raiding animal research laboratories and splashing red paint—symbolizing blood—on people who wear fur. The group's campaign against the dairy industry takes a different tack, employing humor

think Why do advocacy groups sometimes employ confrontational public relations tactics?

and parody on the website www.milksucks.com.

Social Issue Organizations

Social issue organizations are similar to activist groups in structure, but often have more broadly defined social and behavioral goals. Social issue organizations focus on social issues in an effort to change human behaviors by targeting individuals. They tend to use softer tactics to persuade others to support their cause, but are nevertheless often highly visible and politically active. Mothers Against Drunk Driving (MADD) is one such group. Environmental groups such as the Nature Conservancy spent a total of about $22 million on lobbying and public outreach at their recent height in 2009.

Social service ORGANIZATIONS

Social service organizations include social service, philanthropic, cultural, and religious groups that serve the public in various ways. These organizations require active and creative public relations programs.

Prominent national organizations of this type are Goodwill Industries, the American Red Cross, the Boy Scouts and Girl Scouts of America, and the YMCA. Their advocacy is rooted in

> Social service organizations frequently have dual roles—both service and advocacy—and serve the needs of individuals, families, and society in many ways.

a sense of social purpose and the betterment of society as a whole. Local chapters carry out national programs. Service clubs such as the Rotary Club, Kiwanis Club, Lions Club, and Exchange Club raise significant amounts of money for charitable projects. The New York Philharmonic and Metropolitan Museum of Art, among many others, serve the interests of the community while advocating for their own existence.

Philanthropic Foundations

Hundreds of tax-free foundations in the United States are collectively responsible for approximately 14 percent of all charitable giving in this country. Money to establish a foundation is typically provided by a wealthy individual or family, a group of contributors, an organization, or a corporation. The foundation's capital is invested, and

earnings from the investments are distributed as grants to qualified applicants.

In addition to large, highly visible national foundations, which make grants to a variety of causes, smaller organizations such as the Susan G. Komen Breast Cancer Foundation, the Annenberg Foundation, and the Avon Foundation have become quite well known. Many smaller foundations—some of them extremely important in their specialized fields—distribute critical funds for research, education, public performances, displays, and similar purposes. Most of these organizations not only dispense money, but also engage in numerous fundraising activities to collect money for foundation efforts.

Cultural Organizations

Generating interest and participation in the cultural aspects of life

The Gates Foundation was already the largest philanthropic foundation in the world in June 2006 when Warren Buffett, the world's second richest man, gave it $30 billion. With the stroke of a pen, the Gates Foundation doubled its assets to $62 billion. In July 2011, Buffet gave an additional $10 billion to the Gates Foundation to continue education and global health projects. Even though a massive amount has been spent, the organization completely eclipses all other foundations in terms of wealth, with nearly $34 billion in assets as of the most recent financial report. The Ford Foundation, the second largest, has only $10.8 billion in assets. Third largest is the J. Paul Getty Foundation, with $9.6 billion; fourth is the Robert Woods Johnson Foundation, with assets of $8.4 billion. The fifth and sixth largest are the William and Flora Hewlett Foundation, with $7.3 billion in assets, and the W. K. Kellogg Foundation, with $7.2 billion.

 think How is corporate giving a win–win situation for communities and corporations?

is often the responsibility of non-profit organizations in the United States. So, too, in many instances, is the operation of libraries; musical organizations, such as symphony orchestras; and museums of art, history, and natural sciences. Such institutions frequently receive at least part of their income from government sources; in fact, many are operated outright by the government. But even government-operated cultural institutions such as the Smithsonian Institution depend on private support to raise supplementary funds.

Cuts to government programs that subsidize the arts at the state and federal levels have caused many affected organizations to turn to private supporters with increased urgency. Not surprisingly, then, cultural organizations have a great need for public relations professionals. Their constant efforts to publicize exhibitions, performances, and events, as well as to support on-going fund-raising, present many

Social Service Organizations: Strategies and Tactics

PUBLICITY. The news media provide well-organized channels for stimulating public interest in nonprofit organizations and are receptive to newsworthy material from them. Public relations practitioners should look for unusual or appealing personal stories.

CREATION OF EVENTS. Events make news and attract crowds and are another way to increase public awareness. Such activities might include an open house in a new hospital wing or a concert by members of the local symphony orchestra for an audience of blind children.

USE OF SERVICES. Closely tied to increasing overall public awareness are efforts to induce individuals and families to use an organization's services. Written and spoken material designed to attract should emphasize ease of participation and privacy of services in matters of health, financial aid, and family.

CREATION OF EDUCATIONAL MATERIALS. Because a website often provides a first impression of an organization, it should be visually appealing and simply written, contain basic information, and answer obvious questions. Organizations also strive to design logos, or symbols, that help make their materials memorable to the public.

NEWSLETTERS. A news bulletin, usually generated monthly or quarterly, is aimed at members, the news media, and a carefully composed list of other interested parties. Periodic newsletters distributed to opinion leaders are a quiet but effective way to tell an organization's story. Today, many organizations distribute newsletters via e-mail or on social networking sites.

opportunities for public relations campaigns. Most cultural institutions have in-house divisions of public relations and marketing, but others, such as the Getty Museum and the New York Philharmonic, employ outside agencies for these purposes.

Religious Organizations

The mission of organized religion, as perceived by many faiths today, includes much more than holding weekly worship services and underwriting parochial schools. Churches distribute charity, conduct personal guidance programs, provide leadership on moral and ethical issues in their

> **An organization's website is its "front door"—whether that organization is a corporation or a charitable or cultural institution.**

communities, and operate social centers where diverse groups gather.

Public relations goals vary depending on the purposes of social service organizations. In general, nonprofit social service organizations design their public relations to achieve the following objectives:

- Develop public awareness of their missions and activities
- Encourage individuals to use their services
- Recruit and train volunteer workers
- Obtain operating funds

Health ORGANIZATIONS

There are two types of organizations in the health sector. The first type is hospitals, some of which are nonprofit organizations and some of which are for-profit businesses. The second type of health sector organization comprises private and government health agencies, which serve the public interest by providing health care, funding for health initiatives, and oversight.

Hospitals

Because hospitals sell a product (improved health), parallels exist between their public relations objectives and those of other corporations. They focus on four major publics: patients and their families, physicians and medical staff, news media, and the community as a whole.

Hospital administrators and their public relations personnel involve themselves in public affairs and legislation because they operate under a maze of government regulations; and stress consumer relations, which involves keeping patients and their families satisfied, as well as seeking new clients. Hospitals produce publications and publicity for both external and internal audiences. They also have another need that other

corporate public relations practitioners don't handle—the development and nurturing of volunteer networks.

think Which publics make up the audience for hospital public relations efforts?

Health Agencies

The most familiar private and government health agencies are administered at the federal and state levels, such as Medicare, Medicaid, and the Children's Health Insurance Program (CHIP). Nonprofit health agencies range from national organizations such as the American Heart Association, the American Cancer Society, and the National Multiple Sclerosis Society to smaller groups such as the Conservation, Food & Health Foundation in Boston.

The Department of Health and Human Services (HHS) is the federal government's leading health agency. It provides more than 300 programs, including emergency preparedness, Head Start for

> Public relations professionals working for health agencies deal with an enormous amount of public information, and they need to be prepared to handle crisis situations.

preschoolers, maternity and infant programs, disease prevention and immunizations, and insurance programs such as Medicaid and Medicare. Divisions include major initiatives such as the Food and Drug Administration, Centers for Disease Control and Prevention (CDC), and the National Institutes for Health (NIH) as well as smaller services such as the Administration on Aging and the Agency for Health Care Research and Quality.

In addition to federal health initiatives, each state has a statewide health agency. Within the states, many regions, counties, and cities provide taxpayer-supported health services as well. HHS provides funds and guidance to state and local health agencies. With the assistance of private nonprofit foundations, they provide a coordinated network of free or low-cost health services.

Public relations professionals should build working relationships with these government agencies not only to secure funding but also to build coalitions for health campaigns or programs. Public relations professionals must understand both the technical aspects of a public health risk such as a chemical spill or disease outbreak and the needs of the community in order to facilitate effective dialogue between emergency responders, affected members of the public, and the media.

Public relations professionals who specialize in health communication have an impact on all Americans who are concerned about both their personal health risks and threats to their financial security from burdensome medical costs. Essentially, health communicators strive to convey health information, prevention measures, and emergency response information as a means of reducing health risks. Because personal health and the related costs are so important to Americans, health issues and related policies often are leading stories in the news.

Medical breakthroughs, the introduction of high-profile drugs such as Viagra, the graying of 76 million baby boomers, and the ongoing controversies over health costs, medical malpractice reform, and claims of excessive profits for

Health information and advice are omnipresent on the Internet. WebMD is a leading site for consumers, and many physicians now communicate with patients through electronic means. According to International World Stats, 84 percent of North Americans have access to the Internet, and the Office of International Information Programs, U.S. Department of States, found that 67 percent of Americans believed that they could find reliable health care information on the web. Public relations companies produce video and audio programming on the web for their health care clients in an effort to provide doctors, medical reporters, investors, and patients with medical and pharmaceutical information.

doctors and health care companies guarantee robust opportunities to practice sophisticated public relations. Similarly, the Affordable Care Act offers new challenges and opportunities for public relations professionals in the field of health care.

Health Campaigns: Strategies and Tactics

Health campaigns to prevent and respond to diseases, and to promote health and quality of life, began applying social marketing practices in the late 1980s. A number of public relations strategies and

techniques have been implemented for these initiatives, mainly by federal and state governments and private health agencies.

Campaigns to promote breast cancer awareness and the importance of diet, exercise, and screenings for cancer are examples of recent health promotion efforts sponsored by government and nonprofit health organizations. The American College of Emergency Physicians (ACEP), for instance, sponsors the Risky Drinking Campaign, an alcohol awareness program; Failure Is Not an Option, a project to alert the public to the symptoms of heart failure; and the Partnership for Anthrax Vaccine Education, a partnership with George Washington University to provide the latest information about vaccination initiatives. In addition to having altruistic motives, the ACEP sponsors these campaigns as a public relations tool to build goodwill and a positive public image.

The Healthy People Initiative is among the most ambitious and comprehensive health campaigns. Initiated in 1979 by the Department of Health and Human Services, Healthy People was designed to assess the health status of the nation. Healthy People 2020, the latest iteration of the program, focuses on setting health goals and providing clinically based disease-prevention services. According to the Healthy People website (http://www.healthypeople. gov), the campaign represents an unprecedented partnership between more than 350 private and nonprofit organizations and 270 state agencies.

Publicity and educational materials available on the Healthy People website are targeted to both consumers and health care professionals. A fundamental question about all of these public relations efforts is how best to use this information and measure health outcomes to create more effective campaigns. Public relations professionals particularly need well-developed research skills if they are working in this area.

Educational ORGANIZATIONS

Educational institutions include programs that provide childcare, instruction for primary and secondary students, colleges, universities, trade schools, and schools for students with special needs. These organizations are often licensed or regulated by state and federal agencies, as in the case of primary and secondary schools, or by private accreditation bodies such as the Southern Association of Colleges and Schools. Most educational institutions have nonprofit status. Educational institutions demonstrate a staggering array of organizational structures and functions. Like other nonprofit organizations, educational institutions are often supported to some degree by government agencies, but also usually depend on donations from alumni or other donors for supplemental support.

Colleges and Universities

Higher education is big business in the United States. California, the most populous state with 37.3 million residents, spent $2.6 billion in 2011 on the University of California System—2 percent of the state's budget. Key publics for colleges and universities include faculty and staff; students; alumni and other donors; federal, state, and local governments; local community members; and prospective students.

Higher education is also a business that has millions of customers—namely, students. In the United States, more than 20 million students are enrolled at more than 4,000 colleges and universities. Almost every one of these institutions has personnel working in such activities as public relations, marketing communications, and fund-raising.

In large universities, the vice president for development and university relations (or a person with a similar title) supervises the office of development, which includes a division for alumni relations and an office of public relations; these functions are often combined in smaller institutions. Development and alumni personnel seek to enhance the prestige and financial support of the institution. Among other activities, they conduct meetings and seminars, publish newsletters and magazines, and arrange tours of the campus. Their primary responsibilities are to build alumni loyalty and generate funding from private sources.

The public relations director, generally aided by one or more chief assistants, supervises the information news service, publications, and special events. Depending on the size of the institution, perhaps a dozen or more employees will carry out functions supporting these efforts, including writing, photography, graphic design, broadcasting, and computer networking. The most visible aspect of a university public relations program is its news bureau. An active bureau produces hundreds of news releases, photographs, and special columns and articles for print and other media.

To carry out their complex functions, development and public relations specialists must be a part of the management team of the college or university.

Fund-raising has increased dramatically at most public and private universities in recent years as costs have risen and allocations from state legislatures and federal agencies have shrunk dramatically. Moody's financial projected a negative outlook for colleges and universities dependent on state appropriations through 2012. However, colleges and universities that have a strong philanthropic base and less dependence on state legislatures have a stable outlook.

Elementary and Secondary Schools

Competition among districts for students—particularly given new initiatives focused on charter schools development and voucher programs to subsidize private school education—has led many school systems to confront the need for strategic outreach plans to communicate with their constituents, which include students, parents, teachers, voters, and taxpayers. Adding to this pressure, various ballot initiatives in many states have made it necessary for individual schools to present a good case to the public about their

achievements to justify additional funding, attract students, and maintain their reputations in the district.

A handful of individual schools—mostly private—now have public information officers. Otherwise, public relations are the responsibility of principals, teachers, and guidance counselors, who are often advised regarding contentious

 think When do universities and colleges compete outside their sporting arenas?

issues by school district staff. Parent–teacher associations (PTA) frequently assume public relations duties as well, serving as boosters for the school by giving media interviews, generating news stories, and sponsoring events.

Individual elementary and secondary schools have websites that provide updates about events, performance data, personnel, student accomplishments, team scores, and so forth. Websites are also a good way for schools to provide links to assignments and allow the school to interact with parents and students.

School Districts

Public relations initiatives that affect the entire district are typically administered at the district level. This is generally true of public schools, but similar coordination takes place among parochial schools that are part of a larger organizational body such as an archdiocese. Public information officers, and administrators who serve that function in smaller districts, are utilized by most school districts in the United States. This person is typically the face of the school district to the press and public, or the advisor to those who interact with the public. In the best cases, his or her work complements and coordinates public relations functions, and often builds on the work of individual schools.

Crisis communications is another area of public relations undertaken by school districts. The most famous example of effective communications during a crisis came in the wake of the shooting death of 12 students at Columbine High School in Colorado. The district's skillful handling of media and community relations earned it a Silver Anvil Award from the PRSA.

 **APPLY YOUR KNOWLEDGE**

What Would You Do?

Find the Fun

The Pinellas County Health Department developed its first major health awareness campaign in 2011. Working with the Centers for Disease Control (CDC), the health department's goal is to improve the health of the nearly 1 million citizens living in the St. Petersburg, Florida, region. The campaign was dubbed "Find the Fun Now," emphasizing its lighthearted approach to fitness and nutrition.

The campaign focuses on fun activities. In addition to social media outreach initiatives, flash

mobs aimed at getting bystanders to do jumping jacks or dance have been incorporated into the campaign.

Imagine that you work for the Pinellas County Health Department and have been assigned to this campaign team. How would you go about identifying the characteristic of the target audience, creating a message to help its members understand the importance of the issue, and researching the best communication channels to reach the target audience? Write a short summary of your plans.

summary

What Are the Basic Purposes and Functions of Public Relations in Nonprofit, Health, and Education Organizations?

- Although a broad range of nonprofit organizations exist, most nonprofit, health, and education organizations create communications campaigns and programs, require a staff (including volunteers) to handle their work, and are involved in fund-raising.

What Role Does Public Relations Play in the Fund-Raising Efforts of Nonprofit Organizations?

- Depending on their mission and strategy, nonprofits may seek major donations from large corporations or foundations and smaller contributions from individuals. Recruiting volunteer labor is often crucial to make up for lack of operating funds and involve the community to reach the nonprofit's goals.

Which Public Relations Goals and Tactics Do Nonprofit Advocacy Groups and Social Service Organizations Pursue?

- Public relations goals for advocacy groups, service groups, and philanthropic, cultural, and religious organizations include developing public awareness, getting individuals to use their services, creating educational materials, recruiting volunteers, and fund-raising.

Which Public Relations Goals and Tactics Do Health and Education Organizations Employ?

- In health organizations, public relations professionals help communicate information about medical advances, the availability of health services, and potential health risks. Public relations for hospitals focuses on enhancing the public's perception of the institutions and marketing their services.

- The audience for education institution communications include alumni, students, prospective students, faculty and staff, government, and the general public.

questions
FOR REVIEW AND DISCUSSION

1 Identify public relations strategies and tactics that advocacy groups use to further their causes.

2 Name and describe some types of social service agencies.

3 List and describe some commonly used fund-raising tactics.

4 What are the major roles of public relations professionals in health organizations?

5 List some key components of successful health campaigns.

6 With which primary public does a sound university public relations program begin? What other constituents must be addressed when designing a higher education public relations campaign?

Mattel Says Yes to Greenpeace, No to Rainforest Destruction

www.triplepundit.com

By Raz Godelnik | October 10th, 2011

Last week, Greenpeace made another impressive victory in its ongoing battle against paper company Asia Pulp and Paper (APP). After a four month Greenpeace campaign, Mattel, the largest toy company in the world and maker of the famed Barbie doll line announced a new paper policy. One of their decisions was to direct their printers not to contract with controversial sources, including APP. This was not just a huge win for Greenpeace, but also an important reminder to APP and other companies: rainforest destruction is bad for business.

As we reported here on June, the campaign's goal was to draw attention to the toy industry's use of glossy cardboard packaging whose pulp is partly sourced from Indonesian rainforests. Greenpeace International investigations have also established links between leading toy brands, such Mattel, Disney and Lego and APP, which Greenpeace describes as "the largest and most notorious pulp and paper company operating in Indonesia."

Greenpeace focused its efforts on Mattel in a brilliant and creative campaign that used one of Mattel's most famous toys – Barbie and Ken — to draw attention to Mattel's relationship with APP. They produced a funny 'Barbie, It's Over' campaign, which included **a shocking interview with Ken, a public Twitter feud** between the former couple, inappropriate photos of Barbie with a chainsaw and so on. And there was some activism offline as well, including a banner of Ken protesting Mattel's actions in the Indonesian rainforest Greenpeace protesters hung on Mattel headquarters in California.

Conflict often emerges between activist groups advocating issues such as protection of the environment and the policies of corporations that make consumer products.

By avoiding strident accusations and channeling criticism through the Ken doll, Greenpeace was able to minimize the mistrust that can arise when persuasion gets too pushy. Humor disarms the audience and spurs the urge to share with friends.

Social media has become an important tool for non-profit organizations to launch advocacy campaigns. Social media is an effective tool not only because it has the potential to reach into the lives of millions, but also because its use is cost efficient.

Traditional publicity strategies tend to complement social media efforts. Sometimes the coverage on nightly news or in a major newspaper about a viral video or a wildly sensational tweet, for example, generates greater public pressure on a company than the social media is able to achieve on its own.

The result was not just a lot of media attention, but also attention from consumers who participated in the campaign online, on Facebook, Twitter and other channels and also sent, according to Greenpeace, over 500,000 emails to Mattel, expressing their dissatisfaction with Mattel's relationship with APP and asking the company to "immediately implement a new procurement policy for all pulp and paper products, including packaging, and make sure that its products are made in ways that don't damage the environment."

And Mattel indeed listened. They have come up with a new and quite impressive list of **sustainable sourcing principles**, focusing on three fundamental steps to advance sustainability: maximizing postconsumer recycled content where possible, avoiding virgin fiber from controversial sources, and seeking to increase the percentage of fiber that is certified by a credible third party. Mattel has also announced it is establishing aggressive goals to measure progress on packaging as the focus of the company's initial implementation phase: By the end of 2011, 70 percent of Mattel's paper packaging will be composed of recycled material or sustainable fiber. By the end of 2015, it will increase to 85 percent. Last but not least, Mattel will show preference, when feasible, for FSC-certified fiber.

Mattel didn't name names in their announcement, but it's very clear which company they refer to when talking about "controversial sources." For those who want it in writing, Mattel's spokesperson Jules Andres has no problem to say it loud and clear, telling the **Los Angeles Times** "Mattel's new policy "directs our printers not to contract with controversial sources" and that Mattel considers Asia Pulp & Paper "a controversial source." Mattel, by the way, directed its suppliers already in June, to put a freeze on purchases from APP, following the Greenpeace campaign.

.....

Raz Godelnik is the co-founder and CEO of **Eco-Libris**, *a green company working to green up the book industry in the digital age. He is also an adjunct professor in the University of Delaware's Alfred Lerner College of Business and Economics*

Mattel could not "throw APP under the bus" by naming the supplier because paper suppliers are an essential part of the company's supply chain. In this instance, Mattel successfully balanced the rising expectations of their customers with the need to maintain good relations with the overall paper industry.

Many times the wise public relations person will provide an exclusive interview with the back story—more detail, more disclosure, and more persuasive arguments—to a favored and powerful journalist after the general news release.

Responsiveness to the public groundswell goes a long way in restoring the reputation of a company in the eyes of key publics such as customers and activist groups.

When a company takes corrective action with concrete steps and outcomes, key publics may actually increase their brand loyalty for the company after a problem. This is why crisis consultants say that a crisis is an opportunity for renewal when handled well.

TACTICS

Text Credits

Photo Credits

Index

Page references followed by "f" indicate illustrated figures or photographs; followed by "t" indicates a table.

1

1984, 37, 304

A

Accommodation, 6, 182-183, 185, 190, 193
  conflict and, 183, 185
Accuracy, 37, 200, 213, 394
Acronyms, 133
Action, 9, 20, 33-34, 47, 71, 79-80, 116, 128-129, 137, 142-144, 149, 152, 157, 163-164, 170-172, 181, 186, 190, 192, 202-203, 207, 215, 277-278, 281, 298, 349-351, 364, 411-413
Active listening, 297
Adaptation, 345
Advice, 10, 22, 33, 36, 79, 85, 87, 91, 136, 228, 384, 418
advocacy, 33, 37, 79, 183-185, 192-193, 198-200, 224, 298, 337, 370, 373, 403-404, 406, 411, 415, 421
Affection, 165
Age, 23, 29-30, 32-33, 35, 42, 48, 51, 55, 61, 66, 102, 107-108, 110, 115, 120, 156-157, 227-229, 234-235, 261, 268, 276, 394-395, 398, 400
Agenda, 152, 155-156, 171, 333
Agenda setting, 156
Aggressive, 159, 296, 351, 359, 399, 407, 412, 423
Amazon.com, 280
Ambiguity, 343
Ambiguous messages, 365
Analysis, 4, 6, 8-9, 33, 36, 44, 63, 66, 85, 97, 102, 104-105, 111, 113, 118, 120, 138, 141-143, 163-164, 171, 235, 339
  of audience, 138, 143, 163
Anderson, Peter, 174
Anecdotes, 159
Anonymity, 108, 233
Apology, 7, 185, 190, 192, 206, 291
Appearance, 6, 24, 52, 71, 93, 142, 182, 220, 264, 303, 331-332, 363
Argentina, 340, 345
Argument, 47, 160, 345, 350-351, 355
Arguments, 40, 46, 48, 58, 132, 158, 169-170, 185, 373, 423
Aristotle, 160, 374
Armstrong, Lance, 390
Arrangement, 322-323
Artifacts, 281
Assertive, 6
Attack, 143, 179, 189-190, 205, 276, 374
  personal, 276, 374
Attention, 3, 29, 35, 89, 102, 113, 120, 128-129, 132, 135, 142-144, 167-168, 170, 191-193, 208, 227, 229, 231-232, 238-239, 285, 303, 319-320, 327-328, 330, 332, 340, 422-423
  gaining, 77, 168, 239
  of audience, 143
  selective, 170
Attitude, 9, 34, 47, 127-128, 138, 142-143, 160, 166
  of audience, 138, 143, 145, 166
Attitude change, 9, 127-128, 138, 145
Attitudes, 6, 9-10, 12, 33, 37, 41, 55, 70, 76-77, 101, 105-108, 114, 127, 130, 136-138, 142-143, 145, 150-152, 157-158, 160-161, 163-164, 168-171, 223-224, 230, 338, 349, 411
Attraction, 29, 393-394
Attribution, 209, 258, 412
Audience, 6-7, 12-13, 17, 19, 33, 92, 100, 105-107, 110-113, 115, 117-120, 125, 127-134, 136-138, 140, 142-145, 156, 158, 162-164, 166-171, 223-224, 227, 229-232, 235-236, 238-241, 246-247, 255-256, 258, 260-261, 268, 271-273, 275, 277, 349, 370, 387-388,

416-417, 420-421
  age of, 33, 115, 120, 156, 268
  analysis of, 33, 105, 118, 143
  analyzing, 111, 120
  attention of, 129, 238
  attitudes of, 41, 183, 230
  challenges to, 100, 238
  challenging, 158, 272
  concern for, 229
  culture, 19, 224, 235, 275
  defined, 13, 17, 19, 115, 129, 240
  definition of, 6, 143, 183
  demographics, 100, 120, 163, 387
  diversity of, 227, 235
  feedback, 6, 37, 105, 128-129, 136, 145, 239, 268, 271, 285
  feedback from, 6
  immediate, 120, 128, 162, 167, 230, 301
  information about, 100, 112, 142, 158, 239, 241, 247, 319, 347, 349, 370
  interviewing, 36, 105-106, 258
  knowledge of, 41, 156
  motivation, 19
  needs of, 131, 134, 231
  perceptions, 33, 113, 118, 134, 143, 156, 162
  relating to, 272
  secondary, 112, 119, 137, 144, 420
  self-interest, 7, 112, 163, 170-171, 229
  size of, 92, 318-319
  target, 6, 13, 36, 105-107, 110-112, 115, 120, 125, 131-132, 136-137, 142-144, 162, 164, 167-168, 227, 230-232, 235-236, 239-241, 246, 272, 299, 388, 420
  values of, 112, 169, 224
Audience analysis, 36, 163, 171
  demographics, 163
  knowledge of audience, 163
  process in, 171
Audiences, 12-15, 18-19, 36, 41, 44, 56, 77, 82, 85, 90, 100, 103, 105-106, 114-115, 120-121, 126-132, 136-138, 144-145, 162, 167, 169, 221, 223-241, 245, 302-303, 342, 348, 385, 397
Augustine, 191
Authority, 28, 52, 78-79, 81-82, 158, 201, 208, 226, 229, 240, 317, 381
  decision by, 79
Avoidance, 145, 343
  uncertainty, 343

B

Baby Boomers, 163, 227-229, 241, 418
Bar graphs, 112
Behavior, 9, 46, 112, 114, 127, 134, 137-138, 145, 160-161, 187, 200, 202, 223, 275
Belief, 6, 135, 160, 168-169
Beliefs, 127, 150, 152, 157, 163-164, 166, 168-170, 201
  of audience, 163, 166
Berelson, Bernard, 152
Berra, Yogi, 192
Bias, 108, 131, 294
Biographical material, 250
Blame, 189
Blogs, 3, 11-12, 43, 61, 102, 104, 112, 126-127, 159, 169-170, 191, 208, 225, 273-276, 285, 349-350, 411
body, 46, 108, 192, 240, 248, 280, 303, 355, 391
Books, 36, 61, 102-104, 127, 170, 238-239, 249, 257, 282, 325, 348
Brainstorming, 3, 18, 65
Bridge, 99, 351
Brin, Sergey, 302
bulleted lists, 250
Bureaucracy, 84
Business, 13, 15, 18, 24, 27, 30, 32-33, 36-39, 42-45, 47, 51, 59, 61-62, 66, 70-71, 76-77, 82, 84,

86-90, 92-93, 99, 103-105, 111-113, 141, 155, 157, 172, 188-189, 216, 237-238, 249-250, 272-274, 280, 291-295, 305, 309-311, 316, 319-321, 328-332, 339-342, 347-348, 366-368, 394-395, 405-406, 411-412, 422-424

C

Capitalism, 5, 160, 237, 346
Case studies, 57
CDs, 44, 250
Cell phones, 109, 203, 308, 367
Certainty, 170
Changes, 6-7, 34, 39, 50, 58, 136, 138, 143, 145, 173, 183, 185-186, 232, 238, 269, 291, 325-326, 338, 345, 397
Channel, 13, 112, 128-129, 163, 170, 240, 263, 280-281, 286, 307, 326, 409
  organizational, 128, 326
Channels, 6, 12-13, 18, 20, 39, 59, 115, 130, 134, 145, 162-163, 171, 185, 223, 239, 268, 344, 375-377, 387, 416
Channels of communication, 167, 239, 376
Character, 35, 170, 210, 227, 230, 262, 274-275, 297, 315, 386
Charisma, 166
Charts, 88, 112, 117, 270, 323, 326, 333
Chronological order, 270
Claim, 35, 64, 173, 212, 214, 310, 388, 394
Claims, 43, 140, 170, 185, 189, 191-192, 199, 214, 337, 348-350, 399
Clarity, 112, 133, 145, 161, 163, 167, 171
Climate, 16, 129, 161, 203, 230, 345, 351, 403, 412, 414
  group, 161, 351, 403, 414
  organizational, 414
Clinton, Bill, 362-363
Clinton, Hillary, 403
Closed-ended questions, 103
Closure, 188
Colbert, Stephen, 371
Colleagues, 3, 61-62, 104-105, 152, 411
Collectivism, 343
commentary, 121, 159, 274
Commitment, 89, 93, 127, 133-135, 149, 166, 183, 300-301, 304, 311, 391
Commitments, 127, 345, 354
Committees, 82, 350, 374, 411-412
Common ground, 131, 188
Communicate information, 187, 421
Communication, 4, 6-7, 9, 12, 14-15, 17-20, 32-33, 36-40, 42, 44-46, 50, 57-59, 62-66, 68-69, 76-79, 81-83, 85, 87-89, 98-100, 102, 105, 109, 111-112, 118-119, 123, 125-146, 149, 153, 160-164, 167-171, 182-190, 192-193, 207-208, 216-217, 236, 239, 252, 284-285, 288, 300-302, 311, 340-343, 348-350, 362, 375-376, 395, 405, 420
  and feedback, 6, 271
  assertive, 6, 178
  barriers to, 128
  careers in, 57-59, 62-66, 68-69
  channels of, 167, 239, 376
  competence, 46, 59
  components of, 20, 128, 184
  confidence in, 33, 341
  context, 14, 20, 57, 100, 131, 145, 163, 167-168, 171, 207, 227
  defensive, 190, 192, 252
  defined, 17, 19, 114-115, 129, 143, 178
  definition, 6-7, 143, 160, 170, 178, 183
  definition of, 6, 143, 160, 183
  definitions of, 6, 20
  effective, 6, 12, 14, 59, 65, 77, 82, 98, 109, 111, 118-119, 125-126, 128-130, 133-137, 142, 145, 161-162, 164, 167-168, 182, 187-188, 190, 193, 285

ethical, 7, 46, 89, 133, 164, 170, 178, 183, 217, 301, 350, 353
ethics and, 201, 207-208, 216-217, 390
evaluative, 37, 98, 105, 141
forms of, 9, 68, 133, 167
formula, 131
foundations of, 190
functions of, 20, 79, 187, 193
goals of, 126, 145, 192
good, 12, 42, 58-59, 62, 64-65, 68, 76, 87, 100, 105, 111, 114, 116, 118, 131, 141-142, 163-164, 189-190, 201, 216-217, 277-278, 300-302, 307, 311, 348, 405
human, 81-82, 160, 178, 184, 192, 232, 301, 307, 350, 365
impersonal, 167
in workplace, 350
intentional, 6
intercultural, 343, 352, 390
interpersonal, 4, 39, 127-128, 167
language and, 129-130, 343, 353
leadership and, 19, 63
listening and, 40, 50
mass, 12, 14, 20, 36-37, 39, 50, 65-66, 89, 115-116, 126-131, 135, 149, 153, 171, 239, 252, 260, 268, 284-285, 350
mediated, 33, 158
models of, 37, 128, 137
nonverbal, 112, 301, 343
persuasive, 36-37, 78, 98, 132, 149, 160-161, 163-164, 167-171, 190, 260
power of, 33, 38, 42, 44, 76, 115, 161, 227, 232, 375
public, 4, 6-7, 9, 12, 14-15, 17-20, 32-33, 36-40, 42, 44-46, 50, 57-59, 62-66, 68-69, 76-79, 81-83, 85, 87-89, 98-100, 102, 105, 109, 111-112, 118-119, 123, 125-145, 149, 153, 160-164, 167-171, 182-190, 192-193, 207-208, 216-217, 236, 239, 252, 284-285, 300-302, 311, 340-343, 348-350, 362, 375-376, 395, 405, 420
public communication, 46
small group, 376
supportive, 36
types of, 77, 98, 128, 130, 162, 409
unintentional, 192
verbal, 127, 187, 343
Communication models, 128
Communication process, 9, 38, 82, 128-129, 135, 163
    message and, 128, 163
communication skills, 7, 40
communicator, 37-38, 59, 126-131, 134, 145, 160, 168-169, 225, 239, 362
Communities, 15, 30, 106, 116, 166, 280, 309, 342, 351, 405, 416-417
    communication and, 144, 158
Competence, 46-47, 59, 70, 166
Competition, 6-8, 12, 18-20, 29, 45-46, 56, 58, 68, 70, 97, 101-102, 113, 129, 160, 175, 177-193, 231, 371, 391, 405-406, 408, 420
Compliance, 211
Compromise, 76, 163, 167, 184, 190, 201
Computer software, 157
Computers, 43, 168, 240, 268, 272, 279, 282, 395
Conflict, 6-7, 12, 20, 28-29, 32, 38-39, 56-58, 68, 70, 129, 149-152, 168, 171, 175, 177-193, 200, 224, 343, 349, 405-406, 412-413
    active, 29, 38, 187-188
    competition in, 178
    content, 20, 102, 168, 171, 232, 372
    culture and, 190, 224
    defined, 129, 178, 193
    elements of, 6
    ethics and, 200
    force in, 160
    goals of, 192
    group, 32, 56-57, 70, 150-152, 160-161, 168, 179, 181-183, 185, 200, 232, 343, 372
    issues of, 188
    management of, 6-7, 20, 57, 129, 178, 183, 193
    online, 58, 102, 191, 372
    process of, 158
    relationship, 6, 38-39, 192, 405
    status and, 232
    strategy and, 32, 190
    styles of, 343
Conflict management, 20, 38, 56, 70, 180-181, 185-188, 190, 192-193

Connotation, 346
Consensus, 141, 152, 158, 235
Constraints, 99, 190
Construct, 332
Contamination, 189
Content analysis, 97, 102, 104-105, 297
Context, 14, 20, 57, 100, 117, 131, 163, 167-168, 171, 197, 207, 210, 227, 343-344
    characteristics of, 131
    of communication, 14, 128, 145, 167, 227
    of messages, 145, 163, 168, 171
    words and, 108
Contrast, 13-14, 33, 39, 66, 76, 78, 80, 82, 102-103, 107, 134, 168, 210, 237, 239, 249, 293
Control, 14, 82, 110, 114, 121, 128, 140, 159, 186, 189, 211, 229, 261, 292, 342, 363
Control group, 121
Conversation, 11, 51, 58, 61, 120-121, 233, 252, 273-274, 278, 287
    advice and, 233
Conversation analysis, 120
Conversational style, 256
Cooperation, 91, 185, 308, 405
Coordination, 82, 89, 420
Core beliefs, 168
Couric, Katie, 332
Cover letter, 109
Credibility, 17, 38, 46, 80, 99, 125, 131-133, 140, 145, 163-167, 171, 173, 180, 190, 202-203, 273-274, 292-293, 302-303, 341
    appeals to, 163, 165
    culture and, 190
Criticism, 31, 45, 80, 99, 157, 177, 276-277, 280-281, 363-364, 394
    objectivity and, 295
Cues, 132, 136, 343
Cultural diversity, 39, 234
Cultural values, 201, 225
Culture, 19, 40, 61, 93, 224, 235, 237, 262, 275, 341-342, 352-353, 381, 408
    conversation and, 61
    defined, 19, 237, 341
    gender and, 40
    groups and, 235
    language and, 353
    leadership and, 19
    listening, 40, 275
    listening and, 40
    organizational, 40, 93, 275
    time and, 237

D

Dalai Lama, 157
Data, 4, 50, 63, 65, 75, 79, 84, 89, 97-99, 102-104, 106-108, 121, 141, 164, 166, 189, 225, 229, 234, 241, 320
    audience, 106-107, 111, 164, 166, 229, 241, 391
    organization of, 89
Databases, 3, 59, 102-103, 112, 141, 209, 211, 225
Dating, 228, 232, 240, 268, 350, 369
Debates, 177
Deception, 215
Decision-making, 78, 166, 227
Definition, 6-7, 13, 22-23, 106, 143, 160, 170, 178, 183, 372
Definitions, 6, 20-21, 178
    contrast, 178
    research, 6, 20
DeGeneres, Ellen, 16, 140, 307, 320
Delivery, 7, 103, 108, 238, 296, 337
    importance of, 7
    methods of, 108
democracy, 33, 164, 225, 348, 350-351
Democratic leadership, 245
Democrats, 245, 375
Demographics, 100, 103, 120, 163, 302
Denial, 189-190, 192
Description, 3, 37, 39, 68, 168
Diagrams, 323
Dialogue, 37-39, 49, 128, 159, 188, 271, 273, 275, 286, 311, 418
Directories, 104, 107, 127, 209
Discounting, 167
Discourse, 149, 158, 171, 177-178
Discrimination, 51, 71, 203, 412
Dissatisfaction, 423
Distractions, 132
Diversity, 10, 39, 41-42, 224, 227, 234-235, 301, 342
    audience and, 224

cultural, 10, 39, 41, 224, 234-235, 342
Dominance, 109, 306, 342, 370
Doublespeak, 133
Drawings, 209, 250
Dress, 224, 319
Drucker, Peter, 167
DVDs, 44, 127, 384
Dynamism, 185

E

E-books, 239
Effective communicator, 126
Electronic databases, 102, 211
E-mail, 3, 7, 44, 102, 106, 108, 110-111, 116, 119, 127, 203, 207-208, 210, 226-227, 239, 246-248, 257, 260, 263, 267-268, 318, 351
Email, 23, 111, 219, 409
Emotion, 170
Emotional appeals, 168, 170
Emotions, 390-391
Empathy, 50, 164, 166
    listening and, 50
Emphasis, 32, 39, 43, 59, 65, 76, 111, 138, 143, 200, 248-249, 256, 321, 411
Enlightenment, 165
Enthusiasm, 362, 390
Environment, 5, 7, 10, 13, 15, 40, 55, 58, 76, 130, 173, 186-187, 193, 205, 216-217, 240, 251, 287, 308-309, 351
Episode, 286
Episodes, 34, 75, 192, 296
Equality, 232
ethical standards, 201, 311
Ethics, 11, 46-47, 57, 80, 170, 181, 195, 197-220, 255, 267, 273, 355, 390, 394, 396
    communication and, 46, 207
    competence and, 46-47
    defined, 204
    definition, 170, 372
    listening and, 273
    organizational, 47, 206, 209, 212, 215
    relationship, 197, 202, 216, 390
Ethnicity, 61, 164, 224
Ethos, 160
Euphemisms, 133
Evaluating, 63, 89, 137, 141-142, 145, 188
evaluation, 9, 20, 30, 43, 57, 85, 97-99, 116, 118, 137-142, 144-145, 154-155, 326
Evidence, 40, 55, 105, 156, 170, 202, 206, 226, 310, 351, 353, 392
Exaggeration, 30
Examples, 64, 80-81, 111, 114-115, 127, 149, 159, 168, 170, 185, 193, 210, 212, 227, 230, 272, 280-281, 283-284, 303, 311, 377, 382
    brief, 191
    using, 149, 170, 185, 230, 280-281, 284, 377
Expression, 35, 37, 200

F

Face, 51, 103, 128, 149, 159, 165, 167, 187-188, 192, 199, 204, 240-241, 291-292, 305, 316, 342, 346, 350-351, 420
Facebook, 10, 22, 42-43, 61, 69, 80, 86, 90, 100-101, 118, 125-126, 139-141, 159, 162, 167, 205, 218-219, 223, 239, 248, 269, 273-274, 276-279, 282-287, 298-299, 368, 423
Face-to-face communication, 128
Facial expressions, 121, 128, 136
Fact, 12, 30, 37, 42, 44, 56, 61, 77, 79-80, 87, 102, 105, 121, 141, 150-151, 171, 191, 197-198, 205-207, 213-214, 234, 245, 252, 258-259, 263, 271, 280
facts, 12, 35, 58, 99, 103, 112, 144, 156, 161, 171, 181, 207, 215, 240, 350, 364
Family, 8-9, 18, 32, 34, 51, 66, 135, 152, 162, 165, 169, 197, 227, 232, 235, 262, 281, 286, 321, 345, 383, 394-395, 406-407, 415-416
    types of, 162, 238
Feedback, 6, 9, 21, 37, 63, 99, 108, 128-129, 135-136, 141, 145, 268, 271, 291
    interpersonal, 128
Fields, 12, 17, 34, 37, 40, 44, 50, 65-66, 70, 129, 340, 415
films, 214, 227, 239, 348, 387-388, 393
Flexibility, 51, 239, 256, 258, 409
Focus group, 8, 75, 100, 106, 317
Focus groups, 4, 97, 102-106, 120-121, 143, 188
Followers, 28, 86, 125, 141-142, 167, 262, 274, 279,

281, 296, 299, 331, 385-386, 390
Force, 137, 143, 150, 159-160, 267, 376, 413
    in conflict, 150, 413
Ford, Henry, 31, 48, 262
Forum, 45, 224, 233
Forums, 101, 104, 127
Frame of reference, 62
Frames, 158
free speech, 201, 207, 372

G

Gaming, 231
Gatekeepers, 14, 20, 43, 127-128, 131, 139-141, 156, 168-169, 171, 249, 268-269
    media, 14, 20, 43, 127-128, 131, 139-141, 156, 168-169, 171, 249, 268-269
    organizational, 128, 131, 156
Gender, 40, 50-51, 66-67, 70-71, 111, 133, 164, 169, 203, 227, 241
    and conflict, 70
    listening and, 40, 50
    terms for, 133
General public, 13, 30, 77, 108, 110, 112, 114-115, 211, 224, 421
Generation X, 163, 227-228, 230
Generation Y, 227-228
Geographic location, 65, 376
Gesture, 32
Gestures, 128
Giving advice, 348
Grammar, 58, 256
Graphs, 112, 258, 270
    pie, 112
Group, 8, 14, 41, 56-57, 65, 70, 75, 79, 82, 87-88, 92, 100, 106-108, 110, 116, 119, 121, 131-132, 143, 150-152, 159-162, 164-165, 167-168, 170, 179, 181-183, 185, 231-232, 234-237, 240-241, 246, 254, 279, 286-287, 307, 321, 414-415
    characteristics of, 107, 110, 131, 165, 228-229, 241
    conflict, 32, 56-57, 70, 150-152, 160-161, 168, 179, 181-183, 185, 200, 232, 343, 372
    definition of, 143, 160, 183, 372
    focus group, 8, 75, 100, 106, 317
    leadership, 116, 200, 321, 372
    primary, 75, 92, 107-108, 119, 128, 135, 161, 167, 246, 307, 339, 348, 387
    secondary, 119
    size of, 65, 92, 318
    think, 8, 14, 57, 65, 75, 82, 87-88, 100, 116, 131-132, 143, 150, 159-161, 170, 173, 181-182, 227, 236, 254, 279, 281, 284, 307, 343, 396, 411
Groups, 4, 10, 14-15, 23, 36-37, 40-43, 45, 87-88, 97, 100, 102-106, 120-121, 127, 130-131, 138, 142-144, 149-152, 163-164, 166, 168, 171, 173, 181-182, 188, 197-198, 201, 206, 229, 231-232, 234-236, 240-241, 277, 280-282, 298-299, 350-351, 369-370, 406-407, 411-415, 417
    focus, 4, 23, 36, 40, 97, 100, 102-106, 120-121, 143, 188, 280-281, 322, 415, 417
    virtual, 106, 240, 372

H

Hamilton, James, 29
Hate speech, 277, 287
Hearing, 16, 58, 316
Hierarchy, 63, 89, 165-166
Hierarchy of needs, 165
Hofstede, Geert, 343
Home decoration, 113
Honesty, 7, 170, 200, 202, 278, 355
Hostile environment, 301
Human resources, 81-82, 107, 276, 282
Humor, 132, 144, 275, 277, 280, 415

I

Identification, 19, 37, 62, 318
Identity, 76, 158, 191, 212, 235, 331-332
Illustration, 164, 180, 307, 369, 392
Illustrations, 130
Immediacy, 120
Independents, 149, 375
Index, 43, 103, 149, 235, 347, 399
Indexing, 276
Individualism, 343
Influence, 6, 10-11, 33-34, 37, 40, 43, 57, 66, 68-69, 75-79, 82, 93, 101, 105, 107-108, 121, 125, 145, 151-153, 161, 168, 170, 178-180, 183, 192, 227-228, 238-239, 276, 292, 353-354
Information, 3, 6-8, 12, 14, 16, 19, 32-34, 37, 39, 43-45, 47-48, 58, 60, 62-63, 68-69, 77, 82, 89, 98-100, 102-106, 108-109, 111-112, 114, 116-119, 121, 126-135, 140, 142-145, 153-158, 166-172, 185, 187-188, 199-201, 203-210, 213-217, 219, 223-224, 238-239, 241, 254-256, 268-273, 275-276, 282-285, 311, 316, 318-319, 321, 327-330, 347-350, 360-363, 365-370, 376-377, 387-388, 416-421
    definition of, 6, 143, 160
    ignoring, 210
    negative, 34, 47, 80, 135, 140, 155-156, 158, 200, 205, 219, 273, 278, 353, 420
    power and, 160, 228, 241, 327
    sources of, 44, 112, 228, 252, 294, 302
Information overload, 44, 316
Information seekers, 130
Ingratiation, 189-190, 286
Innovations, 134, 181
    diffusion of, 134
Inputs, 9, 114
Instant messaging, 225
Interaction, 18, 68, 143, 145, 152, 203, 223, 228, 233, 239, 252
Interactivity, 269-270, 285
Intercultural communication, 343
    language and, 343
    meaning, 343
    nonverbal, 343
Interest, 6-7, 10-12, 18-20, 32-34, 36, 40, 45-47, 61, 76, 104, 109, 112, 115, 117, 135, 142, 151-152, 160, 163, 165, 170-171, 200, 213-214, 216-217, 249-250, 269, 278-280, 352-353, 369-370, 372-373, 385, 389, 393-394, 404-405, 414-417
Internalization, 143
Internet, 3, 13, 17, 39, 44, 59, 62, 84, 102, 104-106, 110, 119, 140, 150, 157, 165, 203, 208, 217, 225, 228-229, 232-233, 239-240, 265, 267-288
    databases, 3, 59, 102, 225
    directories, 104
    e-mail, 3, 44, 102, 106, 110, 119, 203, 208, 239, 267-268, 270-271, 351
    listservs, 239-240
    privacy and, 233
    search engines, 104, 269
Internet sources, 13, 119
Interpersonal communication, 4, 127
interpretation, 37, 119, 156, 167, 210-211
Interpreting, 77, 260
Interrupting, 40
Interruptions, 66, 298
Interviewees, 105
Interviewers, 109, 261
Interviewing, 36, 105-106, 109, 258
    survey, 105-106, 109, 258
Interviews, 18, 28, 32, 92, 97, 102-105, 107-109, 111, 119, 121, 188, 252-253, 257-258, 294, 328, 385, 390, 397
    informational, 119
    of audience, 260
    preparation for, 294
Intimacy, 128
Introductions, 319
Invasion, 217, 364
Invention, 35, 268
iPod, 251
Issues, 3, 10, 12, 18-19, 31, 36-39, 41, 43, 45, 47, 56, 61, 68, 79-80, 99, 102-103, 120, 150-153, 159, 161, 168, 171, 180, 186-190, 197-198, 208, 216-217, 232-233, 257-258, 272, 275-276, 304-305, 308, 345, 364-367, 374, 417-418

J

Jargon, 133, 247, 303
Jewelry, 352
Jokes, 207, 386
Journals, 12, 46, 102-103
Judgment, 30, 45, 170, 183, 210, 386

K

Kerry, John, 376
Key words, 6
knowledge, 7, 18, 41, 44, 46-47, 56, 58, 61-62, 64, 68, 77, 86, 92-93, 97, 115, 118, 144, 156, 183, 187, 192-193, 209, 323, 342
    of audience, 163
Knowledge of audience, 163
Kutcher, Ashton, 386

L

Language, 13, 30, 41-42, 55, 61, 121, 129-130, 133, 145, 160, 167, 206-207, 234-235, 238, 286-287, 310, 342-344, 352-353
    accurate, 55, 130, 145, 206
    appropriate, 133, 235, 238
    components, 121
    courses in, 352
    culture and, 352-353
    definition of, 160
    doublespeak, 133
    euphemisms and, 133
    immediate, 167
    importance of, 41-42, 61, 121, 129, 167
    jargon, 133
    meaning, 121, 133, 343, 353
    power and, 160
    power of, 42
    sounds, 121, 352
    styles of, 343
    technical, 129, 133
    technology, 121, 342, 353
    words, 129-130, 133, 206-207, 343-344
Lazarsfeld, Paul, 152
Leader, 28, 38, 152-155, 157, 191, 197, 225, 239-240, 252, 365, 372, 374, 399
Leaders, 6, 11, 13-14, 17-18, 28, 30-32, 34-35, 37, 41, 50, 61, 75, 134, 136, 152-156, 162, 171, 184, 225-226, 238-241, 295, 317, 350-351
    types of, 97, 156, 162, 238, 317
Leadership, 19, 27, 45-46, 63, 68, 77, 116, 166, 200, 208, 321, 417
    communication and, 45-46, 63, 77
    democratic, 245, 365
    ethics and, 200, 208
    group, 116, 200, 321, 372
    mentoring and, 45
Leading questions, 108
Liaison, 19, 407
Libraries, 416
Lighting, 149, 318, 332
Liking, 4
LinkedIn, 208, 269, 273, 280, 285, 299, 368
Links, 43, 103, 130, 144, 247-248, 274, 276, 279, 372, 420
listeners, 12, 104, 152, 268, 387-388
Listening, 10, 33, 40, 50, 98, 186, 275
    active, 33
    critical, 186, 365
    effective, 10, 98
    evaluative, 98
    forced, 275
    gender and, 40
    importance of, 98
    information and, 273
    objective, 98
    perceptions and, 33
    process of, 98
    types of, 98
Listservs, 239-240
Logical argument, 160
Logos, 133, 160, 210, 330
Love, 115, 166, 204, 208, 286, 303, 305, 347
Lying, 181, 197
    ethics of, 181

M

Mad Men, 230
MADD, 404, 415
Madison, James, 29
Magazines, 10, 12, 16, 59-61, 103, 105, 126-127, 161, 165, 169, 197, 226, 237-240, 246, 249, 254-255, 284, 348, 383-384
Management, 6-7, 9-10, 12, 15, 18-20, 30, 33, 36-40, 43, 47-49, 56-57, 59, 62-65, 68, 70, 76-81, 85, 89, 93, 102-103, 111-112, 114, 119, 136-137, 145, 160, 166-167, 177-183, 185-190, 192-193, 197, 296, 339-340, 361-363
    of conflict, 57, 177-178, 190, 193

Mania, 381, 384, 389, 397
Maps, 30, 284
Marriage, 151, 177, 406, 413
Marriages, 228, 235
    interracial, 235
Marx, Karl, 157
Maslow, Abraham, 165
Mass communication, 50, 66, 127
    magazines, 127
    newspapers, 127
    radio, 66, 127
    television, 66, 127
Matrix, 117, 190, 284
McLuhan, Marshall, 342
Mean, 45, 55, 114, 187, 216, 229-230, 236, 321, 323, 397
Meaning, 101, 121, 133, 322, 343, 353
Media, 3, 6, 8-14, 16-18, 20-24, 27-29, 32-33, 36-39, 42-44, 47-48, 55-56, 58-65, 67-71, 76-80, 82-86, 88-92, 100-105, 111-112, 114-116, 119-121, 125-131, 134-136, 138-145, 152-160, 162-163, 165, 167-171, 183-186, 188, 191-193, 205-206, 215-217, 227, 230-231, 233, 235-236, 238-241, 243, 245-264, 267-288, 293-297, 310-311, 317, 321, 323, 326-332, 337-344, 347-353, 355-356, 361-366, 368, 372-377, 383-390, 393, 409-411, 413-414, 423
    and children, 202, 235, 238
    books and magazines, 348
    content analysis, 97, 102, 104-105, 297
    individual and, 134, 302
    messages, 3, 6, 10, 12-14, 17-18, 20, 23, 33, 39, 43, 48, 77, 85, 90, 104-105, 115, 126-127, 129-131, 134, 140-143, 159-160, 163, 167-171, 202-203, 223-224, 227, 231, 235-236, 239-240, 256, 272, 284-285, 302-303, 350-351
    movies, 90, 165, 262-263, 364-365, 387, 389
    relationships and, 20, 274
    study of, 17, 76, 230
Media effects, 156
    cognitive, 156
media interactions, 102
Median, 55, 65-67, 229-230, 232
Mediated communication, 158
Memory, 301, 327
Men, 36, 39-40, 50, 57, 60, 66-68, 70, 76, 115, 159, 227, 230-231, 235, 238-239, 305, 345, 387
Mentoring, 45
Message, 8, 14, 17, 20, 22, 35, 37, 62, 75, 77, 98, 100, 105-106, 110, 112, 114-116, 118, 125-135, 137-138, 140-145, 158-163, 166-171, 238-239, 246-248, 254, 256-257, 271, 273, 285, 298-299, 307, 376-377
    asynchronous, 127
Messages, 3, 6, 10, 12-14, 17-18, 20, 23, 33, 39, 41, 43, 48, 77, 85, 90, 97-98, 104-106, 110, 115, 126-127, 129-132, 134, 140-143, 159-161, 163-171, 202-203, 223-225, 227-228, 231-232, 235-237, 239-240, 256, 272, 284-285, 302-303, 350-351, 363, 411
    ambiguous, 23, 365
    content, 3, 18, 20, 104-106, 127, 130-131, 140-141, 163, 165, 167-168, 170-171, 228, 232, 236, 279, 344
    context of, 117, 131, 167
    creation, 160
    levels of, 134, 282
    mixed, 235, 351
    relationship, 6, 39, 131, 202, 237
    solution, 160, 166, 168
Metaphor, 347
Methods of delivery, 108
Mindful, 386
Mobile phones, 42, 203, 236, 240, 279
Mode, 37, 81
Models, 37, 39-41, 48-49, 98, 112, 128, 137, 153, 171, 365, 390
    of communication, 128, 137, 153, 365
    of listening, 98
    psychological, 128
monitors, 3, 183, 193, 214, 276, 316, 318, 326
Motivation, 19, 310, 351
Movement, 29, 31, 36, 47, 56, 116, 142, 182, 192, 226, 239, 267, 274, 372, 413, 415
Movies, 90, 165, 262-263, 364-365, 387, 389
Multimedia presentations, 127
MySpace, 43, 269

N
Name-calling, 365
Narrative, 191
Needs, 11, 13, 58-59, 61-62, 68, 77, 81, 87, 89, 98, 113, 121, 129, 134-135, 144, 165-166, 180, 186, 188, 198-199, 263, 287, 319-320, 322, 352, 414-415, 418-419
    establishing, 188, 320
    hierarchy of, 165
    satisfying, 302
negative comments, 278
Network analysis, 44
Networking, 45, 48, 59, 91, 127, 136, 272-274, 276-277, 280-281, 299, 344, 416
New media, 11, 17, 43, 238, 268, 285
    characteristics of, 285
    defined, 17
    ethics, 11
News sources, 103-104
Newsgroups, 273
Newspapers, 3, 10, 12, 14, 16, 27-28, 44, 59, 61, 103-105, 126-127, 138-139, 144, 155-156, 165, 167-169, 207, 218, 237-240, 252-255, 270, 361, 393-394
Nielsen Media Research, 256, 258
Noise, 121, 132-133, 189
Nonverbal behavior, 301, 343
Nonverbal communication, 343
Norms, 61, 135, 157, 168, 170
    group, 135, 168, 170
Notes, 13, 38, 60, 69, 138, 142, 172, 227, 317, 371

O
Obama, Barack, 61, 140, 151, 235, 245, 363, 374-375
Obama, Michelle, 150, 359, 369
Objectivity, 89, 168, 295, 394
Online surveys, 110, 121
Open-ended questions, 103
opening statement, 181, 252
Openness, 191
Opinion leaders, 11, 17, 28, 30, 34-35, 75, 134, 136, 152-156, 162, 171, 238-241
Orator, 363
Organization, 3, 6-7, 10-23, 28-29, 37-39, 41, 45, 47, 56-58, 61-66, 68, 71, 75-82, 84, 86, 98-107, 109-115, 120, 128-131, 138-141, 159, 163-164, 166, 170, 173, 177-190, 192-193, 198-201, 203-204, 206-210, 212, 215-217, 225-226, 250, 253-254, 257, 269, 271, 275, 277-281, 284-285, 293-295, 300-301, 304-305, 317-320, 322-324, 359-360, 404, 406-412, 414-417
    characteristics of, 105, 107, 110, 112, 131, 136, 226, 285, 404
    culture and, 190, 352
    definition of, 6, 22-23, 143, 183
    of data, 104
    of ideas, 192, 351
Organizational chart, 79
Others, 8, 41, 46, 58, 63, 68, 76, 78-79, 86, 93, 101, 104, 134, 151-153, 161, 164, 166, 171-172, 212-213, 233, 307, 343
    perceptions of, 76, 93
Outlines, 144, 250
Outlining, 250, 262
Outputs, 23

P
Pace, 65, 225, 236
Palin, Sarah, 320
Panel, 38, 47, 103, 120, 200
Panel discussion, 120
Panels, 308, 361
Paraphrase, 192
Pathos, 160
Peers, 47, 65, 91, 152, 157, 161, 163, 230
Perception, 22-23, 28, 37, 78-79, 97, 168, 170-171, 309, 350
    analysis of, 97
    awareness, 37, 168, 399
    communication, 28, 37, 78-79, 149, 168, 170-171, 350
    definition of, 22-23
    formation, 171
    interpretation, 37
    interpretation of, 37
    media, 22-23, 28, 37, 78-79, 97, 168, 170-171, 350, 399
    organization, 22-23, 28, 37, 78-79, 149, 170, 309
    organization of, 22
    person, 170
    selection, 168, 171
    stages of, 78
    understanding of, 28, 79, 168
Perceptions, 8, 33, 51, 76-77, 85, 93, 113, 118, 126, 134, 156, 162, 192, 234, 293
Periodicals, 117
Persona, 136, 219
Personal experience, 161
Personality, 31, 58, 134, 207, 212-213, 229, 239, 257, 260, 320, 331-332, 381, 383
Perspective, 17, 40, 62, 83, 120, 142, 158-160, 178, 199, 216, 229, 233, 342
    definition of, 160
Persuasion, 6, 28, 33, 37, 39, 48, 111, 134, 147, 149-174, 350, 370, 411
    ethical criteria for, 170
    importance of, 128, 162, 167
persuasive communication, 36, 160-161, 163-164, 170-171
Photographs, 52, 63, 112, 168, 206, 209, 239, 249, 269, 414
Play, 3, 43, 48, 97-98, 116, 119, 157-158, 160, 163, 183, 186, 200, 217, 259-260, 282, 304, 363, 367, 369, 399
Podcasting, 59
Polarization, 159
policy changes, 34
Political economy, 342
Political power, 160, 241
Polls and surveys, 102, 107, 164
Population, 41, 44, 84, 88, 102, 105-108, 115, 119, 121, 151-152, 164-165, 223, 229, 234-237, 282, 338-339
Position, 19, 28, 58, 68, 81, 158-159, 163, 170, 187, 199, 239-240, 250, 295, 359-360, 368, 370
Posters, 10, 12, 32-33, 116, 126-127, 368-369
Posture, 253
Power, 5, 13, 33, 35-36, 38, 40-42, 44, 76-77, 79-80, 104, 115, 149, 152, 157, 160-161, 165-166, 171, 224, 226-229, 237, 300, 327, 375, 395-396
    and organizations, 76, 227, 231
    competence and, 166
    culture and, 224
    expert, 166
    information, 33, 44, 77, 80, 104, 149, 157, 160-161, 171, 208, 224, 226, 241, 327, 395
    language and, 343
    legitimate, 115, 411
    reward, 343
    sources of, 44, 228
    types of, 77, 204, 253
Power distance, 343
PowerPoint, 272, 282
Practicing, 216
Prediction, 247
premises, 323
Presentation, 47, 225, 258, 319-320, 327-328
    movement, 47
Presentations, 89, 91, 127, 130, 282, 302, 328, 366, 393
Pressure, 36, 76, 91, 138, 163, 179, 183, 188, 407, 411, 420
Presumption, 209
Preview, 47, 254, 387
Print media, 62, 89, 91, 238-239, 255, 263
Problem solving, 4, 6, 45, 63, 77, 166
    process of, 166
Problem-solving, 12, 59, 62, 89
Production, 8-9, 57, 62, 78, 81, 91, 139, 192, 257-258, 304, 309, 323, 363-364, 387-388
Professionalism, 46-47, 156, 190, 411
projectors, 318
Proof, 69, 143, 276
Psychological needs, 165
Psychology, 33, 44
Public communication, 46
    credibility and, 46
    ethics, 46
    topic, 46
Public hearings, 370
Public speaking, 166
Public sphere, 233
Purpose, 12, 15, 20, 30, 33, 37, 49, 105, 107-108, 111-112, 118, 201, 224, 307, 317-320, 322,

324-325, 328, 364, 392
general, 30, 105, 107-108, 111-112, 224, 317, 364
goals and, 12, 20
of communication, 118
specific, 108, 111-112, 118, 224
statement, 254

Q

questionnaire, 47, 108-110
Questionnaires, 108-109
Questions, 21, 49, 71, 99, 103, 106, 108-113, 119-120,
    126, 136-137, 145, 192, 201-204, 209, 230,
    250, 271-273, 294, 317-319, 332-333,
    351-352, 416
    closed, 103, 108
    follow-up, 327
    of value, 269
    open-ended, 103
    responding to, 203
    survey, 99, 103, 106, 108-111, 119-120, 143, 230,
        271, 294, 351

R

Race, 7, 20, 107, 116, 141, 169, 215, 321,
    331-332, 391-392
Racism, 413
Radio, 12, 16, 62, 66, 104-105, 126-127, 129-130,
    135, 140, 144, 152-153, 155, 165, 167, 170,
    235, 239-240, 245, 255-263, 268, 270, 272,
    332, 363, 383
Reagan, Ronald, 159, 362-363
Reality TV, 226, 298, 350
Reasoning, 170
Receiver, 128-130, 132-133, 163, 270, 390
Receivers, 135, 169, 238, 343
Receiving, 31, 179, 409, 411
Reconstruction, 409
References, 105
Regional differences, 65, 130
Regulators, 179, 370
Reinforcement, 128, 130, 163, 168
Relationships, 6, 10, 15-16, 20, 23, 36, 38-39, 49, 69,
    76, 197, 216-217, 228, 285, 341, 343, 389,
    391, 393, 414, 418
    building of, 6
    definition of, 6, 23
    development of, 341
    ethical, 178, 197, 217
    family and, 184, 197
    media and, 20, 62, 216, 341
    messages in, 6
    online, 62, 78, 216, 228, 276, 285, 414
    primary, 20, 36, 311
    stages of, 78, 216
    workplace, 10, 36
Relaxation, 261, 370
Religion, 107, 169, 224, 408, 417
Remembering, 6
Renaissance, 29
Repeating, 134
Repetition, 132
Reporting, 9, 78, 160, 209, 386
Representations, 235
Reproach, 337
Reproduction, 249
Research, 4, 6-10, 13, 17-20, 33-38, 44, 46-47, 50,
    57-59, 63-64, 68, 70, 75-77, 79, 83, 85-87,
    89, 95, 97-122, 128-129, 132, 134-138,
    140-144, 161-162, 168, 186, 188-189, 200,
    203, 225-228, 230-231, 249-251, 255-256,
    263, 303, 308-309, 326, 331, 359, 375-376,
    408
    books, 33, 36, 102-104, 249, 282
    documents, 58, 104, 181
    electronic databases, 102, 211
    e-mail and, 106, 226
    examples, 64, 102-103, 111, 114-115, 168, 227,
        230, 280, 303
    goals of, 126
    interviews, 18, 97, 102-105, 107-109, 111, 119,
        121, 188, 258, 294
    news sources, 103-104
    newspapers, 10, 44, 59, 103-105, 126, 138, 144,
        203, 255, 270, 393-394
    online, 8-9, 13, 44, 47, 58, 79, 97, 102-106,
        110-111, 119-121, 136, 138, 144, 191,
        225, 227-228, 249-251, 263, 273, 282,
        298, 375

patterns in, 107, 184
periodicals, 117
primary and secondary sources of, 112
search engines, 104
statistics, 4, 40, 58, 102-103, 107, 168, 225, 249
testimony, 85, 164
topic, 46, 101, 104, 106, 250, 258, 260, 273, 326
websites and, 143, 270, 282
Research methods, 99, 102, 121, 143
    surveys, 102, 121
Reservation, 317-318
Resonance, 136
Responding, 10, 59-60, 191, 200, 203, 370
Response, 69, 79-80, 108-110, 116, 149-150, 183,
    191-192, 278, 284, 291, 296, 347, 362, 418
Responsiveness, 190
Retention, 41, 125, 134, 138, 145
Retrieval, 102
Rhetoric, 132, 149, 160, 412
Robots, 80
Rodriguez, Alex, 150
Role models, 40-41, 153, 171, 390
Roles, 36, 50, 55, 63, 66, 70, 77, 93, 193, 230, 393
    individual, 167, 415
    research, 36, 50, 63, 70, 75, 77, 230, 393
Rules, 101, 120, 157, 161, 173, 210, 255, 302, 355,
    359, 373
Rumor, 237, 279-280, 301

S

Satisfaction, 32, 57, 68, 168, 297, 302, 311, 407
Scholarly journals, 46
Scripts, 104, 365
Search engines, 104, 224, 247
Secondary sources, 112
Self, 6-7, 57, 86, 109, 112, 120, 157, 163, 165-166,
    168, 170-171, 187, 202, 229, 252, 311, 337,
    353, 355, 363, 394
    material, 161, 252
    open, 6, 311
    social, 86, 120, 157, 161, 163, 166, 168, 170, 229,
        311, 337, 353
Self-actualization, 166
Self-censorship, 157
Self-esteem, 165, 202
Self-interest, 7, 112, 163, 165, 170-171, 229
Self-perception, 168, 170-171
Semantic noise, 133
Separation, 36, 291
Sequence, 115, 117
Seuss, Dr., 210
Sex, 18, 107, 151, 177-179, 232-233, 278, 350, 390
Sexual harassment, 189, 207
Short sentences, 256
Short-term orientation, 343
Signs, 187, 212, 227, 320, 323-324, 327, 332
Silence, 238
Simplicity, 133, 145, 291, 369
Sincerity, 166
Slippery slope, 159
Smiling, 277
Social networking, 59, 127, 136, 167, 272-274, 276,
    280-281, 344, 416
Social networking sites, 127, 167, 208, 272-274, 280,
    344
Social power, 231
Social presence, 127
Social space, 223
Sound bites, 225, 257-258, 362
Source, 16, 41, 44, 61, 63, 65-67, 79, 82-83, 87-88,
    128, 131-133, 135, 145, 160, 163-167, 171,
    189, 268-270, 282, 334, 361, 366
Source credibility, 131-132, 145, 160, 163-166, 171
Sources, 9, 13, 34, 44, 58, 88, 103-104, 111-112, 119,
    141, 149, 153-155, 160-161, 167, 209, 228,
    246, 256, 269, 422-423
Space, 14, 20, 55, 61, 87, 90, 106, 140-141, 168, 247,
    249, 253, 277, 285, 316, 322, 327-328, 375
    personal, 55, 108
    power and, 327
Speaker, 128, 143, 260, 317-320, 322, 326, 332-333
Speakers, 97, 234, 240, 317-319, 333, 343
speaking, 97, 166-167, 240, 252, 319-320, 330, 342
specific purpose, 111
Speech, 56, 85, 89, 103, 157, 197, 201, 213, 217, 272,
    322, 346, 354, 372, 374-375
    hate, 277, 287
Speeches, 14, 28, 31, 103-104, 111, 126-127, 130,
    322, 362-363

informative, 281
persuasive, 181
purpose of, 111
Spelling, 58
Stakeholders, 7, 15, 18, 21, 23, 43, 48, 69, 178, 180,
    187, 190, 292-293, 310, 348
Star, 133, 146, 167, 226, 232, 258, 281, 293, 298,
    308, 320, 330, 337, 385, 387-388, 391, 397
statements, 23, 30, 34, 103-104, 115, 135, 167-168,
    204-207, 214, 216, 261, 341, 343, 350, 414
Statistical Abstract of the United States, 103
Statistics, 4, 39-40, 58, 102-103, 107, 155, 168, 170,
    225, 249, 299, 390
    use of, 170
    using, 100, 107, 170, 299
Status, 46-47, 61, 65, 75, 80, 93, 138, 163-164, 191,
    206, 224, 234, 419
Stereotype, 259
Stimuli, 152
Stories, 3, 14, 19, 32, 58, 62, 85, 89, 138-140,
    142-143, 158, 162, 168, 185, 218, 249-250,
    272-274, 287, 293-295, 303, 330, 341, 361,
    387-388, 420
Strategic planning, 36-37, 91, 111-112, 119, 143, 238,
    340, 347
    defined, 143
Stress, 417
Style, 12, 14, 27, 145, 174, 237, 247, 263, 343, 362,
    374
    ambiguity, 343
    defined, 237
    language and, 343
    level of, 145
Submission, 110
Substituting, 133
Summarizing, 68, 261
Superiority, 17
Support, 6, 10-11, 15-16, 18, 29, 32-33, 38, 48, 56, 85,
    97, 103-105, 112-117, 150-152, 157, 162,
    167-168, 179-181, 184, 186, 193, 203, 216,
    232-233, 241, 284, 301-305, 310-311,
    348-349, 351, 364, 374-375, 411-416
Surprise, 11, 30, 61, 197, 236, 254, 332
Surveillance, 130
Survey research, 87, 114, 120, 142-143
Surveys, 40, 65, 97, 102-103, 105-111, 118-121, 144,
    152, 164, 170, 188, 274, 294-295, 297, 300,
    302-303, 353
    online, 85, 97, 102-103, 105-106, 110-111,
        119-121, 144, 326
Surveys and polls, 168, 170
Symbol, 133, 211, 217
Symbols, 130, 133, 209, 416
Sympathy, 150, 253, 278
Symposiums, 130
System, 3, 29, 32, 48, 76, 116, 129, 135, 137, 160,
    217, 268-269, 298, 317-318, 340, 359-360,
    409, 419

T

tables, 67, 136, 139, 219, 317-318, 320, 345
Taboo, 233, 339
Target audience, 6, 105-107, 110, 115, 131-132,
    142-143, 164, 168, 231-232, 235, 239-241,
    246, 272, 420
Team, 9, 19, 51, 65, 68, 89-90, 97, 116, 162-163, 279,
    306, 309, 351, 382, 385, 390-391, 419-420
Technological advances, 36, 121, 141
Technology, 22-23, 43, 57, 62, 67, 69, 75, 80, 85, 90,
    92, 121, 219, 224, 271, 276-277, 326, 362,
    377
    communication and, 62
    groups and, 121
    nonverbal, 112
    organizational, 326
Telephone, 3, 14, 92, 102-103, 107-109, 119, 121,
    127, 132, 257, 260, 263, 318, 385, 411
Television, 6, 10, 12, 14, 16, 44, 61-62, 69, 88-89,
    103-105, 112, 126-127, 129-130, 135, 143,
    150, 152-153, 161, 166-170, 181, 203, 213,
    225-226, 228-230, 238-240, 245, 250,
    254-258, 260-263, 303-304, 362-365, 383,
    387-390
Temperature, 251
Territory, 30
Test, 47, 90, 101, 106, 110, 131, 144, 204, 303
Testimonials, 159, 165, 170, 214, 414
Testimony, 85, 127, 164, 370
Texting, 75, 90, 143, 167-168, 236

Thought, 6, 11, 31, 51, 68, 111, 141, 150, 184-185,
	189, 197, 277, 398-399
Time, 3, 5-6, 14, 20, 22, 28-30, 33, 35-36, 38-39,
	41-44, 48-50, 65, 68-69, 80-81, 87, 89-93,
	102, 106-108, 112-113, 115, 117-118,
	120-121, 132-134, 139, 141, 151, 153, 157,
	167-168, 170, 182-186, 198, 209-210,
	214-215, 228-231, 246-247, 251-252, 254,
	258, 271-272, 276-277, 282, 298, 304-307,
	316-319, 321-327, 347-348, 368-371,
	406-407
Time of day, 107
Topic, 46, 55, 101, 104, 106, 150, 166, 172-173, 233,
	250, 257-258, 260, 273, 326
	choosing, 326
Topics, 157, 160, 168, 178, 206, 215, 256-257, 274,
	317, 319, 403
Touch, 42, 273, 316, 345, 375, 393, 398
Trust, 13-14, 16, 19, 36, 132, 188, 202-203, 226, 228,
	286, 291-293, 300-301, 311, 351, 376, 404
Twitter, 22, 42-43, 69, 80, 86, 93, 101, 104, 125-126,
	141-142, 159, 162, 169, 185, 203-204, 206,
	223, 248, 260, 262, 269, 279-280, 282-285,
	321, 331, 362-363, 385-386, 410-411,
	422-423

U
Uncertainty, 188, 191, 228-229, 301, 343, 388
Uncertainty avoidance, 343
Understanding, 6, 10, 16-17, 23, 28, 32, 36-38, 61-62,
	79, 108, 113, 115, 128-130, 133, 135, 151,
	164, 168, 190, 197, 206, 349
	audience attitudes, 143, 145
	barriers to, 128
United States, 5, 20, 22, 29-32, 41, 47-48, 61, 65-66,
	76, 84, 150-151, 182, 213, 227-229, 231,
	234-235, 241, 257, 267, 311, 341, 345-346,
	351-353, 391, 393-394, 406, 410-411,
	419-420

V
Values, 41, 47, 112, 134, 157-158, 163-164, 168-171,
	181, 183, 198, 200-201, 224-225, 228, 234,
	241, 332, 347, 353, 403-404, 406
	of audience, 163
Variety, 4, 6-7, 13, 17, 20, 48, 56-58, 61, 70-71, 87, 91,
	108, 127-130, 134, 143-145, 156, 215,
	235-236, 249-250, 269, 272, 297-298,
	309-310, 340, 366-368, 389
Video, 3, 7, 43, 62, 69, 103-104, 106, 117-118, 127,
	130, 141-142, 144, 159, 210, 215, 247-248,
	250-251, 257-260, 270-272, 280-281,
	284-285, 316, 318, 321, 326-327, 330, 392,
	411
	videos, 8, 38, 42, 106, 112-113, 117, 185, 213,
	225-227, 248, 259, 274, 280-282, 285, 332,
	363, 372, 381, 393
Videotapes, 209
Violation, 192, 206, 210, 214
Violence, 34, 159, 211, 340, 398-399
Vividness, 239
Voice, 18, 23, 101, 115, 128, 182, 184, 236, 256, 273,
	275, 292, 351
Volume, 80, 141

W
Warhol, Andy, 225
Websites, 3, 12, 39, 44, 102, 110, 136, 143, 159, 165,
	169, 205, 225, 237, 249, 260, 269-272, 274,
	284-285, 372-373
	database, 102
	employment, 372
	Google, 102, 205, 269, 279
	museum, 3
	research and, 102, 110, 270
	search engines, 269
Wikipedia, 273, 372
Winfrey, Oprah, 140
Women, 27, 31, 34-36, 39-40, 48, 50-51, 57, 60,
	66-68, 70, 79-80, 115-116, 136, 165, 180,
	223-224, 229-231, 233, 235, 240-241, 309,
	345, 376, 388, 390
Words, 6, 12, 14, 22-23, 40, 47, 115, 128-131, 133,
	140, 156, 163, 182, 188-189, 206-207,
	247-248, 273, 343-344, 400
	characteristics of, 131
	power of, 115
Workplace, 10, 36, 207, 275-276, 350

World Wide Web, 39, 240, 268-269
Worldview, 181

Y
Yahoo!, 104, 157, 247-248
YouTube, 8-10, 42-43, 69, 101, 106, 113, 117, 126,
	258-260, 267, 284-285, 296, 321, 326, 332,
	362-363, 399, 411